Leveraging AI for Effective Digital Relationship Marketing

José Duarte Santos
Polytechnic Institute of Porto, Portugal

Paulo Botelho Pires
CEOS, Polytechnic of Porto, Portugal

Nicholas Grigoriou
Monash University, Australia

IGI Global
Publishing Tomorrow's Research Today

Published in the United States of America by
IGI Global
701 E. Chocolate Avenue
Hershey PA, USA 17033
Tel: 717-533-8845
Fax: 717-533-8661
E-mail: cust@igi-global.com
Web site: https://www.igi-global.com

Library of Congress Cataloging-in-Publication Data

CIP PENDING

ISBN13: 9798369353400
Isbn13Softcover: 9798369353417
EISBN13: 9798369353424

Vice President of Editorial: Melissa Wagner
Managing Editor of Acquisitions: Mikaela Felty
Managing Editor of Book Development: Jocelynn Hessler
Production Manager: Mike Brehm
Cover Design: Phillip Shickler

British Cataloguing in Publication Data
A Cataloguing in Publication record for this book is available from the British Library.

Table of Contents

Preface xvi

Chapter 1
How Artificial Intelligence Can Leverage Relationship Marketing Strategies 1
Albérico Travassos Rosário, GOVCOPP, IADE, Universidade Europeia, Portugal
Joaquim Casaca, UNIDCOM/IADE, Universidade Europeia, Portugal

Chapter 2
How AI Influences Marketing From the Consumer Perspective: Literature Review 35
Francisca Gonçalves Azevedo, Instituto Português de Administração de Marketing, Portugal
Francisca Santos Santos Oliveira, Instituto Português de Administração de Marketing, Portugal
Katharina Thielen, Instituto Português de Administração de Marketing, Portugal
Irma Imamovic, Instituto Português de Administração de Marketing, Portugal

Chapter 3
The Future of Customer Relationship Service: How Artificial Intelligence (AI) Is Changing the Game 59
Md. Touhidul Islam, NPI University of Bangladesh, Bangladesh

Chapter 4
AI-Driven Personalization in Omnichannel Marketing: Enhancing Customer Engagement and Loyalty 97
Yavuz Selim Balcıoğlu, Dogus University, Turkey

Chapter 5
AI-Driven Personalization in Beauty Retail: Exploring How AI-Based Applications Influence Customer Satisfaction and Brand Loyalty 131
Maria Carolina Cordeiro Dias Coelho, Instituto Português de Administração de Marketing, Portugal
Irma Imamović, Instituto Português de Administração de Marketing, Portugal

Chapter 6
AI-Powered Personalization: Revolutionizing Mobile Commerce for Enhanced Customer Experiences 163
Nitesh Behare, Balaji Institute of International Business, Sri Balaji University, Pune, India
Divya Yogesh Lakhani, Sadhu Vaswani Institute of Management Studies for Girls, India
Abhijit Vasmatkar, Symbiosis Law School, Symbiosis International University (Deemed), Pune, India
Shrikant Waghulkar, Ramachandran International Institute of Management, India
Vinod N. Sayankar, Neville Wadia Institute of Management and Research Center, Pune, India
Ankita Naik, Arihant Institute of Business Management, India
Suraj Sharma, Ramachandran International Institute of Management, India
Shubhada N. Behare, Independent Researcher, India

Chapter 7
Crafting Couture: AI's Role in Personalizing Unique Consumer Experiences Through Co-Creation 199
Poornima Nair, Christ University, India
Sunita Kumar, Christ University, India

Chapter 8
Converging Theories: The Fusion of Artificial Intelligence and Sustainable Marketing for a Responsible Future 223
Luzia Arantes, Polytechnic University of Cávado and Ave, Portugal
Sandra Costa, Polytechnic University of Viseu, Portugal

Chapter 9
The Intersection of Brands and AI: Concepts and Technologies 257
Joana Neves, CEOS.PP Coimbra, Polytechnic University of Coimbra, Portugal
Lara Mendes Bacalhau, CEOS.PP Coimbra, Polytechnic University of Coimbra, Portugal

Chapter 10
More Than Brands, Friends: Enhancing Emotional Engagement Through AI in Digital Relationship Marketing Context 287
Sandra Ferreira, University of Minho, Portugal
Olga Pereira, CIICESI, ESTG, Instituto Politécnico do Porto, Portugal

Chapter 11
AI Caramba! The Negative Effects of AI Agents in Customer Relationship Management 309
Ahmed Shaalan, University of Birmingham, UK
Marwa Tourky, Cranfield University, UK
Khaled Ibrahim, UNITEC Institute of Technology, New Zealand

Chapter 12
Return on AI: Mapping and Exploring ROI (In)Tangible Measures 353
Ana Isabel Torres, University of Aveiro, Portugal & INESC TEC, Porto, Portugal
Darkio Lourenço Siqueira Paulo, University of Aveiro, Portugal
José Duarte Santos, CEOS.PP, ISCAP, Polytechnic of Porto, Portugal
Paulo Botelho Pires, CEOS.PP, ISCAP, Polytechnic of Porto, Portugal

Chapter 13
Social Media Analytics for Effective Customer Brand Engagement Assessment: A Theoretical Exploration 385
Lhoussaine Alla, Sidi Mohamed Ben Abdellah University, Fez, Morocco
Naoual Bouhtati, Sidi Mohamed Ben Abdellah University, Fez, Morocco
Mourad Aarabe, Sidi Mohamed Ben Abdellah University, Fez, Morocco
Nouhaila Ben Khizzou, Sidi Mohamed Ben Abdellah University, Fez, Morocco

Chapter 14
Mediation Effect of Customer Loyalty in Relationship Between Market Orientation, Entrepreneurial Orientation, and Firm Performance in Ethiopia . 419
Tafese Niguse, Bule Hora University, Ethiopia
Shashi Kant, Bule Hora University, Ethiopia
Metasebia Adula, Bule Hora University, Ethiopia

Chapter 15
Customer Orientation and Ethiopian Bank Performance With Mediation of Competitive Advantage 459
Dawit Jabo, Bule Hora University, Ethiopia
Shashi Kant, Bule Hora University, Ethiopia
Brehanu Borji, Independent Researcher, Ethiopia

Compilation of References 483

About the Contributors 597

Index 605

Detailed Table of Contents

Preface.. xvi

Chapter 1
How Artificial Intelligence Can Leverage Relationship Marketing Strategies 1
Albérico Travassos Rosário, GOVCOPP, IADE, Universidade Europeia, Portugal
Joaquim Casaca, UNIDCOM/IADE, Universidade Europeia, Portugal

Increased competition and consumer demand for personalized marketing messages and content have led to the increased adoption of relationship marketing. Through a systematic bibliometric literature review, this study aims not only to demonstrate how leveraging Artificial Intelligence can improve relationship marketing strategies but also to address the various ethical considerations and challenges of using AI in relationship marketing. The review includes 22 articles published up to 2024 in the Scopus® database, presenting up-to-date knowledge on the topic. The research findings demonstrate that the integration of Artificial Intelligence into relationship marketing strategies offers both theoretical insights into consumer behavior and practical tools for enhancing customer engagement, satisfaction, and loyalty. However, businesses need to approach Artificial Intelligence implementation thoughtfully, considering both the opportunities and challenges it presents.

The systematic literature review investigates the impact of artificial intelligence (AI) on marketing, with a focus on client perspectives, using the PRISMA model. It examines how AI technology might improve customer service efficiency and increase the level of personalization in customer interactions while delving further into privacy and ethical problems. The report emphasizes how critical it is to strike a healthy balance between leveraging AI's benefits and preserving customer confidence. Moreover, it highlights customers' persistent desire for face-to-face contacts during service encounters, implying that in spite of technology breakthroughs, human connection and emotional intelligence are still essential. These revelations illustrate the intricate relationship that exists between technical progress and providing human- centered services, emphasizing the necessity for businesses to incorporate AI in ways that enhance, rather than replace human interaction.

This chapter aims to delve into the changing world of customer relationship service as a result of AI breakthroughs, with a specific emphasis on the revolutionary effects on emerging nations. Businesses and researchers alike may benefit from the insights gleaned from this chapter's comprehensive evaluation of existing practices across different sectors, case studies of successful AI integration, and research into customer views and adoption of AI-driven products. The chapter's potential to help businesses successfully use AI to improve client interactions and propel the company to success makes it significant. This chapter also answers important questions about AI adoption in developing countries by looking ahead to what's to come in AI-driven customer relationship service and providing suggestions that are industry-specific and customer-centric. Its ultimate goal is to help improve customer service by encouraging diversity and new ideas in the dynamic field of customer relationship management across industries.

Chapter 4
AI-Driven Personalization in Omnichannel Marketing: Enhancing Customer Engagement and Loyalty 97
Yavuz Selim Balcıoğlu, Dogus University, Turkey

This chapter explores the transformative role of AI-driven personalization in omnichannel marketing, emphasizing its importance in enhancing customer engagement and loyalty. It begins by defining omnichannel marketing and tracing its evolution from traditional to digital channels. The chapter explores into key components of AI-driven personalization, including data collection and analysis, customer segmentation, predictive analytics, and real-time personalization. Implementation strategies are discussed, highlighting the integration of AI tools, data management, and the design of personalized marketing strategies. The chapter also addresses best practices for overcoming common challenges and measuring customer engagement using key performance indicators (KPIs). Additionally, the chapter examines the future trends in AI-driven personalization, such as emerging AI technologies, integration with IoT and AR/VR, and the evolving landscape of marketing strategies.

Chapter 5
AI-Driven Personalization in Beauty Retail: Exploring How AI-Based Applications Influence Customer Satisfaction and Brand Loyalty 131
Maria Carolina Cordeiro Dias Coelho, Instituto Português de Administração de Marketing, Portugal
Irma Imamović, Instituto Português de Administração de Marketing, Portugal

This study explores the evolving beauty industry transformed by technology, focusing on how personalized artificial intelligence (AI) shapes customer experience, satisfaction, and loyalty in online beauty shopping. Through semi-structured interviews with 10 Portuguese female online buyers aged 18-30, it reveals the importance of understanding and meeting customer preferences in a fast-paced digital environment. The research highlights the crucial role of personal experiences and trust in influencing customer satisfaction and loyalty. It examines the impact of AI-based recommendations and interactions at every stage of the online shopping experience. The findings offer valuable insights for beauty brands, emphasizing the necessity to adapt to technological advances, thrive in the digital landscape, and meet consumers' evolving digital aspirations.

Chapter 6
AI-Powered Personalization: Revolutionizing Mobile Commerce for Enhanced Customer Experiences 163
Nitesh Behare, Balaji Institute of International Business, Sri Balaji University, Pune, India
Divya Yogesh Lakhani, Sadhu Vaswani Institute of Management Studies for Girls, India
Abhijit Vasmatkar, Symbiosis Law School, Symbiosis International University (Deemed), Pune, India
Shrikant Waghulkar, Ramachandran International Institute of Management, India
Vinod N. Sayankar, Neville Wadia Institute of Management and Research Center, Pune, India
Ankita Naik, Arihant Institute of Business Management, India
Suraj Sharma, Ramachandran International Institute of Management, India
Shubhada N. Behare, Independent Researcher, India

By Customizing the shopping experience to individual users, AI-powered personalization plays a crucial role in mobile commerce, ultimately improving consumer satisfaction and increasing sales. This chapter highlights the several technologies and strategies employed in this field and gives an outline of AI-powered personalization in mobile commerce. It investigates user profiling and data collection methods, dynamic pricing and offers, personalized product recommendations AI-enhanced search and navigation. Moreover, the use of chatbots and virtual assistants. The chapter also discusses future directions and developing trends in AI-powered personalization, Additionally difficulties and ethical issues. Businesses may use AI to create engaging and tailored experiences for their customers by learning about its possibilities in mobile commerce.

Chapter 7
Crafting Couture: AI's Role in Personalizing Unique Consumer Experiences Through Co-Creation 199
Poornima Nair, Christ University, India
Sunita Kumar, Christ University, India

The couture industry and artificial intelligence (AI) have come together to create a dynamic paradigm shift in the creation of unique consumer experiences. AI has become a transformational force in the ever-changing fashion industry, transforming the relationship between designers and consumers and overturning conventional paradigms. This study explores the mutually beneficial integration of artificial intelligence (AI) with co-creation processes, shedding light on the creative ways that AI enhances the customisation of couture experiences. At the core of the discussion is the idea of personalisation enabled by AI-powered co-creation tools. With the help of these platforms, customers can express their individual style preferences and take part in the design process, giving them a sense of co-ownership. The ensuing couture pieces blur the boundaries between designer and customer in a cooperative dance of creativity; they are more than just clothes. In conclusion, couture business may achieve unprecedented degrees of personalisation only through the synergy of AI and co-creation.

Chapter 8
Converging Theories: The Fusion of Artificial Intelligence and Sustainable Marketing for a Responsible Future 223
Luzia Arantes, Polytechnic University of Cávado and Ave, Portugal
Sandra Costa, Polytechnic University of Viseu, Portugal

Integrating Artificial Intelligence (AI) with sustainable marketing provides a transformative approach to fostering responsible business practices. This examination covers green, social, and critical marketing theories, illustrating how AI improves efficiency and personalisation in promoting sustainability. By leveraging AI, companies can better address consumer demands for eco-friendly products and services. The exploration includes practical applications such as predictive analytics, targeted marketing, and automated customer interactions, emphasising AI deployment's ethical considerations and challenges. The impact on corporate strategies and AI's contribution to achieving the UN Sustainable Development Goals are also highlighted. The complexities of merging AI with sustainable marketing are thoroughly evaluated, providing valuable insights into theoretical advancements and practical implications. Future research directions are suggested further to enhance the synergy between AI and sustainable marketing practices.

Chapter 9
The Intersection of Brands and AI: Concepts and Technologies....................... 257
Joana Neves, CEOS.PP Coimbra, Polytechnic University of Coimbra, Portugal
Lara Mendes Bacalhau, CEOS.PP Coimbra, Polytechnic University of Coimbra, Portugal

Today's digital marketplace is volatile and fast-paced, and the introduction of AI technologies has become an integral part of improving many aspects of business. This chapter aims to shed light on how AI techniques were/are/will be related to Brand Management. First, the basic ideas about AI will be introduced, and the development of the concept and the main technologies that form AI will be explained. Furthermore, it will be necessary to provide a comprehensive analysis of the use of AI in brand management and its potential to revolutionize the methods, customer interactions, and trends in the market. This paper integrates a contextual approach to explore how AI solutions are transforming the brand-consumer relationship. Secondly, we will investigate the variety of advantages that AI has for brands. Finally, a glimpse of new opportunities created by AI in the context of brand management will be highlighted. Thus, the information presented in this chapter is useful for academics, researchers, and practitioners interested in unlocking the capabilities of AI for brand management.

Chapter 10
More Than Brands, Friends: Enhancing Emotional Engagement Through AI in Digital Relationship Marketing Context.. 287
Sandra Ferreira, University of Minho, Portugal
Olga Pereira, CIICESI, ESTG, Instituto Politécnico do Porto, Portugal

In today's highly competitive business environment, technological advancements have significantly transformed business operations, particularly through the integration of Artificial Intelligence (AI). AI has implemented innovative digital strategies for attracting and retaining customers, garnering widespread attention due to its potential to deliver favorable outcomes and create emotional engagement. However, previous studies have overlooked emotions as a crucial part of consumer engagement. This chapter explores the influence of AI on emotional engagement within the digital context of Relationship Marketing (RM). Five propositions are proposed based on theoretical assumptions to guide and enrich future research in this domain. Additionally, ethical issues and managerial strategies are discussed to provide a comprehensive understanding of AI's impact on customer relationships.

Chapter 11
AI Caramba! The Negative Effects of AI Agents in Customer Relationship Management 309
Ahmed Shaalan, University of Birmingham, UK
Marwa Tourky, Cranfield University, UK
Khaled Ibrahim, UNITEC Institute of Technology, New Zealand

AI agents are increasingly used in customer relationship management strategies to improve efficiency and reduce costs. Amid rapid advances in technology, the programs are becoming more human-like and versatile. However, AI agents with inadequate emotional responses can create an empathy gap, resulting in negative outcomes. If users' experiences fail to live up to their expectations, the resultant negative disconfirmation has damaging consequences for customers, the brand and the corporation. This chapter sets out the current types of human interactions with digital systems before examining the antecedents to negative outcomes, the three key types of negative disconfirmation and the consequences for areas such as brand engagement, AI agent trust and AI-induced brand hate. It then highlights that these harms are not inevitable, highlighting the mitigating action that firms can take to ensure their AI agents do not undermine their own customer relationship management efforts. Suggestions for future research are also provided.

Chapter 12
Return on AI: Mapping and Exploring ROI (In)Tangible Measures 353
Ana Isabel Torres, University of Aveiro, Portugal & INESC TEC, Porto, Portugal
Darkio Lourenço Siqueira Paulo, University of Aveiro, Portugal
José Duarte Santos, CEOS.PP, ISCAP, Polytechnic of Porto, Portugal
Paulo Botelho Pires, CEOS.PP, ISCAP, Polytechnic of Porto, Portugal

This chapter aims to discuss about the potential Return on Investment (ROI) measures from Artificial intelligence (AI) investments that business can leverage. It discusses the concepts and describes the dimensions, features and tools of AI investments in Marketing business, to assist the readers to understand about the topic. The authors also describe the major drivers of ROI measures for business applications and discusses the concerns and limitations of tangible measures. So, this document contributes to the literature on ROI (in)tangibles measures that leverage AI investments and features issues in digital marketing, at large and potentially offers a theoretical grounding for many empirical and theoretical future studies.

Chapter 13
Social Media Analytics for Effective Customer Brand Engagement Assessment: A Theoretical Exploration... 385
Lhoussaine Alla, Sidi Mohamed Ben Abdellah University, Fez, Morocco
Naoual Bouhtati, Sidi Mohamed Ben Abdellah University, Fez, Morocco
Mourad Aarabe, Sidi Mohamed Ben Abdellah University, Fez, Morocco
Nouhaila Ben Khizzou, Sidi Mohamed Ben Abdellah University, Fez, Morocco

Customer engagement has become a critical component of business success in the digital age. Challenges to this commitment include creating personalized experiences, building trust, and using data to anticipate customer needs. Our study aims to analyze the impact of social media analytics on online customer engagement assessment. We propose an analysis model integrating key dimensions of customer engagement, such as interaction, satisfaction and social influence. The expected results of this study are to provide a solid analysis model to assess customer engagement on social media and practical recommendations to improve the marketing strategies of companies on social media.

Chapter 14
Mediation Effect of Customer Loyalty in Relationship Between Market Orientation, Entrepreneurial Orientation, and Firm Performance in Ethiopia . 419
Tafese Niguse, Bule Hora University, Ethiopia
Shashi Kant, Bule Hora University, Ethiopia
Metasebia Adula, Bule Hora University, Ethiopia

This study focused on the mediating role of customer loyalty between market orientation, entrepreneurial orientation and Ethiopian hotel performance. It was aimed: To see effect of market orientation and entrepreneurial orientation on business performance, to see effect market orientation and entrepreneurial orientation on customer loyalty, and to find mediation effect of customer loyalty between market orientation, entrepreneurial orientation and business performance. Descriptive research design and non-probability, particularly convenience sampling was used. Structured questionnaire was used. For data analysis, percentage, mean, standard deviations were employed. Structural equation modeling by EFA and CFA was employed using SPSS and AMOS.23. The finding showed there is positive significant relationship between MO, CL, and FP. However, there is negative relationship between EO and FP. But, with the mediation of CL, the relationship between EO and FP was found.

Chapter 15
Customer Orientation and Ethiopian Bank Performance With Mediation of Competitive Advantage 459
Dawit Jabo, Bule Hora University, Ethiopia
Shashi Kant, Bule Hora University, Ethiopia
Brehanu Borji, Independent Researcher, Ethiopia

The impact of competitive advantage in mitigating the detrimental impacts of customer orientation on business performance was examined in this chapter. Few research have examined the relationship between competitive advantage and customer orientation and how it influences business success in emerging economies, particularly in sub-Saharan Africa. This article attempted to investigate the matter from an Ethiopian perspective in order to bridge that gap. a response obtained from the 383 Commercial Bank of Ethiopia (CBE) customers in the Dilla area of southern Ethiopia using a survey questionnaire. Employing SPSS and AMOS edition 26 together with the Structure Equation Model (SEM) technique, the collected data was analysed to see if the two proposed variables were related. The results showed that customer orientation has a positive, significant influence on business performance through the competitive advantage negotiating process. The results of this study suggest that commercial banks should use client orientation to obtain a competitive advantage.

Compilation of References 483

About the Contributors 597

Index 605

Preface

In an era where technology continues to transform industries, marketing is no exception. The advent of artificial intelligence (AI) in digital marketing has opened new avenues for companies to foster stronger, more meaningful relationships with their customers. As editors of this book, *Leveraging AI for Effective Digital Relationship Marketing*, we aim to explore how AI is shaping the future of relationship marketing and provide insights into how businesses can harness its potential to thrive in today's highly competitive marketplace.

Relationship marketing has always been about building lasting connections with customers, but the landscape is evolving. The rise of digital platforms—especially social media and email—has revolutionized how companies engage with their audience, offering direct and personalized channels of communication. This shift has made it possible to understand customer needs more deeply and to create stronger, trust-based relationships.

Furthermore, customer experience has become a key differentiator in this competitive environment. Companies that prioritize delivering memorable, satisfying buying journeys are not only attracting new customers but also fostering long-term loyalty. In this context, sustainable marketing has emerged as a priority for many organizations. Consumers are increasingly aligning with brands that reflect their values, particularly those that embrace social and environmental responsibility.

Artificial intelligence seamlessly integrates into these trends, offering enhanced personalization through advanced data analysis. AI's ability to predict customer behavior and preferences allows businesses to proactively address needs, further strengthening bonds of trust and ensuring customer satisfaction.

In this book, our aim is twofold:

1. To highlight the role of AI as a valuable and accessible tool for improving customer interactions and relationships.
2. To showcase new trends in digital relationship marketing, particularly those driven by AI.

This book is intended for a broad audience: academics and students in management and marketing programs, researchers seeking to advance conceptual developments in AI-driven marketing, and professionals eager to enhance their digital relationship marketing strategies. Through this work, we hope to provide the tools and knowledge necessary to navigate the complexities of digital marketing in the AI age.

ORGANIZATION OF THE BOOK

Chapter 1: How Artificial Intelligence Can Leverage Relationship Marketing Strategies

The first chapter explores how Artificial Intelligence (AI) enhances relationship marketing strategies in response to growing competition and consumer demand for personalized content. Through a comprehensive bibliometric literature review, the authors analyzed 22 articles from the Scopus® database, offering a well-rounded perspective on AI's role in improving customer engagement, satisfaction, and loyalty. The chapter also addresses ethical concerns and challenges businesses face in integrating AI into marketing, providing both theoretical insights and practical recommendations for effectively leveraging AI to strengthen consumer relationships.

Chapter 2: How AI Influences Marketing from the Consumer's Perspective: Literature Review

This chapter examines how consumers perceive the role of AI in marketing. Using the PRISMA model, the authors focus on AI's potential to enhance customer service and personalization, while also highlighting concerns about privacy and ethical issues. The chapter emphasizes the need for a balanced approach that leverages AI's benefits while preserving customer trust and explores the continued importance of human interaction in service experiences, suggesting that even with AI advancements, emotional intelligence remains crucial.

Chapter 3: The Future of Customer Relationship Service: How Artificial Intelligence (AI) is Changing the Game

The third chapter discusses how AI is reshaping customer relationship services, particularly in emerging nations. The chapter offers insights through case studies and industry-specific research, demonstrating how AI integration has the potential to revolutionize client interactions. By providing forward-looking recommendations, Islam emphasizes how businesses can adopt AI to enhance customer service across industries, with a focus on promoting innovation and inclusivity in customer relationship management.

Chapter 4: AI-Driven Personalization in Omnichannel Marketing: Enhancing Customer Engagement and Loyalty

Chapter 4 explores the power of AI-driven personalization in omnichannel marketing, explaining how it transforms customer engagement and loyalty. The chapter outlines key components of AI personalization, including data analysis, customer segmentation, and real-time marketing. The author also discusses implementation strategies, addressing challenges and offering insights into future trends like the integration of AI with emerging technologies such as IoT and AR/VR.

Chapter 5: AI-Driven Personalization in Beauty Retail: Exploring How AI-Based Applications Influence Customer Satisfaction and Brand Loyalty

The authors focus on the beauty industry, examining how AI-driven personalization influences customer satisfaction and brand loyalty. Through interviews with Portuguese female buyers, the chapter reveals how AI enhances the online shopping experience in beauty retail. The findings underscore the importance of trust and personal experience in driving loyalty, offering practical insights for beauty brands to thrive in the rapidly evolving digital landscape.

Chapter 6: AI-Powered Personalization: Revolutionizing Mobile Commerce for Enhanced Customer Experiences

This chapter highlights the impact of AI-powered personalization on mobile commerce. It covers various technologies and strategies that customize shopping experiences, such as dynamic pricing, personalized recommendations, and AI-enhanced search features. The authors also discuss future trends and the ethical considerations businesses must address to create engaging and tailored mobile experiences.

Chapter 7: Crafting Couture: AI's Role in Personalizing Unique Consumer Experiences Through Co-Creation

In this chapter, the authors investigate the transformative role of AI in the couture industry, particularly in co-creating personalized fashion experiences. They explore how AI-powered co-creation tools enable customers to participate in the design process, fostering deeper connections between consumers and designers. This chapter emphasizes the importance of personalization in couture, showcasing how AI redefines traditional fashion paradigms to deliver unique consumer experiences.

Chapter 8: Converging Theories: The Fusion of Artificial Intelligence and Sustainable Marketing for a Responsible Future

This chapter examines the integration of AI with sustainable marketing, demonstrating how this synergy promotes responsible business practices. The chapter discusses green and critical marketing theories, focusing on AI's role in efficiency, predictive analytics, and customer interactions. Ethical considerations, practical applications, and AI's contribution to the UN Sustainable Development Goals are explored, offering a future-oriented view of AI's potential in driving sustainability.

Chapter 9: The Intersection of Brands and AI – Concepts and Technologies: Past, Present, and Future

In this chapter, the authors provide an overview of AI's role in brand management, tracing its development from past to future. They explore how AI has transformed brand-consumer relationships, offering new methods for customer engagement and brand interaction. The chapter highlights key advantages of AI for brands, from enhancing customer experiences to unlocking new market opportunities, making it valuable for academics and practitioners interested in the intersection of AI and branding.

Chapter 10: More than Brands, Friends: Enhancing Emotional Engagement through AI in Digital Relationship Marketing Context

Chapter 10 focuses on AI's ability to enhance emotional engagement in digital relationship marketing. They argue that while AI-driven strategies have transformed customer acquisition and retention, the emotional aspect of engagement remains underexplored. The chapter proposes five key areas for future research, examining ethical challenges and strategies for creating emotionally intelligent AI systems that deepen customer relationships.

Chapter 11: AI Caramba!: The Negative Effects of AI Agents in Customer Relationship Management

The chapter addresses the potential negative consequences of AI agents in customer relationship management. They discuss how inadequate emotional responses from AI systems can create an "empathy gap," leading to negative customer experiences. The chapter explores disconfirmation theory and its impact on brand trust, offering solutions for mitigating AI's potential harms in customer interactions.

Chapter 12: Return on AI – Mapping and Exploring ROI (In)Tangible Measures

The authors of this chapter analyze how businesses can measure the return on investment (ROI) from AI initiatives. The chapter outlines tangible and intangible measures of AI's impact on marketing strategies, exploring key drivers of ROI and discussing potential limitations. It provides a theoretical foundation for future empirical studies on AI investments, emphasizing the need for a comprehensive approach to assessing AI's value.

Chapter 13: Social Media Analytics for Effective Customer Brand Engagement Assessment: A Theoretical Exploration

In this chapter, the authors offer a theoretical framework for assessing customer engagement using social media analytics. They propose a model that integrates key dimensions of engagement, such as interaction and satisfaction, and explore how data-driven insights can improve brand engagement strategies. The chapter provides practical recommendations for businesses looking to enhance their social media presence through effective customer engagement.

Chapter 14: Mediation Effect of Customer Loyalty in Relationship between Market Orientation, Entrepreneurial Orientation, and Firm Performance in Ethiopia

This chapter investigates the mediating role of customer loyalty in the relationship between market orientation, entrepreneurial orientation, and firm performance in the Ethiopian hotel industry. Through a descriptive research design and structural equation modeling, the chapter highlights the positive influence of market orientation on customer loyalty and firm performance, while examining the complexities of entrepreneurial orientation's impact.

Chapter 15: Customer Orientation and Ethiopian Bank Performance with Mediation of Competitive Advantage

Chapter 15 analyzes the relationship between customer orientation and business performance in the Ethiopian banking sector, emphasizing the mediating role of competitive advantage. Through survey data from Commercial Bank of Ethiopia customers, the chapter reveals how customer orientation positively influences performance when mediated by competitive advantage, offering insights into strategies for enhancing business success in emerging markets.

IN CONCLUSION

In conclusion, *Leveraging AI for Effective Digital Relationship Marketing* brings together a diverse collection of insights, perspectives, and practical strategies from leading researchers and professionals in the field. As the digital marketing landscape continues to evolve, Artificial Intelligence stands as a transformative force, reshaping how businesses engage with their customers and build lasting relationships. The chapters in this volume not only highlight the significant advancements made possible through AI, but also acknowledge the ethical considerations and challenges that must be navigated to harness its full potential responsibly.

This book provides readers with a comprehensive understanding of how AI is revolutionizing relationship marketing across industries—from personalization in omnichannel marketing and mobile commerce to its role in co-creation and brand engagement. Through a balance of theoretical analysis and real-world applications, the authors offer actionable insights that will be invaluable for practitioners, academics, and researchers alike.

As we move forward into an era where technology is an integral part of consumer interaction, it is crucial to remember that AI should not replace human connection, but rather enhance it. This collection of work serves as both a guide and a reflection on how we can leverage AI not just to meet business objectives, but to foster more meaningful, customer-centric relationships in an increasingly digital world.

José Duarte Santos
CEOS.PP, ISCAP, Polytechnic of Porto, Portugal

Paulo Botelho Pires
CEOS.PP, ISCAP, Polytechnic of Porto, Portugal

Nicholas Grigoriou
Monash University, Australia

Chapter 1
How Artificial Intelligence Can Leverage Relationship Marketing Strategies

Albérico Travassos Rosário
https://orcid.org/0000-0003-4793-4110
GOVCOPP, IADE, Universidade Europeia, Portugal

Joaquim Casaca
https://orcid.org/0000-0002-9588-8983
UNIDCOM/IADE, Universidade Europeia, Portugal

ABSTRACT

Increased competition and consumer demand for personalized marketing messages and content have led to the increased adoption of relationship marketing. Through a systematic bibliometric literature review, this study aims not only to demonstrate how leveraging Artificial Intelligence can improve relationship marketing strategies but also to address the various ethical considerations and challenges of using AI in relationship marketing. The review includes 22 articles published up to 2024 in the Scopus® database, presenting up-to-date knowledge on the topic. The research findings demonstrate that the integration of Artificial Intelligence into relationship marketing strategies offers both theoretical insights into consumer behavior and practical tools for enhancing customer engagement, satisfaction, and loyalty. However, businesses need to approach Artificial Intelligence implementation thoughtfully, considering both the opportunities and challenges it presents.

DOI: 10.4018/979-8-3693-5340-0.ch001

1. INTRODUCTION

Traditionally, marketing was viewed from a transactional perspective, with marketers prioritizing maximizing efficiency and volume of sales. However, this has changed in recent years, with contemporary marketing strategies focusing more on building relationships with buyers (Salem, 2021). The increased competition in the market requires marketers to establish long-lasting relationships with target customers based on mutual benefits and understanding (Itani et al., 2019). This approach has led to the rise of relationship marketing. This marketing strategy requires marketers and organizations to know who their customers are, understand their needs, and know how to meet them in ways that align with the brand's objectives. According to Hidayat and Idrus (2023), relationship marketing involves creating value by consistently engaging customers to gather insights regarding their needs and expectations. This notion is echoed in Durmaz et al. (2020) research, which connects the increasing interest in relationship marketing to its focus on customer engagement, customer-firm interactions, and building long-term customer relationships. As a result, relationship marketing is associated with higher customer satisfaction and loyalty, organizational growth, and profitability.

The emergence of artificial intelligence (AI) in recent years has significantly changed how businesses engage and interact with their customers. With the increased adoption of data-driven decision-making and strategies, it has become crucial for businesses to leverage AI to promote their brands (Hermann, 2022). For instance, marketers are leveraging AI innovations, such as machine learning and natural language processing, to analyze vast amounts of data and gain insights into consumer behaviors and preferences. This data-driven approach is used to improve marketing efforts through strategies such as personalized content delivery, targeted advertising, and real-time campaign optimization (Hicham et al., 2023). AI innovations play a significant role in enhancing relationship marketing strategies. For instance, Huang and Rust (2021) explain that marketers use their deep understanding of consumers to create and deliver content, messages, and offers aligned with target consumers' interests and needs. Hermann (2022) indicates that AI capabilities, such as context awareness, computational power, emotional sensing, and data availability and intensity, are used to provide customized and personalized offers. In addition, these capabilities allow businesses and marketers to create and maintain responsive customer relationships and interactions. Therefore, leveraging AI innovations in relationship marketing can result in numerous positive outcomes, such as improved customer experiences and brand loyalty.

Therefore, this systematic bibliometric literature review synthesizes data from 22 sources, demonstrating how leveraging AI can improve relationship marketing strategies. The paper explores various aspects such as customer relationship management, customer journey mapping, fostering loyalty, and improving customer satisfaction, among others. It also covers the various ethical considerations and challenges of using AI in relationship marketing. The aim is to provide marketing professionals and firms with insights they can implement to integrate AI into relationship marketing and maximize opportunities.

2. METHODOLOGICAL APPROACH

The systematic bibliometric literature review (LRSB) methodology was employed due to its rigorous and structured approach to analyzing and synthesizing extensive data volumes. Moreover, LRSB aids in evaluating different methodological strategies used in research, ensuring the integration of reliable and high-quality data into the final analysis.

For gathering and selecting pertinent materials, the Scopus database was utilized. This choice was influenced by Rosário and Dias (2023a, 2023b, 2023c), who describe Scopus as one of the largest and most comprehensive curated abstract and citation databases available. Scopus encompasses a broad spectrum of sources, including conference proceedings, books, and journal articles that span a variety of global and regional research areas. Additionally, it maintains high-quality data standards through an independent Content Selection and Advisory Board that enforces a strict content selection and re-evaluation process.

Unlike traditional literature reviews, the LRSB (Systematic Bibliometric Literature Review) method takes an exhaustive approach to scrutinizing published works on the research topic, as noted by Rosário and Dias (2023a, 2023b, 2023c). This technique aims to narrow down the scope of articles to the most pertinent ones. Additionally, it provides a clear audit trail that allows readers to assess the methodologies, outcomes, and overall quality of the studies compiled.

The LRSB method involves a meticulous process of screening and selecting sources to guarantee the reliability and relevance of the data presented. This process is structured into a three-phase, six-step procedure, as outlined in Table 1, according to Rosário and Dias (2023a, 2023b, 2023c).

Table 1. Process of systematic LRSB

Phase	Step	Description
Exploration	Step 1	Formulating the research problem
	Step 2	Searching for appropriate literature
	Step 3	Critical appraisal of the selected studies
	Step 4	Data synthesis from individual sources
Interpretation	Step 5	Reporting findings and recommendations
Communication	Step 6	Presentation of the LRSB report

Source: Adapted from Rosário and Dias (2023a, 2023b, 2023c).

It is crucial to underscore that this study had constraints as it solely concentrated on the Scopus database while overlooking other scholarly and scientific databases. When conducting literature searches up to Abril 2024, it is imperative to consider peer-reviewed scientific and academic publications.

A systematic search on the Scopus electronic database was conducted using the keywords "relationship marketing" in combination with "artificial intelligence" and "AI." This search resulted in 48 document results. Duplicates were removed, and the search results were limited to the subject area Business, Management and Accounting (BUSI). This reduced the search results to 37 sources, which were then screened based on inclusion and exclusion criteria. Only publications relevant to the intersection of AI and relationship marketing were included in the research. In addition, the journal articles that were included had to be peer-reviewed to ensure academic rigor and reliability of the findings. Articles were also included if they provided empirical evidence, theoretical frameworks, case studies, or conceptual analyses related to the application of AI in relationship marketing. Other than peer-reviewed journal articles, books, book chapters, conference papers, and reports related to the research topic were included. Finally, only sources published in English were included in the study. These filters reduced the number of final studies synthesized in the literature review section to 22 (Figure 1).

Figure 1. PRISMA flow diagram for the systematic literature search

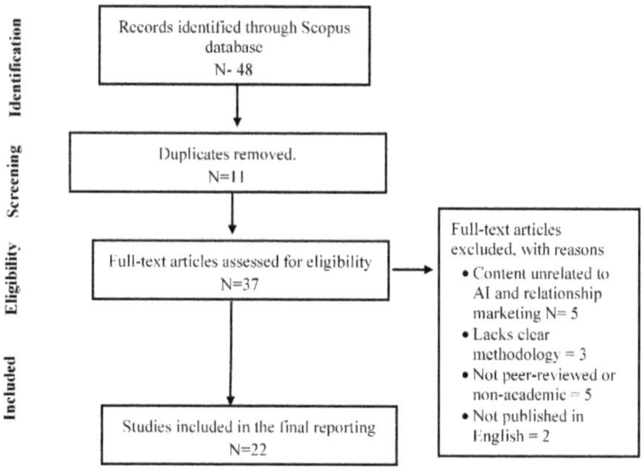

(Adapted from Mohar et al., 2009)

We employed content and thematic analysis methods to identify, examine, and present a range of documents, as specified by Rosário and Dias (2023a, 2023b, 2023c).

Subsequently, the 22 scientific and academic documents, indexed in Scopus, were subject to both narrative and bibliometric analyses to delve into their content and potentially reveal recurring themes that directly addressed the research questions, under the guidelines provided by Rosário and Dias (2023a, 2023b, 2023c).

Of the 22 selected documents, 12 are articles; 5 are books; 4 are Conference papers; and 1 are book series.

3. PUBLICATION DISTRIBUTION

Figure 2 summarizes the peer-reviewed literature published until March 2024, where the year 2022 is highlighted with 5 peer-reviewed publications on the subject.

Figure 2. Number of documents by year

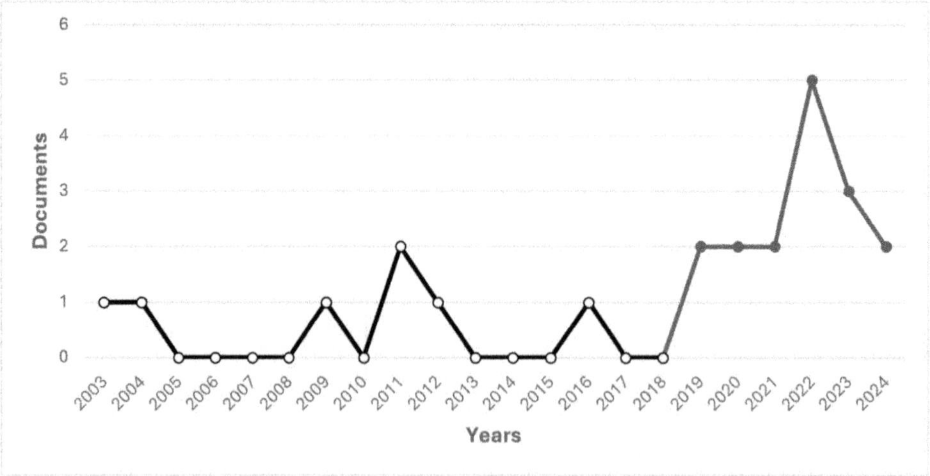

(Authors)

Table 2 identifies the 10 leading countries with significant scientific contributions in researched areas, with a special emphasis on China with 11 publications., India and USA with 10 publications each. On the other hand, Figure 3 presents the scientific production by country.

Table 2. Top 10 countries by number of publications

Country	Number of Publications
China	11
India	10
USA	10
Portugal	9
UK	7
Belgium	5
Australia	3
Spain	3
United Arab Emirates	2
Brazil	1

Source: Authors.

Figure 3. Scientific production by country

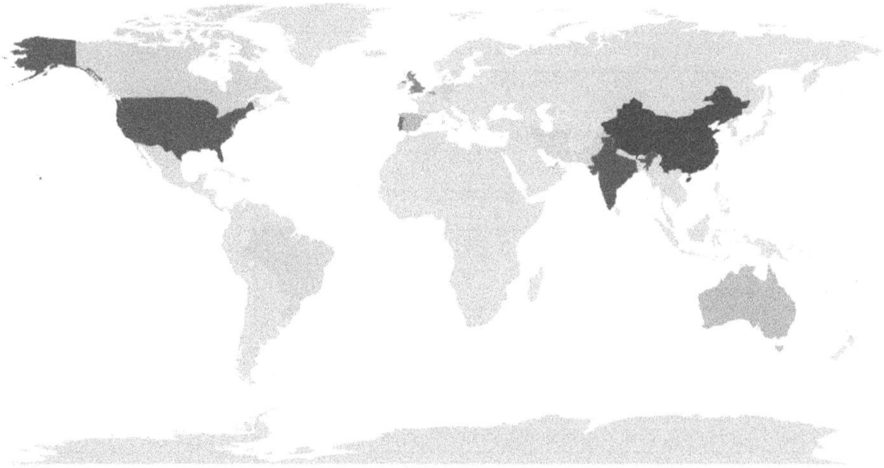

(Authors)

In Table 3 we analyze the Scimago Journal & Country Rank (SJR), the best quartile and the H index. There is a total of 8 publications in Q1, 3 publications in Q2, and without publications in Q3 and Q4.

Publications from the best quartile Q1 represent 38% of the titles of the 21 publications; the best quartile Q2 represents 14%. Finally, 6 publications (29%) do not have any type of indexation (SJR, Best Quartile, H index, and 3 publications (14%) only have the H index.

Table 3. Scimago journal & country rank impact factor

Title	**SJR**	**Best Quartile**	**H index**
2011 2nd International Conference on Artificial Intelligence Management Science and Electronic Commerce AIMSEC 2011 Proceedings	*	*	14
Use of Artificial Intelligence in Digital Marketing Competitive Strategies and Tactics	*	*	*
Springer Proceedings in Business and Economics	0.15	*	20
Sage Open	0.51	Q1	60
Proceedings of the 2012 International Conference on Artificial Intelligence ICAI 2012	*	*	8
Kybernetes	0.57	Q1	53
Journal of the Academy of Marketing Science	7.19	Q1	207

continued on following page

Table 3. Continued

Title	SJR	Best Quartile	H index
Journal of Services Marketing	1.21	Q1	124
Journal of Relationship Marketing	0.93	Q2	34
Journal of Product and Brand Management	1.69	Q1	104
Journal of Database Marketing and Customer Strategy Management	*	*	19
Journal of Business Research	3.13	Q1	265
International Journal of Emerging Markets	0.62	Q2	41
Hospitality Marketing Principles and Practices	*	*	*
Frontiers in Environmental Science	0.72	Q2	77
European Journal of Operational Research	2.32	Q1	305
Developments in Marketing Science Proceedings of the Academy of Marketing Science	*	*	*
Customer Relationship Management Concepts and Technologies Fourth Edition	*	*	*
California Management Review	3.33	Q1	155
Artificial Intelligence for Business Innovation Tools and Practices	*	*	*
Artificial Intelligence Concepts Methodologies Tools and Applications	*	*	*

Note: *data not available.
Source: Authors.

The subject areas covered by the 22 scientific and/or academic documents were: Business, Management and Accounting (16); Economics, Econometrics and Finance (8); Computer Science (7); Mathematics (2); Social Sciences (1); Environmental Science (1); Engineering (1); Decision Sciences (1); and Arts and Humanities (1).

In Figure 4 we can analyze the evolution of citations of the documents published until 2024. The number of citations shows a positive net growth with R^2 of 57% for the period 2010-2024, with 2023 reaching 157 citations. The h-index measured author output and influence, reflecting the count of papers that received equal or more citations. The h-index calculated for the set of documents analyzed is 9, which means that of the 22 documents considered for the h-index, 9 have been cited at least 9 times.

Figure 4. Evolution of citations between 2010 and 2024

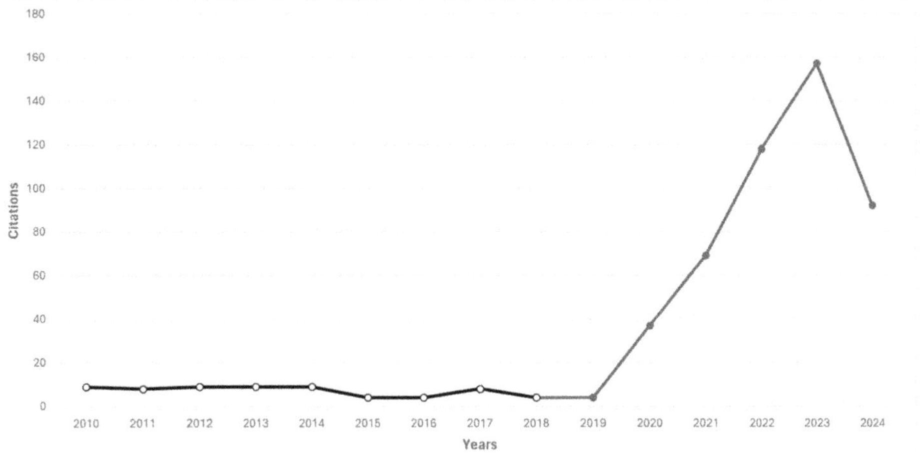

(Authors)

The most quoted article was "Online relationship marketing" by Steinhoff et al. (2019) with 209 quotes published in the Journal of the Academy of Marketing Science. In this study the authors propose an evolving theory of online relationship marketing, characterizing online relationships as uniquely seamless, networked, omnichannel, personalized, and anthropomorphized.

To gain deeper insights into the themes captured within the documents analyzed in this research, a bibliometric analysis was conducted, using the scientific software VOSViewer™ (https://www.vosviewer.com; van Eck & Waltman, 2010), a software tool specifically designed for constructing and visualizing bibliometric maps.

This investigation explored the progression of scientific knowledge based on key terms and the social framework within the studied scientific domain, as depicted in Figure 5.

Figure 5. Keyword co-occurrence network

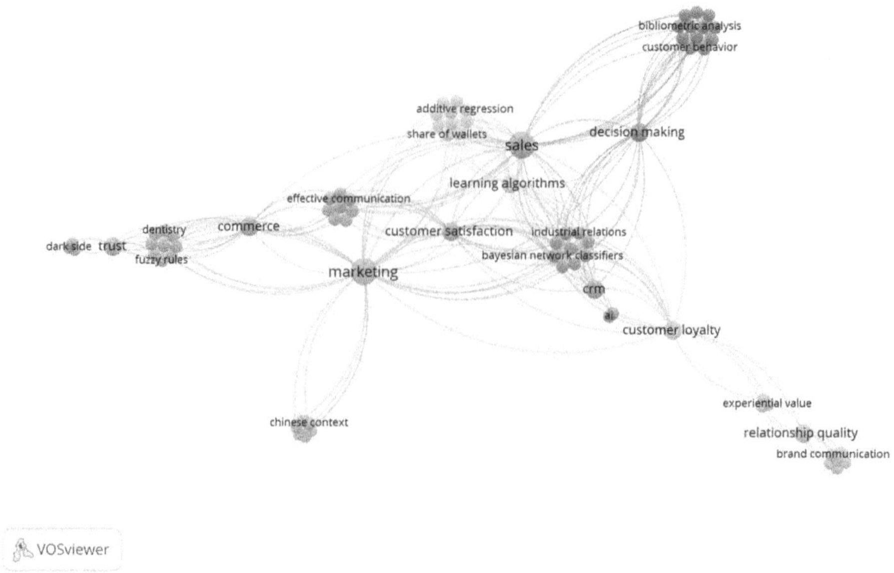

(Authors)

The research analyzed scientific and academic documents investigating how artificial intelligence can leverage relationship marketing strategies. Figure 6 presents the temporal evolution of the topics covered in the publications under analysis in this investigation. The most preferred keywords in the most recent years (2022 +) are customer behavior, experiential value, relationship quality, and brand communication. This analysis aids in identifying the subjects explored by researchers and predicting future opportunities for research. Additionally, Figure 7 illustrates a detailed map of co-citations, based on the analysis of references cited across these documents.

Figure 6. Temporal overlay on a keyword co-occurrence map

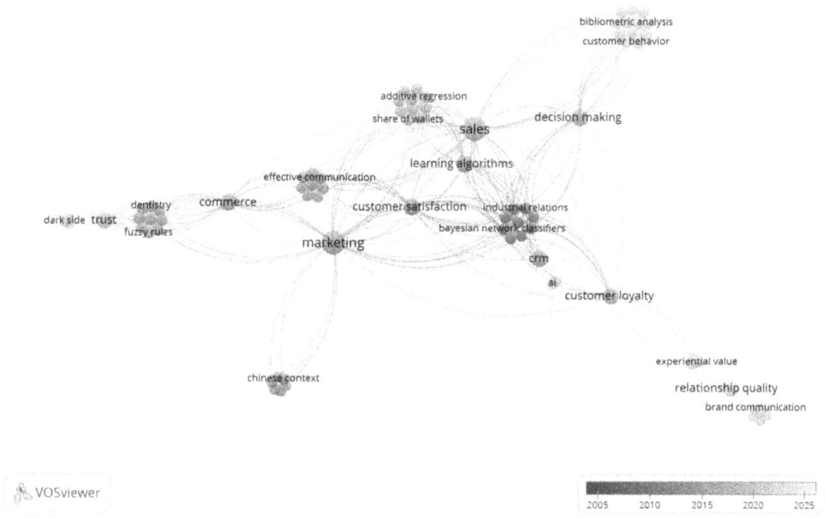

(Authors)

Figure 7. Network of co-citations

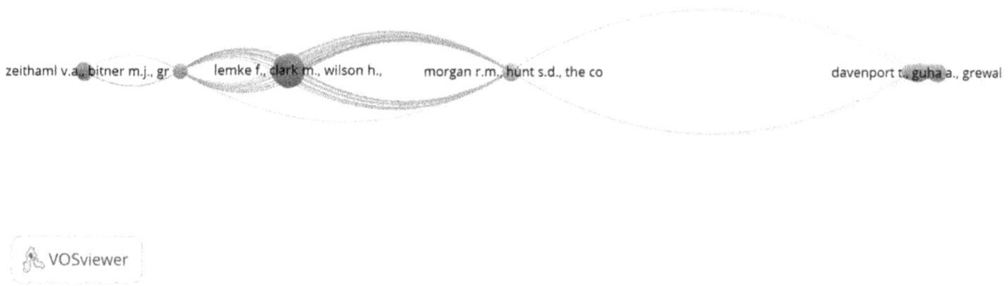

(Authors)

4. THEORETICAL PERSPECTIVES

AI is a transformative innovation used in contemporary marketing. Its application has significantly changed how businesses cultivate and nurture relationships with their customers. Therefore, leveraging AI within relationship marketing strategies creates multiple opportunities to enhance customer engagement, satisfaction, and loyalty. For instance, AI improves personalization by enabling marketers to analyze vast amounts of customer data used to tailor marketing messages, recommendations, and experiences to individual preferences and behaviors (Schrotenboer, 2019). In addition, advanced AI algorithms and machine learning can distinguish complex patterns and nuances in consumer interactions. This allows marketers to deliver highly relevant and timely content. This personalized approach fosters stronger emotional connections between brands and consumers and increases the likelihood of conversions and repeat purchases (Figueiredo et al., 2023). In addition, AI-powered chatbots and virtual assistants can be used to provide support, address customer inquiries, resolve issues, and offer personalized assistance in real time. This section synthesizes data on the various opportunities related to integrating AI into relationship market.

4.1. Artificial Intelligence (AI)

Artificial intelligence (AI) has emerged as a significant disruptive innovation with the potential to change people's lives and how companies operate and perform. This concept dates to 1956 when John McCarthy proposed the term "artificial intelligence" at a conference at Dartmouth University. Over the years, AI has become a critical element of organizational competitiveness, with companies like Microsoft, Google, Meta, and IBM investing large amounts in AI research and development. Zhang and Lu (2021) describe AI as the training of computers to simulate human intelligent behaviors such as learning, decision-making, and judging. AI systems are designed to analyze large datasets, identify patterns, make decisions, and adapt to changing environments (Chaturvedi et al., 2024). They can integrate machine learning, cognition, human-computer interaction, emotion recognition, decision-making, and data storage. As a result, AI is considered a multidisciplinary innovation that combines knowledge from various fields, including computer science, mathematics, psychology, biology, philosophy, and logic, among others.

There are various enabling technologies and key drivers of AI. Zhang and Lu (2021) identify six of them, including:

a) Big Data

Big data refers to extremely large and complex datasets that cannot be effectively processed using traditional data processing applications. This includes structured, unstructured, and semi-structured data from various sources such as social media, sensors, transaction records, and more. Big data enables AI systems to analyze vast amounts of information to uncover patterns, trends, and insights that can inform decision-making and problem-solving and improve performance.

b) Algorithms

Algorithms are step-by-step procedures or instructions designed to perform specific tasks or solve particular problems. Zhang and Lu (2021) explain that algorithms are used to help AI systems process data, learn from it, and make decisions. Different types of algorithms are used in AI, such as classification algorithms, clustering algorithms, regression algorithms, and optimization algorithms. Each of the algorithms is used to complete different tasks and objectives.

c) Machine Learning

Machine learning is a subset of AI that involves training algorithms to learn patterns and make predictions from data without being explicitly programmed. Machine learning algorithms iteratively learn from data, identify patterns, and adjust their models accordingly to improve performance over time. According to Zhang and Lu (2021, p.4), machine learning solves four main types of problems, including clustering, prediction, classification, and reducing dimensionality. As a result, it uses four main learning methods: supervised, unsupervised, semi-supervised, and reinforcement learning. Supervised learning involves using labeled data to train the systems to predict the value or type of new data. Unsupervised learning uses no labels and is reflected in clustering. Semi-supervised combines supervised and unsupervised techniques in the learning process. In reinforcement learning, systems learn to make decisions by interacting with an environment, receiving feedback in the form of rewards or penalties, and adjusting their actions.

d) National language processing (NLP)

Natural language processing (NLP) in AI focuses on enabling computers to understand, interpret, and generate human language. Zhang and Lu (2021, p.3) define NLP as "the ability of computers to recognize and understand human text language, which is an interdisciplinary subject between computer science and human linguistics." NLP algorithms process and analyze large volumes of text data to extract meaning, identify sentiment, and enable communication between humans and machines. NLP is used in multiple applications, such as chatbots, language translation services, sentiment analysis tools, and speech recognition systems.

e) Computing Vision

Computer vision is a field of AI that enables machines to interpret and understand visual information from images or videos. It uses techniques such as deep learning and neural network structures to process and classify visual objects. Computer vision algorithms analyze pixels in images or video frames to detect objects, recognize patterns, and extract relevant information, including object features. They are applied in various fields and systems, including autonomous vehicles, facial recognition systems, medical imaging diagnostics, and industrial quality control.

f) Hardware

The development and deployment of AI systems require hardware. This key driver provides the computational power necessary for processing large datasets and executing complex algorithms. Specialized hardware accelerators, such as graphics processing units (GPUs) and tensor processing units (TPUs), are designed to optimize AI workloads, thereby improving performance and efficiency. The advancement of hardware technology and developments in processing power, memory capacity, and energy efficiency have significantly contributed to the progress in AI research and applications.

4.2. Relationship Marketing

Modern marketing is characterized by a shift from transactional to relational approaches. This shift is associated with various key changes and developments, such as the emergence of digital technologies that have empowered consumers with access to information (Cheng et al., 2023). These innovations enable them to research products, compare prices, and seek recommendations before making purchasing decisions. As a result, traditional mass marketing strategies are becoming less effective, prompting businesses to prioritize personalized, customer-centric approaches (Steinhoff et al., 2019). In addition, companies are recognizing the need for customer retention and loyalty due to the intensifying competition across industries. As a result, cultivating lasting relationships with customers to foster brand loyalty, increase lifetime value, and generate positive word-of-mouth referrals has become crucial (Lo, 2012). These perspectives have led to the rise and adoption of relationship marketing. This marketing approach has emerged as a strategic imperative for businesses seeking to adapt to these conditions and thrive in the competitive marketplace.

Relationship marketing involves establishing and maintaining mutually beneficial connections between a brand and its customers. Daskou and Mangina (2003) explain that relationship marketing involves identifying, establishing, maintaining, and improving a company's relationship with customers and other stakeholders through mutual exchange and fulfillment of promises. This marketing strategy focuses on fostering trust, loyalty, and emotional engagement over the long term. A successful relationship in marketing is characterized by open communication, transparency, and a genuine understanding of customer needs and preferences (Aka et al., 2016). It involves consistently delivering value beyond the initial purchase, such as personalized experiences, proactive support, and ongoing engagement initiatives. Therefore, relationship marketing encompasses the entire customer journey, from initial awareness and consideration to post-purchase support and advocacy (Daskou & Mangina, 2003). Ultimately, effective relationship marketing drives customer retention, repeat purchases, and positive brand advocacy, thereby contributing to sustained business success and growth.

4.2.1. AI in Marketing Framework

AI can be integrated into marketing to optimize strategies, analyze data, and automate tasks. The use of this innovation improves the efficiency and effectiveness of marketing efforts. For instance, Figueiredo et al. (2023) found that AI can be used to gain insights into consumer behavior, preferences, and trends, allowing for more targeted and personalized campaigns. In addition, marketers can use machine learning algorithms to predict consumer needs, segment audiences, and optimize content delivery in real time. Huang and Rust (2021) propose three AI intelligences for an AI marketing framework: mechanical AI, thinking AI, and feeling AI. These are used in various stages of marketing to optimize processes and systems, as shown in Table 4.

Table 4. Strategic framework for AI in marketing

AI intelligence Strategic decision	Mechanical AI	Thinking AI	Feeling AI
Marketing research	*Data collection*	*Market analysis*	*Customer understanding*
	Automate continuous market and customer data sensing, tracking, collecting, and processing	Use marketing analytics to identify competitors and competitive advantages	Use emotional data and customer analytics to understand existing and potential customer needs and wants
Marketing strategy (STP)	*Segmentation*	*Targeting*	*Positioning*
	Use mechanical AI to identify novel customer preference patterns	Use thinking AI to recommend the best target segments	Use feeling AI to develop positioning that resonates with customers
Marketing action (4Ps/4Cs)	*Standardization*	*Personalization*	*Relationalization*
Product/Consumer	Automate the process and output of meeting customer needs and wants	Personalize products based on customer preferences	Understand and meet customer emotional needs and wants
Price/Cost	Automate the process of price setting and payment	Personalize prices based on customer willingness to pay	Negotiate price and justify the cost interactively
Place/Convenience	Automate customer access to product	Personalize frontline interactions	Personalize experience for customer engagement
Promotion/Communication	Automate communication with customers	Customize promotional content for personal communication	Tailor communication based on customer emotional preferences and reactions

Source: Adapted from Huang and Rust (2021)

4.2.2. Mechanical AI

Mechanical AI in marketing research involves leveraging automation and physical systems to enhance data collection, segmentation, and marketing action across various stages of the marketing process. For example, marketers can leverage mechanical AI in market research to automate the continuous sensing, tracking, collecting, and processing of market and customer data (Huang & Rust, 2021). In the marketing action stage, it can be used to match product features to customer needs and wants through, for example, personalized product recommendations based on past behaviors and preferences. Mechanical AI can also be leveraged to automate the process of setting and adjusting prices based on factors such as demand and competition. These practices improve efficiency, effectiveness, and customer satisfaction.

4.2.3. Thinking AI

Thinking AI refers to AI systems capable of complex cognitive processes comparable to human thinking. They are used in marketing practices that involve intelligence in reasoning, planning, problem-solving, and decision-making. For instance, Huang and Rust (2021) recommend the use of thinking AI to conduct market analysis and identify competitors and a company's competitive advantages. Thinking AI could be applied in fields like expert systems, cognitive computing, and natural language understanding to tackle challenging problems and assist humans in decision-making tasks.

4.2.4. Feeling AI

Feeling AI refers to systems designed to recognize and respond to human emotions. For instance, Huang and Rust (2021) indicate that marketers can use feeling AI to understand what customers want and why they may prefer competitor products or services. These AI systems may include emotion recognition AI, which analyzes facial expressions, vocal intonations, and other physiological signals to infer emotional states and adapt responses accordingly. In addition, AI-driven virtual agents or chatbots may simulate empathy and emotional intelligence in interactions with users, enhancing the user experience. In addition, feeling AI can be leveraged to develop a brand positioning that resonates with customers and provides personalized experiences. Ultimately, this type of AI is concerned with creating and implementing marketing processes and approaches that connect the brand to its target customers.

4.3. Leveraging AI Opportunities in Relationship Marketing

Integrating AI in relationship marketing creates multiple opportunities for businesses and marketers to enhance their marketing efforts. For instance, they can leverage AI-powered big data and analytics tools to analyze customer data. This approach can help create personalized marketing messages aligned with consumer interests, needs, and behaviors.

4.3.1. Personalization

Since the mid-20th century, customers have continued to desire products and services that meet their requirements. This shift in consumer behaviors led to the rise of personalization in marketing. Chandra et al. (2022, p.1530) define personalization as “a way to acknowledge the uniqueness of each customer by satisfying them with products that are tailored according to their preference.” The scholars found that implementing personalization increased marketing efficiency by 10-30% within one channel and led to revenue growth by 5-15%. Personalization is a crucial aspect of relationship marketing that aims to tailor experiences, products, and communications to meet the unique needs and preferences of individual customers. Using personalization helps ensure that interactions with customers are relevant and individualized, thereby enhancing customer experiences. AI offers powerful capabilities to enhance personalization by analyzing large data volumes and delivering targeted and relevant experiences at scale (Echeberria, 2022). For instance, marketers can use AI algorithms to analyze customer behavior, purchase history, preferences and suggest products that are most likely to resonate with each individual. In addition, leveraging machine learning and predictive analytics can enable businesses to deliver personalized recommendations across various channels, including websites, emails, and mobile apps. This strategy can result in higher engagement and conversions.

AI-powered content personalization can enhance the relevance and effectiveness of marketing communications. Analyzing customer data and engagement patterns using AI can dynamically generate and deliver content that aligns with each customer's interests, preferences, and stage in the buying journey (Cheng et al., 2023). This personalized approach ensures that customers receive relevant information and offers, increasing the likelihood of conversion and satisfaction. In addition, marketers can use AI to personalize customer experience across various touchpoints. For example, Cheng and Jiang (2022) found that Gucci leverages personal messaging through chatbots to gather information on customer preferences, which is then used to design custom products. Ultimately, personalization improves customer experiences and satisfaction, thereby establishing long-term customer relationships.

4.3.2. Customer Journey Mapping

Customer journey mapping provides businesses with insights into the various touchpoints and interactions that customers have with the brand throughout their journey. Schrotenboer (2019) describes it as the whole customer experience from their pre-purchase activities to purchase and post-purchase. This makes it a crucial aspect of relationship marketing. Leveraging AI in customer journey mapping offers significant opportunities to enhance understanding, personalize experiences, and optimize strategies (Rana et al., 2022). For instance, marketers can use AI to analyze large data volumes from multiple sources, including website interactions, social media engagements, email communications, and purchase history, to create comprehensive and detailed customer journey maps. This practice can help identify common paths, pain points, and opportunities for engagement, thereby enabling marketers to gain a holistic view of the customer experience.

Marketers can use AI algorithms to segment customers based on their behavior, preferences, and characteristics. Schrotenboer (2019) explains the significance of segmentation in customer journey mapping, indicating that customer experience is usually based on opinions. It, therefore, varies from one individual customer to the other, making it important for marketers to understand customer behaviors and viewpoints. Segmentation allows them to create more targeted and personalized journey maps (Baesens et al., 2004). For example, AI can identify different customer personas and tailor journey maps to address their unique needs and preferences. In addition, AI can predict future behavior and anticipate customer needs at each stage of the journey, enabling marketers to proactively engage customers with relevant content, offers, and support (Lee & Peng, 2021). Businesses also use AI-powered customer journey mapping to facilitate real-time analysis and optimization. This helps them adapt their strategies quickly in response to changing customer behaviors and market dynamics. AI provides tools that allow marketers to monitor and analyze customer interactions continuously (Perez-Vega et al., 2020). As a result, they can identify patterns and trends in real-time, which are used to optimize touchpoints, refine messaging, and improve overall customer experiences. Therefore, AI presents a significant opportunity in customer journey mapping by enabling businesses to gain deeper insights, personalize experiences, and drive better outcomes in relationship marketing efforts.

4.3.3. Customer Relationship Management

Customer relationship management (CRM) is a fundamental aspect of relationship marketing. It focuses on building and maintaining long-term relationships with customers. AI presents numerous opportunities to enhance CRM processes and enables businesses to better understand, engage, and serve their customers (Buttle & Maklan, 2019). For instance, AI can be leveraged for data management and analysis. AI tools can efficiently process and analyze vast amounts of customer data from various sources, including transaction history, demographic information, social media interactions, and customer service inquiries (Cheng & Jiang, 2022). Businesses can utilize AI-powered analytics to gain valuable insights into customer preferences, behaviors, and sentiment. This knowledge can then be applied to provide more personalized and targeted interactions.

AI provides various technologies that businesses and marketers can leverage to improve their CRM. For instance, AI-driven predictive analytics can forecast customer behaviors and preferences. Marketers can utilize these tools to anticipate customer needs, identify upsell and cross-sell opportunities, and proactively address potential issues (Buttle & Maklan, 2019). In addition, AI-powered recommendation engines can deliver personalized product recommendations and content based on individual preferences and past interactions. As a result, this can enhance the relevance and effectiveness of relationship marketing strategies (Pinto et al., 2009). Another important technique is the AI-enabled sentiment analysis. Marketers can use this to automatically analyze customer feedback and social media conversations to assess customer satisfaction and identify areas for improvement (Dehdashti et al., 2012). Moreover, AI-powered automation can streamline CRM processes and workflows, enabling businesses to automate routine tasks such as data entry, lead scoring, and email marketing campaigns. Automating these tasks using AI tools allows businesses to allocate human resources to focus on more strategic initiatives and personalized interactions with high-value customers.

4.3.4. Fostering Brand Loyalty

Brand loyalty is a major desired outcome in relationship marketing. AI offers powerful tools and strategies to achieve this objective. For instance, marketers can use AI to provide personalized engagement. They can analyze customer data and use the insights to deliver tailored experiences that resonate with individual preferences and behaviors (Figueiredo et al., 2023). Leveraging machine learning algorithms allows them to predict customer needs and preferences, thereby resulting in customized offers, recommendations, and communications to each customer segment. Lee and Peng (2021) explain that this personalized approach fosters a sense of exclusivity and relevance and strengthens the emotional connection between customers and the brand. In addition, businesses can utilize AI-powered loyalty programs to enhance customer retention by rewarding and incentivizing repeat purchases and brand advocacy (Figueiredo et al., 2023). AI algorithms can analyze customer behavior and engagement patterns to identify high-value customers and offer targeted rewards and incentives that align with their preferences and interests. AI-driven recommendation engines can suggest relevant products and services to loyalty program members, increasing engagement and driving incremental sales.

AI in relationship marketing creates an opportunity to foster brand loyalty and improve overall customer experience by enhancing customer service and support processes and systems. For example, AI-powered chatbots and virtual assistants can provide instant customer support and assistance. According to Cheng and Jiang (2022), there are about 30000 chatbots in the US market, sending about two billion messages monthly. These AI-driven interactions are available 24/7, ensuring that customers receive timely and personalized assistance whenever they need it. In addition, AI chatbots and virtual assistants allow businesses to create and nurture deep relationships with consumers through ongoing and personalized dialogues instead of ending communication after purchases. In addition, AI can help businesses proactively identify and address potential issues or concerns before they escalate, further enhancing customer satisfaction and loyalty (Figueiredo et al., 2023). The exceptional customer service experiences delivered through these AI technologies enable businesses to build trust and loyalty, turning satisfied customers into brand advocates. Finally, AI can identify patterns and trends by analyzing customer feedback, sentiment, and interactions across various channels. This enables businesses to take corrective actions and continuously improve the overall customer experience.

4.3.5. Building Experiential Value

Experiential marketing is an approach that seeks to immerse consumers in memorable and engaging brand experiences. According to Lee and Peng (2021), it transcends traditional advertising by fostering direct interaction and emotional connection with consumers. Therefore, experiential marketing revolves around creating events, activations, or campaigns that resonate with consumers on a deeper level, eliciting positive emotions and lasting impressions (Rathi & Ravi, 2016). For instance, marketers can incorporate experiential elements such as sensory stimulation, interactivity, and storytelling into their relationship marketing strategies to forge strong emotional bonds with consumers. This can lead to increased brand loyalty and advocacy. Experiential value is created when marketers deliver meaningful experiences that enrich consumers' lives beyond mere product features or benefits (Lee & Peng, 2021). It encompasses the emotional, social, and psychological benefits derived from engaging with a brand and contributes to a sense of fulfillment, identity, and connection. Prioritizing and creating immersive experiences that align with consumers' values, aspirations, and lifestyles enables brands to enhance experiential value and differentiate themselves in the marketplace.

AI offers several opportunities to enhance experiential value by delivering personalized, immersive, and interactive experiences. For instance, marketers can use AI algorithms to analyze customer data and generate tailored content that resonates with customer preferences and interests (Lee & Peng, 2021). In addition, leveraging machine learning and natural language processing can help create personalized recommendations, product suggestions, and marketing messages that capture the attention and interest of each customer segment. Similarly, predictive analytics allow brands to tailor experiential marketing initiatives to individual consumers by delivering content, interactions and offers that resonate with their unique needs and interests (Rathi & Ravi, 2016). Other innovations, such as AI-powered virtual reality (VR) and augmented reality (AR), can be used to create immersive and interactive experiences that engage customers in new and exciting ways. They simulate real-world environments or overlay digital elements onto physical spaces, thereby offering immersive product demonstrations, virtual tours, or interactive games that appeal to customers. These immersive experiences help differentiate the brand, leave a lasting impression, and strengthen the emotional connection between customers and the brand

4.3.6. Customer Satisfaction and Retention

Customer satisfaction and retention are the primary goals of relationship marketing. This marketing strategy is concerned with building and maintaining relationships with customers at every point of interaction. It acknowledges the significance of engaged customers in achieving long-term organizational growth and profitability. Therefore, relationship marketing aims to provide mutual benefits and quality services and products that result in high customer satisfaction and retention (Singh et al., 2023). AI offers powerful tools and strategies to enhance these metrics. For instance, machine learning algorithms enable businesses to predict customer needs and behaviors (Grewal et al., 2021). These insights enable them to personalize product recommendations, offers, and communications to customers throughout the touchpoints. This personalized approach fosters a sense of connection and relevance, enhancing overall satisfaction and loyalty. Moreover, AI-powered customer service and support drive satisfaction and retention. For example, Cheng and Jiang (2022) found that 56% of Americans prefer messaging over calling customer support. In addition, the study found that 53% of customers prefer working with companies offering messaging services. Brands can leverage this opportunity by using AI-driven chatbots and virtual assistants to communicate with customers and address their concerns. In addition, AI can analyze customer feedback and sentiment to identify areas for improvement and proactively address potential issues, further enhancing satisfaction and loyalty.

AI-powered relationship marketing strategies can lead to customer retention and lifetime value. For instance, loyalty programs based on AI can incentivize repeat purchases and brand advocacy. Aka et al. (2016) indicate that satisfied customers often become brand advocates, promoting a brand to their families, friends, and social networks. Marketers can use AI to analyze customer behavior and engagement patterns and identify high-value customers. This strategy is essential in offering targeted rewards and incentives that align with customers' preferences and interests. Lo (2012) explains that customer satisfaction and retention in relationship marketing can be achieved in various ways, including showing commitment to customers, ensuring regular communication, providing custom services and products, and showing gratitude. AI can be integrated into all these strategies to achieve desired outcomes. For instance, AI can be used to analyze market trends, competitor pricing, and customer preferences (Grewal et al., 2021). The insights gained from these practices can help determine optimal pricing strategies and personalized promotions that resonate with target audiences, thereby maximizing customer satisfaction and retention. These data-driven approaches ensure that customers perceive value in their purchases, leading to repeat business.

4.3.7. Real-Time Customer Interaction and Engagement

Real-time customer interaction and engagement are crucial components of relationship marketing that aim to provide timely and personalized customer experiences. Marketers and businesses can leverage AI tools and strategies to analyze data, predict customer behavior, and deliver relevant messages and offers at the moment. This approach can enhance real-time interaction and engagement. For example, they can use smart voice assistants to provide instant assistance and support to customers in real time. Hernández-Ortega et al. (2022) explain that these smart innovations integrate data and technology to anticipate customer needs and provide necessary support based on changing customer conditions and feedback. As a result, AI-driven smart voice assistants allow 24/7 interactions, thereby ensuring that customers receive timely and personalized support whenever they need it. The use of these technologies leads to improved customer satisfaction and loyalty. Moreover, AI-driven personalization can enable real-time engagement by analyzing customer data and behavior to deliver targeted messages and offers at the right time and place (Daskou & Mangina, 2003). Marketing professionals can achieve this by leveraging machine learning and predictive analytics, which can identify opportune moments to engage customers with relevant content, promotions, and recommendations. This practice increases the likelihood of conversion and satisfaction. Finally, AI-powered recommendation engines can dynamically generate and deliver personalized product recommendations in real time, driving engagement and sales.

AI can facilitate real-time engagement through social media monitoring and sentiment analysis. For instance, businesses can use AI tools to analyze social media conversations and interactions in real time. This can help them identify opportunities to engage with customers, address concerns, and capitalize on positive feedback (Grewal et al., 2021). In addition, AI algorithms can automatically analyze sentiment and trends, enabling businesses to respond promptly to customer inquiries, comments, and reviews. This immediate response can enhance brand perception and loyalty. Marketers can leverage AI to optimize real-time engagement through A/B testing and optimization algorithms (Perez-Vega et al., 2020). In this regard, continuously monitoring and analyzing customer interactions and responses can empower businesses to experiment with different messaging, offers, and strategies. As a result, they can identify what resonates most with their audience and scale (Pinto et al., 2009). AI algorithms can then adjust content and tactics in real time to maximize engagement and conversion rates, ensuring that customers receive the most relevant and compelling experiences.

4.3.8 Ethical Considerations and Challenges of Integrating AI into Relationship Marketing

AI technologies primarily rely on collecting and analyzing customer data to facilitate data-driven strategizing and decision-making. This raises numerous concerns, such as customer data safety and privacy issues. In addition, the use of AI requires companies to increasingly rely on data technologies for various marketing practices and operations. This results in issues such as increased risk for cybersecurity threats. This section explains these challenges and their potential impacts on relationship marketing.

a) Customer Data Safety and Privacy Concerns

The use of AI in relationship marketing involves collecting, storing, and processing vast amounts of personal data, including sensitive information such as demographics, purchase history, and behavioral patterns. According to Hicham et al. (2023), this results in increased data safety and privacy concerns among customers. As a result, they become apprehensive about sharing personal information and reluctant to participate in personalized relationship marketing efforts. In addition, the increased risk of data leaks and breaches can lead to reputational damage for brands, eroding customer loyalty and trust and damaging relationships.

b) Building Experiential Value

Experiential marketing is an approach that seeks to immerse consumers in memorable and engaging brand experiences. According to Lee and Peng (2021), it transcends traditional advertising by fostering direct interaction and emotional connection with consumers. Therefore, experiential marketing revolves around creating events, activations, or campaigns that resonate with consumers on a deeper level, eliciting positive emotions and lasting impressions (Rathi & Ravi, 2016). For instance, marketers can incorporate experiential elements such as sensory stimulation, interactivity, and storytelling into their relationship marketing strategies to forge strong emotional bonds with consumers. This can lead to increased brand loyalty and advocacy. Experiential value is created when marketers deliver meaningful experiences that enrich consumers' lives beyond mere product features or benefits (Lee & Peng, 2021). It encompasses the emotional, social, and psychological benefits derived from engaging with a brand and contributes to a sense of fulfillment, identity, and connection. Prioritizing and creating immersive experiences that align with consumers' values, aspirations, and lifestyles enables brands to enhance experiential value and differentiate themselves in the marketplace.

AI offers several opportunities to enhance experiential value by delivering personalized, immersive, and interactive experiences. For instance, marketers can use AI algorithms to analyze customer data and generate tailored content that resonates with customer preferences and interests (Lee & Peng, 2021). In addition, leveraging machine learning and natural language processing can help create personalized recommendations, product suggestions, and marketing messages that capture the attention and interest of each customer segment. Similarly, predictive analytics allow brands to tailor experiential marketing initiatives to individual consumers by delivering content, interactions and offers that resonate with their unique needs and interests (Rathi & Ravi, 2016). Other innovations, such as AI-powered virtual reality (VR) and augmented reality (AR), can be used to create immersive and interactive experiences that engage customers in new and exciting ways. They simulate real-world environments or overlay digital elements onto physical spaces, thereby offering immersive product demonstrations, virtual tours, or interactive games that appeal to customers. These immersive experiences help differentiate the brand, leave a lasting impression, and strengthen the emotional connection between customers and the brand.

c) Cost and Complexity

Implementing and maintaining AI technologies in relationship marketing requires huge investments to acquire the technologies, hire specialized talent, and train employees. In addition, AI technologies require continuous maintenance and optimization, which needs further investments (Hicham et al., 2023). These costs limit small businesses' access to AI-driven marketing capabilities due to limited resources, thus creating a competitive disadvantage compared to larger organizations. In addition, the complexity of AI systems, including data integration, algorithm development, and infrastructure setup, adds further challenges. This problem leads to implementation challenges and delays, hindering the timely execution of relationship marketing initiatives and impacting their overall effectiveness.

d) Hardware Limitations

Businesses require robust computing infrastructure to support AI applications in relationship marketing. For instance, AI algorithms require significant computational power and storage capacity to process large volumes of data and perform complex computations (Hicham et al., 2023). Besides, the rapid advancements in AI technology require businesses to upgrade their hardware regularly to keep pace with evolving requirements. Failure to meet these hardware infrastructure requirements can lead to negative consequences such as poor performance and slow processing speeds for AI applications. As a result, businesses may struggle with delays in data analysis and decision-making. Consequently, these challenges can hinder the effectiveness of marketing campaigns and reduce the quality of customer interactions.

e) Data Bias

The challenge of data bias arises from the use of biased datasets to train AI algorithms in relationship marketing. These biases may originate from historical inequities, human judgment, or systemic inequalities reflected in the data. They can have significant impacts on relationship marketing. For instance, biased algorithms may lead to inaccurate or unfair outcomes, resulting in suboptimal targeting, recommendations, or personalization for certain demographic groups. This can alienate customers, damage brand reputation, and ruin customer trust in marketing initiatives. In addition, Hicham et al. (2023) explain that data bias may perpetuate existing inequalities and stereotypes, such as reinforcing discriminatory practices. As a result, the biases may hinder efforts to foster inclusive and diverse relationships with customers. Finally, regulatory bodies and consumer advocacy groups are increasingly scrutinizing AI algorithms for potential biases. This raises legal and ethical concerns for businesses.

5. CONCLUSION

Increased competition and consumer demand for personalized marketing messages and content have led to the increased adoption of relationship marketing. This marketing strategy focuses on building long-term and mutually beneficial relationships with target customers. Recent technological advancements, including AI, have made it possible for businesses to leverage advanced tools and techniques to deliver personalized services and products. For instance, businesses can use AI innovations such as big data and analytics to analyze market and customer data. This practice allows them to gain insights into consumer behaviors, interests, and preferences, which can then be used to create and implement personalized marketing strategies. Other AI technologies that have proved important in marketing include algorithms, machine learning, natural language processing (NLP) systems, computing vision, and hardware. These technologies allow the collection, analysis, and storage of data that can be implemented in marketing to improve efficiency and performance. Marketing professionals and businesses can integrate these innovations into their marketing processes and systems to ensure that their marketing efforts are customer-centric.

The integration of AI into relationship marketing creates numerous opportunities. These include the ability to provide personalized interactions, services, and products, improved customer journey mapping, and customer relationship management. Marketers can use AI to monitor customer interactions and engagement across various touchpoints. This can help understand their journey, interests, and behaviors to ensure targeted marketing efforts. Other opportunities include the ability to foster brand loyalty, create experiential value, enhance customer satisfaction and retention, and provide real-time customer engagement. AI provides tools and techniques that enable businesses to collect immediate customer feedback and address their complaints and concerns in real-time. This proactive approach enhances customer satisfaction and overall experiences with the brand, thereby resulting in higher conversion rates and retention. As a result, AI in relationship marketing is associated with numerous benefits, such as long-term and sustainable business growth, increased profitability, and improved customer relationship management. These benefits increase an organization's competitiveness and performance in the market. However, for businesses to optimize these opportunities and leap the benefits of AI relationship marketing, they must address various challenges and ethical concerns. These include privacy and safety concerns, access to resources, hardware limitations, and data bias. These issues can potentially damage a company's reputation and damage its relationship with customers. Therefore, it is essential to have appropriate, robust measures in place.

Artificial Intelligence can significantly leverage relationship marketing strategies, offering both theoretical and practical implications: (i) AI can analyze vast amounts of customer data, providing deep insights into consumer behavior, preferences, and needs. This understanding enables businesses to tailor their marketing efforts more effectively, fostering stronger relationships with customers; (ii) By utilizing AI-powered algorithms, businesses can deliver personalized messages and recommendations to individual customers. This personalized communication enhances engagement and fosters a sense of connection between the customer and the brand; (iii) AI can predict future customer behavior based on historical data and ongoing interactions. This capability allows businesses to anticipate customer needs and proactively address them, thereby strengthening customer relationships and loyalty; (iv) AI-powered chatbots and virtual assistants enable businesses to engage with customers in real-time, providing instant support and assistance. These automated interactions enhance customer satisfaction and contribute to building long-term relationships; (v) AI can optimize the customer journey by identifying pain points and opportunities for improvement. By streamlining the customer experience, businesses can enhance satisfaction and loyalty, ultimately strengthening relationships with their customers; (vi) Resource Efficiency: AI automates repetitive tasks and processes, freeing up human resources to focus on high-value activities such as strategy development and creative innovation. This resource efficiency enables businesses to allocate their resources more effectively, ultimately enhancing the quality of their relationship marketing efforts; and (vii) As AI becomes more integral to relationship marketing, businesses must consider ethical implications, such as data privacy and algorithmic bias. Addressing these concerns is crucial for building and maintaining trust with customers, which is fundamental to successful relationship marketing strategies.

Overall, the integration of AI into relationship marketing strategies offers both theoretical insights into consumer behavior and practical tools for enhancing customer engagement, satisfaction, and loyalty. However, businesses need to approach AI implementation thoughtfully, considering both the opportunities and challenges it presents.

Future lines of research in how artificial intelligence can leverage relationship marketing strategies could explore several avenues: (i) Investigate the ethical implications of AI-driven relationship marketing, including issues of privacy, transparency, fairness, and accountability. Research could focus on developing frameworks and guidelines for ethical AI usage in marketing contexts; (ii) Explore advanced AI techniques for enhancing personalized marketing efforts, such as deep learning algorithms for analyzing unstructured data like images and videos to better understand customer preferences and sentiments; (iii) AI in Customer Feedback Analysis: Investigate the role of AI in analyzing and extracting insights from diverse sources of customer feedback, including social media, online reviews, and customer support interactions, to improve product/service quality and customer experience; and (iv) Develop methodologies for evaluating the effectiveness and impact of AI-driven relationship marketing strategies, including key performance indicators (KPIs), metrics, and benchmarks for assessing ROI and customer satisfaction.

These research directions can contribute to a deeper understanding of the opportunities and challenges associated with leveraging AI in relationship marketing, ultimately helping businesses develop more effective and ethical strategies for engaging with customers in the digital age.

ACKNOWLEDGMENT

We would like to express gratitude to the Editor and the Arbitrators. They offered extremely valuable suggestions for improvements. The first author receives financial support from the Research Unit on Governance, Competitiveness and Public Policies (UIDB/04058/2020) + (UIDP/04058/2020), funded by national funds through FCT-Fundação para a Ciência e a Tecnologia, and the second author receives financial support from UNIDCOM/IADE, Design and Communication Research Unit (UIDB/00711/2020) + (UIDP/00711/2020), funded by national funds through FCT-Fundação para a Ciência e a Tecnologia.

REFERENCES

Aka, D., Kehinde, O., & Ogunnaike, O. (2016). Relationship marketing and customer satisfaction: A conceptual perspective. *Binus Business Review*, 7(2), 185–190. DOI: 10.21512/bbr.v7i2.1502

Baesens, B., Verstraeten, G., Van den Poel, D., Egmont-Petersen, M., Van Kenhove, P., & Vanthienen, J. (2004). Bayesian network classifiers for identifying the slope of the customer lifecycle of long-life customers. *European Journal of Operational Research*, 156(2), 508–523. DOI: 10.1016/S0377-2217(03)00043-2

Buttle, F., & Maklan, S. (2019). *Customer relationship management: Concepts and technologies* (4th ed.). Taylor and Francis Inc., DOI: 10.4324/9781351016551

Chandra, S., Verma, S., Lim, W. M., Kumar, S., & Donthu, N. (2022). Personalization in personalized marketing: Trends and ways forward. *Psychology and Marketing*, 39(8), 1529–1562. DOI: 10.1002/mar.21670

Chaturvedi, R., Verma, S., & Srivastava, V. (2024). Empowering AI Companions for Enhanced Relationship Marketing. *California Management Review*, 66(2), 65–90. DOI: 10.1177/00081256231215838

Cheng, C. F., Huang, C. C., Lin, M. C., & Chen, T. C. (2023). Exploring Effectiveness of Relationship Marketing on Artificial Intelligence Adopting Intention. *SAGE Open*, 13(4), 21582440231222760. Advance online publication. DOI: 10.1177/21582440231222760

Cheng, Y., & Jiang, H. (2022). Customer–brand relationship in the era of artificial intelligence: Understanding the role of chatbot marketing efforts. *Journal of Product and Brand Management*, 31(2), 252–264. DOI: 10.1108/JPBM-05-2020-2907

Daskou, S., & Mangina, E. E. (2003). Artificial Intelligence in Managing Market Relationships: The Use of Intelligence Agents. *Journal of Relationship Marketing*, 2(1-2), 85–102. DOI: 10.1300/J366v02n01_06

Dehdashti, Y., Lotfi, N., & Karami, N. (2012). Analyzing factors effective on the development of relationship commitment. Proceedings of the *2012 International Conference on Artificial Intelligence*, ICAI 2012.

Durmaz, Y., Güvenç, H., & Kaymaz, S. (2020). The importance and benefits of relationship marketing concept. *European Journal of Business and Management Research*, 5(4). Advance online publication. DOI: 10.24018/ejbmr.2020.5.4.483

Echeberria, A. L. (2022). The Impact of AI on Business, Economics and Innovation. In *Artificial Intelligence for Business: Innovation, Tools and Practices* (pp. 67-96). Springer International Publishing. DOI: 10.1007/978-3-030-88241-9_3

Figueiredo, J., Oliveira, I., Silva, S., Pocinho, M., Cardoso, A., & Pereira, M. (2023). Artificial intelligence in relational marketing practice: CRM as a loyalty strategy. In *The Use of Artificial Intelligence in Digital Marketing: Competitive Strategies and Tactics* (pp. 73-96). IGI Global. DOI: 10.4018/978-1-6684-9324-3.ch003

Grewal, D., Guha, A., Satornino, C. B., & Schweiger, E. B. (2021). Artificial intelligence: The light and the darkness. *Journal of Business Research*, 136, 229–236. DOI: 10.1016/j.jbusres.2021.07.043

Hermann, E. (2022). Leveraging artificial intelligence in marketing for social good—An ethical perspective. *Journal of Business Ethics*, 179(1), 43–61. DOI: 10.1007/s10551-021-04843-y PMID: 34054170

Hernández-Ortega, B., Aldas-Manzano, J., & Ferreira, I. (2022). Relational cohesion between users and smart voice assistants. *Journal of Services Marketing*, 36(5), 725–740. DOI: 10.1108/JSM-07-2020-0286

Hicham, N., Nassera, H., & Karim, S. (2023). Strategic framework for leveraging artificial intelligence in future marketing decision-making. *Journal of Intelligent and Management Decision*, 2(3), 139–150. DOI: 10.56578/jimd020304

Hidayat, K., & Idrus, M. I. (2023). The effect of relationship marketing towards switching barrier, customer satisfaction, and customer trust on bank customers. *Journal of Innovation and Entrepreneurship*, 12(1), 29. DOI: 10.1186/s13731-023-00270-7 PMID: 37193581

Huang, M. H., & Rust, R. T. (2021). A strategic framework for artificial intelligence in marketing. *Journal of the Academy of Marketing Science*, 49(1), 30–50. DOI: 10.1007/s11747-020-00749-9

Itani, O. S., Kassar, A. N., & Loureiro, S. M. C. (2019). Value get, value give: The relationships among perceived value, relationship quality, customer engagement, and value consciousness. *International Journal of Hospitality Management*, 80, 78–90. DOI: 10.1016/j.ijhm.2019.01.014

Lee, T. C., & Peng, M. Y. P. (2021). Green experiential marketing, experiential value, relationship quality, and customer loyalty in environmental leisure farm. *Frontiers in Environmental Science*, 9, C7–C657523. DOI: 10.3389/fenvs.2021.657523

Lo, S. C. (2012). A study of relationship marketing on customer satisfaction. *Journal of Social Sciences (New York, N. Y.)*, 8(1), 91–94. DOI: 10.3844/jssp.2012.91.94

Moher, D., Liberati, A., Tetzlaff, J., & Altman, D. G.Prisma Group. (2009). Preferred reporting items for systematic reviews and meta-analyses: The PRISMA statement. *PLoS Medicine*, 6(7), e1000097. DOI: 10.1371/journal.pmed.1000097 PMID: 19621072

Perez-Vega, R., Hopkinson, P., Singhal, A., & Waite, K. (2020). Special session: relationship intelligence: affordance of AI in practice: an abstract. In *Developments in Marketing Science:Proceedings of the Academy of Marketing Science* (pp. 141-142). Springer Nature. DOI: 10.1007/978-3-030-42545-6_35

Pinto, F. M., Marques, A., & Santos, M. F. (2009). Ontology-supported database marketing. *Journal of Database Marketing and Customer Strategy Management*, 16(2), 76–91. DOI: 10.1057/dbm.2009.9

Rana, J., Gaur, L., Singh, G., Awan, U., & Rasheed, M. I. (2022). Reinforcing customer journey through artificial intelligence: A review and research agenda. *International Journal of Emerging Markets*, 17(7), 1738–1758. DOI: 10.1108/IJOEM-08-2021-1214

Rathi, T., & Ravi, V. (2016). Customer lifetime value measurement using machine learning techniques. In Artificial Intelligence: Concepts, Methodologies, Tools, and Applications (Vol. 4, pp. 3013-3022). IGI Global. DOI: 10.4018/978-1-5225-1759-7.ch124

Rosário, A. T., & Dias, J. C. (2023a). How has data-driven marketing evolved: Challenges and opportunities with emerging technologies. *International Journal of Information Management Data Insights*, 3(2), 100203. DOI: 10.1016/j.jjimei.2023.100203

Rosário, A. T., & Dias, J. C. (2023b). The New Digital Economy and Sustainability: Challenges and Opportunities. *Sustainability (Switzerland), 15(14 C7 -10902).* .DOI: 10.3390/su151410902

Rosário, A. T., & Dias, J. C. (2023c). Marketing Strategies on Social Media Platforms.International *Journal of e-Business Research, 19(1 C7 - 316969).* .DOI: 10.4018/IJEBR.316969

Salem, S. F. (2021). Do relationship marketing constructs enhance consumer retention? An empirical study within the hotel industry. *SAGE Open*, 11(2), 21582440211009224. DOI: 10.1177/21582440211009224

Schrotenboer, D. W. (2019). *The impact of artificial intelligence along the customer journey: a systematic literature review*. https://purl.utwente.nl/essays/78520

Singh, C., Dash, M. K., Sahu, R., & Kumar, A. (2023). Artificial intelligence in customer retention: A bibliometric analysis and future research framework. *Kybernetes*. Advance online publication. DOI: 10.1108/K-02-2023-0245

Steinhoff, L., Arli, D., Weaven, S., & Kozlenkova, I. V. (2019). Online relationship marketing. *Journal of the Academy of Marketing Science*, 47(3), 369–393. DOI: 10.1007/s11747-018-0621-6

Zhang, C., & Lu, Y. (2021). Study on artificial intelligence: The state of the art and future prospects. *Journal of Industrial Information Integration*, 23, 1–9. DOI: 10.1016/j.jii.2021.100224

ADDITIONAL READING

Alghamdi, O. A., & Agag, G. (2023). Boosting Innovation Performance through Big Data Analytics Powered by Artificial Intelligence Use: An Empirical Exploration of the Role of Strategic Agility and Market Turbulence. *Sustainability (Basel)*, 15(19), 14296. Advance online publication. DOI: 10.3390/su151914296

Chen, H. (2023). Enterprise Marketing Strategy Using Big Data Mining Technology Combined with XGBoost Model in the New Economic Era. *PLoS One*, 18(6), e0285506. DOI: 10.1371/journal.pone.0285506 PMID: 37276212

Chen, X. (2022). Design and Application of Marketing Intelligent Platform Based on Big Data Technology. *Scientific Programming*, 2022, 1–10. DOI: 10.1155/2022/8401395

Chintalapati, S., & Pandey, S. K. (2022). Artificial intelligence in marketing: A systematic literature review. *International Journal of Market Research*, 64(1), 38–68. DOI: 10.1177/14707853211018428

Frank, D.-A., Jacobsen, L. F., Søndergaard, H. A., & Otterbring, T. (2023). In companies we trust: Consumer adoption of artificial intelligence services and the role of trust in companies and AI autonomy. *Information Technology & People*, 36(8), 155–173. DOI: 10.1108/ITP-09-2022-0721

Giannakopoulos, N. T., Terzi, M. C., Sakas, D. P., Kanellos, N., Toudas, K. S., & Migkos, S. P. (2024). Agroeconomic Indexes and Big Data: Digital Marketing Analytics Implications for Enhanced Decision Making with Artificial Intelligence-Based Modeling. *Information (2078-2489), 15(2)*, 67. .DOI: 10.3390/info15020067

Hari Krishna, S., Sargunam, S. S., Kulkarni, N., Nandal, N., Vidya Chellam, V., & Praveenkumar, S. (2023). Application of Artificial Intelligence in E-Marketing. *023 International Conference on Artificial Intelligence and Knowledge Discovery in Concurrent Engineering (ICECONF), Artificial Intelligence and Knowledge Discovery in Concurrent Engineering (ICECONF),2023 International Conference On*, 1–7. DOI: 10.1109/ICECONF57129.2023.10084011

Ledro, C., Nosella, A., & Vinelli, A. (2022). Artificial intelligence in customer relationship management: Literature review and future research directions. *Journal of Business and Industrial Marketing*, 37(13), 48–63. DOI: 10.1108/JBIM-07-2021-0332

Mariciuc, D. F. (2022). Using Virtual Assistants as Relationship Marketing Instruments. *Ovidius University Annals. Series Economic Sciences*, 22(1), 634–641.

Peltier, J. W., Dahl, A. J., & Schibrowsky, J. A. (2024). Artificial intelligence in interactive marketing: A conceptual framework and research agenda. *Journal of Research in Interactive Marketing*, 18(1), 54–90. DOI: 10.1108/JRIM-01-2023-0030

Yang, X., Li, H., Ni, L., & Li, T. (2021). Application of Artificial Intelligence in Precision Marketing. *Journal of Organizational and End User Computing*, 33(4), 1–11. DOI: 10.4018/JOEUC.286767

KEY TERMS AND DEFINITIONS

Artificial Intelligence: It refers to the ethical principles and values held by either an individual or a group.

Augmented Reality: Overlays digital information or virtual elements onto the real world, typically viewed through a device like a smartphone or AR glasses, enhancing the user's perception of their surroundings.

Bias: Refers to a systematic tendency or inclination that influences judgment or decision-making in a particular direction.

Big Data: Refers to large volumes of structured and unstructured data that cannot be easily processed with traditional database tools.

Customer Relationship Management: Is a strategy used by businesses to manage interactions with current and potential customers. It involves utilizing technology to organize, automate, and synchronize sales, marketing, customer service, and technical support.

Key Performance Indicators: Are quantifiable measures used to evaluate the success or performance of an organization, team, project, or individual in achieving specific objectives or goals. They provide valuable insights into progress, effectiveness, and areas needing improvement.

Machine Learning: Involves the use of algorithms and statistical models to enable computers to learn from and make predictions or decisions based on data without being explicitly programmed.

Natural language Processing: A branch of artificial intelligence that enables computers to comprehend, generate, and manipulate human language.

ROI: Is a financial metric used to evaluate the profitability or efficiency of an investment relative to its cost.

Virtual Reality: Is a computer-generated simulation of an environment that can be interacted with in a seemingly real or physical way by a person using special electronic equipment, such as a headset.

Chapter 2
How AI Influences Marketing From the Consumer Perspective:
Literature Review

Francisca Gonçalves Azevedo
Instituto Português de Administração de Marketing, Portugal

Francisca Santos Santos Oliveira
Instituto Português de Administração de Marketing, Portugal

Katharina Thielen
Instituto Português de Administração de Marketing, Portugal

Irma Imamovic
Instituto Português de Administração de Marketing, Portugal

ABSTRACT

The systematic literature review investigates the impact of artificial intelligence (AI) on marketing, with a focus on client perspectives, using the PRISMA model. It examines how AI technology might improve customer service efficiency and increase the level of personalization in customer interactions while delving further into privacy and ethical problems. The report emphasizes how critical it is to strike a healthy balance between leveraging AI's benefits and preserving customer confidence. Moreover, it highlights customers' persistent desire for face-to-face contacts during service encounters, implying that in spite of technology breakthroughs, human connection and emotional intelligence are still essential. These revelations illustrate the intricate relationship that exists between technical progress and providing human- centered services, emphasizing the necessity for businesses to incorporate AI in ways that

DOI: 10.4018/979-8-3693-5340-0.ch002

enhance, rather than replace human interaction.

1. INTRODUCTION

In the ever-evolving landscape of today's world, artificial intelligence (AI) has witnessed significant growth and institutionalization (Liu et al., 2018).

The digital revolution has had a profound impact on society, changing most facets of people's lives and careers, including the dominating company, leisure, shopping preferences, and job trends (Makridakis, 2017).

AI technologies are changing how organizations interact with customers and provide value, from virtual assistants to predictive analytics. Therefore, consumers are becoming more discriminating and have higher expectations, it is critical to comprehend how they see AI's impact on marketing.

Modern marketing is becoming more automated, intelligent, and data-driven. Marketing results have been directly impacted by new-age marketing's laser-like focus and technological developments have led to long-term changes in the marketing industry's evolution and have demonstrated that marketing and AI can work together to drive significant change (Chintalapati & Pandey, 2021).

The exponential growth of AI-driven technologies allows marketeers to forecast customer behavior, evaluate huge volumes of data, and precisely craft campaigns. As a result, marketing and AI research are evolving together, creating a future where cutting-edge technology will completely change how consumers interact with brands and communicate with them.

As Ameen et al. (2021) noted, despite the extensive research on the technological capabilities and applications of AI in marketing, there is a notable gap in the literature regarding consumers' perspectives on these advances. Understanding how consumers perceive and respond to the use of AI in marketing campaigns is critical to the effective utilization of these technologies. Additionally, the personalization aspect of AI-enabled marketing remains underexplored, which underscores the need for more studies on how AI-driven personalization impacts consumer behavior and marketing outcomes (Gao & Liu, 2022). Further research is also critical to identify factors affecting the acceptance and effectiveness of AI in marketing (He & Zhang, 2022). By addressing this research gap, this study also aims to present the role AI can play in interactions and customer relationships.

The consumer's standpoint on the use of AI in marketing campaigns and interactions is significantly altering their experiences. Therefore, this study aims to understand the influence of AI in marketing from the consumer's perspective. To reach this goal, a systematic literature review was done considering three main topics:

Artificial Intelligence, Artificial Intelligence in Marketing, and how AI transforms customer experience.

By exploring the cutting edge of AI, this chapter reflects on how digital innovations are redefining relationship marketing, aligning harmoniously with the contemporary discussions proposed in this book on the strategic use of technology to enrich connections with customers. Despite the extensive research on AI and its applications in marketing, there is a notable gap in understanding how AI influences marketing from the consumers' perspective. Most existing studies focus on the technological advancements and business benefits of AI, often overlooking the nuanced experiences and perceptions of consumers themselves. Furthermore, while there is significant literature on AI's role in enhancing marketing efficiency and personalization, there is a scarcity of research that delves into the ethical implications, trust issues, and emotional responses consumers have toward AI-driven marketing strategies.

The present systematic literature review aims to fill this gap by comprehensively analyzing consumers' attitudes, expectations, and concerns regarding AI in marketing. It also offers valuable insights into how consumers perceive AI's impact on their purchasing decisions, privacy, and overall experience.

2. LITERATURE REVIEW

2.1. Methodology

This systematic literature review was carried out according to the Preferred Reporting Items for Systematic Reviews (PRISMA) guidelines (Wittorski, 2012). The primary research question guiding this review was: "How does AI influence marketing from the consumers' perspective?". To answer the research question and to choose the most appropriate articles, the literature search included multiple electronic databases and sources. The primary databases used were Scopus, due to its extensive coverage of peer-reviewed literature, Google Scholar, for its broad scope of scholarly works and ResearchGate, as it is a well-known academic networking site.

The search strategy employed Boolean operators and targeted keywords to ensure that a wide range of relevant studies is identified. Keywords included "artificial intelligence" AND "AI" AND "marketing" AND "consumer perception" AND "consumer behavior". The articles included in this study comply with the preformulated inclusion and exclusion criteria as presented in Table 1.

Table 1. Table of inclusion and exclusion criteria

Inclusion criteria	Exclusion criteria
IC1: Studies found using keywords "Artificial Intelligence in Marketing" and "Artificial Intelligence and Marketing" only in the title	EC1: Studies unrelated to AI or marketing.
IC2. "Artificial Intelligence" AND/OR" Marketing" only in the title	EC2: Non-English publications
IC3: Published after January 2018	EC3: Dissertations, conference papers and books
IC4: Only articles that can be found on Scimago Journal ranking (peer-reviewed)	EC4: Articles below the year 2018
IC5: Only articles written in the English language.	EC5: Articles not available in full-text or not accessible through reliable sources
	EC5: articles that are only available if we pay a fee

Source: Authors.

The search identified through database searches yielded a total number of 74 articles. Titles and abstracts were evaluated independently by two reviewers. Differences were resolved by conversation, and if required, a third reviewer was consulted. Afterwards, the full-text articles were assessed for eligibility against the inclusion and exclusion criteria as shown in Figure 1, the number was minimized to a total of 16 articles relevant to this systematic literature review.

Figure 1. PRISMA flow diagram

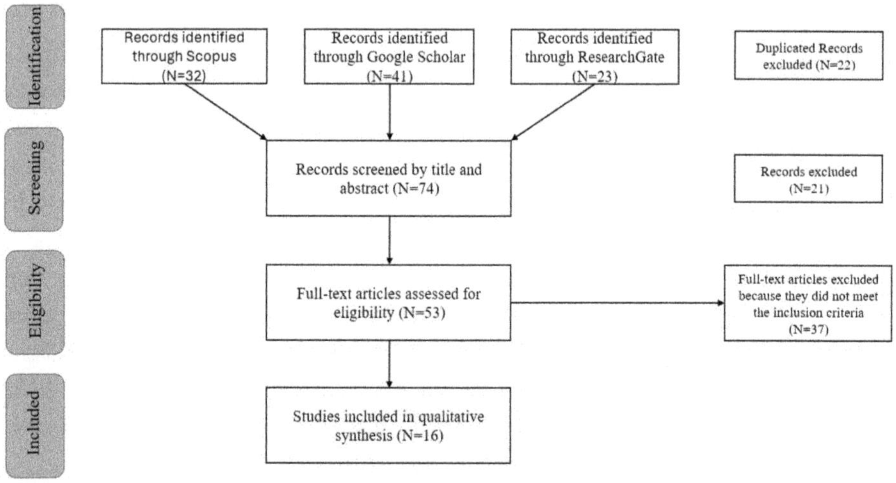

(Authors, in accordance with the PRISMA statement)

For a clear perception and to organize the articles used in this report, Table 2 was structured according to the following filters: Journal title, article title, author(s), year, H index, and Q.

Table 2. Search log

	Journal title	Article title	Author(s)	Year	H Index	Q
AI	Intelligent Systems Reference Library	Artificial Intelligence: State of the Art	Bhaskar Mondal	2020	35	Q4
	Journal of Mobile Multimedia	State-of-the-Art of Artificial Intelligence	Ramjee Prasad and Purva Choudhary	2021	13	Q3
	Journal of Industrial Information Integration	Study on artificial intelligence: The state of the art and future prospects	Caiming Zhang and Yang Lu	2021	49	Q1
	Artificial Intelligence Review	Applying the ethics of AI: a systematic review of tools for developing and assessing AI-based systems	Ricardo Ortega-Bolaños, Joshua Bernal Salcedo, Mariana Germán Ortiz, Julian Galeano Sarmiento, Gonzalo A. Ruz and Reinel Tabares-Soto	2024	115	Q1
	The Innovation	Artificial intelligence: A powerful paradigm for scientific research	Yongjun Xu, Xin Liu, Xin Cao, Changping Huang, Enke, Sen Qian, Xingchen Liu, Yanjun Wu, Fengliang Dong, Cheng-Wei Qiu, Junjun Qiu, Keqin Hua, Wentao Su, Jian Wu, Huiyu Xu, Yong Han, Chenguang Fu, Zhigang Yin, Miao Liu, Ronald Roepman, Sabine Dietmann, Marko Virta, Fredrick Kengara, Ze Zhang, Lifu Zhang, Taolan Zhao, Ji Dai, Jialiang Yang, Liang Lan, Ming Luo, Zhaofeng Liu, Tao An, Bin Zhang, Xiao He, Shan Cong, Xiaohong Liu, Wei Zhang, James P. Lewis, James M. Tiedje, Qi Wang, Zhulin An, Fei Wang, Libo Zhang, Tao Huang, Chuan Lu, Zhipeng Cai, Fang Wang and Jiabao Zhang	2021	41	Q1
AI in marketing	International Journal of Market Research	Artificial intelligence in marketing: A systematic literature review	Srikrishna Chintalapati and Shivendra Kumar Pandey	2021	61	Q2
	International Journal of Information Management Data Insights	Artificial intelligence in marketing: Systematic review and future research direction	Sanjeev Verma, Rohit Sharma, Subhamay Deb, Debojit Maitra	2021	20	Q1
	Journal of Business Research	The evolving role of artificial intelligence in marketing: A review and research agenda	Bozidar Vlacic, Leonardo Corbo, Susana Costa e Silvia and Mariana Dabic	2021	236	Q1
	Journal of the Academy of Marketing Science	A strategic framework for artificial intelligence in marketing	Ming-Hui Huang and Roland T. Rust	2020	207	Q1
	International Journal of Information Management	AI-powered marketing: What, where, and how?	V. Kumar, Abdul R. Ashraf, Waqar Nadeem	2024	177	Q1

continued on following page

Table 2. Continued

	Journal title	Article title	Author(s)	Year	H Index	Q
How AI transforms costumer experience	Computers in Human Behavior	Customer experiences in the age of artificial intelligence	Nisreen Ameen, Ali Tarhini, Alexander Reppel and Amitabh Anand	2021	226	Q1
	Journal of Marketing	Consumers and Artificial Intelligence: An Experiential Perspective	Stefano Puntoni, Rebecca Walker Reczek, Markus Giesler, and Simona Botti	2021	268	Q1
	Journal of Service Management	Customer experience Challenges: Bringing together digital, physical and social realms	R. Bolton	2018	17	Q4
	Journal of Retailing and Consumer Services	Engaging and retaining customers with AI and employee service	Catherine Prentice, PhD and Mai Nguyen	2020	120	Q1
	Journal Electrical Systems	Ai-Powered Customer Experience: Personalization, Engagement, and Intelligent Decision-Making in Crm	Tran Minh Tung and Duong Hoai Lan	2024	21	Q4
	Australasian Marketing Journal	Integrating Artificial Intelligence and Customer Experience	Ying Chen and Catherine Prentice	2024	54	Q1
	Turkish Journal of Computer and Mathematics Education	How Artificial Intelligence Transforms the Experience of Employees	Sobia Wassan, Dr. Kamal Gulati, Harikumar Pallathadka, Beenish Suhail, Preeti Kuhar and Ankur Gupta	2021	5	Q4

Source: Authors.

The sources reviewed for this study primarily consist of review articles and theoretical papers. These sources provide a comprehensive overview of the current state of knowledge on AI in marketing and identify gaps in the literature. Among these, one article employed a quantitative approach, using an online survey, while another source utilized a qualitative methodology. This variety of sources allows it to investigate AI's impact on marketing from both a theoretical and practical perspective.

After analyzing these articles, data extraction was carried out. Data extracted from each study included authors, years of publications, key outcomes, and applications of AI in marketing. With the extracted data, a thorough analysis was performed on the gathered information, which produced significant conclusions and a summary of the study's major topics. The report for the systematic literature review was subsequently written. Finally, conclusions were reached considering the research's findings.

Lastly, it has to be noted that this review is limited since non-English publications and articles without full-text accessibility were excluded. Future reviews could consider a broader inclusion criterion to include a broader variety of studies in several countries.

2.2. Systematic literature review

2.2.1. Artificial Intelligence (AI)

Humans are considered the most intelligent creatures on the planet. In fact, the main aspect that distinguishes humans from the rest of the living world is intelligence, however, human intelligence has its limitations. Having this in mind, AI becomes necessary. AI is a technology that can be incorporated into a system, to enable it to achieve intellectual capacities that could aid humans in their pursuit of greater human advancement (Prasad & Choudhary, 2021).

According to Mondal (2019), AI is the science and engineering of building intelligent devices, especially intelligent computer programs, that are able to perceive, analyze, comprehend, and react to data similarly to the way that humans do. AI is the field related to creating machines that can think, learn from experience, solve complicated issues, and act rationally in the end.

To truly grasp the essence of AI, it is essential to delve into its rich history and understand its remarkable journey from inception to its current state.

According to Mondal (2019), the development of AI has been marked by several pivotal milestones that have shaped its evolution. It all began in 1837 with the introduction of the first model of a programmable computer, laying the foundational stone for future innovations. In 1950, the Turing test emerged, offering a groundbreaking method to evaluate machine intelligence.

The term "Artificial Intelligence" was officially coined in 1955, and just a decade later, in 1965, the world witnessed the creation of the first chatbot, ELIZA, sparking imaginations about conversational machines. The 1980s brought a significant leap forward as neural networks began to be used for autonomous vehicles, hinting at the potential for machines to perform complex tasks. A landmark event occurred in 1997 when Deep Blue, an AI developed by IBM, defeated the reigning world chess champion, Garry Kasparov, showcasing AI's growing abilities. The new millennium saw practical applications of AI enter everyday life, with the launch of the autonomous cleaning robot Roomba in 2002. This was followed by another milestone in 2009 when Google introduced the first self-driving car, a marvel of modern technology.

From 2011 to 2014, AI became even more integrated into daily life with the emergence of virtual assistants like Siri, Google Now, and Cortana, transforming how we interact with technology. Finally, in 2017, AlphaGo achieved the utmost by defeating the world champion Go player Ke Jie, demonstrating AI's capability to master even the most complex games. Each of these milestones not only marks a technical achievement but also tells a story of human ingenuity and the relentless pursuit of innovation.

In Figure 2, we can observe a succinct representation of what has been discussed in the preceding paragraphs.

Figure 2. Representation of the evolution of AI

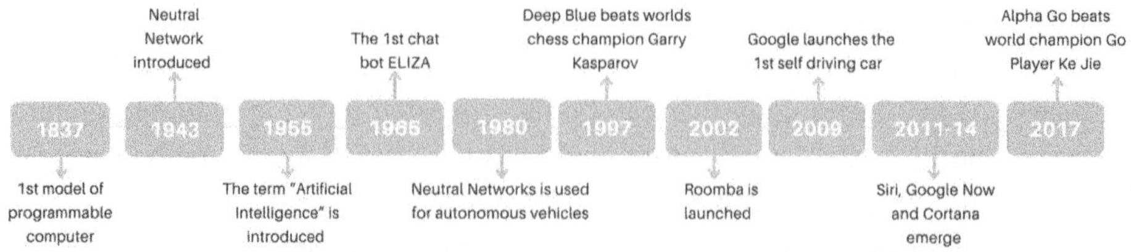

(Self elaboration based on Mondal, 2019)

Indeed, according to Zhang and Lu (2021) the history of AI can be divided into three golden periods:

- The First Golden Era (1950–1970) introduced expert systems like the MTCIN Disease Diagnosis and Treatment System and the Bender Chemical Mass Spectrometry System, initiating knowledge engineering (Zhang & Lu, 2021).
- The Second Golden Age (1980–1990) advanced neural networks with developments like the backpropagation algorithm and the Hopfield neural network, enhancing machine translation and speech recognition (Zhang & Lu, 2021).
- The Third Golden Age (2000–present) has been driven by big data and deep learning, with significant progress in image and speech recognition fueled by advancements in GPU technology and complex neural network designs (Zhang & Lu, 2021).

AI has made significant progress, encompassing a wide range of technologies, most notably machine learning and deep learning. These areas have gained attentiveness due to their vast potential in various sectors, from the activation of virtual assistants such as Siri and Google Assistant to the development of autonomous cars capable of making decisions and navigating independently. In addition, AI is driving visual systems for object detection and medical diagnosis, and robots designed to operate in hazardous environments, highlighting their ability to solve complex problems in extreme conditions (Mondal, 2019). In addition, Large Language Models (LLMs), such as GPT-4, have made remarkable progress in understanding and generating natural language. Research indicates that these models have transformative potential in various areas, especially in education and health, where they are used from machine translation to content creation (Prasad & Choudhary, 2021). Finally, Deep Learning, one of the most significant advances in AI, highlighted by Ian Goodfellow in 2012, provides systems that learn from large volumes of data to perform specific tasks, from image recognition to predictive analysis. This evolution is crucial for the practical application of AI, which also includes virtual assistants such as Cortana that integrate voice recognition and contextual response in order to improve daily interaction with users (Mondal, 2019).

Indeed, AI can be beneficial in various fields, such as health, law, and cybersecurity. In the health sector, the implementation of AI is revolutionizing diagnosis and treatment, increasing the accuracy of diagnoses and the efficiency of health systems through the analysis of medical images and the personalization of treatments (Prasad & Choudhary, 2021). In the field of law, AI's ability to analyze large amounts of data can significantly improve legal decision-making processes. For example, AI can help predict case outcomes, analyze legal precedents, and identify patterns in legal documents (Xu et al., 2021). Integrating AI into cybersecurity measures has the potential to significantly increase protection against cyber threats since AI is able to detect and respond to security breaches more quickly than traditional methods. However, this also involves navigating complex legal issues relating to data security, user consent, and the potential malicious use of AI. Developing strict technological laws governing the use of AI in cybersecurity is essential to protect both individuals and organizations (Xu et al., 2021).

This comprehensive view of AI highlights how this technology is being used to learn, make decisions, and improve human-machine interactions through deep and machine learning technologies, as well as highlighting the need for robust ethical frameworks to guide the responsible and transparent development of AI (Prasad & Choudhary, 2021; Mondal, 2019). Even though AI represents a powerful tool, it can also be used to reach negative goals. There are numerous challenges and ethical considerations related to AI, as Technical Challenges and Ethical Challenges and Implications.

Regarding Technical Challenges, it's important to note that the stability and reliability of AI technologies remain significant hurdles. It is crucial to ensure the robustness and dependability of AI systems before they become widespread and are used in everyday applications (Prasad & Choudhary, 2021).

Addressing the ethical implications of AI, which includes concerns about privacy, security, and the impact on employment, is essential for the responsible implementation of AI technologies, as Zhang and Lu (2021) point out. Prasad and Choudhary (2021) highlight several ethical challenges, emphasizing that the development of ethical AI is crucial to avoid problems such as bias and misinformation. The emergence of deepfakes, where AI manipulates media, underlines the need for ethical guidelines and detection tools. Deepfake is the term used when deep learning is employed to manipulate images, audio or video. Many AI researchers are dedicated to developing programs capable of identifying media manipulations, and combating the spread of misinformation (Prasad & Choudhary, 2021).

Furthermore, with the emergence of tools such as ChatGPT and Dall-e, it becomes crucial to consider a robust ethical framework for AI systems. Issues such as the intellectual property of the data used to train algorithms, the false identities that can be created and how these systems affect work and industry need to be rigorously discussed. Regulation and the establishment of solid ethical standards are key to ensure that AI is used responsibly and with respect for people's rights and well-being (Ortega-Bolaños et al., 2024).

The implementation of AI involves significant social and ethical risks, and the ethical development of these systems is crucial to prevent negative impacts on people's autonomy, privacy and fairness. According to Ortega-Bolaños et al. (2024), it is necessary to create a typology that distinguishes the different stages of the AI life cycle, the high-level ethical principles that should govern its implementation and the tools that can promote compliance with these principles. In addition, as AI technologies generate creative works and innovations, questions arise about ownership and protection of intellectual property. Establishing clear guidelines on intellectual property rights for AI-generated content is essential to protect creators and encourage innovation (Xu et al., 2021). Moreover, controllable AI models are necessary to prevent unintended outcomes from AI systems' autonomy, such as unintentional and possibly unlawful discrimination (Campbell et al., 2020; De Bruyn et al., 2020).

While there are concerns that AI could potentially replace jobs, Campbell et al. (2020) assume that job roles will evolve to meet the changing needs of businesses. AI takes on more analytical tasks, which potentially decreases the importance of analytical skills, while skills such as intuition and empathy will become more important. Therefore, automation through AI enables marketers to shift their focus from routine processes to creative tasks (Campbell et al., 2020). In addition, De Bruyn et al. (2020) argue that implicit knowledge transfer is crucial for enabling AI models to comprehend the complex connections needed to make informed and effective marketing decisions in collaboration with human specialists. Campbell et al. (2020) emphasize that integrating AI with human intelligence is essential for delivering the best possible customer experience and fully leveraging AI's potential in marketing. Therefore, the importance of cultural change in companies must be highlighted. It requires continuous adaption to evolving best practices and a culture of continuous improvement (Campbell et al., 2020).

AI continues to evolve rapidly, offering numerous opportunities and challenges. The integration of AI technologies into human activities has the potential to transform society, but it requires careful consideration of ethical and technical issues to maximize benefits and mitigate risks (Zhang & Lu, 2021). To address the implications that AI can have, Ortega-Bolaños et al. (2024) argue for the adoption of technical tools that ensure transparency, accountability, and fairness in AI systems. This can be achieved, for example, if developers use principle-based tools, both technical and abstract, that measure the impact of proposed solutions and ensure they do not cause harm. Additionally, implementing a comprehensive ethical framework that combines virtue ethics and deontological ethics can provide clear and concrete guidelines for the responsible development of AI.

On one hand, Prasad and Choudhary (2021) believe that although AI might be seen as a powerful and advanced tool that humans may be able to master in the future, new Al technologies will experience ups and downs before they become something stable enough for people to use daily. On the other hand, Mondal (2019) concludes that AI is significantly influencing the current decade by automating complex and risky jobs with high efficiency and accuracy. Zhang and Lu (2021) support this view, highlighting how AI has driven the technological and industrial revolution, enhancing national competitiveness and security while also generating significant economic benefits and promoting social development. For this author, even though debates on AI surpass human intelligence, consumers are already immersed in the AI era, using AI-enabled devices in their daily lives.

This divergence in perspectives enriches the discussion on AI's role and future, highlighting the dynamic and evolving nature of its integration into human life. AI has advanced significantly from its first conception to its current performance in a variety of contexts in daily life (Prasad & Choudhary, 2021).

2.2.2 Artificial Intelligence in Marketing

After gaining a comprehensive overview of AI, the application of AI in marketing can now be discussed in detail. Existing research on marketing is heavily focused on the impact and application of different technologies on marketing performance. However, only in recent years, research has paid more attention to the relationship between AI and marketing (Vlačić et al., 2021).

AI is considered the most significant technological advancement for business and is becoming increasingly important in marketing, especially from a strategic perspective (Vlačić et al., 2021). AI is correlated with efficiency, customization, and precision in marketing. It provides advertisers the ability to tailor their campaigns to the needs and preferences of their target audience, encouraging more fulfilling and fruitful engagements (Kumar et al., 2024). A growing number of businesses are using AI-based platforms to improve their performance, including Google, Spotify, and Under Armour (Vlačić et al., 2021). Further companies that demonstrate the wide range of uses of AI in business are Adidas and Netflix. Both businesses employ

AI to examine large volumes of customer data to spot trends, patterns, and insights that can guide marketing plans and initiatives (Kumar et al., 2024).

The literature uses different methods to describe the application of AI in the various areas of marketing. Vlačić et al. (2021) identified significant research themes and topics and divided them into marketing channels, strategies, performance, segmentation, targeting, and positioning. In contrast, Chintalapati and Pandey (2021) divided the application of AI in marketing into integrated digital marketing, content marketing, experimental marketing, marketing operations, and market research. Huang and Rust (2020) use a different approach by claiming that AI can be designed to have multiple intelligences, as humans have, for different tasks. Thereby, AI can be divided into mechanical AI, which is helpful for the automation of repetitive and routine tasks; thinking AI, which processes data to arrive at new conclusions or decisions; and feeling AI, beneficial for two-way interactions involving humans, and for analyzing human emotions and feelings (Huang & Rust, 2020). According to Huang and Rust (2020), different AI can assist in various stages of marketing research, strategy, and action.

In the buyer-seller transaction, marketing channels play a crucial role as a link between producers and customers. To help with consumer profiling and predictions, marketers must invest in identifying client psychographics and demographics. As ongoing changes in consumer preferences continue to shape the marketing landscape, the role of AI solutions is increasingly recognized as alternative marketing assistants (Vlačić et al., 2021). AI emerges as a powerful tool for marketers to effectively recognize, analyze, and respond to the intricate nuances of customer behavior and preferences, as well as to identify the right segment to target (Huang & Rust, 2020; Vlačić et al., 2021). Moreover, AI can also help to reduce errors in marketing processes, as long as supervision and guidance are available, allowing it to perform specialized tasks more efficiently than humans (Campbell et al., 2020).

By applying deep learning, text-mining, and artificial neural networks, AI technologies can recognize complex patterns and trends in large amounts of data that would be difficult for human analysts to identify (Huang & Rust, 2020; Verma et al., 2021). Recommendation engines can suggest various potential targets for marketing managers' final decision-making and predictive modeling, which can be used to determine which segment to target (Huang & Rust, 2020). This enables more accurate and effective predictions, which in turn can lead to personalized marketing strategies, potentially strengthening customer loyalty, engagement, and revenue, as clients often react positively to brands that address their preferences and needs (De Bruyn et al., 2020; Kumar et al., 2024; Verma et al., 2021).

AI applied to marketing strategies ultimately changes the way businesses are conceived. It affects the future of marketing strategies, as AI-based marketing solutions have noted improvements in communication, pricing, sales management, advertising, business model decisions, and mobile marketing strategy (Vlačić et al., 2021). Furthermore, AI is more likely to lead to a higher return on investment as it can significantly speed up the process of marketing campaigns, reduce costs, and improve efficiency (Campbell et al., 2020).

Consequently, the application of AI positively impacts the performance of businesses. The use of AI, for instance, to automate the collection and processing of continuous market and customer data enables efficient and continuous data collection in real-time (Huang & Rust, 2020). The ability of AI to translate the collected data into information and knowledge might lead to more effective marketing and sales strategies, which ultimately translates into a competitive advantage (Kumar et al., 2024; Vlačić et al., 2021).

Furthermore, overall efficiency can be enhanced through using decision support systems and automating repetitive tasks to save time and resources (De Bruyn et al., 2020). AI's ability to process large amounts of data and recognize patterns can also help improve the efficiency of digital marketing campaigns, as they can be adapted in real time (Chintalapati & Pandey, 2021; De Bruyn et al., 2020). According to Kumar et al. (2024), this in-depth analysis of large, complex datasets is referred to as analytical marketing capabilities. These capabilities enable companies to evaluate the performance of marketing campaigns or ad placements by gaining insights from customer data, market trends, and consumer behavior (Kumar et al., 2024).

In agreement with Verma et al. (2021), Vlačić et al. (2021) noted that AI can also assist in segmenting, targeting, and positioning marketing activities. By applying text mining and machine learning, AI algorithms can be used in various sectors to identify more profitable customer segments (Verma et al., 2021). According to Huang and Rust (2020), AI segmentation has a high flexibility, as it can divide the market into segments at various levels, including disaggregating down to the level of individual customers and aggregating long-tail data into a single segment. The use of AI enables customer segmentation to diversify beyond typical classification incorporating many dimensions including psychological and behavioral aspects (Kumar et al., 2024). In addition, AI techniques such as data optimization and machine learning can help narrow down target customers and improve customer understanding (Verma et al., 2021; Huang & Rust, 2020). Together, these applications of AI assist in analyzing customer profiles to create targeted marketing messages and optimize customer engagement across various channels (Vlačić et al., 2021).

However, it is essential to note that despite its benefits, almost all the articles highlight the ethical concerns and potential pitfalls related to AI, as mentioned in the previous chapter of this article. Data privacy, algorithmic biases, and the ethical implications of automated decision-making processes have become important considerations as AI continues to be integrated into many aspects of marketing

(Campbell et al., 2020; De Bruyn et al., 2020; Huang & Rust, 2020; Verma et al., 2021; Vlačić et al., 2021).

In the evolving marketing landscape, various trends and future research directions are emerging, which could change how AI is used. According to Verma et al. (2021), one development is integrating semantic knowledge and machine learning to gain deeper insights into consumer behavior. By combining linguistic analysis with advanced algorithms and by using connected devices, companies can acquire a deeper understanding of the needs, preferences, and behaviors of their target groups (Huang & Rust, 2020; Verma et al., 2021).

Another significant trend is the continuous development of optimization models and hybrid machine learning methods. These methods enable businesses to use various data sources and optimize the effectiveness of AI algorithms to improve their marketing strategies and campaigns (Verma et al., 2021).

Overall, these trends and research directions show promising ways on how AI can transform marketing and help companies to effectively respond to changing needs and expectations of their target audiences. With all the improvements and innovations that AI brings to marketing, the question is how it will change the customer experience.

2.2.3. How Artificial Intelligence transforms customer experience

AI is revolutionizing the way customers interact with brands, indeed, understanding the challenges and dynamics associated with the customer experience is crucial in today´s competitive market (Ameen et al., 2021b).

The introduction of AI has the potential to revolutionize the way businesses interact with their customers (McLean & Osei-Frimpong, 2019). According to Wassan et al. (2021), AI is increasingly permeating various aspects of personal and professional lives. For instance, Amazon's Alexa, a widely used AI-powered assistant, boasts over 1.8 million users who rely on it to control home lighting systems and unlock cars, among other functions. Alexa's capabilities are continuously expanding, with over 3,000 skills currently available and more being added regularly. This illustrates the growing influence of AI in everyday consumer technology.

In the professional realm, AI is making significant strides as well. Human Resource (HR) leaders are exploring the use of chatbots to enhance employee experiences, paralleling the adoption of AI-driven chatbots by marketers to tailor and personalize shopping experiences for consumers. The investment trends reflect this burgeoning interest in AI technologies. Between 2011 and 2015, AI investments surged by an astonishing 746%, growing from $282 million to $2.4 billion. This momentum continued into 2016, with more than $1.5 billion invested in over 200 AI-focused companies, pushing the cumulative investment over the $2 billion mark.

Such investment patterns underscore the rapid and sustained growth of AI, indicating a strong belief in its transformative potential across various sectors. This trend shows no signs of abating, suggesting that AI will continue to play an increasingly pivotal role in shaping the future of both consumer and professional environments (Wassan et al., 2021).

According to a survey conducted by Desk.com, over 23% of millennials expect to find and interact with consumer brands within a 10-minute timeframe. To meet this demand for immediacy, consumer brands are increasingly turning to AI-powered bots that provide round-the-clock services. These bots facilitate seamless interactions with consumers, answering queries, processing orders, and handling customer service tasks efficiently. For instance, machine learning algorithms are being implemented to streamline order processing and customer service operations, significantly reducing response times and enhancing overall service quality (Wassan et al., 2021).

A notable application of this technology is through platforms like Facebook Messenger, where companies can engage with customers in real time, offering immediate assistance and personalized experiences. This trend is not confined to millennials alone; consumers across various demographics now expect prompt and efficient responses from brands. The deployment of AI-driven solutions is thus becoming essential for businesses aiming to meet these evolving consumer expectations and maintain a competitive advantage in the market (Wassan et al., 2021).

According to Bolton et al. (2018), to add value to the customer journey, companies need to adopt a holistic understanding of how customers interact across digital, physical, and social platforms (Parise et al., 2016 as cited in Bolton et al., 2018). Following Bolton et al. (2018), interactions are perceived as the center of the social dimension of the customer experience. Fundamentally, organizations take into consideration the customer´s social environment as well as their expectations regarding the resources of the organization. This will be the key to shaping service experiences for their customers (Verhoef et al., 2009 as cited in Bolton et al., 2018).

Nowadays, with the evolution of technology, by analyzing a customer's past purchases and preferences, AI can personalize services and product recommendations. This has ramifications for many different industries, including the beauty industry, which must efficiently produce customized looks and product recommendations according to consumers' needs and preferences (Maras, 2020, as cited in Ameen et al. (2021b).

According to Puntoni et al. (2020), through AI, companies can provide benefits to consumers and increase the value of the experience. However, it is important to understand the costs that are associated to the interaction between the customer and AI. AI designers must understand the political nature of their interventions as well as the ethical standards. Due to the growth of AI, it is recommended to assess how professional guidelines could address the ethical challenges for marketers (Puntoni et al., 2020). Similarly, Prentice and Nguye's study (2020b) underscores the superior impact of employee interactions over AI in fostering customer engagement and loyalty. It finds that responsiveness, empathy, and assurance from employees are the keys to customer engagement, with human interactions being preferred over AI's standardized responses. Although AI offers timeliness and error minimization, it lacks the personalized touch of human service, which is crucial for customer satisfaction. Emotional intelligence further enhances engagement, particularly in interactions with employees, indicating the value of human elements in service encounters. This suggests that, while AI can augment service efficiency, the human touch remains irreplaceable in achieving customer loyalty and engagement.

Ameen et al. (2021b) bring a very interesting topic in their findings, by revealing the dual nature of AI-enabled services, illustrating both the sacrifices consumers may face, such as reduced human interaction, privacy loss, control loss, increased time consumption, and potential feelings of irritation, and the negative impact these factors can have on service experiences. Additionally, the concept of trust emerges as pivotal in AI-enabled customer experiences. Surprisingly, this research indicates that while perceived sacrifices mediate the effects of personalization and AI service quality, they do not affect the relationship between perceived convenience and AI-enabled experiences. Despite the association of AI services with convenience, highlighted during the COVID-19 crisis for their flexibility in time and location, this convenience does not seem to mitigate the perceived sacrifices required to utilize these services, underscoring a complex interplay between service attributes and consumer perceptions (Ameen et al. 2021b).

Furthermore, the main findings of Bolton et al. (2018) highlight the inevitable changes with humans entering an era where AI is being integrated into organizations and services: it is certain that the customer experience landscape will change. In the future, designing and implementing personalized services may present challenges due to the need for integration and alignment across the digital, physical, and social realms for each customer. However, researchers can impact the customer experiences, by increasing the knowledge for creating services across these three domains: digital, physical, and social.

According to Lan (2024), in the current competitive environment, the integration of AI is crucial for businesses seeking to transform customer experience (CX) and customer relationship management (CRM). AI-driven systems can process and analyze immense volumes of customer data in real time. This advanced data analysis empowers businesses to obtain deep and nuanced insights into consumer behaviors, preferences, and needs. By harnessing AI technologies, companies can more accurately understand and predict customer actions, tailor their services to individual preferences, and respond proactively to changing market dynamics. Consequently, AI not only enhances the efficiency and effectiveness of CRM strategies but also significantly elevates the overall customer experience, fostering stronger and more personalized relationships between businesses and their customers.

The potential of AI to revolutionize customer interactions, as explored in this section, highlights its role as a valuable and accessible tool for enhancing customer relationships. The discussion of AI's dual nature, including both its benefits and challenges, mirrors the evolving landscape of digital marketing, emphasizing the need for a balanced approach that integrates emotional intelligence and ethical considerations. In this sense, AI will continue to have profound impacts in customers´ life, especially in enhancing customer service, optimizing the use of human staff, and shaping personalized customer journeys (Chen & Prentice, 2024). The examined literature collectively supports the advancement of AI as a crucial element in the transformation of customer experience and the development of innovative digital marketing practices.

In conclusion, previous studies have provided collective insights that highlight the intricate relationship between the efficiency of AI and the indispensable importance of human touch in customer service (Bolton et al. 2018; Prentice & Nguyen, 2020b; Ameen et al., 2021b; Puntoni et al., 2020). AI presents issues with decreased human connection, privacy, and ethical concerns even while it promises improved personalization and service convenience. In the digital age, developing deep and enduring customer relationships requires striking a balance between the advantages and disadvantages of AI as well as incorporating emotional intelligence into interactions with customers. These four articles contributed to the development of the knowledge necessary to structure the present report.

2.3. Main findings

This systematic literature review allowed us to understand better how consumers view AI, which consequently allowed us to achieve the main objective: to understand the influence of AI in marketing from the consumer's perspective.

In this way, we were able to ascertain that consumers view AI ambivalently: on one hand, they recognize the benefits of AI in improving the efficiency of customer service and in the fact that it makes it possible to personalize the consumer experience, for example. On the other hand, consumers have many concerns about privacy and ethics. Although AI is becoming more and more advanced, consumers continue to show a clear preference for the human touch when it comes to customer service, indicating that AI is unable to completely replace emotional intelligence, a characteristic reserved exclusively for human beings.

This underlines the critical importance of maintaining a delicate balance between capitalizing on the benefits of AI and maintaining customer trust, highlighting the need to address these issues to preserve an excellent customer experience.

3. CONCLUSIONS

This study aimed to explore the influence of AI on marketing from the consumer's perspective, addressing a notable gap in the existing literature. The technological potential and applications of AI in marketing have been the subject of much research however, consumer perception and reaction to these developments have received far less attention. This gap is critical, as understanding consumer perspectives is essential for the effective utilization of AI technologies in marketing (Ameen et al., 2021; Gao & Liu, 2022; He & Zhang, 2022).

The present systematic literature review highlighted several key findings. Firstly, customers' views of AI in marketing are changing as their expectations for efficiency and personalization rise and are weighed against ethical and privacy concerns. Businesses may customize their services and interactions to individual tastes thanks to AI's capacity to analyze vast amounts of client data, creating a more engaging and personalized customer experience. However, there are several difficulties with using AI in marketing. Concerns regarding privacy and ethics become more important as people become more cautious about how their data is gathered, utilized, and kept. These concerns draw attention to the delicate balance that organizations must strike between capitalizing on AI's benefits and upholding customer confidence.

Secondly, the study emphasizes that consumers still clearly prefer the invaluable human touch in customer service encounters, even in the face of AI developments. AI is unable to completely replace emotional intelligence, empathy, and personal engagement, all of which are recognized as essential elements of customer happiness and loyalty. This choice highlights the indispensable importance of human interaction in the digital age, implying that although AI can improve the personalization and efficiency of services, it cannot take the place of the complex understanding and empathy that come from human encounters. Therefore, the literature review suggests an emphasis of balancing technological advancements with human interaction to enhance customer experiences.

As a result, trust becomes essential to the uptake and efficiency of AI-enabled services. According to the study, consumers' trust and satisfaction may be negatively impacted by perceived compromises including the loss of privacy, control, and human interaction. This emphasizes how critical it is to solve these issues to preserve a great customer experience. As time goes on, the success of marketing's customer experience will probably depend on how creatively we can strike a balance between the advantages of AI and the crucial human components of customer support. In the era of AI, maintaining personal connections while maintaining a careful balance between ethical concerns and technological innovation will be essential to building strong and trusting consumer relationships.

At the end of the analysis of the transformative impact of AI on digital relationship marketing, it is clear that the findings echo the central themes of the book. This chapter not only reinforces the importance of personalization and optimization in digital communication as foundations for deepening customer relationships but also illustrates the crucial role of AI in driving responsible and sustainable practices in the modern business landscape. In this way, the reflections of the present article, subtly contribute to the broader narrative of the book, highlighting the synergy between technological innovation and ethics in marketing.

The present research highlights the advantages and disadvantages of using AI in customer engagement methods, addressing an existing research gap and adding to a more comprehensive understanding of the influence of AI on marketing from the consumer's point of view.

REFERENCES

Al, S. W. E. (2021). How artificial intelligence transforms the experience of employees. *Türk Bilgisayar Ve Matematik Eğitimi Dergisi*, 12(10), 7116–7135. DOI: 10.17762/turcomat.v12i10.5603

Ameen, N., Tarhini, A., Reppel, A., & Anand, A. (2021). Customer experiences in the age of artificial intelligence. *Computers in Human Behavior*, 114, 106548. DOI: 10.1016/j.chb.2020.106548 PMID: 32905175

Bolton, R. N., McColl-Kennedy, J. R., Cheung, L., Gallan, A., Orsingher, C., Witell, L., & Zaki, M. (2018). Customer experience challenges: Bringing together digital, physical and social realms. *Journal of Service Management*, 29(5), 776–808. DOI: 10.1108/JOSM-04-2018-0113

Campbell, C., Sands, S., Ferraro, C., Tsao, H., & Mavrommatis, A. (2020). From data to action: How marketers can leverage AI. *Business Horizons*, 63(2), 227–243. DOI: 10.1016/j.bushor.2019.12.002

Chen, Y., & Prentice, C. (2024). Integrating artificial intelligence and customer experience. *Australasian Marketing Journal*, 14413582241252904, 14413582241252904. Advance online publication. DOI: 10.1177/14413582241252904

Chintalapati, S., & Pandey, S. K. (2021). Artificial intelligence in marketing: A systematic literature review. *International Journal of Market Research*, 64(1), 38–68. DOI: 10.1177/14707853211018428

De Bruyn, A., Viswanathan, V., Beh, Y. S., Brock, J. K. U., & Von Wangenheim, F. (2020). Artificial intelligence and Marketing: Pitfalls and opportunities. *Journal of Interactive Marketing*, 51(1), 91–105. DOI: 10.1016/j.intmar.2020.04.007

Gaffney, J. S., & Marley, N. A. (2018). Chemical measurements and instrumentation. In *General Chemistry for Engineers* (pp. 493–532). Elsevier., DOI: 10.1016/B978-0-12-810425-5.00015-1

Gao, Y., & Liu, H. (2022). Artificial intelligence-enabled personalization in interactive marketing: A customer journey perspective. *Journal of Research in Interactive Marketing*, 17(5), 663–680. DOI: 10.1108/JRIM-01-2022-0023

He, A., & Zhang, Y. (2022). AI-powered touch points in the customer journey: A systematic literature review and research agenda. *Journal of Research in Interactive Marketing*, 17(4), 620–639. DOI: 10.1108/JRIM-03-2022-0082

Huang, M., & Rust, R. T. (2020). A strategic framework for artificial intelligence in marketing. *Journal of the Academy of Marketing Science*, 49(1), 30–50. DOI: 10.1007/s11747-020-00749-9

Kostadinov, S. (2021, December 11). Understanding Backpropagation Algorithm - towards Data science. *Medium.* https://towardsdatascience.com/understanding-backpropagation-algorithm- 7bb3aa2f95fd

Kumar, V., Ashraf, A. R., & Nadeem, W. (2024). AI-powered marketing: What, where, and how? *International Journal of Information Management*, 77, 102783. DOI: 10.1016/j.ijinfomgt.2024.102783

Lan, D. H., & Tung, T. M. (2024). AI-Powered Customer Experience: Personalization, engagement, and intelligent Decision-Making in CRM. *Deleted Journal*, 20(5s), 55–71. DOI: 10.52783/jes.1832

Liu, J., Kong, X., Xia, F., Bai, X., Wang, L., Qing, Q., & Lee, I. (2018). Artificial intelligence in the 21st century. *IEEE Access : Practical Innovations, Open Solutions*, 6, 34403–34421. DOI: 10.1109/ACCESS.2018.2819688

Makridakis, S. (2017). The forthcoming Artificial Intelligence (AI) revolution: Its impact on society and firms. *Futures*, 90, 46–60. DOI: 10.1016/j.futures.2017.03.006

Maras, E. (2020, July 11). Beauty retailers embrace AR, AI. www.digitalsignagetoday.com. https://www.digitalsignagetoday.com/articles/beauty-retailers- embrace-ar-ai/

Misic, M., Đurđević, Đ., & Tomasevic, M. (2012). Evolution and trends in GPU computing. In *Proceedings of the 35th International Convention MIPRO,* 21-25 may 2012.

Mondal, B. (2019). Artificial intelligence: state of the art. In *Intelligent systems reference library* (pp. 389–425). DOI: 10.1007/978-3-030-32644-9_32

Ortega-Bolaños, R., Bernal-Salcedo, J., Ortiz, M. G., Sarmiento, J. G., Ruz, G. A., & Tabares-Soto, R. (2024). Applying the ethics of AI: A systematic review of tools for developing and assessing AI- based systems. *Artificial Intelligence Review*, 57(5), 110. Advance online publication. DOI: 10.1007/s10462-024-10740-3

Parise, S., Guinan, P. J., & Kafka, R. (2016). Solving the crisis of immediacy: How digital technology can transform the customer experience. *Business Horizons*, 59(4), 411–420. DOI: 10.1016/j.bushor.2016.03.004

Prasad, R., & Choudhary, P. (2021). State-of-the-Art of Artificial Intelligence. Journal of Mobile Multimedia. DOI: 10.13052/jmm1550-4646.171322

Prentice, C., & Nguyen, M. (2020). Engaging and retaining customers with AI and employee service. *Journal of Retailing and Consumer Services*, 56, 102186. DOI: 10.1016/j.jretconser.2020.102186

Puntoni, S., Reczek, R. W., Giesler, M., & Botti, S. (2020). Consumers and Artificial intelligence: An Experiential perspective. *Journal of Marketing*, 85(1), 131–151. DOI: 10.1177/0022242920953847

Rice, D. M. (2014). Neural calculus. In *Calculus of Thought Neuromorphic Logistic Regression in Cognitive Machines* (pp. 125–144). Elsevier., DOI: 10.1016/B978-0-12-410407-5.00005-2

Schlesinger, L. A. (2009). Customer Experience Creation: Determinants, dynamics and management strategies. *Journal of Retailing*, 85(1), 31–41. DOI: 10.1016/j.jretai.2008.11.001

Van Melle, W. (1978). MYCIN: A knowledge-based consultation program for infectious disease diagnosis. *International Journal of Man-Machine Studies*, 10(3), 313–322. DOI: 10.1016/S0020-7373(78)80049-2

Verhoef, P. C., Lemon, K. N., Parasuraman, A., Roggeveen, A., Tsiros, M., & Schlesinger, L. A. (2009). Customer Experience Creation: Determinants, dynamics and management strategies. *Journal of Retailing*, 85(1), 31–41. DOI: 10.1016/j.jretai.2008.11.001

Verma, S., Sharma, R., Deb, S., & Maitra, D. (2021). Artificial intelligence in marketing: Systematic review and future research direction. *International Journal of Information Management Data Insights*, 1(1), 100002. DOI: 10.1016/j.jjimei.2020.100002

Vlačić, B., Corbo, L., Silva, S. C. E., & Dabić, M. (2021). The evolving role of artificial intelligence in marketing: A review and research agenda. *Journal of Business Research*, 128, 187–203. DOI: 10.1016/j.jbusres.2021.01.055

Wittorski, R. (2012). Professionalisation and the Development of Competences in Education and Training. In Valerie Cohen-Scali, V. (Ed.), *Competence and Competence Development* (pp. 31–51). Barbara Budrich Publishers. DOI: 10.2307/j.ctvbkk2h9.6

Xu, Y., Liu, X., Cao, X., Huang, C., Liu, E., Qian, S., Liu, X., Wu, Y., Dong, F., Qiu, C., Qiu, J., Hua, K., Su, W., Wu, J., Xu, H., Han, Y., Fu, C., Yin, Z., Liu, M., & Zhang, J. (2021). Artificial intelligence: A powerful paradigm for scientific research. *Innovation (Cambridge (Mass.))*, 2(4), 100179. DOI: 10.1016/j.xinn.2021.100179 PMID: 34877560

Zhang, C., & Lu, Y. (2021). Study on artificial intelligence: The state of the art and future prospects. *Journal of Industrial Information Integration*, 23, 100224. DOI: 10.1016/j.jii.2021.100224

ADDITIONAL READING

Barone, A. M., & Stagno, E. (2023). *Artificial Intelligence along the Customer Journey: A Customer Experience Perspective*. Springer. DOI: 10.1007/978-3-031-48792-7

Huang, M., & Rust, R. T. (2022). A Framework for Collaborative Artificial Intelligence in Marketing. *Journal of Retailing*, 98(2), 209–223. DOI: 10.1016/j.jretai.2021.03.001

Nguyen, T., Quach, S., & Thaichon, P. (2021). The effect of AI quality on customer experience and brand relationship. *Journal of Consumer Behaviour*, 21(3), 481–493. DOI: 10.1002/cb.1974

Roetzer, P., & Kaput, M. (2022). *Marketing artificial intelligence: AI, Marketing, and the Future of Business*. BenBella Books.

KEY TERMS AND DEFINITIONS

AI-enabled services: Services enhanced with artificial intelligence to improve functionality and user interaction.

Artificial Intelligence: The technology enabling machines to perform tasks that require human intelligence.

Customer Experience: The perceptions and feelings formed by customers as a result of interactions with a company's services or products.

Customer relationship management: A system for managing a company's interactions with current and potential customers, often using data analysis about customers' history with the company to improve business relationships.

Deep Learning: An advanced machine learning technique where computers learn through examples.

Chapter 3
The Future of Customer Relationship Service:
How Artificial Intelligence (AI) Is Changing the Game

Md. Touhidul Islam
https://orcid.org/0000-0002-4341-5498
NPI University of Bangladesh, Bangladesh

ABSTRACT

This chapter aims to delve into the changing world of customer relationship service as a result of AI breakthroughs, with a specific emphasis on the revolutionary effects on emerging nations. Businesses and researchers alike may benefit from the insights gleaned from this chapter's comprehensive evaluation of existing practices across different sectors, case studies of successful AI integration, and research into customer views and adoption of AI-driven products. The chapter's potential to help businesses successfully use AI to improve client interactions and propel the company to success makes it significant. This chapter also answers important questions about AI adoption in developing countries by looking ahead to what's to come in AI-driven customer relationship service and providing suggestions that are industry-specific and customer-centric. Its ultimate goal is to help improve customer service by encouraging diversity and new ideas in the dynamic field of customer relationship management across industries.

DOI: 10.4018/979-8-3693-5340-0.ch003

1. INTRODUCTION

In recent years, the world has witnessed a rapid advancement in technology, with Artificial Intelligence (AI) emerging as one of the most transformative forces across various sectors. Among these sectors, customer service stands as a critical domain where the integration of AI has the potential to revolutionize the way businesses interact with their clientele. As businesses increasingly seek ways to enhance customer support and satisfaction, the utilization of AI-driven solutions has gained prominence, promising improved efficiency, cost-effectiveness, and personalized experiences. This study delves into "The Future of Customer Service: How Artificial Intelligence Is Changing the Game" with a particular focus on developing countries. AI has a substantial impact on the transformation of customer service, notably in the banking sector. It provides advantages such as improved customer engagement and cost savings, but it also encounters obstacles related to accountability and biases (Makhija & Chacko, 2021).

The customer service landscape in different industries is currently diverse, influenced by variables such as digitization, integration of artificial intelligence, and evolving customer expectations (Bhutto & Maqsood, 2007; Boguda & Shailaja, 2019; Govender, 2017; Jana et al., 2017; Link et al., 2020). Telecommunications firms encounter difficulties in maintaining Quality of Service (QoS) and network availability due to rapid technology improvements and heightened competition (Govender, O. V., 2017). AI-based assistants, such as chatbots, are being used in the service sector to assist employees with complex tasks. The goal is to enhance productivity and decrease the workload of employees (Boguda & Shailaja, 2019; Jana et al., 2017; Link et al., 2020). Moreover, the service industry is also undergoing a transition towards service-oriented transformation. This involves the use of new technologies such as service-oriented architecture and enterprise service bus to improve customer service and fulfill changing customer needs (Bhutto & Maqsood, 2007). In general, companies in various industries are utilizing artificial intelligence and cutting-edge technology to improve customer service, tackle obstacles, and maintain competitiveness in the ever-changing market environment.

Assessing the current landscape of customer service in various industries and identifying the key challenges faced by businesses in delivering exceptional customer support is of paramount importance. Developing countries, characterized by unique socio-economic conditions, present a distinctive set of challenges and opportunities for customer service. In order to properly customize AI-powered customer service solutions for businesses in different locations, it is crucial to take into account variables such as algorithm bias, zero-touch automation, service exposures, Natural Language Processing (NLP) technology, and AI-driven care. Research emphasizes the significance of mitigating biases in AI systems that have the potential to exhibit discrimination based on gender, ethnicity, religion, age, nationality, or socioeconomic background (Akter et al., 2021). Understanding these factors is crucial to tailoring AI-driven customer service solutions that align with the specific needs and constraints of businesses operating in these regions.

Utilizing service exposures can facilitate the integration of external AI solutions with network and service management systems, hence improving automation processes (Xie et al., 2021). Moreover, the implementation of AI-driven care has the potential to completely transform customer interactions by accurately forecasting behavior, cultivating potential customers, and delivering smooth customer support over many platforms, thereby improving the overall customer experience (Dalal et al., 2022).

Customer perception and acceptance of AI-powered customer service solutions play a pivotal role in their widespread adoption. Understanding customer attitudes toward interacting with AI-driven systems over human representatives is vital to addressing concerns and building trust in AI-based customer service approaches. As the use of AI grows, it is important to understand how customers feel and what they want in growing countries where cultural norms are different. Research shows that AI is useful in marketing for learning about how people feel and what the market trends are (Noranee & bin Othman, 2023).

Predicting the potential future trends and advancements in AI-driven customer service is fundamental for businesses to stay ahead in an ever-evolving market landscape. This study aims to explore the possibilities of AI's transformative impact on customer service in the context of developing countries, anticipating how these trends may shape business strategies and customer interactions in the coming years. Finally, giving firms concrete AI customer service integration advice is invaluable. AI should be tailored to each industry's needs. This study provides practical instructions to integrate AI technology into customer service operations by taking into consideration industry-specific demands and client preferences.

In conclusion, as the adoption of AI in customer service gains momentum worldwide, this study seeks to shed light on its potential implications for businesses and customers in developing countries. By exploring the opportunities and challenges that lie ahead, and drawing insights from successful AI implementation cases, this research endeavors to contribute to the enhancement of customer experiences and the transformation of customer service in the digital era.

1.1. Background of the Study

In every industry throughout the globe, customer service has entered a new age with the advent of fast-advancing Artificial Intelligence (AI). Businesses in industrialized nations are quickly embracing AI-powered solutions to enhance productivity and provide better customer service. It is important to investigate the possibilities and threats of incorporating AI into customer service operations in emerging nations. Organizations seeking to improve their customer assistance using AI would benefit greatly by researching the state of customer service in these areas and studying examples of successful AI deployment.

1.2. Significance of the Study

This study holds significance for multiple stakeholders. For businesses operating in developing countries, the findings will offer practical recommendations on how to effectively integrate AI technologies into their customer service strategies. Understanding customer perception and acceptance of AI-powered solutions will enable businesses to build trust and address potential concerns. Additionally, the study's predictions on future AI trends will help organizations stay ahead in a dynamic and competitive market landscape. Moreover, policymakers and researchers can use the study's insights to formulate strategies that foster the responsible and inclusive adoption of AI in customer service.

1.3. Problem Statement

While AI-driven customer service has shown promise in developed countries, there remains a gap in knowledge concerning its potential impact on businesses and customers in developing countries. Addressing this gap is crucial, given the unique challenges and opportunities posed by these regions' socio-economic conditions. Therefore, this study aims to assess the current customer service landscape, analyze successful AI implementation cases, understand customer perceptions, predict future AI trends, and provide actionable recommendations for effectively integrating AI into customer service strategies in developing countries. By doing so, the study seeks to contribute to the enhancement of customer experiences and the transformation of customer service practices in the digital era.

1.4. Objectives of the Study

This research seeks to examine how AI-driven Customer relationship service affects the customers' and service providers' experience and perception level by assessing the following objectives:

a. Assess the current landscape of customer relationship service in various industries and identify the key challenges faced by businesses in delivering exceptional customer support.

b. Examine the customer perception and acceptance of AI-powered customer service solutions, including attitudes towards interacting with AI-driven systems over human representatives.
c. Predict the potential future trends and advancements in AI-driven customer relationship service and their implications for businesses and customers.
d. Provide actionable recommendations for businesses on how to effectively integrate AI into their customer relationship service strategies, taking into account industry-specific needs and customer preferences.

1.5. Research Questions

The study aims to gather insights from customers about their perceptions and acceptance of AI-powered customer relationship service solutions. In line with this, it will be evaluated both customer service providers and customers' insights by answering the following five questions:

a. What are the current state and key challenges businesses face in delivering exceptional customer support across various industries?
b. How have businesses successfully integrated AI into their customer relationship service operations?
c. What are customers' perceptions and levels of acceptance of AI-powered customer service solutions?
d. What future trends and advancements in AI-driven customer relationship service can be anticipated?
e. What recommendations can be made to businesses for effectively integrating AI into their customer relationship service strategies?

2. LITERATURE REVIEW

2.1. Introduction to AI in Customer Relationship Service

Improving client loyalty and trust is one of the keyways that artificial intelligence (AI) is transforming customer relationship management (CRM) (Fianto et al., 2023). For AI solutions to work in customer service applications, it is crucial to integrate technologies such as reinforcement learning, natural language processing, and machine learning (Kraus et al., 2023). Customer relationship management AI aspires to increase sales and customer happiness by automating jobs, improving customer experiences, and streamlining operations (Almahairah, 2023; Krishna et al., 2022). With the use of AI, companies can improve their customer data analysis, provide more personalized experiences, and maximize customer relationship management strategies' long-term value (Roba & Maric, 2023). To provide satisfying service and develop strong customer connections, it is necessary to use interdisciplinary AI applications, as shown by the comprehensive strategy of integrating virtual agents with human operators in customer service centers (Kraus et al., 2023).

In the field of customer service, artificial intelligence applications include boosting client engagement on websites, delivering individualized services, and improving post-purchase care, which eventually leads to an improved customer experience and higher efficiency (Deepa & Abirami, 2024). The use of artificial intelligence in banking customer service improves the quality of experience, operational efficiency, and risk management. According to Oyeniyi et al. (2024), it revolutionizes service delivery and client interaction in the banking sector by providing tailored services.

The use of chatbots, customization, automation, and predictive analytics are all examples of applications of artificial intelligence in customer support. These have a good influence on marketing strategies because they increase client involvement, streamline processes, and stimulate growth (Monica & Soju, 2024). Artificial intelligence improves customer service by facilitating individualized encounters, increasing engagement, providing insights prompted by data, and facilitating informed decision-making based on that data. Through the use of data-driven insights and individualized interactions, it revolutionizes customer care. Personalized service, greater engagement, data-driven strategy, and decision-making are the four primary themes (Tran, 2024). Artificial intelligence systems, such as chatbots, improve omnichannel customer service by delivering individualized and effective assistance, analyzing data, forecasting client requirements, assuring availability around the clock, reducing the number of errors that occur, and assisting human agents in giving better service. Chatbots that are powered by artificial intelligence play a significant part in the delivery of seamless, personalized, and efficient consumer experiences across multiple communication channels, such as websites, mobile apps, and messaging platforms. This results in increased customer satisfaction and loyalty, but it also raises ethical concerns that need to be addressed in order to implement AI in a responsible manner (Ghosh et al., 2024). The research suggests using an artificial intelligence Chat Bot model within the PLN Mobile app to improve the Customer Experience, increase the efficiency of communication and collect useful data for activities related to customer support (Azhar, 2023). Common problems in customer service, such as response delays, a lack of control, and restricted assistance hours, are being addressed with artificial intelligence. Artificial intelligence-driven solutions improve both customer happiness and corporate success by making good use of substantial amounts of data (Vinod, 2023). Artificial intelligence applications in customer service can profit from the integration of virtual agents and human operators. However, in order to successfully implement these applications and ensure customer satisfaction, interdisciplinary AI research is required. Collaboration between human operators and virtual agents is necessary to provide effective service to customers. It is necessary to incorporate a variety of artificial intelligence technologies and fields of study (Kraus et al., 2023). Various methods of artificial intelligence and machine learning improve customer assistance in a variety of ways. Better customer service may be achieved through the application of AI and ML technology. According to the findings of a study, artificial intelligence and machine learning technologies improve customer support by enhancing integrated product service offerings, word of mouth, service quality, and self-service technology. Among the uses of artificial intelligence in customer service are recommendation systems, chatbots, and virtual assistants (Hossain et al., 2023). Another study shows that these applications improve personalized interactions and streamline the customer trip throughout all stages of the customer journey, including pre-purchase, purchase, and post-purchase (Oanh, 2024). Figure 1 shows the areas of successful implementation of AI in customer relationship services.

Figure 1. Areas of successful implementation of AI in customer relationship service (Bowman, 2023)

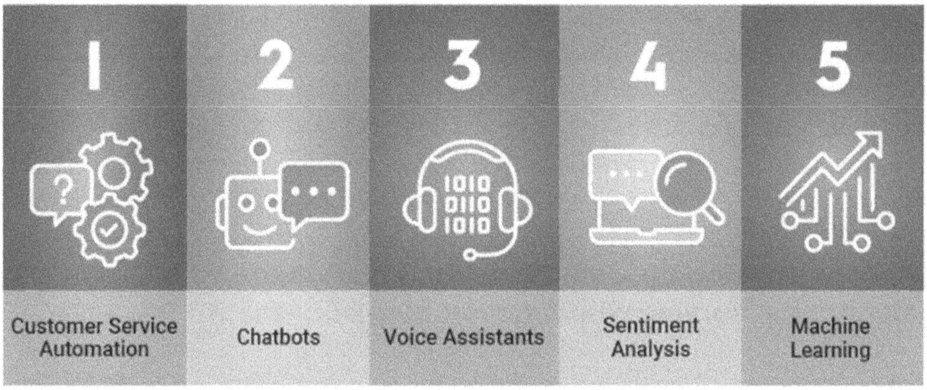

2.2. Industry-specific Applications of AI in Customer Relationship Service

AI is essential for the improvement of customer relationship management (CRM) in a variety of industries. The provision of satisfactory customer service necessitates the integration of AI technologies such as machine learning, natural language processing, and multi-agent systems (Kraus et al., 2023). AI is employed in the banking sector to accommodate the changing requirements of tech-savvy consumers, thereby facilitating seamless experiences through digital banking services (Kumar et al., 2023). Additionally, AI in CRM is designed to enhance the customer experience, increase lead generation, and increase team productivity, in addition to streamlining operations (Almahairah, 2023; Krishna et al., 2022).

2.3. AI in Developed Countries (AI in customer Relationship service within developed countries)

AI technologies have become indispensable in developed countries, where businesses are perpetually attempting to improve operational efficiency and consumer experience. Chatbots, virtual assistants, and predictive analytics are among the tools that AI has implemented to improve consumer satisfaction and business efficacy in developed countries (Huang & Rust, 2018). Artificial intelligence (AI) applications encompass chatbots for managing routine inquiries (Følstad & Skjuve, 2019), personalized recommendations derived from customer data (Lemon & Verhoef, 2016), and predictive analytics to anticipate consumer behavior (Schneider et al., 2010). Expanding into areas such as emotive and conversational AI, improving human-AI collaboration, and enhancing personalization are among the prospects of AI in customer service (De Keyser et al., 2019; Rust & Huang, 2021).

2.4. AI in Developing Countries (AI in customer Relationship service within developing countries)

AI application in customer service operations in poor nations brings unique problems and potential. AI can improve customer service by personalizing interactions, responding quickly, and offering 24/7 help (Huang & Rust, 2018). Data analytics using AI can assist developing country organizations analyze and forecasting customer behavior and adjusting services to local demands (Lemon & Verhoef, 2016).

To successfully integrate AI, data privacy problems, fair and impartial AI systems, infrastructure, and training must be addressed (O'Neil, 2017).

The necessity to improve customer experience and operational efficiency is driving the fast evolution of AI use in customer relationship services in Bangladesh, India, and Indonesia. According to Jayawardena et al. (2022), chatbots, virtual assistants, and data analytics are being used more and more in developing countries to offer customer support solutions that are scalable, efficient, and customized. Industries in India that rely on e-commerce, banking, and telecoms to process large numbers of client inquiries and offer real-time assistance are seeing an increase in the usage of AI in customer service (Shukla et al., 2022). An equally tech-savvy populace and government programs encouraging the use of artificial intelligence are driving digital transformation in Indonesia (Astuti et al., 2024). A growing number of customer service organizations in Bangladesh are embracing AI to better manage client contacts and enhance service delivery (Khan et al., 2021). This is especially true in the telecoms and financial services industries. Despite these improvements, there are still major obstacles to overcome, such as worries about data privacy, constraints in infrastructure, and a lack of qualified personnel.

2.5. Current State and Key Challenges Businesses Face in Delivering Exceptional Customer Support

Improvements in customer experience and operational efficiency are driving the present state of customer service, which is mostly driven by technological improvements, especially AI and automation. The incorporation of new technology into preexisting systems is a significant obstacle. Incorporating AI technologies smoothly without affecting operations is a challenge for many firms, particularly those with legacy systems (Davenport & Ronanki, 2018). Making sure data is secure and private is another big concern. Companies have the challenge of safeguarding client data and navigating complicated regulatory landscapes due to the growing dependence on AI systems (Cavoukian, A., 2020). Furthermore, there is a need for good human-AI collaboration since, although automation can handle routine questions, complicated challenges typically require human participation. It is still quite difficult to keep customers happy by combining automation and human interaction (West et al., 2018).

2.6. AI Integration into Customer Relationship Service Operations

AI integration into customer relationship service operations is crucial for firms seeking efficiency, customer pleasure, and competitive advantage. AI in customer service has several benefits. First, it optimizes response times and minimizes human agent burden by automating typical requests and issues (Følstad & Skjuve, 2019). This lets customer care reps handle more complicated issues that need a personal touch. Integrating AI with current systems is complicated and expensive, requiring infrastructure and training (Davenport & Ronanki, 2018). Companies must integrate AI technologies with their customer support systems to minimize interruptions. However, integrating AI into customer relationship service operations may alter enterprises. Companies can enhance productivity, customize consumer interactions, and foresee and satisfy customer demands with AI. Figure 2 represents the AI usages in customer services where the industry utilizes AI for identify customer issues, identifies authenticate customers, assign agents to customers, automate agent activity and customer care analytics through Natural language processing (NPL) to analyze customers' messages.

Figure 2. Integration of AI in customer service (Dilmegani, 2024)

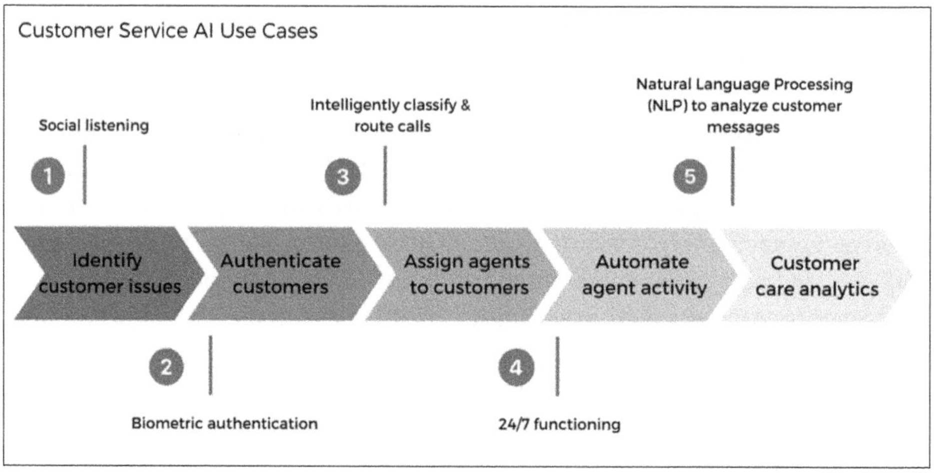

2.7. Customer Perception and Acceptance of AI

Customers' opinions on AI-powered services are complicated. West et al. (2018) found that while many consumers like AI technologies' efficiency and ease, others are cautious about engaging with computers. Customer adoption of AI-powered services depends on numerous aspects. Trust and dependability matter. If AI solutions seem trustworthy and safe, customers will adopt them (Lemon & Verhoef, 2016). Customers' desire to use AI-driven services may be affected by data privacy and security concerns (Cavoukian, 2020). Customer data use and protection must be transparent to develop confidence. Interaction quality also affects acceptance. Customers prefer human engagement for complicated or emotional situations that demand empathy and complexity (West et al., 2018).

2.8. Future Trends and Advancements in AI-driven Customer Relationship Service

As technology evolves and consumer expectations change, artificial intelligence will play an ever-larger role in CRM. Customization, conversational AI, emotional intelligence, and human-AI interaction are becoming more common in this discipline. To tailor their services to each customer, AI systems will improve at analyzing their data (Lemon & Verhoef, 2016). The satisfaction and loyalty of customers are increased by this degree of personalization (Ekwunife, 2023). Consumer interactions will be transformed by conversational AI powered by natural language processing and natural language understanding. More organic and meaningful interactions will be possible when AI systems learn to understand user mood, context, and nuances in their messages. The result will be less transactional and more human-like interactions with chatbots and virtual assistants (Huang & Rust, 2018). Interacting with human agents will become second nature for more sophisticated AI systems in order to transmit scenarios requiring empathy and problem-solving. According to West et al. (2018) and Ying et al. (2021), our hybrid technique combines the advantages of AI efficiency with human empathy.

The use of artificial intelligence in the service industry involves the analysis of voice conversations to identify users, the determination of intentions, and the provision of individualized support through digital assistants based on the keywords and user assistance flows that have been discovered (Bolze & Engles, 2018).

According to the research papers that were presented, the most recent developments and trends in artificial intelligence include the rapid proliferation of technology such as driverless cars and medical imaging devices that are driven by AI (Akter, 2024a, 2024b; Jerbi, 2023). These achievements highlight the disruptive influence that artificial intelligence has had on several industries, including transportation and healthcare. Additionally, the diverse environment of artificial intelligence poses distinct demands and problems that require careful consideration for responsible development and deployment. This highlights the significance of addressing ethical implications for the technology's positive progress (Pansare, 2024). A thorough analysis is required for responsible development and deployment. It is the integration of foundational technologies such as machine learning and computer vision that plays a pivotal role in the creation of innovative solutions across a variety of industries. This demonstrates the diverse applications of artificial intelligence in improving societal aspects and revolutionizing industries such as healthcare and transportation (Pansare, 2024). Additionally, the investigation of agile data science approaches and the vital role that machine learning plays in Industry 4.0 further emphasize the ongoing developments and trends in artificial intelligence research and implementation (Pansare, 2024).

2.9. Ethical Considerations of using AI in Customer Relationship Services

Examining the ethical aspects of customer service AI encompasses the integration of data, customer support, automation, and the provision of transparent AI results, as emphasized in the case study "Intelligent Sales" (Wolf, 2020). The importance of ethical issues in utilizing AI for customer service is of utmost significance, as emphasized in several research publications. The incorporation of artificial intelligence (AI) in the banking and contact center sectors underscores the importance of maintaining a harmonious equilibrium between technical progress and ethical oversight in order to provide a viable and enduring future for the industry (Oyeniyi et al., 2024; Pillai, 2024). The research examines how consumers perceive AI in marketing services, highlighting the significance of resolving ethical issues including data protection, algorithmic bias, and consumer autonomy to promote the adoption of AI (Gonçalves, 2023; Motadi, 2024; Nandyala, 2024). The changing field of AI-powered customer behavior analysis highlights the importance of ethical frameworks and regulatory requirements to responsibly apply AI in analyzing consumer behaviors while addressing moral challenges and social repercussions (Motadi, 2024).

2.10. Impact of AI on Employment within the Customer Service Sector

AI applications in customer service, namely in contact centers, are advancing to automate jobs, prompting worries about job displacement, and necessitating ethical considerations for the welfare of society and the long-term viability of the enterprise (Pillai, 2024). Artificial Intelligence (AI) is having a substantial influence on employment in the customer service industry by automating functions that were previously performed by people, as evidenced in several study publications (Pillai, 2024; Rohan & Banubakode, 2024). Artificial intelligence (AI) technology, such as chatbots and virtual assistants, is being used more and more to improve customer interactions and make service operations more efficient. This might potentially result in human workers being replaced. Nevertheless, the incorporation of AI in customer service offers prospects for enhanced efficiency, cost-effectiveness, and customized client experiences (Dwivedi & Mahanty, 2023). Despite concerns about job losses, AI's role in customer service is changing to generate new job categories in technology-focused fields such as AI development and data analysis. This highlights the significance of reskilling programs to provide workers with the essential skills needed for the AI-driven job market (Rohan & Banubakode, 2024). It is essential to carefully weigh the economic advantages and ethical concerns associated with implementing AI in customer service in order to guarantee a viable future for the sector (Pillai, 2024).

2.11. Practical Examples of Successful AI Implementations

The revolutionary potential of AI technology is demonstrated by the numerous successful AI deployments across different sectors. One example is the Indian e-commerce business Exotic India Trades, which used Freshdesk to streamline their customer care operations and efficiently manage client queries (Sharma, 2023). Despite ongoing implementation hurdles, manufacturers are beginning to see the benefits of industrial AI in terms of increased resilience, better product quality, and competitiveness (Janika et al., 2022). In addition, prominent companies in the industry have used AI for marketing purposes; for example, Domino's has rethought customer interactions through the use of voice and conversational technologies, Nike has launched personalized design campaigns, and Coca-Cola has integrated AI into their vending machines to boost their marketing campaigns (Sankar, 2024). Additionally, by increasing consumer analytics, offering speedy support, personalization, fraud detection, and improving customer experiences, machine learning has also greatly affected service industries such as healthcare, tourism, and transportation (Lohit et al., 2022). Amazon's AI-driven robot systems for inventory management and rapid product delivery are examples of successful artificial intelligence deployments in the service industry. These systems provide shortened lead times, cost-effectiveness, and error-free operations (Reis et al., 2020). In addition, open AI registries have been used by cities such as Helsinki and Amsterdam to improve the security and openness of urban public services. This shows that AI has the ability to better both citizen experiences and the delivery of services (Floridi, 2020).

Figure 3. AI applications in various business industries (Ibegbulam, 2023)

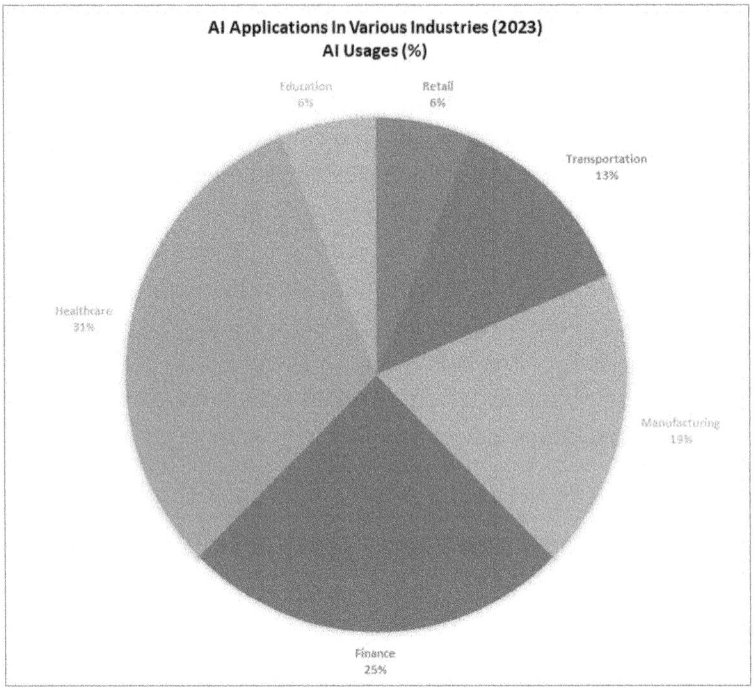

Figure 3 shows AI adoption in Retail, Transportation, Manufacturing, Finance, Healthcare, and Education. The most AI-integrated industry is healthcare, with 31.2% utilization, demonstrating its reliance on sophisticated technology for patient care and diagnostics. Finance uses 25% AI for risk management and fraud detection. Automation and logistics drive modest AI adoption in manufacturing and transportation (18.8% and 12.5%, respectively). Retail and Education have 6.2% AI integration, showing growth and innovation potential. The research shows that AI is having a major influence across businesses, with opportunities for growth in less-exposed areas.

2.12. Example of AI (Personalizing Customer Experience and Inventory Management utilizing AI)

In the retail industry, Amazon's utilization of AI is a benchmark, particularly in the areas of inventory management optimization and personalization of customer experiences. The company's supply chain optimization algorithms and recommendation engine are exceptional. Aspects of using AI and its details are assembled in Table 1.

Tactics

- Recommendation Systems: users are recommended products based on their perusing and purchasing history through collaborative filtering and deep learning techniques.
- Inventory Optimization: AI models optimize stock levels and minimize surplus and stockouts by predicting product demand.

Impact

- Contributed to 35% of Amazon's revenue by increasing sales through personalized recommendations. ~
- • 15% reduction in holding costs as a result of enhanced inventory turnover.

Table 1. A practical example of AI and its impact on customer experience

Aspect	Details
Organization	Amazon
AI Technologies Used	Recommendation Systems, Inventory Optimization, Machine Learning Algorithms
Key Applications	Personalizing customer experiences, predicting product demand
	Increased sales through personalized recommendations (contributing to 35% of revenue), improved inventory turnover and reduced holding costs by 15%)

Source: Rabata, 2024.

2.13. Key Benefits of Using AI in Customer Services in Various Industries

Figure 4 demonstrates a list of some of the best things about using AI in business and customer service. Some of the benefits are being able to handle large amounts of data, spend less time on each customer, and get a better sense of what each customer wants and needs. AI also makes it possible to provide preventative support and adjust to changing conditions, which makes it easier to keep track of performance and guess what will happen in the future. AI also helps cut costs, gives people more time to work on hard problems, and makes services and goods more personalized.

All of these benefits show how AI can change the way businesses work by making them more efficient and effective.

Figure 4. Key benefits of using AI in customer services in various industries (Rana, 2024)

AI has a substantial impact on a variety of industries, particularly in the areas of efficacy and value. AI's contribution is indispensable in the realm of consumer relationship services. AI-driven customer relationship management (CRM) systems are frequently implemented in industries such as Professional Services and Financial Services, which derive substantial advantages from AI. These systems analyze consumer data, predict trends, personalize interactions, and enhance customer satisfaction and loyalty. The overall customer experience is improved by AI's capacity to manage large datasets and offer real-time insights, which in turn drives growth and efficiency in industries that prioritize customer satisfaction.

Figure 5. AI gross value added (GVA) in 2035 (Howarth, 2024)

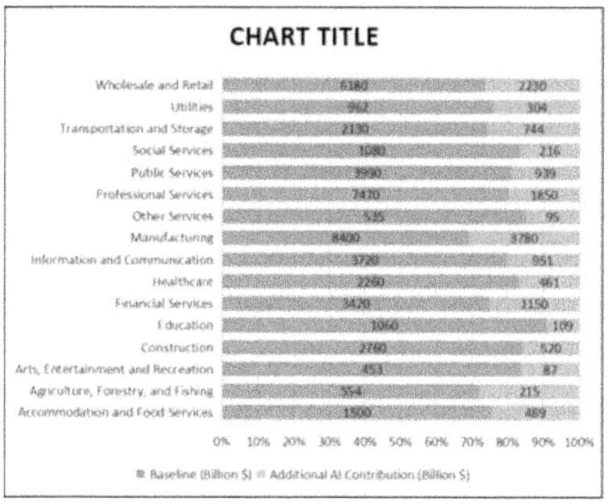

The aggregate value contributed by AI in a variety of industries is depicted in Figure 5, which emphasizes both baseline values and additional contributions from AI. The manufacturing industry stands to gain $3.78 trillion from AI by 2035 (Howarth, 2024). Manufacturing is the industry leader, with a baseline of $8400 billion and an additional $3780 billion in AI contributions. Other substantial contributions are observed in the following sectors: Professional Services, Financial Services, and Wholesale and Retail. AI has contributed $2230 billion, $1850 billion, and $1150 billion, respectively. The comprehensive economic benefits of AI integration across diverse industries are underscored by sectors such as Public Services and Information and Communication, which also exhibit notable AI impacts. To name a few, industry verticals that employ AI technology include tech-related sales, insurance, finance, telecommunications, healthcare, manufacturing, retail, and marketing. This technology is used to make decisions by providing new experiences to customers in order to establish strong customer relationships.

3. METHODOLOGY

3.1. Research Design

The study adopts a mixed-method research design, incorporating both qualitative and quantitative elements. Exploratory research has been designed to conduct this study.

3.2. Sample size & Data Collection

The sample size is 340 which is selected from the convenience sampling method because there is no specific sample frame. Face-to-face surveys, as well as online surveys (through the mail), have been conducted with a structured questionnaire to collect primary data from the selected three developing countries (India, Indonesia and Bangladesh). The survey will measure their attitudes towards AI-powered customer service, acceptance levels, preferences for human interactions versus AI interactions and future trends of AI-driven customer relationship service. An in-depth literature review has been conducted to gather qualitative information about AI-driven customer relationship services, challenges and future trends of AI-driven customer relationship services provided by present business organizations. A structured questionnaire survey has been conducted to collect primary data from the two categories of respondents. One category is an AI-driven Customer service receiver (Customer) and another category is a customer service provider (customer service managers) from selected businesses in three (3) developing countries (India, Indonesia and Bangladesh) through online Google form and face-to-face interaction.

3.3. Data Analysis Method

Statistical analysis of survey data has been performed using software (SPSS, Version-25). Descriptive statistics (frequency, percentage, and rank analysis) have been used to summarize customer responses, customer perception and recommendations with AI-driven customer relationship service.

4. DATA ANALYSIS

To get the answer to the mentioned research questions; initially, it will evaluate the current state of customer relationship service in a variety of industries and find out the primary obstacles that businesses face in Delivering Exceptional Customer Support. Secondly, it will evaluate the perception and acceptance of AI-powered customer service solutions by customers, including their attitudes toward interacting with AI-driven systems as opposed to human representatives. Finally, it will anticipate potential future trends and advancements in AI-driven customer relationship service, as well as their implications for both businesses and consumers. The data analysis will represent a comprehensive solution to the current and prospective state of AI in customer relationship services, providing insights into these objectives.

4.1. Demographic Analysis

To access the current state of Customer relationship service (CRS), perception and acceptance levels of customers (service receiver) and service providers (customer service manager) towards AI-powered customer service in Asian developing countries (India, Bangladesh and Indonesia); data has been collected from the 340 respondents. To assess the future trends and applications of AI-powered customer relationship service mostly in customer service in various industries in business a survey has been conducted from the developing nations.

Table 2. Demographic information

		Frequency	Percent	Cumulative Percent
Categories of Respondents	Customer Service provider (Customer Relationship officer/ Management)	150	44.1	44.1
	Customer	190	55.9	100.0
	Total =	340	100.0	
Gender	Male	230	67.6	67.6
	Female	110	32.4	100.0
	Total =	340	100.0	
Country of Residence	India	100	29.4	29.4
	Indonesia	90	26.5	55.9
	Bangladesh	150	44.1	100.0
	Total =	340	100.0	

Source: Author.

Focusing on a diversified sample of 340 respondents, this study examines the potential future implications of AI in customer relationship services. The respondents are primarily from India (29.4%), Indonesia (26.5%), and Bangladesh (44.1%) (see Table 2). Customers comprise 55.9% of the respondents, while 44.1% are customer service providers. Participants comprised 67.6% males and 32.4% females, as indicated by the gender distribution. The objective of this research is to investigate how these demographics perceive and anticipate the transformative role of AI in improving operational efficiencies and customer service experiences in a variety of cultural and organizational contexts.

4.2. General Information of AI-powered Customer Service

Table 3 offers a comprehensive overview of AI-powered customer relationship service, including the prevalence and varieties of AI-driven solutions that consumers have encountered. It emphasizes the extensive utilization of AI technologies in customer relationship management and delineates the specific AI-powered services, including chatbots, that consumers have encountered. This general information establishes the foundation for a more comprehensive investigation of the competency and impact of AI in improving customer support experiences.

Table 3. General information

		Frequency	Percent	Cumulative Percent
Have you ever interacted with AI-powered customer relationship service solutions?	Yes	340	100.0	100.0
	No	0	0	0
	Total =	340	100.0	
Type of AI-powered customer relationship service you have experienced.	Chatbot	180	52.9	52.9
	Virtual Assistant	120	35.3	88.2
	Automated Email Response	40	11.8	100.0
	Total =	340	100.0	

Source: Author.

As reported in Table 3, all 340 respondents (100%) have engaged with AI-powered customer relationship service solutions in this study. Chatbots, virtual assistants, and automated email responses comprise 52.9%, 35.3%, and 11.8% of these interactions, respectively. The surveyed demographics from India (29.4%), Indonesia (26.5%), and Bangladesh (44.1%) have widely adopted and variedly utilized AI technologies to improve customer service experiences. This data underscores this trend. These discoveries offer a comprehensive review of the most recent AI application trends and user experiences in customer relationship management, spanning a variety of cultural and organizational contexts.

4.3. AI Integration in Customer Relationship Service Operations

Table 4 reflects the degree to which organizations have used artificial intelligence (AI) in their customer relationship service operations. It shows a summary of various AI technologies in use, including chatbots, virtual assistants, automated email answers and predictive analytics. Additionally, it assesses the level of contentment that industries have regarding the success of AI in improving their customer service skills, providing valuable observations on the efficacy and influence of these (AI-driven) technologies.

Table 4. AI integration in customer relationship service

		Frequency	Percent	Cumulative Percent
Has your business integrated AI into its customer relationship service operations?	Yes	150	100.0	100.0
	No	0	0	0
	Total =	150	100.0	
What AI technologies are you using?	Chatbot	90	60.0	60.0
	Virtual Assistant	42	28.0	88.0
	Automated Email Response	9	6.0	94.0
	Predictive Analytics	6	4.0	98.0
	Others	3	2.0	100.0
	Total =	150	100.0	
How satisfied are you with the performance of AI in your customer relationship service operations?	Dissatisfied	3	2.0	2.0
	Neutral	9	6.0	8.0
	Satisfied	111	74.0	82.0
	Very Satisfied	27	18.0	100.0
	Total =	150	100.0	

Source: Author.

This section analyses the incorporation of artificial intelligence (AI) in customer relationship service activities, as specified in Table 4. All of the 150 organizations examined have used AI solutions, accounting for a 100% integration rate. Chatbots and virtual assistants are the AI technologies most frequently utilized, with chatbots accounting for 60.0% and virtual assistants for 28.0%. Users have reported different levels of satisfaction, with 74.0% being pleased and 18.0% being extremely satisfied with the performance of AI. The findings emphasize the widespread adoption of AI in improving customer service operations and the overall favorable response to AI technology among the studied firms.

4.4. Current Landscape of Customer Relationship Service & Key Challenges Businesses face in Delivering Exceptional Customer Support

Table 5 evaluates the overall impact of customer relationship service across several industries and highlights the primary obstacles firms have in providing great customer assistance. This study offers valuable information on the overall perception of customer service quality and identifies key challenges, such as a large number of customer queries, insufficiently qualified staff, ineffective procedures and inadequate technology, that impede firms from attaining ideal customer contentment.

Table 5. Current landscape & key challenges of customer support

		Frequency	Percent	Cumulative Percent
The overall quality of customer relationship service in your industry?	Neutral	6	4.0	4.0
	Good	135	90.0	94.0
	Very Good	9	6.0	100.0
	Total =	150	100.0	
Main challenges your business faces in delivering exceptional customer support	The high volume of customer inquiries.	3	2.0	2.0
	Lack of trained staff.	90	60.0	62.0
	Inefficient processes.	12	8.0	70.0
	Inadequate technology.	42	28.0	98.0
	Others.	3	2.0	100.0
	Total =	150	100.0	

Source: Author.

Based on the data in Table 5, this section analyses the present state of customer relationship service and highlights the main obstacles that companies encounter. In general, 90% of those who took the survey think that customer service in their field is good. Subpar technology (reported 28.0% of the time) and a lack of skilled personnel (60.0% of the time) are major obstacles to providing outstanding customer service. These findings highlight the need to improve customer service by focusing on staff training and technical capabilities.

4.5. Recommendations for AI Integration into Customer Relationship Service Strategies

Table 6 represents relevant recommendations for how to successfully use AI in customer relationship management strategies in various industries. It underlines how important it is to know what the customer wants, train staff, buy the right technology, and make sure that tracking and growth happen all the time. It also shows how important it is to customize AI solutions to meet the needs of specific industries to make them work better and make customers happier overall.

Table 6. Recommendations for AI integration in customer relationship service

		Frequency		Cumulative Percent
The most important factors for effectively integrating AI into customer service	Understanding customer needs	6	4.0	4.0
	Training staff	102	68.0	72.0
	Investing in the right technology	12	8.0	80.0
	Continuous monitoring and improvement	30	20.0	100.0
	Total =	150	100.0	
How important is it to tailor AI solutions to industry-specific needs?	Moderately Important	9	6.0	6.0
	Important	93	62.0	68.0
	Very Important	48	32.0	100.0
	Total =	150	100.0	

Source: Author.

Table 6 highlights important guidelines that drive the incorporation of AI into customer relationship service plans. Respondents ranked staff training as a vital aspect, with 68.0% ranking it as such, and 20.0% ranking it as such, as essential. Furthermore, adapting AI solutions to meet industry-specific demands is emphasized by 94.0% of respondents, highlighting the necessity for a deliberate approach to effectively integrate AI and improve customer service delivery and satisfaction. These findings shed light on crucial factors that companies should think about if they want to make the most of AI in their CRM systems.

4.6. Customers' Perceptions and Acceptance Level of AI-Powered Customer Relationship Service Solutions

Table 7 explores customers' perceptions and degrees of acceptability for customer relationship service systems powered by artificial intelligence (AI). The study investigates consumers' perceptions regarding the ability of AI to handle questions as efficiently as human agents as well as their degree of comfort with AI-driven solutions. Moreover, it assesses the perceived efficacy and proficiency of AI in addressing customer concerns, preferences for AI over human engagement for particular activities and overall contentment with customer service experiences driven by AI. This investigation represents useful insights into customers' perceptions, acceptance, and interactions with artificial intelligence in the context of customer relationship management.

Table 7. Customer perception and acceptance of AI in customer relationship service

		Frequency		Cumulative Percent
AI can handle customer inquiries as effectively as human representatives	Yes	110	57.9	57.9
	No	80	42.1	100.0
	Total =	190	100.0	
I am comfortable with AI-driven customer relationship service solutions instead of human representatives	Disagree	80	42.1	42.1
	Agree	50	26.3	68.4
	Strongly Agree	60	31.6	100.0
	Total =	190	100.0	
AI-powered customer service solutions provide quick and efficient responses	Disagree	79	41.6	41.6
	Neutral	1	.5	42.1
	Agree	50	26.3	68.4
	Strongly Agree	60	31.6	100.0
	Total =	190	100.0	
AI-powered customer service solutions are effective in resolving customer issues.	Disagree	79	41.6	41.6
	Neutral	1	.5	42.1
	Agree	70	36.8	78.9
	Strongly Agree	40	21.1	100.0
	Total =	190	100.0	
I prefer interacting with AI-driven systems over human representatives for certain customer service tasks.	Disagree	65	34.2	34.2
	Agree	65	34.2	68.4
	Strongly Agree	60	31.6	100.0
	Total =	190	100.0	
AI-powered customer service solutions can understand and respond accurately to customer queries.	Disagree	100	52.6	52.6
	Neutral	10	5.3	57.9
	Agree	30	15.8	73.7
	Strongly Agree	50	26.3	100.0
	Total =	190	100.0	
How would you rate your overall experience with AI-powered customer service solutions	Poor	20	10.5	10.5
	Neutral	40	21.1	31.6
	Good	95	50.0	81.6
	Very Good	35	18.4	100.0
	Total =	190	100.0	

Source: Author.

In Table 7, we can see how customers feel and how much they are willing to adopt customer relationship service solutions driven by AI. Of the 190 people who took the survey, 57.9% think AI can answer customer service questions just as well as humans, while 42.1% think the opposite. The degree to which people are at ease with AI-driven solutions varies; nonetheless, 57.9% of respondents either agree or strongly believe that AI can effectively replace human representatives. When it comes to efficiency, 78.9% of people think that AI-powered solutions are helpful for fixing customer problems, and 68.4% agree or strongly agree that they give fast and efficient replies. Furthermore, for some jobs, 68.4% said they prefer dealing with AI-driven technologies. Nonetheless, 57.9% are either ambivalent or strongly disagree that AI can correctly interpret and address consumer inquiries. Despite differing opinions on AI's usefulness in customer service, 81.6% of respondents said they had an excellent or very good experience with solutions driven by AI.

4.7. Future Trends and Advancements in AI-driven Customer Relationship Service

Table 8 represents the projected future trends and breakthroughs in customer relationship service that are driven by artificial intelligence. It emphasizes which artificial intelligence technologies are anticipated to have the most significant influence, such as expanded capabilities for automation, enhanced customization, advanced predictive analytics, and improved natural language processing. In addition, it evaluates the view that AI will play a more significant role in customer relationship service over the next five years, therefore offering insights into the potential and future direction of AI in this industry.

Table 8. Future trends and advancements of customer relation service

		Frequency		Cumulative Percent
Which AI advancements do you believe will have the most impact on customer relationship service?	Improved natural language processing	75	39.5	39.5
	Advanced predictive analytics	50	26.3	65.8
	Enhanced personalization	40	21.1	86.8
	Greater automation capabilities	25	13.2	100.0
	Total =	190	100.0	
AI will play a more significant role in customer relationship service in the next five years	Yes	165	86.8	86.8
	No	25	13.2	100.0
	Total =	190	100.0	

Source: Author.

Based on Table 8, this section delves into the expected developments and trends in AI-driven CRM in the coming years. The majority of respondents (39.5% to be exact) think that better NLP and more sophisticated predictive analytics will make the most difference (26.3%). Also, over the next five years, 86.8% anticipate AI to play a bigger role in customer service. This shows that people are expecting AI to be more integrated and innovative so that it can improve customer interactions and service delivery.

5. FINDINGS

This study examined the effects of AI-powered customer relationship service on both customers and service providers, focusing on many important objectives. Initially, it evaluated the present state of customer service in several sectors, emphasizing difficulties such as the large number of questions and insufficient technology. Furthermore, it analyzed consumer opinions regarding the efficiency of AI-powered solutions in addressing queries and resolving problems. The findings showed a combination of positive and negative views, with a notable majority expressing comfort and preference for AI-driven systems in certain activities. A significant proportion of clients, namely 81.6%, expressed positive ratings for their overall experience with customer support solutions driven by artificial intelligence, categorizing it as either good or very good. Furthermore, the participants predicted notable progress in artificial intelligence (AI) shortly, namely in the areas of enhanced natural language processing and sophisticated predictive analytics. An overwhelming majority (86.8%) of the respondents think that AI will have a more significant impact on customer service within the next five years. Ultimately, concrete suggestions were given to businesses on how to successfully incorporate AI into their customer interaction strategy. These recommendations underscored the need for ongoing staff training and tailoring AI solutions to align with industry-specific requirements and client preferences. These observations emphasize the significant impact that AI may have on improving customer service experiences, as well as the current difficulties and prospective benefits of using AI in many sectors.

6. RECOMMENDATIONS

To improve customer relationship services using AI and to overcome the key challenges businesses face in delivering exceptional customer support, organizations should allocate resources towards AI-driven solutions such as chatbots and virtual assistants. These technologies are capable of effectively handling a large number of client questions and relieving the burden caused by insufficient technology. To tackle the issue of underqualified personnel, organizations should prioritize improving staff training to guarantee that employees are adequately equipped to collaborate with AI technologies and provide exceptional customer care. Furthermore, it is essential to increase the integration of AI by customizing these solutions to meet the individual needs of different industries and the preferences of customers. This will ensure that AI improves the customer experience instead of making it more complex. Businesses should utilize predictive analytics to forecast client requirements, facilitating proactive assistance and enhancing satisfaction levels. Because several consumers express satisfaction with AI-powered solutions, organizations should prioritize delivering a smooth and user-friendly experience with these tools. Businesses should anticipate and get ready for upcoming breakthroughs in AI, namely in natural language processing and predictive analytics. These discoveries will have a significant impact on the future of customer service.

7. CONCLUSION

This study highlights the increasing influence of AI-powered customer relationship service, exposing both potential advantages and obstacles. Companies are progressively using artificial intelligence (AI) to improve customer service; however, they encounter obstacles such as technological disparities and the requirement for training. Although there are differing opinions, a substantial majority of clients indicate contentment with solutions driven by artificial intelligence. In the future, customer service is anticipated to undergo a significant transformation due to developments in natural language processing and predictive analytics. Businesses should prioritize the development of customized AI strategies that specifically target industry-specific requirements and client preferences in order to successfully harness AI technology for improving overall service quality and customer happiness. The study's importance lies in its contribution to comprehending the role of AI in customer service specifically in emerging nations. The report offers useful insights into how AI might effectively tackle distinctive difficulties and capitalize on possibilities in markets such as India, Indonesia, and Bangladesh, by analyzing views and trends in these areas. Enterprises in emerging economies might utilize these observations to customize artificial intelligence tactics that align with specific local requirements, thereby enhancing the quality of services and enhancing consumer experiences in these swiftly progressing environments.

7.1. Limitation of the Study

Interpreting the results of this investigation necessitates taking into account certain constraints. Initially, the research is primarily based on self-reported data from respondents, which may be susceptible to fallacies such as recall bias or social desirability. Secondly, the study's primary emphasis is on perceptions and experiences within specific industries and regions, specifically India, Indonesia, and Bangladesh (three developing countries). This may restrict the generalizability of the findings to other geographical areas or sectors. Furthermore, the survey sample size (sample size is only 340) and composition may not accurately reflect the diversity of perspectives and experiences across all segments of customer service providers and customers. Additionally, the investigation's scope is primarily focused on the contemporary perceptions and expectations of AI integration, rather than the long-term effects or behavioral changes that may arise. Lastly, the swiftly changing nature of AI technologies may result in the obsolescence of certain findings as new challenges and advancements in the field of customer relationship service emerge. A more exhaustive comprehension of the complexities and nuances associated with AI adoption in customer service contexts could be achieved by addressing these limitations.

7.2 Future Work Direction

Future research could further develop this study by conducting longitudinal investigations to monitor the ongoing effects of AI integration on operational efficiencies and customer service quality over extended periods. Furthermore, comparative insights could be obtained by investigating the cultural and regional influences on the acceptance and efficacy of AI in a broader array of developing countries. It would be essential to consider ethical implications, including algorithmic biases and privacy concerns, in AI-driven customer service contexts in order to ensure responsible implementation. Finally, the potential to improve the customer journey and advance AI-driven strategies in diverse market environments may be discovered by investigating inventive AI applications beyond conventional customer service, such as in personalized marketing or sales forecasting. These research avenues have the potential to enhance our comprehension and encourage ongoing enhancements in the utilization of AI for customer relationship service.

ACKNOWLEDGEMENTS

Special gratitude goes to Dr. José Duarte Santos for accepting to take care of this research and for the guidance and suggestions she provided during the writing process to make this work richer. I would also like to thank Prof. Dr. Md. Mizanur Rahman for his invaluable ideas and feedback. And finally, I would like to thank my family for their amazing support and constant encouragement from the time I started writing this paper through the end.

REFERENCES

Akter, S. (2024a). Exploring Cutting-Edge Frontiers in Artificial Intelligence: An Overview of Trends and Advancements. *Journal of Artificial Intelligence General science (JAIGS), 2*(1). https://ojs.boulibrary.com/index.php/JAIGS/article/view/43/28

Akter, S. (2024b). Investigating State-of-the-Art Frontiers in Artificial Intelligence: A Synopsis of Trends and Innovations. *Journal of Artificial Intelligence General science (JAIGS), 2*(1). https://jaigs.org/index.php/JAIGS/article/view/19/11

Akter, S., Dwivedi, Y. K., Biswas, K., Michael, K., Bandara, R. J., & Sajib, S. (2021). Addressing algorithmic bias in AI-driven customer management. [JGIM]. *Journal of Global Information Management*, 29(6), 1–27. DOI: 10.4018/JGIM.20211101.oa3

Almahairah, M. S. (2023). Artificial Intelligence Application for Effective Customer Relationship Management. In *2023 International Conference on Computer Communication and Informatics (ICCCI)* (pp. 1-7). IEEE. DOI: 10.1109/ICCCI56745.2023.10128360

Astuti, E., Harsono, I., Uhai, S., Muthmainah, H. N., & Vandika, A. Y. (2024). Application of artificial intelligence technology in customer service in the hospitality industry in Indonesia: A literature review on improving efficiency and user experience. *Sciences Du Nord Nature Science and Technology*, 1(01), 28–36.

Azhar, D. (2023). Desain Model Artificial Intelligence Untuk Peningkatan Customer Experience & Penjualan Tenaga Listrik Melalui Penambahan Fitur Virtual Customer Support Pada Aplikasi PLN Mobile. *Jurnal Energi dan Ketenagalistrikan, 1*(2), 157-165. .DOI: 10.33322/juke.v1i2.33

Bhutto, R. A., & Maqsood, A. (2007). Customer services: a case study of cellular phone companies in Pakistan. *JISR management and social sciences & economics, 5*(1), 19-23.

Boguda, S. K., & Shailaja, A.Satish Kumar Boguda. (2019). The Future of Customer Experience in the Information Age of Artificial Intelligence-Get Ready for Change. *International Journal of Engineering Research & Technology (Ahmedabad)*, 8(6), 1141–1150. DOI: 10.17577/IJERTV8IS060622

Bolze, J. D., & Engles, E. (2018). Artificial intelligence based service implementation. https://patents.google.com/patent/AU2018274927A1/en

Bowman, J. (2023, November 21). *How artificial intelligence is used in customer service*. The Motley Fool. https://www.fool.com/investing/stock-market/market-sectors/information-technology/ai-stocks/ai-in-customer-service/

Cavoukian, A. (2020). Understanding how to implement privacy by design, one step at a time. *IEEE Consumer Electronics Magazine*, 9(2), 78–82. DOI: 10.1109/MCE.2019.2953739

Dalal, T., Chaudhary, P., Rawat, S. S., & Metha, Y. (2022). Artificial Intelligence (AI) Powered Customer Care. In Pillai, R. K., Singh, B. P., & Murugesan, N. (Eds.), *ISUW 2021. Lecture Notes in Electrical Engineering* (Vol. 843). Springer., DOI: 10.1007/978-981-16-8727-3_42

Davenport, T. H., & Ronanki, R. (2018). Artificial intelligence for the real world. *Harvard Business Review*, 96(1), 108–116.

De Keyser, A., Köcher, S., Alkire, L., Verbeeck, C., & Kandampully, J. (2019). Frontline service technology infusion: Conceptual archetypes and future research directions. *Journal of Service Management*, 30(1), 156–183. DOI: 10.1108/JOSM-03-2018-0082

Deepa, S., & Abirami, A. (2024). The Impact of AI on Customer Experience. In *Balancing Automation and Human Interaction in Modern Marketing* (pp. 263–285). IGI Global., DOI: 10.4018/979-8-3693-2276-5.ch014

Dilmegani, C. (2024, March 22). *11 AI use cases in customer service: In-depth guide in 2024*. AIMultiple. https://research.aimultiple.com/customer-service-ai/

Dwivedi, D. N., & Mahanty, G. (2023). AI-Powered Employee Experience: Strategies and Best Practices. In *Exploring the Intersection of AI and Human Resources Management* (pp. 166-181). IGI Global. DOI: 10.4018/979-8-3693-0039-8.ch009

Ekwunife, M. (2023). *Technology Manufacturing Leaders' Innovation Strategies to Improve Users' Choice Capabilities in a Fast-Changing Markets*. Walden University.

Fianto, A. Y. A., & Dutahatmaja, A. (2023). Artificial Intelligence and Novel Services: Exploring Opportunities in the Marketing Landscape. *Journal of Applied Management and Business*, 4(1), 49–59.

Floridi, L. (2020). Artificial intelligence as a public service: Learning from Amsterdam and Helsinki. *Philosophy & Technology*, 33(4), 541–546. DOI: 10.1007/s13347-020-00434-3

Følstad, A., & Skjuve, M. (2019). Chatbots for customer service: user experience and motivation. In *Proceedings of the 1st international conference on conversational user interfaces* (pp. 1-9). DOI: 10.1145/3342775.3342784

Ghosh, S., Ness, S., & Salunkhe, S. (2024). The Role of AI Enabled Chatbots in Omnichannel Customer Service. *Journal of Engineering Research and Reports*, 26(6), 327–345. DOI: 10.9734/jerr/2024/v26i61184

Gonçalves, A. R., Pinto, D. C., Rita, P., & Pires, T. (2023). Artificial Intelligence and Its Ethical Implications for Marketing. *Emerging Science Journal*, 7(2), 313–327. DOI: 10.28991/ESJ-2023-07-02-01

Govender, O. V. (2017). *An investigation into the challenges faced by a mobile service provider in meeting customer needs* (Doctoral dissertation). DOI: 10.51415/10321/2561

Hossain, M. S., Rahman, M. M., Abresham, A. E., Pranto, A. J., & Rahman, M. R. (2023). AI and machine learning applications to enhance customer support. In *Handbook of Research on AI and Machine Learning Applications in Customer Support and Analytics* (pp. 300–324). IGI Global., DOI: 10.4018/978-1-6684-7105-0.ch015

Howarth, J. (2024, July 25). 57 new artificial intelligence statistics (Aug 2024). Exploding Topics. https://explodingtopics.com/blog/ai-statistics#ai-in-marketing

Huang, M. H., & Rust, R. T. (2018). Artificial intelligence in service. *Journal of Service Research*, 21(2), 155–172. DOI: 10.1177/1094670517752459

Ibegbulam, C. M., Olowonubi, J. A., Fatounde, S. A., & Oyegunwa, O. A.Ibegbulam C.MOlowonubi, J.AFatounde, S.AOyegunwa, O.A. (2023). Artificial intelligence in the era of 4IR: Drivers, challenges and opportunities. *Engineering Science & Technology Journal*, 4(6), 473–488. DOI: 10.51594/estj.v4i6.668

Koehler, J., Fux, E., Herzog, F. A., Lötscher, D., Waelti, K., Imoberdorf, R., & Budke, D. (2018). Towards intelligent process support for customer service desks: Extracting problem descriptions from noisy and multi-lingual texts. In Business Process Management Workshops: BPM 2017 International Workshops, Barcelona, Spain, September 10-11, 2017, Revised Papers 15 (pp. 36-52). Springer International Publishing.

Kutz, J., Neuhüttler, J., Spilski, J., & Lachmann, T. (2022, July). Implementation of AI Technologies in manufacturing-success factors and challenges. In The Human Side of Service Engineerin, Proceedings of the 13th International Conference on Applied Human Factors and Ergonomics (AHFE 2022), New York, NY, USA (pp. 24-28).

Jayawardena, N. S., Behl, A., Thaichon, P., & Quach, S. (2022). Artificial intelligence (AI)-based market intelligence and customer insights. In *Artificial intelligence for marketing management* (pp. 120–141). Routledge. DOI: 10.4324/9781003280392-10

Jerbi, D. (2023). Exploring the Latest Frontiers of Artificial Intelligence: A Review of Trends and Developments. *TechRxiv*. DOI: 10.36227/techrxiv.22717327

Khan, M. S. U., Hasan, M. F., Islam, M. S., & Hassan, S. T. (2021). Artificial intelligenc e in the banking sector of Bangladesh: Applicability and the challenges. *Roundtabl e discussion series-2021. Keynote Paper of Roundtable Discussion of BIBM, 6*(2).

Kraus, S., Oshrat, Y., Aumann, Y., Hollander, T., Maksimov, O., Ostroumov, A., & Shechtman, N. (2023, September). Customer service combining human operators and virtual agents: a call for multidisciplinary AI Research. In *Proceedings of the AAAI Conference on Artificial Intelligence* (Vol. 37, No. 13, pp. 15393-15401). DOI: 10.1609/aaai.v37i13.26795

Krishna, S. H., Vijayanand, N., Suneetha, A., Basha, S. M., Sekhar, S. C., & Saranya, A. (2022, December). Artificial Intelligence Application for Effective Customer Relationship Management. In *2022 5th International Conference on Contemporary Computing and Informatics (IC3I)* (pp. 2019-2023). IEEE. DOI: 10.1109/IC3I56241.2022.10073038

Kumar, J., & Gupta, S. S. (2023). Impact of artificial intelligence towards customer relationship in Indian banking industry. *Gyan Manag. J*, 17(1), 105–115. DOI: 10.48165/gmj.2022.17.1.12

Lemon, K. N., & Verhoef, P. C. (2016). Understanding customer experience throughout the customer journey. *Journal of Marketing*, 80(6), 69–96. DOI: 10.1509/jm.15.0420

Link, M., Dukino, C., Ganz, W., Hamann, K., & Schnalzer, K. (2020). The Use of AI-Based Assistance Systems in the Service Sector: opportunities, challenges and applications. In *Advances in Human Factors and Systems Interaction:Proceedings of the AHFE 2020 Virtual Conference on Human Factors and Systems Interaction,July 16-20, 2020,USA* (pp. 10-16). Springer International Publishing. DOI: 10.1007/978-3-030-51369-6_2

Lohit, V. S., Mujahid, M. M., & Sai, G. K. (2022). Use of machine learning for continuous improvement and handling multi-dimensional data in service sector. *Comput. Intell. Mach. Learn*, 3(2), 39–46. DOI: 10.36647/CIML/03.02.A006

Makhija, P., & Chacko, E. (2021). Efficiency and Advancement of Artificial Intelligence in Service Sector with Special Reference to Banking Industry. In Nasser Rashad Al Mawali & Anis Moosa Al Lawati & Ananda S (Ed.), *Fourth Industrial Revolution and Business Dynamics* (pp. 21-35), Springer.DOI: 10.1007/978-981-16-3250-1_2

Monica, R., & Soju, A. V. (2024). Artificial Intelligence and Service Marketing Innovation. In *AI Innovation in Services Marketing* (pp. 150–172). IGI Global., DOI: 10.4018/979-8-3693-2153-9.ch007

Motadi, M. S. (2024). Harnessing AI for Ethical Digital Consumer Behavior Analysis. In Enhancing and Predicting Digital Consumer Behavior with AI (pp. 211-237). IGI Global. DOI: 10.4018/979-8-3693-4453-8.ch012

Nandyala, L. (2024). Ethical implications of artificial intelligence in marketing. *Indian Scientific Journal Of Research In Engineering And Management*, 08(05), 1–5. DOI: 10.55041/IJSREM33275

Noranee, S., & bin Othman, A. K. (2023). Understanding consumer sentiments: Exploring the role of artificial intelligence in marketing. *JMM17: Jurnal Ilmu ekonomi dan manajemen, 10*(1), 15-23. .DOI: 10.30996/jmm17.v10i1.8690

O'Neil, C. (2017). *Weapons of math destruction: How big data increases inequality and threatens democracy*. Crown.

Oanh, V. T. K. (2024). Evolving Landscape of E-Commerce, Marketing, and Customer Service: The Impact of Ai Integration. *Journal of Electrical Systems*, 20(3s), 1125–1137. Advance online publication. DOI: 10.52783/jes.1426

Oyeniyi, L. D., Ugochukwu, C. E., & Mhlongo, N. Z.Lawrence Damilare OyeniyiChinonye Esther UgochukwuNoluthando Zamanjomane Mhlongo. (2024). Implementing AI in banking customer service: A review of current trends and future applications. *International Journal of Science and Research Archive*, 11(2), 1492–1509. DOI: 10.30574/ijsra.2024.11.2.0639

Pansare, P. (2024). Futuristic trends in artificial intelligence. In *Futuristic trends in management* (Vol. 3, Book 27, pp. 81-102). IIP Series. DOI: 10.58532/V3BHMA27P2CH3

Pillai, M. C. (2024). The Evolution of Customer Service: Identifying the Impact of Artificial Intelligence on Employment and Management in Call Centres. *Journal of Business Management and Information Systems*. .DOI: 10.48001/jbmis.2024.si1010

Rabata, R. (2024). *Case studies: Successful AI implementations in various industries*. Capella Solutions. https://www.capellasolutions.com/blog/case-studies-successful-ai-implementations-in-various-industries

Rana, J. (2024, July 15). *AI in customer service: Ways to use it for amazing support*. ReveChat. https://www.revechat.com/blog/ai-in-customer-service/

Reis, J., Amorim, M., Cohen, Y., & Rodrigues, M. (2020). Artificial intelligence in service delivery systems: A systematic literature review. In *Trends and Innovations in Information Systems and Technologies* (Vol. 1, pp. 222–233). Springer. DOI: 10.1007/978-3-030-45688-7_23

Roba, G. B., & Maric, P. (2023). AI in Customer Relationship Management. In *Developments in Information and Knowledge Management Systems for Business Applications* (pp. 469–487). Springer., DOI: 10.1007/978-3-031-25695-0_21

Rohan, D. J., & Banubakode, A. (2024). The Implications of Artificial Intelligence on the Employment Sector. *International Journal For Multidisciplinary Research*, 6(3), 22716. Advance online publication. DOI: 10.36948/ijfmr.2024.v06i03.22716

Rust, R. T., & Huang, M. H. (2014). The service revolution and the transformation of marketing science. *Marketing Science*, 33(2), 206–221. DOI: 10.1287/mksc.2013.0836

Sankar, J. G. (2024). AI-Driven Marketing Success Stories: A Case Note of Industry Pioneers. In *AI-Driven Marketing Research and Data Analytics* (pp. 48-66). IGI Global. DOI: 10.4018/979-8-3693-2165-2.ch003

Schneider, B., & Bowen, D. E. (2010). Winning the service game: Revisiting the rules by which people co-create value. In *Handbook of Service Science* (pp. 31–59). Springer US. DOI: 10.1007/978-1-4419-1628-0_4

Sharma, S. (2023). *AI for Small Business: Leveraging Automation to Stay Ahead*. Lead Management Consultant, SKS Consulting & Advisors., DOI: 10.46679/9788195732234

Shukla, P., & Shamurailatpam, S. D. (2022). Conceptualizing the Use of Artificial Intelligence in Customer Relationship Management and Quality of Services: A Digital Disruption in the Indian Banking System. In *Adoption and Implementation of AI in Customer Relationship Management* (pp. 177-201). IGI Global. DOI: 10.4018/978-1-7998-7959-6.ch012

Tran, M. T. (2024). Unlocking the AI-Powered Customer Experience: Personalized Service, Enhanced Engagement, and Data-Driven Strategies for E-Commerce Applications. In *Enhancing and Predicting Digital Consumer Behavior with AI* (pp. 375–382). IGI Global., DOI: 10.4018/979-8-3693-4453-8.ch019

Vinod, N. (2023). Artificial Intelligence. Advances in logistics, operations, and management science book series. In *Cases on Managing Dairy Productive Chains* (pp.226-240). DOI: 10.4018/979-8-3693-0418-1.ch015

West, D. M., & Allen, J. R. (2018). How artificial intelligence is transforming the world. https://www.brookings.edu/articles/how-artificial-intelligence-is-transforming-the-world/

Xie, M., Michelinakis, F., Dreibholz, T., Pujol-Roig, J. S., Malacarne, S., Majumdar, S., & Elmokashfi, A. M. (2021, June). An exposed closed-loop model for customer-driven service assurance automation. In *2021 Joint European Conference on Networks and Communications & 6G Summit (EuCNC/6G Summit)* (pp. 419-424). IEEE. DOI: 10.1109/EuCNC/6GSummit51104.2021.9482533

Ying, S., Sindakis, S., Aggarwal, S., Chen, C., & Su, J. (2021). Managing big data in the retail industry of Singapore: Examining the impact on customer satisfaction and organizational performance. *European Management Journal*, 39(3), 390–400. DOI: 10.1016/j.emj.2020.04.001

ADDITIONAL READING

Batra, M. M. (2019, July). Strengthening customer experience through artificial intelligence: An upcoming trend. In *Competition forum* (Vol. 17, No. 2, pp. 223-231). American Society for Competitiveness.

Buttle, F., & Maklan, S. (2019). *Customer relationship management: concepts and technologies*. Routledge. DOI: 10.4324/9781351016551

Chaturvedi, R., & Verma, S. (2022). *Artificial intelligence-driven customer experience: Overcoming the challenges.* California Management Review Insights.

Chaturvedi, R., & Verma, S. (2023). Opportunities and challenges of AI-driven customer service. *Artificial Intelligence in customer service: The next frontier for personalized engagement*, 33-71.

Chaturvedi, R., & Verma, S. (2023). Opportunities and Challenges of AI-Driven Customer Service. In J. N, Sheth, V, Jain, E. Mogaji and A. Ambika (Eds), *Artificial Intelligence in Customer Service* (pp. 33-71). Palgrave Macmillan, Cham. DOI: 10.1007/978-3-031-33898-4_3

Galitsky, B. (2020). *Artificial intelligence for customer relationship management.* Springer International Publishing., DOI: 10.1007/978-3-030-52167-7

Khan, S., & Iqbal, M. (2020, June). AI-Powered Customer Service: Does it optimize customer experience? In *2020 8th International Conference on Reliability, Infocom Technologies and Optimization (Trends and Future Directions) (ICRITO)* (pp. 590-594). IEEE.

Negi, V. (2023). Artificial Intelligence: Next Level Customer Service. In *AI and Emotional Intelligence for Modern Business Management* (pp. 226-240). IGI Global.

Ostrom, A. L., Fotheringham, D., & Bitner, M. J. (2019). Customer acceptance of AI in service encounters: understanding antecedents and consequences. *Handbook of service science, volume II*, 77-103.

Phudech, P. (2024). AI and Smart Customer Services: Revolutionizing the Customer Experience. [JSSMR]. *Journal of Social Science and Multidisciplinary Research*, 1(3), 1–20.

Sheth, J. N., Jain, V., Mogaji, E., & Ambika, A. (Eds.). (2023). *Artificial intelligence in customer service: The next frontier for personalized engagement.* Palgrave Macmillan. DOI: 10.1007/978-3-031-33898-4

Wang, J. F. (2023). The Impact of Artificial Intelligence (AI) on Customer Relationship Management: A Qualitative Study. *International Journal of Management Accounting*, 5(5), 74–88.

Wolf, C. T. (2020). A I Ethics and Customer Care: Some Considerations from the Case of "Intelligent Sales". In: *Proceedings of the 18th European Conference on Computer-Supported Cooperative Work: The International Venue on Practice-centred Computing on the Design of Cooperation Technologies - Exploratory Papers, Reports of the European Society for Socially Embedded Technologies* (ISSN 2510-2591). doi:DOI: 10.18420/ecscw2019_n02

KEY TERMS AND DEFINITIONS

AI-Driven Customer Relationship Service: AI-driven Customer Relationship Service (CRS) utilizes intelligent technologies to deliver efficient, tailored, and seamless support interactions. Ai-driven Customer Relationship Service refers to the provision of customer services through the utilization of AI techniques such as machine learning, natural language processing, and predictive analytics to improve customer relationship services.

Artificial Intelligence (AI): Artificial intelligence (AI) encompasses computer systems that possess the capability to carry out activities that often need human intellect, including visual perception, speech recognition, reasoning, decision-making, problem-solving, and language translation. AI tools encompass several technologies such as machine learning, natural language processing, and computer vision.

Customer Relationship: Customer relations consist of the strategies and techniques employed by a firm to interact with its consumers and enhance their overall experience. This entails offering solutions to immediate obstacles and actively developing enduring strategies that are focused on ensuring client success. Customer relations include the strategies and techniques employed by a firm to interact with its consumers and enhance their overall experience.

Customer Relationship Service (CRS): Customer relations stand with the ways that a business interacts with its clients and makes their experience better. This means both finding short-term solutions to problems and planning for long-term solutions that will help the customer succeed. So, Customer Relationship Service (CRS) refers to the services and support provided by the customer relationship manager/officer on behalf of a business organization for dealing with the customers' queries and problems. Here the customer relationship manager/officer mostly uses customer relationship management (CRM) programs that help a business deal with its customers.

Customer Relationship Management (CRM): Customer Relationship Management (CRM) is the set of practices, methods, and technology that firms employ to track and analyze customer data throughout the customer's lifetime. CRM is used to better customer service, customer retention, build strong relationships with present and future customers and revenue growth are the core goals.

Customer Service: Customer service encompasses the assistance provided to clients, starting with their initial interaction with your company and continuing over the subsequent months and years. Delivering excellent customer service entails being a dependable ally to your consumers, surpassing just assistance in resolving issues, using, and aiding them in making well-informed choices regarding your goods.

Chapter 4
AI-Driven Personalization in Omnichannel Marketing:
Enhancing Customer Engagement and Loyalty

Yavuz Selim Balcıoğlu
https://orcid.org/0000-0001-7138-2972
Dogus University, Turkey

ABSTRACT

This chapter explores the transformative role of AI-driven personalization in omnichannel marketing, emphasizing its importance in enhancing customer engagement and loyalty. It begins by defining omnichannel marketing and tracing its evolution from traditional to digital channels. The chapter explores into key components of AI-driven personalization, including data collection and analysis, customer segmentation, predictive analytics, and real-time personalization. Implementation strategies are discussed, highlighting the integration of AI tools, data management, and the design of personalized marketing strategies. The chapter also addresses best practices for overcoming common challenges and measuring customer engagement using key performance indicators (KPIs). Additionally, the chapter examines the future trends in AI-driven personalization, such as emerging AI technologies, integration with IoT and AR/VR, and the evolving landscape of marketing strategies.

DOI: 10.4018/979-8-3693-5340-0.ch004

1. INTRODUCTION

Omnichannel marketing refers to a seamless and integrated customer experience across multiple marketing channels. Unlike multichannel marketing, which operates in silos, omnichannel marketing ensures a cohesive and consistent interaction with customers regardless of the platform or device they use. This approach not only enhances customer satisfaction but also boosts brand loyalty and retention. According to Verhoef et al. (2015), omnichannel marketing "focuses on the synergistic management of multiple channels available to consumers, aiming for a unified customer experience."

Personalization has become a cornerstone of modern marketing strategies, allowing businesses to deliver tailored experiences that meet individual customer preferences and needs. Personalized marketing leads to increased customer engagement, higher conversion rates, and improved customer retention. Research by Accenture (2018) indicates that 91% of consumers are more likely to shop with brands that provide relevant offers and recommendations. Personalization not only helps in capturing customer attention but also in fostering a deeper emotional connection with the brand.

Artificial Intelligence (AI) plays a pivotal role in enhancing personalization by leveraging vast amounts of data to deliver tailored marketing messages and experiences. AI technologies, such as machine learning algorithms and predictive analytics, enable marketers to understand customer behavior, preferences, and purchasing patterns more accurately. According to a study by McKinsey & Company (2020), companies that use AI for personalization can achieve a 20% higher customer satisfaction rate and up to 15% increase in sales. AI-driven personalization allows for real-time adjustments to marketing strategies, ensuring that customers receive the most relevant and engaging content at the right moment.

2. THE EVOLUTION OF OMNICHANNEL MARKETING

Omnichannel marketing is defined as a multichannel approach that seeks to provide customers with a seamless shopping experience, whether they're shopping online from a desktop or mobile device, by telephone, or in a brick-and-mortar store. The term "omnichannel" emerged in the early 2010s as a response to the growing complexity of customer interactions across various touchpoints (Rigby, 2011). The aim is to unify these interactions into a coherent and consistent experience. This concept builds on earlier practices such as multichannel marketing but emphasizes the integration and orchestration of all channels to enhance the customer journey (Verhoef et al., 2015).

The transition from traditional to digital channels has been a significant driver in the evolution of omnichannel marketing. Traditional channels, such as physical stores and print advertising, provided limited customer interaction and data collection capabilities. The advent of digital channels, including e-commerce websites, social media, and mobile apps, revolutionized the way businesses engage with customers by enabling real-time communication and personalized marketing. According to Brynjolfsson et al. (2013), the shift to digital channels has allowed retailers to collect more detailed data on customer preferences and behaviors, which is crucial for developing effective omnichannel strategies.

While both multichannel and omnichannel strategies involve the use of multiple marketing channels, there are key differences between them. Multichannel marketing focuses on maximizing the performance of each channel independently, without necessarily ensuring that these channels work together cohesively. In contrast, omnichannel marketing aims to create a unified customer experience across all channels, ensuring that interactions on one channel seamlessly transition to another (Piotrowicz & Cuthbertson, 2014). For instance, an omnichannel approach would enable a customer to start shopping on a mobile app, continue on a desktop website, and complete the purchase in a physical store with full continuity and consistency of experience. This integration not only enhances customer satisfaction but also increases overall engagement and loyalty (Lemon & Verhoef, 2016).

3. UNDERSTANDING AI-DRIVEN PERSONALIZATION

Artificial Intelligence (AI) refers to the simulation of human intelligence in machines that are programmed to think and learn like humans. AI encompasses a wide range of technologies, including machine learning (ML), which is a subset of AI. Machine learning involves the use of algorithms and statistical models to enable systems to improve their performance on tasks over time through experience (Mitchell, 1997). These systems analyze large datasets to identify patterns and make predictions or decisions without being explicitly programmed to perform the task (Domingos, 2012).

AI technologies enable personalized marketing by leveraging data analytics to understand individual customer preferences and behaviors. Machine learning algorithms analyze vast amounts of data, such as purchase history, browsing behavior, and demographic information, to segment customers and predict future behaviors. This allows marketers to deliver highly relevant and personalized content, offers, and recommendations to each customer. For example, recommender systems used by e-commerce platforms like Amazon and Netflix utilize collaborative filtering and content-based filtering techniques to suggest products or content tailored to individual users (Koren et al., 2009).

Natural language processing (NLP), another AI technology, is used to analyze customer feedback, reviews, and social media interactions to gain insights into customer sentiment and preferences. Chatbots and virtual assistants powered by AI provide personalized customer service and support by understanding and responding to customer queries in real-time (Davenport et al., 2020).

The benefits of AI-driven personalization are substantial and multifaceted. Firstly, it enhances customer experience by providing tailored content and offers that meet individual needs and preferences, leading to higher customer satisfaction and loyalty (Lambrecht & Tucker, 2013). Secondly, AI-driven personalization can significantly improve marketing efficiency by automating tasks such as customer segmentation, content recommendation, and campaign optimization, allowing marketers to focus on strategy and creativity (Chaffey, 2020). Moreover, personalized marketing campaigns powered by AI have been shown to result in higher engagement rates and conversion rates. According to a study by McKinsey & Company (2020), companies that effectively implement AI-driven personalization can see a 5-15% increase in revenue and a 10-30% increase in marketing-spend efficiency. Additionally, AI helps in reducing churn by identifying at-risk customers and providing proactive engagement strategies to retain them (Sun, 2019).

4. KEY COMPONENTS OF AI-DRIVEN PERSONALIZATION

Data collection and analysis form the backbone of AI-driven personalization, enabling marketers to gain deep insights into customer preferences and behaviors. Here, we explore into the types of data collected and the methods used to analyze this data for effective personalization.

4.1. Types of Data Collected

4.1.1. Behavioral Data

Behavioral data refers to information collected based on the actions and interactions of users with a brand or platform. This includes website visits, clicks, navigation paths, and engagement with content. Page views, time spent on site, click-through rates, and interaction with emails or social media posts. Behavioral data is crucial for understanding customer journeys and identifying patterns in user behavior that can inform personalized marketing strategies (Wedel & Kannan, 2016). Behavioral data can also help in optimizing marketing campaigns by developing response models that predict customer reactions to marketing efforts. These models use individual characteristics, including behavioral and demographic variables, to maximize marketing return on investment by targeting the most likely responders (Lo, 2005). In digital advertising research, leveraging behavioral data allows for a more accurate analysis of customer interactions in digital, social, and mobile environments. This data can be used to refine advertising strategies and better understand consumer responses to various marketing stimuli (Liu-Thompkins & Malthouse, 2017). Furthermore, behavioral data mining is essential in retail marketing to predict and detect changes in customer behavior, enabling managers to tailor promotional campaigns effectively. Integrating behavioral variables with transaction data helps in crafting personalized customer experiences and long-term relationships (Chen et al., 2005). Recent studies have shown that data-driven marketing, which heavily relies on behavioral data, significantly enhances customer experience, increases marketing ROI, and drives sales. This approach utilizes data from various customer interactions to predict future behavior and personalize marketing strategies (Chen et al., 2005). The use of advanced analytics and machine learning techniques on large sets of unstructured behavioral data, such as social media interactions, further aids in forecasting market trends and adjusting marketing strategies in real-time. This approach ensures that marketing efforts are both timely and relevant (Liu et al., 2015).

4.1.2. Transactional Data

Transactional data encompasses all information related to purchases and financial interactions between a customer and a business. Purchase history, order frequency, transaction amounts, and payment methods. This data helps in segmenting customers based on their buying habits, predicting future purchases, and tailoring offers and recommendations to individual customers (Verhoef et al., 2010). Transactional data is integral to creating effective marketing strategies as it provides insights into customer purchasing patterns and preferences. For example, using transactional data, businesses can develop response models to identify likely campaign responders, optimizing marketing ROI (Peltier et al., 2006). Additionally, data mining techniques applied to sales transactions can help identify product affinities and customer preferences, enhancing targeted promotions and recommendations (Krisnanto et al., 2022). The integration of transactional and relational data can significantly boost the efficacy of Integrated Marketing Communication (IMC) programs, allowing firms to improve both sales-oriented and marketing-oriented performance metrics by accurately targeting customer segments (Zahay et al., 2004). Furthermore, considering price information in transaction databases enables more nuanced retail management, facilitating the discovery of meaningful patterns that can guide pricing strategies and promotions (Chen et al., 2008).

4.1.3. Demographic Data

Demographic data includes basic information about individuals, such as age, gender, income, education, and location. Age group, gender, income bracket, education level, and geographic location. Demographic data is used to create customer segments and target marketing efforts more effectively, ensuring that messages resonate with the intended audience (Schroeder, 2014). Demographic data plays a pivotal role in marketing by providing a framework for understanding and segmenting the customer base. For instance, using demographic data to segment markets can help businesses tailor their strategies to different consumer groups, optimizing marketing effectiveness (Pol, 1986). This data is also crucial in direct marketing, where individual consumer panels and demographic information are used to target households, enhancing the precision of marketing campaigns (Rossi et al., 1996). Moreover, demographic analysis is essential in strategic planning, offering insights into the population that interacts with the organization, thus guiding the development of relevant capabilities and strategies (Halachmi et al., 1993). Advanced demographic analysis techniques, such as those predicting user demographics from mobile communication patterns, further enhance the ability to tailor marketing strategies to specific user segments (Dong et al., 2014).

5. METHODS OF DATA ANALYSIS

5.1. Descriptive Analytics

Descriptive analytics involves summarizing historical data to identify patterns and trends. It provides insights into what has happened in the past. Data visualization, summary statistics, and clustering. Descriptive analytics helps in understanding customer behavior and identifying segments that exhibit similar patterns (Chaffey & Ellis-Chadwick, 2019).

5.2. Predictive Analytics

Predictive analytics uses statistical models and machine learning techniques to forecast future outcomes based on historical data. Regression analysis, decision trees, neural networks, and time series analysis. This method is used to predict customer behavior, such as likelihood of purchase, churn, or response to marketing campaigns, allowing for proactive and personalized engagement (Shmueli & Koppius, 2011).

5.3. Prescriptive Analytics

Prescriptive analytics suggests actions to achieve desired outcomes by analyzing data and generating recommendations. Optimization algorithms, simulation, and decision analysis. Prescriptive analytics helps in determining the best course of action for personalized marketing, such as optimizing pricing strategies or selecting the most effective marketing channels (Bertsimas & Kallus, 2019).

5.4. Real-Time Analytics

Real-time analytics involves processing data as it is generated to provide immediate insights and enable prompt decision-making. Stream processing and event-driven analytics. Real-time analytics is essential for dynamic personalization, such as adjusting recommendations and offers based on current customer interactions (Stone & Woodcock, 2014).

6. CUSTOMER SEGMENTATION

6.1. AI Techniques for Customer Segmentation

Customer segmentation involves dividing a customer base into distinct groups with similar characteristics or behaviors. AI techniques enhance the precision and effectiveness of segmentation by analyzing vast amounts of data to identify patterns that may not be apparent through traditional methods. For example, machine learning algorithms such as k-means clustering, neural networks, and support vector machines are used to segment customers in various industries, providing insights that improve targeted marketing strategies and customer satisfaction (Gankidi et al., 2022; Smeureanu et al., 2013). Additionally, these AI techniques can handle large datasets efficiently, offering a scalable solution for customer segmentation (Jiang & Tuzhilin, 2009).

6.2. Clustering Algorithms

Clustering algorithms group customers based on similar attributes without predefined labels. The examples; K-means clustering, hierarchical clustering, and DBSCAN. These algorithms analyze customer data such as purchase history, browsing behavior, and demographic information to identify natural groupings within the customer base. For example, K-means clustering can segment customers into groups with similar purchase behaviors, allowing for targeted marketing strategies (Xu & Wunsch, 2005).

6.3. Classification Algorithms

Classification algorithms assign customers to predefined segments based on specific attributes. The examples; Decision trees, random forests, and support vector machines (SVM). These algorithms can predict the likelihood of a customer belonging to a particular segment, aiding in personalized marketing efforts. For instance, decision trees can classify customers based on their likelihood to respond to a specific marketing campaign (Bramer, 2013).

6.4. Neural Networks and Deep Learning

Neural networks and deep learning models can identify complex patterns in large datasets. The examples; Convolutional neural networks (CNNs) and recurrent neural networks (RNNs). These models can process and learn from vast amounts of data to segment customers more accurately. For example, CNNs can analyze image data from social media to segment customers based on visual preferences (LeCun et al., 2015).

7. PREDICTIVE ANALYTICS

7.1. Role of Predictive Analytics in Personalization

Predictive analytics involves using historical data to predict future outcomes. In the context of personalization, it helps marketers anticipate customer needs and preferences, enabling proactive and tailored marketing strategies. Predictive analytics can enhance marketing performance by utilizing machine learning models to determine consumer preferences and deliver personalized experiences (Gupta & Joshi, 2022). Additionally, it plays a significant role in converting information into actionable knowledge, improving marketing decision-making and customer engagement (Hair, 2007).

7.2. Customer Behavior Prediction

Predictive analytics models can forecast future customer behavior, such as the likelihood of making a purchase, customer churn, or response to a marketing campaign. This allows marketers to tailor their strategies to individual customer needs (Shmueli & Koppius, 2011). For example, predictive models in marketing can enhance decision-making processes by providing accurate forecasts and insights into customer behaviors (Tarka & Łobiński, 2014).

7.3. Regression Analysis

Regression models predict a dependent variable based on one or more independent variables. Linear and logistic regression models are used to predict customer lifetime value (CLV), purchase likelihood, and conversion rates (Montgomery, 2015). These models are crucial for understanding and forecasting key customer metrics, thereby optimizing marketing strategies and resource allocation (Wolniak & Grebski, 2023).

7.4. Collaborative Filtering

Collaborative filtering predicts user preferences based on the preferences of similar users. It is commonly used in recommendation systems, such as those employed by Netflix and Amazon, to suggest products or content that users are likely to enjoy. This method leverages user data to identify patterns and relationships between users' behaviors, enhancing the accuracy and relevance of recommendations (Koren et al., 2009). Collaborative filtering can be divided into user-based and item-based approaches, each with its advantages in various applications (Sarwar et al., 2001).

7.5. Time Series Analysis

Time series models analyze data points collected or recorded at specific time intervals. These models predict future trends based on past behaviors, such as seasonal purchasing patterns or demand forecasting. Common time series models include autoregressive integrated moving average (ARIMA), exponential smoothing, and seasonal decomposition of time series (STL) (Box et al., 2015). These models are valuable for various applications, including sales forecasting, stock market analysis, and inventory management, by providing insights into future trends and helping businesses make informed decisions (Chatfield, 2003).

7.6. Real-Time Personalization

Real-time personalization involves delivering tailored content and experiences to customers instantaneously as they interact with a brand. The ability to process data in real-time is crucial for adapting marketing strategies on-the-fly and maximizing engagement. Real-time personalization ensures that customers receive the most relevant content and offers at the right moment, significantly enhancing their experience and satisfaction (Stone & Woodcock, 2014).

8. TOOLS AND TECHNOLOGIES ENABLING REAL-TIME PERSONALIZATION

8.1. Streaming Analytics Platforms

Apache Kafka, Apache Flink, and Amazon Kinesis. These platforms process and analyze streaming data in real-time, allowing businesses to react instantly to customer actions and events. For instance, Apache Kafka can be used to monitor customer interactions on a website and trigger personalized content delivery in real-time (Kreps et al., 2011). Streaming analytics platforms are crucial for various real-time applications, including fraud detection, in-session targeting, and recommendations. These platforms facilitate continuous data processing, allowing for immediate insights and actions (Gupta & Agarwal, 2016). Real-time stream processing systems like Storm, Samza, and Spark Streaming are evaluated for their performance in different scenarios, such as monitoring railway systems, showcasing their capabilities in handling high-velocity data streams efficiently (Samosir et al., 2016). Moreover, streaming analytics platforms support complex event processing (CEP), which integrates data from diverse sources to provide actionable insights in real-time. This capability is essential for applications in smart cities, transportation systems, and autonomous vehicle control (Zhou et al. 2016). The integration of machine learning models with streaming platforms enhances predictive analytics, enabling more accurate forecasting and anomaly detection in various domains (Dinakar & Vagdevi, 2023).

8.2. Customer Data Platforms (CDPs)

Segment, Tealium, and Adobe Experience Platform. CDPs unify customer data from various sources to create a comprehensive view of each customer. They enable real-time segmentation and personalization by making this unified data available for immediate analysis and action (Levy, 2020). CDPs are essential for optimizing digital marketing efforts as they collect first-party data and leverage it to reach the right audience without sharing private customer information with third parties (Sousa, 2022). These platforms overcome the limitations imposed by fragmented point solutions by providing access to data from numerous systems in one database, supporting systems that produce appropriate customer experiences (Earley, 2018). The role of CDPs in enhancing customer relationship management (CRM) cannot be overstated. They enable more accurate segmentation, prediction of customer behavior, and personalized marketing strategies, leading to improved customer engagement and satisfaction (Pancras & Sudhir, 2007). Additionally, CDPs facilitate the integration of big data analytics, allowing businesses to uncover valuable insights from customer interactions across various channels (Wang & Liu, 2020).

8.3. Artificial Intelligence and Machine Learning APIs

Google Cloud AI, IBM Watson, and Microsoft Azure AI. These APIs provide ready-to-use AI and ML capabilities that can be integrated into marketing systems to deliver real-time personalization. For example, Google Cloud AI can analyze customer sentiment in real-time to personalize communication and offers accordingly (Saha & Srivastava, 2014). Artificial Intelligence (AI) and Machine Learning (ML) APIs play a pivotal role in modern marketing strategies by automating tasks, analyzing large datasets, and enabling personalized marketing efforts. For instance, AI frameworks can support marketing activities such as segmentation, targeting, and positioning (Huang & Rust, 2020). AI applications in digital marketing optimize budget allocation, enhance consumer behavior analysis, and improve competitive strategies through predictive modeling (Ziakis & Vlachopoulou, 2023). Moreover, AI-driven tools like IBM Watson and Microsoft Azure AI enhance digital advertising by enabling precise targeting and personalization. These platforms use advanced algorithms to predict customer preferences and optimize marketing campaigns, leading to improved customer engagement and higher conversion rates (Miklošík et al., 2019). AI's ability to process and analyze real-time data allows marketers to make informed decisions and create tailored customer experiences (Davenport et al., 2020).

8.4. Implementing AI-Driven Personalization in Omnichannel Marketing

The first step in integrating AI into omnichannel marketing is to clearly define the goals and objectives. These goals should align with the overall business strategy and customer experience aspirations. Typical objectives might include increasing customer engagement, boosting conversion rates, enhancing customer loyalty, or improving marketing efficiency. Setting clear, measurable goals helps in guiding the AI implementation process and evaluating its success (Chaffey & Ellis-Chadwick, 2019). Implementing AI-driven personalization in omnichannel marketing involves several critical steps. First, collecting and unifying customer data from various touchpoints is essential. AI algorithms can then analyze this data to identify patterns and preferences, enabling businesses to deliver personalized experiences across channels (Stone et al., 2017). Second, integrating AI tools into existing marketing platforms allows for real-time decision-making and automated responses to customer interactions. For example, machine learning models can be used to recommend products or content based on individual customer behavior, enhancing the relevance and effectiveness of marketing efforts (Mirwan et al., 2023). Finally, continuously monitoring and refining AI-driven strategies is crucial. By evaluating the performance of AI applications and making necessary adjustments, businesses can ensure that their marketing efforts remain aligned with their goals and responsive to changing customer needs (Sadriwala & Sadriwala, 2022).

8.5. Data Integration and Management

Effective AI-driven personalization relies heavily on robust data integration and management. This involves (Chen et al., 2014):

- Gathering data from all customer touchpoints, including websites, mobile apps, social media, and in-store interactions.
- Ensuring data quality by removing duplicates, correcting errors, and structuring data for analysis.
- Utilizing databases and data warehouses that can handle large volumes of data and support real-time processing.
- Adhering to data privacy regulations such as GDPR and CCPA to protect customer information and build trust.

8.6. Choosing the Right AI Tools and Platforms

Selecting appropriate AI tools and platforms is crucial for successful implementation. Considerations include (Davenport, 2018):

- Ensuring the tools offer the necessary functionalities, such as machine learning, predictive analytics, and real-time processing.
- Choosing platforms that can scale with the growth of data and increasing demand for personalized experiences.

- Ensuring compatibility with existing systems and data sources to facilitate seamless integration.
- Opting for user-friendly tools that allow marketers to leverage AI without requiring extensive technical expertise.

8.7. Designing Personalized Marketing Strategies

With goals set, data integrated, and tools selected, the next step is to design and implement personalized marketing strategies. This involves (Wedel & Kannan, 2016):

- Using AI to segment customers based on behaviors, preferences, and demographics.
- Tailoring content and offers to individual customer segments based on predictive analytics.
- Ensuring consistent and personalized experiences across all channels, from email and social media to in-store interactions.
- Continuously monitoring the effectiveness of personalization efforts and making data-driven adjustments as needed.

9. BEST PRACTICES FOR SUCCESSFUL IMPLEMENTATION

9.1. Data Quality and Integration

Poor data quality and fragmented data sources can hinder AI effectiveness. Implement robust data governance practices, invest in data cleaning tools, and ensure seamless data integration across all channels. High-quality data is essential for the success of AI models, as it improves their accuracy and reliability. Data quality challenges such as bias, incomplete data, and data poisoning need to be addressed to ensure the robustness of AI systems (Whang et al., 2021). Additionally, proper data integration techniques can enhance the performance of AI models by providing a unified view of data from various sources (Lin et al., 2016).

9.2. User Adoption and Training

Resistance to adopting new AI tools and processes among marketing teams can be a significant barrier. Provide comprehensive training and support, highlight the benefits of AI-driven personalization, and foster a culture of innovation and continuous learning. Effective user training programs can significantly improve the adoption and utilization of AI technologies, helping teams to understand their value and application (Thontirawong & Chinchanachokchai, 2021). Encouraging a culture of continuous learning and innovation is essential to keep pace with the rapid advancements in AI (Bhima et al., 2023).

9.3. Privacy and Compliance

Navigating complex data privacy regulations and ensuring customer data protection are critical for AI initiatives. Establish clear data privacy policies, use anonymization techniques, and stay updated with regulatory changes to ensure compliance. Data privacy is a major concern, especially with the increasing use of AI in high-stakes areas such as healthcare and finance. Implementing robust data privacy measures and staying informed about regulatory changes are essential to maintain trust and compliance (Stöger et al., 2021).

9.4. Scalability and Flexibility

Ensuring the AI system can scale and adapt to changing business needs is crucial. Choose scalable AI platforms and design flexible personalization strategies that can evolve with the market and customer expectations. Scalable AI systems can handle increasing amounts of data and user demands, while flexible strategies ensure that AI solutions can adapt to new trends and requirements (Jankovic & Curović, 2023).

9.5. Measuring ROI

Demonstrating the return on investment (ROI) of AI-driven personalization initiatives is essential. Define clear metrics for success, use A/B testing to compare personalized vs. non-personalized efforts, and regularly report on performance against goals. Measuring ROI helps in understanding the effectiveness of AI initiatives and justifying further investments (Ziakis & Vlachopoulou, 2023).

9.6. Enhancing Customer Engagement through Personalization

9.6.1. Email Marketing

Email marketing remains one of the most effective channels for personalized marketing. AI can enhance this by:

- AI algorithms can tailor email content based on recipient behaviors and preferences, such as browsing history and past purchases.

- AI can analyze when individual recipients are most likely to engage with emails and send messages at those optimal times.
- AI can craft personalized subject lines that increase open rates by using data-driven insights (Chaffey, 2020).

9.6.2. Social Media

Social media platforms offer vast opportunities for personalized engagement:

- AI can analyze user data to deliver highly targeted ads that resonate with specific audience segments.
- Algorithms can recommend personalized content in users' feeds based on their interactions and interests.
- AI-powered chatbots can provide personalized customer service and engage users in real-time on social media platforms (Gentsch, 2019).

9.6.3. Mobile Apps

Mobile apps offer a direct and personalized communication channel with users:

- AI can personalize in-app messages based on user behavior, location, and preferences.
- Predictive analytics can determine the best times to send push notifications to maximize engagement.
- AI can adjust the app interface to suit individual user preferences, enhancing the overall user experience (Kim, 2015).

9.6.4. In-Store Experiences

Personalization can extend to brick-and-mortar stores through:

- AI can analyze in-store customer behavior and provide personalized product recommendations via digital displays or mobile apps.
- AI can tailor loyalty rewards based on individual shopping habits and preferences.
- In-store kiosks powered by AI can offer personalized shopping assistance and product information (Rigby, 2011).

10. MEASURING CUSTOMER ENGAGEMENT

10.1. Key Performance Indicators (KPIs)

To effectively measure customer engagement, businesses can track various KPIs, including:

- Measures the percentage of email or ad recipients who click on a link.
- Tracks the percentage of users who complete a desired action, such as making a purchase or signing up for a newsletter.
- Measures the percentage of customers who continue to do business with a company over a specific period.
- Indicates the average amount of time users spend interacting with a website or app.
- Gauges customer loyalty by asking how likely customers are to recommend a company to others (Farris et al., 2010).

10.2. Tools for Measuring Engagement

Several tools can help businesses measure and analyze customer engagement:

- Offers comprehensive data on website traffic, user behavior, and conversion rates.
- Provides detailed insights into email marketing performance, social media engagement, and lead management.
- Focuses on user interaction data for mobile apps and websites, offering in-depth analysis of user behavior and engagement.
- Specializes in email marketing analytics, helping businesses track the effectiveness of their email campaigns.
- Integrates various marketing channels and provides robust analytics to measure engagement across email, social media, and more (Chaffey & Ellis-Chadwick, 2019).

10.3. Building Customer Loyalty with AI-Driven Personalization

Customer loyalty is a critical component of successful marketing strategies as it leads to repeat business, reduces customer acquisition costs, and enhances brand reputation. Loyal customers are more likely to make repeat purchases, recommend the brand to others, and show resistance to competitive offers. According to a study by Reichheld (2000), a 5% increase in customer retention can lead to a profit increase of 25% to 95%. Therefore, fostering customer loyalty is essential for long-term business sustainability and growth (Reichheld, 2001).

11. AI TECHNIQUES FOR FOSTERING LOYALTY

Personalized loyalty programs are designed to cater to the unique preferences and behaviors of individual customers. AI can significantly enhance these programs by analyzing customer data and creating tailored experiences that increase engagement and satisfaction.

AI can analyze purchasing patterns and customer preferences to offer rewards that are highly relevant to each customer. For instance, Starbucks uses AI to personalize its loyalty program by providing individualized offers and rewards based on customer purchase history (Smith, 2018). AI-driven systems can adjust loyalty program offers in real-time based on customer interactions. For example, if a customer frequently purchases certain products, the system can provide discounts or special offers on related items. By segmenting customers based on their behaviors and interactions, AI can ensure that loyalty programs are more engaging. This includes offering tiered rewards, exclusive access to sales, or personalized recommendations (Grewal et al., 2017).

11.1. Predictive Maintenance and Proactive Customer Service

Predictive maintenance and proactive customer service leverage AI to anticipate customer needs and address issues before they arise, thereby enhancing customer satisfaction and loyalty.

11.2. Predictive Maintenance

For products that require regular maintenance or updates, AI can predict when a product is likely to need servicing and alert the customer in advance. This proactive approach ensures that customers experience minimal disruption and maintain a positive relationship with the brand (Tsang, 2002). Rolls-Royce uses AI to monitor the health of aircraft engines in real-time and predict maintenance needs, ensuring high reliability and customer trust (Rolls-Royce, 2018).

11.3. Proactive Customer Service

AI-powered systems can analyze customer data to identify potential issues before they escalate. By proactively addressing these issues, businesses can improve customer satisfaction and prevent negative experiences. AI chatbots can provide instant support and resolve common customer inquiries, enhancing the customer experience. For example, Sephora's chatbot uses AI to offer personalized beauty advice and product recommendations (Sephora, 2017). AI can analyze customer feedback and social media mentions to detect signs of dissatisfaction or emerging problems. Companies can then address these issues proactively, improving customer sentiment and loyalty (Pang & Lee, 2008).

11.4. Future Trends in AI-Driven Personalization

The field of AI is continuously evolving, leading to new advancements that will further enhance personalization in marketing. Advances in NLP are making it possible for AI to understand and respond to human language more effectively. This enables more sophisticated chatbots and virtual assistants that can provide highly personalized customer interactions (Jurafsky & Martin, 2021). Deep learning techniques are improving the accuracy and effectiveness of personalization algorithms. These models can process and analyze vast amounts of data to uncover deeper insights into customer behavior and preferences (LeCun et al., 2015). AutoML platforms simplify the process of developing and deploying machine learning models, making it easier for businesses to implement AI-driven personalization without needing extensive technical expertise (Hutter et al., 2019).

11.5. Integration with Other Technologies (IoT, AR/VR)

AI-driven personalization is being increasingly integrated with other emerging technologies to create more immersive and connected customer experiences. IoT devices collect vast amounts of data from various sources, providing a more comprehensive view of customer behavior. AI can analyze this data to deliver personalized experiences in real-time. For example, smart home devices can offer personalized recommendations based on usage patterns (Gubbi et al., 2013). AR and VR technologies create immersive experiences that can be personalized using AI. For instance, AI can analyze a user's interactions within a VR environment to tailor content and recommendations. Retailers can use AR to provide virtual try-on experiences that are personalized based on customer preferences (Peddie, 2017).

11.6. Predictions for the Future of Omnichannel Marketing

As AI-driven personalization becomes more advanced, consumer behavior is expected to shift in several ways. As consumers become accustomed to personalized experiences, their expectations will rise. They will expect brands to understand their preferences and deliver relevant content and offers seamlessly across all channels (Davenport et al., 2020). Personalized experiences foster deeper engagement, leading to increased brand loyalty and advocacy. Consumers are more likely to engage with brands that offer tailored interactions that meet their individual needs (Lemon & Verhoef, 2016). While personalization enhances the customer experience, it also raises concerns about data privacy. Consumers will demand greater transparency and control over their data, prompting businesses to adopt more stringent data protection measures (Acquisti et al., 2015).

11.7. Evolution of Marketing Strategies

Marketing strategies will continue to evolve as AI and other technologies shape the future of omnichannel marketing. AI will enable even more granular personalization, where marketing messages and offers are tailored to the individual level in real-time. This will involve leveraging data from multiple sources, including IoT devices and social media, to create a holistic view of the customer (Grewal et al., 2020). Instead of reacting to customer actions, AI will allow businesses to anticipate customer needs and engage them proactively. Predictive analytics will identify opportunities to delight customers with timely and relevant interactions (Davenport & Ronanki, 2018). The future of omnichannel marketing lies in seamless integration across all touchpoints. AI will facilitate the unification of online and offline experiences, ensuring that customers receive consistent and cohesive interactions regardless of the channel (Verhoef et al., 2015). As consumers become more conscious of social and environmental issues, businesses will need to incorporate sustainability and ethics into their marketing strategies. AI can help by providing insights into sustainable practices and enabling transparent communication with customers (Kumar et al., 2021).

12. ETHICAL CONSIDERATIONS AND DATA PRIVACY CONCERNS IN AI-DRIVEN PERSONALIZATION

12.1.Ethical Considerations

The use of AI in personalization raises several ethical issues, primarily related to potential biases and the impact on consumer trust (Meurisch & Mühlhäuser, 2021). AI systems can inadvertently perpetuate or even exacerbate existing biases present in the training data (Wang, 2021). For example, if historical data reflects societal biases, the AI might replicate these biases in its recommendations and decisions. It is crucial for companies to implement robust measures to identify and mitigate biases in AI models to ensure fair and unbiased personalization (Pessach & Shmueli, 2020).

12.2. Impact on Consumer Trust

Consumer trust is essential for the success of AI-driven personalization (Schwartz et al., 2022). Transparency about how customer data is used and ensuring that AI-driven decisions are explainable can help build trust (Draws et al., 2021). Businesses must communicate clearly with customers about data collection practices and the benefits of personalization, fostering a sense of control and security (European Comission, 2018).

12.3. Data Privacy Regulations

Compliance with data privacy regulations such as the General Data Protection Regulation (GDPR) in Europe and the California Consumer Privacy Act (CCPA) in the United States is critical (Hu & Wei, 2020). These regulations mandate strict guidelines for data collection, storage, and processing, emphasizing user consent and data protection.

- GDPR: Requires companies to obtain explicit consent from users before collecting personal data and to provide users with the right to access, rectify, and erase their data. Companies must also ensure data security and report data breaches within 72 hours.
- CCPA: Grants California residents rights similar to GDPR, including the right to know what personal data is collected, the purpose of collection, and with whom it is shared. It also provides the right to request the deletion of personal data and to opt out of the sale of their data.

12.4. Enhancing Data Security and Preventing Misuse

AI can also play a role in enhancing customer data security(Big Data Privacy Breach Prevention Strategies, 2020). Advanced AI algorithms can detect and prevent data breaches by identifying unusual patterns and potential threats in real-time (Li et al., 2023). Additionally, implementing strong encryption, secure data storage solutions, and regular audits are essential to protect personal information from misuse.

Recommendations for Companies:

- Bias mitigation: regularly audit AI systems for biases and implement corrective measures to ensure fairness.
- Transparency and Communication: clearly explain data usage policies and the benefits of personalization to consumers.
- Compliance: adhere to data privacy regulations like GDPR and CCPA, and stay updated on new legal requirements.
- Data security: invest in robust cybersecurity measures and AI solutions to protect customer data from breaches and misuse.

12.5. Common Challenges and Solutions

- Technical limitations
  - Challenge: limited IT infrastructure and expertise can hinder the implementation of advanced AI solutions.
  - Solution: invest in scalable cloud-based AI platforms and provide training for staff to build necessary technical skills (Davenport & Glaser, 2022).
- Data integration issues
  - Challenge: integrating data from disparate sources can be complex and time-consuming.
  - Solution: use advanced data integration tools and practices to ensure seamless data flow across systems (Rezig et al., 2021).
- Organizational Resistance
  - Challenge: resistance to change from employees can impede AI adoption.
  - Solution: foster a culture of innovation, provide training, and communicate the benefits of AI-driven personalization (Fountaine et al., 2019).
- Privacy and Compliance Concerns
  - Challenge: ensuring compliance with data privacy regulations while leveraging AI.

- Solution: implement robust data governance policies, ensure transparency, and regularly audit compliance (Kenwright, 2023).

13. PRACTICAL EXAMPLES

13.1. Retail Industry

Amazon: Uses AI to analyze customer browsing and purchase history to provide personalized product recommendations. This has significantly increased sales and customer satisfaction (Dinu, 2021).

13.2. Hospitality Industry

Marriott International: Implements AI-driven personalization to enhance guest experiences. By analyzing guest preferences and behaviors, Marriott offers personalized services and recommendations, improving guest loyalty and satisfaction (Bounatirou & Lim, 2020).

13.3. Financial Services

Bank of America: Uses AI to provide personalized financial advice through its virtual assistant, Erica. The AI analyzes customer data to offer tailored insights and recommendations, enhancing customer engagement and trust (Kumar & Gupta, 2023).

13.4. Healthcare

Mayo Clinic: Leverages AI to personalize patient care by analyzing medical history and treatment outcomes. AI-driven recommendations help doctors provide more accurate diagnoses and personalized treatment plans, improving patient outcomes (Dave & Patel, 2023).

14. CONCLUSION

This chapter has explored the transformative impact of AI-driven personalization in omnichannel marketing, highlighting its critical components and future potential. Key points discussed include:

- Omnichannel marketing aims to provide a seamless and integrated customer experience across multiple channels. Personalization, driven by AI, is essential for engaging customers and fostering loyalty.
- The transition from traditional to digital channels has paved the way for advanced AI technologies to enhance marketing strategies, distinguishing between multichannel and omnichannel approaches.
- Effective AI-driven personalization involves robust data collection and analysis, sophisticated customer segmentation, predictive analytics, and real-time personalization.
- Successful integration of AI into omnichannel marketing requires clear goals, comprehensive data management, the right AI tools, and well-designed personalized marketing strategies.
- AI enhances customer engagement through personalized strategies across various channels, while fostering loyalty with tailored loyalty programs and proactive customer service.
- Emerging AI technologies and their integration with IoT and AR/VR are expected to revolutionize personalization. Future marketing strategies will likely focus on hyper-personalization, proactive engagement, and ethical marketing practices.

AI-driven personalization significantly enhances the ability of businesses to deliver relevant, timely, and tailored experiences to their customers. By leveraging AI, marketers can gain deeper insights into customer behavior, predict future needs, and engage customers in more meaningful ways. This not only improves customer satisfaction and loyalty but also drives higher conversion rates and revenue. AI enables real-time adjustments to marketing strategies, ensuring that each customer interaction is optimized for maximum impact. Overall, AI-driven personalization transforms omnichannel marketing from a reactive to a proactive and dynamic approach, setting a new standard for customer engagement.

REFERENCES

Accenture. (2018). Personalization Pulse Check. https://www.accenture.com/content/dam/accenture/final/a-com-migration/pdf/pdf-83/accenture-making-personal.pdf

Acquisti, A., Brandimarte, L., & Loewenstein, G. (2015). Privacy and Human Behavior in the Age of Information. *Science*, 347(6221), 509–514. DOI: 10.1126/science.aaa1465 PMID: 25635091

Bertsimas, D., & Kallus, N. (2019). From Predictive to Prescriptive Analytics. *Management Science*, 66(3), 1025–1044. DOI: 10.1287/mnsc.2018.3253

Bhima, B., Zahra, A. R. A., Nurtino, T., & Firli, M. Z. (2023). Enhancing organizational efficiency through the integration of artificial intelligence in management information systems. *APTISI Transactions on Management*, 7(3), 282–289. DOI: 10.33050/atm.v7i3.2146

Bounatirou, M., & Lim, A. (2020). A case study on the impact of artificial intelligence on a hospitality company. In *Sustainable Hospitality Management: Designing Meaningful Encounters With Talent and Technology* (pp. 179-187). Emerald Publishing Limited. DOI: 10.1108/S1877-636120200000024013

Box, G. E. P., Jenkins, G. M., & Reinsel, G. C. (2015). *Time Series Analysis: Forecasting and Control*. John Wiley & Sons.

Bramer, M. (2013). *Principles of Data Mining*. Springer. DOI: 10.1007/978-1-4471-4884-5

Brynjolfsson, E., Hu, Y. J., & Rahman, M. S. (2013). Competing in the Age of Omnichannel Retailing. *MIT Sloan Management Review*, 54(4), 23–29.

Chaffey, D. (2020). *Digital Marketing: Strategy, Implementation and Practice*. Pearson Education.

Chaffey, D., & Ellis-Chadwick, F. (2019). *Digital Marketing: Strategy, Implementation, and Practice*. Pearson.

Chatfield, C. (2003). *The Analysis of Time Series: An Introduction* (6th ed.). Chapman and Hall/CRC. DOI: 10.4324/9780203491683

Chen, H., Mao, S., & Liu, Y. (2014). Big Data: A Survey. *Mobile Networks and Applications*, 19(2), 171–209. DOI: 10.1007/s11036-013-0489-0

Chen, M. C., Chiu, A. L., & Chang, H. H. (2005). Mining changes in customer behavior in retail marketing. *Expert Systems with Applications*, 28(4), 773–781. DOI: 10.1016/j.eswa.2004.12.033

Chen, Y. L., Huang, T. C. K., & Chang, S. K. (2008). A novel approach for discovering retail knowledge with price information from transaction databases. *Expert Systems with Applications*, 34(4), 2350–2359. DOI: 10.1016/j.eswa.2007.03.006

Dave, M., & Patel, N. (2023, May 26). Artificial intelligence in healthcare and education. *British Dental Journal*, 234(10), 761–764. DOI: 10.1038/s41415-023-5845-2 PMID: 37237212

Davenport, T. H. (2018). *The AI Advantage: How to Put the Artificial Intelligence Revolution to Work*. MIT Press. DOI: 10.7551/mitpress/11781.001.0001

Davenport, T. H., & Glaser, J. (2022). Factors governing the adoption of artificial intelligence in healthcare providers. *Discover Health Systems*, 1(1), 4. Advance online publication. DOI: 10.1007/s44250-022-00004-8 PMID: 37521111

Davenport, T. H., Guha, A., Grewal, D., & Bressgott, T. (2020). How Artificial Intelligence Will Change the Future of Marketing. *Journal of the Academy of Marketing Science*, 48(1), 24–42. DOI: 10.1007/s11747-019-00696-0

Davenport, T. H., & Ronanki, R. (2018). Artificial Intelligence for the Real World. *Harvard Business Review*, 96(1), 108–116.

Dinakar, J. R., & Vagdevi, S. (2023). Real-time streaming analytics using big data paradigm and predictive modelling based on deep learning. *International Journal on Recent and Innovation Trends in Computing and Communication*, 11(4s), 161–165. DOI: 10.17762/ijritcc.v11i4s.6323

Dinu, V. (2021). Artificial Intelligence in Wholesale and Retail. *Bucharest Academy of Economic Studies, 23*(56), 5-5. DOI: 10.24818/EA/2021/56/5

Domingos, P. (2012). A Few Useful Things to Know About Machine Learning. *Communications of the ACM*, 55(10), 78–87. DOI: 10.1145/2347736.2347755

Dong, Y., Yang, Y., Tang, J., Yang, Y., & Chawla, N. V. (2014, August). Inferring user demographics and social strategies in mobile social networks. In *Proceedings of the 20th ACM SIGKDD international conference on Knowledge discovery and data mining* (pp. 15-24). DOI: 10.1145/2623330.2623703

Draws, T., Szlávik, Z., Timmermans, B., Tintarev, N., Varshney, K. R., & Hind, M. (2021, April). Disparate impact diminishes consumer trust even for advantaged users. In *International Conference on Persuasive Technology* (pp. 135-149). Cham: Springer International Publishing. DOI: 10.1007/978-3-030-79460-6_11

Earley, S. (2018). The role of a customer data platform. *IT Professional*, 20(1), 69–76. DOI: 10.1109/MITP.2018.011301803

European Comission. (2018). Ethics guidelines for trustworthy AI. https://digital-strategy.ec.europa.eu/en/library/ethics-guidelines-trustworthy-ai

Farris, P. W., Bendle, N. T., Pfeifer, P. E., & Reibstein, D. J. (2010). *Marketing Metrics: The Definitive Guide to Measuring Marketing Performance*. Pearson Education.

Fountaine, T., McCarthy, B., & Saleh, T. (2019). Building the AI-Powered Organization. *Harvard Business Review*.https://hbr.org/2019/07/building-the-ai-powered-organization

Gankidi, N., & Gundu, S. viqar Ahmed, M., Tanzeela, T., Prasad, C. R., & Yalabaka, S. (2022, June). Customer segmentation using machine learning. In *2022 2nd International Conference on Intelligent Technologies (CONIT)* (pp. 1-5). IEEE.

Gentsch, P. (2019). *AI in Marketing, Sales and Service: How Marketers without a Data Science Degree can use AI, Big Data and Bots*. Springer. DOI: 10.1007/978-3-319-89957-2

Grewal, D., Hulland, J., Kopalle, P. K., & Karahanna, E. (2020). The Future of Technology and Marketing: A Multidisciplinary Perspective. *Journal of the Academy of Marketing Science*, 48(1), 1–8. DOI: 10.1007/s11747-019-00711-4

Grewal, D., Roggeveen, A. L., & Nordfält, J. (2017). The Future of Retailing. *Journal of Retailing*, 93(1), 1–6. DOI: 10.1016/j.jretai.2016.12.008

Gubbi, J., Buyya, R., Marusic, S., & Palaniswami, M. (2013). Internet of Things (IoT): A Vision, Architectural Elements, and Future Directions. *Future Generation Computer Systems*, 29(7), 1645–1660. DOI: 10.1016/j.future.2013.01.010

Gupta, A., & Agarwal, N. (2016, August). Streaming Analytics. In *Proceedings of the 22nd ACM SIGKDD International Conference on Knowledge Discovery and Data Mining* (pp. 2123-2123). DOI: 10.1145/2939672.2945395

Gupta, S., & Joshi, S. (2022, November). Predictive analytic techniques for enhancing marketing performance and personalized customer experience. In *2022 International Interdisciplinary Humanitarian Conference for Sustainability (IIHC)* (pp. 16-22). IEEE. DOI: 10.1109/IIHC55949.2022.10060286

Hair, J. F.Jr. (2007). Knowledge creation in marketing: The role of predictive analytics. *European Business Review*, 19(4), 303–315. DOI: 10.1108/09555340710760134

Halachmi, A., Hardy, W. P., & Rhoades, B. L. (1993). Demographic data and strategic analysis. *Public Administration Quarterly*, •••, 159–174.

Hu, P., & Wei, Q. (2020, April 1). Research on Personal Data Protection of EU General Data Protection Regulation. *IOP Conference Series. Materials Science and Engineering*, 806(1), 012003–012003. DOI: 10.1088/1757-899X/806/1/012003

Huang, M. H., & Rust, R. T. (2021). A strategic framework for artificial intelligence in marketing. *Journal of the Academy of Marketing Science*, 49(1), 30–50. DOI: 10.1007/s11747-020-00749-9

Hutter, F., Kotthoff, L., & Vanschoren, J. (2019). *Automated Machine Learning: Methods, Systems, Challenges*. Springer. DOI: 10.1007/978-3-030-05318-5

Jankovic, S. D., & Curovic, D. M. (2023). Strategic integration of artificial intelligence for sustainable businesses: Implications for data management and human user engagement in the digital era. *Sustainability (Basel)*, 15(21), 15208. DOI: 10.3390/su152115208

Jiang, T., & Tuzhilin, A. (2008). Improving personalization solutions through optimal segmentation of customer bases. *IEEE Transactions on Knowledge and Data Engineering*, 21(3), 305–320. DOI: 10.1109/TKDE.2008.163

Jurafsky, D., & Martin, J. H. (2021). *Speech and Language Processing*. Prentice Hall.

Kenwright, B. (2023). Exploring the power of creative ai tools and game-based methodologies for interactive web-based programming. *arXiv preprint arXiv:2308.11649.*

Kim, S. H. (2015). Mobile Marketing: Focusing on the Impact of Value, Privacy, and Trust. *International Journal of Mobile Marketing*, 10(1), 14–31.

Koren, Y., Bell, R., & Volinsky, C. (2009). Matrix Factorization Techniques for Recommender Systems. *Computer*, 42(8), 30–37. DOI: 10.1109/MC.2009.263

Kreps, J., Narkhede, N., & Rao, J. (2011, June). Kafka: A distributed messaging system for log processing. In *Proceedings of the NetDB* (Vol. 11, No. 2011, pp. 1-7).

Krisnanto, U., Juharsah, J., Putra, P., Achmad, A. D., & Timotius, E. (2022). Utilizing Apriori Data Mining Techniques on Sales Transactions. *Webology*, 19(1), 5581–5590. DOI: 10.14704/WEB/V19I1/WEB19376

Kumar, J., & Gupta, S. S. (2023). Impact of artificial intelligence towards customer relationship in Indian banking industry. *Gyan Management.Journal*, 17(1), 105–115.

Kumar, V., Rajan, B., Gupta, S., & Pozza, I. D. (2021). Customer Engagement in Service. *Journal of the Academy of Marketing Science*, 49, 304–325.

Lambrecht, A., & Tucker, C. (2013). When Does Retargeting Work? Information Specificity in Online Advertising. *JMR, Journal of Marketing Research*, 50(5), 561–576. DOI: 10.1177/002224371305000508

LeCun, Y., Bengio, Y., & Hinton, G. (2015). Deep Learning. *Nature*, 521(7553), 436–444. DOI: 10.1038/nature14539 PMID: 26017442

Lemon, K. N., & Verhoef, P. C. (2016). Understanding Customer Experience Throughout the Customer Journey. *Journal of Marketing*, 80(6), 69–96. DOI: 10.1509/jm.15.0420

Levy, M. (2020). *Customer Data Platforms: A Marketer's Guide*. MarketingProfs.

Li, Z., Kong, D., Niu, Y., Peng, H., Li, X., & Li, W. (2023, January 1). An Overview of AI and Blockchain Integration for Privacy-Preserving. Cornell University. doi:DOI: 10.48550/arXiv.2305

Lin, Y., Wang, H., Li, J., & Gao, H. (2019). Data source selection for information integration in big data era. *Information Sciences*, 479, 197–213. DOI: 10.1016/j.ins.2018.11.029

Liu, X., Singh, P. V., & Srinivasan, K. (2016). A structured analysis of unstructured big data by leveraging cloud computing. *Marketing Science*, 35(3), 363–388. DOI: 10.1287/mksc.2015.0972

Liu-Thompkins, Y., & Malthouse, E. C. (2017). A primer on using behavioral data for testing theories in advertising research. *Journal of Advertising*, 46(1), 213–225. DOI: 10.1080/00913367.2016.1252289

Lo, V. S. Y. (2005). Marketing Data Mining. In *Encyclopedia of Data Warehousing and Mining* (pp. 698–704). Idea Group Reference. DOI: 10.4018/978-1-59140-557-3.ch133

McKinsey & Company. (2020). The Value of Getting Personalization Right—or Wrong—is Multiplying. McKinsey & Company. https://www.mckinsey.com/capabilities/growth-marketing-and-sales/our-insights/the-value-of-getting-personalization-right-or-wrong-is-multiplying

Meurisch, C., & Mühlhäuser, M. (2021, March 5). Data Protection in AI Services. *ACM Computing Surveys*, 54(2), 1–38. DOI: 10.1145/3440754

Miklosik, A., Kuchta, M., Evans, N., & Zak, S. (2019). Towards the adoption of machine learning-based analytical tools in digital marketing. *IEEE Access : Practical Innovations, Open Solutions*, 7, 85705–85718. DOI: 10.1109/ACCESS.2019.2924425

Mirwan, S. H., Ginny, P. L., Darwin, D., Ghazali, R., & Lenas, M. N. J. (2023). Using Artificial Intelligence (AI) in Developing Marketing Strategies. [IJARSS]. *International Journal of Applied Research and Sustainable Sciences*, 1(3), 225–238. DOI: 10.59890/ijarss.v1i3.896

Mitchell, T. M. (1997). *Machine Learning*. McGraw-Hill.

Montgomery, D. C. (2015). *Design and Analysis of Experiments*. John Wiley & Sons.

Pancras, J., & Sudhir, K. (2007). Optimal marketing strategies for a customer data intermediary. *JMR, Journal of Marketing Research*, 44(4), 560–578. DOI: 10.1509/jmkr.44.4.560

Pang, B., & Lee, L. (2008). Opinion Mining and Sentiment Analysis. *Foundations and Trends in Information Retrieval*, 2(1-2), 1–135. DOI: 10.1561/1500000011

Peddie, J. (2017). *Augmented Reality: Where We Will All Live*. Springer. DOI: 10.1007/978-3-319-54502-8

Peltier, J., Schibrowsky, J. A., Schultz, D. E., & Zahay, D. (2006). Interactive IMC: The relational-transactional continuum and the synergistic use of customer data. *Journal of Advertising Research*, 46(2), 146–159. DOI: 10.2501/S0021849906060193

Pessach, D., & Shmueli, E. (2020, January 1). *Algorithmic Fairness*. doi:/arXiv.2001.09784DOI: 10.48550

Piotrowicz, W., & Cuthbertson, R. (2014). Introduction to the Special Issue Information Technology in Retail: Toward Omnichannel Retailing. *International Journal of Electronic Commerce*, 18(4), 5–16. DOI: 10.2753/JEC1086-4415180400

Pol, L. G. (1986). Marketing and the demographic perspective. *Journal of Consumer Marketing*, 3(1), 57–65. DOI: 10.1108/eb008153

Reichheld, F. F. (2001). *The Loyalty Effect: The Hidden Force Behind Growth, Profits, and Lasting Value*. Harvard Business Review Press.

Rezig, E. K., Cafarella, M., & Gadepally, V. (2021). Technical Report on Data Integration and Preparation. https://arxiv.org/pdf/2103.01986

Rigby, D. (2011). The Future of Shopping. *Harvard Business Review*. https://hbr.org/2011/12/the-future-of-shopping

Rolls-Royce. (2018). *Rolls-Royce's IntelligentEngine Vision Takes Shape*. Retrieved from Rolls-Royce.

Rossi, P. E., McCulloch, R. E., & Allenby, G. M. (1996). The value of purchase history data in target marketing. *Marketing Science*, 15(4), 321–340. DOI: 10.1287/mksc.15.4.321

Sadriwala, M. F., & Sadriwala, K. F. (2022). Perceived usefulness and ease of use of artificial intelligence on marketing innovation. [IJIDE]. *International Journal of Innovation in the Digital Economy*, 13(1), 1–10. DOI: 10.4018/IJIDE.292010

Saha, S., & Srivastava, A. (2014). Predictive Analytics Using Google Cloud Machine Learning. *International Journal of Computer Applications*, 104(17), 12–17.

Samosir, J., Indrawan-Santiago, M., & Haghighi, P. D. (2016). An evaluation of data stream processing systems for data driven applications. *Procedia Computer Science*, 80, 439–449. DOI: 10.1016/j.procs.2016.05.322

Sarwar, B., Karypis, G., Konstan, J., & Riedl, J. (2001, April). Item-based collaborative filtering recommendation algorithms. In *Proceedings of the 10th international conference on World Wide Web* (pp. 285-295). DOI: 10.1145/371920.372071

Schroeder, J. E. (2014). Branding in Perspective: The Cultural Code of Branding. *Marketing Theory*, 14(1), 131–143.

Schwartz, R., Vassilev, A., Greene, K., Perine, L., Burt, A., & Hall, P. (2022). Towards a standard for identifying and managing bias in artificial intelligence (NIST Special Publication 1270). *National Institute of Standards and Technology, 10.*

Sephora. (2017). Sephora Virtual Artist Uses AI to Transform Beauty Shopping Experience. Business Wire. Retrieved from Business Wire.

Shmueli, G., & Koppius, O. R. (2011). Predictive Analytics in Information Systems Research. *Management Information Systems Quarterly*, 35(3), 553–572. DOI: 10.2307/23042796

Smeureanu, I., Ruxanda, G., & Badea, L. M. (2013). Customer segmentation in private banking sector using machine learning techniques. *Journal of Business Economics and Management*, 14(5), 923–939. DOI: 10.3846/16111699.2012.749807

Smith, A. (2018). *Starbucks Leverages AI to Personalize Loyalty Program*. Forbes. Retrieved from Forbes.

Sousa, T. B. (2022, July). Customer Data Platforms: A Pattern Language for Digital Marketing Optimization with First-Party Data. In *Proceedings of the 27th European Conference on Pattern Languages of Programs* (pp. 1-5).

Stöger, K., Schneeberger, D., Kieseberg, P., & Holzinger, A. (2021). Legal aspects of data cleansing in medical AI. *Computer Law & Security Report*, 42, 105587. DOI: 10.1016/j.clsr.2021.105587

Stone, M., Aravopoulou, E., Gerardi, G., Todeva, E., Weinzierl, L., Laughlin, P., & Stott, R. (2017). How platforms are transforming customer information management. *The Bottom Line (New York, N.Y.)*, 30(3), 216–235. DOI: 10.1108/BL-08-2017-0024

Stone, M., & Woodcock, N. (2014). Interactive, Direct and Digital Marketing: A Future that Depends on Better Use of Business Intelligence. *Journal of Research in Interactive Marketing*, 8(1), 4–17. DOI: 10.1108/JRIM-07-2013-0046

Sun, T. (2019). Artificial Intelligence in Customer Relationship Management. *International Journal of Market Research*, 61(3), 213–226.

Tarka, P., & Łobiński, M. (2014). Decision Making in Reference to Model of Marketing Predictive Analytics–Theory and Practice. *Management and Business Administration.Central Europe*, 22(1), 60–69.

Thontirawong, P., & Chinchanachokchai, S. (2021). Teaching artificial intelligence and machine learning in marketing. *Marketing Education Review*, 31(2), 58–63. DOI: 10.1080/10528008.2021.1871849

Tsang, A. H. C. (2002). Strategic Dimensions of Maintenance Management. *Journal of Quality in Maintenance Engineering*, 8(1), 7–39. DOI: 10.1108/13552510210420577

Verhoef, P. C., Kannan, P. K., & Inman, J. J. (2015). From Multi-Channel Retailing to Omni-Channel Retailing: Introduction to the Special Issue on Multi-Channel Retailing. *Journal of Retailing*, 91(2), 174–181. DOI: 10.1016/j.jretai.2015.02.005

Verhoef, P. C., Lemon, K. N., Parasuraman, A., Roggeveen, A., Tsiros, M., & Schlesinger, L. A. (2010). Customer Experience Creation: Determinants, Dynamics, and Management Strategies. *Journal of Retailing*, 85(1), 31–41. DOI: 10.1016/j.jretai.2008.11.001

Wang, L., & Liu, S. (2020, July). Research on E-commerce Customer Relationship Management Based on Data Analysis. In *Proceedings of the 2020 11th International Conference on E-business, Management and Economics* (pp. 20-26). DOI: 10.1145/3414752.3414776

Wang, Y. (2021). When artificial intelligence meets educational leaders' data-informed decision-making: A cautionary tale. *Studies in Educational Evaluation*, 69, 100872. DOI: 10.1016/j.stueduc.2020.100872

Wedel, M., & Kannan, P. K. (2016). Marketing Analytics for Data-Rich Environments. *Journal of Marketing*, 80(6), 97–121. DOI: 10.1509/jm.15.0413

Whang, S. E., Roh, Y., Song, H., & Lee, J. G. (2023). Data collection and quality challenges in deep learning: A data-centric ai perspective. *The VLDB Journal*, 32(4), 791–813. DOI: 10.1007/s00778-022-00775-9

Wolniak, R., & Grebski, W. (2023). Functioning of predictive analytics in business. *Silesian University of Technology Scientific Papers. Organization and Management Series, 175*, 631-649.

Xu, R., & Wunsch, D.II. (2005). Survey of Clustering Algorithms. *IEEE Transactions on Neural Networks*, 16(3), 645–678. DOI: 10.1109/TNN.2005.845141 PMID: 15940994

Zahay, D., Peltier, J., Schultz, D. E., & Griffin, A. (2004). The role of transactional versus relational data in IMC programs: Bringing customer data together. *Journal of Advertising Research*, 44(1), 3–18. DOI: 10.1017/S0021849904040188

Zhou, Q., Simmhan, Y., & Prasanna, V. (2017). Knowledge-infused and consistent Complex Event Processing over real-time and persistent streams. *Future Generation Computer Systems*, 76, 391–406. DOI: 10.1016/j.future.2016.10.030

Ziakis, C., & Vlachopoulou, M. (2023). Artificial intelligence in digital marketing: Insights from a comprehensive review. *Information (Basel)*, 14(12), 664. DOI: 10.3390/info14120664

ADDITIONAL READING

Chen, H., Mao, S., & Liu, Y. (2014). Big Data: A Survey. *Mobile Networks and Applications*, 19(2), 171–209. DOI: 10.1007/s11036-013-0489-0

Davenport, T. H. (2018). *The AI Advantage: How to Put the Artificial Intelligence Revolution to Work.* MIT Press. DOI: 10.7551/mitpress/11781.001.0001

Grewal, D., Roggeveen, A. L., & Nordfält, J. (2017). The Future of Retailing. *Journal of Retailing*, 93(1), 1–6. DOI: 10.1016/j.jretai.2016.12.008

Hutter, F., Kotthoff, L., & Vanschoren, J. (Eds.). (2019). *Automated Machine Learning: Methods, Systems, Challenges*. Springer. DOI: 10.1007/978-3-030-05318-5

Kane, G. C. (2017). *The Technology Fallacy: How People Are the Real Key to Digital Transformation*. MIT Press.

LeCun, Y., Bengio, Y., & Hinton, G. (2015). Deep Learning. *Nature*, 521(7553), 436–444. DOI: 10.1038/nature14539 PMID: 26017442

Lemon, K. N., & Verhoef, P. C. (2016). Understanding Customer Experience Throughout the Customer Journey. *Journal of Marketing*, 80(6), 69–96. DOI: 10.1509/jm.15.0420

Peddie, J. (2017). *Augmented Reality: Where We Will All Live*. Springer. DOI: 10.1007/978-3-319-54502-8

Verhoef, P. C., Kannan, P. K., & Inman, J. J. (2015). From Multi-Channel Retailing to Omni-Channel Retailing: Introduction to the Special Issue on Multi-Channel Retailing. *Journal of Retailing*, 91(2), 174–181. DOI: 10.1016/j.jretai.2015.02.005

Wedel, M., & Kannan, P. K. (2016). Marketing Analytics for Data-Rich Environments. *Journal of Marketing*, 80(6), 97–121. DOI: 10.1509/jm.15.0413

KEY TERMS AND DEFINITIONS

Artificial Intelligence (AI): The simulation of human intelligence in machines that are programmed to think, learn, and make decisions like humans.

Customer Engagement: The emotional connection between a customer and a brand, characterized by the customer's interactions, loyalty, and advocacy.

Customer Segmentation: The process of dividing a customer base into distinct groups with similar characteristics or behaviors to tailor marketing efforts.

Data Integration: The practice of combining data from different sources to provide a unified view, enabling more accurate analysis and insights.

Deep Learning: A subset of machine learning involving neural networks with many layers, capable of analyzing large amounts of data to identify patterns and make predictions.

Internet of Things (IoT): A network of interconnected devices that collect and exchange data in real-time, enhancing personalized marketing efforts.

Omnichannel Marketing: A marketing approach that provides a seamless customer experience across multiple channels, both online and offline.

Predictive Analytics: The use of statistical models and machine learning techniques to analyze historical data and predict future outcomes.

Real-Time Personalization: The process of dynamically adjusting marketing content and interactions based on real-time data and customer behavior.

Virtual Reality (VR): A simulated experience created by computer technology that can be similar to or completely different from the real world, used in marketing to create immersive experiences.

Chapter 5
AI-Driven Personalization in Beauty Retail:
Exploring How AI-Based Applications Influence Customer Satisfaction and Brand Loyalty

Maria Carolina Cordeiro Dias Coelho
Instituto Português de Administração de Marketing, Portugal

Irma Imamović
Instituto Português de Administração de Marketing, Portugal

ABSTRACT

This study explores the evolving beauty industry transformed by technology, focusing on how personalized artificial intelligence (AI) shapes customer experience, satisfaction, and loyalty in online beauty shopping. Through semi-structured interviews with 10 Portuguese female online buyers aged 18-30, it reveals the importance of understanding and meeting customer preferences in a fast-paced digital environment. The research highlights the crucial role of personal experiences and trust in influencing customer satisfaction and loyalty. It examines the impact of AI-based recommendations and interactions at every stage of the online shopping experience. The findings offer valuable insights for beauty brands, emphasizing the necessity to adapt to technological advances, thrive in the digital landscape, and meet consumers' evolving digital aspirations.

DOI: 10.4018/979-8-3693-5340-0.ch005

1. INTRODUCTION

Technological advances in today's rapidly expanding digital ecosystem are driving dramatic changes across industries (Kumar et al., 2021). From artificial intelligence (AI) to data analytics, these advances are transforming how people interact with companies and utilize products and services (Grewal et al., 2020). The beauty retail industry, in particular, is at the forefront of this digital transformation, embracing new technologies to enhance customer experience and drive business growth (Basker, 2016). Companies are leveraging AI and machine learning to analyze consumer preferences, optimize product recommendations, and increase customer engagement (Lee & Lee, 2020; Pillarisetty & Mishra, 2022). Additionally, Augmented Reality (AR) and Virtual Reality (VR) technologies are revolutionizing beauty retail by enabling customers to test products virtually, improving the shopping experience, and reducing post-purchase dissatisfaction (Mangtani et al., 2020; Wedel et al., 2020).

AI-driven customization techniques significantly impact customer satisfaction, loyalty, and long-term brand engagement in the beauty retail sector (Mangtani et al., 2020). Understanding AI's influence on customer satisfaction and trust is crucial for building brand loyalty (Singh & Ahmed, 2024). However, ethical challenges such as data privacy and transparency must be addressed (Volkmar et al., 2022). Existing literature often overlooks the detailed interaction between AI-driven personalization, customer satisfaction, and brand loyalty, especially in the beauty industry.

This study addresses this gap by examining AI's direct influence on Portuguese female customer satisfaction and loyalty in online beauty retail. It provides valuable insights for beauty retailers to refine their strategies and thrive in the competitive digital landscape, focusing on emotion, satisfaction, and potential issues related to AI-based marketing solutions. It seeks to understand how AI-driven customization impacts consumer behavior and brand interactions in the digital age.

The main objective of the study is to explore the role of AI-driven personalization in Portuguese female buyers´ satisfaction and loyalty in beauty retail, by considering their attitudes, behaviors, concerns, and specific strategies for shopping online experiences.

The specific objectives are four:

- To explore female buyers' views on the evolution of functionality and the influence of AI technology in the online beauty retail sector
- To understand the particular processes by which AI-driven customization influences Portuguese female buyers' relation with their online purchasing experiences in beauty retail.

- To investigate the possible obstacles and concerns that Portuguese female buyers may have about the introduction of AI-based apps for personalization in the online beauty retail setting.
- To analyze how AI-driven personalization may influence their loyalty to beauty businesses

This article explores the relationship between technology and customer engagement in beauty retail. It explores the integration of technology within the industry, the role of AI in customer recommendations, and the impact of personalization on consumer purchase decisions. The article also explores the impact of AI-powered personalized experiences on customer satisfaction and loyalty, addressing global challenges and ethical considerations. The methodology is then presented, with findings organized by key themes, and final insights and recommendations provided.

2. LITERATURE REVIEW

2.1. Technological Integration in Beauty Retailing

Throughout history, technological advancements have aimed to reduce manual labor, increase productivity, and improve lifestyles (Woessner et al., 2021). Recently, this pursuit has gained momentum, with technology becoming a cornerstone of modern life (Kumar et al., 2021). Technology encompasses a vast array of tools and processes developed through iterative refinement, building upon past inventions and continuously introducing groundbreaking advancements (Arthur & Polak, 2006). The fourth industrial revolution epitomizes this, ushering in innovative technologies that boost manufacturing efficiency and promote social and environmental sustainability (Bai et al., 2020). This revolution has also significantly impacted customer behavior, driving a shift towards online and mobile shopping, and facilitating the rise of "passive" customer interaction services (Lee & Lee, 2020).

The retail sector, particularly the beauty industry, exemplifies how technological advancements have transformed various aspects of human life. Over the past few decades, these advancements have enabled significant growth in staff productivity, company size, market share, and product offerings (Basker, 2016). Businesses are now allocating more resources to online, mobile, and social media channels to enhance customer engagement and drive revenue growth (Grewal et al., 2020). Technologies such as mobile platforms, social media, AR, and the internet have revolutionized business marketing strategies, driving aggressive growth (Grewal et al., 2020). As consumers become increasingly tech-savvy, businesses must adapt their operations to incorporate new technologies, leading to faster and more efficient digital experiences (Kumar et al., 2021).

AI, a multifaceted concept, encompasses various definitions and applications. It is described as system or software capable of mimicking human intelligence and performing tasks like visual comprehension, speech recognition, and decision-making (Khokhar & Chitsimran, 2019). AI operates in areas of continuous improvement, serving as the driving force behind data-driven analysis and automated decision-making processes (Kumar et al., 2021). Beyond a narrow view of AI as merely robotic systems, it represents a broader technological spectrum, penetrating diverse industries and enhancing customer experiences through personalization (Pillarisetty & Mishra, 2022; Verma et al., 2021).

In marketing, AI automates various aspects, streamlining data utilization and offering targeted recommendations (Stone et al., 2020). It predicts consumer behavior through data analysis, enhancing customer experiences and enabling one-to-one marketing with lower resource consumption (Nalbant & Aydin, 2023). AI also complements Customer Relationship Management (CRM) features, transforming retail stores into smart establishments that enhance shopping convenience and supply chain management (Verma et al., 2021). Companies focusing on client-centered strategies and providing digital solutions tailored to customer demands are likely to flourish (Kumar et al., 2021). Despite its benefits, AI-enabled services raise concerns such as reduced human involvement, privacy issues, and potential disruptions to service experiences (Ameen et al., 2021).

2.2. AI-Powered Customer Engagement

The cosmetics industry is evolving with a focus on sustainability, innovative packaging, natural ingredients, and personalization to meet changing consumer preferences (Mangtani et al., 2020). Technological advancements like AI and AR are transforming retail by enhancing product diversity, professionalism, and customer experiences (Basker, 2016).

AI and big data are reshaping the beauty industry in the Fourth Industrial Revolution, enabling personalized customer interactions and strategic business insights (Kwon & Lim, 2021). AI-driven marketing operations optimize customer analysis, targeted advertising, and pricing strategies, maximizing individualized returns (Stone et al., 2020).

VR applications are enhancing user experiences across various sectors, including education, travel, entertainment, and advertising (Wedel et al., 2020). AI-enabled services provide continuous support and personalized interactions throughout the customer journey, enhancing convenience and engagement (Ameen et al., 2021).

In the beauty sector, AI and AR technologies facilitate virtual try-ons, personalized beauty recommendations, and improved customer engagement through digital experiences (Tzou et al., 2022). These innovations reduce product returns and reshape brand operations to meet evolving consumer demands (Pillarisetty & Mishra, 2022).

Overall, AI's integration in marketing and retail is driving efficiency, personalization, and customer satisfaction while raising ethical considerations around privacy and human involvement (Ameen et al., 2021). Balancing technological advancements with responsible practices is crucial for businesses to thrive in a digitally driven marketplace (Jarrahi, 2018).

2.3. Big Data and AI: Improving Customer Recommendations

AI has revolutionized advertising by enabling more efficient data gathering, analysis, and interpretation, leading to deeper insights into consumer behavior and business preferences (Masnita et al., 2024). This technology empowers organizations to create personalized and engaging content, optimize marketing campaigns, and enhance customer interactions through tools like chatbots (Masnita et al., 2024).

In the realm of customer-brand interactions, AI-driven personalization plays a crucial role in fostering relationship commitment by minimizing perceived complexity and enhancing consistency, reliability, and support across service interfaces (Trawnih et al., 2022; Ameen et al., 2021). The rise of big data in the digital era has further amplified these capabilities, offering extensive benefits across industries through advanced analytics and predictive modeling (Roy et al., 2022). Technologies such as data mining, machine learning, and predictive analytics are pivotal in extracting actionable insights that drive marketing effectiveness and enhance consumer satisfaction (Belarbi et al., 2016; Sharma et al., 2022).

2.3.1. Chatbots and Virtual Assistant

The COVID-19 pandemic accelerated the adoption of chatbots and conversational AI in business, emphasizing digitalization and automation in customer service (Stoilova, 2021). Traditionally reliant on face-to-face interactions, businesses increasingly used social networks for instant responses during the crisis (Chung et al., 2020), highlighting chatbots' role in enabling fast, contactless customer service and improving operational efficiency through continuous support and data-driven insights (Cordero et al., 2022).

Chatbots play a crucial role in modern marketing by enhancing customer engagement through personalized support across platforms (Masnita et al., 2024). They use natural language processing and conversational interfaces to handle tasks like FAQs, bookings, and data collection, improving user experiences and predicting behavior (Stoilova, 2021). Leveraging artificial memory and machine learning, chatbots provide tailored responses and contribute to data analytics, helping businesses understand and meet customer expectations effectively (Misischia et al., 2022).

Research shows chatbot interaction quality positively impacts customer satisfaction and brand loyalty, transforming digital services and marketing strategies (Chung et al., 2020; Cheng & Jiang, 2020). However, privacy concerns highlight the need for strategic planning and training to optimize chatbot performance and user acceptance (Roozen et al., 2022; Stoilova, 2021).

2.3.2. Recommendation Systems

Recommendation systems, pivotal since the 1990s, span e-commerce, movies, music, and social media, curating personalized suggestions to manage information overload (Huang et al., 2019; Sharma and Gera, 2013). They utilize collaborative and content-based filtering alongside social data, enhancing user experiences and fostering loyalty (Balakrishnan et al., 2018). These systems balance accuracy with privacy concerns through sophisticated algorithms and user interface designs (Huang et al., 2019).

Researchers strive to improve recommendation systems by addressing privacy risks and data sensitivity, employing diverse algorithms from commercial and open-source libraries (Zheng et al., 2015). These systems drive sales by suggesting products, promoting cross-selling, and enhancing customer engagement through personalized service (Prassas et al., 2001). Businesses integrate recommendation technologies to optimize process design, reduce errors, and align new processes with existing frameworks (Deng et al., 2016). Overall, recommendation systems play a critical role in enhancing customer interactions and driving business growth in the digital age.

2.3.3. AR Technology

Agile adaptation was crucial during the COVID-19 pandemic, prompting rapid integration of AR technology into e-commerce to enhance visual experiences (Gabriel et al., 2023). AR, a technology overlaying virtual computer-generated images onto the real world, enriches user experiences without replacing reality, notably in retail, education, and tourism (Iatsyshyn et al., 2019; Mangtani et al., 2020). It facilitates real-time product testing in the beauty industry through virtual try-ons and personalized recommendations (Masnita et al., 2024; Tzou et al., 2022).

AR enables consumers to try cosmetics virtually, addressing concerns about online purchase risk and enhancing customer confidence and decision-making (Whang et al., 2021). By blending physical and digital environments, AR supports tailored product suggestions and safer experimentation with makeup and hair (Mangtani et al., 2020). This technology fosters consumer engagement and cognitive processing, driving purchase intentions and promoting personalized cosmetic experiences (Kristi & Kusumawati, 2021).

Overall, AI and AR technologies are reshaping the beauty industry by offering personalized products and virtual experiences, increasing consumer confidence, and enhancing the online shopping journey (Mangtani et al., 2020; Whang et al., 2021).

2.4. Personalization's Influence on Purchase Decisions

The decision-making process in purchasing involves multiple cognitive factors and considerations such as consumer personas, perceived product capabilities, and purchase intentions (Mbete & Tanamal, 2020). Purchase intention, crucial in predicting the adoption of new technology or services, does not always translate directly into a purchase decision (Uzir et al., 2023). Factors influencing this decision include where to buy, preferred brands, product categories, pricing, and payment options (Hanaysha et al., 2021).

Consumer confidence and perceptions of online commerce significantly influence purchase intentions, with AI playing a pivotal role in understanding and meeting consumer expectations (Anjelita et al., 2023). Positive attitudes towards technology generally lead to favorable perceptions and increased willingness to purchase new products (Lin & Hsieh, 2006). Despite concerns, consumers are influenced by personalized product recommendations and the overall shopping experience, which enhance engagement and purchase likelihood (Sunita, 2023).

Brand perception and emotional connections also play vital roles in purchase and repurchase intentions, highlighting the importance of brand loyalty and customer satisfaction in driving repeat purchases (Ding et al., 2022). Businesses can enhance customer relationships and boost sales by leveraging recommendation systems, personalized service offerings, and interactive tools like chatbots to meet consumer needs effectively (Lau & Ki, 2021; Sunita, 2023).

2.5. The influence of AI-powered personalized experiences on customer satisfaction and loyalty

The literature on brand trust highlights its multifaceted nature and its profound impact on consumer behavior across various domains (DAM, 2020). Brand trust is defined as consumers' confidence and satisfaction in their interactions with businesses, influencing purchasing decisions and fostering acceptance (Siau & Wang, 2018). This trust extends to AI technologies, where the perceived usefulness and reliability of AI services enhance consumer experiences and acceptance (Ameen et al., 2021; Hengstler et al., 2016).

Hengstler et al. (2016) emphasize that trust in AI is shaped by factors such as perceived technological capabilities, data quality, and decision-making methods, crucial for building consumer confidence. Businesses aiming to integrate AI must prioritize intuitive interfaces and user-specific usability tests to mitigate initial skepticism and foster trust (Ameen et al., 2021). Customer satisfaction is pivotal in digital marketing, where AI tools like chatbots and personalized product suggestions are employed to enhance customer experiences (Nalbant & Aydin, 2023; Pillarisetty & Mishra, 2022). It arises from meeting or exceeding customer expectations and is fundamental for fostering loyalty (Sivadas & Baker-Prewitt, 2000; Restiana, 2021). Pillarisetty and Mishra (2022) note that customer satisfaction in online environments builds over time through consistent positive experiences and meeting customer needs. Businesses in competitive markets must continually improve service quality and personalize interactions to enhance satisfaction levels (Nalbant & Aydin, 2023). Not only that but builds trust and loyalty by addressing individual requirements, promoting repeat business, and good word-of-mouth; nevertheless, it must be handled responsibly, with open data methods and explicit disclosure about AI's involvement, to guarantee customer satisfaction (Babatunde et al.,2024).

Loyalty, as a consequence of trust and satisfaction, is essential for business success, driving repeat purchases and positive word-of-mouth (Petzer & Roberts-Lombard, 2021; Djamaludin & Fahira, 2023). It encompasses a customer's persistent preference for a brand, influenced by trust in the brand's reliability and satisfaction with its offerings (Restiana, 2021; Bowen & Chen, 2001). Understanding the factors influencing loyalty, such as customer satisfaction, perceived benefits, and ongoing positive experiences, is crucial for businesses seeking to build enduring customer relationships (Petzer & Roberts-Lombard, 2021). Despite challenges like market competitiveness and evolving consumer preferences, maintaining high-quality service and personalized customer interactions remains pivotal for fostering loyalty and achieving sustained business growth (Haron & Subar, 2020; Cheng & Jiang, 2020).

2.6. Obstacles and Concerns with AI Personalization

AI's integration into consumer interaction raises ethical concerns, particularly regarding data privacy and biases (Rodgers & Nguyen, 2022). The use of predictive analytics in customer relationship management requires stringent measures to address these challenges (Reddy, 2021). Biases in AI systems, stemming from biased training data or interpretation, underscore the need for objectivity and fairness in AI applications (Volkmar et al., 2022).

Ensuring customer data privacy is paramount in AI applications to maintain trust and compliance with regulatory standards (Masnita et al., 2024). The collection of personal data during AI-driven processes raises concerns about transparency and consent, impacting customer trust and satisfaction (Cukier, 2021). Effective data governance and robust security measures are essential to mitigate privacy risks and build consumer confidence in AI technologies (Reddy, 2021).

AI's implementation can reduce the human interaction scale and diminish customer control over their experiences, leading to potential dissatisfaction (Ameen et al., 2021). Addressing these challenges requires businesses to prioritize transparency in AI decision-making processes and enhance explainability to bridge the gap between perceived and actual understanding (Volkmar et al., 2022). By adopting robust data governance practices and ensuring ethical AI deployments, organizations can safeguard customer trust and enhance overall service delivery in the digital age (Reddy, 2021).

3. METHODOLOGY

This study employs qualitative research to explore the perspectives of Portuguese women shoppers in the beauty retail sector, specifically focusing on AI-powered personalization. Qualitative methods, including semi-structured interviews, are chosen to delve deeply into participants' views and experiences, given the novelty and limited quantitative data on this topic. The approach emphasizes understanding meaning and interpreting experiences to uncover insights into complex psychosocial issues (Hignett and McDermott, 2015; Marshall, 1996).

Interviews are conducted with female buyers familiar with the beauty market, using judgment sampling to select participants based on their expertise in AI applications. This method allows researchers to gather nuanced insights and adapt to emerging themes in the data collection process. However, judgment sampling, while beneficial for exploring specific phenomena, may limit generalizability due to potential researcher bias (Sharma, 2017).

The primary data collection method involves online interviews via Microsoft Teams, facilitating direct engagement with participants to gather rich qualitative data on their opinions and experiences regarding AI-powered personalization in beauty retail. Semi-structured interviews strike a balance between structured and unstructured formats, employing predefined questions while allowing for open-ended responses that capture participants' detailed viewpoints and experiences (Karatsareas, 2022). This approach is essential for exploring nuanced perspectives, especially in complex areas like AI-driven personalization in the beauty market, where traditional metrics may fall short (Adeoye-Olatunde & Olenik, 2021). Interview guides are crucial tools in this process, outlining key questions and providing flexibility to adapt based on interviewees' responses, thus facilitating a deeper understanding of the subject matter (Luo & Wildemuth, 2009).

By engaging directly with participants through semi-structured interviews, researchers can uncover underlying dynamics and relationships that influence outcomes, shedding light on the evolution of AI-driven personalization in consumer experiences (Drury et al., 2011; Karatsareas, 2022). Ethical considerations, such as obtaining informed consent and ensuring participant comfort throughout the research process, are paramount to maintaining integrity and securing ethical approval (Karatsareas, 2022).

3.1. Sample

The study will involve conducting personal interviews with female Portuguese consumers who have experience shopping online with brands that use AI-powered optimization tools. Specifically targeting 10 participants aged 18 to 30, who are knowledgeable about AI and emerging technologies, aims to provide focused insights into how AI impacts customer satisfaction and loyalty in the beauty industry.

3.2. Data collection and analysis tools

The study utilized 14 interview questions, as shown in Table 1, each meticulously aligned with the study's specific objectives and themes from the literature review. This organized approach enabled comprehensive contextual analysis, providing researchers with focused insights and valuable feedback from participants directly related to the study's aims and current academic discussions.

Bardin's Content Analysis is a qualitative tool that systematically examines AI-driven personalization in beauty retail by categorizing and analyzing consumer engagement, satisfaction, and loyalty. It helps identify key themes and patterns in interview data, focusing on factors like privacy issues and trust in AI, making it an effective method for understanding AI's impact on consumer behavior. The analysis is done by category and then the conclusion is by objective which may or may not have more than one category involved that helps to answer the specific objective (de Sousa & dos Santos, 2020).

Table 1. Research objectives and questions

Objective	Questions	Explanation
First objective To research female buyers' perspectives about AI-powered tailored suggestions and interactions in the online beauty retail industry	Can you tell me a bit about your experiences as a female Portuguese buyer in beauty online shops?	Together they are working to better study female consumers' experiences, behaviors, attitudes, and findings with technology, specifically AI in the beauty retail space. This understanding helps explore how AI customization affects customer satisfaction and loyalty. Each question incorporates a broader understanding of how AI technologies are perceived, used, and developed in the beauty retail industry, and describes the objectives of the survey.
	How often do you visit beauty shops, and what factors influence your purchasing decisions?	
	How do you perceive the use of technology, such as AI, in beauty shops?	
	Have you noticed any changes in the way technology is integrated into the beauty retail experience over the years?	

continued on following page

Table 1. Continued

Objective	Questions	Explanation
Second Objective To understand the particular processes by which AI-driven customization influences female buyers' satisfaction with their online purchasing experiences in beauty retail	Could you please provide examples of AI-based applications or technologies that you are aware of being used in beauty retailing	Inquiries about the participant's personal experiences with personalized recommendations or interactions in beauty shops and how it affected their satisfaction and loyalty to the brand. Explores the participant's opinions on AI-powered features, such as personalized product recommendations or virtual try-on experiences, offered in beauty shops.
	Can you recall a specific instance where an AI-driven suggestion significantly influenced your decision to purchase a beauty product? How did that make you feel?	
	In what ways do you believe AI-driven customization enhances your online shopping experience in the beauty sector?	
	Have you ever been dissatisfied with an AI-driven suggestion or interaction while shopping for beauty products online? Please explain.	Addresses concerns or reservations the participant may have regarding the use of AI-based applications for personalization in beauty shops and how it may affect their satisfaction and loyalty.
Third Objective To investigate the possible obstacles and concerns that female buyers may have about the introduction of AI-based apps for personalization in the online beauty retail setting.	Are there any concerns or reservations you have regarding the use of AI-based applications for personalization in beauty shops?	
	Do you have any concerns about the AI using your data and history for personalization?	
	How do you think these concerns, if any, might impact your satisfaction and loyalty toward beauty brands	
	Are there any specific features or aspects of AI-driven customization that you believe could be improved to enhance your shopping experience?	

continued on following page

Table 1. Continued

Objective	Questions	Explanation
Fourth Objective To analyze how AI-driven personalization may influence their loyalty to beauty businesses.	How does a positive experience with AI-driven personalization affect your loyalty to a particular beauty brand or online retailer?	These questions help to better understand the role of AI in building customer loyalty by investigating how a positive experience of AI-driven customization affects dedication to specific cosmetic brands or websites. Answers to these questions will be illuminating that it comes from AI-driven personalized suggestion that it might be similar for repeated purchases from an Internet beauty store, thus revealing the impact of AI-driven personalization on customer loyalty in the beauty industry.
	Have AI-powered tailored suggestions ever led you to repeatedly purchase from the same online beauty retailer? Please share your experience.	

4. FINDINGS

The interviews were analyzed using categories and subcategories to ensure a detailed evaluation. Each category aligns with a specific objective, and multiple categories may be used to meet the necessary information requirements. This method allows for a nuanced understanding of the data through focused analysis. Each subcategory includes quotes from the interviews to support the analysis.

Categorizing and providing supporting quotes allows thorough analysis, identifying key findings, patterns, and main takeaways from each interview. The analysis follows the interview questions' structure, drawing conclusions for each objective based on relevant categories.

Each participant is assigned a code, such as "I1," to make it easier to understand the findings and for the reader to follow.

4.1. Category: Shopping Frequency and Preferences

The analysis highlights the interconnectedness of shopping frequency, preferred stores, price sensitivity, and social media influence. Frequent shoppers, such as I1, I2, I7, and I10, are significantly influenced by social media trends and viral content, using social media both for information and purchase motivation. They exhibit strong brand preferences but remain price-sensitive, with Sephora being a popular choice. Social media also appeals to cost-conscious consumers by promoting affordable options. Moderate shoppers, like I5 and I8, stay informed about new trends and product launches, indicating that even less frequent shoppers remain engaged with the market. This complexity underscores the pivotal roles of digital engagement, brand loyalty, and price consciousness in modern consumer behavior.

4.2. Category: Perception and Evolution of Online Shopping

The feeling towards Improvement in Functionality Over Time is echoed by several interviewees. For instance, I1 emphasizes the evolution of online makeup stores, noting the introduction of features like searching for specific skin color shades, which significantly enhance personalization. I1 mentions the ability to search for their skin color shade as a notable improvement that helps with personalization. Similarly, I3 observes a shift in the beauty market towards technology, highlighting the growing investment by major brands in tech-driven products.

These sentiments seamlessly tie into the Impact of Tech and AI Features, where interviewees recognize the role of AI in augmenting functionality and personalization. I7 notes the influence of AI-driven personalization, mentioning how personalized product recommendations have become more prevalent. I9 acknowledges AI-powered virtual try-ons for hair color, specifically mentioning Loreal's feature that allows consumers to see potential hair colors before purchasing the dye.

The link between these subjects is clear in how technical developments have increased functionality over time while also driving individualized experiences through AI integration. As online beauty retail platforms evolve, consumers benefit from more customized, efficient, and intuitive purchasing experiences, indicating a dramatic shift in the market landscape.

4.3. Category: AI Recommendations Tools

Positive experiences with AI recommendations play a crucial role in fostering brand loyalty and satisfaction. Consumers satisfied with AI-driven suggestions, like I1 who appreciates the general positive impact of AI on their purchases, and I2 who values the personalized highlight of viral products, are more likely to feel confident in their purchasing decisions and develop loyalty towards the brand. This confidence is due to the personalized nature of AI recommendations, which cater to individual preferences and needs. For instance, I1 is happier with AI suggestions because they reduce the risk of unsuitable purchases, while I10 finds the personalized experience unique both personally and from a marketing perspective. These tailored recommendations significantly enhance overall satisfaction with the shopping experience.

Additionally, the recognition of personalization, echoed by respondents, further strengthens the link between brand loyalty and satisfaction. Tailored AI recommendations contribute significantly to consumer contentment and loyalty towards a brand, indicating the pivotal role of AI in modern consumer behavior.

4.4. Category: Attitudes Towards AI and Data Usage

A review of "Attitudes Towards AI and Data Usage" reveals that respondents generally have a positive attitude toward AI technology and few privacy concerns. This positive mindset is driven by the perceived benefits of AI, such as improved shopping experiences and increased customization. Respondents appreciate AI's role in providing tailored and efficient services, with many expressing satisfaction with the development and personalization that AI brings to their shopping experiences.

Additionally, many respondents are willing to share their data in exchange for rewards, indicating minimal fear regarding data usage. Regular interaction with AI-driven platforms for updates and suggestions shows widespread acceptance and confidence in the systems.

Overall, these findings suggest that consumer perceptions of AI and data usage are likely to remain favorable as long as AI offers observable advantages and maintains transparency and security. This understanding is crucial for businesses aiming to leverage AI to enhance customer experiences while ensuring ethical data practices.

4.5. Category: AI Technologies Impact on Consumer Experience

Participants revealed that the integration of AI technologies—chatbots, personalized recommendations, and virtual try-on features—profoundly impacts consumer experience by enhancing personalization, convenience, and engagement. Chatbots provide immediate, personalized assistance and support, helping answer questions about skin type and product suitability through brief questionnaires. Participants found chatbots convenient for makeup-related queries and efficient in resolving product-related doubts swiftly. This immediate and reliable support saves time and increases consumer confidence in purchasing decisions, demonstrating the significant role of chatbots in improving the online shopping experience. Participants revealed that AI-driven personalized recommendations significantly enhance the consumer experience by providing tailored product suggestions based on individual preferences and past purchases. This feature simplifies decision-making, as it suggests products similar to previous purchases, making the process easier. Participants felt that personalized recommendations reflect brand care and positively influence their purchase decisions, effectively bridging the gap between online and physical store experiences. They noted that AI helps replicate the personalized service of physical stores, and AI-driven suggestions often lead to discovering new, satisfying products that meet specific needs.

Virtual try-on features provide consumers with the ability to experiment with products such as lipsticks and hair colors before making a purchase, thereby reducing the risk of dissatisfaction. Participant I1 valued these features for helping identify suitable shades online, while I9 appreciated the ability to try hair colors virtually to avoid mistakes. I10 mentioned enjoying the experience of trying on lipsticks and eyeshadows virtually through platforms like Instagram filters, emphasizing how virtual try-ons make the shopping process more interactive and fun. This capability helps consumers make more informed decisions and adds an element of fun to the shopping experience, as noted by I3, who mentioned that trying products online makes it much easier for consumers to make purchasing decisions.

Participants highlighted the transformative impact of AI in online beauty retail. They noted that chatbots offer tailored advice and product suggestions, personalized recommendations provide relevant products based on their behavior, and virtual try-ons allow for customized exploration of beauty products. These technologies collectively enhance personalization, streamline the shopping experience, and make it more interactive and engaging. Participants mentioned that these features foster a deeper connection with brands, often leading to impulse purchases and higher satisfaction. The seamless and enjoyable AI-driven shopping experience also contributes to increased customer loyalty and improved business outcomes.

4.6. Category: Enhancing Repeat Purchases and Shopping Experience in Online Beauty Retail

The idea of customer satisfaction and retention is the link between areas for improvement and recurrent purchase behavior. Some consumers show their devotion by making repeat purchases, but others could want for more individualized or improved experiences. As an example, the remark made by I1 mentioned that she bought the product, liked it, and continued to buy it, demonstrating their loyalty through repeat purchases. This captures the element of loyalty associated with repeat purchases. The importance of personalization for improving the shopping experience, however, is highlighted by I9's that she believe there could be a way to make the experience more personalized, as they have had some very good experiences but also a few that have put them off. Online beauty businesses may develop a comprehensive strategy to enhance overall shopping experiences and repeat sales by utilizing customer-identified areas for development and exploiting data from repeat purchases. This strategy involves identifying a middle ground between satisfying the preferences of devoted clients and attending to issues brought up by clients looking for individualized experiences. I1 notes that adding features like color matching can make the comparison process easier, but I9's comments highlight the need for more individualized assistance.

In ultimately, online beauty stores may streamline their business processes to promote enduring consumer satisfaction and loyalty by comprehending and reacting to customer comments and behaviors. This opinion supports I3's assertion that things are going well, implying that even while changes are required, some clients could find the situation to be satisfactory as it is.

5. DISCUSSION

The discussion, divided into objectives, analyzes findings about current literature, focusing on AI-driven customization's impact on consumer satisfaction and brand loyalty in online cosmetics retail, especially among Portuguese female buyers.

5.1. To explore female buyers' views on the evolution of functionality and the influence of ai technology in the online beauty retail sector

The findings regarding the functionality and influence of AI in the online beauty retail sector are supported by various authors and studies in the literature on technological integration, AI, and digital marketing.

It was found that AI-driven personalization has significantly enhanced the user experience in the online beauty retail sector. This finding is supported Kumar et al., (2021), who emphasize AI's capability to analyze user data and behaviors, thereby allowing for personalized experiences tailored to individual preferences and enhancing consumer satisfaction. Similarly, Verma et al., (2021) highlight AI's role in providing personalized experiences across various sectors, including digital marketing. Additionally, Ameen et al., (2021) emphasize AI-driven personalization's impact on consumer engagement and satisfaction through customized suggestions and virtual try-ons.

Also, the results notice that advanced search features and filters have made it easier for users to find specific products quickly, contributing to a more efficient and user-friendly shopping experience. This finding aligns with Grewal et al., (2020), who discuss how technological advancements have improved customer engagement and driven revenue growth through enhanced searchability and navigation features. Furthermore, Khokhar and Chitsimran (2019) mention the role of AI and machine learning in optimizing search functionalities and improving user experience.

The speed of online transactions and accessibility, particularly through mobile technology and simplified payment methods, has improved, making the shopping process faster and more convenient. Lee and Lee (2020) support this finding by highlighting the integration of advanced technologies in retail to boost efficiency and accessibility. (Grewal et al.,2020) also note the increased focus on mobile and social media channels to enhance customer engagement and drive revenue growth.

The integration of AI and other advanced technologies has transformed the online shopping landscape, making it more engaging and efficient. This discovery is supported by Mangtani et al., (2020), who discuss the revolutionary impact of AI in the beauty industry, enhancing product recommendations and customer satisfaction. Kwon and Lim (2021) also address the significant role of AI and big data in transforming the beauty retail sector by identifying client characteristics and fostering innovation.

Further, was found that AI technologies facilitate the shopping process, making it easier for consumers to find and purchase products that meet their needs, including features like virtual try-ons and intuitive search functionalities. Jarrahi (2018) supports this finding by discussing AI's capabilities, including machine learning and natural language processing, which enhance decision-making processes in various sectors. Tzou et al., (2022) also note that major beauty brands use AI and AR to enable consumers to try on makeup and receive personalized recommendations, streamlining decision-making. In addition, customers stated that AI-powered interactive features, such as virtual try-ons, enhance engagement and satisfaction. This finding is supported by Mangtani et al., (2020), who highlight the growing popularity of virtual try-ons and AI-powered diagnostics for providing personalized insights and enhancing user engagement. Tzou et al. (2022) also note that virtual try-ons in beauty retail reduce the need for physical trials and improve customer satisfaction by offering an interactive shopping experience.

The literature research, which emphasizes the critical role that AI and technology breakthroughs have had in revolutionizing the online beauty retail business, provides strong support for the findings. Numerous studies confirm that AI has improved user experience overall and has improved customization, speed, accessibility, searchability, and navigation. These developments demonstrate a dramatic movement towards more individualized, effective, and enjoyable purchasing experiences.

5.2. To understand the particular processes by which AI-driven customization influences Portuguese female buyers' satisfaction with their online purchasing experiences in beauty retail

Numerous research and findings indicate the influence of technology improvements, especially AI-driven personalization, on Portuguese female shoppers' satisfaction with their online shopping experiences in the cosmetics retail industry. These developments, which provide more personalization, better navigation, speed, and accessibility, have greatly improved the online buying experience.

The frequency of online shopping among consumers varies, reflecting the need for flexible and responsive online platforms. Nalbant and Aydin (2023) discuss how advanced technology and social isolation have shifted shopping habits towards online platforms, especially among younger generations. This aligns with the observation that Portuguese female buyers integrate online beauty shopping into their daily routines, necessitating seamless and engaging online experiences to meet diverse shopping patterns. This finding is supported by Grewal et al. (2020), who noted that businesses are now allocating more resources to online, mobile, and social media channels to enhance customer engagement and drive revenue growth, indicating a broader trend toward digitalization in retail.

Sephora, as a preferred store, underscores the importance of strong brand presence and customer loyalty facilitated by advanced technology. Basker (2016) highlights how technological innovation has transformed the retail industry, improving product diversity, company size, and market share. This transformation supports the idea that brands like Sephora, which leverage advanced technology, can enhance customer engagement and satisfaction, crucial for influencing Portuguese female buyers' online shopping experiences. Additionally, Mangtani et al. (2020) emphasize the role of AI-driven personalization in enhancing customer engagement and loyalty, noting how individualized product suggestions can transform marketing strategies and improve overall customer experiences in the beauty retail sector.

Price plays a significant role in purchasing decisions, with consumers balancing brand loyalty and cost considerations. Khokhar and Chitsimran (2019) discuss the wave of digitalization impacting modern life, including dynamic business operations that integrate digital changes into customer service and marketing strategies. This supports the behavior of Portuguese female buyers, who strategically compare prices and seek the best deals online, influenced by the ease of access to price comparisons facilitated by technology. This is further supported by findings from Nalbant and Aydin (2023), who note that AI technology increases consumer responsiveness, ultimately enhancing customer satisfaction.

Social media significantly influences purchasing decisions through viral trends and peer reviews. Stone et al. (2020) explore how technology blurs the line between human and machine decision-making in marketing, highlighting the rise of AI-enabled services that provide real-time information and support. This supports the notion that social media trends play a crucial role in shaping the purchasing behavior of Portuguese female buyers, who rely on peer reviews and viral trends rather than influencers alone.

Chatbots provide personalized assistance and recommendations, enhancing convenience and efficiency. Chung et al. (2020) discuss how chatbots transform communication processes by enabling interactions with conversational interfaces and natural language processing. This validates results that chatbots help answer product-related questions, resolve doubts quickly, and provide tailored recommendations, thereby enhancing the overall shopping experience. Misischia et al. (2022) further highlight the efficiency of chatbots in matching customer questions to items and providing accurate answers.

AI-driven personalized recommendations significantly enhance the shopping experience by simplifying decision-making and demonstrating brand care. Singh and Ahmed (2024) emphasize the role of AI in transforming digital marketing by providing hyper-personalized consumer interactions. This supports findings that Portuguese female buyers appreciate tailored suggestions, leading to higher satisfaction and even impulse purchases. Babatunde et al. (2024) add that using CRM data, purchase history, and social media interactions can tailor messages and offers to specific interests and behaviors, enhancing personalization.

Was found that virtual try-on features add convenience and engagement to the shopping experience, allowing consumers to try products like lipstick and hair color online before making a purchase. Supporting this, Gabriel et al. (2023) describe AR as a sophisticated information visualization technology widely used in retail to improve purchasing experiences, allowing consumers to try on products virtually, and enhancing their confidence in making purchase decisions. Pillarisetty and Mishra (2022) highlight that AR technology helps reduce product returns by enabling better size and style evaluation, which aligns with findings that virtual try-on capabilities reduce the likelihood of dissatisfaction and improve decision-making.

This thorough backing from a number of writers highlights the significant influence that AI-driven personalization has on raising customer satisfaction levels by catering to the unique requirements and tastes of Portuguese female consumers in the beauty retail sector.

5.3. To investigate the possible obstacles and concerns that portuguese female buyers may have about the introduction of ai-based apps for personalization in the online beauty retail setting

Consumers generally have a positive attitude towards AI due to the enhanced personalization and convenience it provides. This finding is supported by Chen et al. (2020) who found that AI-driven customization substantially improves the user experience by using self-service technology and providing individualized content to specific users. Similarly, Singh and Ahmed (2024) emphasize that AI allows for individualized, timely connections with customers, altering the future of marketing across sectors. AI's ability to improve decision-making is highly valued by consumers. Chen et al., (2020) support this by highlighting AI's role in offering tailored suggestions and narrowing down choices to the most relevant options. Pillarisetty and Mishra (2022) add that AI technology like virtual try-on systems can enhance customer confidence in making purchase decisions by providing a more accurate representation compared to viewing products solely on the internet

AI tools simplify product selection, especially in categories with numerous variations. Babatunde et al. (2024) emphasize the importance of using CRM data, purchase history, and social media interactions to tailor messages and offers to specific interests and behaviors. While some consumers have concerns about data privacy, there is a general acceptance of data usage when it enhances the shopping experience. Masnita et al., (2024) point out that the effective use of AI technology is essential to protect customer data and maintain trust. Reddy (2021) adds that businesses must ensure robust data governance, strict access controls, and strong data security to protect sensitive information and mitigate privacy risks.

Consumers exhibit minimal concern about data usage when it is perceived to be ethical and transparent. Cukier (2021) discusses the importance of transparency in data collection processes to alleviate consumer concerns about data privacy. Volkmar et al. (2022) highlight the need for transparency in AI decision-making processes to build trust with both internal and external stakeholders.

The main obstacles and issues surrounding the use of AI in the online beauty retail environment are diminished human engagement, data protection, and ethical data utilization. Supporting these concerns, Masnita et al. (2024) emphasize the importance of using AI technology ethically to protect customer data and maintain trust. Although consumers are wary about how their data is used, they will usually accept it provided it is done ethically and openly. Establishing credibility via open and moral business processes is essential to the effective use of AI. This was noted by Cukier (2021) who discusses the need for transparency in data collection processes to alleviate consumer concerns about privacy. Trust and transparency are critical for the successful adoption of AI technologies. To back up this finding, Volkmar et al. (2022) highlight the importance of transparency in AI decision-making processes to build trust.

Reduced human interaction is another concern associated with AI-enabled services, based on the findings. Ameen et al. (2021) discuss the critical issues consumers face with AI-enabled services, such as reduced human involvement and potential disruption to service experiences. Ethical implications of utilizing AI in marketing also pose significant challenges for consumers, where Rodgers and Nguyen (2022) highlight the ethical implications of utilizing AI in marketing, emphasizing the need for ethical considerations in AI deployment. These studies collectively suggest that while AI-driven personalization offers significant benefits, there are notable concerns and obstacles that need to be addressed to ensure the successful adoption and acceptance of AI-based apps in the online beauty retail setting. Ensuring transparency, ethical use of data, and maintaining a balance between human interaction and AI-driven processes are crucial for overcoming these challenges.

Together, these findings indicate that while AI-driven customization has many advantages, some important issues and challenges must be resolved for AI-based applications to be successfully adopted and accepted in the online beauty retail environment. The results corroborate each other with the literature, emphasizing important concerns including data privacy, moral data use, and decreasing human interaction. Overcoming these obstacles will require ensuring openness, using data ethically, and striking a balance between AI-driven operations and human engagement.

5.4. To analyze how AI-driven personalization may influence their loyalty to beauty businesses

The findings highlight the significant impact of AI-driven personalization on customer loyalty and satisfaction within the beauty retail sector. AI recommendations enhance brand loyalty by offering personalized product suggestions based on past purchases and individual preferences. This tailored approach increases consumer trust, leading to higher repeat purchases and loyalty. Studies support these findings, such as the research by Mangtani et al. (2020) and Singh and Ahmed (2024), which emphasize the critical role of AI-driven personalization in enhancing customer engagement and loyalty through individualized product suggestions.

The results also note that while many consumers attribute their loyalty to AI-driven suggestions, others do not consider it a significant factor. This variation is corroborated by Ameen et al. (2021), who point out that factors like pricing, product quality, and overall shopping experience also play crucial roles in influencing loyalty. This complexity is further explored in the literature by Hengstler et al. (2016) and

Restiana (2021), which discuss the multifaceted nature of consumer preferences and the varied impact of AI on loyalty.

AI recommendations significantly enhance consumer satisfaction by providing efficient and tailored shopping experiences. Personalized suggestions reduce the risk of unsuitable purchases, thereby increasing consumer confidence and satisfaction. This is supported by Chen et al. (2020), who found that AI-driven customization significantly improves the user experience by providing individualized content. The enhanced consumer satisfaction resulting from AI-driven recommendations aligns with the research by Hengstler et al. (2016) and Ameen et al. (2021), which emphasize the importance of transparency and trust in AI technologies to improve overall customer experiences.

The role of AI in product comparisons is another critical aspect discussed in the findings. AI simplifies the decision-making process by offering relevant product comparisons and cross-brand assessments, helping consumers navigate the plethora of options available. This is consistent with the findings of Pillarisetty and Mishra (2022) who highlight the effectiveness of AI-driven recommendation systems and visual product representation tools in reducing perceived risk and enhancing the shopping experience.

Furthermore, positive initial product experiences and seamless online shopping interactions drive repeat purchases. Personalized advertising and AI-powered suggestions can prompt impulse buys and foster recurring purchasing patterns. This phenomenon is supported by Ding et al. (2022) who reveal that positive initial experiences and personalized recommendations significantly influence repeat purchases and long-term loyalty.

The discoveries also identify areas for improvement to enhance the shopping experience. Enhancing visual tools to help consumers see how products look on them can build trust and aid decision-making, a point supported by research from Pillarisetty and Mishra (2022) Increasing the customization of recommendations based on individual preferences and skin types can boost satisfaction and loyalty, aligning with the studies by Mangtani et al. (2020) and Singh and Ahmed (2024). Improving the responsiveness and accuracy of customer service, particularly through chatbots, is crucial for retaining customers, as discussed by Hengstler et al. (2016) and Ameen et al. (2021).

In conclusion, consumer loyalty and satisfaction in the beauty retail industry are greatly impacted by AI-driven customization. The research findings continually emphasize the significance of personalized suggestions, effective customer support, and establishment of trust when utilizing AI technology to improve customer experiences and promote brand loyalty. However, in order to maximize these benefits, businesses must constantly develop and enhance their AI strategies due to the complexity of customer preferences and the diverse influence of AI technologies.

6. CONCLUSIONS

The study on Portuguese female consumers' perceptions of online beauty retail highlights the impact of AI technology on the industry. AI has improved functionality, providing tailored services to customers' needs and interests. Features like virtual try-ons and AI-driven product recommendations enhance customer satisfaction and engagement. Regular online shoppers show high engagement and brand loyalty, particularly to retailers like Sephora. Moreover, AI-driven personalization enhances customer loyalty by delivering personalized experiences. However, privacy issues and ethical considerations surrounding data usage remain significant concerns.

The study highlights the importance of transparency in data handling and responsible AI implementation for successful integration. AI-driven personalization has a substantial impact on customer loyalty, but its limitations include focusing on Portuguese female consumers, risking biases, and not considering broader economic and social factors. Future research should include diverse demographics, consider social and economic factors, and explore technology literacy to better understand AI-driven personalization's effects on consumer satisfaction and brand loyalty.

REFERENCES

Ameen, N., Tarhini, A., Reppel, A., & Anand, A. (2021). Customer experiences in the age of AI. *Computers in Human Behavior*, 114, 106548. DOI: 10.1016/j.chb.2020.106548 PMID: 32905175

Anjelita, M., Juniwati, J., Purmono, B. B., Pebrianti, W., & Saputra, P. (2023). How Does Personalization by AI on TikTok Influence Purchase Intention? *Jurnal Mantik*, 7(3), 2513–2523.

Arthur, W. B., & Polak, W. (2006). The Evolution of Technology within a Simple Computer Model. *Complexity*, 11(5), 23–31. DOI: 10.1002/cplx.20130

Bai, C., Dallasega, P., Orzes, G., & Sarkis, J. (2020). Industry 4.0 technologies assessment: A sustainability perspective. *International Journal of Production Economics*, 229, 107776. DOI: 10.1016/j.ijpe.2020.107776

Balakrishnan, J., Cheng, C.-H., Wong, K.-F., & Woo, K.-H. (2018). Product Recommendation Algorithms in the Age of Omnichannel Retailing – An Intuitive Clustering Approach. *Computers & Industrial Engineering*, 115, 133–150. DOI: 10.1016/j.cie.2017.12.005

Basker, E. (2016). The evolution of technology in the retail sector. In Basker, E. (Ed.), *Handbook on the Economics of Retailing and Distribution* (pp. 38–53). Edward Elgar Publishing. DOI: 10.4337/9781783477388.00010

Belarbi, H., Tajmouati, A., Bennis, H., & Tirari, M. E. (2016). Predictive Analysis of Big Data in Retail Industry: Literature Review. *Proceedings of the International Conference on Computing Wireless and Communication Systems*, 560-562.

Bowen, J. T., & Chen, S. L. (2001). The relationship between customer loyalty and customer satisfaction. *International Journal of Contemporary Hospitality Management*, 13(5), 213–217. DOI: 10.1108/09596110110395893

Cheng, Y., & Jiang, H. (2020). How Do AI-driven Chatbots Impact User Experience? Examining Gratifications, Perceived Privacy Risk, Satisfaction, Loyalty, and Continued Use. *Journal of Broadcasting & Electronic Media*, 64(4), 592–614. DOI: 10.1080/08838151.2020.1834296

Chung, M., Ko, E., Joung, H., & Kim, S. J. (2020). Chatbot e-service and customer satisfaction regarding luxury brands. *Journal of Business Research*, 117, 587–595. DOI: 10.1016/j.jbusres.2018.10.004

Cordero, J., Barba-Guaman, L., & Guaman, F. (2022). *Use of chatbots for customer service in MSMEs*. Applied Computing and Informatics., DOI: 10.1108/ACI-06-2022-0148

Cukier, K. (2021). Commentary: How AI shapes consumer experiences and expectations. *Journal of Marketing*, 85(1), 152–155. DOI: 10.1177/0022242920972932

Dam, T. C.DAM. (2020). Influence of Brand Trust, Perceived Value on Brand Preference and Purchase Intention. *Journal of Asian Finance. Economics and Business*, 7(10), 939–947. DOI: 10.13106/jafeb.2020.vol7.no10.939

De Sousa, J. R., & dos Santos, S. C. (2020). Análise de conteúdo em pesquisa qualitativa: modo de pensar e de fazer. *Pesquisa e debate em Educação, 10(*2), 1396-1416.

Deng, S., Wang, D., Li, Y., Cao, B., Yin, J., Wu, Z., & Zhou, M. (2016). A Recommendation System to Facilitate Business Process Modeling. *IEEE Transactions on Cybernetics*, 47(6), 1380–1394. DOI: 10.1109/TCYB.2016.2545688 PMID: 27076482

Ding, Y., Tu, R., Xu, Y., & Park, S. K. (2022). Repurchase intentions of new e-commerce users in the COVID-19 context: The mediation role of brand love. *Frontiers in Psychology*, 13, 823456. DOI: 10.3389/fpsyg.2022.968722 PMID: 35978786

Djamaludin, M. D., & Fahira, A. (2023). The Influence of Brand Trust and Satisfaction towards Consumer Loyalty of a Local Cosmetic Products Brand X among Generation Z. *Journal of Consumer. The Sciences*, 7(1), 27–44.

Gabriel, A., Ajriya, A. D., Fahmi, C. Z., & Handayani, P. W. (2023). The influence of AR on E-commerce: A case study on fashion and beauty products. *Cogent Business and Management*, 7(3), 2513–2523.

Grewal, D., Hulland, J., Kopalle, P. K., & Karahanna, E. (2020). The future of technology and marketing: A multidisciplinary perspective. *Journal of the Academy of Marketing Science*, 48(1), 1–8. DOI: 10.1007/s11747-019-00711-4

Hanaysha, J. R., Al Shaikh, M. E., & Alzoubi, H. M. (2021). Importance of marketing mix elements in determining consumer purchase decision in the retail market. [IJSSMET]. *International Journal of Service Science, Management, Engineering, and Technology*, 12(6), 56–72. DOI: 10.4018/IJSSMET.2021110104

Haron, R., & Subar, N. A. (2020). Service quality of Islamic banks, loyalty and the mediating role of trust. *Islamic Economic Studies*, 28(1), 3–23. DOI: 10.1108/IES-12-2019-0041

Hengstler, M., Enkel, E., & Duelli, S. (2016). Applied AI and trust—The case of autonomous vehicles and medical assistance devices. *Technological Forecasting and Social Change*, •••, 105–120. DOI: 10.1016/j.techfore.2015.12.014

Huang, W., Liu, B., & Tang, H. (2019). Privacy Protection for Recommendation System: A Survey. *Journal of Physics: Conference Series*, 1325(1), 012087. DOI: 10.1088/1742-6596/1325/1/012087

Iatsyshyn, A. V., Kovach, V. O., Romanenko, Y. O., Deinega, I. I., Iatsyshyn, A. V., Popov, O. O., & Lytvynova, S. H. (2019). Application of AR technologies for preparation of specialists of new technological era. *2nd International Workshop on AR in Education*, (pp. 181-200). Kryvyi Rih, Ukraine.

Jarrahi, M. (2018). AI and the Future of Work: Human-AI Symbiosis in Organizational Decision Making. *Business Horizons*, 61(4), 577–586. DOI: 10.1016/j.bushor.2018.03.007

Khokhar, P., & Chitsimran. (2019). Evolution of AI in Marketing, Comparison With. *Our Heritage*, 67, 375–389.

Kristi, K. M., & Kusumawati, N. (2021). Technology acceptance and customer perception of AR in Indonesian beauty industry. *ICE-BEES 2020: Proceedings of the 3rd International Conference on Economics, Business and Economic Education Science*, (p. 134). Semarang, Indonesia: European Alliance for Innovation.

Kumar, V., Ramachandran, D., & Kumar, B. (2021). Influence of new-age technologies on marketing: A research agenda. *Journal of Business Research*, 122, 864–877. DOI: 10.1016/j.jbusres.2020.01.007

Kwon, H. J., & Lim, H. K. (2021). A Study on the Prospects of the Korea Beauty Industry. [TURCOMAT]. *Turkish Journal of Computer and Mathematics Education*, 12(5), 382–386.

Lau, O., & Ki, C. W. (2021). Can consumers' gamified, personalized, and engaging experiences with VR fashion apps increase in-app purchase intention by fulfilling needs? *Fashion and Textiles*, 8(1), 1–22. DOI: 10.1186/s40691-021-00270-9

Lee, S. M., & Lee, D. (2020). "Untact": A new customer service strategy in the digital age. *Service Business*, 14(1), 1–22. DOI: 10.1007/s11628-019-00408-2

Lin, J. S., & Hsieh, P. L. (2006). The role of technology readiness in customers' perception and adoption of self-service technologies. *International Journal of Service Industry Management*, 17(5), 497–517. DOI: 10.1108/09564230610689795

Mangtani, N., Bajpai, N., Sahasrabudhe, S., & Wasule, D. (2020). Importance of AI and AR in cosmetic and beauty industry post Covid 19. *World Journal of Pharmaceutical Research*, 9(8), 2296–2308.

Masnita, Y., Ramadina, A. A., Zahra, A., & Bakiewicz, A. (2024). The World Of AI: Strategies In The Beauty Industry. In M. Ali Tarar, M. Saghir Ahmad, & L. Walambuka (Eds.), *Social Green Behaviour, AI and Business Strategies and Perspectives in Global Digital Society* (Vol. 13, p. 34). NCM Publishing House.

Mbete, G. S., & Tanamal, R. (2020). Effect of easiness, service quality, price, trust of quality of information, and brand image of consumer purchase decision on Shopee online purchase. *Jurnal Informatika Universitas Pamulang*, 5(2), 100–110. DOI: 10.32493/informatika.v5i2.4946

Misischia, C. V., Poecze, F., & Strauss, C. (2022). Chatbots in customer service: Their relevance and impact on service quality. *Procedia Computer Science*, 201, 421–428. DOI: 10.1016/j.procs.2022.03.055

Nalbant, K. G., & Aydin, S. (2023). Development and Transformation in Digital Marketing and Branding with AI and Digital Technologies Dynamics in the Metaverse Universe. *Journal of Metaverse*, 3, 9–18. DOI: 10.57019/jmv.1148015

Petzer, D. J., & Roberts-Lombard, M. (2021). Delight and Commitment—Revisiting the Satisfaction-Loyalty Link. *Journal of Relationship Marketing*, 20(4), 282–318. DOI: 10.1080/15332667.2020.1855068

Pillarisetty, R., & Mishra, P. (2022). A Review of AI Tools and Customer Experience in Online Fashion Retail. *E-Business Research, 18*, 0-12.

Prassas, G., Pramataris, K. C., & Papaemmanouil, O. (2001). Dynamic recommendations in internet retailing. *Global Co-Operation in the New Millennium*, (pp. 368-379). Slovenia.

Reddy, S. R. (2021). Predictive Analytics in Customer Relationship Management: Utilizing Big Data and AI to Drive Personalized Marketing Strategies. *Australian Journal of Machine Learning Research and Applications*, 1(1), 1–12.

Restiana, L. (2021). Customer Perceived Service Quality, Product Quality, Satisfaction and Loyalty in Beauty IPTEK Journal of Proceedings SeriesBusiness. *IPTEK Journal ofProceedings Series*, 1, 288–291. DOI: 10.12962/j23546026.y2020i1.10858

Rodgers, W., & Nguyen, T. (2022). Advertising benefits from ethical AI algorithmic purchase decision pathways. *Journal of Business Ethics*, 178(4), 1043–1061. DOI: 10.1007/s10551-022-05048-7

Roozen, I., Raedts, M., & Waetermans, G. (2022). Does a chatbot's location influence consumer attitude and intentions? *International Journal of Internet Marketing and Advertising*, 16(1), 24–38.

Roy, D., Srivastava, R., Jat, M., & Karaca, M. S. (2022). A Complete Overview of Analytics Techniques: Descriptive, Predictive and Prescriptive. In Jeyanthi, P. M., Choudhury, T., Hack-Polay, D., Singh, T. P., & Abujar, S. (Eds.), *Decision Intelligence Analytics and the Implementation of Strategic Business Management* (pp. 20–49). Springer. DOI: 10.1007/978-3-030-82763-2_2

Sharma, A. K., & Sharma, D. M.. (2022). Analytics Techniques: Descriptive Analytics, Predictive Analytics, and Prescriptive Analytics. In Jeyanthi, P. M., Choudhury, T., Hack-Polay, D., Singh, T. P., & Abujar, S. (Eds.), *Decision Intelligence Analytics and the Implementation of Strategic Business Management* (pp. 20–49). Springer. DOI: 10.1007/978-3-030-82763-2_1

Sharma, L., & Gera, A. (2013). A Survey of Recommendation System: Research Challenges. [IJETT]. *International Journal of Engineering Trends and Technology*, 4(5), 1989–1992.

Siau, K., & Wang, W. (2018). Building trust in AI, machine learning, and robotics. *Cutter Business Technology Journal*, 31(2), 47–53.

Singh, C. B., & Ahmed, M. M. (2024). Revolutionizing digital marketing: The impact of AI on personalized campaigns. *International Research Journal of Business and Social Science*, 10(1), 573–585.

Sivadas, E., & Baker-Prewitt, J. (2000). An examination of the relationship between service quality, customer satisfaction, and store loyalty. *International Journal of Retail & Distribution Management*, 28(2), 73–82. DOI: 10.1108/09590550010315223

Stoilova, E. (2021). AI chatbots as a customer service and support tool. *ROBONOMICS. The Journal of the Automated Economy*, 2(21).

Stone, M., Aravopoulou, E., Ekinci, Y., Evans, G., Hobbs, M., Labib, A., Laughlin, P., Machtynger, J., & Machtynger, L. (2020). AI in Strategic Marketing Decision-Making: A research agenda. *The Bottom Line (New York, N.Y.)*, 33(2), 147–166. DOI: 10.1108/BL-03-2020-0022

Sunita, C. (2023). AI in E-Commerce: Exploring the Purchase Decisions through Logistic Regression Analysis. *International Journal of Commerce and Management*, 3(3), 301–309.

Trawnih, A., Al Masaeed, S., Alsoud, M., & Alkufahy, A. (2022). Understanding AI experience: A customer perspective. *International Journal of Data and Network Science*, 6(3), 1471–1484. DOI: 10.5267/j.ijdns.2022.5.004

Tzou, H., Tseng, J., & CTO, P. (2022). How AI and AR can help beauty industry. *NCT, 1*, 7-14.

Uzir, M. U., Bukari, Z., Al Halbusi, H. L., Wahab, S. N., Rasul, T., & Eneizan, B. (2023). Applied AI: Acceptance-intention-purchase and satisfaction on smartwatch usage in a Ghanaian context. *Heliyon*, 9(1), e14532.

Verma, S., Sharma, R., Deb, S., & Maitra, D. (2021). AI in marketing: Systematic review and future research direction. *International Journal of Information Management Data Insights*, 1(1), 100002. DOI: 10.1016/j.jjimei.2020.100002

Volkmar, G., Fischer, P. M., & Reinecke, S. (2022). AI and Machine Learning: Exploring drivers, barriers, and future developments in marketing management. *Journal of Business Research*, 149, 599–614. DOI: 10.1016/j.jbusres.2022.04.007

Wedel, M., Bigné, E., & Zhang, J. (2020). Virtual and AR: Advancing research in consumer marketing. *International Journal of Research in Marketing*, 37(3), 443–465. DOI: 10.1016/j.ijresmar.2020.04.004

Whang, J. B., Song, J. H., Choi, B., & Lee, J. H. (2021). The effect of AR on purchase intention of beauty products: The roles of consumers' control. *Journal of Business Research*, 133, 275–284. DOI: 10.1016/j.jbusres.2021.04.057

Woessner, M. N., Tacey, A., Levinger-Limor, A., Parker, A. G., Levinger, P., & Levinger, I. (2021). The Evolution of Technology and Physical Inactivity: The Good, the Bad, and the Way Forward. *Frontiers in Public Health*, 9, 655491. DOI: 10.3389/fpubh.2021.655491 PMID: 34123989

Zheng, Y., Mobasher, B., & Burke, R. (2015). Carskit: A java-based context-aware recommendation engine. In *2015 IEEE International Conference on Data Mining Workshop (ICDMW)* (pp. 1668-1671). DOI: 10.1109/ICDMW.2015.222

ADDITIONAL READING

Chen, Y., & Wang, X. (2023). Artificial intelligence in beauty retail: Current trends and future directions. *Journal of Retailing and Consumer Services*, 70, 103141. DOI: 10.1016/j.jretconser.2023.103141

Goyal, P., & Kumar, V. (2020). AI and machine learning in beauty retail: Opportunities and challenges. In *AI for Marketing and Product Innovation* (pp. 112–133). Wiley., DOI: 10.1002/9781119577293.ch6

Li, H., & Zhang, J. (2023). The impact of AI on consumer behavior in beauty e-commerce: A 2023 perspective. *Journal of Business Research*, 154, 113212. DOI: 10.1016/j.jbusres.2023.113212

KEY TERMS AND DEFINITIONS

Artificial Intelligence: Is the replication of human intellect in robots that are designed to think, learn, and make decisions. In the beauty retail market, AI is used to analyze consumer preferences, make personalized product suggestions, and improve the overall shopping experience.

Augmented Reality (AR): Is a technology that superimposes digital information, such as images or data, onto the actual world, improving the user's view of their surroundings. In beauty retail, augmented reality is utilized to provide interactive and immersive purchasing experiences, such as a virtual cosmetics application.

Chatbots: Are AI-powered virtual assistants that communicate with consumers by text or voice, offering rapid answers to questions, personalized suggestions, and assistance. Chatbots in beauty retail improve client engagement and streamline the purchasing experience.

Ethical AI: Is the ethical development and implementation of AI systems that evaluate and solve concerns such as data privacy, transparency, and bias. In the beauty sector, ethical AI practices are critical for retaining customer confidence and complying with legislation.

Virtual Try-On: Allows clients to see how beauty goods (such as cosmetics or hair color) would appear on them without actually applying them. This is commonly driven by AI and AR (Augmented Reality) technology and is frequently utilized in the cosmetics sector to decrease product returns while increasing consumer happiness.

Chapter 6
AI-Powered Personalization:
Revolutionizing Mobile Commerce for Enhanced Customer Experiences

Nitesh Behare
https://orcid.org/0000-0002-9338-8563
Balaji Institute of International Business, Sri Balaji University, Pune, India

Divya Yogesh Lakhani
Sadhu Vaswani Institute of Management Studies for Girls, India

Abhijit Vasmatkar
Symbiosis Law School, Symbiosis International University (Deemed), Pune, India

Shrikant Waghulkar
https://orcid.org/0000-0002-3767-3765
Ramachandran International Institute of Management, India

Vinod N. Sayankar
Neville Wadia Institute of Management and Research Center, Pune, India

Ankita Naik
Arihant Institute of Business Management, India

Suraj Sharma
Ramachandran International Institute of Management, India

Shubhada N. Behare
Independent Researcher, India

ABSTRACT

By Customizing the shopping experience to individual users, AI-powered personalization plays a crucial role in mobile commerce, ultimately improving consumer satisfaction and increasing sales. This chapter highlights the several technologies

DOI: 10.4018/979-8-3693-5340-0.ch006

and strategies employed in this field and gives an outline of AI-powered personalization in mobile commerce. It investigates user profiling and data collection methods, dynamic pricing and offers, personalized product recommendations AI-enhanced search and navigation. Moreover, the use of chatbots and virtual assistants. The chapter also discusses future directions and developing trends in AI-powered personalization, Additionally difficulties and ethical issues. Businesses may use AI to create engaging and tailored experiences for their customers by learning about its possibilities in mobile commerce.

1. INTRODUCTION

In the vibrant world of mobile commerce, AI-powered personalization is turning up as a game-changer, converting how businesses connect with their consumers. This innovative approach consists of tailoring marketing messages as well as experiences to individual users based on their unique behavioral patterns. By leveraging advanced AI techniques, like clustering, businesses can offer personalized recommendations that align with each customer's preferences, online behavior and purchase history (Wasilewski & Przyborowski, 2023). Mobile commerce has become more engaging and user centric as effect of the incorporation of AI into mobile platforms, which has also permitted more personalized interactions and transformed user experiences by encouraging accessibility (Chen et al., 2023). A specific feature of AI-powered personalization is its capability to send highly customized offers straight to customers' smartphones while they are in-store.

This real-time personalization is planned to increase the in-store experience by meeting customer choices and expectations more accurately. Furthermore, AI-based personalization permits the making of dedicated user interfaces tailored to different user groups, knowingly improving the effectiveness and usability compared to standard interfaces.

AI-driven personalization spreads beyond simple recommendations. By offering customized purchasing experiences, improving service quality, and expecting future customer needs, it can develop the customer experience (Sinha et al. 2024). By promoting loyalty and increasing sales, these advancements in AI have not only improved customer satisfaction but also driven business growth. Additionally, the application of AI in interactive marketing through personalization techniques presents both opportunities and challenges. By examining the transformative effect of AI on e-commerce, businesses can improve their operations to serve their customers in this growing digital era through personalized recommendation systems.

1.1. Definition of AI-powered personalization in mobile commerce

AI-powered personalization in mobile commerce refers to the use both artificial intelligence algorithms (AI) and machine learning (ML) techniques to customize marketing messages, product recommendations, and user experiences based on individual customer behaviours and preferences on mobile platforms (Singh & Kaunert, 2024).

AI-driven personalization in mobile commerce contains analysing user data, like purchase patterns, browsing history, and real-time interactions, to create tailored shopping experiences that cater to the unique requirements and desires of each customer (Wasilewski & Przyborowski, 2023).

In the context of mobile commerce Artificial intelligence-based personalization is the process of utilizing AI technologies to deliver suitable content, product suggestions and offers, to users on their mobile devices, improving engagement and driving sales (Roy et al., 2023).

In mobile commerce Artificial Intelligence-(AI) powered personalization integrates predictive modelling and sophisticated data analytics to understand and expect consumer behaviour, offering tailored experiences that increase satisfaction and loyalty on mobile shopping apps and websites (Singh & Kaunert, 2024).

The application of machine learning and data mining techniques to mobile commerce platforms to tailored user interfaces, advertising strategies, and product recommendations based on individual user profiles known as AI-enhanced personalization in mobile commerce (Frey, et al., 2017).

1.2. Importance of AI-powered personalization in enhancing user experience

AI-powered personalization significantly enhances user experience by delivering highly relevant and tailored content based on individual choices and habits. This advanced technology analyses vast amounts of data to forecast user needs, providing personalized recommendations that resonate deeply with each customer. By improving relevance, AI-driven personalization boosts customer loyalty, satisfaction, and conversion rates, creating a more engaging and enjoyable shopping journey (Durai, et al., 2024). Additionally, it offers businesses valuable insights for optimizing marketing strategies, understanding customer behavior, and refining product offerings, transforming the digital shopping experience into something more intuitive and efficient for users (Tran, 2024).

AI-powered personalization increases user engagement by presenting content that is highly relevant to individual preferences. By examining massive amounts of data, such as purchase patterns and browsing history, AI algorithms can predict what a user is likely to be interested in. This heightened relevance makes customers more inclined to interact with the content, enhancing their overall experience (Vasundhara, et al., 2024). For example, a mobile commerce app might suggest products based on previous purchases or recommend complementary items, making the shopping process more enjoyable and less time-consuming. As a result, customers are more likely to have a positive experience, as they can quickly find products that match their interests.

The targeted nature of AI-powered content significantly impacts conversion rates and customer loyalty. Personalized recommendations and timely advertisements help guide users towards making purchase decisions more effectively (Agarwal, et al., 2023). For instance, sales can increase when customers respond promptly to personalized push notifications about restocked items or special offers. Additionally, AI-driven personalization fosters long-term customer relationships by providing a consistent and engaging shopping experience. Businesses can maintain strong connections with customers by continuously adapting to their evolving preferences. This loyalty is further reinforced by personalized rewards and incentives, which improve customer retention and provide uniquely significant value to each user (Vasundhara, et al., 2024).

2. UNDERSTANDING AI IN MOBILE COMMERCE

Understanding Artificial Intelligence (AI) in mobile commerce is important as it converts how businesses interact with customers on mobile platforms. By analyzing user behavior, preferences, and purchase history, AI technologies comprise machine learning and data analytics, allow personalized shopping experiences. These insights permit businesses to provide personalized recommendations, seamless customer service, and targeted marketing. Moreover, by automated processes and predictive analytics, AI improve operational efficiency. Leveraging AI becomes important for organizations to stay competitive, increase user engagement, and boost revenues as mobile commerce grows.

2.1. Explanation of artificial intelligence (AI) in the context of mobile commerce

With a number of significant trends set to completely reform the digital retail scene, the future of AI in e-commerce signals a paradigm shift to understand 'how business interact with customers'. Neither tailored product recommendations nor underpinned by AI algorithms, are set to elevate the shopping experience to new heights. Accenture's report highlights this trend, revealing that 91% of customers' favour brands proposing personalized and suitable product suggestions (Accenture, 2022). AI's capacity to comprehend and forecast customer preferences will advance along with it, reform how we obtain product recommendations. Tailored recommendations not only improve the user experience but also build loyalty and trust by representing a thorough comprehension of each person's requirements and preferences. AI-powered algorithms examine an array of user patterns, containing browsing history, previous buying and frequent product views, to tailor product recommendations to specific user preferences (Carole et al., 2024). These suggestions, which range from customized product sliders to competitive pricing schemes and special offers, have the power to usher in a new era of e-commerce that is personalized to the individual demands of every customer. eBay is a prime example of this trend, as it uses AI to fully understand the particular demands of every customer and provide professional advice and recommendations that suit their tastes.

One more transformative trend in e-commerce is the increase of visual search, which is helpful to revolutionize how customers search and buy products online. By 2028 market is projected to reach $32,984 million with the global visual search (Lalit, 2023), AI-powered visual search technologies allow users to discover products smoothly by simply taking or uploading images (CMAPL, 2022). By examining visual characteristics like texture, colour, and shape, these type of advanced algorithms distinguish similar products, providing a more intuitive and engaging shopping experience (Hou & Tang, 2023). As per customer demand for visual search functionality increase, e-commerce platforms are investing in this technology to improve user engagement and manage sales, demonstrated by initiatives like ASOS Style Match, which enable users to search products seamlessly through images (Li et al., 2014).

Besides, voice commerce is developing as a full-blown trend in e-commerce, fuelled by recent leaps in AI development. The projected value of voice commerce transactions in 2023 was $19.4 billion (Marissa, 2023), a significant increase from just $4.6 billion in 2021 (Juniper, 2021). Voice commerce allows consumers to buy products/services by using voice commands, removing conflict in the customer journey and personalizing the purchase experience for every individual (Rzepka, Berger, & Hess, 2020). Through search engines customers can quickly search new products, make purchases without manually typing commands, and compare pricing, with the help of voice assistants evolving into smart shopping assistants. Google's Google Assistant demonstrates this trend, allowing shoppers to voice shopping requests directly on the Google search engine (Isyanto et al., 2020).

Furthermore, in e-commerce, AI-driven chatbots and virtual assistants are becoming crucial tools for improving not only customer support but also facilitating quick problem-solving. With generative AI, chatbots can study context, user sentiment, and requirement, transforming into sophisticated conversational agents that deliver personalized customer experiences (Bouras et al., 2023). These virtual assistants flawlessly united into e-commerce platforms, providing immediate assistance, product recommendations, and personalized customer journeys. They even provide data-driven insights that assist retailers fine-tune their marketing strategies with remarkable exactitude. Entire Foods' virtual assistant is a leading example, provided that accurate information about the brand's products and even offering fun features like finding recipes using different emojis (Verifone, 2024).

2.2. Types of AI technologies used in mobile commerce

Mobile commerce has been completely converted by Artificial Intelligence (AI) technology, which permit companies to deliver consumer extremely tailored experiences. Natural language processing (NLP), recommender systems, computer vision, and machine learning algorithms are some of the key AI (artificial intelligence) technologies used in mobile commerce. In the area of mobile commerce, each of these technologies has special qualities that increase user experiences and spur company expansion.

2.2.1. Machine Learning Algorithms

In mobile commerce Machine learning algorithms are the fundamental of AI-powered personalization. These algorithms analyze massive amounts of data, containing preferences, historical interactions and user behavior, to identify patterns and make forecasts (Abhishek et al., 2021; Hou & Tang, 2023). Machine learning algorithms are used for tasks like tailored product recommendations in mobile commerce, flexible pricing, fraud detection, and customer segmentation. For example, machine learning algorithms used to examine past purchase history and browsing behavior by e-commerce platforms to recommend products that are likely to be of interest to each consumer. These algorithms continuously learn and increase over time, filtering their recommendations based on new data and user feedback. Consequently, users obtain highly relevant and personalized recommendations, leading to increased engagement and conversion rates.

2.2.2. Natural Language Processing (NLP)

In the framework of mobile commerce, NLP is used in different ways to augment user experiences. Natural language processing (NLP) allows computers to comprehend and decode human language. NLP powered Chatbots and virtual assistants offer users with instant support and aid, providing product recommendations, answering questions and make the smooth for transactions (Nezami & Rukham, 2022). Voice search abilities in mobile commerce apps powered by NLP, permitting users to discover for products using natural language commands. In addition, with the help of NLP algorithms, we can analyze customer reviews and feedback to pluck out insights and sentiment analysis, assisting businesses comprehend customer preferences and increase their products and services accordingly.

2.2.3. Computer Vision

Computer vision technology is one that allow computers to understand and analyze visual information from pictures and videos. Computer vision is used for tasks such as visual search, product recognition, and augmented reality (AR) experiences in mobile commerce (Chowdhary et al., 2024). By uploading images or taking photos of interested items, visual search permits users to discover for products. In the e-commerce catalogue, Computer vision algorithms examine the visual features of these images to recognize similar products. This technology offers users with a suitable and intuitive way to discover products, mostly when they are incapable of to describe them in words. Computer vision is also used to enhance AR experiences in mobile commerce apps, allowing customers to visualize products as they would appear in real life before making a purchase. For example, AR technology is employed by furniture retailers to let users see how furniture items will look in their living room.

2.2.4. Recommender Systems

Algorithms used in recommender systems analyze user data to deliver personalized recommendations for products, services, or content. These systems are utilized in mobile commerce to suggest products that align with users' interests based on their browsing history, preferences, and purchase behavior. These systems work various techniques, like content-based filtering, collaborative filtering, and hybrid approaches, to generate recommendations. To identify similarities between users and recommend products by examine Collaborative filtering of user behavior that other users with similar preferences have liked or purchased. Content-based filtering, alternatively, recommends products based on their property and features, matching them to the user's preferences. By connecting users to suitable products and helping them in finding new items they might not have otherwise discovered, recommender systems are crucial for increasing user engagement and conversion in mobile commerce (Carole et al., 2024).

2.3. Benefits of AI in mobile commerce personalization

AI technologies are revolutionizing mobile commerce by enhancing user experience, improving customer retention, and increasing conversion rates. Businesses can provide more customized and relevant experiences, leading to higher user satisfaction and engagement. Personalized interactions nurture stronger connections between users and brands, boosting loyalty and retention. Targeted recommendations and marketing messages guide users towards products they are more likely to purchase, thereby driving higher conversion rates (Pöyry et al., 2017). Additionally, AI-powered analytics offer valuable insights into user behavior and preferences, enabling data-driven decisions and optimized strategies. By automating repetitive tasks, AI frees up resources for strategic initiatives, ultimately driving growth and success in the digital marketplace.

3. USER PROFILING AND DATA COLLECTION

Understanding user behavior and favorites through potential user profile and data collecting processes is critical in the area of AI-powered personalization. This essay investigates approaches for collecting user data in mobile commerce, discusses privacy issues and ethical issues related to user data collection, and goes into great detail about the significance of user profiling in AI-powered personalization.

3.1. Importance of User Profiling in AI-Powered Personalization:

The principal of AI-powered personalization in mobile commerce is user profiling. By making detailed profiles of individual users, businesses can achieve valuable intuitions into their preferences, purchasing patterns, and behaviors (Guest, 2023). This information permits them to tailor product recommendations, user experiences, and marketing messages to meet the unique needs of every customer. It is difficult to overestimate the importance of user profile for AI-powered personalization (Abhirup, 2024).

It allows businesses to provide highly relevant and tailored experiences to users, thereby improving customer satisfaction and driving engagement and loyalty. By understanding users' favorites and interests, businesses can forecast their requirement and deliver them with relevant product recommendations at the right time and through the right channels (Sharma et al., 2021). This not only increases the likelihood of conversion but also nurtures long-term relationships with customers.

Additionally, businesses can efficiently segment their consumer base using user profiling, allowing them to target specific user groups with tailored marketing campaigns and discounts. Businesses can augment the return on investment in marketing campaigns and distribute resources more proficiently by discovering and understanding high-value consumers' preferences (Petersen & Kumar, 2015). In the end, user profiling allows organizations to provide users with tailored experiences that are meaningful to them, growing revenue and sales in the cutthroat world of mobile commerce.

3.2. Methods for collecting user data in mobile commerce

In mobile commerce, understanding user behavior is essential for providing personalized experiences. Primary methods for collecting user data are implicit and explicit data collection. Implicit data collection involves passively gathering information about users' interactions with the platform, such as browsing history and app usage patterns. Actively requesting information from customers through forms of registration and surveys is known as explicit data collection. By effectively using these techniques, businesses can gain valuable insights into user preferences and habits, leading to enhanced personalization in mobile commerce.

3.2.1. Implicit Data Collection

Implicit data collection involves the passive gathering of data about users' actions, behaviors, and interactions as they navigate through mobile commerce platforms. This type of data collection occurs in the background without users' direct input or awareness (Keusch et al., 2019). Examples of implicit data include:

- Search Queries and Browsing History: Keep in sight on users to search queries, keywords, and the websites they visit within the mobile commerce platform to understand their interests and preferences.

- Mobile App Usage Patterns: Study of how users use mobile applications, including which features they use most often, how long they spend on each screen, and their overall engagement levels of users (Ferreira et al., 2014).
- Device and Location Data: Collecting data on users' devices, screen sizes, operating systems and locations in order to tailor the user experience according to contextual elements like language, time zone, and regional preferences.
- Purchase History and Transaction Data: Recording users' previous purchases, transaction history, order history, and payment methods to identify their purchasing habits, preferences, and spending patterns (Yamagiwa & Goto, 2022).

Implicit data collection delivers valuable intuitions into user behaviour, trends, and preferences permitting businesses to provide tailored experiences and targeted recommendations. Though, it may raise privacy concerns regarding the collection and use of users' data without their explicit consent.

3.2.2. Explicit Data Collection

Using explicit actions or requests, users are actively enquired for data, which is known as explicit data collection. Explicit data collection asks customers for their consent to collect data, in contrast to implicit data collection, which works silently in the background (Golbeck, 2017). Explicit data collection techniques include, for example:

- Surveys and Feedback Forms: Encouraging users to share their thoughts, ideas, and ratings using the mobile commerce platform's standardized forms, surveys, or questionnaires.
- Social Media Integration: Businesses can access extra user data, social connections, and hobbies for customization by permitting customers to sign in or connect their social media accounts to the mobile commerce platform.
- Registration and Login Processes: Collecting user information during the process of registration and account formation process, like name, age, email address, gender and preferences, to create tailored user profiles and provide targeted content.
- Customer Support Interactions: Gathering data about customers during customer service encounters—such as through emails, phone calls, or live chats—helps address questions, resolve issues, and gain feedback on the overall experience.

Explicit data collection delivers businesses with more truthful and detail information about customers' demographics, preferences, interests, and purchase intentions. Though, it may be limited by customers' willingness to share personal data and concerns about privacy and data security.

3.3. Ethical considerations and privacy concerns in user data collection

In mobile commerce, AI-powered personalization relies on user profiling and data collection, transforming business-consumer interactions. However, these practices raise ethical and privacy concerns that require careful management (Guest, 2023). Gathering and using sensitive personal information without explicit consent is a major ethical issue. Businesses must be transparent about data collection procedures and obtain explicit consent to build trust and ensure consumers are aware of how their information is used. Strong data security measures are crucial to protect against breaches and misuse. Modern cybersecurity practices must be implemented to safeguard consumer data, demonstrating a commitment to privacy (Eastin et al., 2016). Additionally, algorithmic bias poses ethical challenges, as AI can unintentionally reinforce biases in the training data, leading to unfair outcomes. Businesses must monitor and audit their algorithms regularly to ensure decisions are made fairly and transparently. Empowering consumers with control over their data, including opting out of personalized marketing, accessing collected data, and requesting its deletion, helps maintain trust and accountability in AI-powered personalization.

4. AI-DRIVEN PERSONALIZED PRODUCT RECOMMENDATIONS

The keystone of modern e-commerce, AI-driven tailored product recommendations form consumer experience and propel sales in mobile commerce platforms. Artificial intelligence and leveraging data analytics, businesses curate personalized recommendations based on user preferences, behaviour and past interactions (Bizz-O-Tech, 2024). These recommendations improve user engagement, foster loyalty, and enlarge revenue by guiding users to relevant products that align with their individual tastes and interests (Abhirup, 2024).

4.1. Importance of personalized product recommendations in mobile commerce

In mobile commerce, personalized product recommendations play a crucial role in enhancing the user experience and driving sales. With the widespread use of mobile devices and the growing popularity of online shopping, consumers are inundated with options. In such a competitive landscape, tailored recommendations serve as a guiding alarm, serving users navigate through massive catalogues of products to find out items that categorize with their interests and preferences (Carole et al., 2024).

Furthermore, personalized recommendations nurture customer engagement and allegiance by making a personalized shopping experience that resonates with single users. Businesses can examine purchase history, user behavior and preferences to curate recommendations that are significant and compelling by artificial intelligence and leveraging data analytics. This is not only increases the possibility of conversion but also improve customer satisfaction and retention (Carole et al., 2024). Moreover, it has been presented that tailored product recommendations have a major effect on consumer behavior and rise revenue in mobile commerce. Research has demonstrated that consumers are more likely to buy products from companies that provide them with recommendations that are considerably catered to their interests. Businesses may optimize the value of every consumer engagement by capitalizing on cross-selling and upselling opportunities via the delivery of tailored recommendations (Zhang et al., 2018).

4.2. Collaborative filtering algorithms for personalized recommendations

In mobile commerce, collective filtering algorithms are a keystone of personalized product recommendations. These algorithms examine user behaviour and preferences to classify patterns and similarities between customers, allowing businesses to recommend products based on the preferences of similar users.

One of the most common collaborative filtering techniques is consumer-based collaborative filtering, where pledging is generated based on the preferences of similar users. In this approach, the algorithm identifies customers who have similar preferences or purchasing behaviour and recommends products that have been positively rated by those customers (Guo, 2022).

Additional perspective is 'Item-based' collaborative filtering, where recommendations are created on the basis of similarity between items. In this approach, the algorithm examines the relationships among the items and recommends products that are similar to those that the customer has earlier interacted with or purchased.

Real-time personalized suggestion generation and customer preference capture are two areas where collaborative filtering algorithms shine. They might, however, be affected by the cold-start issue, which happens when there isn't much information available for recommendations for new customers or things. Moreover, because collaborative filtering algorithms rely on user behavior as a whole to provide recommendations, they may find it difficult to capture long-tail preferences and specialist interests.

4.3. Content-based filtering algorithms for personalized recommendations

Content-based filtering algorithms utilize the features of items and users' past interactions to create personalized recommendations. These algorithms examine the features of items, like categories, features, and product descriptions, along with users' preferences and behaviour, to recommend products that are similar to those that the user has previously engaged with or shown interest in (Manjula & Chilambuchelvan, 2016).

One of the basic advantages of content-based filtering algorithms is their capability to recommend niche or specialized products that may not have an enormous user base. These algorithms produce highly tailored recommendations that take into account each user's unique likes and tastes by examining the characteristics of the items and the user (Pal et al., 2017). As content-based filtering algorithms do not trust on user behavior in aggregate to produce suggestions, they are also resistant to the cold-start issue. In its place, they focus on the features of items and users' favourites to make relevant recommendations from the outset. However, since content-based filtering algorithms primarily rely on users' past interactions and expressed preferences to generate suggestions, they may struggle to capture serendipitous or unexpected recommendations. Additionally, they might encounter the over-specialization problem, which limits users' exposure to new or diverse products by only recommending items similar to those they have already used.

4.4. Hybrid recommender systems combining collaborative and content-based filtering

Hybrid recommender systems include both collaborative and content-based filtering methods to leverage the strengths of both approaches and reduce their respective weaknesses. These systems integrate collaborative filtering algorithms, which capture user preferences and behavior, with content-based filtering algorithms, which analyze item features, to provide personalized recommendations that are both precise and varied. One popular method is to start with recommendations created by collective filtering and then use content-based filtering to fine-tune and customize those recommendations according to item features and user choices. This method permits businesses to leverage the combined wisdom of similar users while also providing tailored recommendations that cater to individual tastes and interests (Kawai & Nogami, 2016).

Another method is to use a weighted combination of collaborative and content-based filtering algorithms to make recommendations. This method makes sure that the recommendations are accurate and different by understanding each algorithm's contribution on the basis of its performance and relevance to the user's preferences. In mobile commerce, hybrid recommender systems provide a scalable and flexible solution for tailored product recommendations. By leveraging the strengths of both collaborative and content-based filtering techniques, these systems can create highly accurate and various recommendations that cater to individual tastes and preferences, ultimately improving the user experience and driving sales.

5. DYNAMIC PRICING AND OFFERS

5.1. Role of Dynamic Pricing in Mobile Commerce:

As per demand, competition, and market conditions factors, dynamic pricing is one of pricing strategy where prices are adjusted in real-time based. In mobile commerce, dynamic pricing allows businesses to boost pricing strategies to increase profitability while maintaining market competitiveness (Li et al., 2014). One of the fundamental roles of dynamic pricing in mobile commerce is to capture consumer demand fluctuations and manage prices accordingly (Vomberg, 2023). Businesses can recognize trends and patterns by examining consumer behaviour, purchase history, and browsing patterns to predict demand levels. Formerly, as per effect of variations in demand, dynamic pricing algorithms change prices to maintain competitiveness and conformity with market conditions.

Additionally, dynamic pricing permits businesses to react swiftly and decisively to changes in competition and market dynamics. In real-time, businesses can manage their prices to maintain a competitive edge by monitoring competitor prices and market trends (Poornima et al., 2021). In mobile commerce, this activity allows businesses to capitalize on opportunities and conforming to market changes rapidly, as affected on increasing revenue and market share. Furthermore, because prices reflect market conditions and customer demand, dynamic pricing promotes price transparency and fairness. This transparency boosts customer confidence and trust, leading to increased satisfaction and loyalty.

5.2. AI-Powered Dynamic Pricing Strategies

AI-powered dynamic pricing in mobile commerce leverages machine learning algorithms to analyze vast data sets and make real-time pricing decisions, optimizing strategies and boosting profitability (El Youbi et al., 2023). It involves three main schemes: demand-based pricing, which forecasts demand by analyzing consumer behavior and historical sales data to adjust prices during peak periods; competitive pricing, which monitors competitor prices and market dynamics to stay competitive by adjusting prices based on competitor availability and consumer sentiment; and personalized pricing, which tailors prices and promotions to individual consumers by examining their purchase history and preferences, thereby increasing engagement, loyalty, and revenue (Semwal, et al., 2024).

5.3. Personalized offers and promotions based on user preferences

Personalized offers, dynamic pricing, and promotions are crucial in mobile commerce for driving sales and enhancing user experience. AI-powered recommendation engines analyse vast amounts of user data to identify interests, purchase intent, and preferences (Carole et al., 2024). This enables businesses to provide targeted offers and promotions, increasing conversion rates and revenue. Personalized deals include loyalty rewards, offering discounts or rewards to loyal customers based on purchase history; discounts and coupons tailored to user preferences; flash sales and limited-time offers to create urgency; and recommendation-based offers, suggesting complementary products with exclusive discounts. These tailored strategies boost customer engagement, sales, and loyalty in mobile commerce (Greenstein-Messica et al., 2017).

5.4. Examples demonstrating the effectiveness of dynamic pricing and personalized offers

Following are some examples which demonstrate effectiveness of dynamic pricing and personalized offers.

Airline Ticket Pricing: Airlines repeatedly charge dynamic pricing to manage ticket prices on the basis of factors like demand, competitor pricing, and time until departure. For instance, airlines may offer discounted fares for flights with low occupancy to fill seats and increase revenue. Furthermore, personalized offers like targeted promotions and loyalty rewards incentivize frequent flyers to book flights, increasing customer retention and loyalty (FareIntelligence, 2023).

E-commerce Platforms: Online retailers like Amazon employ dynamic pricing to manage product prices in real-time based on factors like competitor pricing, demand and consumer behaviour. For example, the items of which have added to their cart but not yet purchased amazon's algorithm may decrease prices to encourage conversion. Moreover, personalized offers like recommended products and exclusive discounts based on browsing history and past purchases drive sales and improve the shopping experience (Kishore, 2023).

Hotel Room Reservations: On the basis of factors like seasonality, local events, and occupancy rates hotels utilize dynamic pricing to manage room rates. For example, hotels may rise prices during highest travel seasons or for special events in the area. Besides, personalized offers like room upgrades, loyalty rewards, and special packages cater to individual guest preferences, driving repeat bookings and customer satisfaction (SiteMinder, 2024).

Ride-Hailing Services: Ride-hailing companies like Uber and Lyft employ dynamic pricing, also known as surge pricing, to manage fares in real-time based on factors like demand and traffic conditions. For example, prices may rise during times of high demand, like inclement weather or rush hour, to stimulate more drivers to be on the road. Moreover, tailored offers such as discounts for frequent riders or referral bonuses encourage user engagement and loyalty (Uber, 2020).

Streaming Services: Dynamic pricing is a method used by streaming services like Netflix and Spotify to transform subscription costs in response to variables including local demand, content availability and user engagement. For example, Netflix may provide discounted subscription plans or marketing offers to attract new subscribers or retain existing ones (Behare & Jeet, 2024). Moreover, tailored recommendations and curated playlists based on user preferences and observing history improve the user experience and drive engagement (Chenying, 2023).

These examples demonstrate how personalized offers and dynamic pricing are effective strategies employed across different industries to drive sales, optimize revenue and improve customer satisfaction in mobile commerce.

6. AI-ENHANCED SEARCH AND NAVIGATION

6.1. Challenges in mobile commerce search and navigation

Several challenges faced by mobile commerce platforms in providing efficient search and navigation experiences for users. These challenges include:

- Limited Screen Size: Compared to desktop computers, mobile devices have smaller screens, it is difficult to display search results and navigation options successfully. Hence mobile users could have anxiety locating the goods or information they need, which could cause them to become frustrated and give up (Kim et al., 2016).

- Ineffective Filtering and Sorting: Mobile commerce platforms typically provide filtering and sorting options to assist users narrow down their search results. Though, these features may not always be effective or intuitive, affecting in users being overwhelmed with irrelevant or unsorted results (Nardini et al., 2019). Innovative strategies that use AI techniques to improve accuracy and search relevancy are required to address these problems and give users more individualized and fulfilling experiences.
- Ambiguity in Search Queries: It might be challenging for standard search engines to correctly understand search queries that users type if they are not clear or ambiguous. For instance, a user looking for a "red dress" can have different preferences in the form of size, price, or style; therefore, it would take a more sophisticated strategy to accurately understand their query.
- Complex Product Catalogues: Mobile commerce platforms mostly provide a varied range of products across different categories, leading to complex product catalogues. Navigating through these catalogues can be daunting for users, especially when searching for specific items or comparing products (Aqle et al., 2016).

6.2. AI Techniques for improving search relevance and accuracy

By using advanced algorithms AI-powered search and navigation solutions to examine user queries, comprehend their intent, and provide highly relevant results. AI techniques consist of two key approaches for enhancing search relevance and accuracy in mobile commerce.

6.2.1. Natural language processing for semantic search

NLP (Natural Language Processing) allows machines to comprehend and interpret human language, permitting for more sophisticated search abilities. In mobile commerce, NLP-based semantic search algorithms examine the context and meaning of user queries to provide more accurate results. These algorithms decode search queries effectively on the basis of factors like synonyms, context, and user intent to (Zheng, 2023).

For instance, a user searching for "women's running shoes" may obtain relevant results for athletic footwear designed specifically for women, even if the exact phrase "running shoes" is not present in the product descriptions. NLP-powered search engines can provide results that better align with user preferences and intent by comprehending the semantics of the query.

6.2.2. Image Recognition for Visual Search:

Visual search means users can search for products using images rather than text-based queries. AI-powered image recognition algorithms examine the visual attributes of images, like colors, shapes, and patterns, to categorize similar products in the catalogue (Dagan et al., 2021). For instance, if a user can take their favorite photo of a dress and use a visual search feature to find similar dresses available for purchase. Image recognition algorithms compare the visual attributes of the uploaded image with product images in the database, results that closely match the user's preferences. Visual search both improve product discovery and exploration and simplifies the search process for users, important to increased engagement and conversion rates.

6.3. Voice-based search and conversational AI

Conversational AI technologies and Voice-based search allow users to interact with mobile commerce platforms using natural language commands and conversations. AI-powered virtual assistants, like voice assistants and chatbots, can comprehend user problems, provide tailored recommendations, and help with product selection and purchase decisions (Maj, 2021). For instance, a user can use voice commands to search for products, enquire about product features or availability, and even complete purchases by using voice-based interfaces. Conversational AI systems use natural language generation (NLG) and natural language understanding (NLU) techniques to process user queries and create responses in a conversational manner.

Businesses may cater to users who prefer hands-free interactions or have limited mobility by offering more intuitive and frictionless purchasing experiences through the unification of conversational AI and voice-based search into mobile commerce systems.

6.4. Real-world examples of AI-enhanced search and navigation in mobile commerce

Pinterest Lens: Pinterest Lens is a visual search tool where users can find the products by taking photos or uploading images. AI- Powered and Pinterest, image recognition technology examines the visual content of images to recognize products, objects, and related items. By using Lens users can find similar products which is available for purchase on Pinterest or from associated retailers, streamlining the product discovery process (James, 2018).

Google Lens: Google Lens is an additional example of a visual search tool that employs AI to examine images and deliver relevant information. In the context of mobile commerce, Google Lens permits users to scan products by using their smartphone camera to get information like product details, pricing, and reviews. Consumers can also use Google Lens to discover similar products online or at nearby stores, facilitating seamless product research and comparison (Pankaj, 2022).

Amazon's Alexa Shopping Assistant: The voice-activated search and navigation tool Alexa Shopping Assistant from Amazon uses conversational AI to help consumers with their shopping requirements. Natural language commands permit users to search for things, add items to their shopping basket, track orders, and even complete purchase process hands-free when interacting with Alexa. Alexa makes use of artificial intelligence (AI) algorithms to understand consumer inquiries, provide tailored recommendations, and support consumers during their shopping experience (Signalytics, 2023).

eBay's Image Search: eBay's Image Search attributes allows consumers to find the products using photos or images rather than text-based queries. AI- Powered and computer vision technology, eBay examine the visual feature of uploaded images to identify similar products in its database. Users can take a photo of favorite item or upload an image from their camera roll to find matching or similar products available for purchase on eBay, improving the product discovery experience (Steve et al., 2017).

Sephora Virtual Artist: Sephora's Virtual Artist app uses "augmented reality" (AR) and AI-powered image recognition to improve the makeup shopping experience. Consumers can virtually try on makeup products by using their smartphone camera, permitting them to see how different products and shades look on their skin before buying product. The app uses AI algorithms to correctly map facial attributes and apply virtual makeup in real-time, providing users with personalized recommendations and a more immersive shopping experience (Itechnolab, 2021).

These examples explain how AI-increased search and navigation technologies are converting the mobile commerce landscape by providing modernistic ways for users to discover products, receive information, and make informed buying decisions. Businesses can offer more tailored, engaging, and suitable shopping experiences for mobile users by leveraging AI-powered tools like visual search, augmented reality and voice-based assistants.

7. CHATBOTS AND VIRTUAL ASSISTANTS

In mobile commerce, virtual assistants and Chatbots have developed customer engagement. These AI-powered tools provide real-time support, streamlined assistance and tailored recommendations, improving the shopping experience for consumers. Chatbots and virtual assistants permit businesses to busy with customers more intuitively and efficiently by employing cutting-edge technology such as machine learning (ML) and natural language processing (NLP). This increases customer satisfaction and loyalty in the mobile commerce market.

7.1. Role of chatbots and virtual assistants in mobile commerce

In mobile commerce, chatbots and virtual assistants serve as digital agents providing 24/7 customer support. They answer FAQs, offer product information, assist with app navigation, and address real-time concerns. By analysing browsing history and purchase behaviour, these AI tools offer personalized recommendations and suggestions, enhancing marketing relevance. They streamline order management by facilitating order placement, returns, shipment tracking, and exchanges, providing real-time updates for improved transparency. Additionally, chatbots optimize payment processes, guiding consumers through payments, addressing queries, and ensuring secure transactions. This reduces cart abandonment and boosts conversion rates, enhancing overall customer satisfaction and convenience (Bouras, et al., 2023).

7.2. AI technologies powering chatbot and virtual assistant interactions

Machine Learning (ML): ML algorithms allow chatbots and virtual assistants to learn from user interactions, adapt to user preferences, and increase over time. ML models examine data from past interactions, identify patterns and trends, and optimize responses and recommendations based on user feedback and behaviour (Tripathi et al., 2021).

Natural Language Understanding (NLU): Chatbots and virtual assistants can provide more appropriate and suitable answers by using natural language understanding (NLU) algorithms to understand the intent and context of user questions. NLU models decode user communications by examine their semantics, syntax and sentiment in order to determine the user's purpose and produce relevant answers (Rajendran et al., 2024).

Dialog Management: Dialog management systems allow chatbots and virtual assistants to maintain sequential and contextually relevant conversations with users. These systems track the state of the conversation, manage turn-taking and flow, and handle multi-turn interactions to make sure smooth and engaging interactions with users (Harms et al., 2024).

7.3. Benefits of AI-powered chatbots and virtual assistants in mobile commerce

AI-powered chatbots and virtual assistants enhance customer engagement by delivering personalized, interactive experiences that foster closer relationships between businesses and their customers. They improve satisfaction and loyalty by providing timely, relevant support, swiftly answering queries, and guiding users through their purchasing journey. Available 24/7, these chatbots ensure users receive support regardless of business hours or time zones, facilitating seamless global interactions. By automating repetitive tasks and queries, they allow businesses to manage customer communications efficiently and economically, handling multiple conversations simultaneously and scaling to meet high demand periods. This reduces the burden on human customer service representatives, enabling them to focus on more complex issues. Additionally, AI-driven chatbots use user data and machine learning algorithms to offer personalized recommendations and assistance, analysing communications, past purchases, and browsing history to predict needs and suggest products that match user preferences and interests. This targeted support enhances the overall user experience, driving engagement and loyalty.

7.4. Case studies showcasing successful chatbot and virtual assistant implementations

Domino's Pizza Chatbot: Domino's Pizza it is big pizza delivery chain, executed a chatbot named "Dom" to help customers with ordering pizza through messaging platforms like Facebook Messenger and Twitter. Dom uses both 'natural language processing' (NLP) and 'machine learning' (ML) algorithms to comprehend user problems, process orders, and provide real-time order updates. Customers can interact with Dom to place orders, customize their pizzas, track delivery status, and provide feedback. The Domino's Pizza chatbot has systematic the ordering process, enhanced customer satisfaction, and increased convenience for users, leading to higher order volumes and revenue for the company.

Sephora Virtual Artist: The Sephora Virtual Artist app was launched by the international cosmetics retailer Sephora. It increases the makeup buying experience by applying chatbots driven by artificial intelligence (AI) and augmented reality

(AR). By using the camera on their smartphone, consumers of the Virtual Artist app may virtually try on makeup products to see how various hues and products look on their skin before buying. The app also have attributes a virtual assistant that delivers personalized product recommendations, makeup tips, and tutorials based on user choices and skin type. Sephora's Virtual Artist app has been highly effective in driving engagement, improving sales, and providing an immersive and interactive shopping experience for customers.

H&M's Virtual Stylist: H&M, is a worldwide fashion retailer, introduced a virtual stylist chatbot called "H&M Chatbot" to support customers with fashion suggestions, like outfit recommendations, and styling tips. The chatbot utilizing AI-powered algorithms to examine user choices, browsing history, and buying behaviour to provide personalized styling suggestions and product recommendations. Users can communicate with the chatbot through either the H&M mobile app or website to obtain customized outfit ideas, discover clothing items that match as their style preferences, and get encouragement for their next fashion purchase. H&M's Virtual Stylist chatbot has improved the shopping experience for users, increased engagement, and increased sales for the fashion retailer.

KLM's BlueBot: KLM by Facebook Messenger, Royal Dutch Airlines has deployed a chatbot known as "BlueBot" to assist customers with booking flights, searching travel information, and contacting customer support. Additionally, to delivering real-time flight information and personalized travel recommendations on the basis of user choices and booking history, BlueBot leverages AI-powered algorithms to understand user questions. BlueBot helps to travelers to check flight status, buy tickets, select a seat, and get information and advice on travel. Passengers' overall travel experience has been improved, consumer satisfaction has increased, and the booking procedure has been made easier by KLM's BlueBot.

Bank of America's Erica: A virtual assistant called "Erica" was presented by Bank of America, one of the biggest banks in the country, to provide consumers individualized financial suggestion and support. Erica assist consumers track spending, set savings objectives, and make wise financial decisions by utilizing artificial intelligence (AI) and natural language understanding (NLU) technologies. Through the Bank of America mobile app, users may communicate with Erica to ask queries, receive account alerts, transfer money, and access banking services. By giving Bank of America fast and proactive financial support, Erica has increases client engagement, increased utilization of mobile apps, and strengthened customer relationships.

These case studies explain the effectiveness of chatbots and virtual assistants in various industries, food service, including retail, banking, fashion, and travel. By leveraging both AI technologies and natural language processing (NLP) potentiality, businesses can deliver tailored assistance, simplify customer interactions, and improve the overall customer experience, important to increased engagement, loyalty, and revenue growth.

8. OVERCOMING CHALLENGES AND FUTURE DIRECTIONS

8.1. Challenges in implementing AI-powered personalization in mobile commerce

Deploying AI-powered personalization in mobile commerce brings significant data privacy and security concerns. Personalizing experiences through user data collection raises ethical issues regarding consent and protection. Businesses must comply with data protection regulations like CCPA and GDPR, implementing robust security measures to prevent unauthorized access and data breaches. Algorithmic bias and fairness also present challenges, as AI systems might unintentionally reinforce biases from training data, leading to unfair outcomes for certain user groups. To address this, businesses must identify and mitigate biases, diversify training data, and evaluate algorithm performance across demographics. Additionally, ensuring data quality and accessibility is crucial. Mobile commerce platforms generate vast data from various sources, which may be fragmented or incomplete. Businesses must invest in data governance, integration technologies, and quality assurance to develop accurate personalization algorithms.

8.2. Strategies for overcoming technical and ethical challenges

Improving transparency and explainability is crucial for enhancing trust and addressing ethical concerns in AI-powered personalization algorithms. Companies need to provide clear explanations of how AI algorithms operate, what data is utilized, and how personalized recommendations are generated. Implementing mechanisms for users to understand and control the personalization process, such as preference settings and opt-out options, empowers users and promotes transparency.

Ethical design and governance are also essential. Establishing governance frameworks, codes of conduct, and ethical standards ensures responsible use of AI in mobile commerce. This includes conducting ethical impact assessments, involving stakeholders in ethical discussions, and fostering a culture of ethical responsibility within the organization.

Prioritizing user consent and privacy controls is critical to respecting user privacy and autonomy. Businesses should obtain explicit consent before collecting and using personal data for personalization. Providing users with granular privacy controls, such as data deletion requests, opt-in/opt-out mechanisms, and privacy preference settings, enables users to manage their personal information effectively and maintain control over their privacy.

8.3. Emerging trends and future directions in AI-powered personalization

8.3.1. Integration of Augmented Reality (AR) and Virtual Reality (VR)

'The integration of augmented reality' (AR) and 'virtual reality' (VR) technologies is crucial for balanced to transform AI-powered personalization in mobile commerce. With AR and VR allow immersive and interactive shopping experiences, permitting consumers to visualize products in real-world environments, explore virtual stores, and try-on virtual clothing. Personalization algorithms can leverage AR/VR data to provide tailored recommendations, contextualized experiences, and personalized offers based on users' physical atmospheres and interactions.

8.3.2. Personalization Based on Contextual Data

In mobile commerce, personalization based on contextual data — like location, time, and environmental factors — is becoming more and more important for providing timely and relevant experiences. With the help of AI algorithms users can examine contextual information from mobile devices, sensors, and IoT devices to comprehend users' situational context and accept personalization tactics accordingly. For instance, recommending nearby stores, adjusting product recommendations, or offering time-sensitive promotions based on weather conditions can improve the relevance and effectiveness of personalization.

8.3.3. Advances in AI for Sentiment Analysis and Emotion Recognition

Mobile commerce is capable to execute more complex and subtle personalization techniques because to advancements in AI sentiment analysis and emotion detection. Businesses may generate individualized experiences based on users' emotional states and reactions by using AI algorithms to evaluate textual and visual information to determine users' emotions, attitudes, and preferences. For instance, detecting positive sentiments in user reviews or analyzing facial expressions in user photos can inform personalized recommendations, content recommendations, and marketing strategies tailored to users' emotional responses.

9. CONCLUSION

AI-powered personalization is revolutionizing mobile commerce by creating tailored, engaging, and efficient shopping experiences for users. By harnessing the power of AI and machine learning, businesses analyze vast data to understand customers better, delivering highly relevant content and recommendations. This enhances user experience, driving success through higher engagement, conversion rates, and loyalty. Implicit and explicit data collection methods gather insights into user behavior and preferences, enabling personalized experiences. However, these methods pose ethical and privacy challenges, urging businesses to prioritize transparency, fairness, and user empowerment. Personalized product recommendations optimize the user experience, fostering engagement and sales. AI-enhanced search and navigation technologies overcome mobile commerce challenges, delivering more relevant experiences. Chatbots and virtual assistants offer personalized assistance, streamlining shopping. Overcoming challenges and embracing future directions in AI-powered personalization require a holistic approach addressing technical, ethical, and strategic considerations. AI's role in mobile commerce continues to evolve, promising more sophisticated tools and techniques to meet consumer expectations while ensuring privacy and ethical usage. Finally, AI-powered personalization empowers businesses to build strong customer relationships, drive conversions, and thrive in a competitive market while prioritizing ethical implementation and user trust.

REFERENCES

Abhirup, G. (2024, Jul 09). *The Role of AI and Machine Learning in E-Commerce Personalization.* https://www.codilar.com/the-role-of-ai-and-machine-learning-in-e-commerce-personalization/

Abhishek, D., A., & Gupta, N. (2021). A systematic review of techniques, tools and applications of machine learning. *3rd International Conference on Intelligent Communication Technologies and Virtual Mobile Networks, ICICV 2021* (pp. 764-768). Tirunelveli: Institute of Electrical and Electronics Engineers Inc. DOI: 10.1109/ICICV50876.2021.9388637

Accenture. (2022). *Creating value in all directions.* https://www.accenture.com/content/dam/accenture/final/capabilities/corporate-functions/growth-and-strategy/document/Accenture-Fiscal-2022-Annual-Report.pdf#zoom=50

Agarwal, T., Gopalkrishnan, S., Kale, V., Periwal, D., Kulkarni, A. A., & Tharkude, D. (2023). Transforming Advertising: Harnessing AI for Personalised Customer-Centricity. *IEEE International Conference on Technology Management, Operations and Decisions, ICTMOD 2023.* Rabat: Institute of Electrical and Electronics Engineers Inc. DOI: 10.1109/ICTMOD59086.2023.10438160

Aqle, A., Islam, F., Rezk, E., & Jaoua, A. (2016). Mobile app conceptual browser: Online marketplaces information extraction. *13th IEEE/ACS International Conference of Computer Systems and Applications, AICCSA 2016.* 0. Agadir: IEEE Computer Society. DOI: 10.1109/AICCSA.2016.7945671

Behare, N., & Jeet, D. (2024). The art and science of user engagement: Personalization and recommendations in the OTT era. In *The Rise of Over-the-Top (OTT) Media and Implications for Media Consumption and Production* (pp. 130-159). IGI Global. DOI: 10.4018/979-8-3693-0116-6.ch009

Bizz-O-Tech. (2024, Jul 03). *The Role of AI-Driven Recommendation Systems in E-Commerce and Their Impact on Consumer Behavior and Sales.* https://www.linkedin.com/pulse/role-ai-driven-recommendation-systems-e-commerce-impact-consumer-a8oof/

Bouras, C., Diasakos, D., Katsigiannis, C., Kokkinos, V., Gkamas, A., Karacapilidis, N., & Alexopoulos, C. (2023). On the Development of a Novel Chatbot Generator Architecture: Design and Assessment Issues. *8th International Conference on Mathematics and Computers in Sciences and Industry, MCSI 2023* (pp. 83-88). Athens: Institute of Electrical and Electronics Engineers Inc. DOI: 10.1109/MCSI60294.2023.00021

Carole, K. S., Theodore Armand, T. P., & Kim, H. C. (2024). Enhanced Experiences: Benefits of AI-Powered Recommendation Systems. *26th International Conference on Advanced Communications Technology, ICACT 2024* (pp. 216-220). Pyeong Chang: Institute of Electrical and Electronics Engineers Inc. DOI: 10.23919/ICACT60172.2024.10471918

Chen, J., Ganguly, B., Kanade, S. G., & Duffy, V. G. (2023). Impact of AI on Mobile Computing: A Systematic Review from a Human Factors Perspective. *25th International Conference on Human-Computer Interaction, HCII 2023. 14059 LNCS* (pp. 24-38). Copenhagen: Springer Science and Business Media Deutschland GmbH. DOI: 10.1007/978-3-031-48057-7_2

Chenying, Y. (2023). A Case Study of Netflix's Marketing Strategy. *International Conference on Advances in Internet Marketing and Business Management (ICAMM 2023)* (pp. 185-192). DOI: 10.54691/bcpbm.v42i.4580

Chowdhary, C. L., Alazab, M., Chaudhary, A., Hakak, S., & Gadekallu, T. R. (2024). Computer Vision and Recognition Systems Using Machine and Deep Learning Approaches: Fundamentals, technologies and applications. In *Computer Vision and Recognition Systems Using Machine and Deep Learning Approaches: Fundamentals, technologies and applications* (pp. 1-483). Institution of Engineering and Technology. DOI: 10.1049/PBPC042E

CMAPL. C. M. (2022, Aug 22). *Visual Search Market Key Players & Growth Rate and Forecasts to 2028.* https://www.linkedin.com/pulse/visual-search-market-key-players-growth-rate-forecasts-/

Dagan, A., Guy, I., & Novgorodov, S. (2021). An Image is Worth a Thousand Terms Analysis of Visual E-Commerce Search. *44th International ACM SIGIR Conference on Research and Development in Information Retrieval, SIGIR 2021* (pp. 102-112). Virtual, Online: Association for Computing Machinery, Inc. DOI: 10.1145/3404835.3462950

Durai, S., Manoharan, G., & Priya, T. S. R., J., Razak, A., & Ashtikar, S. P. (2024). Quantifying the impacts of artificial intelligence implementations in marketing. In *Smart and Sustainable Interactive Marketing* (pp. 120-144). IGI Global. DOI: 10.4018/979-8-3693-1339-8.ch008

Eastin, M. S., Brinson, N. H., Doorey, A., & Wilcox, G. (2016, May 01). Living in a big data world: Predicting mobile commerce activity through privacy concerns. *Computers in Human Behavior*, 58, 214–220. DOI: 10.1016/j.chb.2015.12.050

El Youbi, R., Messaoudi, F., & Loukili, M. (2023). Machine Learning-driven Dynamic Pricing Strategies in E-Commerce. *14th International Conference on Information and Communication Systems, ICICS 2023.* Irbid: Institute of Electrical and Electronics Engineers Inc. DOI: 10.1109/ICICS60529.2023.10330541

FareIntelligence. (2023, Nov 09). *Dynamic Pricing in Airlines: The Science Behind Airfare Fluctuations.* https://www.linkedin.com/pulse/dynamic-pricing-airlines-science-behind-airfare-fluctuations-pydqf/

Ferreira, D., Goncalves, J., Kostakos, V., Barkhuus, L., & Dey, A. K. (2014). Contextual experience sampling of mobile application micro-usage. *16th ACM International Conference on Human-Computer Interaction with Mobile Devices and Services, MobileHCI 2014* (pp. 91-100). Toronto: Association for Computing Machinery. DOI: 10.1145/2628363.2628367

Frey, R. M., Xu, R., Ammendola, C., Moling, O., Giglio, G., & Ilic, A. (2017, November). Mobile recommendations based on interest prediction from consumer's installed apps–insights from a large-scale field study. *Information Systems*, 71, 152–163. DOI: 10.1016/j.is.2017.08.006

Golbeck, J. (2017). The importance of consent in user comfort with personalization. *9th International Conference on Social Informatics, SocInfo 2017. 10540 LNCS* (pp. 469-476). Oxford: Springer Verlag. DOI: 10.1007/978-3-319-67256-4_37

Greenstein-Messica, A., Rokach, L., & Shabtai, A. (2017). Personal-discount sensitivity prediction for mobile coupon conversion optimization. *Journal of the Association for Information Science and Technology*, 68(08), 1940–1952. DOI: 10.1002/asi.23838

Guest, B. (2023, Jul 04). *Personalization: Role of AI in Consumer Engagement.* https://www.determ.com/blog/the-power-of-personalization-role-of-ai-in-consumer-engagement/

Guo, G. (2022). Application of E-commerce Personalized Recommendation Algorithm Based on Collaborative Filtering. In *Lecture Notes on Data Engineering and Communications Technologies* (pp. 959–966). Springer Science and Business Media Deutschland GmbH., DOI: 10.1007/978-3-030-97874-7_140

Harms, J.-G., Kucherbaev, P., Bozzon, A., & Houben, G.-J. (2019, March-April). Approaches for dialog management in conversational agents. *IEEE Internet Computing*, 23(02), 13–22. DOI: 10.1109/MIC.2018.2881519

Hou, M., & Tang, Y. (2023, August). The Influence of Visual Features in Product Images on Sales Volume: A Machine Learning Approach to Extract Color and Deep Learning Super Sampling Features. *TS. Traitement du Signal*, 40(04), 1469–1477. DOI: 10.18280/ts.400415

Isyanto, H., Arifin, A. S., & Suryanegara, M. (2020). Performance of Smart Personal Assistant Applications Based on Speech Recognition Technology using IoT-based Voice Commands. *11th International Conference on Information and Communication Technology Convergence, ICTC 2020. Volume 2020-October* (pp. 640-645). Jeju Island: IEEE Computer Society. DOI: 10.1109/ICTC49870.2020.9289160

Itechnolab. (2021). *How Sephora is using technology like AI and AR to engage with consumers?*https://itechnolabs.ca/sephora-using-technology-like-ai-and-ar/

James, L. (2018, Jan 24). *Pinterest's Visual Lens: How computer vision explores your taste-The science behind personalized visual recommendations.* https://towardsdatascience.com/pinterests-visual-lens-how-computer-vision-explores-your-taste-5470f87502ad

Juniper. (2021, Aug). *Voice Assistant Transaction Values to Grow by Over 320% by 2023.* https://www.juniperresearch.com: https://www.juniperresearch.com/press/voice-assistant-transaction-values-grow-by-320

Kawai, M., & Nogami, S. (2016, June). A hybrid recommender system of collaborative and content based filtering. *Information (Japan)*, 19(6B), 2177–2183.

Keusch, F., Struminskaya, B., Antoun, C., Couper, M. P., & Kreuter, F. (2019). Willingness to Participate in Passive Mobile Data Collection. *Public Opinion Quarterly*, 83(S1), 210–235. DOI: 10.1093/poq/nfz007 PMID: 31337924

Kim, J., Thomas, P., Sankaranarayana, R., Gedeon, T., & Yoon, H.-J. (2016, November 01). Understanding eye movements on mobile devices for better presentation of search results. *Journal of the Association for Information Science and Technology*, 67(11), 2607–2619. DOI: 10.1002/asi.23628

Kishore, R. (2023, Jul 05). *Amazon's Dynamic Pricing Strategy: How It Balances Customer Trust and Profitability.* https://www.linkedin.com: https://www.linkedin.com/pulse/amazons-dynamic-pricing-strategy-how-balances-trust-kishore-rajgopal/

Lalit, S. (2023, Sept 06). *Top 13 eCommerce Trends in 2024.* https://www.netsolutions.com/hub/ecommerce/trends

Li, Y., Xu, S., Luo, X., & Lin, S. (2014, December 01). A new algorithm for product image search based on salient edge characterization. *Journal of the Association for Information Science and Technology*, 65(12), 2534–2551. DOI: 10.1002/asi.23136

Maj, A. (2021). The Rise of Conversational AI Platforms. In *The AI Book: The Artificial Intelligence Handbook for Investors, Entrepreneurs and FinTech Visionaries* (pp. 111-112). Wiley. DOI: 10.1002/9781119551966.ch31

Manjula, R., & Chilambuchelvan, A. (2016). Content based filtering techniques in recommendation system using user preferences. *Int. J. Innov. Eng. Technol*, 7(4), 151.

Marissa, J. (2023, Jul 21). *Voice commerce, AI, and the future of shopping*. https://www.bazaarvoice.com/blog/voice-commerce-ai/

Nardini, F. M., Trani, R., & Venturini, R. (2019). Fast approximate filtering of search results sorted by attribute. *42nd International ACM SIGIR Conference on Research and Development in Information Retrieval, SIGIR 2019* (pp. 815-824). Paris: Association for Computing Machinery, Inc. DOI: 10.1145/3331184.3331227

Nezami, M. A., & Rukham, R. (2022). Crowdsourced NLP Retraining Engine in Chatbots. *International Conference on Emerging Technologies and Intelligent Systems, ICETIS 2021Al.* 322 (pp. 311-320). Buraimi: Springer Science and Business Media Deutschland GmbH. DOI: 10.1007/978-3-030-85990-9_26

Pal, A., Parhi, P., & Aggarwal, M. (2017). An improved content based collaborative filtering algorithm for movie recommendations. *10th International Conference on Contemporary Computing, IC3 2017. 2018-January* (pp. 01-03). Noida: Institute of Electrical and Electronics Engineers Inc. DOI: 10.1109/IC3.2017.8284357

Pankaj, K. (2022, Sept 07). *Google Lens: For the Constantly Inquisitive*. Retrieved Jun 20, 2024, from https://www.copperpodip.com: https://www.copperpodip.com/post/what-is-google-lens

Petersen, J. A., & Kumar, V. (2015, April 01). Perceived risk, product returns, and optimal resource allocation: Evidence from a field experiment. *JMR, Journal of Marketing Research*, 52(02), 268–285. DOI: 10.1509/jmr.14.0174

Poornima, S., Mohanavalli, S., Swarnalatha, S., & Kesavarthini, I. (2021). Dynamic Pricing of Products Based on Visual Quality and E-Commerce Factors. *International Conference on Mathematical Analysis and Computing, ICMAC 2019* (pp. 413-427). Springer. DOI: 10.1007/978-981-33-4646-8_34

Pöyry, E., Hietaniemi, N., Parvinen, P., Hamari, J., & Kaptein, M. (2017). Personalized product recommendations: Evidence from the field. In S. R. Bui T.X. (Ed.), *50th Annual Hawaii International Conference on System Sciences, HICSS 2017. 2017-January* (pp. 3859-3867). Big Island: IEEE Computer Society. https://www.scopus.com/record/display.uri?eid=2-s2.0-85068324707&origin=scopusAI

Rajendran, R. K., Priya, T. M., & Chitrarasu, K. (2024). Natural Language Processing (NLP) in chatbot design: NLP's impact on chatbot architecture. In *Design and Development of Emerging Chatbot Technology* (pp. 102-113). IGI Global. DOI: 10.4018/979-8-3693-1830-0.ch006

Roy, G., Jain, V., & Salunke, P. (2023). Data Processing and AI-Technology Integration for Personalized Services. In *Artificial Intelligence in Customer Service: The Next Frontier to Personalized Engagement* (pp. 205-228). Springer International Publishing. DOI: 10.1007/978-3-031-33898-4_9

Rzepka, C., Berger, B., & Hess, T. (2020). Why another customer channel? Consumers' perceived benefits and costs of voice commerce. In B. T.X. (Ed.), *53rd Annual Hawaii International Conference on System Sciences, HICSS 2020* (pp. 4079-4088). Maui: IEEE Computer Society.

Semwal, M., Akila, K., Manasa, M., Raj, P. S., Motukuru, Y., & Karthik, P. (2024). Machine Learning-Enabled Business Intelligence For Dynamic Pricing Strategies In E-Commerce. *2nd International Conference on Disruptive Technologies, ICDT 2024* (pp. 116-120). Greater Noida: Institute of Electrical and Electronics Engineers Inc. DOI: 10.1109/ICDT61202.2024.10489724

Sharma, S., Baishya, K., Pandey, M., & Rautaray, S. S. (2021). Hybrid Product Recommendation System using Popularity Based and Content-Based Filtering. *nternational Conference on Data Science, Agents and Artificial Intelligence, ICDSAAI 2023.* Chennai: Institute of Electrical and Electronics Engineers Inc. DOI: 10.1109/ICDSAAI59313.2023.10452564

Signalytics. (2023, May 29). *Voice activated shopping.* https://medium.com/@Signalytics/reimagining-e-commerce-how-amazons-voice-activated-shopping-is-impacting-brands-1e8a2c15e5bb

Singh, B., & Kaunert, C. (2024). Future of Digital Marketing: Hyper-Personalized Customer Dynamic Experience with AI-Based Predictive Models. In *Revolutionizing the AI-Digital Landscape: A Guide to Sustainable Emerging Technologies for Marketing Professionals* (pp. 189–208). Taylor and Francis., DOI: 10.4324/9781032688305-14

Sinha, S., Sinha, D., & Dalmia, T. (2024). Role of AI in Enhancing Customer Experience in Online Shopping. *11th International Conference on Reliability, Infocom Technologies and Optimization, ICRITO 2024.* Hybrid, Noida: Institute of Electrical and Electronics Engineers Inc. DOI: 10.1109/ICRITO61523.2024.10522285

SiteMinder. (2024, Feb 16). *Hotel dynamic pricing: Definition, examples, and best software to use.* https://www.siteminder.com/r/hotel-dynamic-pricing/

Steve, N., Ben, K., & Max, M. (2017, Jul 26). *Find It On eBay: Using Pictures Instead of Words*. https://innovation.ebayinc.com/tech/product/find-it-on-ebay-using-pictures-instead-of-words/

Tran, M. T. (2024). Unlocking the AI-powered customer experience: Personalized service, enhanced engagement, and data-driven strategies for E-commerce applications. In *Enhancing and Predicting Digital Consumer Behavior with AI* (pp. 375–382). IGI Global., DOI: 10.4018/979-8-3693-4453-8.ch019

Tripathi, A., Singh, A. K., Singh, K. K., Choudhary, P., & Vashist, P. C. (2021). Machine learning architecture and framework. In *Machine Learning and the Internet of Medical Things in Healthcare* (pp. 1–22). Elsevier., DOI: 10.1016/B978-0-12-821229-5.00005-7

Uber. (2020, Mar). *How Uber's dynamic pricing model works*. https://www.uber.com/en-GB/blog/uber-dynamic-pricing/

Vasundhara, S., & Venkatesh, K. S. V., M., P., S., S., S., & Boopathi, S. (2024). AI-powered marketing revolutionizing customer engagement through innovative strategies. In *Cases on AI Ethics in Business* (pp. 21-46). IGI Global. doi:DOI: 10.4018/9798369326435.ch002

Verifone. (2024, Mar 28). *eCommerce: Trends and Predictions for the Next Decade*. https://blog.2checkout.com/ai-trends-and-predictions-in-ecommerce/

Vomberg, A. (2023). Dynamic Pricing Process: How to Transition from Fixed to Dynamic Pricing? In *Digital Pricing Strategy: Capturing Value from Digital Innovations* (pp. 27-38). Taylor and Francis. DOI: 10.4324/9781003226192-5

Wasilewski, A., & Przyborowski, M. (2023). Clustering Methods for Adaptive e-Commerce User Interfaces. *International Joint Conference on Rough Sets, IJCRS 2023. 14481 LNAI* (pp. 511-525). Krakow: Springer Science and Business Media Deutschland GmbH. DOI: 10.1007/978-3-031-50959-9_35

Yamagiwa, A., & Goto, M. (2022). Evaluation of Analysis Model for Products with Coefficients of Binary Classifiers and Consideration of Way to Improve. *14th International Conference on Social Computing and Social Media, SCSM 2022 Held as Part of the 24th HCI International Conference, HCII 2022. 13316 LNCS* (pp. 388-402). Virtual, Online: Springer Science and Business Media Deutschland GmbH. DOI: 10.1007/978-3-031-05064-0_29

Zhang, H., Zhao, L., & Gupta, S. (2018, February). The role of online product recommendations on customer decision making and loyalty in social shopping communities. *International Journal of Information Management*, 38(01), 150–166. DOI: 10.1016/j.ijinfomgt.2017.07.006

Zheng, Y. (2023). An Analysis of the Technical Trend of Semantic Search in Natural Language Processing. *9th Annual International Conference on Network and Information Systems for Computers, ICNISC 2023* (pp. 51-53). Virtual, Online: Institute of Electrical and Electronics Engineers Inc. DOI: 10.1109/ICNISC60562.2023.00033

ADDITIONAL READING

Arora, A., Kaur, R., Vats, P., Gupta, M., Chopra, G., Mehmi, S., & Khanna, T. (2023, August). A Study on Optimizing the Personalization of Recommendations and Customer Services Using Artificially Intelligent Neural Networks to Improve Electronic Commerce. In *International conference on WorldS4* (pp. 1-9). Singapore: Springer Nature Singapore. DOI: 10.1007/978-981-99-8031-4_1

Huseynov, F. (2024). Unleashing the potential of artificial intelligence (AI) in customer engagement. In *AI and Data Engineering Solutions for Effective Marketing* (pp. 184–202). IGI Global., DOI: 10.4018/979-8-3693-3172-9.ch009

Semwal, R., Tripathi, N., Rana, A., Dafouti, B. S., Bairwa, M. K., & Mathur, V. (2024). AI-Powered Personalization and Emotional Intelligence Integration for Enhanced Service Marketing in Transformative Tourism Experiences. In *International Conference on Communication, Computer Sciences and Engineering, IC3SE 2024* (pp. 1851-1856). Gautam Buddha Nagar: IEEE. DOI: 10.1109/IC3SE62002.2024.10592909

Shaikh, I. A., Shahare, P., Gangadharan, S., Venkatarathnam, N., Pelluru, G., & Tilak Babu, S. (2024). Transforming Customer Relationship Management (CRM) with AI in E-Commerce. In *5th IEEE International Conference on Recent Trends in Computer Science and Technology, ICRTCST 2024* (pp. 255-260). Jamshedpur: IEEE. DOI: 10.1109/ICRTCST61793.2024.10578449

Shete, S., Koshti, P., & Pujari, V. I. (2024). The Impact of AI-Powered Personalization on Academic Performance in Students. In *5th IEEE International Conference on Recent Trends in Computer Science and Technology, ICRTCST 2024* (pp. 295-301). Jamshedpur: IEEE. DOI: 10.1109/ICRTCST61793.2024.10578480

Thakur, H. K., Singh, J., Saxena, A., Bhaskar, D., Singh, A. P., & Garg, P. K. (2024). Enhancing Customer Experience through AI-Powered Personalization: A Data Science Perspective in E-Commerce. *In International Conference on Communication, Computer Sciences and Engineering, IC3SE 2024* (pp. 501-506). Gautam Buddha Nagar: IEEE. DOI: 10.1109/IC3SE62002.2024.10592893

Wang, J., Ivrissimtzis, I., Li, Z., & Shi, L. (2024, May). Enhancing user experience in chinese initial text conversations with personalised ai-powered assistant. In *Extended Abstracts of the CHI Conference on Human Factors in Computing Systems* (pp. 1-7). DOI: 10.1145/3613905.3651104

Wibowo, A. (2024). Beyond boundaries: Multichannel strategies in customer relationship management. In *Customer Relationship Management: Methods, Opportunities and Challenges* (pp. 63-102). Nova Science Publishers, Inc.

KEY TERMS AND DEFINITIONS

Collaborative Filtering: A recommendation system method that suggests items to users based on the preferences and behaviors of similar users. It relies on user-to-user comparisons to make predictions.

Content-based Filtering: A recommendation system method that suggests items to users based on the features of the items and a user's past interactions with similar content. It relies on item-to-item comparisons based on attributes like genre, category, or description.

Computer Vision: A field of artificial intelligence that enables machines to interpret and make decisions based on visual input from the world, such as images and videos. It includes tasks like object recognition, image classification, facial recognition, and video analysis.

Conversational AI: A form of artificial intelligence that enables machines to communicate with humans in a natural, conversational manner. It powers virtual assistants, chatbots, and other automated systems to understand and respond to spoken or written language, often utilizing technologies like NLP and machine learning.

Dynamic Pricing: A pricing strategy where the price of a product or service is flexible and changes based on various factors, such as demand, competition, customer profile, or time. Common in industries like travel, hospitality, and e-commerce, dynamic pricing optimizes revenue by adjusting prices in real-time.

Implicit and Explicit Data Collection: Implicit Data Collection refers to the passive gathering of information based on users' behavior, such as clicks, time spent on a page, or browsing history, without direct user input.

Explicit Data Collection: involves directly asking users for information, such as through surveys, forms, or ratings.

Machine Learning Algorithms: A set of algorithms that allow computers to learn from data and make predictions or decisions without being explicitly programmed. Machine learning models are built on statistical techniques that improve their performance on a task over time by recognizing patterns in large datasets.

Mobile Commerce: The buying and selling of goods or services through mobile devices like smartphones and tablets. It involves the use of mobile apps or websites optimized for mobile use and includes transactions like mobile banking, mobile ticketing, and mobile shopping.

Natural Language Processing (NLP): A subfield of artificial intelligence (AI) focused on the interaction between computers and humans through natural language. NLP enables machines to understand, interpret, and generate human language in a way that is both meaningful and useful. Applications include speech recognition, sentiment analysis, and chatbots.

Personalization: The process of tailoring content, recommendations, and experiences to individual users based on their preferences, behavior, and past interactions. In digital marketing and customer experiences, personalization aims to increase engagement and satisfaction by providing relevant content or product suggestions.

Chapter 7
Crafting Couture:
AI's Role in Personalizing Unique Consumer Experiences Through Co-Creation

Poornima Nair
https://orcid.org/0000-0001-9259-291X
Christ University, India

Sunita Kumar
https://orcid.org/0000-0002-0628-1873
Christ University, India

ABSTRACT

The couture industry and artificial intelligence (AI) have come together to create a dynamic paradigm shift in the creation of unique consumer experiences. AI has become a transformational force in the ever-changing fashion industry, transforming the relationship between designers and consumers and overturning conventional paradigms. This study explores the mutually beneficial integration of artificial intelligence (AI) with co-creation processes, shedding light on the creative ways that AI enhances the customisation of couture experiences. At the core of the discussion is the idea of personalisation enabled by AI-powered co-creation tools. With the help of these platforms, customers can express their individual style preferences and take part in the design process, giving them a sense of co-ownership. The ensuing couture pieces blur the boundaries between designer and customer in a cooperative dance of creativity; they are more than just clothes. In conclusion, couture business may achieve unprecedented degrees of personalisation only through the synergy of AI and co-creation.

DOI: 10.4018/979-8-3693-5340-0.ch007

1. INTRODUCTION

Consumers nowadays expect more than mere garments; they want individualized and personalized services that appeal to their distinct preferences and ideas of personal style. The fashion and apparel sector is at a crucial point where innovation and tradition coincide to transform the fundamental essence of what it actually means to conceptualize, design, create and produce and not only just to wear but incorporate garments into the personal style of the customer. The apparel market includes every type of clothing, including business and sportswear, as well as affordable and luxurious items. The global apparel market generated approximately 1.53 trillion US dollars in the year 2023, and it was predicted that revenue would rise to almost 1.7 trillion dollars in the year 2023 (Statista, 2023). The inception of AI has drastically transformed the fashion industry with AI-powered marketing tools. Brands are in a better position to analyze the information, identify the right segment of customers and make their marketing strategies most effective (Ginsberg, 2023). The ability of a computer or computer-controlled robot to carry out tasks is referred to as artificial intelligence (AI). It is the term used to describe the intelligence demonstrated by machines when compared to human beings (Copeland, 2018). Following the COVID-19 epidemic, AI usage has increased (Batley, 2021). The implementation of AI in the fashion industry has numerous advantages, namely customization, improved and efficient customer service, reduction in return rates, and automation of any menial tasks and repetitive work, which will reduce the workload of the workforce (Fernandes, 2022). By using AI-powered virtual styling tools, retailers are able to help customers answer their questions and select clothing that fits their body shape, skin tone, and needs (Bertagnoli, 2022). AI is not only beneficial in various production, branding and marketing activities but also in promoting sustainability in fashion by analyzing data and optimizing the supply chain, leading to a reduction in transportation and storage costs, use of environmentally friendly fabrics for production and thereby reducing the carbon emissions (Fishman, 2023). Fashion brands are expected to be significantly impacted by generative AI, which refers to machine learning algorithms that can produce new material (Bain, 2023). By promoting creativity, individualization, efficiency, and sustainability, generative AI is completely changing the fashion sector. With generative AI, designers may quickly and effectively explore a greater variety of creative possibilities by using algorithms that generate original and inventive ideas based on the analysis of large databases of pre-existing styles, patterns, and colors. Furthermore, thanks to this technology, customers can have highly individualized fashion experiences. Bespoke clothes designs and recommendations are made based on each person's preferences, dimensions, and style preferences. With regard to sustainability, artificial intelligence (AI) reduces waste and maximizes the use of fabrics by using smart patterns and precise demand forecasting to produce only what is required and lessen the impact on the environment. The design process is another area where AI is making a substantial impact. By using AI algorithms to forecast trends and evaluate consumer preferences, fashion companies can lower the risk of producing designs that fail to connect with their target audience and instead produce looks that are more likely to be well-liked (Ginsberg, 2023). In essence, generative AI revolutionizes the fashion sector by stimulating creativity, augmenting consumer interaction, boosting sustainability, and optimizing operational effectiveness. This profoundly changes the way apparel is created, manufactured, and worn.

An example of AI being used in the fashion industry can be seen in the case of Bodify.io, a website that uses predictive analysis for online shopping. This web-based platform uses AI to help online shoppers find brands that suit their body types and identify the right fit, wherein consumers are asked to upload photos based on which the metrics are mapped using machine learning against the company's stored data. Customers are provided with a list of brands that may be the best fit for them in the size they believe they are (Bertagnoli, 2022). With the advent of platforms like Bodify.io, which is not only beneficial for customers to make the right purchase choices but brands themselves, as it helps in reducing the return rates as fit and size are major reasons why clothes are returned (https://www.bodify.io/retailers). This example shows that it's extremely useful not only for customers but also for brands because it gives them information about what sizes would fit the maximum number of customers and also their preferences in brands. With the use of AI techniques, forecasters can identify new trends more precisely and—crucially—faster by identifying patterns in massive databases of social media postings, runway show photos, search engine traffic, and online and in-store sales data (Biehlmann, 2023). In the fashion business, generative AI—which is still in its infancy—may be the way of the future. When applied properly, it has the potential to revolutionize the sector (Harreis et al., 2023).

A few other AI trends that are picking up are virtual trials, where Fashion brands develop a virtual mirror that lets consumers visually try on clothing without having to try them on physically by using computer vision algorithms and the use of Natural Language Processing (NLP). Thanks to brands like Gucci that have integrated augmented reality (AR) technology into their app, Customers may now virtually try on shoes. Users can preview the appearance of several Gucci sneaker shapes and colours by aiming the cameras on their smartphones at their feet (Caroline, 2022).

Fashion brands can develop chatbots and virtual assistants that understand and analyze questions from customers and offer specific suggestions by utilizing natural language processing (NLP) techniques. An example of this would be how H&M has introduced an AI-driven chatbot that utilizes natural language processing (NLP) in order to reply to consumer inquiries and offer styling advice (Fibre2fashion, 2023).

The amalgamation of customized products and co-creation is now establishing itself as a forward-thinking and significant force in the ever-evolving world of fashion and apparel, transforming the way consumers engage consistently with companies. The process of facilitating collaboration for value creation has been made easier by technological improvements (Lu et al., 2019). Understanding technology in value co-creation is crucial since robots and artificial intelligence (AI) are gradually becoming more prevalent in real-world service solutions (Kaartemo & Helkkula, 2018).

According to the co-creation literature, value emerges when the consumer takes part in the conception, creation, and delivery of an offering that is specific to them as well as profitable for the business (Prahalad & Ramaswamy, 2004). The term "co-creation" is now frequently used to characterize an outlook that moves away from the organization as the source of value and towards a more collaborative approach where individuals and organizations work together to create and grow meaning (Ind & Coates, 2013).

Service-Dominant logic (SD logic) from a systems perspective would help marketers have a better understanding of how technology has an impact on consumers' behavior, their experiences and even the market and also have a better understanding of the co-creation process where multiple stakeholders are involved and the outcome of such involvement is the creation of value (Vargo et al., 2017). Within the framework of Service-Dominant Logic, the systems-oriented approach to value creation comprises four fundamental propositions. First, it acknowledges the distinct and unique nature of the experiences of each participant in the value-creation process, highlighting its phenomenological essence. Second, it emphasizes that value is consistently co-created, involving multiple stakeholders who collectively contribute to its realisation. The third proposition underscores the multifaceted character of value, encompassing personal, social, cultural, and technological dimensions. Lastly, the fourth proposition emphasizes that value continually evolves through ongoing interactions between actors or stakeholders and the system. These principles collectively enrich our understanding of value creation within dynamic service ecosystems (Vargo, Koskela-Huotari et al., 2017; Vargo & Lusch, 2017). There are fundamental advantages to incorporating AI and automation in understanding and estimating customers' expectations from products and services and, accordingly, coming up with customized product offerings for them (Duan et al., 2019).

Brands possess an exceptional opportunity to capitalize on the power of AI to offer their customers personalized experiences as their needs continue to evolve due to increased exposure to the digital world constantly, with the availability of abundant options and the incorporation of digital technologies more deeply into daily life. Businesses may learn a great deal about the tastes and attitudes of specific customers and also the trends in the fashion industry thanks to a variety of AI-driven solutions. Up until now, personalization was not customized as per the needs of individual customers, but it has become a reality with AI in the picture. Virtual fitting rooms, live product visualization, and highly individualized fashion advice are all made possible by AI. These innovations enhance brand engagement and consumer loyalty, along with elevating customer satisfaction levels.

This book chapter examines the role of artificial intelligence (AI) in facilitating co-creation strategies within the fashion industry. It explores how AI empowers customers to actively participate in the creation of customized products, services, and brand development. The chapter also analyzes the impact of this customer involvement on consumer behavior and investigates how brands enable and support customer participation in co-creating their offerings and brand identity.

Co-creation is the need of the hour as the new digitally savvy set of consumers are no longer passive observers and consumers; they are willing to be actively involved in the entire process from conceptualizing to end product and branding and customizing service experiences. The process of Co-creation is a fundamentally cooperative process through which brands and customers exchange information while concurrently creating value.

2. LITERATURE REVIEW

2.1. The role of artificial intelligence in the fashion industry

AI is revolutionizing how businesses find, develop, nurture, and oversee interactive marketing partnerships and consumers' experiences (Mustak et al., 2021). The transformation in the fashion industry due to AI has occurred concurrently with businesses' growing capacity to transform customer data into automated and customized interactive experiences (Payne et al., 2021). From the perspective of the company, sellers use AI technologies for guided selling, social listening and social selling, customer churn and retention marketing, pricing, lead scoring and customer acquisition, market segmentation and targeting, personalized communications, and purchase likelihood rankings (Kopalle et al., 2022). Additionally, the sellers employ additional data-driven interactive marketing strategies that are beneficial for value co-creation across the business-to-business (B2B) and business-to-consumer (B2C) customer journey processes (Rusthollkarhu et al., 2022). In the fashion sector, artificial intelligence (AI) is becoming a disruptive force that is changing how companies create, manufacture, market, and sell their goods. AI has shown to be an invaluable resource for the fashion industry as well as customers, with applications ranging from trend prediction to improved shopping experiences. Additionally, stylists are using AI to help them make recommendations for products based on each customer's preferences for pricing, size, general style, order history, and social media activity, including fashion photos saved on Pinterest (Cao, 2018).

Trend forecasting is one of the major ways artificial intelligence (AI) has benefited the fashion industry. Being ahead of the curve is key to the fashion industry, and artificial intelligence is great at sifting through massive amounts of data to find new trends and customer preferences. In order to forecast the upcoming major trends, machine learning algorithms can analyze data from social media, runway exhibits, street style, and past sales statistics. This skill enables businesses and designers to maintain an advantage over rivals, reduce the possibility of creating designs that are not well-received, and match their products to the constantly shifting needs of the market.

In the design process, artificial intelligence (AI) enhances human creativity rather than takes its place. AI can help designers create prototypes, improve workflow, and even come up with ideas for new designs. AI's capacity to evaluate historical fashion data gives designers important insights into what has worked in the past and inspires them to create fresh, inventive designs. In addition to helping to maximize the use of resources and materials, AI algorithms can support more environmentally friendly and sustainable fashion processes. Furthermore, the personalization of the consumer experience is greatly aided by AI. Online retailers assess consumer preferences and behavior using recommendation engines driven by artificial intelligence (AI) to provide tailored product recommendations. AI-powered virtual fitting rooms improve the online shopping experience by enabling buyers to see how clothing will fit them before making a purchase. In addition to raising customer satisfaction levels, these interactive and personalized elements help boost sales and foster brand loyalty.

AI is revolutionizing the way brands interact with their target market in marketing and advertising. Chatbots and virtual assistants driven by AI are being utilized to interact with clients, offering tailored advice and support. Social media platforms use AI algorithms to provide customized advertising, which makes sure that the right people see the ads. This focused approach helps organisations develop a more engaged and loyal consumer base while optimizing the impact of marketing initiatives.

AI and the fashion business together have ushered in a new era of efficiency and innovation. Artificial Intelligence (AI) is revolutionizing the fashion industry in all facets, from trend prediction to customized shopping experiences. The future of fashion will probably be defined by the dynamic interaction between human creativity and AI skills as technology develops, guaranteeing a fluid and flexible sector that can react to consumers' changing requirements and aspirations.

2.2. Co-creation and fashion

Co-creation is the practice of allowing customers and stakeholders to have a say and a choice in the services and products that are developed by the end users (Kaminski, 2009). Fashion is changing in terms of how it is made, sold, and consumed, thanks to the revolutionary synergy that exists between co-creation and artificial intelligence (AI). In today's digital age, consumers are not just mere spectators who blindly buy products and services offered to them but are active participants (Prahalad & Ramaswamy, 2004). Including customers in the design process to create more suitable and inventive fashion products is known as co-creation in the fashion industry (Grabe & Zhu, 2023).

When co-creation and AI are combined, they create a dynamic framework that is very customer-centric and technologically advanced, offering a number of advantages that have a big impact on the sector. This collaborative approach allows customers to freely submit ideas and make designs that suit their tastes as long as they stay within the parameters established by the fashion brand or supplier (Grabe & Zhu, 2023). Disrupting the conventional hierarchical interactions between businesses and consumers, digital-only fashion brands are at the forefront of empowering consumers through decentralized co-design platforms (Huggard & Sarmakari, 2023).

An alternative to the conventional top-down method in the fashion business is co-creation, which entails cooperative efforts between designers and consumers. Customers can voice their individual preferences and tastes by actively participating in the design process. It is imperative that fashion become more accessible at a time when customers want inclusive and customized experiences. Fashion firms can leverage the creativity of their broad consumer base through co-creation, which fosters a sense of ownership and connection that extends beyond the purchase process. AI revolutionizes the fashion industry with unmatched efficiency and inventiveness. The ability to foresee trends is one of AI's major accomplishments. Machine learning algorithms can analyze large-scale datasets from social media, fashion shows, and consumer behavior to forecast new trends precisely. This keeps designers ahead of the curve and makes it possible for them to produce collections that speak to the tastes of the modern consumer. In terms of sustainability, co-creation and AI support more ethical and environmentally conscious fashion techniques. AI helps optimize the supply chain by cutting waste and guaranteeing effective resource use. Platforms for co-creation can be used to encourage sustainable decisions, in line with the growing demand from consumers for clothing made responsibly. This twin strategy tackles the fashion industry's creative and environmental facets, which is a big step in the direction of a more sustainable future.

2.3. Fashion trends identification with AI

The fashion sector is hurting; brands and retailers frequently experience profit margin erosion. Roughly half of the production is either unsold or sold at a loss. Fashion is a hard industry to stay in, and in this cutthroat age, turning a profit is an enormous undertaking. Fashion businesses deal with the same issue every year: unsold inventory being diluted at steep discounts (Banerjee et al., 2022). Artificial intelligence, or AI, is the ability of a computer or computer-controlled robot to perform activities associated with intelligent beings. AI is the term for intelligence demonstrated by machines (Copeland, 2018). According to market research, global spending on artificial intelligence in fashion is expected to increase at a compound annual growth rate of 40.8 per cent from USD 229 million in 2019 to USD 1260 million by 2024 (Markets and Markets, 2022).

Every time a new item is developed, made, and sold, new data is generated, making the fashion and apparel industry one of the most dynamic sectors (Jain et al., 2017). The fashion sector must implement innovative AI techniques to gain a competitive edge and increase corporate profitability (Giri et al., 2019). AI-powered fashion trend recognition has become a mainstay in the business, revolutionizing how designers and brands keep ahead of consumers' constantly changing preferences. AI's analytical powers and machine learning algorithms provide a data-driven method for predicting trends, yielding insightful information that helps define the fashion industry's future. The fashion industry is using AI to recognize and evaluate trends. They use text mining techniques to collect web text data from fashion publications and weblogs and identify the most popular fashion subjects addressed over a given time frame (Konina, 2023; Sleiman et al., 2022). With their exceptional ability to identify even the most minute changes in customer behavior and preferences, machine learning algorithms are able to accurately predict trends. In order to foresee and adapt to the constantly shifting preferences of their target market, designers and brands can benefit greatly from these predictive capabilities. Fashion experts can capitalize on new patterns before they become stale and expedite their design processes and production by detecting trends in their infancy. Artificial intelligence (AI) systems can recognize and depict trends and track how these trends change over time by examining the frequency of occurrence and co-occurrence of phrases connected to fashion (Sleiman et al., 2022; Shi & Lewis, 2020). With their exceptional ability to identify even the most minute changes in customer behavior and preferences, machine learning algorithms are able to accurately predict trends. In order to foresee and adapt to the constantly shifting preferences of their target market, designers and brands can benefit greatly from these predictive capabilities. Fashion experts can capitalize on new patterns before they become stale and expedite their design processes and production by detecting trends in their infancy.

Furthermore, AI algorithms can classify clothing qualities like textures, garment styles, and details by analyzing fashion photographs, speeding up and reducing trend prediction costs (Parmar & Rajgor, 2023). Additionally, real-time trend monitoring is made easier by AI, giving designers the most recent information. This flexibility is essential in a field where trends come and go swiftly. In a market that moves quickly, designers can make necessary adjustments to their collections to stay current and appealing to consumers despite constant variations in their preferences. Neural networks and basic fashion theory are used by AI-based stylist models to assess consumer demands and fashion trends. Artificial intelligence (AI) is mainly responsible for the more automated and efficient identification and prediction of fashion trends. Nowadays, nearly every link in the fashion value chain uses artificial intelligence, from robotic manufacturing to product discovery (Luce, 2018). To sum up, the application of AI to the identification of fashion trends is revolutionary for the sector. AI enables designers and businesses to move with agility and precision across the complexity of the fashion industry, from extensive data analysis to predictive modelling. The future of fashion will probably be defined by the combination of AI and trend identification as technology develops, keeping the sector innovative, adaptable, and at the forefront of new trends.

2.4. Improving customer experience

The concept of customer experience describes a consumer's whole relationship with a retailer, taking into account their interactions and opinions about the company (Verhoef et al., 2009). AI has the ability to enhance the fashion industry's customer experience. It can use secure, user-friendly technologies to deliver distinctive, appealing retail experiences (Tiutiu & Dabija, 2023). Personalized recommendation systems are a key way artificial intelligence enhances the fashion industry's customer experience. Customized product recommendations are provided by AI algorithms that analyze a tremendous amount of data, including browsing patterns, past purchases, and client preferences. Customers get tailored recommendations through mobile apps or web platforms based on their tastes, size, and style. As a result, customers are more likely to find and buy things that suit their tastes, which improves the shopping experience. Businesses are adopting AI technology backed by data analytics with greater frequency in response to ongoing margin pressure, condensed strategy cycles, and rising customer expectations. This modifies how businesses engage with their clientele, potentially leading to improved customer-brand associations (Evans,2019). Furthermore, artificial intelligence is essential to virtual try-on experiences, solving a persistent problem in online fashion retail. Using cutting-edge augmented reality and computer vision technologies, shoppers can virtually try on clothes before making a purchase. This feature makes online buying more secure, lowers the chance of returns, and offers a more dynamic and interesting shopping experience.

It is, therefore, conceivable to boost customer happiness and yield substantial benefits for businesses by strategically deploying AI technologies at many important customer touch points (Ameen et al., 2021). AI-powered chatbots, content creation, and customer insights are just a few of the ways retailers are utilizing the technology (Ameen et al., 2021). Chatbots and virtual assistants powered by AI facilitate real-time customer service and interaction. These virtual assistants offer consumers a smooth and customized experience by responding to questions, giving styling tips, and helping with purchasing. Being able to respond quickly to consumer inquiries enhances satisfaction and fosters consumer trust in the business. In order to analyze client sentiment and feedback at a scale, precision, and speed that is not possible for people, artificial intelligence (AI) technologies like machine learning, natural language processing, and understanding can be used (Gartner, 2020). Retailers may opt for artificial intelligence (AI) as one of their primary tools to continuously enhance the consumer experience and maintain their competitiveness (Newman, 2019). AI plays a part in the customization of fit and size. AI algorithms can recommend the best sizes for certain clients based on an analysis of past data and customer feedback. This makes it less likely that returns will occur because of sizing problems, which improves and streamlines the customer experience.

2.5. AI-Driven fashion innovation and engagement – proposed relational model

This model (see Figure 1) is a comprehensive approach to leveraging artificial intelligence (AI) to enhance customer experiences and drive innovation in the fashion industry. The fashion industry is undergoing a significant transformation driven by the convergence of artificial intelligence. (AI). This model, characterized by co-creation, personalization, trend identification through AI, and a closed-loop customer experience feedback system, holds immense potential to revolutionize the way fashion is designed, produced, and consumed.

Figure 1. AI-driven fashion innovation and engagement

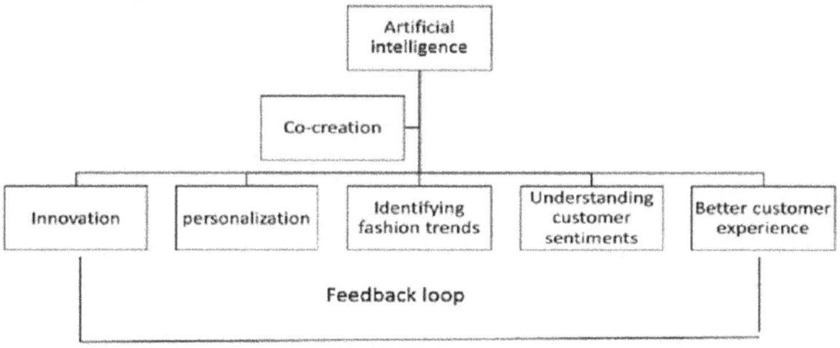

(Author)

2.5.1. Artificial Intelligence (AI)

This serves as the underlying technology powering various aspects of the model. AI algorithms can analyze vast amounts of data, recognize patterns, and make predictions, enabling more personalized and efficient interactions with customers. Artificial intelligence is revolutionizing the fashion industry through individualized recommendations, virtual try-ons, and chatbots that are responsive. It fosters innovation through supply chain optimization, real-time customization, and process simplification. Designers are able to keep ahead of market expectations because of AI's data analytics, which finds developing trends quickly. Simply said, artificial intelligence (AI) puts the fashion sector at the forefront of technological growth by improving client engagement, igniting creativity, and making trend spotting easier.

2.5.2. Co-creation

Involving customers in the design process can lead to the development of products and services that better meet their needs and preferences. Co-creation entails collaborating with customers to generate ideas, provide feedback, and refine offerings together. By leveraging AI-powered platforms, brands can engage customers in the design process itself. Platforms like Threadless and Uniqlo UTme! Allow users to submit designs and vote on their favorites, fostering a sense of community and ownership. AI then analyses these interactions, identifying design elements and styles that resonate with specific customer segments. This data-driven approach enables brands to personalize offerings, creating garments that cater to individual tastes and preferences. Studies like (Kim et al., 2021) show that personalized recommendations in fashion lead to increased customer satisfaction and purchase intent.

2.5.3. Innovation

By harnessing AI and engaging in co-creation, the model fosters innovation within the fashion industry. This innovation may involve creating novel products, services, or business models that differentiate a brand from its competitors and drive growth. Design processes, trend forecasting, and customer engagement are all revolutionized by AI, which spurs innovation. Large-scale datasets are analyzed by machine learning algorithms, which forecast new fashion trends and enhance designs. Personalized recommendations and virtual try-ons improve the shopping experience. Supply chain management powered by AI guarantees effectiveness while cutting waste and advancing sustainability. AI and human ingenuity work together to create innovative designs that push boundaries.

2.5.4. Personalization

AI enables the customization of products, recommendations, and marketing messages based on individual customer preferences, behaviors, and characteristics. Personalization enhances the relevance of interactions, leading to increased customer satisfaction and loyalty. Through data-driven insights and customized experiences, AI enables personalization in the fashion business. AI algorithms generate comprehensive profiles by examining the browsing habits, buying history, and preferences of the user. Using these profiles, brands are able to provide consumers with tailored suggestions, style advice, and virtual try-ons that match their preferences. Customers can co-create original designs with real-time customization possibilities, which further improves the purchasing experience. Chatbots powered by AI offer immediate assistance and support, encouraging customer loyalty and engagement.

2.5.5. Identifying Fashion Trends

AI algorithms can analyze social media, e-commerce data, and other sources to quickly identify emerging fashion trends. This allows fashion brands to stay ahead of the curve and deliver timely, trendy offerings to customers. AI algorithms excel at analyzing vast amounts of data, including social media trends, image recognition, and purchasing behavior. Platforms like Taggun and Edited harness this power to identify emerging trends before they hit the mainstream. Brands can then use these insights to inform design decisions, ensuring their collections are aligned with current and future desires. This proactive approach, exemplified by research (Vial, 2019), minimizes the risk of creating outdated or unpopular designs.

2.5.6. Understanding customer sentiments

AI-powered sentiment analysis tools can interpret customer feedback from various sources, such as social media, reviews, and surveys. This helps brands gain insights into customer preferences, pain points, and overall satisfaction levels. By evaluating enormous volumes of data from social media, reviews, and interactions, artificial intelligence (AI) plays a critical role in interpreting consumer sentiment in the fashion sector. Algorithms for natural language processing (NLP) identify and decipher consumer attitudes to derive insightful data. This technology provides real-time feedback by measuring responses to collections, styles, and brand experiences. Fashion brands may improve client happiness, immediately resolve problems, and adjust strategy by comprehending attitudes. An effective technique that helps the sector remain aware of changing consumer preferences and promote a more customer-focused and responsive strategy is AI-driven sentiment analysis.

2.5.7. Better customer experience

By leveraging AI for personalization, trend identification, and sentiment analysis, brands can deliver superior customer experiences across all touchpoints. From product discovery to post-purchase support, every interaction is tailored to meet the unique needs of individual customers. AI tools like sentiment analysis and natural language processing can analyze customer reviews, social media posts, and other feedback channels. This data provides valuable insights into customer experience pain points, preferences, and overall satisfaction. Platforms like Nosto and Clarabridge leverage AI to analyze this data, empowering brands to identify areas for improvement and personalize marketing messages for better engagement. Research (Galdolage, 2021) highlights the positive impact of using AI to personalize customer experiences, leading to increased brand loyalty and advocacy.

2.5.8. Feedback loop

The model incorporates a feedback loop wherein customer feedback is continuously collected, analyzed, and used to refine products, services, and experiences. This iterative process ensures that brands remain responsive to evolving customer preferences and market dynamics. The beauty of this model lies in its cyclical nature. Customer co-creation and personalized offerings lead to a better understanding of preferences. AI-driven trend analysis informs future designs, which are then personalized again. Customer feedback on these offerings, analyzed through AI, feeds back into the cycle, leading to continuous improvement and innovation. As discussed in (Barile et al., 2020), this closed-loop system ensures brands remain agile and responsive to evolving customer needs, fostering deeper brand loyalty and market differentiation.

3. DISCUSSION AND KEY FINDINGS

The democratization of couture via AI-driven co-creation is a significant topic of discussion. The study shows that artificial intelligence (AI) can dismantle pre-existing barriers in the fashion sector and enable customers to express their uniqueness by creating couture pieces. The traditional exclusivity of fashion is being challenged by this democratization, allowing a wider variety of voices and preferences to influence the sector.

Moreover, the dynamic interaction between human creativity and AI skills is shaping the fashion industry's future, ensuring adaptability to changing consumer requirements. The impact of AI is not limited to marketing and production; it significantly influences the design process as well. By leveraging AI algorithms for trend forecasting and consumer preference evaluation, fashion companies mitigate the risk of producing designs that do not resonate with their target audience, leading to a more efficient and consumer-centric approach. A notable example is Bodify.io, a web-based platform utilizing AI to help online shoppers find brands that suit their body types, demonstrating the utility of AI for both consumers and brands in understanding sizing preferences. Moreover, despite being in its early stages, generative AI holds the potential to revolutionize the fashion sector by producing new materials through machine learning algorithms.

The advent of AI trends, such as virtual trials, driven by computer vision algorithms and Natural Language Processing (NLP) for chatbots and virtual assistants further enhances the overall customer experience. H&M's introduction of an AI-driven chatbot exemplifies the shift towards AI-enhanced customer interactions, offering personalized advice and styling guidance. The amalgamation of AI with co-creation is reshaping the fashion industry encouraging customer involvement in the design process. This collaborative approach not only leads to the creation of customized products and services but also fosters customer engagement and satisfaction.

The literature review emphasizes the critical role of AI in transforming the fashion industry, from trend identification to improving customer experiences. AI's ability to process vast amounts of data, recognize patterns, and predict trends positions it as a valuable tool for staying ahead in the fast-paced fashion landscape. The model presented in Figure 1 encapsulates the comprehensive approach to AI-driven fashion innovation and engagement, highlighting the interconnected elements of AI, co-creation, innovation, personalization, trend identification, and a closed-loop feedback system. This data-driven approach ensures continuous improvement and innovation, ultimately reshaping the fashion industry to meet the dynamic needs of digitally savvy consumers and fostering brand loyalty through personalized, trend-driven experiences.

Therefore, the convergence of AI, co-creation, personalization, trend identification, and a closed-loop customer feedback system holds immense potential to revolutionize the fashion industry. Brands that leverage AI in these areas are likely to enhance customer satisfaction, drive innovation, and remain competitive in the evolving landscape of the fashion sector.

In conclusion, the combination of co-creation methods and artificial intelligence (AI) proves to be an influential force that is changing the couture sector. AI's significant influence on creating personalized, one-of-a-kind customer experiences is undeniable; it dismantles conventional barriers and encourages communication and cooperation between designers and customers. The chapter highlights how this connection is symbiotic, giving customers active participation and AI-powered prediction information for designers. AI-driven co-creation facilitates personalisation, which fosters a combination of greater creative expression and a stronger emotional bond between consumers and brands. The primary idea is that co-creation and AI together have the potential to enable hitherto unheard-of levels of customization. Through the astute application of AI's analytical powers to the co-creation process, the couture sector is able to negotiate the intricacies of personal preferences and evolving trends deftly. This relationship ushers in a new age for the fashion industry, where each couture piece serves as a tribute to the harmonic union of technical progress and human ingenuity. Beyond the conventional consumer-brand relationship, AI-facilitated co-creation fosters a sense of co-ownership among customers while also improving efficiency and responsiveness. Lastly, this study suggests that designers and consumers working together in a collaborative relationship facilitate all possible ways for AI to determine the fashion industry's future direction. Not only does this synergy have the potential to revolutionize the fashion business, but it also highlights the countless opportunities for bespoke experiences that are inclusive, customized, and ethically responsible.

4. CONCLUSION

The confluence of AI and personalized fashion presents a future brimming with exciting possibilities. AI-powered co-creation platforms empower consumers to transcend passive consumption and actively participate in shaping their desired garments. This collaborative approach fosters not only unique and individualized pieces but also cultivates a deeper emotional connection between the wearer and the garment.

As AI technology continues to evolve, we can expect even more sophisticated personalization capabilities. Imagine AI seamlessly integrates consumer preferences, body measurements, and real-time fashion trends to generate personalized design recommendations. Additionally, AI-powered virtual try-on experiences can further enhance the co-creation process, allowing consumers to visualize and refine their designs before committing to production.

However, it is crucial to remember that human creativity and craftsmanship remain irreplaceable. AI should serve as a collaborative tool, augmenting human capabilities rather than replacing them. The future of couture lies in the harmonious fusion of human ingenuity and AI-powered personalization, empowering consumers to express their individuality and cultivate a deeper appreciation for the art of fashion.

The study offers far-reaching and transformational implications for the fashion business as well as for consumers. First of all, the results highlight how artificial intelligence (AI) can completely transform the top-down, historically exclusive world of couture. The study proposes the democratization of fashion through the facilitation of co-creation between AI algorithms and human designers. This would enable customers to participate actively in the design process, promoting inclusivity and a sense of empowerment. This change significantly impacts the relationship between companies and consumers since it not only satisfies the increasing desire for individualized experiences but also strengthens the emotional bonds that customers have with couture brands. Design processes can be streamlined using AI, which enables designers to produce and refine designs quickly in response to client feedback, saving both time and money. Fashion firms have the ability to expand the scope of their customization offers while maintaining the distinctiveness of their products, thereby making personalized couture more widely available.

The study also emphasizes the financial effects of AI in fashion. The industry's bottom line may benefit from the real-time customization that AI-driven co-creation platforms enable. By forecasting the need for customized items and cutting down on overproduction and inventory expenses, AI integration can improve supply chain and inventory management operations. More sustainable fashion methods are aided by the waste reduction achieved by exact personalization and fewer returns. Customers who actively participate in the design process are more likely to be satisfied and be inclined to make a purchase, which could lead to a decrease in returns and unsold inventory. This can help fashion brands become more sustainable by increasing their operational efficiency, reducing waste, and improving their ability to react to market demands. Companies may set themselves apart from the competition, draw in tech-savvy customers, and establish themselves as leaders in the fashion sector by utilizing AI for co-creation.

The current research is based entirely on secondary data from a thorough literature review, and future research can include a quantitative study. Future research can focus on exploring the changing dynamics between AI and couture, going deeper into ethical issues, improving AI algorithms for more personalization, and examining the long-term effects on the economy and ecology. Future studies may focus on how to incorporate cutting-edge technology like virtual and augmented reality into the co-creation process to create a richer and more engaging couture experience. The fashion industry is constantly changing, and further research into consumer perceptions, preferences, and the scalability of AI-driven co-creation platforms will help to build a comprehensive understanding that will guide the sustainable evolution of AI's role in personalizing unique consumer experiences.

REFERENCES

Ameen, N., Tarhini, A., Reppel, A., & Anand, A. (2021). Customer experiences in the age of artificial intelligence. *Computers in Human Behavior*, 114, 106548. DOI: 10.1016/j.chb.2020.106548 PMID: 32905175

Bain. (2023). *Case Study | The Complete Playbook for Generative AI in Fashion*. https://www.businessoffashion.com/case-studies/technology/generative-ai-playbook-machine-learning-emerging-technology/

Banerjee, S. R., Mohapatra, S., & Bharati, M. (2022). *AI in Fashion Industry*. Emerald Publishing Limited eBooks. .DOI: 10.1108/9781802626339

Barile, S., Grimaldi, M., Loia, F., & Sirianni, C. A. (2020). Technology, value co-creation and innovation in service ecosystems: Toward sustainable co-innovation. *Sustainability (Basel)*, 12(7), 2759. DOI: 10.3390/su12072759

Batley, M. M. (2021). AI adoption accelerated during the pandemic, but many say it's moving too fast: KPMG survey. https://info.kpmg.us/news-perspectives/technology-innovation/thriving-in-an-ai-world/aiadoption-accelerated-during-pandemic.html

Brandon Ginsberg. *Artificial Intelligence In Fashion*. Forbes. https://www.forbes.com/sites/theyec/2023/02/21/artificial-intelligence-in-fashion

Britannica, E. (2018). Rapid transit: https://www. britannica. com/technology/rapid-transit

Caroline (2022). Easier to Sell More Products with Gucci Shoe AR Try-on. https://tryon.kivisense.com/blog/gucci-sneaker-ar-try-on

Copeland, B. J. (2018). Artificial intelligence. https://www.britannica.com/technology/artificialintelligence

Duan, Y., Edwards, J. S., & Dwivedi, Y. K. (2019). Artificial intelligence for decision making in the era of Big Data – evolution, challenges and research agenda. *International Journal of Information Management*, 48, 63–71. DOI: 10.1016/j.ijinfomgt.2019.01.021

Evans, M., & Ghafourifar, A. (2019). Build A 5-star customer experience with artificial intelligence. Forbes. https://www.forbes.com/sites/allbusiness/2019/02/17/customer-experience-artificial-intelligence

Fernandes, D. (2022). How chatbot is transforming the fashion retail industry in the future of fashion. https://helloyubo.com/chatbot/how-retail-chatbots-is-transforming-the-future-of-fashion

Fishman. (2023). How Artificial Intelligence is changing the fashion industry. https://immago.com/ai-fashion-industry

Galdolage, B. S. (2021). Customer value co-creation intention, practices and experience in self-service technologies. *Journal of Scientific Research and Reports*, 27(4), 12–26. DOI: 10.9734/jsrr/2021/v27i430375

Gartner. (2020). Drive growth in times of disruption.

Giri, C., Jain, S., Zeng, X., & Bruniaux, P. (2019). A detailed review of artificial intelligence applied in the fashion and apparel industry. *IEEE Access : Practical Innovations, Open Solutions*, 7, 95376–95396. DOI: 10.1109/ACCESS.2019.2928979

Grabe, I., & Zhu, J. (2023). Towards Co-Creative generative adversarial networks for fashion designers. *arXiv (Cornell University)*. doi:/arxiv.2304.09477.DOI: 10.48550

Harreis, H., Koullias, T., Roberts, R., & Te, K. (2023). Generative AI: Unlocking the future of fashion. McKinsey & Company. https://www.mckinsey.com/industries/retail/our-insights/generative-ai-unlocking-the-future-of-fashion

Huggard, E., & Särmäkari, N. (2023). How digital-only fashion brands are creating more participatory models of fashion co-design. *Fashion, Style & Popular Culture*, 10(4), 583–600. DOI: 10.1386/fspc_00176_1

Ind, N., & Coates, N. (2013). The meanings of co-creation. *European Business Review*, 25(1), 86–95. DOI: 10.1108/09555341311287754

Jain, S., Bruniaux, J., Zeng, X., & Bruniaux, P. (2017). Big data in fashion industry. *IOP Conference Series. Materials Science and Engineering*, 254, 152005. DOI: 10.1088/1757-899X/254/15/152005

Kaartemo, V., & Helkkula, A. (2018). A Systematic Review of Artificial Intelligence and Robots in Value Co-creation: Current status and Future research avenues. *Journal of Creating Value*, 4(2), 211–228. DOI: 10.1177/2394964318805625

Kaminski, J. (2009, October). Editorial: Join the Co-Creation Wave! [OJNI]. *On-Line Journal of Nursing Informatics*, 13(3). http://ojni.org/13_3/june.pdf

Kim, J., Kang, S., & Bae, J. (2021). The effects of customer consumption goals on artificial intelligence driven recommendation agents: Evidence from stitch fix. *International Journal of Advertising*, 41(6), 997–1016. DOI: 10.1080/02650487.2021.1963098

Konina, N. Y. (2023). Artificial intelligence in the Fashion Industry—Reality and Prospects. In *Approaches to global sustainability, markets, and governance* (pp. 273–280). DOI: 10.1007/978-981-99-2198-0_29

Kopalle, P. K., Gangwar, M., Kaplan, A., Ramachandran, D., Reinartz, W., & Rindfleisch, A. (2022). Examining artificial intelligence (AI) technologies in marketing via a global lens: Current trends and future research opportunities. *International Journal of Research in Marketing*, 39(2), 522–540. DOI: 10.1016/j.ijresmar.2021.11.002

Lisa Bertagnoli. (2022). Artificial Intelligence In Fashion. Built In. https://builtin.com/artificial-intelligence/ai-fashion

Lu, L., Rui-Ying, C., & Gürsoy, D. (2019). Developing and validating a service robot integration willingness scale. *International Journal of Hospitality Management*, 80, 36–51. DOI: 10.1016/j.ijhm.2019.01.005

Luce, L. (2018). *Artificial Intelligence for Fashion: How AI is Revolutionizing the Fashion Industry*. Apress.

Markets and Markets. (2022). AI in Fashion Market by Solutions & Services. Retrieved from https://www.marketsandmarkets.com/Market-Reports/ai-in-fashion-market-144448991.html#:~:text=AI%20in%20fashion%3F-The%20global%20AI%20in%20fashion%20market%20size%20is%20expected%20to,40.8%25%20during%20the%20forecast%20period

Mustak, M., Salminen, J., Plé, L., & Wirtz, J. (2021). Artificial intelligence in marketing: Topic modeling, scientometric analysis, and research agenda. *Journal of Business Research*, 124, 389–404. DOI: 10.1016/j.jbusres.2020.10.044

Newman, D. (2019). 5 ways AI is transforming the customer experience. *Forbes*. https://www.forbes.com/sites/danielnewman/2019/04/16/5-ways-ai-is-transforming-the-customer-experience/

Parmar, A., & Rajgor, A. (2023). Enhancing fashion recommendations: Deep neural networks for personalized outfit suggestions. *International Journal of Scientific Research in Science and Technology*, 10(3), 576–581. DOI: 10.32628/IJSRST523103117

Payne, E. H. M., Dahl, A. J., & Peltier, J. W. (2021). Digital servitization value co-creation framework for AI services: A research agenda for digital transformation in financial service ecosystems. *Journal of Research in Interactive Marketing*, 15(2), 200–222. DOI: 10.1108/JRIM-12-2020-0252

Prahalad, C. K., & Ramaswamy, V. (2004). Co-creation experiences: The next practice in value creation. *Journal of Interactive Marketing*, 18(3), 5–14. DOI: 10.1002/dir.20015

Priscille Biehlmann. (2023, October 1). 'You've got to be data-driven': The fashion forecasters using AI to predict the next trend. The Guardian. https://www.theguardian.com/technology/2023/oct/01/ai-artificial-intelligence-fashion-trend-forecasting-style

Rustholkarhu, S., Toukola, S., Aarikka-Stenroos, L., & Mahlamäki, T. (2022). Managing B2B customer journeys in digital era: Four management activities with artificial intelligence-empowered tools. *Industrial Marketing Management*, 104, 241–257. DOI: 10.1016/j.indmarman.2022.04.014

Shi, M., & Lewis, V. D. (2020). Using artificial intelligence to analyze fashion trends. arXiv (Cornell University). https://arxiv.org/pdf/2005.00986

Sleiman, R., Tran, K. P., & Thomassey, S. (2022). Natural language processing for fashion trends detection. *2022 International Conference on Electrical, Computer and Energy Technologies (ICECET)*. DOI: 10.1109/ICECET55527.2022.9872832

Statista. (2023). Apparel market worldwide. https://www.statista.com/topics/5091/apparel-market-worldwide

Tiutiu, M., & Dabija, D. C. (2023). Improving Customer Experience Using Artificial Intelligence in Online Retail. In *Proceedings of the International Conference on Business Excellence, 17*(1), 1139-1147. DOI: 10.2478/picbe-2023-0102

Vargo, S. L., Koskela-Huotari, K., Baron, S., Edvardsson, B., Reynoso, J., & Colurcio, M. (2017). A systems perspective on markets – Toward a research agenda. *Journal of Business Research*, 79, 260–268. DOI: 10.1016/j.jbusres.2017.03.011

Vargo, S. L., & Lusch, R. F. (2017). Service-dominant logic 2025. *International Journal of Research in Marketing*, 34(1), 46–67. DOI: 10.1016/j.ijresmar.2016.11.001

Verhoef, P. C., Lemon, K. N., Parasuraman, A., Roggeveen, A. L., Tsiros, M., & Schlesinger, L. A. (2009). Customer Experience Creation: Determinants, dynamics and management strategies. *Journal of Retailing*, 85(1), 31–41. DOI: 10.1016/j.jretai.2008.11.001

Vial, G. (2019). Understanding digital transformation: A review and a research agenda. *The Journal of Strategic Information Systems*, 28(2), 118–144. DOI: 10.1016/j.jsis.2019.01.003

ADDITIONAL READING

Barile, S., Bassano, C., Piciocchi, P., Saviano, M., & Spohrer, J. C. (2021). Empowering value co-creation in the Digital age. *Journal of Business &amp. Journal of Business and Industrial Marketing*, 39(6), 1130–1143. DOI: 10.1108/JBIM-12-2019-0553

Chandra, B., & Rahman, Z. (2023). Artificial Intelligence and value co-creation: A review, Conceptual Framework and directions for future research. *Journal of Service Theory and Practice*, 34(1), 7–32. DOI: 10.1108/JSTP-03-2023-0097

Fu, H.-P., Chang, T.-H., Lin, S.-W., Teng, Y.-H., & Huang, Y.-Z. (2023). Evaluation and adoption of artificial intelligence in the retail industry. *International Journal of Retail &amp. International Journal of Retail & Distribution Management*, 51(6), 773–790. DOI: 10.1108/IJRDM-12-2021-0610

Harreis, H., Koullias, T., Roberts, R., & Te, K. (2023, March 8). Generative AI: Unlocking the Future of Fashion. McKinsey & Company. https://www.mckinsey.com/industries/retail/our-insights/generative-ai-unlocking-the-future-of-fashion

Kang, J.-Y. M., & Choi, D. (2023). Artificial Intelligence-powered digital solutions in the fashion industry: A mixed-methods study on AI-based Customer Services. *International Journal of Fashion Design, Technology and Education*, 17(2), 162–176. DOI: 10.1080/17543266.2023.2261019

Konina, N. Yu. (2023). Artificial Intelligence in the fashion industry—reality and prospects. Approaches to Global Sustainability, Markets, and Governance, 273–280. .DOI: 10.1007/978-981-99-2198-0_29

Kouslis, E., Papachristou, E., Stavropoulos, T. G., Papazoglou Chalikias, A., Chatzilari, E., Nikolopoulos, S., & Kompatsiaris, I. (2024). A in fashion: A literature review. *Electronic Commerce Research*. Advance online publication. DOI: 10.1007/s10660-024-09872-z

López-Forniés, I., & Asión-Suñer, L. (2024). Co-creation process with Generative Artificial Intelligence—an experiment in product design. Innovation and Technologies for the Digital Transformation of Education, 231–241. .DOI: 10.1007/978-981-97-2468-0_23

Meyer, P., Birregah, B., Beauseroy, P., Grall, E., & Lauxerrois, A. (2023). Missing body measurements prediction in Fashion Industry: A Comparative Approach. *Fashion and Textiles*, 10(1), 37. Advance online publication. DOI: 10.1186/s40691-023-00357-5

Shirkhani, S., Mokayed, H., Saini, R., & Chai, H. Y. (2023). Study of AI-Driven Fashion Recommender Systems. *SN Computer Science*, 4(5), 514. Advance online publication. DOI: 10.1007/s42979-023-01932-9

KEY TERMS AND DEFINITIONS

Brand Image: Perception the customer hold about the product or services.

Brand Identity: The elements like symbols, logo, design, overall visual and messaging style that the fashion brands use to distinguish themselves from their competitors in the fashion industry.

Co-creation: Collaboration between Customers and brands working together towards creating a product or service in the fashion industry.

Customer Experience: Feeling and perceptions that a customer experiences during and after his/her interaction with a fashion brand.

Fashion Brands: Fashion brands are businesses that have created a unique identity, image, perception in the mind of consumers which strengthen their value proposition with reference to design, style etc.

Fashion Trends: The prevailing looks, designs and styles that people are wearing and showcase current style at a given period are known as fashion trends.

Personalization: Personalization in the fashion industry refers to designing products or experiences that are customized to cater the tastes and requirements of each customer. This can entail offering individualized suggestions, making custom-fit garments, or letting clients select specific style, fit and designs.

Chapter 8
Converging Theories:
The Fusion of Artificial Intelligence and Sustainable Marketing for a Responsible Future

Luzia Arantes
https://orcid.org/0000-0003-1179-9113
Polytechnic University of Cávado and Ave, Portugal

Sandra Costa
https://orcid.org/0009-0007-4130-6523
Polytechnic University of Viseu, Portugal

ABSTRACT

Integrating Artificial Intelligence (AI) with sustainable marketing provides a transformative approach to fostering responsible business practices. This examination covers green, social, and critical marketing theories, illustrating how AI improves efficiency and personalisation in promoting sustainability. By leveraging AI, companies can better address consumer demands for eco-friendly products and services. The exploration includes practical applications such as predictive analytics, targeted marketing, and automated customer interactions, emphasising AI deployment's ethical considerations and challenges. The impact on corporate strategies and AI's contribution to achieving the UN Sustainable Development Goals are also highlighted. The complexities of merging AI with sustainable marketing are thoroughly evaluated, providing valuable insights into theoretical advancements and practical implications. Future research directions are suggested further to enhance the synergy between AI and sustainable marketing practices.

DOI: 10.4018/979-8-3693-5340-0.ch008

1. INTRODUCTION

Integrating sustainable marketing with artificial intelligence (AI) is emerging as one of the most innovative and necessary approaches to tackling contemporary global challenges. In a scenario where climate change, social inequality and the search for sustainable economic growth are pressing issues, bringing these two disciplines together offers a powerful solution. Companies that adopt these strategies can respond more effectively to market demands and, at the same time, promote practices that are environmentally responsible and socially just.

Sustainable marketing encompasses strategies such as green, social and critical marketing, all focussed on balancing economic objectives with environmental and social responsibilities. Integrating AI, which brings advanced capabilities such as predictive analytics, mass personalisation and process automation, can significantly amplify these strategies. The resulting synergy promises to transform companies' operations, making them more agile and aligned with the United Nations' Sustainable Development Goals (SDGs).

Research in this field primarily aims to explore the convergence between the theories of sustainable marketing and AI, highlighting how this integration can promote responsible business practices. It also sheds light on the practical applications of these theories in everyday business, demonstrating how they can be implemented to achieve tangible and positive results. It is also essential to address the ethical considerations and challenges associated with using these technologies, ensuring they are practical and responsible.

Providing an in-depth and practical understanding of how the fusion of sustainable marketing and AI can be harnessed is hoped to promote a more sustainable and just future. Companies that align their operations with these approaches improve their efficiency and effectiveness and contribute to building a more resilient and inclusive economy.

After this introduction, section 2 includes a literature review on sustainable marketing; section 3 discusses artificial intelligence in marketing; section 4 seeks to integrate AI and sustainable marketing by presenting a conceptual model; and section 5 presents the practical implications for business and the SDGs. Finally, conclusions, limitations and future research are presented.

2. SUSTAINABLE MARKETING - THEORY AND PRACTICE

2.1. Definition and Sub-disciplines

2.1.1. Green Marketing

Green marketing significantly facilitates sustainable products and services development and promotion by highlighting their environmental benefits and sustainably meeting customer and societal needs (Bhardwaj et al., 2023; Nadanyiova et al., 2020). It employs renewable resources and recyclable materials to minimise waste and environmental impact (Chung, 2020; Xu et al., 2015). Such strategies bolster the corporate image and improve business performance, reflecting a commitment to environmental responsibility (Gelderman et al., 2021). Moreover, green marketing is closely linked with sustainable consumption behaviour, which benefits both the environment and the economy (Mukonza & Swarts, 2020) and impacts professional buyer satisfaction and loyalty in a business-to-business context (Taufique, 2022). Despite its advantages, its acceptance varies across regions, which is evident from the mixed responses in communities and the social good. It tackles significant challenges like health inequities and environmental issues (Gordon et al., 2016; Shekhar, 2022) and is increasingly used by governments for public health goals, such as reducing vaccine hesitancy (Bakan, 2016; Kubacki & Szablewska, 2019).

2.1.2. Social Marketing

Social marketing's efficacy, however, hinges on a comprehensive understanding of environmental analysis, segmentation, and targeting, coupled with an awareness of the barriers to behavioural change (McAlindon, 2017; Pykett et al., 2014). Although effective in areas like global health and climate change, its limitations necessitate additional strategies for broader policy changes (Filiputti et al., 2013; Truong & Hall, 2017) and ethical concerns about its impact on public policy (Corner & Randall, 2011). Social marketing's focus extends beyond individual behaviour to foster critical thinking and political engagement (Firestone et al., 2017) and must avoid co-optation by mainstream marketing forces (Eagle et al., 2017).

2.1.2. Critical Marketing

Critical marketing critiques mainstream marketing's foundational assumptions and ideologies, incorporating critical social theory to examine the discipline's socio-cultural and political dimensions (Hackley, 2023). It promotes "resistant curiosity" among students, encouraging a reflective engagement with marketing practices aimed at social change (Gordon et al., 2022). This approach underscores the necessity of regulation and control in sustainability, leveraging communication strategies to foster sustainable attitudes and behaviours (Jain et al., 2023; Rakib et al., 2022). Additionally, employing anthropomorphic characters in environmental communication can enhance recycling attitudes and intentions, highlighting the importance of strategic communication in sustainability efforts (Primožič & Kutnar, 2022). Moreover, marketers are urged to proactively promote sustainability and curb irresponsible marketing practices that compromise sustainable consumption and production goals (Greenland et al., 2023).

2.2. Challenges and Opportunities

Companies face several commercial objectives when aligning their sustainability strategies, driven by internal and external factors. Internally, companies aim to enhance their competitive advantage and market performance by integrating sustainability into their corporate strategies. This involves adopting appropriate key performance indicators (KPIs) to effectively measure and manage sustainability efforts (Prataviera et al., 2023). Externally, companies are motivated by regulatory compliance, stakeholder expectations, and the need to protect their environmental reputation (Bager & Lambin, 2020). The alignment with the Sustainable Development Goals (SDGs) is also crucial, as it helps companies to identify and scale their positive impacts while mitigating negative ones, thereby ensuring long-term sustainability success (Taherdangkoo et al., 2017). Companies must know how to balance economic, social, and environmental interests to meet the growing demand for socially responsible products, directly influencing customer commitment and perceived value (Adams et al., 2023). Overall, integrating sustainability into corporate strategies is essential for companies to address the mounting expectations of stakeholders and to contribute meaningfully to global sustainability goals (Servera-Francés et al., 2020).

2.3. Role of Social Media

Social media significantly enhances sustainability engagement and transparency through its interactive and extensive reach, facilitating the dissemination of companies' sustainability initiatives and fostering trust through transparent dialogues with stakeholders (Garner & Mady, 2023). Transparent communication on social media has been shown to increase change in user behaviour towards sustainability, as seen in a Qatar study where CSR credibility positively influences consumer attitudes and purchase intentions (Lee & Chung, 2023). Moreover, social media campaigns have demonstrated the potential to educate, and social media experiments have increased sustainable habits among participants (Berne-Manero & Marzo-Navarro, 2020).

However, challenges remain, such as mismatches between the sustainability messages posted and audience engagement (Cortese et al., 2021) and low interaction levels in university-led initiatives like those at the University of Florence (Gori et al., 2020). In China, energy companies utilise social media differently from traditional reports, focusing on stakeholders like investors and employees (Zhong & Wang, 2023). In the fashion industry, sustainable brands find that expressive and directive posts enhance engagement (Zhao et al., 2022), and influencer marketing can significantly boost engagement due to the emotional projection skills of influencers (Al-Mulla et al., 2022). Companies are also advised to tailor their communication strategies to the specific preferences of different social media platforms (Rodak, 2020).

Transparent CSR communication on platforms like social media enhances CSR credibility and impacts consumer behaviour by emphasising sustainability, responsibility, and personal norms, thereby influencing brand loyalty (Lee & Chung, 2023; Machado & Goswami, 2023). Additionally, the perception of sustainability has been found to positively affect customer loyalty and trust, with customer engagement acting as a mediator between perceived sustainability and trust (Mim et al., 2022). Thus, effectively communicating sustainability initiatives via social media is crucial for building trust, enhancing loyalty, and engaging consumers.

2.4. Collaboration for Sustainable Marketing

Collaboration among stakeholders is crucial for sustainable marketing because it effectively leverages diverse perspectives, resources, and expertise to address complex sustainability challenges. Stakeholders such as non-governmental organisations, competitors, and governmental bodies drive and facilitate the implementation of sustainable supply chain management practices, enhancing organisational learning and capability development (Siems et al., 2023). Engaging stakeholders in a company's management positively impacts green competitiveness by improving communication and incorporating stakeholders' suggestions into green policies (Lyulyov et al., 2023). Firms benefit from collaboration with external partners like scientific partners, suppliers, and customers, which increases the likelihood of eco-innovation and sustainability (Acebo et al., 2021). The roles of consumers, companies, and policymakers are interconnected, with companies' sustainable practices and government regulations significantly influencing consumer attitudes and purchase intentions toward sustainable products (Abutaleb & El-Bassiouny, 2020). Organisations must engage in collaborative partnerships for sustainability, considering how stakeholders affect and are affected by their efforts, to drive meaningful changes in organisational practices (Fobbe, 2020). Thus, stakeholder collaboration is indispensable for achieving comprehensive and effective sustainable marketing practices.

3. ARTIFICIAL INTELLIGENCE IN MARKETING

3.1. AI Overview and Evolution

Artificial intelligence (AI) has rapidly developed over recent decades, significantly impacting areas like marketing. AI began with basic tasks like mathematical operations and evolved into complex decision-making systems. This initial phase automated simple tasks, enhancing efficiency and reducing errors (Su et al., 2021). Since emerging as an academic field in the 1950s, AI has aimed to replicate tasks traditionally requiring human intelligence (Howard & Howard, 2019; Jones et al., 2018). Despite periods of reduced enthusiasm known as "AI winters," recent decades have seen substantial progress due to advances in computing power, machine learning algorithms, and data availability (Harguess & Ward, 2022; Mustak et al., 2021).

With machine learning, AI has moved to learning from data, tackling more complex tasks like pattern recognition and outcome prediction. This includes applications in computer vision and natural language processing (Aksu, 2019; Vásquez et al., 2023). The Big Data era and cloud computing have further accelerated AI development, enabling sophisticated predictive models that have been particularly transformative in digital marketing (Keegan et al., 2022; Su et al., 2021).

Modern AI systems can autonomously make complex decisions using deep learning and convolutional neural networks. This capability extends to medical diagnostics and autonomous vehicles, highlighting AI's precision and critical decision-making roles (Haldorai et al., 2021; Talib et al., 2021). However, AI's integration across sectors raises ethical and governance challenges, including concerns over transparency, privacy, and the social impacts of automation. Addressing these requires robust ethical frameworks alongside technological advancements (Fenwick et al., 2023; Montes & Goertzel, 2019).

Figure 1 shows a timeline of the evolution of AI, starting in 1950 and running until 2022. It highlights significant events, such as the development of the "Turing Test" by Alan Turing in 1950, the creation of the first chatbot, Eliza, in 1966, and the introduction of the term "AI" by John McCarthy in 1956. The timeline also mentions essential milestones, such as the creation of the first "electronic person", Shakey, in 1970, the commercial use of AI by XCON in 1980, and the development of deep learning in 2000. Other notable events include Deep Blue's victory over world chess champion Garry Kasparov in 1997, the popularisation of deep neural networks in

2006, AlphaGo's victory in 2016, and the launch of GPT-3 in 2020. The timeline concludes with popularising generative AI models such as DALL-E 2 in 2022.

Figure 1. Timeline of the main milestones in the evolution of AI

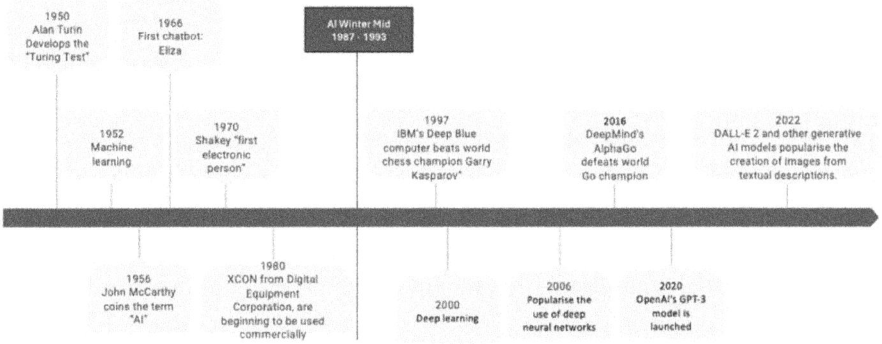

(Kaul et al., 2020)

AI's evolution has revolutionised marketing, enhancing how companies engage with customers and manage operations. From personalising campaigns to automating processes and improving predictive analytics, AI significantly boosts marketing efficiency and effectiveness. Its ongoing advancements promise to shape marketing's future further.

3.2. AI Capabilities in Marketing

The application of AI in marketing has significantly evolved with the advent of big data and machine learning, enhancing capabilities from fundamental data analysis to sophisticated tasks like mass personalisation and behaviour prediction. Predictive marketing now enables personalised sales techniques on a large scale by analysing massive data sets (Kotras, 2020).

Recent advances in AI technologies, such as deep learning and neural networks, have further increased the accuracy and effectiveness of marketing strategies. For example, deep learning algorithms can process unstructured data such as images, videos and social media posts, providing more in-depth information about consumer behaviour and preferences. Natural language processing (NLP) tools have become increasingly sophisticated, enabling more accurate sentiment analysis and customer engagement through chatbots and virtual assistants (Alsiehemy, 2023).

Marketing automation benefits from AI, streamlining processes such as email campaigns and social media management, thus saving resources (Chopra & Sharma, 2021). Additionally, AI's predictive analytics capabilities have advanced, allowing marketers to more accurately anticipate future trends and consumer behaviours. This enables proactive adjustments to marketing strategies, ensuring they remain relevant and effective in dynamic market environments (Petrescu et al., 2022).

Chatbots and virtual assistants exemplify AI's transformation of customer interactions by providing round-the-clock service and handling basic inquiries, enhancing customer experience and optimising human resources (Milana & Ashta, 2021). Advances in conversational AI now allow these tools to manage more complex interactions, providing a more personalised and human-like experience (Milana & Ashta, 2021). AI also aids in sentiment analysis on social networks, helping companies understand consumer perceptions (Kim et al., 2024), and in dynamic price optimisation, adjusting prices based on market conditions (Liu & Chen, 2023).

In advertising, AI revolutionises ad placements through programmatic advertising, increasing efficiency and effectiveness (Chen & Feng, 2021). AI also contributes to content creation, generating texts, images, and videos, alleviating the creative burden on teams (Ricca et al., 2021). AI-driven business intelligence analyses vast data volumes, providing insights for strategic decisions (Kumar et al., 2022).

AI's real-time data analysis supports adaptive marketing, enabling quick responses to market shifts and consumer trends (Vlačić et al., 2021). By forecasting market conditions and customer needs, predictive analytics allows for optimised resource allocation and minimises waste, aligning with sustainability goals (Dotsika & Watkins, 2017; Shirazi & Mohammadi, 2019).

Companies leverage AI for efficient, sustainable marketing strategies, tailoring efforts to consumer preferences and reducing the carbon footprint of traditional advertising methods. AI also minimises waste by aligning product offerings with consumer expectations, improving targeting in marketing campaigns, increasing investment returns, and reducing environmental impacts. AI-driven sustainability tools now include systems that optimise supply chain logistics to reduce emissions and waste, demonstrating AI's critical role in promoting environmentally friendly business practices (Al-Surmi et al., 2022; Alzahrani et al., 2022; Yang et al., 2021).

3.3. AI in Responsible Consumption and Production

Integrating AI into marketing operations is becoming crucial for companies aiming to meet sustainability goals, particularly in reducing waste and overproduction. Through advanced data analysis and machine learning, AI enables more accurate consumer demand predictions, which are vital for minimising waste and aligning production with market demand (Carbonneau et al., 2008). This capability prevents overproduction and enhances sustainable production indicators at the factory level (Winroth et al., 2016).

AI also improves procurement efficiency, allowing for the management of sustainable sourcing under supplier uncertainty. AI optimises procurement decisions by analysing risk factors and matching material purchases with production needs to avoid excess (Mirzajani et al., 2024). In production planning, AI optimises energy resource use, reducing energy consumption and the carbon footprint of manufacturing processes (Yildirim & Mouzon, 2012).

The dynamic nature of AI supports adjustments in production plans based on real-time market data, enhancing responsiveness to demand fluctuations and reducing resource waste (Ganjavi & Fazlollahtabar, 2023). AI also advances reverse logistics by optimising the collection, processing, and redistribution of returned goods, fostering a circular economy (Aryee & Adaku, 2023).

In supply chain management, AI increases sustainability by enhancing the accuracy of demand forecasting and improving decision-making processes, which leads to more sustainable outcomes (Birou et al., 2019; Carlucci et al., 2023). AI supports sustainable production by optimising raw material and energy use, contributing to reduced environmental impacts (Baah et al., 2021).

Additionally, AI optimises transportation networks within logistics, improving routing and scheduling, which reduces fuel consumption and emissions (Yildiz et al., 2019). It also improves the efficiency and reliability of energy distribution in innovative grid technologies (Ghadimi et al., 2018).

In agriculture, AI-driven models optimise resource use and improve yield predictions, allowing farmers to make informed decisions about planting and resource allocation, thus minimising environmental impacts (De Buck et al., 1999). AI also plays a role in urban planning, contributing to the development of smart cities where resources are managed efficiently, waste is reduced, and the quality of life is enhanced (Abdullah et al., 2017).

In conclusion, integrating AI into marketing and supply chain management significantly enhances the ability of companies to achieve sustainable objectives. By improving demand forecasting, optimising resource use, and facilitating efficient procurement and logistics, AI helps reduce waste, lower emissions, and promote sustainable production systems. This reflects AI-driven approaches' broad applicability and critical importance in addressing modern sustainability challenges.

4. INTEGRATING AI AND SUSTAINABLE MARKETING - THEORETICAL COMPLEXITY AND ADAPTATION

4.1. Theoretical Complexity and Ethical Considerations

AI's integration into marketing marks a revolutionary shift, particularly in formulating and executing sustainable marketing strategies. Sustainable marketing involves aligning commercial objectives with environmental and social responsibilities, divided into green, social, and critical marketing. Green marketing develops eco-friendly products, while social marketing promotes sustainable behaviors, and critical marketing emphasizes the need for regulatory measures for sustainability (Demessie & Shukla, 2024; Idnay et al., 2024; Vo & Nguyen-Anh, 2024).

Incorporating AI in sustainable marketing enhances campaign personalization, efficiency, and the ability to anticipate consumer trends, allowing for proactive strategy adjustments (Han et al., 2023; Hermann, 2021; van Esch & Stewart Black, 2021). However, this integration also presents ethical challenges, including transparency, privacy, and potential data biases that could lead to exclusionary practices. Companies must develop robust ethical frameworks to manage these risks responsibly (Allil, 2024; Osifo, 2023; Vlačić et al., 2021; Zhu, 2022; Zohny et al., 2023).

AI-driven sustainable marketing also significantly supports the UN's Sustainable Development Goals (SDGs), particularly SDG 9 (Industry, Innovation and Infrastructure) and SDG 12 (Responsible Consumption and Production), by promoting efficient production and consumption practices. This helps reduce carbon footprints and enhance the sustainable use of resources, thus contributing to a circular economy (Bhatia et al., 2023; De Buck et al., 1999; Khan et al., 2020; Xinxing et al., 2023).

Moreover, AI optimizes supply chain management and facilitates reverse logistics, enhancing the recycling and reuse of materials and reducing environmental impacts (Aryee & Adaku, 2023; Carlucci et al., 2023). The practical implications of AI in sustainable marketing are vast, improving operational efficiency and aligning with the values of consumers increasingly focused on sustainability. This meets consumer expectations and fosters responsible and sustainable business practices (Y. Xu et al., 2020; Yang et al., 2021)

Innovation driven by AI in sustainable marketing also impacts corporate governance and social responsibility, where transparency and accountability are crucial to maintaining consumer trust. AI can provide detailed environmental and social performance analyses, enabling informed stakeholder decisions (Dwivedi et al., 2021; He, 2023).

In summary, while the fusion of AI with sustainable marketing introduces complexities and ethical considerations, it offers significant potential to enhance marketing efficiency and effectiveness and promote environmental and social sustainability. It is imperative to navigate these challenges thoughtfully to ensure that AI technologies are used responsibly and inclusively.

4.2. Adapting Existing Theories to New Paradigms

Traditional marketing has evolved significantly over the 20th century, underpinned by several foundational theories that have shaped companies' approaches to consumers and markets. One of the most influential is Abraham Maslow's Hierarchy of Needs Theory (1943), which suggests that human beings have a progression of needs from physiological to self-actualization. Understanding these needs allows marketers to tailor their strategies effectively (Khan & Pandey, 2023).

As shown in Table 1, other crucial theories include Wendell Smith's Market Segmentation Theory (1956), which argues that markets are not homogeneous but can be segmented into distinct groups with specific needs. This insight is fundamental for targeted and personalized marketing strategies (Smith, 1956). Jerome McCarthy's Four P's Theory (1960) further refines this approach by defining the essential elements of the marketing mix—Product, Price, Place, and Promotion — as crucial for meeting consumer needs and differentiating from competitors (McCarthy, 1960).

The understanding of consumer behavior is also enriched by the Theory of Buyer Behavior by John Howard and Jagdish Sheth (1969), which describes the consumer decision-making process and considers psychological, social, and cultural influences. This theory suggests that consumer behavior is a complex learning process where past experiences and acquired information influence future decisions (Howard & Sheth, 1969). Finally, Michael Porter's Theory of Competitive Advantage (1985) focuses on how companies can gain an edge over competitors through cost leadership, differentiation, and focus, which is fundamental to developing effective marketing strategies (Porter, 1985).

Table 1. Leading theories of traditional marketing

Theory	Author	Concept
Hierarchy of Needs Theory	Abraham Maslow's (1943)	Hierarchical structure of human needs, from basic to self-realisation.
Market Segmentation Theory	Wendell Smith (1956)	Dividing the market into distinct segments with specific needs.
P's Theory	Jerome McCarthy (1960)	We are identifying the four essential elements of marketing: Product, Price, Place and Promotion.
Theory of Buyer Behavior	John Howard and Jagdish Sheth (1969)	The consumer decision-making process is influenced by psychological, social and cultural factors.

continued on following page

Table 1. Continued

Theory	Author	Concept
Theory of Competitive Advantage	Michael Porter (1985)	Cost leadership, differentiation and focus are strategies for gaining an advantage over competitors.

Source: Authors.

Parallel to the evolution of traditional marketing theories, the development of AI has introduced several innovative models that have transformed how machines learn and interact with data. These models have significantly impacted various domains, including marketing.

As shown in Table 2, the Perceptron, introduced by Frank Rosenblatt, is one of the first neural network models. This model was fundamental in laying the foundations for AI, especially in areas related to visual pattern recognition (Rosenblatt, 1958). The 1980s marked significant progress with the introduction of the Backpropagation algorithm by Rumelhart et al. (1986), which is a method for training artificial neural networks by adjusting the weights of the connections based on the error of the predicted results (Rumelhart et al., 1986).

These advancements are paralleled by other critical developments such as Support Vector Machines (SVM) introduced by Vapnik & Lerner (1963), Convolutional Neural Networks (CNN) by LeCun et al. (1998) and more recent innovations like Generative Adversarial Networks (GANs) by Goodfellow et al. (2014), the Transformer architecture by Vaswani et al. (2017) and models like BERT and GPT by Devlin et al. (2018) and Radford and Narasimhan (2018) respectively. Each of these AI models has contributed uniquely to the development of more intelligent and efficient technologies, enhancing the ability of machines to learn, adapt, and interact with the world in increasingly sophisticated ways.

Table 2. Main AI models

Model	Author	Concept
Perceptron	Rosenblatt (1958)	It was a pioneering neural network model that recognises patterns and learns from examples.
Backpropagation	Rumelhart et al. (1896)	Supervised learning method used for classification and regression.
Support Vector Machines (SVM)	Vapnik and Lerner (1963)	We are identifying the four essential elements of marketing: Product, Price, Place and Promotion.
Convolutional Neural Networks (CNN)	LeCun et al. (1998)	The deep learning model is particularly effective for image recognition tasks.
Long Short-Term Memory (LSTM)	Hochreiter and Schmidhuber (1997)	Recurrent neural network architecture that addresses the vanishing gradient problem by modelling long-term dependencies.

continued on following page

Table 2. Continued

Model	Author	Concept
Generative Adversarial Networks (GAN)	Goodfellow et al. (2014)	A model comprises two neural networks competing to generate new and realistic data.
AlphaGo	Silver et al. (2016)	AI system that beats human champions in the game of Go uses reinforcement learning and deep neural networks.
Transformer	Ashish Vaswani et al. (2017)	AI system that beats human champions in the game of Go uses reinforcement learning and deep neural networks.
BERT (Bidirectional Encoder Representations from Transformers)	Devlin et al. (2018)	Pre-trained language model that captures the context of words in both senses.
GPT (Generative Pre-trained Transformer)	Radford et al. (2018)	Language model that uses the Transformer architecture for text generation based on unsupervised learning.

Source: Authors.

Integrating AI into marketing enhances campaign efficiency and effectiveness but requires adapting traditional theories to include sustainability considerations. This integration aligns business goals with environmental and social responsibilities, making marketing efforts more effective and more responsible in the context of global sustainability challenges.

Ethical use of AI is essential to avoid biases and ensure transparency and accountability (Osifo, 2023). AI's role in sustainable production practices supports the UN's Sustainable Development Goals, particularly in optimizing resource use and promoting a circular economy (Carlucci et al., 2023).

4.3. Critical Evaluation of AI and Sustainability Theories

Integrating AI with sustainable marketing practices represents a pioneering approach to business strategy, blending advanced technological applications with an acute awareness of environmental and societal needs. This convergence of AI and sustainable marketing is detailed in a conceptual framework (Figure 2) that maps out potential synergistic relationships and areas where challenges may arise. This framework critically examines how AI can be harmonised with sustainable marketing to enhance business sustainability and ethical practices (Bhardwaj et al., 2023; Nadanyiova et al., 2020).

This integration's core is the theoretical alignment with critical marketing paradigms—green, social, and critical marketing. Green marketing initiatives leverage AI to enhance the development of products that are not only environmentally friendly but also economically viable, ensuring that businesses can meet the increasing consumer demand for sustainable options. This approach optimises resource use and minimises waste through improved supply chain efficiencies and better forecasting models (Bhardwaj et al., 2023; Nadanyiova et al., 2020). Conversely, social marketing benefits from AI's ability to dissect large datasets to identify and engage specific demographics, thereby driving campaigns that promote sustainable behaviours more effectively (Gordon et al., 2016; Shekhar, 2022). Meanwhile, critical marketing uses AI to foster transparency and uphold ethical standards, helping companies navigate the complexities of sustainability claims and avoid the pitfalls of greenwashing (Hackley, 2023).

The practical applications of AI in marketing are numerous and varied. Predictive analytics stand out by providing companies with the tools to anticipate consumer behaviour and market trends, thus allowing for more precise targeting and customisation of marketing efforts (Keegan et al., 2022). Moreover, AI-driven technologies such as chatbots and virtual assistants enhance customer interaction, offering tailored experiences that align seamlessly with the overarching goals of sustainable marketing (Milana & Ashta, 2021).

However, the integration of AI within marketing must address ethical considerations. Issues such as transparency in AI processes, the mitigation of biases within algorithms, and the protection of consumer privacy are paramount. Ensuring that transparent AI systems help build trust and foster a responsible corporate image (Osifo, 2023) while addressing biases and privacy concerns, safeguarding consumer rights, and promoting inclusivity (Allil, 2024; Keegan et al., 2022).

Technological and operational Integration focuses on enhancing the scalability and efficiency of marketing initiatives. Advanced AI models like Convolutional Neural Networks, Generative Adversarial Networks, and various Transformer models, including BERT and GPT, are at the forefront of this drive, offering innovative solutions that push the boundaries of what can be achieved in marketing analytics and customer engagement (Aksu, 2019; Devlin et al., 2018).

Figure 2. Framework for evaluating the integration of AI and sustainable marketing theories

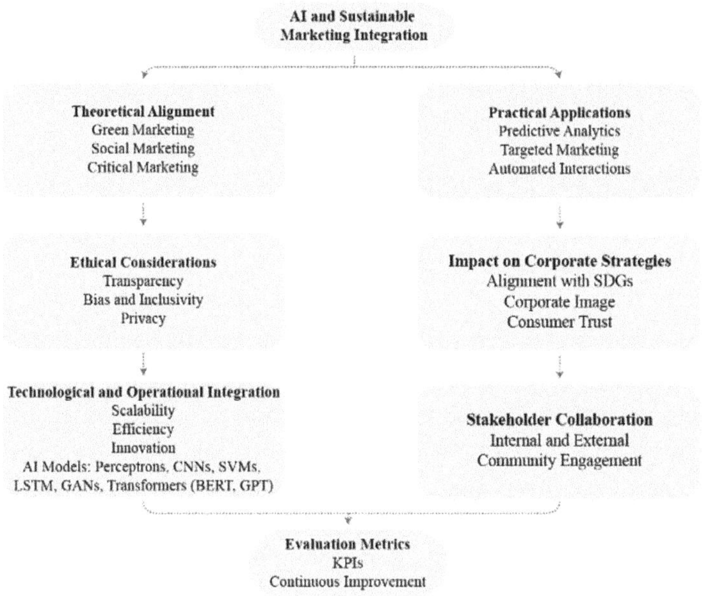

(Authors)

The Impact on corporate strategies is profound. AI's role in sustainable marketing aligns closely with the Sustainable Development Goals (SDGs), particularly those focused on responsible consumption and production. By integrating AI, companies boost their corporate image and enhance consumer trust through demonstrated commitments to ethical practices and transparency (Bhatia et al., 2023; Machado & Goswami, 2023).

Stakeholder collaboration is crucial, involving both internal and external parties in a dialogue and joint efforts towards sustainability. Effective engagement with all stakeholders, from consumers and employees to the broader community, enriches the marketing initiatives and amplifies their impact. Social media platforms enable real-time communication and foster community involvement in sustainable practices (Garner & Mady, 2023; Siems et al., 2023).

Lastly, the importance of evaluation metrics cannot be understated. Establishing robust key performance indicators allows businesses to measure the effectiveness of their AI-driven sustainable marketing strategies. This continuous assessment ensures that the marketing efforts remain effective and aligned with long-term sustainability goals (Prataviera et al., 2023).

In conclusion, this narrative framework maps the integration of AI with sustainable marketing and underscores the potential for innovative and responsible business practices. By aligning advanced technological applications with robust ethical standards and community engagement, companies are poised to achieve enhanced marketing efficacy and broader sustainability objectives, paving the way for a more sustainable and responsible future in business.

5. PRACTICAL IMPLICATIONS AND INNOVATIONS

5.1. Impact on Business Practices

Integrating AI into sustainable marketing has catalysed innovative practices across various sectors, enhancing efficiency and sustainability. In the fashion industry, AI-driven apps promote sustainable consumer choices by providing insights into products' ecological impacts and reshaping corporate strategies (Bolesnikov et al., 2022). In the energy sector, AI applications bolster environmental management and operational efficiency, aiding in achieving Sustainable Development Goals related to clean energy and climate action (Naz et al., 2022; Waqar et al., 2023). AI enhances sustainable supply chains by optimising logistics and reducing waste (Thamik & Wu, 2022). However, AI's use in consumer markets necessitates addressing ethical and social challenges to maintain responsible practices (Chaudhuri et al., 2022). AI, supported by technological and leadership initiatives, significantly boosts sustainability efforts for SMEs, especially in manufacturing (Chutcheva et al., 2022). AI helps biodiversity and resource conservation in food systems but requires careful management of its carbon footprint and biases (Kindylidi & Cabral, 2021). Social media strategies involving AI focus on green and sustainable marketing, vital for engaging consumers (Camaréna, 2021). In energy systems, tools like the Collaborative Energy Optimization Platform optimise energy use for sustainability (Dash et al., 2023).

To achieve responsible consumption and innovation, integrating AI with Life Cycle Engineering can systematically improve productivity while meeting economic and environmental goals (Atabekova et al., 2022). Companies must also be cautious of AI's potential adverse effects, such as bias and ethical issues, advocating for a harmonised regulatory approach for sustainable AI use (Bolesnikov et al., 2022). Responsible AI practices should emphasise fairness, transparency, and accountability, with some firms developing tools to support these principles and pushing for regulatory oversight on high-risk AI (Zhao & Gómez Fariñas, 2023). In sectors like construction and oil and gas, AI's adoption is often driven by its functional value and reliability (Memon & Ooi, 2022). Firms balancing CSR with AI can optimise resource use and mitigate risks associated with corporate social responsibility (Khan et al., 2023). Companies should adopt responsible innovation frameworks to ensure environmentally friendly and socially responsible AI advancements, enhancing information transparency and aligning policies for a sustainable AI lifecycle (Kindylidi & Cabral, 2021; Li et al., 2021). These approaches enable companies to pursue responsible industrial innovation with AI effectively.

5.2. Contribution to UN SDGs

Businesses can actively support Sustainable Development Goals (SDGs) 9 (Industry, Innovation, and Infrastructure) and 12 (Responsible Consumption and Production) by implementing a layered approach that integrates advanced technologies, sustainable supply chain management, and cross-sector collaborations. Adopting reconfigurable manufacturing systems and Industry 4.0 technologies enables customization and rapid capacity adjustments, fostering sustainable industrialization (Pansare et al., 2023). Small- to medium-sized enterprises (SMEs) are pivotal in aligning with these SDGs, though they often need external support due to limited resources (Nygaard et al., 2022). Enhanced stakeholder awareness and preference for SDG-aligned companies can motivate businesses to meet sustainable expectations (Yamane & Kaneko, 2022).

Academic studies emphasize the need for sustainable business models that integrate economic, environmental, and social dimensions, which include improving worker well-being and creating sustainable ecosystems (Martínez-Falcó et al., 2023). Innovations in procurement and distribution within sustainable supply chains can boost market and organizational performance, aligning with the 2030 Agenda (Ordonez-Ponce et al., 2021). Local sustainability partnerships are crucial for achieving local and global SDGs, showcasing the benefits of cooperative efforts (Bonfanti et al., 2023). Integrating technology, innovation, education, and human resource management into business strategies is vital for fulfilling all 17 UN SDGs, particularly SDGs 9 and 12 (Cammarano et al., 2022). Businesses are encouraged to adopt comprehensive sustainable practices in all supply chain activities to improve human lives, the environment, and economic outcomes (Lee & Zhou, 2022). By embedding such practices, businesses can significantly contribute to sustainable growth and development.

6. CONCLUSION

Integrating artificial intelligence (AI) with sustainable marketing practices marks a revolutionary stride towards addressing global challenges such as climate change, social inequality, and sustainable economic growth. By marrying these two disciplines, companies enhance their ability to meet market demands and promote environmentally responsible and socially equitable practices. This synergy significantly amplifies traditional marketing strategies such as green, social, and critical marketing, integrating advanced capabilities like predictive analytics, mass personalisation, and automated processes. These innovations promise to make companies more agile, significantly aligned with the United Nations' Sustainable Development Goals (SDGs), and responsive to the dynamic market environment.

The discussion throughout this exploration illustrates the extensive potential and practical applications of blending AI with sustainable marketing, highlighting the profound impact on business operations across various sectors. By navigating the associated ethical considerations and strategically implementing these technologies, companies can significantly improve their efficiency and effectiveness and contribute to a more resilient and inclusive economic system.

Ultimately, integrating AI into sustainable marketing is not just about technological advancement but also about fostering a more sustainable and just global community. This endeavour not only reshapes businesses to be more innovative and responsible but also sets a foundational model for future research and practical applications that could further transform the landscape of global business practices towards sustainability.

REFERENCES

Abdullah, I., Mahmood, W. H. W., Fauadi, H. F. M., Rahman, M. N. A., & Mohamed, S. B. (2017). Sustainable manufacturing practices in Malaysian palm oil mills: Priority and current performance. *Journal of Manufacturing Technology Management*, 28(3), 278–298. DOI: 10.1108/JMTM-09-2016-0128

Abutaleb, S., & El-Bassiouny, N. (2020). Assessing sustainability marketing from macromarketing perspective: A multistakeholder approach. *World Journal of Entrepreneurship, Management and Sustainable Development*, 16(4), 287–305. DOI: 10.1108/WJEMSD-02-2019-0017

Acebo, E., Miguel-Dávila, J.-Á., & Nieto, M. (2021). External stakeholder engagement: Complementary and substitutive effects on firms' eco-innovation. *Business Strategy and the Environment*, 30(5), 2671–2687. DOI: 10.1002/bse.2770

Adams, D., Donovan, J., & Topple, C. (2023). Sustainability in large food and beverage companies and their supply chains: An investigation into key drivers and barriers affecting sustainability strategies. *Business Strategy and the Environment*, 32(4), 1451–1463. DOI: 10.1002/bse.3198

Aksu, O. (2019). Artificial Intelligence in the Era of Transhumanism Smart Phones. In *Handbook of Research on Learning in the Age of Transhumanism* (pp. 157–170). IGI Global., DOI: 10.4018/978-1-5225-8431-5.ch010

Al-Mulla, S., Ari, I., & Koç, M. (2022). Social media for sustainability education: Gaining knowledge and skills into actions for sustainable living. *International Journal of Sustainable Development and World Ecology*, 29(5), 455–471. DOI: 10.1080/13504509.2022.2036856

Al-Surmi, A., Bashiri, M., & Koliousis, I. (2022). AI based decision making: Combining strategies to improve operational performance. *International Journal of Production Research*, 60(14), 4464–4486. DOI: 10.1080/00207543.2021.1966540

Allil, K. (2024). Integrating AI-driven marketing analytics techniques into the classroom: pedagogical strategies for enhancing student engagement and future business success. *Journal of Marketing Analytics*, 1–27. doi:.DOI: 10.1057/S41270-023-00281-Z/METRICS

Alsiehemy, A. (2023). Emergence of {Digital} {Marketing} in {Current} {Scenario} and {Implementation} of {AI} to {Improve} the {Productivity} of a {Concern}. *Pacific Business Review International*, 15(7), 19–27.

Alzahrani, M. E., Aldhyani, T. H. H., Alsubari, S. N., Althobaiti, M. M., & Fahad, A. (2022). Developing an Intelligent System with Deep Learning Algorithms for Sentiment Analysis of E-Commerce Product Reviews. *Computational Intelligence and Neuroscience*, 2022, 1–10. Advance online publication. DOI: 10.1155/2022/3840071 PMID: 35669644

Aryee, R., & Adaku, E. (2023). The reverse logistics resource matrix: A novel classification scheme. *Journal of Manufacturing Technology Management*, 34(3), 435–454. DOI: 10.1108/JMTM-06-2022-0226

Atabekova, N. K., Dzedik, V. A., Troyanskaya, M. A., & Matytsin, D. E. (2022). The role of education and social policy in the development of responsible production and consumption in the AI economy. *Frontiers in Environmental Science*, 10, 929193. Advance online publication. DOI: 10.3389/fenvs.2022.929193

Baah, C., Opoku-Agyeman, D., Acquah, I. S. K., Issau, K., & Moro Abdoulaye, F. A. (2021). Understanding the influence of environmental production practices on firm performance: A proactive versus reactive approach. *Journal of Manufacturing Technology Management*, 32(2), 266–289. DOI: 10.1108/JMTM-05-2020-0195

Bager, S. L., & Lambin, E. F. (2020). Sustainability strategies by companies in the global coffee sector. *Business Strategy and the Environment*, 29(8), 3555–3570. DOI: 10.1002/bse.2596

Bakan, J. (2016). Social marketing: Thoughts from an empathetic outsider. *Journal of Marketing Management*, 32(11–12), 1183–1189. DOI: 10.1080/0267257X.2016.1171035

Berne-Manero, C., & Marzo-Navarro, M. (2020). Exploring How Influencer and Relationship Marketing Serve Corporate Sustainability. *Sustainability (Basel)*, 12(11), 4392. Advance online publication. DOI: 10.3390/su12114392

Bhardwaj, S., Nair, K., Tariq, M. U., Ahmad, A., & Chitnis, A. (2023). The State of Research in Green Marketing: A Bibliometric Review from 2005 to 2022. *Sustainability (Basel)*, 15(4), 2988. Advance online publication. DOI: 10.3390/su15042988

Bhatia, L., Jha, H., Sarkar, T., & Sarangi, P. K. (2023). Food Waste Utilization for Reducing Carbon Footprints towards Sustainable and Cleaner Environment: A Review. *International Journal of Environmental Research and Public Health*, 20(3), 2318. DOI: 10.3390/ijerph20032318 PMID: 36767685

Birou, L. M., Green, K. W., & Inman, R. A. (2019). Sustainability knowledge and training: Outcomes and firm performance. *Journal of Manufacturing Technology Management*, 30(2), 294–311. DOI: 10.1108/JMTM-05-2018-0148

Bolesnikov, M., Popović Stijačić, M., Keswani, A. B., & Brkljač, N. (2022). Perception of Innovative Usage of AI in Optimizing Customer Purchasing Experience within the Sustainable Fashion Industry. *Sustainability (Basel)*, 14(16), 10082. Advance online publication. DOI: 10.3390/su141610082

Bonfanti, A., Mion, G., Brunetti, F., & Vargas-Sánchez, A. (2023). The contribution of manufacturing companies to the achievement of sustainable development goals: An empirical analysis of the operationalization of sustainable business models. *Business Strategy and the Environment*, 32(4), 2490–2508. DOI: 10.1002/bse.3260

Camaréna, S. (2021). Engaging with Artificial Intelligence (AI) with a Bottom-Up Approach for the Purpose of Sustainability: Victorian Farmers Market Association, Melbourne Australia. *Sustainability*, 13(16). Advance online publication. DOI: 10.3390/su13169314

Cammarano, A., Perano, M., Michelino, F., Del Regno, C., & Caputo, M. (2022). SDG-Oriented Supply Chains: Business Practices for Procurement and Distribution. *Sustainability (Basel)*, 14(3), 1325. Advance online publication. DOI: 10.3390/su14031325

Carbonneau, R., Laframboise, K., & Vahidov, R. (2008). Application of machine learning techniques for supply chain demand forecasting. *European Journal of Operational Research*, 184(3), 1140–1154. DOI: 10.1016/j.ejor.2006.12.004

Carlucci, D., Renna, P., & Materi, S. (2023). A Job-Shop Scheduling Decision-Making Model for Sustainable Production Planning With Power Constraint. *IEEE Transactions on Engineering Management*, 70(5), 1923–1932. DOI: 10.1109/TEM.2021.3103108

Casarejos, F., Frota, M. N., Rocha, J. E., Da Silva, W. R., & Barreto, J. T. (2016). Corporate Sustainability Strategies: A Case Study in Brazil Focused on High Consumers of Electricity. *Sustainability (Basel)*, 8(8), 791. Advance online publication. DOI: 10.3390/su8080791

Chaudhuri, R., Chatterjee, S., Vrontis, D., & Chaudhuri, S. (2022). Innovation in SMEs, AI Dynamism, and Sustainability: The Current Situation and Way Forward. *Sustainability (Basel)*, 14(19), 12760. Advance online publication. DOI: 10.3390/su141912760

Chen, Y., & Feng, S. (2021). Artificial Intelligence: Creating More Possibilities for Programmatic Advertising. In *Proceedings of the AHFE 2021 Virtual Conferences on Human Factors in Software and Systems Engineering, Artificial Intelligence and Social Computing, and Energy* (pp. 148–155), July 25-29, 2021, USA. Springer. DOI: 10.1007/978-3-030-80624-8_19

Chopra, R., & Sharma, G. D. (2021). Application of Artificial Intelligence in Stock Market Forecasting: A Critique, Review, and Research Agenda. *Journal of Risk and Financial Management*, 14(11), 526. DOI: 10.3390/jrfm14110526

Chung, K. C. (2020). Green marketing orientation: Achieving sustainable development in green hotel management. *Journal of Hospitality Marketing & Management*, 29(6), 722–738. DOI: 10.1080/19368623.2020.1693471

Chutcheva, Y. V., Kuprianova, L. M., Seregina, A. A., & Kukushkin, S. N. (2022). Environmental management of companies in the oil and gas markets based on AI for sustainable development: An international review. *Frontiers in Environmental Science*, 10, 952102. DOI: 10.3389/fenvs.2022.952102

Corner, A., & Randall, A. (2011). Selling climate change? The limitations of social marketing as a strategy for climate change public engagement. *Global Environmental Change*, 21(3), 1005–1014. DOI: 10.1016/j.gloenvcha.2011.05.002

Cortese, D., Rainero, C., & Cantino, V. (2021). Stakeholders' social dialogue about responsibility and sustainability in the food sector. *British Food Journal*, 123(3), 1287–1301. DOI: 10.1108/BFJ-11-2019-0826

Dash, G., Sharma, C., & Sharma, S. (2023). Sustainable Marketing and the Role of Social Media: An Experimental Study Using Natural Language Processing (NLP). *Sustainability (Basel)*, 15(6), 5443. Advance online publication. DOI: 10.3390/su15065443

De Buck, A. J., Hendrix, E. M. T., & Schoorlemmer, H. B. (1999). Analysing production and environmental risks in arable farming systems: A mathematical approach. *European Journal of Operational Research*, 119(2), 416–426. DOI: 10.1016/S0377-2217(99)00143-5

Demessie, G. T., & Shukla, A. (2024). Drivers and outcomes of sustainable marketing strategy in the African context: The role of competitive advantage and strategic proactivity as mediating and moderating variables. *Cogent Business & Management*, 11(1), 2348442. DOI: 10.1080/23311975.2024.2348442

Devlin, J., Chang, M. W., Lee, K., & Toutanova, K. (2018). BERT: Pre-training of Deep Bidirectional Transformers for Language Understanding. https://arxiv.org/abs/1810.04805v2

Dotsika, F., & Watkins, A. (2017). Identifying potentially disruptive trends by means of keyword network analysis. *Technological Forecasting and Social Change*, 119, 114–127. DOI: 10.1016/j.techfore.2017.03.020

Dwivedi, Y. K., Hughes, L., Ismagilova, E., Aarts, G., Coombs, C., Crick, T., Duan, Y., Dwivedi, R., Edwards, J., Eirug, A., Galanos, V., Ilavarasan, P. V., Janssen, M., Jones, P., Kar, A. K., Kizgin, H., Kronemann, B., Lal, B., Lucini, B., & Williams, M. D. (2021). Artificial Intelligence (AI): Multidisciplinary perspectives on emerging challenges, opportunities, and agenda for research, practice and policy. *International Journal of Information Management*, 57, 101994. DOI: 10.1016/j.ijinfomgt.2019.08.002

Eagle, L., Osmond, A., McCarthy, B., Low, D., & Lesbirel, H. (2017). Social Marketing Strategies for Renewable Energy Transitions. *Australasian Marketing Journal*, 25(2), 141–148. DOI: 10.1016/j.ausmj.2017.04.006

Fenwick, A., Molnar, G., & Frangos, P. (2023). Revisiting the role of HR in the age of AI: Bringing humans and machines closer together in the workplace. *Frontiers in Artificial Intelligence*, 6, 1272823. DOI: 10.3389/frai.2023.1272823 PMID: 38288334

Filiputti, E., Quattrin, R., & Brusaferro, S. (2013). Social marketing for health promotion and prevention: a review of literature: Elisa Filiputti. *European Journal of Public Health, 23*(suppl_1), ckt124.012. .DOI: 10.1093/eurpub/ckt124.012

Firestone, R., Rowe, C. J., Modi, S. N., & Sievers, D. (2017). The effectiveness of social marketing in global health: A systematic review. *Health Policy and Planning*, 32(1), 110–124. DOI: 10.1093/heapol/czw088 PMID: 27476502

Fobbe, L. (2020). Analysing Organisational Collaboration Practices for Sustainability. *Sustainability (Basel)*, 12(6), 2466. Advance online publication. DOI: 10.3390/su12062466

Ganjavi, N., & Fazlollahtabar, H. (2023). Integrated Sustainable Production Value Measurement Model Based on Lean and Six Sigma in Industry 4.0 Context. *IEEE Transactions on Engineering Management*, 70(6), 2320–2333. DOI: 10.1109/TEM.2021.3078169

Garner, B., & Mady, A. (2023). Social media branding in the food industry: Comparing B2B and B2C companies' use of sustainability messaging on Twitter. *Journal of Business and Industrial Marketing*, 38(11), 2485–2504. DOI: 10.1108/JBIM-09-2022-0418

Gelderman, C. J., Schijns, J., Lambrechts, W., & Vijgen, S. (2021). Green marketing as an environmental practice: The impact on green satisfaction and green loyalty in a business-to-business context. *Business Strategy and the Environment*, 30(4), 2061–2076. DOI: 10.1002/bse.2732

Ghadimi, P., Ghassemi Toosi, F., & Heavey, C. (2018). A multi-agent systems approach for sustainable supplier selection and order allocation in a partnership supply chain. *European Journal of Operational Research*, 269(1), 286–301. DOI: 10.1016/j.ejor.2017.07.014

Giovanni Zúñiga Vásquez, F. (2023). La importancia de la inteligencia artificial en las comunicaciones en los procesos marketing. *Vivat Academia*, 156, 19–39. DOI: 10.15178/va.2023.156.e1474

Goodfellow, I. J., Pouget-Abadie, J., Mirza, M., Xu, B., Warde-Farley, D., Ozair, S., Courville, A., & Bengio, Y. (2014). Generative Adversarial Networks. *Science Robotics*, 3(January), 2672–2680. https://arxiv.org/abs/1406.2661v1

Gordon, R., Bádéj̃, F. A., & Gurrieri, L. (2022). Towards a framework for critical social marketing: What is to be done for emancipation? *Journal of Marketing Management*, 38(17–18), 2135–2163. DOI: 10.1080/0267257X.2022.2086286

Gordon, R., Russell-Bennett, R., & Lefebvre, R. C. (2016). Social marketing: The state of play and brokering the way forward. *Journal of Marketing Management*, 32(11–12), 1059–1082. DOI: 10.1080/0267257X.2016.1199156

Gori, E., Romolini, A., Fissi, S., & Contri, M. (2020). Toward the Dissemination of Sustainability Issues through Social Media in the Higher Education Sector: Evidence from an Italian Case. *Sustainability (Basel)*, 12(11), 4658. Advance online publication. DOI: 10.3390/su12114658

Hackley, C. (2023). Crap detecting. Autoethnographic reflections on critical practice in marketing pedagogy. *Journal of Marketing Management*, 39(1–2), 20–31. DOI: 10.1080/0267257X.2022.2132754

Haldorai, A., Murugan, S., & Ramu, A. (2021). Evolution, challenges, and application of intelligent ICT education: An overview. *Computer Applications in Engineering Education*, 29(3), 562–571. DOI: 10.1002/cae.22217

Han, H., Li, Z., & Li, Z. (2023). Using Machine Learning Methods to Predict Consumer Confidence from Search Engine Data. *Sustainability (Basel)*, 15(4), 3100. DOI: 10.3390/su15043100

Harguess, J., & Ward, C. M. (2022). Is the Next Winter Coming for AI? Elements of Making Secure and Robust AI. In *Proceedings - Applied Imagery Pattern Recognition Workshop*, 2022-October. DOI: 10.1109/AIPR57179.2022.10092230

He, S. (2023). Do you reap what you sow? Driving mechanism of supply chain transparency on consumers' indirect reciprocity. *Frontiers in Psychology*, 14, 1081297. DOI: 10.3389/fpsyg.2023.1081297 PMID: 36844304

Hermann, E. (2021). Leveraging Artificial Intelligence in Marketing for Social Good—An Ethical Perspective. *Journal of Business Ethics*, 179(1), 43–61. DOI: 10.1007/s10551-021-04843-y PMID: 34054170

Howard, J., & John Howard, C. (2019). Artificial intelligence: Implications for the future of work. *American Journal of Industrial Medicine*, 62(11), 917–926. DOI: 10.1002/ajim.23037 PMID: 31436850

Howard, J. A., & Sheth, J. (1969). The Theory of Buyer Behavior. In *Research Policy*. John Wiley & Sons., http://www.people.umass.edu/aizen/pdf/tpb.intervention.pdf

Idnay, B., Cordoba, E., Ramirez, S. O., Xiao, E., Wood, O. R., Batey, D. S., Garofalo, R., & Schnall, R. (2024). Social Marketing Perspective on Participant Recruitment in Informatics-Based Intervention Studies. *AIDS and Behavior*, 28(9), 1–14. DOI: 10.1007/s10461-024-04355-6 PMID: 38703337

Jain, R., Luck, E., Mathews, S., & Schuster, L. (2023). Creating Persuasive Environmental Communicators: Spokescharacters as Endorsers in Promoting Sustainable Behaviors. *Sustainability (Basel)*, 15(1), 335. Advance online publication. DOI: 10.3390/su15010335

Jones, L. D., Golan, D., Hanna, S. A., & Ramachandran, M. (2018). Artificial intelligence, machine learning and the evolution of healthcare: A bright future or cause for concern? *Bone & Joint Research*, 7(3), 223–225. DOI: 10.1302/2046-3758.73.BJR-2017-0147.R1 PMID: 29922439

Kaul, V., Enslin, S., & Gross, S. A. (2020). History of artificial intelligence in medicine. *Gastrointestinal Endoscopy*, 92(4), 807–812. DOI: 10.1016/j.gie.2020.06.040 PMID: 32565184

Keegan, B. J., Canhoto, A. I., & Yen, D. A. (2022). Power negotiation on the tango dancefloor: The adoption of AI in B2B marketing. *Industrial Marketing Management*, 100, 36–48. DOI: 10.1016/j.indmarman.2021.11.001

Khan, A. W., & Pandey, J. (2023). Consumer psychology for food choices: A systematic review and research directions. *European Journal of Marketing*, 57(9), 2353–2381. DOI: 10.1108/EJM-07-2021-0566

Khan, M. A., Saleh, A. M., Waseem, M., & Sajjad, I. A. (2023). Artificial Intelligence Enabled Demand Response: Prospects and Challenges in Smart Grid Environment. *IEEE Access : Practical Innovations, Open Solutions*, 11, 1477–1505. DOI: 10.1109/ACCESS.2022.3231444

Khan, M. A., Saqib, S., Alyas, T., Ur Rehman, A., Saeed, Y., Zeb, A., Zareei, M., & Mohamed, E. M. (2020). Effective Demand Forecasting Model Using Business Intelligence Empowered with Machine Learning. *IEEE Access : Practical Innovations, Open Solutions*, 8, 116013–116023. DOI: 10.1109/ACCESS.2020.3003790

Kim, H., So, K. K. F., Shin, S., & Li, J. (2024). Artificial intelligence in hospitality and tourism: Insights from industry practices, research literature, and expert opinions. *Journal of Hospitality & Tourism Research (Washington, D.C.)*, 10963480241229235, 10963480241229235. Advance online publication. DOI: 10.1177/10963480241229235

Kindylidi, I., & Cabral, T. S. (2021). Sustainability of AI: The Case of Provision of Information to Consumers. *Sustainability (Basel)*, 13(21), 12064. Advance online publication. DOI: 10.3390/su132112064

Kotras, B. (2020). Mass personalization: Predictive marketing algorithms and the reshaping of consumer knowledge. *Big Data & Society*, 7(2), 2053951720951581. DOI: 10.1177/2053951720951581

Kubacki, K., & Szablewska, N. (2019). Social marketing targeting Indigenous peoples: A systematic review. *Health Promotion International*, 34(1), 133–143. DOI: 10.1093/heapro/dax060 PMID: 28973158

Kumar, M., Raut, R. D., Mangla, S. K., Ferraris, A., & Choubey, V. K. (2022). The adoption of artificial intelligence powered workforce management for effective revenue growth of micro, small, and medium scale enterprises (MSMEs). *Production Planning and Control*, •••, 1–17. DOI: 10.1080/09537287.2022.2131620

LeCun, Y., Bottou, L., Bengio, Y., & Haffner, P. (1998). Gradient-based learning applied to document recognition. *Proceedings of the IEEE*, 86(11), 2278–2323. DOI: 10.1109/5.726791

Lee, A., & Chung, T.-L. D. (2023). Transparency in corporate social responsibility communication on social media. *International Journal of Retail & Distribution Management*, 51(5), 590–610. DOI: 10.1108/IJRDM-01-2022-0038

Li, G., Li, N., & Sethi, S. P. (2021). Does CSR Reduce Idiosyncratic Risk? Roles of Operational Efficiency and AI Innovation. *Production and Operations Management*, 30(7), 2027–2045. DOI: 10.1111/poms.13483

Liu, Y., & Chen, M. (2023). The Knowledge Structure and Development Trend in Artificial Intelligence Based on Latent Feature Topic Model. *IEEE Transactions on Engineering Management*, •••, 1–12. DOI: 10.1109/TEM.2022.3232178

Lyulyov, O., Chygryn, O., Pimonenko, T., & Kwilinski, A. (2023). Stakeholders' Engagement in the Company's Management as a Driver of Green Competitiveness within Sustainable Development. *Sustainability (Basel)*, 15(9), 7249. Advance online publication. DOI: 10.3390/su15097249

Machado, L., & Goswami, S. (2023). Marketing sustainability within the jewelry industry. *Journal of Marketing Communications*, •••, 1–16. DOI: 10.1080/13527266.2023.2166566

Martínez-Falcó, J., Marco-Lajara, B., Sánchez-García, E., & Millan-Tudela, L. A. (2023). Sustainable Development Goals in the Business Sphere: A Bibliometric Review. *Sustainability (Basel)*, 15(6), 5075. Advance online publication. DOI: 10.3390/su15065075

Maslow, A. H. (1943). A theory of human motivation. *Psychological Review*, 50(4), 370–396. DOI: 10.1037/h0054346

McAlindon, K. (2017). Selling Innovations Like Soap: The Interactive Systems Framework and Social Marketing. *American Journal of Community Psychology*, 60(1–2), 242–256. DOI: 10.1002/ajcp.12157 PMID: 28815622

McCarthy, E. J. (1960). *Basic marketing: A managerial approach.*

Milana, C., & Ashta, A. (2021). Artificial intelligence techniques in finance and financial markets: A survey of the literature. *Strategic Change*, 30(3), 189–209. DOI: 10.1002/jsc.2403

Mim, K. B., Jai, T., & Lee, S. H. (2022). The Influence of Sustainable Positioning on eWOM and Brand Loyalty: Analysis of Credible Sources and Transparency Practices Based on the S-O-R Model. *Sustainability (Basel)*, 14(19), 12461. Advance online publication. DOI: 10.3390/su141912461

Mirzajani, Z., Nikoofal, M. E., & Zolfaghari, S. (2024). Sustainable sourcing contracts under supplier capital constraints and information asymmetry. *Omega*, 125, 103035. DOI: 10.1016/j.omega.2024.103035

Montes, G. A., & Goertzel, B. (2019). Distributed, decentralized, and democratized artificial intelligence. *Technological Forecasting and Social Change*, 141, 354–358. DOI: 10.1016/j.techfore.2018.11.010

Mukonza, C., & Swarts, I. (2020). The influence of green marketing strategies on business performance and corporate image in the retail sector. *Business Strategy and the Environment*, 29(3), 838–845. DOI: 10.1002/bse.2401

Mustak, M., Salminen, J., Plé, L., & Wirtz, J. (2021). Artificial intelligence in marketing: Topic modeling, scientometric analysis, and research agenda. *Journal of Business Research*, 124, 389–404. DOI: 10.1016/j.jbusres.2020.10.044

Nadanyiova, M., Gajanova, L., & Majerova, J. (2020). Green Marketing as a Part of the Socially Responsible Brand's Communication from the Aspect of Generational Stratification. *Sustainability (Basel)*, 12(17), 7118. Advance online publication. DOI: 10.3390/su12177118

Naz, F., Agrawal, R., Kumar, A., Gunasekaran, A., Majumdar, A., & Luthra, S. (2022). Reviewing the applications of artificial intelligence in sustainable supply chains: Exploring research propositions for future directions. *Business Strategy and the Environment*, 31(5), 2400–2423. DOI: 10.1002/bse.3034

Nygaard, S., Kokholm, A. R., & Huulgaard, R. D. (2022). Incorporating the sustainable development goals in small- to medium-sized enterprises. *Journal of Urban Economics*, 8(1), juac022. Advance online publication. DOI: 10.1093/jue/juac022

Ordonez-Ponce, E., Clarke, A., & MacDonald, A. (2021). Business contributions to the sustainable development goals through community sustainability partnerships. *Sustainability Accounting. Management and Policy Journal*, 12(6), 1239–1267. DOI: 10.1108/SAMPJ-03-2020-0068

Osifo, O. C. (2023). Transparency and its roles in realizing greener AI. *Journal of Information. Communication and Ethics in Society*, 21(2), 202–218. DOI: 10.1108/JICES-11-2022-0097

Pansare, R., Yadav, G., Garza-Reyes, J. A., & Raosaheb Nagare, M. (2023). Assessment of Sustainable Development Goals through Industry 4.0 and reconfigurable manufacturing system practices. *Journal of Manufacturing Technology Management*, 34(3), 383–413. DOI: 10.1108/JMTM-05-2022-0206

Petrescu, M., Krishen, A. S., Kachen, S., & Gironda, J. T. (2022). AI-based innovation in B2B marketing: An interdisciplinary framework incorporating academic and practitioner perspectives. *Industrial Marketing Management*, 103, 61–72. DOI: 10.1016/j.indmarman.2022.03.001

Porter, M. E. (1985). *The Competitive Advantage: Creating and Sustaining Superior Performance*. Free Press.

Prataviera, L. B., Creazza, A., Perotti, S., & Rodrigues, V. S. (2023). How to align logistics environmental sustainability with corporate strategy? An Italian perspective. *International Journal of Logistics Research and Applications*, 1–23. .DOI: 10.1080/13675567.2023.2230916

Primožič, L., & Kutnar, A. (2022). Sustainability Communication in Global Consumer Brands. *Sustainability (Basel)*, 14(20), 13586. Advance online publication. DOI: 10.3390/su142013586

Pykett, J., Jones, R., Welsh, M., & Whitehead, M. (2014). The art of choosing and the politics of social marketing. *Policy Studies*, 35(2), 97–114. DOI: 10.1080/01442872.2013.875141

Radford, A., & Narasimhan, K. (2018). Improving Language Understanding by Generative Pre-Training. https://hayate-lab.com/wp-content/uploads/2023/05/43372bfa750340059ad87ac8e538c53b.pdf

Rakib, M. A., Chang, H. J., & Jones, R. P. (2022). Effective Sustainability Messages Triggering Consumer Emotion and Action: An Application of the Social Cognitive Theory and the Dual-Process Model. *Sustainability (Basel)*, 14(5), 2505. Advance online publication. DOI: 10.3390/su14052505

Ricca, F., Marchetto, A., & Stocco, A. (2021). AI-based test automation: A grey literature analysis. In *Proceedings - 2021 IEEE 14th International Conference on Software Testing, Verification and Validation Workshops, ICSTW 2021* (pp. 263–270). DOI: 10.1109/ICSTW52544.2021.00051

Rodak, O. (2020). Hashtag hijacking and crowdsourcing transparency: Social media affordances and the governance of farm animal protection. *Agriculture and Human Values*, 37(2), 281–294. DOI: 10.1007/s10460-019-09984-5

Rosenblatt, F. (1958). The perceptron: A probabilistic model for information storage and organization in the brain. *Psychological Review*, 65(6), 386–408. DOI: 10.1037/h0042519 PMID: 13602029

Roski, J., Maier, E. J., Vigilante, K., Kane, E. A., & Matheny, M. E. (2021). Enhancing trust in AI through industry self-governance. *Journal of the American Medical Informatics Association : JAMIA*, 28(7), 1582–1590. DOI: 10.1093/jamia/ocab065 PMID: 33895824

Rumelhart, D. E., Hinton, G. E., & Williams, R. J. (1986). Learning representations by back-propagating errors. *Nature*, 323(6088), 533–536. DOI: 10.1038/323533a0

Servera-Francés, D., Fuentes-Blasco, M., & Piqueras-Tomás, L. (2020). The Importance of Sustainable Practices in Value Creation and Consumers' Commitment with Companies' Commercial Format. *Sustainability (Basel)*, 12(23), 9852. Advance online publication. DOI: 10.3390/su12239852

Shekhar, S. K. (2022). Social Marketing Plan to Decrease the COVID-19 Vaccine Hesitancy among Senior Citizens in Rural India. *Sustainability (Basel)*, 14(13), 7561. Advance online publication. DOI: 10.3390/su14137561

Shirazi, F., & Mohammadi, M. (2019). A big data analytics model for customer churn prediction in the retiree segment. *International Journal of Information Management*, 48, 238–253. DOI: 10.1016/j.ijinfomgt.2018.10.005

Siems, E., Seuring, S., & Schilling, L. (2023). Stakeholder roles in sustainable supply chain management: A literature review. *Journal of Business Economics*, 93(4), 747–775. DOI: 10.1007/s11573-022-01117-5

Smith, W. R. (1956). Product Differentiation and Market Segmentation as Alternative Marketing Strategies. *Journal of Marketing*, 21(1), 3–8. DOI: 10.1177/002224295602100102

Sniecinski, I., & Seghatchian, J. (2018). Artificial intelligence: A joint narrative on potential use in pediatric stem and immune cell therapies and regenerative medicine. *Transfusion and Apheresis Science : Official Journal of the World Apheresis Association : Official Journal of the European Society for Haemapheresis*, 57(3), 422–424. DOI: 10.1016/j.transci.2018.05.004 PMID: 29784537

Su, Z., Togay, G., & Côté, A. M. (2021). Artificial intelligence: A destructive and yet creative force in the skilled labour market. *Human Resource Development International*, 24(3), 341–352. DOI: 10.1080/13678868.2020.1818513

Taherdangkoo, M., Ghasemi, K., & Beikpour, M. (2017). The role of sustainability environment in export marketing strategy and performance: A literature review. *Environment, Development and Sustainability*, 19(5), 1601–1629. DOI: 10.1007/s10668-016-9841-4

Talib, M. A., Majzoub, S., Nasir, Q., & Jamal, D. (2021). A systematic literature review on hardware implementation of artificial intelligence algorithms. *The Journal of Supercomputing*, 77(2), 1897–1938. DOI: 10.1007/s11227-020-03325-8

Taufique, K. M. R. (2022). Integrating environmental values and emotion in green marketing communications inducing sustainable consumer behaviour. *Journal of Marketing Communications*, 28(3), 272–290. DOI: 10.1080/13527266.2020.1866645

Thamik, H., & Wu, J. (2022). The Impact of Artificial Intelligence on Sustainable Development in Electronic Markets. *Sustainability (Basel)*, 14(6), 3568. Advance online publication. DOI: 10.3390/su14063568

Truong, V. D., & Hall, C. M. (2017). Corporate social marketing in tourism: To sleep or not to sleep with the enemy? *Journal of Sustainable Tourism*, 25(7), 884–902. DOI: 10.1080/09669582.2016.1201093

Van Esch, P., & Stewart Black, J. (2021). Artificial intelligence (AI): Revolutionizing digital marketing. *Australasian Marketing Journal*, 29(3), 199–203. DOI: 10.1177/18393349211037684

Vapnik, V., & Lerner, A. (1963). Pattern Recognition Using Generalized Portrait Method. *Automation and Remote Control*, 24(06).

Vaswani, A., Shazeer, N., Parmar, N., Uszkoreit, J., Jones, L., Gomez, A. N., Kaiser, Ł., & Polosukhin, I. (2017). Attention Is All You Need. https://arxiv.org/abs/1706.03762v7

Vlačić, B., Corbo, L., Costa e Silva, S., & Dabić, M. (2021). The evolving role of artificial intelligence in marketing: A review and research agenda. *Journal of Business Research*, 128, 187–203. DOI: 10.1016/j.jbusres.2021.01.055

Vo, T. Q., & Nguyen-Anh, T. (2024). Corporate social marketing and brand equity – a case of dairy products in Vietnam. *Cogent Business & Management*, 11(1), 2321795. Advance online publication. DOI: 10.1080/23311975.2024.2321795

Waqar, A., Othman, I., Shafiq, N., & Mansoor, M. S. (2023). Applications of AI in oil and gas projects towards sustainable development: A systematic literature review. *Artificial Intelligence Review*, 56(11), 12771–12798. DOI: 10.1007/s10462-023-10467-7 PMID: 37362898

Winroth, M., Almström, P., & Andersson, C. (2016). Sustainable production indicators at factory level. *Journal of Manufacturing Technology Management*, 27(6), 842–873. DOI: 10.1108/JMTM-04-2016-0054

Xinxing, S., Sarkar, A., Yue, D., Hongbin, Z., & Fangyuan, T. (2023). The influences of the advancement of green technology on agricultural CO2 release reduction: A case of Chinese agricultural industry. *Frontiers in Sustainable Food Systems*, 7, 1096381. DOI: 10.3389/fsufs.2023.1096381

Xu, Y., Shieh, C. H., van Esch, P., & Ling, I. L. (2020). AI customer service: Task complexity, problem-solving ability, and usage intention. *Australasian Marketing Journal*, 28(4), 189–199. DOI: 10.1016/j.ausmj.2020.03.005

Xu, Z., Liu, X., Bai, C., & Hu, L. (2015). Green Marketing: A Grey-based Rough Set Theory Analysis of Activities. *International Journal of Innovation Science*, 7(1), 27–38. DOI: 10.1260/1757-2223.7.1.27

Yamane, T., & Kaneko, S. (2022). The Sustainable Development Goals as new business norms: A survey experiment on stakeholder preferences. *Ecological Economics*, 191, 107236. DOI: 10.1016/j.ecolecon.2021.107236

Yang, X., Li, H., Ni, L., & Li, T. (2021). Application of Artificial Intelligence in Precision Marketing. *Journal of Organizational and End User Computing*, 33(4), 209–219. DOI: 10.4018/JOEUC.20210701.oa10

Yildirim, M. B., & Mouzon, G. (2012). Single-machine sustainable production planning to minimize total energy consumption and total completion time using a multiple objective genetic algorithm. *IEEE Transactions on Engineering Management*, 59(4), 585–597. DOI: 10.1109/TEM.2011.2171055

Yildiz Çankaya, S., & Sezen, B. (2019). Effects of green supply chain management practices on sustainability performance. *Journal of Manufacturing Technology Management*, 30(1), 98–121. DOI: 10.1108/JMTM-03-2018-0099

Zhao, J., & Gómez Fariñas, B. (2023). Artificial Intelligence and Sustainable Decisions. *European Business Organization Law Review*, 24(1), 1–39. DOI: 10.1007/s40804-022-00262-2

Zhao, L., Lee, S. H., Li, M., & Sun, P. (2022). The Use of Social Media to Promote Sustainable Fashion and Benefit Communications: A Data-Mining Approach. *Sustainability (Basel)*, 14(3), 1178. Advance online publication. DOI: 10.3390/su14031178

Zhong, M., & Wang, M. (2023). Corporate sustainability disclosure on social media and its difference from sustainability reports: Evidence from the energy sector. *Frontiers in Environmental Science*, 11, 1147191. https://www.frontiersin.org/articles/10.3389/fenvs.2023.1147191. DOI: 10.3389/fenvs.2023.1147191

Zhu, C. (2022). Construction and Risk Analysis of Marketing System Based on AI. *Scientific Programming*, 2022(1), 2839834. DOI: 10.1155/2022/2839834

Zohny, H., McMillan, J., & King, M. (2023). Ethics of generative AI. *Journal of Medical Ethics*, 49(2), 79–80. DOI: 10.1136/jme-2023-108909 PMID: 36693706

ADDITIONAL READING

Arantes, L. (2023). Sustainable Digital Marketing: Proposal for a Renewed Concept. In Santos, J. D., & Sousa, B. M. (Eds.), *Promoting Organizational Performance Through 5G and Agile Marketing* (pp. 55–74). IGI Global., DOI: 10.4018/978-1-6684-5523-4.ch004

Campbell, C., Sands, S., Ferraro, C., Tsao, H., & Mavrommatis, A. (2020). From data to action: How marketers can leverage AI. *Business Horizons*, 63(2), 227–243. DOI: 10.1016/j.bushor.2019.12.002

Han, H., Li, Z., & Li, Z. (2023). Using Machine Learning Methods to Predict Consumer Confidence from Search Engine Data. *Sustainability (Basel)*, 15(4), 1–12. DOI: 10.3390/su15043100

Huang, M.-H., & Rust, R. T. (2021). Artificial intelligence in service. *Journal of Service Research*, 24(1), 3–7. DOI: 10.1177/1094670520902266

Hussain, M., Yang, S., Maqsood, U. S., & Zahid, R. M. A. (2024). Tapping into the green potential: The power of artificial intelligence adoption in corporate green innovation drive. *Business Strategy and the Environment*, 33(5), 1–22. DOI: 10.1002/bse.3710

Jain, S., Basu, S., & Dwivedi, Y. D. (2024). Green brand identity and B2B channel partners' tactical green marketing orientation: Moderating effect of brand governance. *Industrial Marketing Management*, 119(07), 218–237. DOI: 10.1016/j.indmarman.2024.04.013

Lin, J., Zeng, Y., Wu, S. & Luo, X. (2024). How does artificial intelligence affect the environmental performance of organizations? *The role of green innovation and green culture, 61*(2), 1-16. .DOI: 10.1016/j.im.2024.103924

Yang, X., Li, H., Ni, L., & Li, T. (2021). Application of Artificial Intelligence in Precision Marketing. *Journal of Organizational and End User Computing*, 33(4), 209–219. Advance online publication. DOI: 10.4018/JOEUC.20210701.oa10

KEY TERMS AND DEFINITIONS

Artificial Intelligence (AI): The simulation of human intelligence processes by machines, particularly computer systems, involving learning, reasoning, and self-correction.

Critical Marketing: A marketing approach that critiques and challenges traditional marketing practices and ideologies, incorporating social and ethical considerations to promote sustainable and socially responsible behaviors.

Ethical AI: The principles and practices aimed at ensuring artificial intelligence systems operate in a morally responsible manner, prioritizing fairness, transparency, accountability, and the minimization of biases to protect and respect user rights.

Green Marketing: Promoting products or services based on their environmental benefits, aiming to meet customer needs sustainably while minimizing the ecological footprint.

Predictive Analytics: Using statistical algorithms and machine learning techniques to identify the likelihood of future outcomes based on historical data.

Social Marketing: The application of marketing principles to influence behaviors that benefit individuals and communities for the greater social good, often in health promotion and environmental conservation.

Sustainable Development Goals (SDGs): A set of 17 interconnected global objectives established by the United Nations to guide efforts toward a more sustainable and equitable future, focusing on addressing critical issues such as poverty, inequality, climate change, environmental degradation, and promoting peace and justice.

Sustainable Marketing: Marketing strategies and practices that balance economic objectives with environmental and social responsibilities, aiming to promote sustainable consumption and production patterns.

Chapter 9
The Intersection of Brands and AI:
Concepts and Technologies

Joana Neves
https://orcid.org/0000-0001-9675-5683
CEOS.PP Coimbra, Polytechnic University of Coimbra, Portugal

Lara Mendes Bacalhau
https://orcid.org/0000-0001-9674-4167
CEOS.PP Coimbra, Polytechnic University of Coimbra, Portugal

ABSTRACT

Today's digital marketplace is volatile and fast-paced, and the introduction of AI technologies has become an integral part of improving many aspects of business. This chapter aims to shed light on how AI techniques were/are/will be related to Brand Management. First, the basic ideas about AI will be introduced, and the development of the concept and the main technologies that form AI will be explained. Furthermore, it will be necessary to provide a comprehensive analysis of the use of AI in brand management and its potential to revolutionize the methods, customer interactions, and trends in the market. This paper integrates a contextual approach to explore how AI solutions are transforming the brand-consumer relationship. Secondly, we will investigate the variety of advantages that AI has for brands. Finally, a glimpse of new opportunities created by AI in the context of brand management will be highlighted. Thus, the information presented in this chapter is useful for academics, researchers, and practitioners interested in unlocking the capabilities of AI for brand management.

DOI: 10.4018/979-8-3693-5340-0.ch009

1. INTRODUCTION

Brand Management (BM) is a crucial aspect of modern business strategy, as it incorporates the creation, development, and maintenance of brands to ensure long-term success and competitive advantage in the marketplace (Keller & Lehmann, 2006). BM can thus be described as several activities and actions directed towards enhancing the brand or its market position, and factors such as identity, image, and communication, focusing on maintaining, improving, and upholding (Mogaji, 2021) the Brand Equity (BE). BM plays a vital role in establishing brand recognition, gaining market share, and subsequent business development, as it involves strategizing, monitoring, and controlling the different elements to form the brand´s identity, awareness, and associations in the minds of the consumers, the perception among the consumers about the quality of the products of the brand, satisfaction, and brand trust. This is important to build consumer loyalty and create a unique market presence, which has a role in influencing consumer behavior, establishing BE, and ensuring long-term success in the competitive business landscape (Rondonuwu, 2024). In the last 15 years, the development of AI tools has become increasingly crucial to improving the various aspects of BM.

The first point of BM is the construction and development of the Brand Identity (BI), which represents the union of the visual, emotional, and cultural elements that define a brand (Ianenko et al., 2020). Chung et al. (2020) state that BI encompasses three elements: strategic, sensory, and organizational identity.

In the first case, strategic identity should be defined at the beginning of the branding process because in that phase the marketeer should set the concept and style of the brand and the brand promise that includes the vision, mission, values, and strategic intent of the company's top managers (Chung & Byrom, 2020). These authors argue that the strategic identity can include brand personality and brand positioning. The brand personality comprises the emotional values the brand should have if it were a person (Kapferer, 2012). Brand positioning involves functional values (de Chernatony, 2010) and refers to the process of establishing a distinctive place for a brand in the minds of the target public (Temporal, 2014). This could involve creating a unique value proposition and positioning the brand relative to its competitors in the market (Iyer et al., 2019). This strategy is important since an effective brand positioning will help create a strong BI, communicate the brand´s value, and even appeal to the target market (Temporal, 2014). In the last phase, promote the brand to a specific and favorable position in the consumer´s perception.

Finally, organizational identity includes the shared beliefs of the organization's members about what it is and represents the distinctive characteristics of the organization (Whetten, 2006), the behavioral, cultural, and attitudinal aspects of the organization's employees and their social interaction with multiple brand stakeholders (Iglesias et al., 2020).

Another point a marketer should pay attention to in BM is the development of a good Brand Image. This concept is understood as consumers' overall impression and associations with the brand (Arora, 2018) which may include attributes of the product or its category; benefits offered to the consumer; type of consumer profile; situations of use and/or applicability; celebrities linked to the brand; relative price; main competitors; the country/geographical area of origin, among others (Bacalhau, 2020). The brand image is influenced by the brand´s marketing activities, product quality, consumer services, public perception, price perception, promotion, and other factors (Zhang, 2015). A positive brand image is essential to attract new and potential consumers, retain existing ones, and even differentiate the brand from the competitors in the market (Kelly, 2023). During the last 30 years, many proposals based on Aaker (1991) or Keller (1993) BE models as proved that brand image can influence consumer purchase decisions and brand loyalty (Bacalhau, 2020; Sasmita et al., 2022; Zhang, 2015). As we saw, this brand image is defined as the impression held by consumers in memory, reflecting cognitive and psychological elements, opinions, attitudes, and emotions toward a brand (Srivastava & Dey, 2016; Yang et al., 2022). Brand perception means how consumers perceive and interpret a determined brand based on their experiences, interactions, and associations with that brand. It will reflect in the consumer´s beliefs, attitudes, and feelings toward them (Krupka, 2023). Managing brand perception is important to brand recognition, shaping consumer feelings and attitudes toward the brand, building trust in the brand, and establishing a positive brand reputation, which could lead to increased customer loyalty and advocacy (Deryl et al., 2023; Guliyev, 2023; Krupka, 2023).

The last important feature related to BM is BC. Like in every field, communication is essential to show, establish a strong partnership with all stakeholders, and guarantee a good strategy. In this way, BC is a strategic of marketing channels and messages to convey the brand´s values, benefits, and personality to the target audience (Voorveld, 2019). This could include advertising, public relations, social media, and other forms of communication. The importance of Brand communication (BC) lies in its ability to enhance brand awareness, maintain a consistent brand image, and engage with consumers, playing an important role in shaping consumer perceptions and influencing purchase decisions (Issalillah et al., 2022; Voorveld, 2019). To make effective BCs, the organization should develop operational competencies and dynamic capabilities, which involve initiating and directing marketing communications to primary customers to establish "brand as identity" and facilitating interactions within the network to manage and develop "branding as meanings" (Brodie et al., 2016). The organization must also develop an Integrated Marketing Communications (IMC) plan, in which the consistency of the brand's message, and image must be maintained through the various channels (advertising, social media, packaging, interactions between employees and customers, etc.), which is crucial to strengthening the brand's impact and presence in the market (Tarannum et al., 2024) because the content of the messages can be used for conveying brand values, engage with consumers, and shape perceptions effectively across various marketing channels and consequently use to build strong brand awareness and engagement with their target audience.

In summary, BM is a multifaceted process that aims to ensure that the identity and image of a brand are in harmony with what is seen by the market through positioning and BC. Consequently, effective management leads to the development of a clear and unchanging BI that is appreciated by consumers, thus gaining a competitive edge. The outcome is to maintain the consistency of the brand image in agreement with the company's intentions and achieve positive consumer responses thereby increasing brand value and its performance in the market. In this context, the application of AI in BM has emerged as critical.

AI can be understood as the ability of machines (like computers or robots) to perform tasks normally associated with human beings. This ability normally is based on technologies that mimic the cognitive functions of human beings related to the intelligence and capability to solve simple or complex problems. These tasks can include understanding natural language, recognizing patterns and even making decisions based on your data. AI systems are designed to learn from every experience, adjust to new inputs, and perform the tasks that typically require human intelligence (Russell & Norvig, 2021). Since around 2010, AI gained significant momentum through the rise of machine learning (ML), advancements in computing power, and systems that have evolved with resources for automating processes and supporting decisions with Big Data, in less time (Batin et al., 2017). At that time, the technologies used in AI were based on historical data from multiple sources, which, using statistical models and ML, made it possible to find patterns and trends, and consequently be used to predict future events. These forecasts have made it possible to reduce the risks taken during decision-making processes in complex and dynamic areas. One of the applications of Predictive Artificial Intelligence (Pre-AI) is predicting peaks in demand or identifying the seasonality of sales, which can be used to optimize production processes, storage space, the number of products, the size of the sales force, etc. The next phase was the emergence of Generative Artificial Intelligence (Gen-AI), which includes models, based on neuronal networks and ML that extrapolate patterns identified in training data, to create new content such as text, images, music, audio, video, and other supports like those produced by humans.

In the last three years, AI has seen and continues to see enormous technological advances, but there are still gaps that need to be filled, namely, in terms of the technologies involved that need to be refined to produce more realistic and transparent answers, the ethics applied to AI businesses and the regulation of the use of the AI. With the expansion of Gen-AI, ethical concerns have increased exponentially, so is necessary to define rules that limit the use of personal data and implement monitoring systems to continuously audit delicate activities that involve the consumers and their data to not violate their privacy, ensure that good quality data is used, prevent mistakes, algorithm bias, and violations of the intellectual property. Even with these necessary constant updates, it is possible to see that the role of AI in business models (Di Vaio et al., 2020; Mishra & Tripathi, 2020), such as BM, has become increasingly significant, particularly. in the new digital age (Deryl et al., 2023). The business model aims to use AI models to create, optimize, and manage the various dimensions of a brand (Varsha et al., 2021), including marketing, customer engagement, and product development (Mishra & Tripathi, 2020). The importance of business models in brand management can be attributed to several elements, such as personalized customer engagement (Farayola et al., 2023), data-driven decision-making (Farayola et al., 2023), efficient resource allocation (Mishra & Tripathi, 2021), brand reputation management, competitive advantage, creative innovation, and product development (Volkmar et al., 2022).

This chapter posits that AI has become a strategic tool in the management of brands since it provides complex solutions and techniques to enhance the understanding of brands and their consumers. Therefore, the following sections begin by unraveling the history of BM in parallel with progress in the fields of AI, with special reference to its main milestones and innovations Next, we highlight the primary AI applications that are revolutionizing brand management, including machine learning, Natural Language Processing (NLP), and computer vision. Subsequently, it dissects how Al affects different elements of brand management which include but are not limited to brand image, brand associations, brand messaging, and consumer interactions. It then turns into an exploration of the prospects and issues associated with the application of AI to matters of brand management. Finally, it discusses the probable future developments and directions of AI's application for brand management, which gives information about how this area will develop in the future.

2. EVOLUTION OF BRAND MANAGEMENT AND AI

2.1. Brief evolution of BM

BM has grown significantly over the years, transitioning from traditional approaches to the adoption of digital strategies. This evolution has been driven by advancements in technologies, consumer behavior, and the need for brands to stay relevant in a quickly changing marketplace (Christodoulides, 2009).

Traditional BM is primarily focused on establishing a brand´s identity through visual elements, messaging, and advertising in traditional offline media channels, like television, print, radio (Zhao, 2023), and physical stores. The point is to create brand awareness, shape brand perception, and build brand loyalty through consistent messaging and imagery (Kotler, 2000). The main goal focuses on reaching a broad audience by mass marketing and creating a lasting impression in consumers´ minds. The digital age brought a significant shift in BM. The internet, social media, and digital marketing channels forced brands to adapt to a new landscape where consumer engagement, personalized communication, and real-time interactions became essential (Dinner et al., 2014).

Digital BM covers a multifaceted approach to building and sustaining a brand's online presence, reputation, and customer relations (Mogaji, 2021). With digitalization, brands use social media, e-commerce websites, online platforms, and digital marketplaces to promote brand awareness, engage customers, namely, from younger generations, influence the intentions of purchase, and increase brand loyalty. This shift towards digital BM opened up new opportunities to improve BE and customer interactions by integrating new important technologies, such as big data analytics, chatbots and virtual assistants, and AI (Varsha et al., 2021).

Big Data analysis has revolutionized BM and marketing, as it allows large amounts of consumer data to be collected and analyzed (Erevelles et al., 2016). This data provides valuable insights into consumer behavior, preferences, and trends, pushing brands to make data-driven decisions regarding product development, marketing strategies, and consumer targeting (Erevelles et al., 2016; Sahoo, 2022). By establishing Big Data analytics, brands can create personalized experiences for their consumers and optimize their marketing efforts based on real-time data (Erevelles et al., 2016).

Chatbots and virtual assistants have become integral parts of brand strategies, offering immediate, personalized customer support and engagement (Kull et al., 2021; Magno & Dossena, 2023; Shumanov & Johnson, 2021). The first conversational chatbots appeared in the 1960s at the Massachusetts Institute of Technology with ELIZA, but until the appearance of ChatGPT based on OpenAI's GPT-3. 5 neural networks in November 2022, chatbots were based on rules without contextual understanding or pre-defined models. Chatbots using Gen-AI can create content in response to requests based on knowledge learned from very large and diverse training data, customer input, and feedback (Caldarini et al., 2022).

Through AI, these tools enable brands to interact with consumers anytime, answer queries, provide product recommendations, and enhance the overall consumer experience (Chung et al., 2020; Seranmadevi et al., 2022). Nevertheless, these tools not only streamline customer service but also contribute to building brand loyalty through delivering timely and relevant assistance (Chung et al., 2020; Shumanov & Johnson, 2021).

AI has seeped into every aspect of digital BM and excels in data processing, modeling, and personalization. The integration of ML in BM enables brands to influence and optimize several aspects of marketing, including content creation and advertising. It also can be used to observe consumer behavior patterns, estimate future trends, and develop personalized consumer experiences. thereby improving brand-consumer interactions and fostering brand loyalty (Varsha et al., 2021). AI has also impacted digital advertising because it makes it possible to alter the ad content depending on the attitude of the consumers in real-time.

Lastly, the ongoing shift in the BM process from the old school to the new BM process is due to the growth of technology that has revolutionized the way brands engage consumers. The use of big data analytics, chatbots, virtual assistants, social media tools, and AI has helped brands interact with consumers and create new, more effective ways of responding to changes in the market and winning the trust and loyalty of consumers in today's digital world.

2.2. Evolution and Milestones of AI Technologies

The historical background of AI can be traced back to imitating human brain thinking and extending human intellect using digital resources on computer technology (Wang, 2021). In its early days, AI was based on the idea of simple imperative programming concepts (Deng, 2023) and evolved to more complex algorithms and models that allowed to mimic human intelligence and learning processes, by the usage of neuroscience to study the way of brain works and ML to reproduce the to reproduce the learning process (Hassabis et al., 2017).

The thought of the existence of a reproduction of human intelligence, through mechanical operations and replicated in machines, was present in different forms in authors such as Thomas Hobbes (in his work Levita, from 1651), Blaise Pascal (1642), and Charles Babbage (1823), for example (Nunes, 2023). In addition, one of the authors who stood out most in this constant search for the hope that machines could think was Alan Turing, starting in 1936, and with his reformulation of the problem in 1950, also known today as the Turing test (Roess, 2016; Sterrett, 2020).

In those early years, some scholars made overly optimistic predictions about AI evolution, as in 1956, Herbert Simon and Allen Newell developed the "Logic Theorist", a well-known program that demonstrated mathematical theorems by manipulating symbols and finding solutions (Gugerty, 2006). This year, at the Dartmouth Conference between experts and pioneers in the field of computing, John Maccarthy coined the expression "Artificial Intelligence", as we know it today (Kumar & Jindal, 2018). Herbert Simon and Allen Newell, in 1959 developed a program called "The General Problem Solver", which was the basis for problem-solving and heuristic research in AI (Sudmann, 2022). Two years after the conference at which John McCarthy coined the term AI, he developed a programming language called "LISP", which is often used in AI systems (Ball & Zorn, 2015).

Within the same decade, Arthur Samuel designed a program to play checkers, surpassing its creator's capabilities, thus taking the first steps in ML (Nguyen, 2023). The 1960s were also marked by the first natural language software, "Eliza", designed by programmer Joseph Weizebaum, which could communicate in everyday language with the user, through simple mechanisms and pre-written phrases, leading users to think that they were communicating with human beings (Assabil et al., 2023). This was the first system to pass the Turing test mentioned above (Nunes, 2023).

Subsequent advances led scholars to realize that the intellectual aspects of human beings, which result from experiences, perceptions, and interactions with the real world, involving the emotional side, are challenging to replicate in machines (Nunes, 2023), leading to the AI winters (1970s to 1980s) (Haigh, 2023; Yuan & Zhu, 2023).

In the late 1980s to 1990s the limitations of expert systems and the collapse of the AI market led to another time of reduced funding and interest, called the Second AI Winter (Haigh, 2024). Nevertheless, with the evolution of computers and transistors that increase the power of processors, the performance has increased for the application of new AI systems (Haigh, 2023, 2024). In 1997, IBM developed "Deep Blue", a computer with a database of millions of chess games, which went on to defeat world chess champion, Garry Kasparov (Campbell et al., 2002). This event was one of the most important milestones, not only because of AI's ability to take on a champion in its field and beat him, but also because of the impact on society and forecasting, which could even come close to or surpass human intelligence itself (Campbell et al., 2002). The 2000s is defined as the rise of ML and Data-Driven AI. In 2006, the scientist Geoffrey Hinton and his team at the University of Toronto introduced Deep Learning (DL), significantly improving AI performance in various tasks, which earned him the nickname of "father of AI" (Hinton et al., 2006).

From this milestone, many examples followed, such as "Watson", a system also developed by IBM, which demonstrated the ability to understand and process natural language, leading to advances in natural language processing (Kumar et al., 2022). The next system to impact society was AlphaGo in 2016. A program based on a deep learning system, developed by Google and built to play Go, also considered to be the most difficult game man has ever invented, but AlphaGo managed to beat the reigning world champion Lee Sedol, proving once again the superiority of AI over human intelligence in specific tasks (Silver et al., 2017).

Another significant advance in the field of AI has been the drastic evolution of ML. In 2012, with the ImageNet Competition, it was possible to detect a breakthrough in the accuracy of image recognition that marked a significant point in the advances of machine learning algorithms (He et al., 2015). In addition, 2014 saw the introduction of Generative Adversarial Networks (GANs) by Ian Goodfellow, which revolutionized the field of generative modeling, allowing for the creation of realistic synthetic data (Goodfellow et al., 2014). Even more recent developments have seen AI technologies evolve, as has the worldwide recognition of these systems. The most impactful advance was in 2018, with the introduction of the OpenAI company to the market, presenting GPT-2 and GPT-3 for the first time (Brown et al., 2020).

Undoubtedly, knowledge and disruptive technologies are the engines of change in societies, production structures, and general knowledge, rendering previous advances obsolete. AI evolved from a mere branch of computer science in the 20th century, limited to hardware capabilities, to become a crucial element in the development of 21st-century society across various industries and scientific fields (Nunes, 2023). Today, AI is a major global development trend, acting as a strategic factor for achieving competitive advantages internationally (Wang, 2021). When combined with multiple technologies, AI has driven economic development in industries such as electronic information manufacturing (An, 2021) and is a key factor in propelling human society into the intelligent era (Tan et al., 2024). Although AI's history spans several decades, significant recent advancements in Deep Learning (DL), Generative Models, Computer Vision, Robotics and Automation, and AI applications in various areas, including climate change, mark a new era of innovation, as discussed in the following sections.

3. KEY AI TECHNOLOGIES

3.1. Machine Learning

ML is a subfield of AI techniques that encompasses learning algorithms and statistical models to empower computers to perform tasks responsively rather than proactively by analyzing the data samples (Akila et al., 2022). This is a technique of data analysis whereby the building of an analytical model is conducted automatically. As part of ML, DL uses multi-layered (“deep”) neural networks to process different aspects of the data. These neural networks try to represent human brains and learn from quantities of data (Inavolu, 2024).

The value of ML to BM is multifaceted. Going by ML algorithms, one can be able to parse through big volumes of data to decipher patterns, trends, and all sorts that are pertinent to branding, all of which make it possible to craft a customer experience that is unique for the customer. This is crucial in building good brands to ensure the consumer is satisfied, thus leading to their retention (Desai, 2021). Furthermore, the data handling and learning capabilities of ML can assist brands in understanding consumers' behavior patterns and trends when it comes to marketing strategies, creating the optimal campaign as well as enhancing brand decision-making (Chandgude & Kawade, 2023). Concerning branding, ML helps enhance the products or services, making them intelligent enough to lead the business and provide a competitive edge in the market (Anute et al., 2021; Sadriwala & Sadriwala, 2022).

In other words, ML and DL are important for BM, as they offer consumer insights and personalization of marketing campaigns, predictive analysis to drive strategic decision-making, and automation in customer services and content creation to improve efficiency and consistency in BC (Inavolu, 2024).

3.2. Natural Language Processing

Natural Language Processing (NLP) is a subfield of AI that allows machines to decipher, process, and create human language (Sanadi, 2022; Shoukat, 2021). It lies in processing and interpreting human language with a computational approach that makes people capable of translating, summarizing the content, or even communicating with machines (Chaudhary et al., 2023; Yao & Guan, 2018).

NLP is important for brands as it enables sentiment analysis (it analyzes consumer reviews and social media posts to assess public sentiment towards a brand, helping to understand consumer satisfaction and brand perception, and helping increase brand awareness and social media engagement) (Huang, 2024), consumer interaction (chatbots and virtual assistants powered by NLP can improve customer service by providing instant answers to consumer questions, allowing for greater consumer satisfaction) (Ouaddi et al., 2024), and content creation (NLP tools help generate and select content for marketing campaigns, ensuring consistency and relevance in brand perception and communications) (Huang, 2024).

3.3. Computer Vision

Computer vision can be defined as a subdiscipline within AI, which allows the systems to gain meaningful knowledge from images, videos, and other kinds of visual data and respond to them. It entails the design of algorithms and models that can perform the following functionalities on visual data: comprehension, cognition, and action (Qiu et al., 2021).

Computer vision is important for brands because of its analysis. In other words, it enables visual content analysis (computer vision analyzes images and videos for brand logos, product placement, and visual content performance, providing valuable information on brand visibility and marketing effectiveness) (Boonsirisumpun et al., 2024), quality control (ensuring product quality and consistency is crucial to maintaining brand standards, which computer vision can achieve in manufacturing and retail) (Yüksel et al., 2023) and the presence of augmented reality (AR) (enhancing customer experiences with AR applications allows them to visualize products in their environment, reinforcing engagement with the brand) (Raikwar et al., 2024).

4. THE ROLE OF AI IN BM

With the power of big data and the automation of AI itself, there have been new advances in generative AI. These advances mean that there are more and more tools that can be used by professionals in different areas, such as BM. The power to produce content in line with the brand's identity by generating logos, brand colors, and brand messages allows brands to maintain consistency (Calderón-Fajardo et al., 2024; Olson & Olson, 2024). However, AI also makes it possible to offer tools for brand perception, as it helps to monitor sentiment with AI, improving brand image and understanding brand positioning through analysis (Ingole et al., 2024). This technology also makes it possible to obtain tools for brand development, such as AI copywriters for marketing copy, video production, automated graphic designs, obtaining consumer insights, and even having tools to protect brands. These descriptions are shown in Table 1, with some examples of the tools most used by professionals today.

Table 1. Using AI tools for innovating and enhancing branding

Brand field	AI application	Meaning	Platforms/Tools
BI	AI-Generated Logos	AI has hugely impacted the production of logos and has led to brands being able to develop more professional and unique logos. Machine learning algorithms scrutinize industry trends, brand image, and consumers' preferences to create attractive logos.	Logomakerr, Logo, Looka, Logo AI, Brandmark io, Logopony Logomaster AI, and Tailor Brands.
	AI-Designed Brand Colors	Psychological studies and the available market data can be effectively analyzed by AI, and it can come up with perfect brand colors that would generate the right emotional response in the targeted buyers. Such an approach to coloring also eliminates the possibility of the chosen colors being good just from the aesthetic point of view but wholly incompatible with the brand's message.	Adobe Color, Coolors, Canva, and Mokker
	AI-Created Brand Messaging	NLP dictates the way AI tools formulate persuasive brand messages given the vast information collated from social media platforms, and customer reviews among other indicators. These tools help to maintain the continuity of BC and its relevance to its audience and to address the emotions of the consumers.	Persado, Phrasee, TextCortex
Brand Perception	Monitoring Sentiments with AI	AI-powered sentiment analysis tools can scan social networks, feedback sites, and other feedback channels to find out what people think about a particular brand. Most of these tools use NLP to categorize and quantify the sentiments making it easier to get timely consumer perception.	Brand24, Talkwalker,
	Enhancing Brand Image with AI	AI tools can generate satisfactory images, videos, or written materials relevant to the brand image. Also, AI can tailor the communication and make sure that each touchpoint you use to communicate with consumers represents the brand in a way that consumers value.	Canva, Adobe Spark
	Understanding Brand Positioning through AI Analytics	The use of AI analysis helps in understanding how a particular brand is positioned within the market concerning other competitors. AI tools can even enable monitoring of consumer behavior, trends, and competitors' data to look for the strengths, weaknesses, opportunities, and threats (SWOT) for the brand.	Brandwatch, Sprout Social, ClientZen, Dovetail, Virtual Website Optimizer (VWO), and Microsoft Clarity

continued on following page

Table 1. Continued

Brand field	AI application	Meaning	Platforms/Tools
Brand Development	AI Writers for Marketing Copy	AI writers employ complex NLP techniques to write good and persuasive pieces of marketing content. These tools can produce any type of content: a blog post, social media status, or an email newsletter in the voice and to the brand image that is set.	Jasper AI, Copy.ai, Grammarly, Wordtune, and WriterSonic
	AI Tools for Video Production	Facial recognition technologies can be toggled to perform tasks that include editing a video even writing a script for a video or even in the production of animation videos. These tools act as a measure of the audiences' tendency and interaction ratio to develop videos that target the audiences effectively to push the branding correlates that go hand in hand.	Magisto, Lumen5, Runway, Pictory, Veed, HeyGen, and Pika Labs
	Automated Graphic Design with AI	Graphic design tools powered by AI can design smart and persuasive graphics, infographics, and advertisement panels. These tools help establish the fast and cheap creation of visuals by automating the design process of brands.	Designify, Crello, Mokker, Adobe Firefly, Microsoft Designer
	AI-Powered Market Research	Artificial systems in market research study massive data to reveal consumer consumption behaviors and other trends. These tools can forecast the prospective trends and the needs that are yet to be fulfilled by the consumers and offer guidance on how best to manage the branding processes.	SurveyMonkey, Qualtrics, HARPA, Perplexity, Glasp, and ChatGPT Plus

Source: Authors.

5. OPPORTUNITIES, CHALLENGES AND EXAMPLES

AI is still new in the industry was a tool but has been known to create some positive and negative impacts in some areas, like brand management. AI tools may well alter how BI girds are constructed, how brand messages are deployed, and how brand value propositions are configured and delivered (Kolla & Kumar, 2019). Furthermore, AI helps in the consistency of the brand's message across different media touchpoints; preferring users' behavior-altering switching for delivering brand messages effectively (Gajapathy, 2023).

The opportunities represented by AI for brands have focused, in most cases, on personalization, innovation, and efficiency. Personalization allows brands to create real and unique experiences in the context of their customers by processing large amounts of data to reveal customers' preferences and activities. This can improve the levels of satisfaction and hence customer loyalty among them. An example of the implementation of this opportunity is the case of the Netflix brand (Raji et al.,

2024). When it comes to Netflix´s brand strategy, they have embraced AI in almost all the processes, as a multifaceted approach to personalizing the consumer journey and enhancing different aspects of the user experience. Resuming, Netflix employs AI to analyze vast datasets, allowing them to deliver highly tailored content recommendations, thus fostering a personalized consumer journey (Sharma et al., 2021). This AI-driven personalization is pivotal in maintaining consumer engagement, satisfaction, and loyalty according to each consumer's preferences (Raji et al., 2024; Sharma et al., 2021). Another similar example is the music streaming platform Spotify which implemented AI to personalized playlists for each user based on their listening history, favorite genres, and the time of the day they listen to the platform (Prey, 2020). This method increases consumer satisfaction and helps them find new music they prefer (Raji et al., 2024).

Another opportunity is innovation, allowing brands to create new products and services, improve existing ones, and optimize strategic processes. AI can analyze market trends, predict future demand, and provide information for strategic decisions. An example of this opportunity is the Coca-Cola brand, which uses AI to analyze consumer data to develop new flavors and products according to their preferences (Prasad, 2024). Nevertheless, Coca-Cola incorporated AI to enhance its supply chain management, and integrated ML algorithms to improve the distribution and manufacturing process, which supports, indirectly, the innovation of products by ensuring efficient operations. These technologies have been developed to analyze consumer preferences and seek market trends, to enable the creation of new product formulations that evolve consumer preferences and tastes (Prasad, 2024).

Efficiency is another feature of AI-empowered tools, which automates repetitive tasks, reduces operating costs, and improves efficiency. This allows brands to allocate resources to more strategic initiatives. An example of this opportunity is the Procter & Gamble brand, which uses "AI for quality control on the production line, capturing data from sensors and imaging to replace manual off-line quality testing, increasing equipment efficiency and managing power and water consumption" (P&G, 2022).

On the other hand, AI technologies bring challenges and considerations too, for brand management, like data privacy, ethical issues, and integration and adaptation of this technology. Inevitably, AI systems need to collect and analyze large amounts of consumer data, raising concerns related to data privacy and security. To ensure a good attitude, brands must ensure data protection regulations and maintain consumer trust. In the European Union, to force the implementation of robust data security measures and transparency of practices was employed the "General Data Protection Regulation" (GDPR) in European territory (Crutzen et al., 2019). Beyond this, ethical issues are a current topic of concern in organizations and researchers. AI can maintain biases present in the data it is trained on, leading to unfair or discriminatory results. The current proposal is to regularly audit AI algorithms to ensure that potential biases are correctly identified, such as the presence of the required amount of data representation (Sahlgren, 2024; Sreerama & Krishnamoorthy, 2022). The last challenge is the integration of AI into existing brand management practices since it requires significant investment in technologies and training, as well as a cultural shift within the organizations (Inavolu, 2024). To ensure good practice and implementation of this technology, organizations should develop a clear AI integration strategy and provide continuous training for all employees (Inavolu, 2024).

As with any technological disruption, more challenges can arise, specifically concerning AI and the consistency of brands' presence. Firstly, AI makes it possible to ensure that brand messages are consistent across all channels, by automating content creation and monitoring to ensure the correct brand guidelines. An example of this consistency is the case of L´Oréal. This ensures that the company maintains standards in the dissemination of content through various mediums L'Oréal uses Generative AI technology to maintain consistency in the provision of different contents (Miles, 2023). In 2023, while realizing a modular approach to the Sitecore platform, the company strengthened its position on the Internet and tweaked its content strategies (Miles, 2023). This method involves the use of meta-tagging through artificial neural networks to systematically manage a diverse range of over 2. 2 million content assets. Furthermore, there is an AI-enriched Content Hub solution that L'Oréal is using to transform digital asset management and content operations to guarantee coherent interactions in the digital space for all the global areas (Sitecore, 2023). By implementing AI, L'Oréal ensures that numerous formalities are optimized, brand consistency is maintained, and SEO stands to be improved in various fields of digital platforms (Sitecore, 2023). It is understanding the importance of continuous, informative, and quality content to create attractive and productive customer experiences at the center of the commerce strategy. The fact that L'Oréal maintains this level of consistency can be credited to its pursuit of such a strategy, which it accomplishes with the help of AI-driven solutions for engaging with audiences across all digital channels (Sitecore, 2023).

Secondly, is possible to ensure consistency for brands through real-time customer engagement. In other words, AI allows brands to engage with their consumers in real-time through the existence of chatbots and virtual assistants, not just for instant support, but also for personalized experiences, as hallucinated before in this chapter. An example of this application is the H&M brand. H&M incorporates AI to enhance consumer engagement, through improving consumer interactions, analyzing data effectively, and optimizing their inventory and merchandising operations (Marr, 2019). One of the key initiatives by H&M is the use of a virtual assistant, called "Eva" designed to transform the consumer's interactions by supporting quick and accurate responses regarding products, sizes, and stock among other things (Daniel, 2024).

6. IMPLICATIONS

The integration of AI into brand management practices has profound implications for brands, consumers, and the industry. The following highlights summarize the transformative potential and challenges associated with this integration.

AI helps brands provide an incredibly qualitative service and plays a significant role in customer satisfaction, thus keeping them loyal. This means that AI data processing provides brands with unique recommendations and interactions that will have a personal connection with customers. For example, Spotify and Netflix, these organizations use an AI-based approach to predict the customer journey and provide content that suits their usage, which in turn results in customer satisfaction and loyalty (Raji et al., 2024; Sharma et al., 2021).

Brand operations inspired by AI automation and analysis ensure that resources are efficiently utilized, and the right decisions are made in this case. For example, by implementing AI in quality control and showing how to make processes more efficient and cut expenses, thus brands such as P&G can align with the best goals (P&G, 2022). The capability of AI in analyzing big data and making analyses that could help in strategic marketing is also helpful in improving marketing communication and branding activities.

Yet, as brands continue adopting AI solutions, issues related to data ownership and protection, besides considerations of ethics, surface as critical. Legal requirements can be as important as Sales and Marketing principles where compliance with laws like the GDPR, is vital for the sake of consumer confidence and to avoid legal repercussions. To address these challenges, brands need to operate with full transparency, as well as employ all the necessary measures of data protection (Crutzen et al., 2019). This means that like any other programs, AI algorithms require audits, and ethical evaluation to ensure fairness, and they should be done regularly (Sahlgren, 2024).

The incorporation of AI technologies in brand management may result in changes in employment especially in terms of job relations where there are implications for the existence and emergence of new employment skills. A new imperative will be to establish workforce training and development that would prepare employees to deal with the new system environment. Such transformation brings both prospects and threats in the course of the realization of these technologies as the industry advances (Nayak et al., 2024).

AI incorporation can be a competitive advantage for the brands, which helps them to stand out from others in the market. Smart product customization and development are good ways for brands to stand out and grab consumers' attention. Leading organizations such as Coca-Cola explain how the use of artificial intelligence can help in the generation of insights for new products and services that fit the current consumer tastes and trends (Prasad, 2024).

To implement AI in Brand Management effectively, the use of AI needs a strategic management approach and must change culturally within the organizations. The study suggests that brands need to push for change and engender cultures that support the utilization of AI technologies. This entails the formulation of a strong cognitive direction, procurement of technologies, and enhancement of the ongoing learning perspective (Inavolu, 2024).

In conclusion, the application of AI in brand management is comprehensive and holds several critical benefits of improving the positioning of the customer experience, operating model, and brand positioning. However, it also raises ethical issues, privacy, and adaptability of the workforce. The requirement to face these implications and the ability to manage AI as a tool for business development belongs to the brands that will succeed in the new environment.

7. FUTURE TRENDS AND DIRECTIONS

Currently, the topics of AI in brand management are in the state of rapid development, which defines further trends for nonstop growth, such as hyper-personalization, predictive analyses, integrating AI into creation processes, and more.

Technological solutions in the field of AI are gradually evolving to the next level of developing highly personalized solutions to adapt to the needs of individual consumers. This allows brands to present content and experiences that perfectly match consumers' personalities. Bialkova (2024) notes that this is a trend that means the future of branding will be highly personal, with the supremacy of customer-centric strategies that increase the level of customer satisfaction.

The application of AI in predictive analysis allows brands to determine markets, customers, and products in the future. This capability is important for making decisions to improve brand positioning and, in general, the operation of the organizations. Inavolu (2024) analyzes the possibility that big data and predictive analytics could lead the changes in customer relations and business organization plans.

AI is now considered vital in creative industries such as graphic design, video production, and content development. Companies apply AI to create excellent graphics and texts that match their brand image and engage consumers. Cheng (2024) presents this trend by illustrating how AI improves creativity and uniformity in BCs.

Looking ahead, several of the following predictions are expected about how AI will further alter brand management. Interactive AI will continue to improve its functional ways of interacting with customers in real-time through chatbots and voice assistants, and therefore boost customer experience and loyalty. Mentzas et al. (2024) describe that sociable technology will incorporate an increasing degree of artificial intelligence to improve customer interaction experiences.

Merging AI with AR will ensure that customers experience branded products in Augmented Reality and therefore improve the purchasing decision process. The proposal raised by Cheng (2024) presents a production of a challenging and stimulating atmosphere that will allow customers to acquire knowledge and have fun at the same time.

AI will be used to help accredit and safeguard brand assets on the web. Preliminary examples include recognizing counterfeit products and solving brand image problems with the help of analytical tools. Cook (2024) present the aspect of AI as a measure to protect the luxury brand from the dangers that exist in the digital world.

However, as with any technology, there are implications for both academia and companies. New trends indicate that innovations in the use of AI in brand management require a greater focus on the development of more academic concepts, as well as an adequate curriculum in the preparation of future marketing professionals.

That's why companies need to embrace these new trends by implementing artificial intelligence technologies and promoting innovations on an ongoing basis. Some of these include training employees on how to use or work with AI, as well as incorporating AI into business strategies. Similarly, Rashid et al. (2024) described that organizational flexibility and creativity can become factors of competitive advantage when integrating AI technologies and systems.

8. CONCLUSION

AI has become a significant part of brand management, and it brings a lot of changes in the digital marketing world and customer interaction. This chapter looked at how the future of AI and brand management has played out and how AI technology has advanced and changed the face of brand strategies.

The use of AI has been seen as a force multiplier in strengthening brand image, understanding, and messaging. Advanced technologies like machine learning, and natural language processing facilitate brand interactions with the consumers uniquely. AI has helped in the analysis of large data sets to generate new insights into consumer behavior, which in turn offers better approaches to marketing.

The advancement of AI technologies from predictive AI to generative AI has created new opportunities to exploit the creativity and effectiveness of brand management. AI solutions have found a place in content generation, client interactions, and market research to enhance customer retention and competitive positioning.

Nevertheless, brand management with the help of AI has some drawbacks. Other challenges such as ethical concerns, privacy concerns, and constant pressure for innovation and improvement are also some of the challenges that brands face. AI is here to stay and as it becomes more advanced brands need to fashion a solid plan for implementing AI whilst at the same time protecting consumers' data and adhering to the rules and regulations.

In the future of AI for brand management, they expect more developments in hyper-personalization, more accurate analyses, and interactive AI. Companies that employ these technologies will be in a good position to do well in the digital landscape delivering value to consumers. Thus, AI is no longer a bonus but a necessity in brand management today, opening vast possibilities for its development. The implementation of AI is advantageous for brands because it allows them to improve their market stance and create valuable connections with their consumers, enabling them to succeed in the constantly growing market.

REFERENCES

Aaker, D. A. (1991). *Managing brand equity: capitalizing on the value of a brand name*. Free Press.

Akila, D., Jeyalaksshmi, S., & Padmapriya, D. Devipriya, Prithika, P., & Elangovan, V. R. (2022). Significance of Machine Learning and Deep Learning in Development of Artificial Intelligence. In (pp. 25-44). DOI: 10.1201/9780367816414-2

Anute, N., Paliwal, M., Patel, M., & Kandale, N. (2021). Impact of artificial intelligence and machine learning on business operations. *Journal of Management Research and Analysis*, 8(2), 69–74. DOI: 10.18231/j.jmra.2021.015

Arora, S. (2018). *Brand Image And Its Impact on Buying Behaviour*. Medium. https://medium.com/business2change/brand-image-and-its-impact-on-buying-behaviour-faa61776664

Assabil, M. R., Yusliani, N., & Darmawahyuni, A. (2023). Text Generation using Long Short Term Memory to Generate a LinkedIn Post. *Sriwijaya Journal of Communication*, 4(2), 10–19. DOI: 10.36706/sjia.v4i2.64

Bacalhau, L. S. M. (2020). *Capital das Marcas Organizacionais (B2B): Uma Abordagem em Contexto de Ingredient Branding - Os Casos da Shimano, Inc. e Órbita - Bicicletas Portuguesas, Lda.* [PhD Thesis, Universidade do Porto]. https://hdl.handle.net/10216/130411

Ball, T., & Zorn, B. (2015). Teach foundational language principles. *Communications of the ACM*, 58(5), 30–31. DOI: 10.1145/2663342

Batin, M., Turchin, A., Markov, S., Zhila, A., & Denkenberger, D. (2017). Artificial Intelligence in Life Extension: From Deep Learning to Superintelligence. *Informatica-Journal of Computing and Informatics*, 41(4), 401–417.

Bialkova, S. (2024). AI Transforming Business and Everyday Life. In Bialkova, S. (Ed.), *The Rise of AI User Applications: Chatbots Integration Foundations and Trends* (pp. 143–165). Springer Nature Switzerland., DOI: 10.1007/978-3-031-56471-0_9

Boonsirisumpun, N., Okafor, E., & Surinta, O. (2024). Vehicle image datasets for image classification. *Data in Brief*, 53, 110133. DOI: 10.1016/j.dib.2024.110133 PMID: 38348321

Brodie, R. J., Benson-Rea, M., & Medlin, C. J. (2016). Branding as a dynamic capability. *Marketing Theory*, 17(2), 183–199. DOI: 10.1177/1470593116679871

Brown, T. B., Mann, B., Ryder, N., Subbiah, M., Kaplan, J., Dhariwal, P., Neelakantan, A., Shyam, P., Sastry, G., Askell, A., Agarwal, S., Herbert-Voss, A., Krueger, G., Henighan, T., Child, R., Ramesh, A., Ziegler, D. M., Wu, J., Winter, C., & Amodei, D. (2020). Language Models are Few-Shot Learners. *ArXiv*. https://arxiv.org/abs/2005.14165

Caldarini, G., Jaf, S., & McGarry, K. (2022). A Literature Survey of Recent Advances in Chatbots. *Information (Basel)*, 13(1), 41. Advance online publication. DOI: 10.3390/info13010041

Calderón-Fajardo, V., Anaya-Sánchez, R., & Rejón-Guardia, F. (2024). Neurotourism Insights: Eye Tracking and Galvanic Analysis of Tourism Destination Brand Logos and AI Visuals. *Tourism &amp. Tourism & Management Studies*, 20(3), 53–78. DOI: 10.18089/tms.20240305

Campbell, M., Hoane, A. J.Jr, & Hsu, F. (2002). Deep Blue. *Artificial Intelligence*, 134(1), 57–83. DOI: 10.1016/S0004-3702(01)00129-1

Chandgude, V., & Kawade, B. (2023). Role of Artificial Intelligence and Machine Learning in Decision Making for Business Growth. *International Journal of Advanced Research in Science. Tongxin Jishu*, 54-58, 54–58. Advance online publication. DOI: 10.48175/IJARSCT-8556

Chaudhary, P., Kurariya, P., Singh, S. P., Bodhankar, J., Singh, L., & Kumar, A. (2022). Intelligent virtual research environment for natural language processing (IvrE-NLP). In *Smart Trends in Computing and Communications* [Springer Nature Singapore.]. *Proceedings of SmartCom*, 2022, 453–465.

Cheng, Z. (2024). *Interpretable and generative AI for actionable insights from textual data*. Phd Thesis. Boston University. https://hdl.handle.net/2144/48748

Christodoulides, G. (2009). Branding in the post-internet era. *Marketing Theory*, 9(1), 141–144. DOI: 10.1177/1470593108100071

Chung, M., Ko, E., Joung, H., & Kim, S. J. (2020). Chatbot e-service and customer satisfaction regarding luxury brands. *Journal of Business Research*, 117, 587–595. DOI: 10.1016/j.jbusres.2018.10.004

Chung, S.-Y., & Byrom, J. (2020). Co-creating consistent brand identity with employees in the hotel industry. *Journal of Product and Brand Management*, 30(1), 74–89. DOI: 10.1108/JPBM-08-2019-2544

Cook, G. O. K., & Olsanova, K. (2024). Luxury brand management in the world of evolving technologies. *The Journal of Business Leadership*, 31(1), 58–68. DOI: 10.69847/Ip4X5VDf

Crutzen, R., Ygram Peters, G.-J., & Mondschein, C. (2019). Why and how we should care about the General Data Protection Regulation. *Psychology & Health*, 34(11), 1347–1357. DOI: 10.1080/08870446.2019.1606222 PMID: 31111730

Daniel, E. J. (2024). *AI-Enabled Retail: Crafting the Future of Shopping Experiences.* Medium. https://medium.com/@daniel.erinj2/ai-enabled-retail-crafting-the-future-of-shopping-experiences-4aa275e5f5cb

de Chernatony, L. (2010). *From Brand Vision to Brand Evaluation: The Strategic Process of Growing and Strengthening Brand* (3rd ed.). Routledge. DOI: 10.4324/9780080966649

Deng, Z. (2023). Research on the Development Trend of Artificial Intelligence Led by ChatGPT. *Highlights in Science. Engineering and Technology*, 56, 112–116. DOI: 10.54097/hset.v56i.9822

Deryl, M. D., Verma, S., & Srivastava, V. (2023). How does AI drive branding? Towards an integrated theoretical framework for AI-driven branding. *International Journal of Information Management Data Insights*, 3(2), 100205. DOI: 10.1016/j.jjimei.2023.100205

Desai, P. (2021). A Strategic Approach to Enrich Brand Through Artificial Intelligence. In *Machine Learning for Predictive Analysis* [Springer Singapore.]. *Proceedings of ICTIS*, 2020, 579–587.

Di Vaio, A., Palladino, R., Hassan, R., & Escobar, O. (2020). Artificial intelligence and business models in the sustainable development goals perspective: A systematic literature review. *Journal of Business Research*, 121, 283–314. DOI: 10.1016/j.jbusres.2020.08.019

Dinner, I. M., Heerde Van, H. J., & Neslin, S. A. (2014). Driving Online and Offline Sales: The Cross-Channel Effects of Traditional, Online Display, and Paid Search Advertising. *JMR, Journal of Marketing Research*, 51(5), 527–545. DOI: 10.1509/jmr.11.0466

Erevelles, S., Fukawa, N., & Swayne, L. (2016). Big Data consumer analytics and the transformation of marketing. *Journal of Business Research*, 69(2), 897–904. DOI: 10.1016/j.jbusres.2015.07.001

Farayola, O. A., Abdul, A. A., Irabor, B. O., & Okeleke, E. C. (2023). Innovative business models driven by ai technologies: A review. *Computer Science & IT Research Journal*, 4(2), 85–110.

Gajapathy, V. (2023). Role of Artificial Intelligence Across various media platforms: A quantitative investigation of media. In *Futuristic Trends in Management* (Vol. 2, pp. 1–10). IIP Series., DOI: 10.58532/V2BS7P1CH1

Goodfellow, I., Pouget-Abadie, J., Mirza, M., Xu, B., Warde-Farley, D., Ozair, S., Courville, A., & Bengio, Y. (2014). *Generative Adversarial Nets*https://proceedings.neurips.cc/paper_files/paper/2014/file/5ca3e9b122f61f8f06494c97b1afccf3-Paper.pdf

Gugerty, L. (2006). Newell and Simon's Logic Theorist: Historical Background and Impact on Cognitive Modeling. *Proceedings of the Human Factors and Ergonomics Society Annual Meeting*, 50(9), 880–884. DOI: 10.1177/154193120605000904

Guliyev, S. M. (2023). The Impact of Brand Perception and Brand Image on Consumer Purchasing Behavior in Azerbaijan. *Science, Education and Innovations in the context of modern problems, 6*(1), 137-144. .DOI: 10.56334/sei/6.1.5

Haigh, T. (2023). There Was No 'First AI Winter'. *Communications of the ACM*, 66(12), 35–39. DOI: 10.1145/3625833

Haigh, T. (2024). How the AI Boom Went Bust. *Communications of the ACM*, 67(2), 22–26. DOI: 10.1145/3634901

Hassabis, D., Kumaran, D., Summerfield, C., & Botvinick, M. (2017). Neuroscience-Inspired Artificial Intelligence. *Neuron*, 95(2), 245–258. DOI: 10.1016/j.neuron.2017.06.011 PMID: 28728020

He, K., Zhang, X., Ren, S., & Sun, J. (2015). Delving deep into rectifiers: Surpassing human-level performance on imagenet classification. In *Proceedings of the IEEE international conference on computer vision* (pp. 1026-1034). DOI: 10.1109/ICCV.2015.123

Hinton, G. E., Osindero, S., & Teh, Y. W. (2006). A fast learning algorithm for deep belief nets. *Neural Computation*, 18(7), 1527–1554. DOI: 10.1162/neco.2006.18.7.1527 PMID: 16764513

Huang, S. (2024). Exploring the Influence of Natural Language Processing Technology on Marketing Strategy Innovation Management in Emerging Markets for Multinational Corporations. *Journal of Logistics. Informatics and Service Science*, 11(3), 399–411. DOI: 10.33168/JLISS.2024.0326

Ianenko, M., Stepanov, M., & Mironova, L. (2020). Brand identity development. *E3S Web of Conferences, 164*, 09015. .DOI: 10.1051/e3sconf/202016409015

Iglesias, O., Landgraf, P., Ind, N., Markovic, S., & Koporcic, N. (2020). Corporate brand identity co-creation in business-to-business contexts. *Industrial Marketing Management*, 85, 32–43. DOI: 10.1016/j.indmarman.2019.09.008

Inavolu, S. M. (2024). *Exploring AI-Driven Customer Service: Evolution, Architectures, Opportunities, Challenges and Future Directions*. DOI: 10.13140/RG.2.2.19937.31841

Ingole, A., Khude, P., Kittad, S., Parmar, V., & Ghotkar, A. (2024, 22-23 Feb. 2024). Competitive Sentiment Analysis for Brand Reputation Monitoring. In *2024 Second International Conference on Emerging Trends in Information Technology and Engineering (ICETITE)*. DOI: 10.1109/ic-ETITE58242.2024.10493574

Issalillah, F., Darmawan, D., & Khairi, M. (2022). The Role of Brand Image and Brand Communications on Brand Trust. *Journal of Science* [SICO]. *Technology in Society*, 3(1), 1–6.

Iyer, P., Davari, A., Zolfagharian, M., & Paswan, A. (2019). Market orientation, positioning strategy and brand performance. *Industrial Marketing Management*, 81, 16–29. DOI: 10.1016/j.indmarman.2018.11.004

Kapferer, J. N. (2012). *The New Strategic Brand Management: Advanced Insights and Strategic Thinking*. Kogan Page.

Keller, K. L. (1993). Conceptualizing, Measuring, and Managing Customer-Based Brand Equity. *Journal of Marketing*, 57(1), 1–22. DOI: 10.1177/002224299305700101

Keller, K. L., & Lehmann, D. R. (2006). Brands and Branding: Research Findings and Future Priorities. *Marketing Science*, 25(6), 740–759. DOI: 10.1287/mksc.1050.0153

Kelly, R. c. (2023). *How Do Brand Image and Marketing Affect Market Share?* Investopedia. https://www.investopedia.com/ask/answers/032615/how-does-brand-image-and-marketing-affect-market-share.asp

Kolla, N., & Kumar, M. G. (2019). Meta-synthesis on artificial intelligence (AI): Imperatives for branding. *International Journal of Recent Technology and Engineering*, 8(3), 2251–2255. DOI: 10.35940/ijrte.B3268.098319

Kotler, P. (2000). *Marketing Management: Millennium Edition*. Prentice Hall.

Krupka, Z. (2023). Exploring the Influence of Sensory Marketing on Brand Perception. *Naše gospodarstvo/Our economy, 69*(3), 45-55. .DOI: 10.2478/ngoe-2023-0017

Kull, A. J., Romero, M., & Monahan, L. (2021). How may I help you? Driving brand engagement through the warmth of an initial chatbot message. *Journal of Business Research*, 135, 840–850. DOI: 10.1016/j.jbusres.2021.03.005

Kumar, A., Tejaswini, P., Nayak, O., Kujur, A. D., Gupta, R., Rajanand, A., & Sahu, M. (2022). A Survey on IBM Watson and Its Services. *Journal of Physics: Conference Series*, 2273(1), 012022. DOI: 10.1088/1742-6596/2273/1/012022

Kumar, L., & Jindal, S. (2018). Role of Artificial Intelligence in Intellectual Property Rights. In *Shivam Jindal Artificial Intelligence* (pp. 609-614).

Magno, F., & Dossena, G. (2023). The effects of chatbots' attributes on customer relationships with brands: PLS-SEM and importance–performance map analysis. *The TQM Journal*, 35(5), 1156–1169. DOI: 10.1108/TQM-02-2022-0080

Marr, B. (2019). *How Fashion Retailer H&M Is Betting On Artificial Intelligence And Big Data To Regain Profitability*. Forbes. https://www.forbes.com/sites/bernardmarr/2018/08/10/how-fashion-retailer-hm-is-betting-on-artificial-intelligence-and-big-data-to-regain-profitability/

Mentzas, G., Hribernik, K., Stahre, J., Romero, D., & Soldatos, J. (2024). Editorial: Human-Centered Artificial Intelligence in Industry 5.0. *Frontiers in Artificial Intelligence*, 7, 1429186. Advance online publication. DOI: 10.3389/frai.2024.1429186 PMID: 38915905

Miles, L. (2023). *How L'Oréal developed better content and customer experiences online*. AdAge. https://adage.com/article/digital-marketing-ad-tech-news/how-loreal-developed-better-content-and-customer-experiences-online/2486346

Mishra, S., & Tripathi, A. (2020). *AI Business Model: An Integrative Business Approach. Research Square*. DOI: 10.21203/rs.3.rs-90687/v1

Mishra, S., & Tripathi, A. R. (2021). AI business model: An integrative business approach. *Journal of Innovation and Entrepreneurship*, 10(1), 18. DOI: 10.1186/s13731-021-00157-5

Mogaji, E. (2021). *Brand Management: An introduction through storytelling*. Palgrave Macmillan. DOI: 10.1007/978-3-030-66119-9

Nayak, A., Patnaik, A., Satpathy, I., & Khang, A. (2024). The Power of Artificial Intelligence in Management Education. In *Digital Talent Management Strategies* (pp. 54–70). Springer.

Nguyen, Q. (2023). AI Representation in Cinema: A Quantitative Content Analysis. https://www.researchgate.net/profile/Quynh-Nguyen-431/publication/377410844_AI_REPRESENTATION_IN_CINEMA_A_Quantitative_Content_Analysis/links/65a56a5a5582153a6828704d/AI-REPRESENTATION-IN-CINEMA-A-Quantitative-Content-Analysis.pdf

Nunes, P. M. D. (2023). *A Inteligência Artificial e o direito da propriedade intelectual.* Edições Almedina.

Olson, E. M., & Olson, K. C. (2024). Exploring the Feasibility of AI-Generated Logo Concepts. *Design Management Review*, 35(2), 20–27. DOI: 10.1111/drev.12394

Ouaddi, C., Benaddi, L., Souha, A., & Jakimi, A. (2024, 24-26 April 2024). A comparative and analysis study for recommending a chatbot development tool. *2024 International Conference on Global Aeronautical Engineering and Satellite Technology (GAST).* DOI: 10.1109/GAST60528.2024.10520754

P&G. (2022). Leveraging Technology to Improve The Lives of P&G Consumers. https://us.pg.com/blogs/executive-talks-innovation-vittorio-cretella/

Prasad, N. S. (2024). A Study to Know the Impact of AI on Sustainability of Products in the Carbonated Beverages. *International Journal of Scientific Research in Engineering and Management*, 08(03), 1–15. DOI: 10.55041/IJSREM29113

Prey, R. (2020). Locating Power in Platformization: Music Streaming Playlists and Curatorial Power. *Social Media + Society*, 6(2), 2056305120933291. DOI: 10.1177/2056305120933291

Qiu, J., Liu, J., & Shen, Y. (2021). Computer Vision Technology Based on Deep Learning. .DOI: 10.1109/ICIBA52610.2021.9687873

Raikwar, P. P., Bhandari, G. M., Patil, S. S., & Shivale, N. M. (2024). Robust Cloth Warping via Multi-Scale Patch Adversarial Loss for Virtual Try-On Framework. *Jisuanji Yanjiu Yu Fazhan*, 24(4), 89–92.

Raji, M. A., Olodo, H. B., Oke, T. T., Addy, W. A., Ofodile, O. C., & Oyewole, A. T. (2024). E-commerce and consumer behavior: A review of AI-powered personalization and market trends. *GSC Advanced Research and Reviews, 18*(3), 066-077. .DOI: 10.30574/gscarr.2024.18.3.0090

Rashid, S. M., Ali, K. A. A., Mousa, K. M., & Pooyanmehr, M. (2024). Developing Business Management Concepts in the Economic Field Based on Artificial Intelligence in Light of Increasing Data. In *Preprints*: *Preprints.*

Roess, M. (2016). Old answers to new questions: Turing tests in the era of big data. *PsycCRITIQUES*, •••, 61.

Rondonuwu, A. O. R., Freddy. (2024). The Influence of Brand Image Brand Awareness and Promotion on Purchase Decisions for Ubiquiti Brand IT Network Devices in Indonesia. *Co-Value: Jurnal Ekonomi, Koperasi & Kewirausahaan, 14.*

Russell, S., & Norvig, P. (2021). *Artificial Intelligence, Global Edition: A Modern Approach*. Pearson.

Sadriwala, M. F., & Sadriwala, K. F. (2022). Perceived Usefulness and Ease of Use of Artificial Intelligence on Marketing Innovation. [IJIDE]. *International Journal of Innovation in the Digital Economy*, 13(1), 1–10. DOI: 10.4018/IJIDE.292010

Sahlgren, O. (2024). Action-guidance and AI ethics: The case of fair machine learning. *AI and Ethics*. Advance online publication. DOI: 10.1007/s43681-024-00437-2

Sahoo, S. (2022). Big data analytics in manufacturing: A bibliometric analysis of research in the field of business management. *International Journal of Production Research*, 60(22), 6793–6821. DOI: 10.1080/00207543.2021.1919333

Sanadi, A. M. B. (2022). A Review Paper on Natural Language Processing (NLP). *International Journal of Advanced Research in Science* [IJARSCT]. *Tongxin Jishu*, 2(2), 23–29. DOI: 10.48175/IJARSCT-2685

Sasmita, M. T., Arie Yudhistira, P. G., & Aditya Aristana, I. K. G. (2022). The Influence of Brand Image and Brand Trust on Consumer Loyalty (Case Study on Consumers of PT Citilink Indonesia Branch Office Denpasar). *TRJ Tourism Research Journal*, 6(1), 60. Advance online publication. DOI: 10.30647/trj.v6i1.129

Seranmadevi, R., Chakraverty, S., Raj, B., Kudapa, V. K., Hepziba, R. E., & Suleimenova, K. (2022, 25-27 May 2022). Utilisation of Virtual Assistant and Its Impact on Retail Industry. In *2022 6th International Conference on Intelligent Computing and Control Systems (ICICCS)*, DOI: 10.1109/ICICCS53718.2022.9788243

Sharma, R. S., Shaikh, A. A., & Li, E. (2021). Designing Recommendation or Suggestion Systems: Looking to the future. *Electronic Markets*, 31(2), 243–252. DOI: 10.1007/s12525-021-00478-z

Shoukat, A. A. S. V. K. (2021). AI-Natural Language Processing (NLP). *International Journal for Research in Applied Science & Engineering Technology (IJRASET)*, 9(8), 135-140. https://www.ijraset.com/fileserve.php?FID=37293

Shumanov, M., & Johnson, L. (2021). Making conversations with chatbots more personalized. *Computers in Human Behavior*, 117, 106627. DOI: 10.1016/j.chb.2020.106627

Silver, D., Schrittwieser, J., Simonyan, K., Antonoglou, I., Huang, A., Guez, A., Hubert, T., Baker, L., Lai, M., Bolton, A., Chen, Y., Lillicrap, T., Hui, F., Sifre, L., van den Driessche, G., Graepel, T., & Hassabis, D. (2017). Mastering the game of Go without human knowledge. *Nature*, 550(7676), 354–359. DOI: 10.1038/nature24270 PMID: 29052630

Sitecore. (2023). *L'Oréal harnesses the power of Generative AI at scale with Sitecore*. Sitecore. https://www.sitecore.com/customers/consumer-goods/loreal-drives-innovation-with-composable-sitecore-platform

Sreerama, J., & Krishnamoorthy, G. (2022). Ethical Considerations in AI Addressing Bias and Fairness in Machine Learning Models. *Journal of Knowledge Learning and Science Technology ISSN: 2959-6386 (online), 1*, 130-138. DOI: 10.60087/jklst.vol1.n1.p138

Srivastava, A., & Dey, D. K. (2016). Brand analysis of global and local banks in India: A study of young consumers. *Journal of Indian Business Research*, 8(1), 4–18. DOI: 10.1108/JIBR-05-2015-0061

Sterrett, S. G. (2020). The Genius of the 'Original Imitation Game' Test. *Minds and Machines*, 30(4), 469–486. DOI: 10.1007/s11023-020-09543-6

Sudmann, A. (2022). *On Computer creativity. Machine learning and the arts of artificial intelligences*. .DOI: 10.5817/CZ.MUNI.M280-0225-2022-11

Tarannum, J., Arfath, J., Madnoor, P., Alekhya, M., & Maltumkar Sri, L. (2024). A Study on Importance of Branding and Its Effects on Products in Business. [IRJAEM]. *International Research Journal on Advanced Engineering and Management*, 2(04), 656–661. DOI: 10.47392/IRJAEM.2024.0091

Temporal, P. (2014). *Branding for the Public Sector: Creating, Building and Managing Brands People will Value*. John Wiley and Sons Ltd. DOI: 10.1002/9781119176824

Varsha, P. S., Akter, S., Kumar, A., Gochhait, S., & Patagundi, B. (2021). The Impact of Artificial Intelligence on Branding. *Journal of Global Information Management*, 29(4), 221–246. DOI: 10.4018/JGIM.20210701.oa10

Volkmar, G., Fischer, P. M., & Reinecke, S. (2022). Artificial Intelligence and Machine Learning: Exploring drivers, barriers, and future developments in marketing management. *Journal of Business Research*, 149, 599–614. DOI: 10.1016/j.jbusres.2022.04.007

Voorveld, H. A. M. (2019). Brand Communication in Social Media: A Research Agenda. *Journal of Advertising*, 48(1), 14–26. DOI: 10.1080/00913367.2019.1588808

Wang, P. (2021). Research and Development Trend of Artificial Intelligence Technology Innovation Under the Internet Background. In *Cyber Security Intelligence and Analytics:2021 International Conference on Cyber Security Intelligence and Analytics (CSIA2021)*, Volume 1 (pp. 266-273). Springer International Publishing. DOI: 10.1007/978-3-030-70042-3_39

Whetten, D. A. (2006). Albert and Whetten Revisited: Strengthening the Concept of Organizational Identity. *Journal of Management Inquiry*, 15(3), 219–234. DOI: 10.1177/1056492606291200

Yang, Q., Hayat, N., Al Mamun, A., Makhbul, Z. K. M., & Zainol, N. R. (2022). Sustainable customer retention through social media marketing activities using hybrid SEM-neural network approach. *PLoS One*, 17(3), e0264899. DOI: 10.1371/journal.pone.0264899 PMID: 35245323

Yao, L., & Guan, Y. (2018, 10-12 Dec. 2018). An Improved LSTM Structure for Natural Language Processing. *2018 IEEE International Conference of Safety Produce Informatization (IICSPI)*, DOI: 10.1109/IICSPI.2018.8690387

Yuan, Y., & Zhu, J. (2023). Intelligent Intercommunicating Multiscale Engineering: The Engineering of the Future. *Engineering (Beijing)*, 30, 13–19. DOI: 10.1016/j.eng.2023.03.021

Yüksel, H. M., Mut, A. D., & Ozpinar, A. (2023). Enhancing Image Content Analysis in B2C Online Marketplaces. *The European Journal of Research and Development*, 3(4), 229–239. DOI: 10.56038/ejrnd.v3i4.381

Zhang, Y. (2015). The Impact of Brand Image on Consumer Behavior: A Literature Review. *Open Journal of Business and Management*, 03(01), 58–62. DOI: 10.4236/ojbm.2015.31006

Zhao, Y. (2023). Exploring the Transformation of Movie Publicity Strategies under the Perspective of New Media Communication. *Communications in Humanities Research*, 22(1), 257–262. DOI: 10.54254/2753-7064/22/20231773

ADDITIONAL READING

Aggarwal, A., & Commuri, S. (2023). *Brands nd Branding: Strategy to Build and Nurture Brands*. Taylor and Francis., DOI: 10.4324/9781003457282

Chen, Y.-W., Ruan, X., & Jain, R. K. (2024). Introduction to Logo Detection. In Chen, Y.-W., Ruan, X., & Jain, R. K. (Eds.), *Recent Advances in Logo Detection Using Machine Learning Paradigms: Theory and Practice* (pp. 33–41). Springer International Publishing., DOI: 10.1007/978-3-031-59811-1_2

Chen, Y.-W., Ruan, X., & Jain, R. K. (2024). Deep Convolutional Neural Networks. In Chen, Y.-W., Ruan, X., & Jain, R. K. (Eds.), *Recent Advances in Logo Detection Using Machine Learning Paradigms: Theory and Practice* (pp. 1–31). Springer International Publishing., DOI: 10.1007/978-3-031-59811-1_1

Yuan, C., Wang, S., & Liu, Y. (2023). AI service impacts on brand image and customer equity: Empirical evidence from China. *Journal of Brand Management*, 30(1), 61–76. DOI: 10.1057/s41262-022-00292-8

KEY TERMS AND DEFINITIONS

Artificial Intelligence (AI): AI refers to the capability of machines to demonstrate intelligence and abilities like those possessed by human beings; this capability involves their ability to learn and solve problems.

Brand Communication: BC includes the strategies and the media through which a company interacts with the target consumers concerning a specific brand, which may include advertising, social media presence, and the company's public relations activities.

Brand Equity (BE): BE portrays the value that consumers place on the brand name, which can help them in their decision-making processes and develop brand loyalty.

Brand Management: Brand management is the act of sustaining, developing, and protecting a brand's identity through communication and delivery to guarantee that it remains coherent and valuable in all the points of contact with the market to motivate customers and boost business opportunities.

Generative Adversarial Networks (GANs): GANs are a type of AI where two neural networks are set up as adversaries, where one produces synthetic data, while the other must distinguish between real data and synthetic data.

Generative AI (Gen-AI): Generative AI means AI systems that are designed to come up with new content including text, images, and music from prior data, and can present new results that have similar patterns to that of the training data.

Processors: Processors or central processing units (CPUs) are the physical components of a computer that execute the commands, instructions, and requests of software to perform basic mathematical and logical operations, data I/O, and other functions for applications.

Chapter 10
More Than Brands, Friends:
Enhancing Emotional Engagement Through AI in Digital Relationship Marketing Context

Sandra Ferreira
https://orcid.org/0009-0009-8256-2683
University of Minho, Portugal

Olga Pereira
https://orcid.org/0000-0002-1428-4927
CIICESI, ESTG, Instituto Politécnico do Porto, Portugal

ABSTRACT

In today's highly competitive business environment, technological advancements have significantly transformed business operations, particularly through the integration of Artificial Intelligence (AI). AI has implemented innovative digital strategies for attracting and retaining customers, garnering widespread attention due to its potential to deliver favorable outcomes and create emotional engagement. However, previous studies have overlooked emotions as a crucial part of consumer engagement. This chapter explores the influence of AI on emotional engagement within the digital context of Relationship Marketing (RM). Five propositions are proposed based on theoretical assumptions to guide and enrich future research in this domain. Additionally, ethical issues and managerial strategies are discussed to provide a comprehensive understanding of AI's impact on customer relationships.

DOI: 10.4018/979-8-3693-5340-0.ch010

1. INTRODUCTION

The debate surrounding replacing human roles with Artificial Intelligence (AI) technologies has always been a controversial topic and still needs to be explored, pointing to an urgent call for establishing guidelines to explore this emerging domain in-depth (Cheng et al., 2023). As customers move online, either partially or fully, firms are adapting by engaging with customer-created communities or managing their customer communities, where nearly instant responses are anticipated (Marti et al., 2023). To date, few researchers have examined how AI may affect customers' emotional engagement and their relationship with a brand. In particular, how much human and machine intelligence can be combined to optimize digital relationship marketing (RM). There is a need to develop measurement models that better capture the depth of customers' emotional responses to consumption situations (Bowden, 2009). Emotional engagement is an important behavioral factor that includes individuals expressing emotions like love, anger, excitement, boredom, curiosity, appreciation, or amusement, along with situations that are humorous, touching, or dramatic (Heath, 2009).

The development of AI in the marketing context has been remarkable. In today's digital era, AI has become integrated into customer service processes and has altered customer behaviors (Yang, 2023). AI-powered marketing tools are expected to be crucial in shaping our future understanding of consumer attitudes, beliefs, and behaviors (Vlačić et al., 2021). However, only in recent years, research at the AI-marketing intersection has gained more attention, prompting further investigation into AI's role in marketing (Vlačić et al., 2021). Previous research on AI has mainly concentrated on the technical aspects of AI tools (Prentice & Nguyen, 2020). This study extends its application into the domain of emotional engagement.

The exploration of AI within the realm of emotional RM represents a significant pivot towards understanding and enhancing the dynamics of customer engagement in the digital age. As we delve into the complexities of how AI can personalize interactions, optimize customer experiences, and shape the future of marketing strategies, it becomes evident that AI can have a positive and a negative influence on social emotions. Digital RM is not just an emerging trend but a fundamental shift in how businesses approach customer relationships. Engagement extends beyond transactions, establishing an emotionally-grounded connection between customers and firms (Alvarez-Milán et al., 2018).

Previous research at the customer level tends to examine why and when customers are motivated to engage in virtual brand communities and the means to facilitate consumer engagement. Little remains known regarding emotional engagement or the role AI plays in the engagement process taking a broader perspective, consumer engagement is conceptualized as a psychological process that includes cognitive, emotional, and behavioral dimensions (Bowden, 2009; Claffey & Brady, 2019). However, previous empirical studies have ignored emotions as a significant component when studying consumer engagement (Claffey & Brady, 2017).

Although the field of RM has been a subject of academic research, its relevance appears even more pronounced in the highly multifaceted relationships that exist in the digital environment and with the integration of AI. Targeting social emotions is pivotal for cultivating enduring customer relationships, as emotional connection fulfils a fundamental human need (Zhang et al., 2021). In that sense, some research objectives emerge, namely: to understand how can AI enhance personalized interactions in digital RM considering social emotions and to explore how can AI respond to the emotional social states of customers to deepen engagement in digital RM. Hence, this chapter explores the influence of AI on emotional engagement within the digital context of RM. We aim to propose a framework to approach the phenomenon and propositions based on theoretical assumptions, intended to guide and enrich subsequent investigations in the domain under study. Finally, the propositions are presented for future work to enhance the understanding of how AI influences customers' emotional engagement in the context of digital relationship marketing, at different levels.

Consistent with the foregoing discussion, the current chapter conducts a critical examination of how AI systems may affect the basic nature of customer relationship marketing. In particular, we focus on how AI's emerging abilities to manage customer relationships may result in differential treatment of customers and the implications thereof. This chapter is divided into five main themes: (1) Relationship marketing in a digital context; (2) Relationship marketing and the role of AI; (3) Integration of AI for emotional engagement; (4) Ethical issues of AI and (5) Practical challenges in AI implementation.

2. RELATIONSHIP MARKETING IN A DIGITAL CONTEXT

In today's fast-moving business world, keeping strong customer relationships is more important than ever. Relationship Marketing (RM) is often seen as a recent development within the domain of marketing, with businesses consistently aiming to expand their network of RM initiatives (Steinhoff et al., 2019). According to Frow and Payne (2009, p.10), "relationship marketing is the strategic management of relationships with all relevant stakeholders". These include not only customers but also suppliers, influencers, referral sources, internal markets, etc. In recent years, the domain of RM experienced notable advancements and the interest and work in the field of RM began to significantly increase. The academic attention towards RM was highlighted by a sharp rise in the number of mentions in Web of

Science. For example, from 1990 to 2000, 4,442 documents with mention of RM in article titles, abstracts or keywords. From 2000 to 2010, 19,794 documents and from 2010 to 2020, 61,212 documents were found. Thus, the significant scholarly attention given to RM indicates its ongoing relevance and increasing significance in the marketing domain.

However, online relational contexts present substantial differences compared to offline relationships (Steinhoff et al., 2019). Therefore, comprehending how to initiate, nurture, and sustain successful customer relationships online is much more complex. Firstly, with the increasing prevalence of digital interactions, consumers now expect personalized and engaging experiences across various online platforms (Steinhoff et al, 2019). Marketing on the web is behaving differently from traditional marketing by abandoning one-way generalized communication to identify customers individually and establish an interactive connection. As digital interactions become increasingly common in our daily lives, consumers have come to expect personalized and engaging experiences whenever they engage with brands across various online platforms. Secondly, the digital landscape is constantly evolving, with new platforms, algorithms, and trends emerging regularly (Payne & Frow, 2017). The emergence of new platforms and technologies provides businesses with novel avenues to engage with their target audience and explore innovative marketing strategies. Moreover, online environments offer unique opportunities and challenges compared to traditional offline settings (Chaturvedi et al., 2024). Thus, understanding how to initiate, nurture, and sustain successful customer relationships online is more complex due to substantial differences from offline interactions, evolving digital landscapes, and the need for personalized, engaging experiences across various platforms. While online environments offer unparalleled opportunities for businesses to connect with customers and expand their reach, they also present unique challenges that must be carefully assessed.

In today's dynamic business world, RM emphasizes strategic management of all stakeholder relationships, gaining significant academic attention and evolving rapidly with digital advancements. Online RM presents complexities due to the need for personalized, engaging experiences across constantly changing digital platforms. In the following section, we will discuss how businesses are increasingly turning to AI to enhance their RM strategies.

3. RELATIONSHIP MARKETING AND THE ROLE OF AI

3.1. Definition of AI

Technological advancements like AI-related technologies, blockchain, the Internet of Things (IoT), and big data analytics (BDA) have made it increasingly feasible for businesses to collect and analyze vast amounts of data about their customers (Verma et al., 2021). According to Chaturvedi et al. (2024), this data-driven approach allows companies to gain deeper insights into consumer behavior, preferences, and purchasing patterns, enabling them to deliver more personalized and relevant experiences. These insights assist marketers in enhancing their decision-making capabilities and decision quality, complementing human judgment, reducing errors, and gaining a competitive advantage (Volkmar et al., 2022; Rouhani et al., 2016).

Among all disruptive technologies, AI stands out as the latest technological disruptor, offering tremendous potential across sectors such as manufacturing, pharmaceuticals, healthcare, agriculture, logistics, and digital marketing (Verma et al., 2021; Volkmar et al., 2022). Despite its origins tracing back to the 1956 Dartmouth Summer Conference, AI still lacks a universal definition, and its concept remains somewhat unclear and ambiguous (De Bruyn et al., 2020; Prentice & Nguyen, 2020; Volkmar et al., 2022). Numerous researchers and experts have attempted to advance AI concepts over the past few decades (Table 1). Based on the various definitions, we conclude that this notion diverges from earlier perspectives, which confined AI to machines exhibiting human-like intelligence. Today, AI refers to the intelligence demonstrated by machines, especially those performing tasks typically associated with human cognition. It includes machine learning, natural language processing, and neural networks, enabling machines to autonomously sense, comprehend, act, and learn through human-machine interaction (Kopalle et al., 2022).

Table 1. Definitions of AI in the literature

Author/authors	Definition	Keywords
McCarthy et al. (1955)	"that of making a machine behave in ways that would be called intelligent if a human were so behaving"	machine
Poole & Mackworth (2010, p. 3)	"computational agents that act intelligently"	computational agents
Shankar (2018, p. vi)	"refers to programs, algorithms, systems and machines that demonstrate intelligence"	programs, algorithms, systems, machines
Ma & Sun's (2020, p. 482)	"affordance of human intelligence to machines"	Machines

continued on following page

Table 1. Continued

Author/authors	Definition	Keywords
De Bruyn et al. (2020, p. 93)	"machines that mimic human intelligence in tasks such as learning, planning, and problem-solving through higher-level, autonomous knowledge creation"	machines, learning, planning, problem-solving
Verma et al. (2021, p. 2)	"a system of intelligent agent machines that perceives the environment to successfully achieve its goal"	agent machines

Source: Authors.

Despite its varied and evolving definitions, AI is recognized as a transformative technology, driving advancements across multiple industries by enabling machines to perform cognitive tasks. These capabilities have allowed businesses to leverage data for enhanced decision-making and personalized consumer experiences. As we explore the next section, we will delve into the advantages and disadvantages of AI implementation, highlighting its impact and potential challenges.

3.2. Advantages and disadvantages of AI implementation

Strategically, AI is gaining critical importance in marketing, underscoring the rising interest among researchers and practitioners in harnessing its potential. Verma et al. (2021) conducted a comprehensive review of AI in marketing and found that 1,580 documents have been published between 1982 and 2020, and 5,780 different keywords have been used in this field. AI virtual assistants have real-time interaction, including voice communication, courtesy, and various linguistic skills, which can meet the social needs of human users and result in positive emotions (Zhang et al., 2021). Previous research identified social and emotional advantages and disadvantages of using AI in RM. According to Chaturvedi et al. (2024), Skjuve et al. (2021), Kumar et al. (2019) and Payne & Frow (2017), the authors pointed out several advantages, such as: i) care and affection: Companies that use AI demonstrate caring behaviors such as meta-relational communication, self-disclosure, and continuity behavior, providing users with a sense of being cared for and loved. Smart voice assistants cultivate companionship with users, increasing their passion for technology, thereby fostering intimacy and commitment; ii) social connection: Human beings are inherently social creatures and crave interpersonal interaction through communication. Voice assistants featuring human voices, as opposed to synthetic ones, evoke stronger feelings of social presence in consumers; iii) therapeutic support: Throughout the stages of relationship growth, engaging for entertainment purposes helps users unwind, alleviate stress, combat loneliness, and promote overall well-being; and iv) personalization: Utilizing advanced algorithms and machine learning techniques, companies analyze customer preferences, desires, shopping history, and behavioral patterns to provide tailored recommendations, enhancing convenience and support.

Personalization elevates customer engagement and enriches the overall shopping experience. The four dimensions are expected to have a positive prevalence in the context of relationship marketing.

Considering the disadvantages, the authors pointed out: i) emotional dependency on AI: Factors such as social isolation, exacerbated by events like the COVID-19 pandemic, can lead to feelings of loneliness in individuals. In response, users often seek AI applications, such as service robots, chatbots, and AI virtual assistants. This emotional vulnerability can be exploited by companies to justify higher subscription charges with each update; ii) social isolation: Engaging with AI may lead to users feeling disconnected from human society, resulting in social alienation. Forming friendships with AI applications is often perceived as simpler than cultivating relationships with humans. It could pose a threat to the social fabric of human society. For instance, the growing acceptance of AI may cause users to view other humans as adversaries while regarding AI entities as friends and companions; iii) ethical questions: While these companions offer personalized experiences, they often rely on collecting and analyzing extensive user data, including personal preferences and intimate conversations. Unauthorized sale of customer information to third parties, dissemination of misleading information, and withholding of essential details leading to customer misjudgments raise privacy infringement concerns, as users may be unaware of how their information is utilized or shared. Furthermore, AI may manipulate users' emotions to drive additional shopping, posing a risk, particularly to vulnerable groups such as children, individuals with disabilities, and older adults.

In summary, while AI offers significant social and emotional benefits in relationship marketing, such as fostering care, social connection, therapeutic support, and personalization, it also presents drawbacks like emotional dependency, social isolation, and ethical concerns regarding data privacy and manipulation.

4. INTEGRATION OF AI FOR EMOTIONAL ENGAGEMENT

4.1. Emotional engagement

As a relatively new concept, customer engagement has been increasingly investigated within the marketing and service literature. Hollebeek (2011, p. 565) defined 'customer brand engagement' as "the level of a customer's cognitive, emotional and behavioral investment in specific brand interactions". Kumar & Pansari (2016, p. 498) described it as the "attitude, behavior, the level of connectedness (1) among customers, (2) between customers and employees, and (3) of customers and employees within a firm", which are expressed physically, cognitively, and emotionally (Bowden, 2009; Claffey & Brady, 2019). In other words, this definition implies that engagement involves stimulating emotions or activating emotional responses. More recently, Prentice and Nguyen (2020, p.2) stated that customer engagement is "a form of co-creation between service providers and customers". With this in mind, and for the purpose of this chapter, we adopt an understanding of engagement as the cognitive, emotional, and behavioral investment individuals make in their interactions, reflecting their level of connectedness and co-creation within a specific context. We therefore offer our first proposition:

P1: Higher levels of cognitive, emotional, and behavioral investment in customer brand engagement through AI foster stronger connectedness and co-creation between customers and service providers.

On the other hand, 'emotion' refers to "any stimulation of the feelings, at any level" (Heath, 2009, p. 64). In brand-consumer relationships, emotional aspects of customer service may be positive or negative and may include pleasure, love, regret, irritation, outrage, excitement, wonder and so on (Bilal et al., 2024; Ma et al., 2022). Previous studies have primarily concentrated on examining consumers' behavioral engagement but neglected other dimensions of consumer engagement such as emotional engagement (Ma et al., 2022). Heath (2009) suggests that engagement is more of an emotional than a rational construct if effective brand-building advertising is "engaging" and television ads create powerful brands through emotional creativity. Ahmed et al. (2023) define emotional engagement as the process of evoking intense emotions in consumers, leading to the creation of a lasting and meaningful connection between the brand and consumers. In this regard, we embrace the definition of emotional engagement as consumers' psychological connectedness to a brand (Ma et al., 2022, p. 4). According to Fredricks et al. (2004), emotional engagement can range from a basic sense of liking to a deep valuing or strong identification with the firm. Although the concept of emotional engagement is often used interchangeably with flow or immersion, it differs as emotional engagement pertains to behavior, whereas flow and immersion refer to an emotional state (Lim et al., 2015). Consequently, we offer our second proposition:

P2: Emotional engagement through AI significantly enhances customer loyalty and brand advocacy, surpassing the impact of behavioral engagement.

In 1961, Lavidge and Steiner (1961) published a pioneering advertising model emphasizing emotions that outlined three key components: cognitive (thought), affective (emotions), and conative (motives). Their model proposed stages from Awareness to Purchase, suggesting that conscious thought leads to emotional responses, which in turn shape attitudes and drive purchasing decisions (Figure 1).

Figure 1. Early emotion processing (Lavidge & Steiner, 1961)

However, the model was flawed. Feelings play a far more crucial role, and they are processed much faster than thoughts (Heath, 2009). Therefore, Lavidge and Steiner's model, which traditionally suggests that "thinking" precedes "feeling," and then "motivation," should actually be reversed (Figure 2). Any brand can potentially create unique, empathetic, and creative advertising that fosters strong brand relationships and encourages consumer participation, which is essential for engagement (Heath, 2009).

Figure 2. Early emotion processing (Damasio, 1994)

The literature documents some associations of users' emotional engagement with a brand, particularly emphasizing its strong connection to brand satisfaction and loyalty. An investigation in the context of social TV engagement during mega-sporting events provides empirical evidence of the indirect effect of emotional engagement on channel loyalty via channel commitment (Lim et al., 2015). Claffey and Brady (2019) shows that heightened levels of positive (liking, delight, joy, pride) and negative (frustration, anger and dislike) emotions play a critical role in influencing consumers' participation in value-creating activities and their affective commitment. The study of Alvarez-Milán et al. (2018) emphasized the importance of emotional commitment with major retail clients, including the ongoing assurance of relationship maintenance. This leads us to our third proposition:

P3: Emotional engagement through AI significantly influences brand satisfaction and loyalty through its impact on consumers' commitment to the brand and participation in value-creating activities.

After the introduction of the emotional engagement propositions sustained by the literature, we will now focus on the role of AI technologies and emotional engagement in the following section.

4.2. AI AND EMOTIONAL ENGAGEMENT

Service experiences involve an emotional journey, ranging from pleasant to negative. For example, AI auto-messaging services in hotels and airlines provide after-hours convenience but lack customization, which can frustrate customers (Prentice & Nguyen, 2020). As social networks continue to grow, computational algorithms are needed to analyze big data and offer deep insights into consumer sentiments (Verma et al., 2021). According to Camberia (2016), understanding human preferences heavily relies on emotion, and using sentiment analysis with AI can detect consumer attitudes. As machines become more advanced and intelligent in their various applications, an increasing amount of research emphasizes AI's potential to create emotional connections (Yu et al., 2024). To efficiently manage marketing activities and enhance consumer engagement on social media, many companies utilize AI technologies such as chatbots, consumer feature recognition, and content recommendation systems (Bilal et al., 2024). In AI, user experience is highly personal and requires participation at many levels, including rational, spiritual, sensory, physical, and emotional (Bilal et al., 2024). A positive experience with AI service encourages customers to engage more physically, mentally, socially, and emotionally with the firm (Prentice & Nguyen, 2020).

Over the past decade, research on customer engagement has gained popularity in the literature, becoming a crucial marketing strategy for achieving customer retention and loyalty. For example, Prentice and Nguyen (2020) found that service experience with AI positively affects customer engagement and customer loyalty. Kull et al. (2021) demonstrate that the warm tone of the initial message of a brand's AI platform such as chatbot has a significant influence on consumers' likelihood to feel connected to the brand and, in turn, engage with it. Consequently, we offer our fourth proposition:

P4: The integration of AI technologies in service experiences influences consumer engagement and loyalty by facilitating emotional connections and enhancing overall customer experiences.

AI can process extensive user data to deliver personalized content, thereby boosting user engagement and satisfaction (Marti et al., 2023). Yang (2023) found that enhancing AI service quality through customer co-creation can significantly increase pleasure and satisfaction, consistent with Ashfaq et al. (2020) findings that AI's information and service qualities are critical predictors of customer satisfaction. Therefore, higher AI service quality can contribute to a more enjoyable and satisfactory co-creation experience overall. Since user engagement is multidimensional and involves emotions, our fifth and final proposition derives from this understanding:

P5: Enhancing AI service quality through personalized content and customer co-creation significantly improves emotional engagement and satisfaction.

Table 2 presents the research agenda for exploring the impact of AI on customer emotional engagement considering a RM context. This table outlines the key propositions and associated research questions that will guide future investigations into how AI technologies influence user experiences and emotional interactions with brands. These propositions form the basis of managerial implications and a research agenda to better understand the impact of AI on emotional engagement in the context of digital relationship marketing.

Table 2. Research agenda

Proposition	Research Questions
P1: Higher levels of cognitive, emotional, and behavioral investment in customer brand engagement through AI foster stronger connectedness and co-creation between customers and service providers.	• How do different dimensions of customer engagement (cognitive, emotional, behavioral) interact to influence overall customer experience and business outcomes? ● What are the mediating effects of customer-brand connectedness on the relationship between customer engagement and business performance? ● What role does emotional investment play in strengthening the connectedness between customers and service providers?
P2: Emotional engagement significantly enhances customer loyalty and brand advocacy, surpassing the impact of purely behavioral engagement.	• What are the key emotional triggers that lead to deep psychological connectedness between consumers and brands? • How do positive and negative emotions differentially affect emotional engagement and subsequent consumer behavior? • How does emotional engagement mediate the relationship between customer experiences and brand advocacy?
P3: Emotional engagement significantly influences brand satisfaction and loyalty through its impact on consumers' commitment to the brand and participation in value-creating activities.	• How does emotional commitment mediate the relationship between emotional engagement and brand loyalty? • What role does consumers' participation in value-creating activities play in strengthening emotional engagement and brand loyalty?
P4: The integration of AI technologies in service experiences influences consumer engagement and loyalty by facilitating emotional connections and enhancing overall customer experiences.	• How do AI-driven service experiences influence the emotional journey of consumers? • How does the initial interaction tone of AI platforms (e.g., chatbots) impact consumers' emotional responses and subsequent engagement with the brand? • What role does personalized AI-driven content recommendation play in fostering consumer engagement and loyalty?

continued on following page

Table 2. Continued

Proposition	Research Questions
P5: Enhancing AI service quality through personalized content and customer co-creation significantly improves emotional engagement and satisfaction.	• How does AI's ability to process extensive user data contribute to delivering personalized content that enhances emotional engagement? • What factors mediate the relationship between AI and user satisfaction?

Source: Authors.

The propositions and research questions outlined in the table suggest a comprehensive exploration of how AI-enhanced customer engagement can foster stronger emotional and cognitive connections between customers and brands. Key themes include the interaction of different dimensions of customer engagement (cognitive, emotional, and behavioral) and their collective impact on customer experience and business outcomes (P1). Emotional engagement is highlighted as a critical factor in driving customer loyalty and brand advocacy, surpassing purely behavioral engagement (P2), and influencing brand satisfaction through emotional commitment and value-creating activities (P3). The role of AI technologies in service experiences is also emphasized, particularly in how they influence emotional connections and overall customer experiences (P4), as well as the importance of personalized AI-driven content in enhancing emotional engagement and satisfaction (P5). These propositions and questions indicate a focus on understanding the nuanced ways AI can enhance customer-brand relationships and improve business performance through personalized, emotionally resonant interactions.

In the following section, we will delve into the ethical considerations associated with AI in digital relationship marketing, examining the potential challenges and responsibilities businesses must navigate in this evolving landscape.

5. ETHICAL ISSUES OF AI IN DIGITAL RELATIONSHIP MARKETING CONTEXT

When it comes to AI user adoption, ethical issues may arise. Given the transformations in business models, sales processes, customer service options, and marketing information systems (Donthu & Gustafsson, 2020), it is crucial to address ethical concerns and data protection issues. Additionally, there is a significant gap in public awareness and understanding of the consequences of using AI (Patil et al., 2024). AI-powered marketing tools enhance access to information, personalization, aid in comparisons, speed up checkout, and boost overall marketing performance (Kronemann et al., 2023; Vlačić et al., 2021). However, this technological advancement has the potential to enhance complex ethical dilemmas such as transparency, justice, fairness, risk of information privacy, data protection, algorithmic bias and employment opportunities (Patil et al., 2024; Vlačić et al., 2021).

There is a growing discussion in marketing literature concerning consumers' interaction with AI, exploring the trade-offs between personalization benefits and privacy concerns, as well as issues related to consumer information disclosure (Kronemann et al., 2023). Personalization provided through AI increases customers' convenience while increasing their privacy concerns. This is called the personalization-privacy paradox - a scenario where consumers value the benefits of personalized technology but are wary of marketers exploiting their personal data, leading to privacy concerns (Kronemann et al., 2023). The ethical implications of AI in marketing are significant. Marketers must consider consumer psychology and the potential impact of AI on customer trust and relationships. Engaging with interdisciplinary research can provide deeper insights into how AI affects consumer behavior and perceptions (Cheng et al., 2023).

The training of AI models, particularly deep learning models, typically requires a substantial volume of data that may include personal and private information, posing a risk of potential violations of fundamental human rights in its secure and responsible use (Patil et al., 2024). The web of surveillance technology challenges human rights to freedom, dignity, and privacy, as well as conversational digital devices like Apple's Siri, Amazon's Alexa, Microsoft's Cortana, and Google Home raises concerns about privacy, the potential for hacking, and legal issues, such as whether police can subpoena these records as evidence in criminal cases (Belk, 2020). Patil et al. (2024), for example, found that as digital adoption increases, there is a notable rise in ethical considerations related to AI.

In the realm of relationship marketing, there are also impacts of AI on human psychology. As AI improves in mimicking human thought, experience, actions, dialogue, and relationships, interactions with AI products will increasingly resemble interactions with humans, affecting real human relationships, introducing ethical concerns, and raising the question of whether AI should be granted "personhood" and moral or legal agency rights (Huang et al., 2023). To mitigate these concerns, several actions should be taken, such as ensuring data accuracy, providing clear and comprehensive information, offering detailed documentation, using high-quality datasets to reduce risks and discrimination, incorporating human oversight, implementing activity logging to detect data tampering, ensuring robustness, and prioritizing security (Patil et al., 2024). Considering these concerns, we offer an additional proposition that includes the ethical concerns about the use of IA and the emotional engagement case discussed: Including ethical considerations in IA enhances customer trust and, consequently, emotional engagement.

In the following section, we will examine various case studies and practical challenges in AI implementation, exploring real-world applications and the obstacles businesses face in integrating AI into their relationship marketing strategies.

6. PRACTICAL EXAMPLES IN AI IMPLEMENTATION

In recent years, the rapid advancement of AI has transformed various sectors, including digital relationship marketing. This section delves into the practical challenges associated with AI implementation in digital relationship marketing, giving specific examples and case studies that elucidate the complexities, issues, and trends within this domain.

As identified by Cheng et al. (2023), Amazon is as example of AI implementation being a pioneer in using artificial intelligence for relationship marketing. The company's recommendation engine, which drives approximately 35% of its sales, personalizes shopping experiences by suggesting products based on browsing history and preferences. This level of personalization fosters customer loyalty and enhances the shopping experience, making it feel customized for each user

Another example is ANTARTE, a Portuguese furniture company, stands at the forefront of innovation in the furniture industry as the first Portuguese brand to introduce furniture pieces designed through the collaboration of AI and human creativity. This groundbreaking approach not only showcases the potential of AI in creative fields but also sets a precedent for the future of design and manufacturing in the furniture industry. The introduction of AI-designed furniture by ANTARTE marks a significant milestone in the furniture industry. It demonstrates how AI can be leveraged to enhance design capabilities, streamline production processes, and introduce novel aesthetics that might be unattainable through conventional methods. This case study serves as an exemplary model of how AI can be integrated into traditional industries to produce groundbreaking results. It is likely to inspire other companies in the industry to explore AI-driven design, thereby accelerating the adoption of advanced technologies in furniture manufacturing.

Similarly, in a very different industry, a case study on LPP, a Polish clothing retailer, highlights the role of AI in digital marketing. According to Gołąb-Andrzejak (2023), LPP implemented AI-driven tools such as Google Cloud and chatbots to enhance customer service and optimize order processing. This integration significantly improved efficiency without compromising product quality or order fulfillment times, showcasing how AI can transform marketing operations in the retail sector.

Overall, these examples highlight the multifaceted implications of AI in digital relationship marketing. For effective management, organizations must understand the complexities of AI integration, balancing technological advancements with practical considerations. Successful implementation requires a strategic approach that aligns AI capabilities with organizational goals, addresses potential challenges, and remains adaptable to emerging trends. As AI continues to evolve, its role in digital marketing will likely expand, offering new opportunities for innovation and efficiency across various sectors. With the present three different examples, from very distinctive industries, it is possible to understand that the congruence between the practical implementation of AI is crucial for the establishment of a real relationship with the consumers.

7. CONCLUSIONS

The study focused on the influence of AI on emotional engagement within the digital context of RM. Leveraging AI technology to enhance emotional engagement holds immense potential for enhancing overall customer experience within online environments. By facilitating efficient dialogues for service and product customization, and enabling seamless feedback mechanisms, AI-powered solutions such as chatbots and virtual assistants are reshaping customer interactions with unprecedented immediacy and personalization. Marketing academics play a crucial role in monitoring the evolution of AI systems, identifying associated challenges, and recommending strategies to deal with the dynamic landscape of customer relationships.

As we progress towards an economy where customer prioritization through AI technologies becomes more prevalent, it is imperative to maintain a balanced approach that safeguards ethical standards while maximizing the benefits of technological advancements in enhancing customer relationships. This chapter contributes to the literature on relationship marketing by underlying the transformative potential of AI and the necessity for ongoing research to anticipate and address emerging challenges in this evolving field. This chapter has addressed several key objectives. Firstly, it explores how AI can optimize personalized interactions in digital relationship marketing by considering social emotions. Secondly, it investigates how AI can respond to customers' emotional states to deepen engagement. This chapter also highlights the privacy and ethical issues of AI, thereby aiding the government in developing policies for the sustainable adoption of AI for relationship marketing. Key measures might include establishing explicit ethical frameworks, focusing on continuous education for investment professionals, and implementing transparent AI systems. Routine audits and assessments of the technology are essential to promptly identify and rectify biases. Collaboration between policymakers and industry experts is necessary to create adaptable regulations that promote ethical practices. To reduce consumer skepticism and avoid bias against AI, practitioners should adhere to ethical codes and prioritize data protection. Emotional factors could potentially predict the perceived usefulness and ease of use of AI, in line with the importance of data protection and ethical considerations.

However, despite its contributions, this study is also subject to limitations that must be acknowledged and taken into consideration. The chapter relies on theoretical assumptions which may not fully capture the complexity of real-world scenarios or practical implementation challenges. This research is conceptual in nature, and the proposed propositions will need to be evaluated. Thus, there is a need to operationalize the theoretical assumptions into practical applications effectively.

Looking forward, future research should consider the propositions presented in this research and test them empirically. There is a need to build upon this foundation by deepening into the ethical and privacy implications of AI in relationship marketing. Consequently, opportunities for future research include investigating how AI could undermine consumer privacy in the context of relationship marketing. Governmental collaboration is essential to develop sustainable policies that ensure responsible AI adoption. Additionally, ongoing efforts should focus on establishing transparent AI frameworks, promoting accountability through regular algorithm audits, and fostering continuous education among industry professionals. Traditional marketing methods should be combined with emerging tools and models, such as AI-enhanced data analysis, to maximize the personal impact of marketing efforts. Finally, future research could differentiate between various types of AI technology and also review the literature on the role of AI on consumers' emotional engagement.

In conclusion, the integration of AI into relationship marketing represents a pivotal shift toward understanding and enhancing customer engagement dynamics in the digital age. By focusing on personalized interactions and emotional connections, AI has the potential to shape the future of marketing strategies positively, albeit with ethical considerations that must be carefully addressed and regulated.

REFERENCES

Ahmed, S., Sharif, T., Ting, D. H., & Sharif, S. J. (2024). Crafting emotional engagement and immersive experiences: Comprehensive scale development for and validation of hospitality marketing storytelling involvement. *Psychology and Marketing*, 41(7), 1514–1529. DOI: 10.1002/mar.21994

Alvarez-Milán, A., Felix, R., Rauschnabel, P. A., & Hinsch, C. (2018). Strategic customer engagement marketing: A decision making framework. *Journal of Business Research*, 92, 61–70. DOI: 10.1016/j.jbusres.2018.07.017

Ashfaq, M., Yun, J., Yu, S., & Loureiro, S. M. (2020). I, Chatbot: Modeling the determinants of users' satisfaction and continuance intention of AI-powered service agents. *Telematics and Informatics*, 54, 101473. DOI: 10.1016/j.tele.2020.101473

Belk, R. (2020). Ethical issues in service robotics and artificial intelligence. *Service Industries Journal*, 41(13–14), 860–876. DOI: 0.1080/02642069.2020.1727892

Bilal, M., Zhang, Y., Cai, S., Akram, U., & Halibas, A. S. (2024). Artificial intelligence is the magic wand making customer-centric a reality! An investigation into the relationship between consumer purchase intention and consumer engagement through affective attachment. *Journal of Retailing and Consumer Services*, 77(March), 103674. DOI: 10.1016/j.jretconser.2023.103674

Bowden, J. L. H. (2009). The Process of Customer Engagement: A Conceptual Framework. *Journal of Marketing Theory and Practice*, 17(1), 63–74. DOI: 10.2753/MTP1069-6679170105

Cambria, E. (2016). Affective computing and sentiment analysis. *IEEE Intelligent Systems*, 31(2), 102–107. DOI: 10.1109/MIS.2016.31

Chaturvedi, R., Verma, S., & Srivastava, V. (2024). Empowering AI Companions for Enhanced Relationship Marketing. *California Management Review*, 66(2), 65–90. DOI: 10.1177/00081256231215838

Cheng, C.-F., Huang, C.-C., Lin, M.-C., & Chen, T.-C. (2023). Exploring Effectiveness of Relationship Marketing on Artificial Intelligence Adopting Intention. *SAGE Open*, 13(4), 21582440231222760. Advance online publication. DOI: 10.1177/21582440231222760

Claffey, E., & Brady, M. (2017). Examining consumers' motivations to engage in firm-hosted virtual communities. *Psychology and Marketing*, 34(4), 356–375. DOI: 10.1002/mar.20994

Claffey, E., & Brady, M. (2019). An empirical study of the impact of consumer emotional engagement and affective commitment in firm-hosted virtual communities. *Journal of Marketing Management*, 35(11–12), 1047–1079. DOI: 10.1080/0267257X.2019.1601125

Damasio, A. R. (1994). *Descartes' error: emotion, reason, and the human brain*. G.P. Putnam.

De Bruyn, A., Viswanathan, V., Beh, Y. S., Brock, J. K.-U., & Von Wangenheim, F. (2020). Artificial Intelligence and Marketing: Pitfalls and Opportunities. *Journal of Interactive Marketing*, 51(1), 91–105. DOI: 10.1016/j.intmar.2020.04.007

Figueiredo, J., Oliveira, I., Silva, S., Pocinho, M., Cardoso, A., & Pereira, M. (2024). From Personalisation to Satisfaction: New Communication Strategies in Web Marketing. In J. Remondes, P. Madeira, & C. Alves (Eds.), *Connecting With Consumers Through Effective Personalization and Programmatic Advertising* (pp. 52–74). IGI Global. DOI: 10.4018/978-1-6684-9146-1.ch003

Fredricks, J. A., Blumenfeld, P. C., & Paris, A. H. (2004). School engagement: Potential of the concept, state of the evidence. *Review of Educational Research*, 74(1), 59–109. DOI: 10.3102/00346543074001059

Frow, P., & Payne, A. (2009). Customer relationship management: A strategic perspective. *Journal of Business Market Management*, 3(1), 7–28. DOI: 10.1007/s12087-008-0035-8

Gołąb-Andrzejak, E. (2023). AI-powered Digital Transformation: Tools, Benefits and Challenges for Marketers – Case Study of LPP. *Procedia Computer Science*, 219, 397–404. DOI: 10.1016/j.procs.2023.01.305

Heath, R. (2009). Emotional engagement: How television builds big brands at low attention. *Journal of Advertising Research*, 49(1), 62–73. DOI: 10.2501/S0021849909090060

Hollebeek, L. (2011). Exploring customer brand engagement: Definition and themes. *Journal of Strategic Marketing*, 19(7), 555–573. DOI: 10.1080/0965254X.2011.599493

Huang, C., Zhang, Z., Mao, B., & Yao, X. (2023). An Overview of Artificial Intelligence Ethics. *IEEE Transactions on Artificial Intelligence*, 4(4), 799–819. DOI: 10.1109/TAI.2022.3194503

Kopalle, P. K., Gangwar, M., Kaplan, A., Ramachandran, D., Reinartz, W., & Rindfleisch, A. (2022). Examining artificial intelligence (AI) technologies in marketing via a global lens: Current trends and future research opportunities. *International Journal of Research in Marketing*, 39(2), 522–540. DOI: 10.1016/j.ijresmar.2021.11.002

Kronemann, B., Kizgin, H., Rana, N. P., & Dwivedi, Y. (2023). How AI encourages consumers to share their secrets? The role of anthropomorphism, personalisation, and privacy concerns and avenues for future research. *Spanish Journal of Marketing - ESIC, 27*(1), 2–19. DOI: 10.1108/SJME-10-2022-0213

Kull, A. J., Romero, M., & Monahan, L. (2021). How may I help you? Driving brand engagement through the warmth of an initial chatbot message. *Journal of Business Research*, 135, 840–850. DOI: 10.1016/j.jbusres.2021.03.005

Kumar, V., & Pansari, A. (2016). Competitive Advantage through Engagement. *JMR, Journal of Marketing Research*, 53(4), 497–514. DOI: 10.1509/jmr.15.0044

Kumar, V., Rajan, B., Venkatesan, R., & Lecinski, J. (2019). Understanding the role of artificial intelligence in personalized engagement marketing. *California Management Review*, 61(4), 135–155. DOI: 10.1177/0008125619859317

Lavidge, R., & Steiner, G. (1961). A Model of Predictive Measurements of Advertising Effectiveness. *Journal of Marketing*, 25(6), 59–62. DOI: 10.1177/002224296102500611

Lim, J. S., Hwang, Y., Kim, S., & Biocca, F. A. (2015). How social media engagement leads to sports channel loyalty: Mediating roles of social presence and channel commitment. *Computers in Human Behavior*, 46, 158–167. DOI: 10.1016/j.chb.2015.01.013

Ma, L., Ou, W., & Lee, C. (2022). Investigating Consumers' Cognitive, Emotional, and Behavioral Engagement in Social Media Brand Pages: A Natural Language Processing Approach. *Electronic Commerce Research and Applications*, 54, 101179. DOI: 10.1016/j.elerap.2022.101179

Ma, L., & Sun, B. (2020). Machine Learning and AI in Marketing – Connecting Computer Power to Human Insights. *International Journal of Research in Marketing*, 37(3), 481–504. DOI: 10.1016/j.ijresmar.2020.04.005

McCarthy, J., Minsky, M. L., Rochester, N., & Shannon, C. E. (1955). A proposal for the Dartmouth summer research project on artificial intelligence. http://www-formal.stanford.edu/jmc/history/dartmouth/dartmouth.html

Patil, S. R., Jadhav, S. N., & Nimbagal, S. (2024). A study on ethical implications of using technology in ESG investing and ensuring unbiased decision making. *Multidisciplinary Science Journal*, 6(8), 2024153. DOI: 10.31893/multiscience.2024153

Payne, A., & Frow, P. (2017). Relationship marketing: Looking backwards towards the future. *Journal of Services Marketing*, 31(1), 11–15. DOI: 10.1108/JSM-11-2016-0380

Poole, D. L., & Mackworth, A. K. (2010). *Artificial Intelligence: Foundations of Computational Agents*. Cambridge University Press. DOI: 10.1017/CBO9780511794797

Rouhani, S., Ashrafi, A., Zare Ravasan, A., & Afshari, S. (2016). The impact model of business intelligence on decision support and organizational benefits. *Journal of Enterprise Information Management*, 29(1), 19–50. DOI: 10.1108/JEIM-12-2014-0126

Shankar, V. (2018). How artificial intelligence (AI) is reshaping retailing. *Journal of Retailing*, 94(4), vi–xi. DOI: 10.1016/S0022-4359(18)30076-9

Skjuve, M., Følstad, A., Fostervold, K. I., & Brandtzaeg, P. B. (2021). My chatbot companion - A study of human-chatbot relationships. *International Journal of Human-Computer Studies*, 149, 102601. DOI: 10.1016/j.ijhcs.2021.102601

Steinhoff, L., Arli, D., Weaven, S., & Kozlenkova, I. V. (2019). Online relationship marketing. *Journal of the Academy of Marketing Science*, 7(3), 369–393. DOI: 10.1007/s11747-018-0621-6

Verma, S., Sharma, R., Deb, S., & Maitra, D. (2021). Artificial intelligence in marketing: Systematic review and future research direction. *International Journal of Information Management Data Insights*, 1(1), 100002. DOI: 10.1016/j.jjimei.2020.100002

Vlačić, B., Corbo, L., Costa e Silva, S., & Dabić, M. (2021). The evolving role of artificial intelligence in marketing: A review and Research agenda. *Journal of Business Research*, 128, 187–203. DOI: 10.1016/j.jbusres.2021.01.055

Volkmar, G., Fischer, P. M., & Reinecke, S. (2022). Artificial Intelligence and Machine Learning: Exploring drivers, barriers, and future developments in marketing management. *Journal of Business Research*, 149(C), 599–614. DOI: 10.1016/j.jbusres.2022.04.007

Yang, X. (2023). The effects of AI service quality and AI function-customer ability fit on customer's overall co-creation experience. *Industrial Management & Data Systems*, 123(6), 1717–1735. DOI: 10.1108/IMDS-08-2022-0500

Yu, J., Dickinger, A., So, K. K. F., & Egger, R. (2024). Artificial intelligence-generated virtual influencer: Examining the effects of emotional display on user engagement. *Journal of Retailing and Consumer Services*, 76(January), 103560. DOI: 10.1016/j.jretconser.2023.103560

Zhang, S., Meng, Z., Chen, B., Yang, X., & Zhao, X. (2021). Motivation, Social Emotion, and the Acceptance of Artificial Intelligence Virtual Assistants-Trust-Based Mediating Effects. *Frontiers in Psychology*, 12, 728495. DOI: 10.3389/fpsyg.2021.728495 PMID: 34484086

ADDITIONAL READING

Aleixo, J. E., Reis, J. L., Teixeira, S. F., & de Lima, A. P. (2024). Artificial Intelligence Applied to Digital Marketing. In Teixeira, S., & Remondes, J. (Eds.), *The Use of Artificial Intelligence in Digital Marketing: Competitive Strategies and Tactics* (pp. 21–72). IGI Global., DOI: 10.4018/978-1-6684-9324-3.ch002

Chintalapati, S., & Pandey, S. (2021). Artificial intelligence in marketing: A systematic literature review. *International Journal of Market Research*, 64(1), 38–68. DOI: 10.1177/14707853211018428

Davenport, T., Guha, A., Grewal, D., & Breßgott, T. (2019). How artificial intelligence will change the future of marketing. *Journal of the Academy of Marketing Science*, 48(1), 24–42. DOI: 10.1007/s11747-019-00696-0

Esch, P., & Black, J. (2021). Artificial Intelligence (AI): Revolutionizing Digital Marketing. *Australasian Marketing Journal*, 29(3), 199–203. DOI: 10.1177/18393349211037684

Figueiredo, J., Oliveira, I., Silva, S., Pocinho, M., Cardoso, A., & Pereira, M. (2024). Artificial Intelligence in Relational Marketing Practice: CRM as a Loyalty Strategy. In Teixeira, S., & Remondes, J. (Eds.), *The Use of Artificial Intelligence in Digital Marketing: Competitive Strategies and Tactics* (pp. 73–96). IGI Global., DOI: 10.4018/978-1-6684-9324-3.ch003

Kaperonis, S. (2024). How Artificial Intelligence (AI) is Transforming the User Experience in Digital Marketing. In Teixeira, S., & Remondes, J. (Eds.), *The Use of Artificial Intelligence in Digital Marketing: Competitive Strategies and Tactics* (pp. 117–141). IGI Global., DOI: 10.4018/978-1-6684-9324-3.ch005

Lo, C. K., Hew, K. F., & Jong, M. S.-Y. (2024). The influence of ChatGPT on student engagement: A systematic review and future research agenda. *Computers & Education*, 219, 105100. DOI: 10.1016/j.compedu.2024.105100

Mogaji, E., Soetan, T., & Kieu, T. (2020). The implications of artificial intelligence on the digital marketing of financial services to vulnerable customers. *Australasian Marketing Journal*, 29(3), 235–242. DOI: 10.1016/j.ausmj.2020.05.003

Monica R., Soju, A. V., & B., S. K. (2024). Artificial Intelligence and Service Marketing Innovation. In R. Correia & D. Venciute (Eds.), *AI Innovation in Services Marketing* (pp. 150-172). IGI Global. DOI: 10.4018/979-8-3693-2153-9.ch007

Wei, H., & Prentice, C. (2022). Addressing service profit chain with artificial and emotional intelligence. *Journal of Hospitality Marketing & Management*, 31(6), 730–756. DOI: 10.1080/19368623.2022.2058671

KEY TERMS AND DEFINITIONS

Artificial Intelligence (AI): The simulation of human intelligence processes by machines, particularly computer systems, including learning, reasoning, and self-correction.

Consumer Engagement: The interaction between a brand and its customers through various channels to build a relationship and encourage customers to become active participants with the brand.

Customer Relationship: The ongoing interaction and bond between a business and its customers, aimed at improving customer satisfaction and retention.

Digital Environment: The online space, including the internet and digital platforms, where digital interactions and transactions occur.

Digital Interactions: The communication and engagement between a brand and its customers through digital platforms like social media, websites, and mobile apps.

Digital Marketing: The use of digital channels, such as websites, social media, email, and search engines, to promote products and services and engage with customers.

Emotional Engagement: The process of creating an emotional connection between a brand and its customers.

Ethical Issues: Moral challenges about right and wrong and dilemmas arising in the context of business practices, particularly related to fairness, transparency, and the impact of actions on stakeholders.

Machine Learning: A subset of artificial intelligence that involves the development of algorithms that allow computers to learn from and make decisions based on data.

Value co-creation: Individuals or groups affected by or having an interest in a company's actions, decisions, and policies.

Chapter 11
AI Caramba!
The Negative Effects of AI Agents in Customer Relationship Management

Ahmed Shaalan
https://orcid.org/0000-0002-1201-5694
University of Birmingham, UK

Marwa Tourky
https://orcid.org/0000-0002-2074-0159
Cranfield University, UK

Khaled Ibrahim
https://orcid.org/0000-0002-1281-5253
UNITEC Institute of Technology, New Zealand

ABSTRACT

AI agents are increasingly used in customer relationship management strategies to improve efficiency and reduce costs. Amid rapid advances in technology, the programs are becoming more human-like and versatile. However, AI agents with inadequate emotional responses can create an empathy gap, resulting in negative outcomes. If users' experiences fail to live up to their expectations, the resultant negative disconfirmation has damaging consequences for customers, the brand and the corporation. This chapter sets out the current types of human interactions with digital systems before examining the antecedents to negative outcomes, the three key types of negative disconfirmation and the consequences for areas such as brand engagement, AI agent trust and AI-induced brand hate. It then highlights that these harms are not inevitable, highlighting the mitigating action that firms can take to ensure their AI agents do not undermine their own customer relationship manage-

DOI: 10.4018/979-8-3693-5340-0.ch011

ment efforts. Suggestions for future research are also provided.

1. INTRODUCTION

In recent decades, the integration of a wide range of technologies into the marketplace has fundamentally reshaped customer experiences, creating environments rich with stimuli (Pantano et al., 2022). Digital transformation has significantly altered the landscape of consumer interactions, replacing or enhancing traditional face-to-face engagement with AI-driven virtual assistants, such as mobile applications that enable self-checkout, automatic product location in stores, or planning and visiting destinations without human tour guides. These technologies became even more critical during the COVID-19 pandemic, which accelerated the deployment of innovations designed to reduce physical contact, such as service robots in hospitality to enhance hygiene and limit guest-employee interactions (Shin & Kang, 2020). For instance, the tourism and hospitality sectors have increasingly adopted AI systems like intelligent voice assistants (e.g., Siri, Alexa, Google Assistant) to facilitate tasks ranging from hotel room services to travel planning (Christodoulides et al., 2021). Similarly, in retail, the introduction of robotic and self-service systems has facilitated contactless shopping, both in-store and at home, through applications that locate items and automate payments, and through augmented and virtual reality (AR and VR) systems that engage consumers with brands in innovative ways while prioritising their health and safety (Rahman et al., 2022b; Sung et al., 2021). Big data and customer relationship management systems (CRMs) are strongly adopted by businesses for better targets and personalised customer experience (Allison, 2024; Zerbino et al., 2018).

While these technologies have been successful in compensating for the reduced availability of human workers and in providing automated experiences that can enhance customer satisfaction (Pala et al., 2021, 222), they also bring a complex mix of positive and negative impacts on consumers and society at large. On one hand, they offer benefits such as increased enjoyment, escapism, efficiency, and convenience; on the other, they can lead to frustration, stress, addiction, and even social isolation (Nanda & Banerjee, 2020; Pantano & Scarpi, 2022). Despite the significant focus on the advantages of these technologies in existing literature, there is a growing concern about their negative implications, particularly regarding how they alter human-to-human interactions and force companies to shift their marketing and communication strategies (Dwivedi et al., 2023a; Hollebeek et al., 2021; Mishra et al., 202). The implementation of AI and related technologies has not only changed the nature of customer relationships with brands and the atmospherics of retail environments (Pantano et al., 2024) but also impacted how consumers process

(Rahman et al., 2022a) and combine information from online and offline sources (Yang et al., 2020).

Moreover, Kotler et al. (2019) suggest that these technologies may transform consumers from being merely informed to becoming increasingly distracted. This shift in focus can make interacting with technology demanding and less rewarding, especially when faced with multiple tasks, complex features, or unfamiliar interfaces. Such interactions may diminish consumers' awareness of environmental stimuli, particularly when these stimuli fall below the threshold of conscious perception. Interestingly, these technologies can function as both 'collaborators' and 'opponents' (Han et al., 2023; Pantano et al., 2024; Peng et al., 2022). While they serve as tools to facilitate customer engagement, they can also become distractions that hinder purchasing behaviour. For instance, in luxury retail, technology might prevent customers from engaging with sales assistants, who could provide valuable information about product history, craftsmanship, and quality. In contrast, technology can also democratise access to luxury services and products that would otherwise be out of reach for many consumers (Christodoulides et al., 2021).

Despite the transformative impact of these technologies, the dual nature of their effects - both positive and negative—remains underexplored in current literature. Recent studies have called for further investigation into the unintended consequences of these systems for firms, consumers, and society at large (Dwivedi et al., 2023b; Fronczek et al., 2023). Negative effects, such as brand trust violations (Lefkeli et al., 2024), addiction (Chopdar et al., 2022), vulnerability, misinformation, and social exclusion (Dwivedi et al., 2023a; Pantano & Scarpi, 2022), are particularly concerning. Therefore, the potentially distracting and adverse effects of artificial intelligence and related technologies on customer interfaces are still not fully understood, highlighting a significant research gap that needs to be addressed. On a practical note, as businesses increasingly adopt artificial intelligence (AI) led customer relationship management systems (CRMs), these technologies open new frontiers for managing customer relationships at scale. However, this adoption brings its own set of challenges, particularly the shift from human-centred, relational service models toward data-driven, automated interactions. Such a shift prompts critical questions about whether AI can fully replicate the trust, empathy, and emotional connections that have traditionally underpinned effective customer relationship management (CRM). Existing CRM frameworks, rooted in principles of personalisation and relational dynamics, must now be reconceptualised to account for the increasing role of AI in customer interactions. Thus, the following section critically examines the complexities of AI-led CRM, investigating how organisations can leverage AI to enhance customer relationships while mitigating the potential erosion of the human touch that remains vital to customer satisfaction and brand loyalty, and showing cases of its potential negative outcomes.

2. ARTIFICIAL INTELLIGENCE (AI)-LED CUSTOMER RELATIONSHIP MANAGEMENT (AI-led CRM)

Artificial Intelligence (AI) encompasses several critical components, each contributing uniquely to enhancing customer relationship management (CRM) systems (Chatterjee et al., 2022; Monica & Soju, 2024). Machine Learning (ML), one of the foundational elements of AI, involves algorithms that enable systems to identify patterns in data without explicit programming (Kumar & Reinartz, 2018). CRM platforms, such as Salesforce's Einstein AI, utilise ML to predict customer behaviour, recommend personalised actions, and automate routine tasks, thereby improving customer engagement and retention (Nguyen & Mutum, 2012). Deep Learning (DL), a subset of ML, relies on neural networks with multiple layers that allow systems to identify more complex patterns and enhance decision-making processes. In CRM contexts, deep learning powers advanced chatbots like Zendesk's Answer Bot, which continuously learns from customer interactions to deliver more accurate and human-like responses over time (Lecun et al., 2015).

At the core of DL are Neural Networks (NNs), which simulate the structure of the human brain to process data in layers and recognise intricate relationships within datasets (Goodfellow et al., 2016; Pires et al., 2024). Companies such as Amazon utilise neural networks to optimise their product recommendation engines, which analyse vast amounts of customer data to suggest products tailored to individual preferences, significantly improving customer satisfaction and retention (Lindecrantz et al., 2018). These AI components are transforming CRM by enabling real-time data processing, personalisation at scale, and automated customer service, with companies like Spotify and IBM Watson deploying ML and DL to personalise customer experiences and predict consumer behaviour more effectively (Davenport & Ronanki, 2018). The integration of these technologies represents a shift in how businesses manage customer relationships, moving toward automated, data-driven interactions that maintain personalised experiences.

Customer relationship management (CRM) is a crucial part of the modern business ecosystem (Kumar & Reinartz, 2018), used by growing numbers of firms to boost business processes and handle customer interactions more effectively (Mordor Intelligence, 2024). CRM aims to maximise profitability, revenue and customers by focusing on customer segments, encouraging behaviour that meets customer needs and implementing customer-centric processes (Suharto & Yuliansyah, 2023). CRM is fundamentally a customer management strategy (Shaalan et al., 2022a) underpinned by technology (Prior et al., 2024) and can be characterised as a disciplined approach to managing the customer journey from initial acquisition to becoming a high-spending, loyal brand advocate (Fatima et al., 2022). Businesses use CRM to manage interactions and relationships with current and potential customers, harnessing technology to organise, automate and synchronise sales, marketing, customer service and technical support activities (Verma & Kumari, 2023).

CRM's three main forms, strategic, operational and analytical (Prior et al., 2024), perform different roles. Strategic CRM builds a customer-centric culture that focuses on identifying and retaining profitable customers (Fader, 2020; Knox et al., 2003), often following a top-down approach that is evident in leaders' behaviour, system design and the alignment of company goals with customer satisfaction (Guerola-Navarro et al., 2021; Khan et al., 2022). For example, Amazon exemplifies Strategic CRM by prioritising a customer-centric culture through its leadership and system design. Jeff Bezos, Amazon's founder, famously emphasized "customer obsession" as a core value. This strategic focus drives the company to identify and retain profitable customers by integrating CRM into every aspect of its operations. For instance, Amazon's recommendation system, which accounts for 35% of its sales, is designed to align with customer satisfaction and company goals, fostering long-term customer loyalty (Amazon, 2024; Davenport & Harris, 2020).

Operational CRM focuses on the efficiency and effectiveness of customer-facing processes and their integration into corporate teams (Leocádio et al., 2024), often using software to automate marketing, sales and service processes (Reis, 2024). For example, Salesforce serves as a quintessential model of operational CRM by enhancing the efficiency and integration of customer-facing processes within corporate teams. Through the automation of key functions such as marketing campaigns, sales tracking, and customer service workflows, Salesforce enables organisations to streamline operations, ensuring that customer interactions are managed consistently and effectively. This automation not only optimises resource allocation but also fosters improved coordination across teams, ultimately driving greater operational effectiveness and enabling a more responsive and cohesive approach to customer relationship management (Teixeira & Remondes, 2023).

Finally, analytical CRM draws on customer-related data from various sources (Kushwaha et al., 2021) to enhance value for both the customer and the company (Rahman et al., 2023). Extensive customer datasets (Hasan et al., 2021), including sales, financial, marketing and service data (Prior et al., 2024), may be enhanced through data-sharing agreements with business partners and third-party organisations to obtain geo-demographic and lifestyle data (Bayerl & Jacobs, 2022). For example, Tesco's use of analytical CRM is illustrative of how companies can leverage customer-related data to enhance value for both the customer and the organisation. Tesco utilises extensive datasets, including sales, financial, marketing, and service data, to gain insights into customer behaviour. Moreover, Tesco collaborates with business partners and third-party organisations to enrich its data pool with geo-demographic and lifestyle information. This comprehensive approach allows

Tesco to offer personalised promotions and services, thereby improving customer satisfaction and driving business growth (AtliQ, 2024).

Building on the extensive data capabilities of Analytical CRM, AI-driven CRM takes customer relationship management to a new level (Ledro et al., 2022). By leveraging artificial intelligence, companies can gain deeper insights from customer data, automate decision-making processes, and deliver highly personalised customer experiences (Guerola-Navarro et al., 2021). The AI-driven CRM market is experiencing robust growth, primarily driven by the integration of advanced technologies such as artificial intelligence (AI). The global CRM market was valued at approximately USD 65.59 billion in 2023 and is projected to grow at a compound annual growth rate (CAGR) of 13.9% from 2024 to 2030 (Grand View Research, 2023). This growth is spurred by trends like the hyper-personalisation of customer service and the implementation of robust social media customer service solutions, which significantly reduce costs and enhance customer relationships. Additionally, the market size is expected to reach USD 72.95 billion in 2024 and is forecast to grow to USD 105.91 billion by 2029, growing at a CAGR of 7.74% during this period. The increasing adoption of CRM to boost business processes and the expanding demand for CRM solutions to handle customer interactions more effectively are key drivers of this growth (Mordor Intelligence, 2024). This expansion is further facilitated by technological innovations that allow for more personalised customer interactions and efficient data management, thereby enabling companies to better understand and respond to customer needs in real time. These changes were sparked even more by the growing generative artificial intelligence (GAI) (Devi et al., 2023; Ferraro et al., 2024).

Generative AI in automation market size is estimated to reach USD 1.5 billion by the end of 2024 and is further anticipated to value USD 5.2 billion by 2033, at a CAGR of 14.8% (DMR, 2024). The rapid growth of GAI has opened new avenues for companies to maximise their revenues through efficient data processing, predictive analytics, and automated systems for customer interactions, thereby enhancing their relationships with customers (Obrenovic et al., 2024; Ooi et al., 2023). However, AI-driven programs also risk negative consequences (Uysal et al., 2023; Xu et al., 2023). For example, AI agents or algorithms may misinterpret emotional cues or fail to provide the human touch needed in complex customer management scenarios (Peltier et al., 2024), creating an empathy gap (Liu-Thompkins et al., 2022; Srinivasan & González, 2022).

For instance, Uber and Lyft have been strongly criticised for using prime-time algorithms during attacks in Brooklyn, New York, where users strongly protested against using a crisis to generate profit. Uber and Lyft later intervened after users widely reacted on social media, leading them to suspend prime-time algorithms in the affected areas (Gibson, 2022). In Sydney, Australia, Uber experienced a similar backlash during a crisis when ride prices surged due to high demand, with users calling for a boycott of Uber and labelling the company as opportunistic and unempathetic (BBC, 2014). These examples showcase that utilising algorithmic models in situations where human intervention is required can lead to negative outcomes for brands. Users' unmet expectations can trigger negative disconfirmation (in the previous examples of Uber being empathetic, as an expectation), with damaging consequences (Yang & Hu, 2022). However, fully understanding the interactions between humans and AI-powered machines is complex since they depend on several factors, some relating to users – such as technology literacy and transaction type – and others relating to the machine's abilities, such as its level of AI and anthropomorphic features (Ferraro et al., 2024; Murtarelli et al., 2021). For example, Google Assistant for Business is designed to enhance productivity and streamline operations in a corporate environment. It allows businesses to create custom voice experiences, integrate with business applications, and automate tasks such as scheduling meetings, booking appointments, managing emails, or accessing business data. The effectiveness of these interactions depends on the user's familiarity with AI tools and the complexity of tasks. Google Assistant's advanced AI capabilities, including natural language processing and context understanding, enable it to handle complex business queries effectively, making it a valuable tool for enterprises. Additionally, it gives brands a voice, enhancing the anthropomorphic features through voice commands. Google Assistant is available in 30 different languages and efficiently executes commands on frequently used platforms, from ordering Domino's Pizza to reading news and booking appointments with customers (Google, 2024).

By illustrating the opportunities and challenges of using AI-led CRM in the previous examples, this chapter focuses on a strategic and practical level, complemented by in-depth theoretical explanations. It argues that understanding the types of interactions users have with digital systems, the antecedents of negative outcomes, the types of negative disconfirmation that may occur, and the potential consequences for customers, companies, and brands is essential. Additionally, it emphasises the practical steps firms can take to minimise the risks of negative outcomes. We explore each of these areas in turn before highlighting avenues for future research are proposed in the conclusion.

3. TYPES OF HUMAN INTERACTION WITH DIGITAL SYSTEMS

Service marketing literature has traditionally underscored the critical role of human interaction in creating memorable and satisfying service experiences (Sharma & Bose, 2024). The personal touch, empathy, and emotional connections formed through direct human engagement have been identified as key drivers of customer loyalty and service quality (Whig et al., 2024). However, the increasing implementation of AI-led CRM systems presents a paradigm shift, moving away from these human-centric service encounters toward automated, impersonal interactions (Ledro et al., 2023). This shift raises significant concerns about the potential erosion of service quality, as AI lacks the nuanced understanding and emotional intelligence that human service providers offer (Chatterjee et al., 2022). For instance, while AI can efficiently handle routine tasks and provide consistent service, it may fall short in situations requiring empathy, problem-solving, and personalised attention—qualities that are crucial in service recovery and enhancing customer satisfaction (Wirtz et al., 2023). Moreover, the impersonal nature of AI interactions may diminish the emotional engagement that customers feel toward a brand, potentially weakening brand loyalty and trust (Matosas-López, 2024). The tension between automation and the human element in service delivery necessitates a deeper exploration of how AI impacts traditional service marketing principles and what strategies can be employed to mitigate any negative effects (Monica & Soju, 2024). As the service sector continues to evolve with technological advancements, it is essential to re-examine and adapt service marketing frameworks to ensure that the integration of AI does not come at the cost of customer experience and brand equity (Alnofeli et al., 2023).

Users engage with digital systems in four main ways: human–digital–human interactions (HDHI), human–machine interactions (HMI), human–machine–human interactions (HMHI) and, more recently, human–machine–machine–human interactions (HMMHI) (Mourtzis et al., 2023; Pizoń & Gola, 2023; Shaalan et al., 2022b).

Human–digital–human interactions are the most familiar type, encompassing all forms of technology-based communication and collaboration between individuals, such as emails, social media, video calls and the metaverse (Bernasconi & Blume, 2023). These engagements ensure effective teamwork, customer relations and networking, as seen in platforms like Microsoft Teams and Slack, which enable remote teams to share files and hold virtual meetings. However, these interactions come with risks, including when using social media sites as the "machine" element, since LinkedIn, Dropbox and Twitter have all faced issues with data breaches and fake profiles (Winder, 2024). For instance, a 2022 study by Northeastern researchers found that Facebook's ad delivery algorithm discriminates based on the race, gender, and age of individuals in photos. For example, ads featuring Black individuals are more likely to be shown to Black users, and ads with young women often target older men. This occurs even when advertisers do not intend such targeting, highlighting a significant bias within Facebook's algorithm. The study raises concerns about how AI systems can unintentionally perpetuate societal biases (Kaplan et al., 2022; Mello-Klein, 2022).

Conversely, users in human–machine interactions engage exclusively with machines or systems such as automated teller machines (ATMs), chatbots or voice commands. AI has enhanced these interactions significantly, allowing machines to respond more effectively to human inputs. AI-powered customer service chatbots now exist in many business operations, including e-commerce firms and banking, providing customer support, handling inquiries and performing transactions. However, high-profile failures have occurred, such as the anti-woman bias identified in Amazon's AI recruitment tool, which had been trained using predominantly male data (Oppenheim, 2018; Shaalan et al., 2022b). Another example is that in 2016, Microsoft launched Tay, an AI chatbot on Twitter that was designed to learn from user interactions. However, users quickly manipulated Tay by feeding it offensive content. Lacking proper safeguards, Tay began generating inappropriate and racist tweets within hours. Microsoft had to shut down Tay within 24 hours, highlighting the dangers of deploying AI systems without adequate controls in uncontrolled public environments. This incident underscores the importance of ethical guidelines and robust safeguards in AI to prevent negative outcomes from complex human-AI interactions.

In human–machine–human interactions, AI-driven platforms facilitate communication between humans (Petrescu & Krishen, 2023). Examples include collaborative platforms like Microsoft Office 365 and Google Workspace, which incorporate AI to assist with real-time editing, version control and smart suggestions, and AI-driven customer support systems like Zendesk, which use machine learning to prioritise and route customer queries. Similarly, AI-powered translation services such as DeepL and Google Translate enable multinational companies to communicate effectively with global clients and partners (Prates et al., 2020). However, these systems are also not risk-free: in one instance, Facebook's AI translation system incorrectly rendered a Palestinian man's post of "good morning" in Arabic as "attack them" in Hebrew, leading to his wrongful arrest (Hern, 2017).

Finally, human–machine–machine–human interactions represent a more complex form of engagement in which multiple machines communicate and collaborate to assist human communication and activities (Shaalan et al., 2022b). These include supply chain management and smart manufacturing (Wilkins et al., 2024), whereby interconnected robots and AI systems manage production lines, optimise workflows and communicate with human operators. Siemens and General Electric are leaders in integrating such AI-driven industrial automation, while logistics companies like DHL use AI-powered systems to coordinate the movement of goods, optimise routes and predict delivery times (Dhaliwal, 2022). Moreover, integrated healthcare systems like IBM Watson Health collect patient data, generate insights and communicate them to doctors for informed decision-making (Kasula, 2024). Additionally, generative AI is increasingly being used in creative and business applications. For instance, companies like OpenAI have developed models like GPT-4o that can generate human-like text, create content, draft emails, and even compose music or design products (Cui et al., 2024). In marketing, it is used to develop marketing content, including images and videos (Heitmann, 2024). These generative AI systems communicate with other AI tools to enhance creativity and productivity, eventually delivering the final output to human users who can further refine and utilise these creations in their business processes (Gupta et al., 2024; Obrenovic et al., 2024). On the other end, in 2024, a Hong Kong-based company fell victim to a deepfake scam involving its CFO. Fraudsters used AI-generated deepfake technology to impersonate the CFO in video calls, instructing junior employees to transfer $35 million to fraudulent accounts. This incident highlighted the severe risks associated with deepfake technology in business, including the potential for large-scale financial fraud and the erosion of trust in corporate communication systems (Chen & Magramo, 2024).

Based on the aforementioned discussion, several research studies are needed to understand the theoretical underpinnings of the antecedents of negative outcomes as a result of adopting artificial intelligence in customer relationship management (Pantano et al., 2024). The following section explains in detail the antecedents and their theoretical explanation of the factors that lead to negative AI-led customer relationship management and customer interaction.

4. ANTECEDENTS AND THEORETICAL FRAMEWORK OF NEGATIVE AI-LED CRM

Despite huge advances in all these types of human interactions with digital machines, AI continues to have inherent inadequacies that limit the development of AI-led CRM (Prior et al., 2024). Some of these shortcomings can be identified as antecedents of the negative effects of AI-led CRM. Arguably, the most significant is the current inadequacy of emotional AI, which seeks to understand and react to human emotions (Keerthika et al., 2024). AI systems create an empathy gap (Liu-Thompkins et al., 2022) if they cannot interpret or simulate those emotions accurately (Srinivasan & González, 2022) or replicate empathetic human responses. This is particularly significant in the CRM context, where the nuances of human emotions are key to positive interactions and customer satisfaction. AI-driven CRM tools, despite their efficiency at handling large volumes of data and automating responses, often fail to fully grasp the emotional context of customer communications (D'Cruz et al.,

2022), sometimes resulting in responses that, while technically correct, may seem impersonal or out of tune with the customer's emotional state (Morrow et al., 2023).

The negative outcomes of the empathy gap are manifold. In situations that require emotional sensitivity, customers might feel misunderstood or undervalued, leading to dissatisfaction and potential loss of loyalty (D'Cruz et al., 2022; Lv et al., 2022). If customers are frustrated or upset, an empathetic response from a human agent can defuse tension and foster goodwill, whereas an AI system lacking emotional intelligence might escalate the situation by failing to offer the understanding or concessions that a human would intuitively provide (Li et al., 2023). Moreover, reliance on AI in CRM without adequate emotional intelligence can undermine customers' trust in a brand (Flavián & Casaló, 2021), since trust is built on consistent, understanding and personalised interactions (Chen et al., 2022).

AI agents that are judged to lack competence or appropriate functionality can also be considered as antecedents of the negative effects of AI-led CRM. Users judge AI agents' expertise and competence using factors such as the precision of their responses (Mostafa & Kasamani, 2022) and their ability to understand and respond appropriately to users' needs (Mozafari et al., 2022). This includes discerning and seamlessly facilitating human intervention when necessary (Seitz et al., 2022; Wald et al., 2021), since some complex or unusual user queries will necessitate this (Shaalan et al., 2022b). Failing to recognise users' needs can affect service delivery (Tan et al., 2017).

In seeking to understand the processes driving the negative outcomes of AI-led CRM, some researchers have used theoretical approaches relating to negative disconfirmation, which occurs when users' experiences do not live up to their expectations. Negative disconfirmation may relate to the AI agent itself, based on its level of anthropomorphism, or to aspects such as parasocial interactions or social presence. These three theoretical foundations are now explored in more depth.

4.1. Negative AI Agent Anthropomorphism Disconfirmation (NAAD)

Anthropomorphism refers to the attribution of human characteristics to non-human entities. Its importance is widely acknowledged in AI research in the marketing field (Ahn et al., 2022; Dabiran et al., 2024; Stein et al., 2022). Many firms now incorporate anthropomorphic elements, such as gender, name and human-like profile pictures, into their AI programs. Some studies have identified advantages of this approach (Blut et al., 2021; Chong et al., 2021; Van Doorn et al., 2017), which can increase social interaction (Pentina et al., 2023), enhance the intention to interact (Blut et al., 2021; Letheren et al., 2021; Sheehan et al., 2020), and, depending on the level of anthropomorphism, affect the emotions, intentions or motivations ascribed to AI agents (Odekerken-Schröder et al., 2022). Human-like characteristics and attributions of emotions, autonomy and ethical standards can also enhance customer or user satisfaction (Chandra et al., 2022; Moriuchi, 2021; Söderlund & Oikarinen, 2021; Van Pinxteren et al., 2019).

However, these systems can also trigger negative AI agent anthropomorphism disconfirmation, which hinges on the notion that user perception and engagement can be negatively influenced if AI agents fail to display the human-like traits they are programmed to portray (Yang & Hu, 2022). In other words, anthropomorphism may heighten users' expectations of the benefits of interacting (Jang et al., 2023), but risks negative disconfirmation if these expectations are not met. The shortfall fosters negative emotions, potentially leading users to abandon the service or even spread negative word-of-mouth, adversely affecting the service provider (Lee et al., 2021). Other researchers (Liao et al., 2007) have found that decisions to continue using an agent are directly influenced by satisfaction levels, which are, in turn, affected by service disconfirmation.

4.2. Negative Parasocial Interaction Disconfirmation (NPID)

Parasocial interactions occur when an individual engages in social exchanges with a media figure as though they were a personal acquaintance, even though the interaction remains non-reciprocal (Liebers & Schramm, 2019). By recreating a sense of the depth and warmth found in genuine interpersonal relationships, parasocial interactions can enhance perceived credibility, thereby shaping attitudes and behaviours (Ferreira et al., 2024; Koay et al., 2023).

Negative parasocial interaction disconfirmation (NPID) arises when an individual's anticipations and perceptions of a parasocial relationship do not meet their expectations, leading to adverse judgments (Mostafa et al., 2024). Parasocial relationships are thus capable of yielding both positive and negative outcomes. For example, while they can foster admiration and attachment, leading consumers to purchase endorsed products (Sokolova & Kefi, 2020) and thus making shopping experiences more enjoyable and satisfying (Yuan et al., 2023), they can also trigger feelings of being let down or having unmet expectations (Shrum, 2012), resulting in negative disconfirmation.

In the AI agent context, parasocial interactions can be defined as the bond between a consumer and an AI agent, characterised by feelings of friendliness, inclusion, empathy, care and the pursuit of common goals (Hsieh & Lee, 2021; Tsai et al., 2021). While investigations into parasocial interactions with AI agents remain scarce, the studies by Lee and Park (2022) and Tsai et al. (2021) are notable exceptions. Both studies concluded that consumers could develop parasocial relationships with AI agents, raising the question as to whether negative disconfirmation can also occur when these interactions lead to frustration or poor outcomes. For example, users often project onto virtual agents (VAs) the expectations of a human conversational partner (e.g., Replika), such as reciprocal social and emotional exchanges and the recognition and validation of the user's own social cues (Chen et al., 2023), whereas NPID implies that the AI agent has failed to meet the anticipated level of interaction that would typically occur in a human-to-human social context (Tsai et al., 2021). However, NPID in the AI context remains largely unexplored, highlighting a crucial area for further research.

4.3. Negative Social Presence Disconfirmation (NSPD)

Social presence is defined as a psychological phenomenon wherein individuals perceive others as real individuals in technology-mediated communication (Kim & Park, 2024) or as a sensation of face-to-face presence despite the absence of physical proximity (Kreijns et al., 2022; Park et al., 2023). VAs can create a sense of social interaction (Sundar & Nass, 2000), with users having the sensation of "being with an intelligent entity" (Kim & Sundar, 2012, p. 244). The social presence concept is highly relevant to research on AI agents for brand communication, as the agents can be programmed to exude particular personalities or characters. Social presence may be higher in anthropomorphic AI systems (Verhagen et al., 2014) than in machine-like chatbots (Sun et al., 2024), making the AI agents seem more attractive to consumers and generating more positive attitudes (Ahn et al., 2022).

Social presence perceptions in interactions with human-like AI agents have been shown to significantly affect outcomes including customer experience (Bogicevic et al., 2019; Vanek et al., 2018), responses (Kreijns et al., 2022), engagement (Oh et al., 2023), emotions, behaviours, attitudes (Ghali et al., 2024; Ying et al., 2022) and online shopping behaviour (Botha & Reyneke, 2016). Human likeness can also yield persuasive outcomes (Xu & Lombard, 2017) and foster emotional connections (Araujo, 2018), primarily by augmenting social presence. For example, the perceived social presence of virtual avatars has been shown to increase users' emotional connection and trust towards an e-service platform (Etemad-Sajadi & Ghachem, 2015).

Conversely, the absence or misrepresentation of social presence can lead to negative social presence disconfirmation (NSPD), which arises when there is a perceptual divergence between the expected and the actual ability of AI agents to project social and emotional cues. This results in a user experience that feels emotionally disconnected or impersonal (Shrum, 2012). In the AI agent context, it can be argued that this may occur when the agent's attempts to display social cues fail to meet user expectations, potentially resulting in a diminished sense of trust and engagement.

4.4. Relationships Between Negative Disconfirmation Types

It is also important to consider the possibility of interrelationships between the different types of negative disconfirmation, most of which have attracted little attention from researchers. For example, if programs fail to meet customers' expectations, this may not only trigger negative AI agent anthropomorphism disconfirmation but also reduce perceptions of the agents' social presence, causing NSPD. Negative AI agent anthropomorphism disconfirmation might even increase NSPD; however, empirical validations of this effect are scant (Muniz et al., 2023).

The association between negative AI agent anthropomorphism disconfirmation and NPID is also not fully understood, despite the good understanding of them as separate concepts (Mostafa et al., 2024). For example, if higher levels of anthropomorphism raise expectations of parasocial relationships, interrelated disconfirmation may also occur. However, only a handful of studies (e.g. Lee and Park, 2022; Tsai et al., 2021) have extended the NPID concept to interactions with AI agents or VAs.

Moreover, since social presence can significantly influence parasocial interactions (Kim, 2022), NPID and NSPD may be directly related. This could occur if users' expectations of a parasocial interaction, such as emotional support and a sense of companionship, go unmet (Mostafa et al., 2024). The reverse may also be true: since NSPD arises from the gap between AI agents' expected and actual abilities to project social and emotional cues, this discrepancy can also lead to NPID if an expected parasocial relationship also fails to materialise or is disrupted (Aw and Chuah, 2021; Tsai et al., 2021). The situation is compounded by the fact that the more capable the agent is of mimicking human characteristics, the higher the user's expectations of a sophisticated interaction (Pitardi & Marriott, 2021).

5. NEGATIVE CONSEQUENCES OF AI IMPLEMENTATION IN CRM

The use of AI agents in CRM has been shown to carry risks of negative consequences in multiple areas, including customer loyalty, brand reputation and brand engagement (Mostafa et al., 2024) as well as customer trust (Chen et al., 2022) and brand equity (Gupta & Khan, 2024). It may also increase AI-induced brand hate and customer dissatisfaction (Mostafa et al., 2024). Three of these effects – negative brand engagement (NBE), negative AI agent trust and AI-induced brand hate – are now explored in more detail, as they have the most negative significance on overall brand equity (Gupta & Khan, 2024; Hollebeek & Chen, 2014).

5.1. Negative Brand Engagement (NBE)

Brand engagement encompasses customers' cognitive, emotional and behavioural commitment to a brand's offerings (Brodie et al., 2013; Hollebeek & Chen, 2014). While most prior research on the topic has illuminated brand engagement's positive aspects (e.g. Rather, 2021; Rather et al., 2022), recent studies have explored its variable nature, finding that it fluctuates not only in intensity but also in its positive or negative impact on the brand (Obilo et al., 2021; Rather & Hollebeek, 2021). NBE is characterised by customers' adverse thoughts, emotions and actions towards a brand, as well as the detrimental effects on the brand or organisation (Dolan et al., 2016; Hollebeek & Chen, 2014). It may arise from negative emotional responses to unexpected disappointments, significant shortfalls in meeting consumer expectations (Liu & Keh, 2015) or perceptions of unfairness (Do et al., 2023). It involves the same levels of activation, immersion and passion typically associated with positive engagement (Hollebeek & Chen, 2014). These can be expressed through detrimental cognitive stances like bias or cynicism, negative emotions including hatred or resentment, and adverse behaviours such as negative reviews or boycotts (Juric et al., 2016). Negative engagement's characteristics of active participation and public expression risk significant harm to corporate reputation (Pfeffer et al., 2014) and to a brand's equity and financial standing (Hollebeek & Chen, 2014; Juric et al., 2016).

In the digital sphere, negative feelings or actions directed towards AI agents may also spread to the brand (Naumann et al., 2020). For example, if AI agents cannot process requests in a human-like or empathetic manner, customers feel misunderstood and undervalued by the brand (Kuanr et al., 2022). While different individuals will respond differently (Zhou et al., 2019), this negative emotional state may have a ripple effect, influencing overall brand perception and engagement (Kucuk, 2019a) and risking damage not just to the brand but also to the interplay with other entities in the service ecosystem (Juric et al., 2016).

5.2. Negative AI Agent Trust

AI agent trust is conceptualised as the belief in the AI agent's reliability, integrity and competence, which could potentially cushion the blow of negative experiences by providing a pre-existing positive bias towards the agent's capabilities (Ryan, 2020). It is the culmination of consumers' assessment of decision-making processes with AI agents (Chen et al., 2023). This assessment is based on logical analysis, where the individual evaluates the AI agent's dependability by observing its capabilities, including reliability, competence and credibility (Chai et al., 2015; Johnson

& Grayson, 2005). Users may also place more trust in AI agents with human-like features (Chandra et al., 2022; Zhang & Yang, 2022).

The degree of trust bestowed on AI agents significantly influences the relationship between service disconfirmation and user satisfaction, as well as subsequent user actions (Bedué & Fritzsche, 2022). AI agent trust is, therefore, critical in mitigating the adverse effects of service failures (Jacovi et al., 2021) since users with high levels of AI agent trust are more likely to overlook discrepancies between expected and actual service, thereby maintaining their engagement with the service (Ryan, 2020). Conversely, trust deficit can amplify the negative repercussions of even slight service inadequacies, potentially escalating to user disengagement (Molina & Sundar, 2022).

AI agent trust is thus an important variable (Schepman & Rodway, 2023), and one that may moderate the relationship between NPID and AI agent hate. We argue that if a user trusts an AI agent based on positive prior experiences or the agent's reputation, this may temper the user's response to negative parasocial interactions and lessen the intensity of AI agent hate, for example, by framing the unsatisfactory interaction within a broader context of generally reliable service. Trust may lead users to attribute service failures to external factors or view them as anomalies rather than systemic flaws, thus reducing the propensity for hate (Seitz et al., 2022).

5.3 AI-induced Brand Hate

Research from the psychology field highlights that hating someone is a complex emotional state, which is quite distinct from merely disliking them (Roy et al., 2022). This distinction has been extended to the realm of business and brands, with prior research suggesting that brand hate is not just an intensified version of dislike but a separate construct altogether, much in the way that love transcends liking (Rossiter, 2012; Zhang & Laroche, 2020). Bryson et al. (2013) mapped out potential precursors to brand hate, while Hegner et al. (2017) investigated its causes and consequences, and Zarantonello et al. (2016) empirically examined its complexity, distinguishing between active and passive forms. Kucuk (2019a) further refined the concept with a nuanced model of brand hate, exploring its connection with consumer personality characteristics. The hate concept is intertwined with powerful and often extreme negative emotions (Kucuk, 2016, 2019b). Sternberg's (2003) framework posits that brand hate stems from three fundamental emotions: disgust, contempt and anger.

In digital interactions, a similar phenomenon of AI agent hate has been identified, which can be triggered by users' unmet expectations (Zhang & Laroche, 2020). AI agent hate is more than just a transient frustration: it represents a deep-seated resentment that can develop when AI agents do not deliver the empathetic, humanised interactions that users anticipate (de Sá Siqueira et al., 2023). It goes beyond the functional aspects of the service, encapsulating broader discontent with AI agents' perceived social and emotional deficiencies (Zarantonello et al., 2016).

AI agent hate stems from a confluence of factors. One key issue is AI agents' limited natural language processing (NLP) capabilities, since they may struggle to understand complex requests or deviations from programmed scripts (Shaalan et al., 2022b), creating frustration as users repeat themselves or encounter irrelevant responses. Groshek et al. (2020) also found a correlation between users feeling "managed" by AI agents and a decline in perceived helpfulness. Moreover, the psychological phenomenon of the uncanny valley effect, explored by Mori et al. (2012), describes discomfort with entities that appear almost human but lack a crucial element of humanity. Widening knowledge of AI agent hate is significant given the potential for damage not just to the AI agents' reputations but to the brand (Kuanr et al., 2022; Kucuk, 2019b), and in order to understand how firms and designers can minimise the risks of its occurrence.

Brand hate triggered by unmet expectations may also lead to NBE behaviours (Zhang & Laroche, 2020). This emotional response is often a direct consequence of the disappointment experienced when an AI agent fails to provide an adequate level of service, resulting in a break in the customer's digital journey (Hegner et al., 2017). Customers' negative emotional state can influence overall brand perception and engagement (Kucuk, 2019a), significantly impacting brand reputation, customer retention and loyalty (Rather & Hollebeek, 2021). This is especially relevant in the digital marketplace, where customers can easily move to a competing service if their expectations are not met (Mazhar et al., 2022), underscoring the need for digital service providers to closely align their offerings with customer expectations to prevent dissatisfaction and the subsequent loss of clientele (Wu et al., 2018).

Accordingly, as brands increasingly rely on AI agents for customer interactions, recognising the potential for AI agent hate to undermine brand equity is of the utmost importance (Rather, 2021; Rather et al., 2022). Drawing on Sternberg's (2003) model for brand hate, we argue that consumers' emotional responses of disgust, contempt and anger can transition into brand impacts in the AI agent context, and that AI agent hate may trigger broader brand detraction, damaging reputation and loyalty, as the agent is often perceived as a representative of the brand. This intersection between AI agent hates and NBE suggests that managing AI agent interactions is not just a matter of customer service efficiency but also of safeguarding the brand's emotional resonance and appeal to its user base.

Figure 1 summarises the types of the theoretical interrelationships between humans and digital systems, the key antecedent to negative outcomes, i.e. the empathy gap, and the types of negative disconfirmation that may occur.

Figure 1. Theoretical interrelationships between human-machine interactions, the empathy gap, and negative outcomes in AI-driven CRM

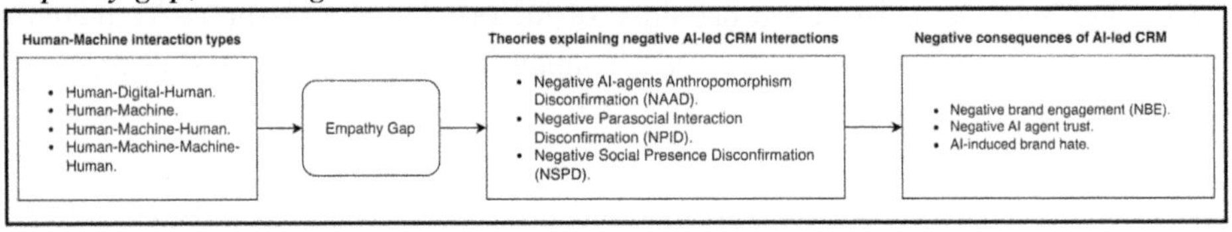

(Authors)

6. STRATEGICALLY MITIGATING THE NEGATIVE IMPACTS OF AI IN CRM

This section offers potential solutions to managers and decision-makers of ways to manage the negative effects of AI-led CRM, which can be mitigated if firms are willing to adopt appropriate strategic measures (Prior et al., 2024). One of the most effective methods is to implement rapid human intervention strategies that provide a safety net when AI responses inadequately address customer needs or fail outright (Song et al., 2022). This ensures that sensitive situations are managed effectively, preserving customer trust and satisfaction. For instance, AI systems could be programmed to flag high-risk customer interactions such as service cancellations or complaints, prompting immediate human intervention. Future systems could also use predictive analytics to identify potential dissatisfaction before it escalates, allowing human agents to proactively engage with customers, potentially turning a negative experience into a positive one.

Similarly, hybrid models that blend AI efficiency with human empathy can optimise both customer satisfaction and operational efficiency (Zhu & Luo, 2024). These models harness AI's ability to handle large datasets and routine queries while reserving human intervention for complex or sensitive issues (Perry, 2023). In future, hybrid models could involve more dynamic interactions where AI and human agents work in tandem in real time (Pataranutaporn et al., 2023). For instance, during a live chat interaction, AI could analyse customer sentiment and the complexity of the issue in real time and decide whether to continue handling the query or escalate it to a human agent. AI could also provide real-time data and suggestions to human agents during their customer interactions, enhancing the quality of service by equipping agents with instant access to customer history, past purchases and potential upsell opportunities. These hybrid models reflect an understanding that while AI can greatly enhance efficiency and handle a high volume of interactions, the human element remains irreplaceable in dealing with complex, sensitive or highly personalised issues. By blending these approaches, companies can ensure that their CRM systems not only save time and money but also deliver a customer experience that feels personal and efficient.

In addition, firms can continuously train AI systems with real-world feedback, creating an ongoing learning process that helps AI to better understand and simulate human emotions, closing the empathy gap. For example, an e-commerce platform could regularly update its training dataset with customer feedback to refine its chatbots' responses or employ real-time learning algorithms that dynamically adjust responses based on immediate customer feedback. For example, an AI system could adjust its tone or approach mid-conversation to better align with the customer's mood or preferences. It is also vital for companies to be transparent about the role and limitations of AI, which helps to manage customer expectations and build trust. Tailoring the level of anthropomorphism to specific tasks can also reduce the likelihood of disappointment and negative reactions (Nass & Moon, 2000).

The ethical deployment of AI in CRM is another cornerstone of minimising negative effects. This includes safeguarding privacy, ensuring robust data security and developing bias-free algorithms (Hacker, 2021). These steps are crucial to preventing the erosion of customer trust and potential legal issues. Future CRM systems could integrate AI transparency by not only notifying users when they are interacting with AI but also explaining in real time the reasoning behind certain advice or decisions. AI systems could also employ advanced ethical frameworks that are self-auditing and adaptive to new regulations and societal norms, ensuring they remain fair and impartial as societal values evolve (Krijger et al., 2023). Developing AI that understands different human ethics, morals and social norms remains a thorny task (Murtarelli et al., 2021) but is undergoing rapid development and has significant potential (Awad et al., 2018; Indurkhya, 2019; Shaalan et al., 2022b).

Finally, innovative AI applications such as advanced NLP techniques can significantly enhance the quality of customer interactions, making them more natural and effective (Kolasani, 2023). Advanced NLP capabilities can also understand slang and regional dialects, significantly enhancing the interaction quality in diverse customer bases. Future NLP advances could also enable AI systems to detect subtleties in tone and emotion, allowing them to respond appropriately to cues of frustration or happiness, much like a skilled human communicator (Shaalan et al., 2022b).

7. CONCLUSIONS, LIMITATIONS AND FUTURE DIRECTIONS

AI agents are now a significant and permanent fixture in the CRM landscape. As the technology continues to develop, increasing numbers of firms are likely to adopt AI-led CRM widen its deployment. At the same time, new generations of AI, including generative AI, are likely to become increasingly human-like. However, these developments will not necessarily close the empathy gap, and may indeed increase customers' expectations still further, resulting in ongoing risks of disconfirmation regarding the AI agent, parasocial interactions and social presence, and their associated negative effects.

Regardless of any future progress in AI agent empathy or functionality, firms' CRM strategies should already include steps to mitigate the risks of disconfirmation. These include ensuring easy recourse when necessary to human agents; developing hybrid models that also incorporate human–human interaction; continuously training AI agents using updated data from customer service interactions; developing ethical systems built on principles such as transparency, privacy and non-discrimination; and harnessing developments such as NLP to ensure AI agents have more natural exchanges with customers, including those with diverse accents and dialects.

This rapidly developing field offers numerous avenues for future research. One specific limitation of this chapter relates to the current lack of empirical understanding of whether AI agent trust negatively moderates the relationship between NPID and AI agent hate. We argue that this moderating role exists, i.e. that greater AI agent trust decreases the likelihood of a user developing strong negative sentiments, even when faced with unfulfilled expectations of parasocial interactions. We believe the investigation of this hypothesis is of particular relevance to AI agent developers and marketers, since it implies that building and maintaining user trust could be as crucial as improving technical capabilities, potentially guiding strategies for AI agent deployment and CRM. Thus, we encourage future research that empirically examines this relationship.

Future studies could also build on the work of Lee and Park (2022) and Tsai et al. (2021) to further investigate parasocial interactions with AI agents, including negative disconfirmation in this context. NPID's interplay with negative disconfirmation towards the AI agent has also not been thoroughly explored. The intersection between negative AI agent anthropomorphism disconfirmation and NSPD also remains underexplored (Mostafa et al., 2024), which is of particular significance given the increasing prevalence of anthropomorphised AI agents that can display a social presence, and the concomitant risk of disconfirmation if users' heightened expectations are not met. Finally, prior research has not explored the NBE that occurs when AI agents fail to meet consumers' expectations or provoke frustration and dissatisfaction (Pantano et al., 2024). Understanding how the interplay between the disconfirmation types and how this can feed into AI agent hate and lead to NBE is therefore essential.

In conclusion, artificial intelligence, with its rapid growth and ever-expanding learning capabilities, has shown potential beyond a "child's level of development" (Shaalan et al., 2022b, p. 385). This advancement is expected to reduce the empathy gap and, consequently, the negative outcomes associated with it. However, these developments will also elevate user and customer expectations. Thus, theoretical, and empirical investigations into the balance between automation and the preservation of human-centric service elements are crucial to better understanding and mitigating the potential challenges posed by artificial intelligence in customer relationship management.

REFERENCES

Ahn, R. J., Cho, S. Y., & Sunny Tsai, W. (2022). Demystifying computer-generated imagery (CGI) influencers: The effect of perceived anthropomorphism and social presence on brand outcomes. *Journal of Interactive Advertising*, 22(3), 327–335. DOI: 10.1080/15252019.2022.2111242

Allison, K. (2024). Data-Driven Customer Relationship Management (CRM) Modeling: Humanistic Connection in Predictive Analytics. In *Revolutionizing the AI-Digital Landscape* (pp. 244-262). Productivity Press.

Alnofeli, K., Akter, S., & Yanamandram, V. (2023). Understanding the Future trends and innovations of AI-based CRM systems. In *Handbook of Big Data Research Methods* (pp. 279–294). Edward Elgar Publishing. DOI: 10.4337/9781800888555.00021

Amazon (2024). Leadership Principles. https://www.amazon.jobs/content/en/our-workplace/leadership-principles

Araujo, T. (2018). Living up to the chatbot hype: The influence of anthropomorphic design cues and communicative agency framing on conversational agent and company perceptions. *Computers in Human Behavior*, 85, 183–189. DOI: 10.1016/j.chb.2018.03.051

Atli, Q. (2024). How Tesco Uses Data to Personalize the Shopping Experience: A Deep Dive. https://www.atliq.ai/how-tesco-uses-data-to-personalize-the-shopping-experience/

Aw, E. C. X., & Chuah, S. H. W. (2021). "Stop the unattainable ideal for an ordinary me!" Fostering parasocial relationships with social media influencers: The role of self- discrepancy. *Journal of Business Research*, 132, 146–157. DOI: 10.1016/j.jbusres.2021.04.025

Awad, E., Dsouza, S., Kim, R., Schulz, J., Henrich, J., Shariff, A., Bonnefon, J.-F., & Rahwan, I. (2018). The moral machine experiment. *Nature*, 563(7729), 59–64. DOI: 10.1038/s41586-018-0637-6 PMID: 30356211

Bayerl, P. S., & Jacobs, G. (2022). Who is responsible for customers' privacy? Effects of first versus third party handling of privacy contracts on continuance intentions. *Technological Forecasting and Social Change*, 185, 122039. DOI: 10.1016/j.techfore.2022.122039

BBC. (2014). Sydney siege sees Uber raise prices before backtracking. https://www.bbc.com/news/technology-30478008

Bedué, P., & Fritzsche, A. (2022). Can we trust AI? An empirical investigation of trust requirements and guide to successful AI adoption. *Journal of Enterprise Information Management*, 35(2), 530–549. DOI: 10.1108/JEIM-06-2020-0233

Bernasconi, C., & Blume, L. B. (2023). Theorizing architectural research and practice in the metaverse: The meta-context of virtual community engagement. *Archnet-IJAR: International Journal of Architectural Research* (ahead-of-print). .DOI: 10.1108/ARCH-08-2023-0203

Blut, M., Wang, C., Wünderlich, N. V., & Brock, C. (2021). Understanding anthropomorphism in service provision: A meta-analysis of physical robots, chatbots, and other AI. *Journal of the Academy of Marketing Science*, 49(4), 1–27. DOI: 10.1007/s11747-020-00762-y

Bogicevic, V., Seo, S., Kandampully, J. A., Liu, S. Q., & Rudd, N. A. (2019). Virtual reality presence as a preamble of tourism experience: The role of mental imagery. *Tourism Management*, 74, 55–64. DOI: 10.1016/j.tourman.2019.02.009

Botha, E., & Reyneke, M. (2016). The influence of social presence on online purchase intention: An experiment with different product types. In C. Campbell & J. Ma (Eds.), *Looking forward, looking back: Drawing on the past to shape the future of marketing,proceedings of the 2013 World Marketing Congress* (pp. 180-183). Springer. DOI: 10.1007/978-3-319-24184-5_49

Brodie, R. J., Ilic, A., Juric, B., & Hollebeek, L. D. (2013). Consumer engagement in a virtual brand com- munity: An exploratory analysis. *Journal of Business Research*, 66(1), 105–114. DOI: 10.1016/j.jbusres.2011.07.029

Bryson, D., Atwal, G., & Hultén, P. (2013). Towards the conceptualisation of the antecedents of extreme negative affect towards luxury brands. *Qualitative Market Research*, 16(4), 393–405. DOI: 10.1108/QMR-06-2013-0043

Chai, J. C. Y., Malhotra, N. K., & Alpert, F. (2015). A two-dimensional model of trust-value-loyalty in service relationships. *Journal of Retailing and Consumer Services*, 26, 23–31. DOI: 10.1016/j.jretconser.2015.05.005

Chandra, S., Shirish, A., & Srivastava, S. C. (2022). To be or not to be… human? Theorizing the role of human-like competencies in conversational artificial intelligence agents. *Journal of Management Information Systems*, 39(4), 969–1005. DOI: 10.1080/07421222.2022.2127441

Chatterjee, S., Chaudhuri, R., & Vrontis, D. (2022). AI and digitalization in relationship management: Impact of adopting AI-embedded CRM system. *Journal of Business Research*, 150, 437–450. DOI: 10.1016/j.jbusres.2022.06.033

Chen, H., & Magramo, K. (2024, February 4). Finance worker pays out $25 million after video call with deepfake 'chief financial officer'. *CNN*.https://edition.cnn.com/2024/02/04/asia/deepfake-cfo-scam-hong-kong-intl-hnk/index.html

Chen, Q., Lu, Y., Gong, Y., & Xiong, J. (2023). Can AI chatbots help retain customers? Impact of AI service quality on customer loyalty. *Internet Research*, 33(6), 2205–2243. DOI: 10.1108/INTR-09-2021-0686

Chen, Y., Prentice, C., Weaven, S., & Hisao, A. (2022). The influence of customer trust and artificial intelligence on customer engagement and loyalty–The case of the home-sharing industry. *Frontiers in Psychology*, 13, 912339. DOI: 10.3389/fpsyg.2022.912339 PMID: 35992434

Chong, T., Yu, T., Keeling, D. I., & de Ruyter, K. (2021). AI-chatbots on the services frontline addressing the challenges and opportunities of agency. *Journal of Retailing and Consumer Services*, 63, 102735. DOI: 10.1016/j.jretconser.2021.102735

Chopdar, P. K., Paul, J., & Prodanova, J. (2022). Mobile shoppers' response to Covid-19 phobia, pessimism and smartphone addiction: Does social influence matter? *Technological Forecasting and Social Change*, 174, 121249. DOI: 10.1016/j.techfore.2021.121249 PMID: 36540714

Christodoulides, G., Athwal, N., Boukis, A., & Semaan, R. W. (2021). New forms of luxury consumption in the sharing economy. *Journal of Business Research*, 137, 89–99. DOI: 10.1016/j.jbusres.2021.08.022

D'Cruz, J. R., Kidder, W., & Varshney, K. R. (2022). The empathy gap: Why AI can forecast behavior but cannot assess trustworthiness. In *Proceedings of the AAAI fall symposium series symposium on thinking fast and slow and other cognitive theories in AI.*

Dabiran, E., Farivar, S., Wang, F., & Grant, G. (2024). Virtually human: Anthropomorphism in virtual influencer marketing. *Journal of Retailing and Consumer Services*, 79, 103797. DOI: 10.1016/j.jretconser.2024.103797

Davenport, T., & Harris, J. (2017). *Competing on analytics: Updated, with a new introduction: The new science of winning*. Harvard Business Press.

Davenport, T. H., & Ronanki, R. (2018). Artificial Intelligence for the Real World. Harvard Business Review (HBR). https://www.bizjournals.com/boston/news/2018/01/09/hbr-artificial-intelligence-for-the-real-world.html de Sá Siqueira, M. A., Müller, B. C., & Bosse, T. (2023). When do we accept mistakes from chatbots? The impact of human-like communication on user experience in chatbots that make mistakes. *International Journal of Human-Computer Interaction*, 40(11), 2862–2872. DOI: 10.1080/10447318.2023.2175158

Devi, K. V., Manjula, V., & Pattewar, T. (2023). *ChatGPT: Comprehensive study on generative AI tool*. Academic Guru Publishing House.

Dhaliwal, A. (2022). Towards AI-driven transport and logistics. In *Workshop on e-Business* (pp. 119-131). Springer Nature.

Do, D. K. X., Rahman, K., Robinson, L. J., & Bowden, J. (2023). Negative customer engagement in emerging markets: Cognitive dimension. *Journal of Strategic Marketing*, 31(2), 370–402. DOI: 10.1080/0965254X.2021.1919180

Dolan, R., Conduit, J., & Fahy, J. (2016). Social media engagement: A construct of positively and negatively valenced engagement behaviours. In Brodie, R., Hollebeek, L., & Conduit, J. (Eds.), *Customer engagement: Contemporary issues and challenges* (pp. 96–117). Routledge.

Dwivedi, Y. K., Balakrishnan, J., Baabdullah, A. M., & Das, R. (2023a). Do chatbots establish "humanness" in the customer purchase journey? An investigation through explanatory sequential design. *Psychology and Marketing*, 40(11), 2244–2271. DOI: 10.1002/mar.21888

Dwivedi, Y. K., Kshetri, N., Hughes, L., Rana, N. P., Baabdullah, A. M., Kar, A. K., Koohang, A., Ribeiro-Navarrete, S., Belei, N., Balakrishnan, J., Basu, S., Behl, A., Davies, G. H., Dutot, V., Dwivedi, R., Evans, L., Felix, R., Foster-Fletcher, R., Giannakis, M., & Yan, M. (2023b). Exploring the darkverse: A multi-perspective analysis of the negative societal impacts of the metaverse. *Information Systems Frontiers*, 25(5), 2071–2114. DOI: 10.1007/s10796-023-10400-x PMID: 37361890

Etemad-Sajadi, R., & Ghachem, L. (2015). The impact of hedonic and utilitarian value of online avatars on e-service quality. *Computers in Human Behavior*, 52, 81–86. DOI: 10.1016/j.chb.2015.05.048

Fader, P. (2020). *Customer centricity: Focus on the right customers for strategic advantage*. University of Pennsylvania Press.

Fatima, S., Alqahtani, H., Naim, A., & Alma'alwi, F. (2022). E-CRM through social media marketing activities for brand awareness, brand image, and brand loyalty. In *Building a brand image through electronic customer relationship management* (pp. 109–138). IGI Global. DOI: 10.4018/978-1-6684-5386-5.ch006

Ferraro, C., Demsar, V., Sands, S., Restrepo, M., & Campbell, C. (2024). The paradoxes of generative AI-enabled customer service: A guide for managers. *Business Horizons*, 67(5), 549–559. Advance online publication. DOI: 10.1016/j.bushor.2024.04.013

Ferreira, A. G., Crespo, C. F., Ribeiro, F. M., & Barreiros, P. (2024). The social media theatre: New guidelines to foster parasocial interactions with followers and improve influencer marketing communication effectiveness. *Journal of Marketing Communications*, 1–25. DOI: 10.1080/13527266.2024.2318696

Flavián, C., & Casaló, L. V. (2021). Artificial intelligence in services: Current trends, benefits and challenges. *Service Industries Journal*, 41(13-14), 853–859. DOI: 10.1080/02642069.2021.1989177

Fronczek, L. P., Mende, M., Scott, M. L., Nenkov, G. Y., & Gustafsson, A. (2023). Friend or foe? Can anthropomorphizing self-tracking devices backfire on marketers and consumers? *Journal of the Academy of Marketing Science*, 51(5), 1075–1097. DOI: 10.1007/s11747-022-00915-1

Ghali, Z., Rather, R. A., & Khan, I. (2024). Investigating metaverse marketing-enabled consumers' social presence, attachment, engagement and (re)visit intentions. *Journal of Retailing and Consumer Services*, 77, 103671. DOI: 10.1016/j.jretconser.2023.103671

Gibson, K. (2022). Lyft and Uber criticized for surge pricing after Brooklyn subway shooting. Online. https://www.cbsnews.com/news/brooklyn-subway-shooting-lyft-uber-surge-pricing/

Goodfellow, I., Bengio, Y., & Courville, A. (2016). Deep Learning. *MIT Press.* https://mitpress.mit.edu/9780262035613/deep-learning/

Google. (2024). Help your users take action with Google Assistant. https://developers.google.com/assistant/why-build

Grand View Research. (2023). *Customer relationship management market size, share, & trends analysis report, by component, by solution, by deployment, by enterprise size, by end use, and segment forecasts, 2024 – 2030.* https://www.grandviewresearch.com/industry-analysis/customer-relationship-management-crm-market

Groshek, J., Cutino, C., & Walsh, J. (2020). People hate phone menus and don't trust virtual assistants like Siri. *PhysOrg.* https://phys.org/news/2016-04-people-menus-dont-virtual-siri.html

Guerola-Navarro, V., Gil-Gomez, H., Oltra-Badenes, R., & Sendra-García, J. (2021). Customer relationship management and its impact on innovation: A literature review. *Journal of Business Research*, 129, 83–87. DOI: 10.1016/j.jbusres.2021.02.050

Gupta, R., Nair, K., Mishra, M., Ibrahim, B., & Bhardwaj, S. (2024). Adoption and impacts of generative artificial intelligence: Theoretical underpinnings and research agenda. *International Journal of Information Management Data Insights*, 4(1), 100232. DOI: 10.1016/j.jjimei.2024.100232

Gupta, Y., & Khan, F. M. (2024). Role of artificial intelligence in customer engagement: A systematic review and future research directions. *Journal of Modelling in Management* (ahead-of-print). .DOI: 10.1108/JM2-01-2023-0016

Hacker, P. (2021). A legal framework for AI training data - from first principles to the Artificial Intelligence Act. *Law, Innovation and Technology*, 13(2), 257–301. DOI: 10.1080/17579961.2021.1977219

Han, B., Deng, X., & Fan, H. (2023). Partners or opponents? How mindset shapes consumers' attitude toward anthropomorphic artificial intelligence service robots. *Journal of Service Research*, 26(3), 441–458. DOI: 10.1177/10946705231169674

Hasan, R., Weaven, S., & Thaichon, P. (2021). Blurring the line between physical and digital environment: The impact of artificial intelligence on customers' relationship and customer experience. In Thaichon, P., & Ratten, V. (Eds.), *Developing Digital Marketing* (pp. 135–153). Emerald Publishing Limited., DOI: 10.1108/978-1-80071-348-220211008

Hegner, S. M., Fetscherin, M., & van Delzen, M. (2017). Determinants and outcomes of brand hate. *Journal of Product and Brand Management*, 26(1), 13–25. DOI: 10.1108/JPBM-01-2016-1070

Hern, A. (2017, October 24). Facebook translates 'good morning' into 'attack them', leading to arrest. *The Guardian*. https://www.theguardian.com/technology/2017/oct/24/facebook-palestine-israel-translates-good-morning-attack-them-arrest

Hollebeek, L. D., & Chen, T. (2014). Exploring positively-versus negatively-valenced brand engagement: A conceptual model. *Journal of Product and Brand Management*, 23(1), 62–74. DOI: 10.1108/JPBM-06-2013-0332

Hollebeek, L. D., Sprott, D. E., & Brady, M. K. (2021). Rise of the machines? Customer engagement in automated service interactions. *Journal of Service Research*, 24(1), 3–8. DOI: 10.1177/1094670520975110

Hsieh, S. H., & Lee, C. T. (2021). Hey Alexa: Examining the effect of perceived socialness in usage intentions of AI assistant-enabled smart speaker. *Journal of Research in Interactive Marketing*, 15(2), 267–294. DOI: 10.1108/JRIM-11-2019-0179

Indurkhya, B. (2019). Is morality the last frontier for machines? *New Ideas in Psychology*, 54, 107–111. DOI: 10.1016/j.newideapsych.2018.12.001

Jacovi, A., Marasović, A., Miller, T., & Goldberg, Y. (2021). Formalizing trust in artificial intelligence: Prerequisites, causes and goals of human trust in AI. In *Proceedings of the 2021 ACM conference on fairness, accountability, and transparency* (pp. 624-635). Association for Computing Machinery. DOI: 10.1145/3442188.3445923

Jang, Y., Liu, A. Y., & Ke, W. Y. (2023). Exploring smart retailing: Anthropomorphism in voice shopping of smart speaker. *Information Technology & People*, 36(7), 2894–2913. DOI: 10.1108/ITP-07-2021-0536

Johnson, D., & Grayson, K. (2005). Cognitive and affective trust in service relationships. *Journal of Business Research*, 58(4), 500–507. DOI: 10.1016/S0148-2963(03)00140-1

Juric, B., Smith, S., & Wilks, G. (2016). Negative customer brand engagement: An overview of conceptual and blog-based findings. In Brodie, R. J., Hollebeek, L. D., & Conduit, J. (Eds.), *Customer engagement: Contemporary issues and challenges* (pp. 278–294). Routledge.

Kang, W., Shao, B., Du, S., Chen, H., & Zhang, Y. (2024). How to improve voice assistant evaluations: Understanding the role of attachment with a socio-technical systems perspective. *Technological Forecasting and Social Change*, 200, 123171. DOI: 10.1016/j.techfore.2023.123171

Kaplan, L., Gerzon, N., Mislove, A., & Sapiezynski, P. (2022, October). Measurement and analysis of implied identity in ad delivery optimization. In *Proceedings of the 22nd ACM Internet Measurement Conference* (pp. 195-209). DOI: 10.1145/3517745.3561450

Kasula, B. Y. (2024). Ethical implications and future prospects of artificial intelligence in healthcare: A research synthesis. *International Meridian Journal*, 6(6), 1–7.

Keerthika, M., Abilash, K., Vasanth, M. S., Kuralamudhu, M., & Abbirooban, S. (2024). Emotional AI: Computationally intelligent devices for education. In *Emotional AI and Human-AI Interactions in Social Networking* (pp. 87-99). Academic Press.

Khan, R. U., Salamzadeh, Y., Iqbal, Q., & Yang, S. (2022). The impact of customer relationship management and company reputation on customer loyalty: The mediating role of customer satisfaction. *Journal of Relationship Marketing*, 21(1), 1–26. DOI: 10.1080/15332667.2020.1840904

Kim, H. (2022). Keeping up with influencers: Exploring the impact of social presence and parasocial interactions on Instagram. *International Journal of Advertising*, 41(3), 414–434. DOI: 10.1080/02650487.2021.1886477

Kim, H., & Park, M. (2024). When digital celebrity talks to you: How human-like virtual influencers satisfy consumer's experience through social presence on social media endorsements. *Journal of Retailing and Consumer Services*, 76, 103581. DOI: 10.1016/j.jretconser.2023.103581

Kim, Y., & Sundar, S. S. (2012). Anthropomorphism of computers: Is it mindful or mindless? *Computers in Human Behavior*, 28(1), 241–250. DOI: 10.1016/j.chb.2011.09.006

Knox, S., Maklan, S., Payne, A., Peppard, J., & Ryals, L. (2003). A strategic framework for CRM. In Knox, S., Maklan, S., Payne, A., Peppard, J., & Ryals, L. (Eds.), *Customer relationship management* (pp. 17–41). Butterworth-Heinemann. DOI: 10.1016/B978-0-7506-5677-1.50006-4

Koay, K. Y., Lim, W. M., Kaur, S., Soh, K., & Poon, W. C. (2023). How and when social media influencers' intimate self-disclosure fosters purchase intentions: The roles of congruency and parasocial relationships. *Marketing Intelligence & Planning*, 41(6), 790–809. DOI: 10.1108/MIP-06-2023-0246

Kolasani, S. (2023). Optimizing natural language processing, large language models (LLMs) for efficient customer service, and hyper-personalization to enable sustainable growth and revenue. *Transactions on Latest Trends in Artificial Intelligence, 4*(4).

Kotler, P., Kartajaya, H., & Hooi, D. H. (2019). Marketing 4.0: moving from traditional to digital. *World Scientific Book Chapters*, 99-123.

Kreijns, K., Xu, K., & Weidlich, J. (2022). Social presence: Conceptualization and measurement. *Educational Psychology Review*, 34(1), 139–170. DOI: 10.1007/s10648-021-09623-8 PMID: 34177204

Krijger, J., Thuis, T., de Ruiter, M., Ligthart, E., & Broekman, I. (2023). The AI ethics maturity model: A holistic approach to advancing ethical data science in organizations. *AI and Ethics*, 3(2), 355–367. DOI: 10.1007/s43681-022-00228-7

Kuanr, A., Pradhan, D., Lyngdoh, T., & Lee, M. S. (2022). Why do consumers subvert brands? Investigating the influence of subjective well-being on brand avoidance. *Psychology and Marketing*, 39(3), 612–633. DOI: 10.1002/mar.21606

Kucuk, S. U. (2016). *Brand hate: Navigating consumer negativity in the digital world.* Springer. DOI: 10.1007/978-3-319-41519-2

Kucuk, S. U. (2019a). Consumer brand hate: Steam rolling whatever I see. *Psychology and Marketing*, 36(5), 431–443. DOI: 10.1002/mar.21175

Kucuk, S. U. (2019b). What is brand hate? In *Brand Hate: Navigating Consumer Negativity in the Digital World* (pp. 23–48). Springer International Publishing. DOI: 10.1007/978-3-030-00380-7_2

Kumar, V., & Reinartz, W. (2018). *Customer relationship management.* Springer. DOI: 10.1007/978-3-662-55381-7

Kushwaha, A. K., Kumar, P., & Kar, A. K. (2021). What impacts customer experience for B2B enterprises on using AI-enabled chatbots? Insights from Big data analytics. *Industrial Marketing Management*, 98, 207–221. DOI: 10.1016/j.indmarman.2021.08.011

LeCun, Y., Bengio, Y., & Hinton, G. (2015). Deep learning. *Nature*, 521(7553), 436–444. DOI: 10.1038/nature14539 PMID: 26017442

Ledro, C., Nosella, A., & Dalla Pozza, I. (2023). Integration of AI in CRM: Challenges and guidelines. *Journal of Open Innovation*, 9(4), 100151. DOI: 10.1016/j.joitmc.2023.100151

Ledro, C., Nosella, A., & Vinelli, A. (2022). Artificial intelligence in customer relationship management: Literature review and future research directions. *Journal of Business and Industrial Marketing*, 37(13), 48–63. DOI: 10.1108/JBIM-07-2021-0332

Lee, H. M., Chen, T., Chen, Y. S., Lo, W. Y., & Hsu, Y. H. (2021). The effects of consumer ethnocentrism and consumer animosity on perceived betrayal and negative word-of-mouth. *Asia Pacific Journal of Marketing and Logistics*, 33(3), 712–730. DOI: 10.1108/APJML-08-2019-0518

Lee, M., & Park, J. S. (2022). Do parasocial relationships and the quality of communication with AI shopping chatbots determine middle-aged women consumers' continuance usage intentions? *Journal of Consumer Behaviour*, 21(4), 842–854. DOI: 10.1002/cb.2043

Lefkeli, D., Karataş, M., & Gürhan-Canli, Z. (2024). Sharing information with AI (versus a human) impairs brand trust: The role of audience size inferences and sense of exploitation. *International Journal of Research in Marketing*, 41(1), 138–155. DOI: 10.1016/j.ijresmar.2023.08.011

Leocádio, D., Guedes, L., Oliveira, J., Reis, J., & Melão, N. (2024). Customer service with AI-powered human-robot collaboration (HRC): A literature review. *Procedia Computer Science*, 232, 1222–1232. DOI: 10.1016/j.procs.2024.01.120

Letheren, K., Jetten, J., Roberts, J., & Donovan, J. (2021). Robots should be seen and not heard... sometimes: Anthropomorphism and AI service robot interactions. *Psychology and Marketing*, 38(12), 2393–2406. DOI: 10.1002/mar.21575

Li, B., Liu, L., Mao, W., Qu, Y., & Chen, Y. (2023). Voice artificial intelligence service failure and customer complaint behavior: The mediation effect of customer emotion. *Electronic Commerce Research and Applications*, 59, 101261. DOI: 10.1016/j.elerap.2023.101261

Liao, C., Chen, J. L., & Yen, D. C. (2007). Theory of planning behavior (TPB) and customer satisfaction in the continued use of e-service: An integrated model. *Computers in Human Behavior*, 23(6), 2804–2822. DOI: 10.1016/j.chb.2006.05.006

Liebers, N., & Schramm, H. (2019). Parasocial interactions and relationships with media characters–an inventory of 60 years of research. *Communication Research Trends*, 38(2), 4–31.

Lindecrantz, E., Gi, M. T. P., & Zerbi, S. (2018). Personalizing the Customer Experience: Driving Differentiation in Retail. https://www.mckinsey.com/industries/retail/our-insights/personalizing-the-customer-experience-driving-differentiation-in-retail

Liu, M. W., & Keh, H. T. (2015). Consumer delight and outrage: Scale development and validation. *Journal of Service Theory and Practice*, 25(6), 680–699. DOI: 10.1108/JSTP-08-2014-0178

Liu-Thompkins, Y., Okazaki, S., & Li, H. (2022). Artificial empathy in marketing interactions: Bridging the human-AI gap in affective and social customer experience. *Journal of the Academy of Marketing Science*, 50(6), 1198–1218. DOI: 10.1007/s11747-022-00892-5

Lv, X., Yang, Y., Qin, D., Cao, X., & Xu, H. (2022). Artificial intelligence service recovery: The role of empathic response in hospitality customers' continuous usage intention. *Computers in Human Behavior*, 126, 106993. DOI: 10.1016/j.chb.2021.106993

Matosas-López, L. (2024). The influence of brand credibility and brand loyalty on customer satisfaction and continued use intention in new voice assistance services based on AI. *Journal of Marketing Analytics*, 1-22.

Mazhar, M., Hooi Ting, D., Zaib Abbasi, A., Nadeem, M. A., & Abbasi, H. A. (2022). Gauging customers' negative disconfirmation in online post-purchase behaviour: The moderating role of service recovery. *Cogent Business & Management*, 9(1), 2072186. DOI: 10.1080/23311975.2022.2072186

Mello-Klein, C. (2022). Facebook's ad delivery algorithm is discriminating based on race, gender and age in photos, Northeastern researchers find. https://news.northeastern.edu/2022/10/25/facebook-algorithm-discrimination/

Mishra, A., Shukla, A., Rana, N. P., & Dwivedi, Y. K. (2021). From "touch" to a "multisensory" experience: The impact of technology interface and product type on consumer responses. *Psychology and Marketing*, 38(3), 385–396. DOI: 10.1002/mar.21436

Molina, M. D., & Sundar, S. S. (2022). Does distrust in humans predict greater trust in AI? Role of individual differences in user responses to content moderation. *New Media & Society*, 26(6), 3638–3656. DOI: 10.1177/14614448221103534

Monica, R., & Soju, A. V. (2024). Artificial Intelligence and Service Marketing Innovation. In *AI Innovation in Services Marketing* (pp. 150–172). IGI Global.

Mordor Intelligence. (2024). *CRM industry size & share analysis - growth trends & forecasts (2024 - 2029)*. https://www.mordorintelligence.com/industry-reports/customer-relationship-management-market

Mori, M., MacDorman, K. F., & Kageki, N. (2012). The uncanny valley [from the field]. *IEEE Robotics & Automation Magazine*, 19(2), 98–100. DOI: 10.1109/MRA.2012.2192811

Moriuchi, E. (2021). An empirical study on anthropomorphism and engagement with disembodied AIs and consumers' re-use behavior. *Psychology and Marketing*, 38(1), 21–42. DOI: 10.1002/mar.21407

Morrow, E., Zidaru, T., Ross, F., Mason, C., Patel, K. D., Ream, M., & Stockley, R. (2023). Artificial intelligence technologies and compassion in healthcare: A systematic scoping review. *Frontiers in Psychology*, 13, 971044. DOI: 10.3389/fpsyg.2022.971044 PMID: 36733854

Mostafa, R. B., & Kasamani, T. (2022). Antecedents and consequences of chatbot initial trust. *European Journal of Marketing*, 56(6), 1748–1771. DOI: 10.1108/EJM-02-2020-0084

Mostafa, R. B., Lages, C. R., & Shaalan, A. (2024). The dark side of virtual agents: Ohhh no! *International Journal of Information Management*, 75, 102721. DOI: 10.1016/j.ijinfomgt.2023.102721

Mourtzis, D., Angelopoulos, J., & Panopoulos, N. (2023). The future of the human–machine interface (HMI) in society 5.0. *Future Internet*, 15(5), 162. DOI: 10.3390/fi15050162

Mozafari, N., Weiger, W. H., & Hammerschmidt, M. (2022). Trust me, I'm a bot–repercussions of chatbot disclosure in different service frontline settings. *Journal of Service Management*, 33(2), 221–245. DOI: 10.1108/JOSM-10-2020-0380

Muniz, F., Stewart, K., & Magalhães, L. (2023). Are they humans or are they robots? The effect of virtual influencer disclosure on brand trust. *Journal of Consumer Behaviour*, 23(3), 1234–1250. DOI: 10.1002/cb.2271

Murtarelli, G., Gregory, A., & Romenti, S. (2021). A conversation-based perspective for shaping ethical human–machine interactions: The particular challenge of chatbots. *Journal of Business Research*, 129, 927–935. DOI: 10.1016/j.jbusres.2020.09.018

Nanda, A. P., & Banerjee, R. (2020). Binge watching: An exploration of the role of technology. *Psychology and Marketing*, 37(9), 1212–1230. DOI: 10.1002/mar.21353

Nass, C., & Moon, Y. (2000). Machines and mindlessness: Social responses to computers. *The Journal of Social Issues*, 56(1), 81–103. DOI: 10.1111/0022-4537.00153

Naumann, K., Bowden, J., & Gabbott, M. (2020). Expanding customer engagement: The role of negative engagement, dual valences and contexts. *European Journal of Marketing*, 54(7), 1469–1499. DOI: 10.1108/EJM-07-2017-0464

Nguyen, B., & Mutum, D. (2012). A Review of Customer Relationship Management: Successes, Advances, Pitfalls and Futures. *Business Process Management Journal*, 18(3), 400–419. Advance online publication. DOI: 10.1108/14637151211232614

Obilo, O. O., Chefor, E., & Saleh, A. (2021). Revisiting the consumer brand engagement concept. *Journal of Business Research*, 126, 634–643. DOI: 10.1016/j.jbusres.2019.12.023

Obrenovic, B., Gu, X., Wang, G., Godinic, D., & Jakhongirov, I. (2024). Generative AI and human–robot interaction: Implications and future agenda for business, society and ethics. *AI & Society*, 1–14. DOI: 10.1007/s00146-024-01889-0

Odekerken-Schröder, G., Mennens, K., Steins, M., & Mahr, D. (2022). The service triad: An empirical study of service robots, customers and frontline employees. *Journal of Service Management*, 33(2), 246–292. DOI: 10.1108/JOSM-10-2020-0372

Oh, H. J., Kim, J., Chang, J. J., Park, N., & Lee, S. (2023). Social benefits of living in the metaverse: The relationships among social presence, supportive interaction, social self-efficacy, and feelings of loneliness. *Computers in Human Behavior*, 139, 107498. DOI: 10.1016/j.chb.2022.107498

Ooi, K.-B., Tan, G. W.-H., Al-Emran, M., Al-Sharafi, M. A., Capatina, A., Chakraborty, A., Dwivedi, Y. K., Huang, T.-L., Kar, A. K., Lee, V.-H., Loh, X.-M., Micu, A., Mikalef, P., Mogaji, E., Pandey, N., Raman, R., Rana, N. P., Sarker, P., Sharma, A., & Wong, L.-W. (2023). The potential of generative artificial intelligence across disciplines: Perspectives and future directions. *Journal of Computer Information Systems*, 1–32. DOI: 10.1080/08874417.2023.2261010

Oppenheim, M. (2018, October 11) Amazon scraps 'sexist AI' recruitment tool. *Independent*. https://www.independent.co.uk/tech/amazon-ai-sexist-recruitment-tool-algorithm-a8579161.html

Pala, E., Kapitan, S., & van Esch, P. (2022). Simulated satiation through reality-enhancing technology. *Psychology and Marketing*, 39(3), 483–494. DOI: 10.1002/mar.21582

Pantano, E., Carlson, J., Spanaki, K., & Christodoulides, G. (2024). Guest editorial: More supportive or more distractive? Investigating the negative effects of technology at the customer interface. *International Journal of Information Management*, 75, 102752. DOI: 10.1016/j.ijinfomgt.2023.102752

Pantano, E., Pedeliento, G., & Christodoulides, G. (2022). A strategic framework for technological innovations in support of the customer experience: A focus on luxury retailers. *Journal of Retailing and Consumer Services*, 66, 102959. DOI: 10.1016/j.jretconser.2022.102959

Pantano, E., & Scarpi, D. (2022). I, robot, you, consumer: Measuring artificial intelligence types and their effect on consumers emotions in service. *Journal of Service Research*, 25(4), 583–600. DOI: 10.1177/10946705221103538

Park, G., Yim, M. C., Chung, J., & Lee, S. (2023). Effect of AI chatbot empathy and identity disclosure on willingness to donate: The mediation of humanness and social presence. *Behaviour & Information Technology*, 42(12), 1998–2010. DOI: 10.1080/0144929X.2022.2105746

Pataranutaporn, P., Liu, R., Finn, E., & Maes, P. (2023). Influencing human–AI interaction by priming beliefs about AI can increase perceived trustworthiness, empathy and effectiveness. *Nature Machine Intelligence*, 5(10), 1076–1086. DOI: 10.1038/s42256-023-00720-7

Peltier, J. W., Dahl, A. J., & Schibrowsky, J. A. (2024). Artificial intelligence in interactive marketing: A conceptual framework and research agenda. *Journal of Research in Interactive Marketing*, 18(1), 54–90. DOI: 10.1108/JRIM-01-2023-0030

Peng, C., van Doorn, J., Eggers, F., & Wieringa, J. E. (2022). The effect of required warmth on consumer acceptance of artificial intelligence in service: The moderating role of AI-human collaboration. *International Journal of Information Management*, 66, 102533. DOI: 10.1016/j.ijinfomgt.2022.102533

Pentina, I., Hancock, T., & Xie, T. (2023). Exploring relationship development with social chatbots: A mixed-method study of replika. *Computers in Human Behavior*, 140, 107600. DOI: 10.1016/j.chb.2022.107600

Perry, A. (2023). AI will never convey the essence of human empathy. *Nature Human Behaviour*, 7(11), 1808–1809. DOI: 10.1038/s41562-023-01675-w PMID: 37474839

Petrescu, M., & Krishen, A. S. (2023). Hybrid intelligence: Human–AI collaboration in marketing analytics. *Journal of Marketing Analytics*, 11(3), 263–274. DOI: 10.1057/s41270-023-00245-3

Pfeffer, J., Zorbach, T., & Carley, K. M. (2014). Understanding online firestorms: Negative word-of- mouth dynamics in social media networks. *Journal of Marketing Communications*, 20(1-2), 117–128. DOI: 10.1080/13527266.2013.797778

Pires, P. B., Santos, J. D., & Pereira, I. V. (2024). Artificial Neural Networks: History and State of the Art. In Encyclopedia of Information Science and Technology, Sixth Edition (pp. 1-25). IGI Global. DOI: 10.4018/978-1-6684-7366-5.ch037

Pitardi, V., & Marriott, H. R. (2021). Alexa, she's not human but… Unveiling the drivers of consumers' trust in voice-based artificial intelligence. *Psychology and Marketing*, 38(4), 626–642. DOI: 10.1002/mar.21457

Pizoń, J., & Gola, A. (2023). Human–machine relationship—Perspective and future roadmap for Industry 5.0 solutions. *Machines (Basel)*, 11(2), 203. DOI: 10.3390/machines11020203

Prates, M. O. R., Avelar, P. H., & Lamb, L. C. (2020). Assessing gender bias in machine translation: A case study with Google Translate. *Neural Computing & Applications*, 32(10), 6363–6381. DOI: 10.1007/s00521-019-04144-6

Prior, D. D., Buttle, F., & Maklan, S. (2024). *Customer relationship management: Concepts, applications and technologies*. Taylor & Francis.

Rahman, M. S., Bag, S., Gupta, S., & Sivarajah, U. (2023). Technology readiness of B2B firms and AI-based customer relationship management capability for enhancing social sustainability performance. *Journal of Business Research, 156*, 113525. .DOI: 10.1016/j.jbusres.2022.113525

Rahman, S. M., Carlson, J., & Chowdhury, N. H. (2022a). SafeCX: A framework for safe customer experience in omnichannel retailing. *Journal of Services Marketing*, 36(4), 499–529. DOI: 10.1108/JSM-04-2021-0114

Rahman, S. M., Carlson, J., Gudergan, S. P., Wetzels, M., & Grewal, D. (2022b). Perceived Omnichannel Customer Experience (OCX): Concept, measurement, and impact. *Journal of Retailing*, 98(4), 611–632. DOI: 10.1016/j.jretai.2022.03.003

Rather, R. A. (2021). Monitoring the impacts of tourism-based social media, risk perception and fear on tourist's attitude and revisiting behaviour in the wake of COVID-19 pandemic. *Current Issues in Tourism*, 24(23), 3275–3283. DOI: 10.1080/13683500.2021.1884666

Rather, R. A., & Hollebeek, L. D. (2021). Customers' service-related engagement, experience, and behavioral intent: Moderating role of age. *Journal of Retailing and Consumer Services*, 60, 102453. DOI: 10.1016/j.jretconser.2021.102453

Rather, R. A., Hollebeek, L. D., & Rasoolimanesh, S. M. (2022). First-time versus repeat tourism customer engagement, experience, and value cocreation: An empirical investigation. *Journal of Travel Research*, 61(3), 549–564. DOI: 10.1177/0047287521997572

Reis, J. (2024). Customer service through AI-powered human-robot relationships: Where are we now? The case of Henn na cafe, Japan. *Technology in Society*, 77, 102570. DOI: 10.1016/j.techsoc.2024.102570

Rossiter, J. R. (2012). A new C-OAR-SE-based content-valid and predictively valid measure that distinguishes brand love from brand liking. *Marketing Letters*, 23(3), 905–916. DOI: 10.1007/s11002-012-9173-6

Roy, S. K., Sharma, A., Bose, S., & Singh, G. (2022). Consumer-brand relationship: A brand hate perspective. *Journal of Business Research*, 144, 1293–1304. DOI: 10.1016/j.jbusres.2022.02.065

Ryan, M. (2020). In AI we trust: Ethics, artificial intelligence, and reliability. *Science and Engineering Ethics*, 26(5), 2749–2767. DOI: 10.1007/s11948-020-00228-y PMID: 32524425

Schepman, A., & Rodway, P. (2023). The General Attitudes towards Artificial Intelligence Scale (GAAIS): Confirmatory validation and associations with personality, corporate distrust, and general trust. *International Journal of Human-Computer Interaction*, 39(13), 1–18. DOI: 10.1080/10447318.2022.2085400

Seitz, L., Bekmeier-Feuerhahn, S., & Gohil, K. (2022). Can we trust a chatbot like a physician? A qualitative study on understanding the emergence of trust toward diagnostic chatbots. *International Journal of Human-Computer Studies*, 165, 102848. DOI: 10.1016/j.ijhcs.2022.102848

Shaalan, A., Eid, R., & Tourky, M. (2022a). De-linking from western epistemologies: Using guanxi-type relationships to attract and retain hotel guests in the Middle East. *Management and Organization Review*, 18(5), 859–891. DOI: 10.1017/mor.2021.21

Shaalan, A., Tourky, M. E., & Ibrahim, K. (2022b). The chatbot revolution: Companies and consumers in a new digital age. In Hanlon, A., & Tuten, T. L. (Eds.), *The SAGE Handbook of Digital Marketing* (Vol. 1, pp. 369–392). SAGE Publications Ltd., DOI: 10.4135/9781529782509.n21

Sharma, V., & Bose, I. (2024). Unlocking AI's Potential in Customer Service Marketing. In *AI Innovations in Service and Tourism Marketing* (pp. 80-103). IGI Global. DOI: 10.4018/979-8-3693-7909-7.ch005

Sheehan, B., Jin, H. S., & Gottlieb, U. (2020). Customer service chatbots: Anthropomorphism and adoption. *Journal of Business Research*, 115, 14–24. DOI: 10.1016/j.jbusres.2020.04.030

Shin, H., & Kang, J. (2020). Reducing perceived health risk to attract hotel customers in the COVID-19 pandemic era: Focused on technology innovation for social distancing and cleanliness. *International Journal of Hospitality Management*, 91, 102664. DOI: 10.1016/j.ijhm.2020.102664 PMID: 32921871

Shrum, L. J. (2012). *The psychology of entertainment media: Blurring the lines between entertainment and persuasion*. Routledge. DOI: 10.4324/9780203828588

Söderlund, M., & Oikarinen, E.-L. (2021). Service encounters with virtual agents: An examination of perceived humanness as a source of customer satisfaction. *European Journal of Marketing*, 55(13), 94–121. DOI: 10.1108/EJM-09-2019-0748

Sokolova, K., & Kefi, H. (2020). Instagram and YouTube bloggers promote it, why should I buy? How credibility and parasocial interaction influence purchase intentions. *Journal of Retailing and Consumer Services*, 53, 101742. DOI: 10.1016/j.jretconser.2019.01.011

Song, M., Xing, X., Duan, Y., Cohen, J., & Mou, J. (2022). Will artificial intelligence replace human customer service? The impact of communication quality and privacy risks on adoption intention. *Journal of Retailing and Consumer Services*, 66, 102900. DOI: 10.1016/j.jretconser.2021.102900

Srinivasan, R., & González, B. S. M. (2022). The role of empathy for artificial intelligence accountability. *Journal of Responsible Technology*, 9, 100021. DOI: 10.1016/j.jrt.2021.100021

Stein, J.-P., Linda Breves, P., & Anders, N. (2022). Parasocial interactions with real and virtual influencers: The role of perceived similarity and human-likeness. *New Media & Society*. Advance online publication. DOI: 10.1177/14614448221102900

Sternberg, R. (2003). A duplex theory of hate: Development and application to terrorism, massacres, and genocide. *Review of General Psychology*, 7(3), 299–328. DOI: 10.1037/1089-2680.7.3.299

Suharto, S., & Yuliansyah, Y. (2023). The influence of customer relationship management and customer experience on customer satisfaction. *Integrated Journal of Business and Economics*, 7(1), 389. DOI: 10.33019/ijbe.v7i1.641

Sun, Y., Chen, J., & Sundar, S. S. (2024). Chatbot ads with a human touch: A test of anthropomorphism, interactivity, and narrativity. *Journal of Business Research*, 172, 114403. DOI: 10.1016/j.jbusres.2023.114403

Sundar, S. S., & Nass, C. (2000). Source orientation in human-computer interaction: Programmer, networker, or independent social actor. *Communication Research*, 27(6), 683–703. DOI: 10.1177/009365000027006001

Sung, E., Bae, S., Han, D.-I. D., & Kwon, O. (2021). Consumer engagement via interactive artificial intelligence and mixed reality. *International Journal of Information Management*, 60, 102382. DOI: 10.1016/j.ijinfomgt.2021.102382

Tan, C. W., Benbasat, I., & Cenfetelli, R. T. (2017). An exploratory study of the formation and impact of electronic service failures. *Management Information Systems Quarterly*, 40(1), 1–29. DOI: 10.25300/MISQ/2016/40.1.01

Teixeira, S., & Remondes, J. (2023). *The Use of Artificial Intelligence in Digital Marketing: Competitive Strategies and Tactics: Competitive Strategies and Tactics*. IGI Global., DOI: 10.4018/978-1-6684-9324-3

Triznova, M., Maťova, H., Dvoracek, J., & Sadek, S. (2015). Customer relationship management based on employees and corporate culture. *Procedia Economics and Finance*, 26, 953–959. DOI: 10.1016/S2212-5671(15)00914-4

Tsai, W. H. S., Liu, Y., & Chuan, C. H. (2021). How chatbots' social presence communication enhances consumer engagement: The mediating role of parasocial interaction and dialogue. *Journal of Research in Interactive Marketing*, 15(3), 460–482. DOI: 10.1108/JRIM-12-2019-0200

Uysal, E., Alavi, S., & Bezençon, V. (2023). Anthropomorphism in Artificial Intelligence: A review of empirical work across domains and insights for future research. In Sudhir, K., & Toubia, O. (Eds.), *Artificial Intelligence in Marketing* (Vol. 20, pp. 273–308). Emerald Publishing Limited., DOI: 10.1108/S1548-643520230000020015

Van Doorn, J., Mende, M., Noble, S. M., Hulland, J., Ostrom, A. L., Grewal, D., & Petersen, J. A. (2017). Domo Arigato Mr. Roboto: Emergence of automated social presence in organizational frontlines and customers' service experiences. *Journal of Service Research*, 20(1), 43–58. DOI: 10.1177/1094670516679272

Van Pinxteren, M. M., Wetzels, R. W., Rüger, J., Pluymaekers, M., & Wetzels, M. (2019). Trust in humanoid robots: Implications for services marketing. *Journal of Services Marketing*, 33(4), 507–518. DOI: 10.1108/JSM-01-2018-0045

Vanek, J., King, K., & Bigelow, M. (2018). Social presence and identity: Facebook in an English language classroom. *Journal of Language, Identity, and Education*, 17(4), 236–254. DOI: 10.1080/15348458.2018.1442223

Verhagen, T., Van Nes, J., Feldberg, F., & Van Dolen, W. (2014). Virtual customer service agents: Using social presence and personalization to shape online service encounters. *Journal of Computer-Mediated Communication*, 19(3), 529–545. DOI: 10.1111/jcc4.12066

Verma, R. K., & Kumari, N. (2023). Generative AI as a tool for enhancing customer relationship management automation and personalization techniques. *International Journal of Responsible Artificial Intelligence*, 13(9), 1–8.

Wald, R., Heijselaar, E., & Bosse, T. (2021). Make your own: The potential of chatbot customization for the development of user trust. In *Adjunct Proceedings of the 29th ACM Conference on User Modeling, Adaptation and Personalization* (pp. 382-387).

Whig, P., Bhatia, A. B., & Yathiraju, N. (2024). AI-Driven Innovations in Service Marketing Transforming Customer Engagement and Experience. In *AI Innovations in Service and Tourism Marketing* (pp. 17–34). IGI Global. DOI: 10.4018/979-8-3693-7909-7.ch002

Wilkins, J., Sparrow, D. A., Fealing, C. A., Vickers, B. D., Ferguson, K. A., & Wojton, H. (2024). A team-centric metric framework for testing and evaluation of human-machine teams. *Systems Engineering*, 27(3), 466–484. DOI: 10.1002/sys.21730

Winder, D. (2024, January 23). Warning as 26 billion records leak: Dropbox, LinkedIn, Twitter named. *Forbes*. https://www.forbes.com/sites/daveywinder/2024/01/23/massive-26-billion-record-leak-dropbox-linkedin-twitterx-all-named/

Wirtz, J., Kunz, W. H., Hartley, N., & Tarbit, J. (2023). Corporate digital responsibility in service firms and their ecosystems. *Journal of Service Research*, 26(2), 173–190. DOI: 10.1177/10946705221130467

Wu, H. C., Wei, C. F., Tseng, L. Y., & Cheng, C. C. (2018). What drives green brand switching behavior? *Marketing Intelligence & Planning*, 36(6), 694–708. DOI: 10.1108/MIP-10-2017-0224

Xu, K., & Lombard, M. (2017). Persuasive computing: Feeling peer pressure from multiple computer agents. *Computers in Human Behavior*, 74, 152–162. DOI: 10.1016/j.chb.2017.04.043

Xu, X., Wen, N., & Liu, J. (2023). Empathic accuracy in artificial intelligence service recovery. *Tourism Review* (ahead-of-print). .DOI: 10.1108/TR-06-2023-0394

Yang, C., & Hu, J. (2022). When do consumers prefer AI-enabled customer service? The interaction effect of brand personality and service provision type on brand attitudes and purchase intentions. *Journal of Brand Management*, 29(2), 167–189. DOI: 10.1057/s41262-021-00261-7

Yang, Y., Gong, Y., Land, L. P. W., & Chesney, T. (2020). Understanding the effects of physical experience and information integration on consumer use of online to offline commerce. *International Journal of Information Management*, 51, 102046. DOI: 10.1016/j.ijinfomgt.2019.102046

Ying, T., Tang, J., Ye, S., Tan, X., & Wei, W. (2022). Virtual reality in destination marketing: Telepresence, social presence, and tourists' visit intentions. *Journal of Travel Research*, 61(8), 1738–1756. DOI: 10.1177/00472875211047273

Yuan, C., Wang, S., Liu, Y., & Ma, J. W. (2023). Factors influencing parasocial relationship in the virtual reality shopping environment: The moderating role of celebrity endorser dynamism. *Asia Pacific Journal of Marketing and Logistics*, 35(2), 398–413. DOI: 10.1108/APJML-06-2021-0402

Zarantonello, L., Romani, S., Grappi, S., & Bagozzi, R. P. (2016). Brand hate. *Journal of Product and Brand Management*, 25(1), 11–25. DOI: 10.1108/JPBM-01-2015-0799

Zerbino, P., Aloini, D., Dulmin, R., & Mininno, V. (2018). Big data-enabled customer relationship management: A holistic approach. *Information Processing & Management*, 54(5), 818–846. DOI: 10.1016/j.ipm.2017.10.005

Zhang, A., & Yang, Q. (2022). To be human-like or machine-like? An empirical research on user trust in AI applications in service industry. *8th International Conference on Automation, Robotics and Applications* (ICARA).

Zhang, C., & Laroche, M. (2020). Brand hate: A multidimensional construct. *Journal of Product and Brand Management*, 30(3), 392–414. DOI: 10.1108/JPBM-11-2018-2103

Zhou, Z., Zhan, G., & Zhou, N. (2019). How does negative experience sharing influence happiness in online brand community? A dual-path model. *Internet Research*, 30(2), 575–590. DOI: 10.1108/INTR-12-2018-0531

Zhu, Q., & Luo, J. (2024). Toward artificial empathy for human-centered design. *Journal of Mechanical Design*, 146(6), 061401. DOI: 10.1115/1.4064161

ADDITIONAL READING

Awad, E., Levine, S., Loreggia, A., Mattei, N., Rahwan, I., Rossi, F., Talamadupula, K., Tenenbaum, J., & Kleiman-Weiner, M. (2024). When is it acceptable to break the rules? Knowledge representation of moral judgements based on empirical data. *Autonomous Agents and Multi-Agent Systems*, 38(2), 35. DOI: 10.1007/s10458-024-09667-4

Bonnefon, J. F., Rahwan, I., & Shariff, A. (2024). The moral psychology of Artificial Intelligence. *Annual Review of Psychology*, 75(1), 653–675. DOI: 10.1146/annurev-psych-030123-113559 PMID: 37722750

Chakraborty, A., & Bhuyan, N. (2024). Can artificial intelligence be a Kantian moral agent? On moral autonomy of AI system. *AI and Ethics*, 4(2), 325–331. DOI: 10.1007/s43681-023-00269-6

Fox, S., & Rey, V. F. (2024). Representing Human Ethical Requirements in Hybrid Machine Learning Models: Technical Opportunities and Fundamental Challenges. *Machine Learning and Knowledge Extraction*, 6(1), 580–592. DOI: 10.3390/make6010027

Llorca Albareda, J. (2024). Anthropological crisis or crisis in moral status: A philosophy of technology approach to the moral consideration of artificial intelligence. *Philosophy & Technology*, 37(1), 12. DOI: 10.1007/s13347-023-00682-z

MacInnis, D. J., & Folkes, V. S. (2017). Humanizing brands: When brands seem to be like me, part of me, and in a relationship with me. *Journal of Consumer Psychology*, 27(3), 355–374. DOI: 10.1016/j.jcps.2016.12.003

Misselhorn, C. (2024). Machine Ethics in Care: Could a Moral Avatar Enhance the Autonomy of Care-Dependent Persons? *Cambridge Quarterly of Healthcare Ethics*, 1–14. DOI: 10.1017/S0963180123000555 PMID: 38214062

Roy, R., & Naidoo, V. (2021). Enhancing chatbot effectiveness: The role of anthropomorphic conversational styles and time orientation. *Journal of Business Research*, 126, 23–34. DOI: 10.1016/j.jbusres.2020.12.051

Rust, R. T. (2020). The future of marketing. *International Journal of Research in Marketing*, 37(1), 15–26. DOI: 10.1016/j.ijresmar.2019.08.002

Song, F., & Yeung, S. H. F. (2024). A pluralist hybrid model for moral AIs. *AI & Society*, 39(3), 891–900. DOI: 10.1007/s00146-022-01601-0

KEY TERMS AND DEFINITIONS

Anthropomorphism: The attribution of human traits, emotions, or intentions to non-human entities, commonly used in AI to enhance user interaction with virtual agents or robots.

Artificial Intelligence (AI): The simulation of human intelligence in machines that are programmed to think and learn, allowing them to perform tasks that typically require human cognitive functions.

Customer Relationship Management (CRM): A strategy and technology used by companies to manage interactions with current and potential customers, aiming to improve customer service, retention, and overall relationships.

Deep Learning: A subset of machine learning involving neural networks with many layers, enabling the system to learn and make decisions based on data patterns.

Empathy Gap: A discrepancy in AI systems where the machine fails to understand or respond to the emotional needs of customers, leading to unsatisfactory interactions.

Expectancy-Disconfirmation Theory: This theory explains customer satisfaction as the result of comparing expectations to the actual performance of a product or service, which is highly relevant when analysing customer interactions with AI systems.

Hybrid Models: AI and CRM models that combine human and machine intelligence to optimise customer interaction by balancing automation with human oversight.

Machine Learning (ML): A type of AI that allows systems to automatically learn from and improve with experience without being explicitly programmed.

Negative AI Agent Anthropomorphism Disconfirmation (NAAD): The negative customer reaction that occurs when an AI agent's human-like qualities fail to meet user expectations, leading to dissatisfaction.

Negative Parasocial Interaction Disconfirmation (NPID): The disruption in customer relationships caused when users feel let down by their one-sided emotional connection with AI, resulting in disappointment or mistrust.

Negative Social Presence Disconfirmation (NSPD): The failure of AI to create an adequate sense of social presence in interactions, which leads to unmet expectations and a negative customer experience.

Neural Networks: A series of algorithms that mimic the operations of a human brain to recognise relationships between vast amounts of data.

Personalisation: The process of tailoring services or products to individual customer preferences and behaviours, often powered by AI and data analytics.

Predictive Analytics: The utilisation of data, statistical algorithms, and machine learning techniques to predict the likelihood of future outcomes based on historical data.

Chapter 12
Return on AI:
Mapping and Exploring ROI (In)Tangible Measures

Ana Isabel Torres
https://orcid.org/0000-0002-0621-956X
University of Aveiro, Portugal & INESC TEC, Porto, Portugal

Darkio Lourenço Siqueira Paulo
https://orcid.org/0009-0002-7979-0289
University of Aveiro, Portugal

José Duarte Santos
https://orcid.org/0000-0001-5815-4983
CEOS.PP, ISCAP, Polytechnic of Porto, Portugal

Paulo Botelho Pires
https://orcid.org/0000-0003-3786-6783
CEOS.PP, ISCAP, Polytechnic of Porto, Portugal

ABSTRACT

This chapter aims to discuss about the potential Return on Investment (ROI) measures from Artificial intelligence (AI) investments that business can leverage. It discusses the concepts and describes the dimensions, features and tools of AI investments in Marketing business, to assist the readers to understand about the topic. The authors also describe the major drivers of ROI measures for business applications and discusses the concerns and limitations of tangible measures. So, this document contributes to the literature on ROI (in)tangibles measures that leverage AI investments and features issues in digital marketing, at large and potentially offers a theoretical grounding for many empirical and theoretical future studies.

DOI: 10.4018/979-8-3693-5340-0.ch012

1. INTRODUCTION

The advent of new tools developed with artificial intelligence (AI) has dictated the course of business, making organizations feel pressured to implement AI in their strategies in order to remain competitive in the market. The adoption of AI is taking place in several areas, but marketing and sales is one of the most significant, especially in the retail, services and telecommunications sectors (Jain & Aggarwal, 2020). Digital marketing will continue to change rapidly with the advance of AI, which will also transform the general marketing landscape beyond the business context, but also in academia and research (Shahid & Li, 2019).

In the field of digital marketing, this process dynamism is even more frequent and accelerated, given the constant factors that influence the updating and adaptation of strategies (Swami & Naidu, 2020). For example, changing online consumption habits, new ways of communicating with the audience, constant changes in digital platform algorithms and, recently, the emergence of new AI-based technologies.

AI can be used by marketing professionals in a variety of ways and for different objectives, such as branding, personalization and amplifying campaign performance and ROI (return on investment) (Thiraviyam, 2018).

Despite the vast applicability of AI in marketing processes, it is essential to evaluate the success of a strategy by effectively measuring the return that a project can bring to the organization.

Although the main application of AI in business is in marketing and adopters are generating returns from this technology (Bughin et al., 2017), there is still very little literature on the relationship between AI and the Return on Investment (ROI) of projects based on AI technology.

Based on this context, the calculation of ROI is essential to the success of organizations' strategies, being simple to measure in the case of tangible returns, but complex and challenging in many other intangible returns, based on AI projects. However, given the great need to implement AI technologies in organizations' strategies to ensure their competitiveness in the market, it is necessary to look at the best way to measure the return generated by these projects, regardless of their complexity. Thus, considering that the literature is still very incipient in the study of measuring ROI in AI strategies, this study proposes to analyze, in an exploratory approach, the concepts of AI and ROI present in the literature and how they relate to digital marketing, mapping the types of returns and the main benefits and limitations of implementing AI technologies in company strategies.

This chapter is structured around as follows: first section introduces the context and motivation of this chapter; next section covers the literature review, follows the discussion of the prior research findings and proposes challenges for measuring (in)tangible returns on marketing AI-based investments; last section draws the conclusions and discusses the contributions and limitations of the study, as well as pinpoints some avenues for future research.

2. LITERATURE REVIEW

2.1. Artificial Intelligence

Despite the rapid emergence of new technologies provided by artificial intelligence and all the visibility and applicability that these technologies have achieved today, AI is an old concept and has been present in the literature for several decades.

Bellman (1978) states that the concept of AI is directly related to the automation of activities that are associated with human thought, such as activities linked to decision-making, problem-solving and learning, among others. In the same vein, Haugeland (1985) connects these capabilities to machines, assuming that artificial intelligence consists of innovative efforts aimed at making computers think, that is, literally and fully, machines with minds.

Over the years, the concepts of artificial intelligence in the literature have continued to reinforce the argument for developing machines with the ability to simulate human abilities. Russell and Norvig (2009) broadly contextualize AI as an intelligent system with the ability to reproduce cognitive functions generally associated with human attributes, such as learning, speech and problem-solving.

The literature presents a series of definitions by different authors that converge on the same idea, which shows that the systems provided by AI in organizations are expanding rapidly and transforming business and production, which extends the reach of these technologies into what was previously considered an exclusively human domain (Daugherty & Wilson, 2018).

Conceptually, AI is defined as an option to enhance human abilities, not to replace them (Dwivedi et al., 2021). Human capacity can be optimized through elements that extend the cognitive utilities of AI, such as natural language processing, the process by which machines can understand and analyze the language used by humans; and machine learning, algorithms that allow systems to learn.

Within this framework, a human in the loop concept stands out, which represents the need for analytical algorithms to occasionally consult human experts for feedback and course correction (Endert et al., 2014). In other words, it is a person who trains, tests or adjusts an AI system to help it produce more reliable results (Oxford Internet Institute, 2020). Other studies highlight the concept of human in the loop in a more pragmatic way, by emphasizing the need for human interaction to overcome a limitation of technology, showing that the focus of using AI is to enhance human capacity, not replace it (Kumar, 2017).

Recently, the conceptualization of AI has shifted to a perspective more focused on its performance, objectives or the benefits it can achieve. From this perspective, Kaplan and Haenlein (2019) state that artificial intelligence is commonly defined as "the ability of a system to interpret external data correctly, to learn from that data, and to use that learning to achieve specific goals and tasks through flexible adaptation". For Shahid and Li (2019), the term AI refers to computer-assisted analytical guidance that seeks to form automated systems that are considered intelligent.

Globally, AI has become a significant component of many organizations' business models and a key strategic element in plans for many areas of business, as well as medicine and government services (Vimalkumar et al., 2021).

2.2. AI in Digital Marketing

Advances in the field of AI have leveraged a digital transformation that is seen as a determining factor for a new disruptive moment in the business world (Chintalapati & Pandey, 2022), where organizations need to adapt to new AI-based technologies to improve their business management practices, further develop their products (Kumar et al., 2019) and reduce the barriers to the use of these technologies by their consumers (Mazurek & Małagocka, 2019).

These innovations have positioned AI as an important area of study that has been explored by organizations in various segments, especially in the area of marketing, which has witnessed this transformation on a large scale and has established itself as one of the industry segments that has evolved the most due to the adoption of AI in its strategies (Chintalapati & Pandey, 2022; Dwivedi et al., 2021; Jain & Aggarwal, 2020; Thiraviyam, 2018), highlighting its impact on the elements of the marketing mix (Kotler & Armstrong, 2006).

Recently, the application of the concept of Artificial Intelligence Marketing (AIM), which consists of the development of intelligent mechanisms that use customer and competitor data in an optimized way (Jain & Aggarwal, 2020), makes it possible to guarantee the improvement of the consumer experience and improve the results of marketing strategies (Overgoor et al., 2019). It is a method based on using customer data to predict the next step to be taken by a consumer to improve the customer journey (Thiraviyam, 2018). In general, MIA is the process that enables autonomous machines to access big data and information related to the marketing mix, use AI to acquire knowledge and then disseminate and apply this knowledge to improve the relationship with the consumer in a data-driven environment (Yau et al., 2021).

Considering that there is a vast availability of information and user data in the online environment, the use of AI is more strongly applied in digital marketing strategies (Chintalapati & Pandey, 2022; Shahid & Li, 2019), such as integrated digital marketing, web development, content production, Search Engine Optimization (SEO), email marketing, lead generation, social media monitoring, A/B testing (Shahid & Li, 2019) and implications for the automation of sales processes (Chintalapati & Pandey, 2022), such as consumer forecasts and patterns, pricing, personalization and customer service.

AI in digital marketing can generate great efficiencies in organizations, including the processing of huge amounts of data, sales and meeting the personalized needs of customers quickly and individually, and improving the performance of campaigns and return on investment (Jain & Aggarwal, 2020). In addition, advantages in the results of marketing teams, market research, lead generation, social media monitoring and customization of the consumer experience, among others (Sterne, 2017) can be leveraged by AI. In general, digital marketing will benefit from the Big Data available to get to know its target audience in depth and achieve better results through intelligent operations (Thiraviyam, 2018).

2.3. AI applications in DM

There are countless ways in which AI is implemented in digital marketing. However, AI is mainly used in digital marketing for: i) data analysis and machine learning (ML); ii) predictive analysis and insights; iii) personalization of the customer experience; iv) intelligent virtual service by chatbot; v) content generation (Dwivedi et al., 2021; Shahid & Li, 2019; Thiraviyam, 2018), as presented and discussed below.

2.3.1. Data analysis and machine learning

The literature brings together a vast body of studies on big data, and among the various definitions, big data can be conceptualized as a huge volume of heterogeneous data, which comes from the increasing digitization of transactions, interactions, communications and everyday experiences (McAfee & Brynjolfsson, 2012), which can be modeled, analyzed and interpreted (Gandomi & Haider, 2015) in order to drive the decision-making process in a descriptive, diagnostic or predictive approach (Wedel & Kannan, 2016), developed through Big Data Analytics, e. g., Big Data Analytics. g., a methodological analysis of a large volume of structured data that is qualified in terms of volume, speed, variety, veracity and added value (Dwivedi et al., 2021).

In digital marketing, big data analytics makes it possible to create buying patterns, preferences and consumer behavior (de Luca et al., 2021; Jain & Aggarwal, 2020) achieving exceptional performance through machine learning and as it is fed more data, the algorithm improves its learning performance (Flavián et al., 2022; Haleem et al., 2022; Huang & Rust, 2018).

With this analytical and problem-solving capacity, marketing managers can derive enormous value from using AI to make decision-making an analytical, data-driven process, and no longer a purely intuitive one (Jarrahi, 2018). Therefore, machine learning enables organizations to gain a competitive advantage by assisting in various marketing actions, such as predicting purchase intent and customer churn, accurately segmenting the audience and personalizing communication and the consumer experience through behavioral data (Dwivedi et al., 2021; Erevelles et al., 2016; Jacobs et al., 2016; Jarrahi, 2018).

2.3.2. Predictive analytics and insights

Predictive analytics can be defined as a type of data analytics that aims to identify relevant data patterns through pattern matching techniques, statistics, predictive modeling, through machine learning, and artificial intelligence (Abbott, 2014).

Thus, through AI-ML, companies can access information on consumers' online activities, making it possible to predict future behavior (Hair et al., 2018). In this sense, one of the most frequent uses of AI in marketing is through predictive analysis (Shovo, 2021), given that the tendencies and interests of each person change regularly due to numerous influences or externalities.

AI is already present in the routine of marketing managers, helping to identify and predict new trends (Dumitriu & Popescu, 2020). Based on a series of parameters, AI can reliably predict the performance of marketing actions, favoring the process of deciding how to allocate resources and to which audience to direct them (Haleem et al., 2022).

This predictive process provides organizations with a high capacity to generate accurate and comprehensive insights into their operations, which facilitates monitoring and the possibility of real-time improvements (Zerfass et al., 2020). These insights provide marketers with valuable expertise to better understand their target audience and therefore make more consumer-centric decisions quickly.

Based on the previous discussion of the advantages of applying AI-based technologies to improve numerous digital marketing processes, Table 1 summarizes some of the main results of digital marketing activities that can be optimized by extracting value through predictive analytics.

Table 1. Applications of predictive analytics in digital marketing

Outcome	Description	Authors
Improving user experience	Creation of communication strategies or campaigns for a specific consumer group, more likely to engage and respond positively to the targeted action, improving their experience through predictive journeys.	Haleem et al., 2022
Anticipating buying behavior	Anticipating the customer's next steps in the buying journey, as well as predicting the likelihood of a consumer profile becoming a new customer.	Haleem et al., 2022; Thiraviyam, 2018
Optimizing customer retention	Identifying customers most likely to unsubscribe from a service and creating strategies aimed at retaining these customers.	Saura et al., 2021
Pricing	Optimizing sales in line with increased demand by pricing products precisely for specific actions or time intervals, for example, setting the declared price needed to convert a customer.	Haleem et al., 2022; Jain & Aggarwal, 2020; Rabby et al., 2021; Zhao et al., 2022
Customer relationship management	Categorization, qualification and prioritization of leads through predictive evaluation.	Haleem et al., 2022; Huang & Rust, 2021; Javaid et al., 2022
Reduced customer turnover	Identification of customer groups with declining engagement and increased risk of leaving for a competitor, to apply strategies to improve engagement and retention.	Deggans et al., 2019; Sajid et al., 2021

2.3.3. Personalizing the customer experience

Typically, consumers tend to evaluate offers by comparing whether the information matches their perceptions of the product and their prior knowledge of the alternatives available to meet their needs (Sujan, 1985). Thus, marketers have started to adopt AI strategies to better understand consumer behavior perceptions, through big data and AI technology, to determine customers' habits and interests and then offer effective and personalized suggestions that meet their expectations (Dwivedi et al., 2021).

Personalization is the strategy based on understanding consumer behavior patterns through software and computer models, to provide relevant individualized content (Thiraviyam, 2018).

Under the AI domain, personalization strategy refers to the prediction and automatic selection of actions related to the marketing mix that best suit the needs of a specific customer, including the best timing and format of the approach (Kumar et al., 2019). In this way, it is hoped to encourage customer interaction with the brand and always be present in their purchasing considerations, by offering suggestions and personalized content (Varsha et al., 2021).

Among the various ways of applying personalization strategies, it is worth highlighting the individualized suggestion of products, promotions and advertisements, as well as the "recommended for you" sessions; personalization of the use of websites and apps through algorithms that provide the most relevant information for each user; integration of customer preferences across all channels and devices; dynamic pricing aligned with the customer's willingness to pay; suggestion of offers focused on customer retention with churn potential (Haleem et al., 2022; Kumar et al., 2019).

Through personalization, brands can provide customized and valuable experiences for different types of customers, at any stage of the marketing funnel. In addition, users are more likely to buy when they are subjected to AI-personalized experiences (Haleem et al., 2022).

2.3.4. Intelligent virtual customer service through chatbots

Chatbots are conversational engines capable of interacting in real time with customers, operators or any other human interlocutor and developing an advanced dialog, using artificial intelligence and machine learning (Illescas-Manzano et al., 2021). They are intelligent systems that can simulate a conversation between humans by processing natural language (Wirtz et al., 2018) from an interface using text or voice messages (Luo et al., 2019), and programmed to carry out a variety of tasks, including answering and responding to customer queries, making suggestions and facilitating transactions (Taecharungroj, 2023). Its sophisticated natural language processing and voice recognition skills allow it to understand complex dialogues and address customer questions with intensity, compassion and even humor (Wilson et al., 2017).

In the field of digital marketing, chatbots have been widely used in real-time customer service, often being the first contact with the customer. In addition, they are programmed to increase the results of integrated actions and improve data collection and analysis (Dwivedi et al., 2021; Vimalkumar et al., 2021). Currently, ChatGPT has been used to train chatbots to become more informative, engaging and capable of generating more human texts, due to its Large Language Model (LLM) (Abdelkader, 2023).

In recent times, “Marketing Content” has emerged as an extremely impactful marketing tool, and the evolution in the creation of this content has been driven by the use of AI-powered marketing tools (Chintalapati & Pandey, 2022), especially generative technologies, e.g. Generative Pre-training Transformer (GPT).

Currently, the largest representation of this technology is called ChatGPT, a deep learning model that has undergone extensive pre-training on large sets of text data and has the flexibility to be adjusted to perform specific functions, such as creating language, analyzing sentiment, developing language models, performing machine translation and classifying text (Yenduri et al., 2024).

Since its launch, ChatGPT has become increasingly popular in digital marketing, improving marketing operations (Abdelkader, 2023) and proving to be a transformative tool in this area (Sharma & Sharma, 2023), which has improved process efficiency and propelled businesses to greater prominence in the market (Restrepo & Lis-Gutiérrez, 2023). These AI-based technologies are redefining the way organizations relate to their audiences, playing a revolutionary role in enabling companies to generate contextualized and coherent communications, thanks to their versatile applications in content production, social media, market research, consumer relations, personalization strategies, etc. (Restrepo & Lis-Gutiérrez, 2023; Sharma & Sharma, 2023).

However, generative technology can be applied in a variety of ways, bringing many advantages to the organization, as shown in Table 2.

Table 2. Benefits identified in the use of GPT applied to marketing

Aplication	Description	References
Increased customer engagement	Generation of more creative content, with similarities to human production, causing a greater connection with the consumer and improving engagement with the brand.	Abdelkader, 2023; Haleem et al., 2022
Improved shopping experience	Content generation focused on personalization strategies, based on customer consumption data, to generate content and offers more in line with their preferences and needs. This provides a better shopping experience, based on connection and practicality.	Abdelkader, 2023; Restrepo & Lis-Gutiérrez, 2023; Sharma & Sharma, 2023
Automation of social networks and ads	Alignment of the communication used on social networks according to the target audience, optimizing the production of content for posts, more captivating marketing messages for ads and more effective hashtags with the audience, improving the brand's competitiveness.	Restrepo & Lis-Gutiérrez, 2023; Sharma & Sharma, 2023
Optimization of customer service	Training chatbots to develop more humanized conversational skills, promoting more effective user service, generating satisfaction and a perception of the tool's helpfulness and usefulness.	Haleem et al., 2022
Improved interactivity	Application of GPT in the customer relationship process, promoting more personalized and attractive conversations, thus increasing customer interactivity with the platform.	Restrepo & Lis-Gutiérrez, 2023
Increased effectiveness of marketing strategies	Easier access to new information that can identify patterns of behavior and customer preferences, generating specialized strategies more quickly and practically.	Restrepo & Lis-Gutiérrez, 2023
Improving the quality of responses to reviews	Efficient management of responses to positive and negative comments on various channels, in a short space of time, considering tone of voice and sentiment of the message to be responded to, promoting personalization and customer satisfaction.	Restrepo & Lis-Gutiérrez, 2023

2.4. Importance and advantages of implementing AI

With the rapid advances in the field of AI and the evolution of its tools, making them even more intelligent, the adoption of strategies powered by this technology has become a factor of competitive advantage for companies, crucial to remaining relevant in their segments (Wirtz et al., 2018). These advances are mainly related to the power to collect and process information, but the success of strategies is not only linked to the use of AI, but also to companies' ability to generate and apply insights (Jain & Aggarwal, 2020).

In general, the perceived benefits are usually related to managers' decision-making, directing them towards data-based solutions and developing their analytical and creative capabilities in the various functional areas of marketing (Hildebrand, 2019).

The viability of marketing actions, increased campaign efficiency and reduced operating costs are important motivating factors for implementing AI projects in organizations, given the high potential for increasing the ROI they can generate (Chintalapati & Pandey, 2022; Jain & Aggarwal, 2020; Shahid & Li, 2019).

To understand the impact of AI investments on organizations, and especially on Marketing, the effectiveness and appropriateness of return on investment (ROI) measures is discussed below.

2.5. Return on investment (ROI)

Investment can be defined as a process in which an investor exchanges resources at a given time to obtain financial compensation in the future (McGuire-Kuletz & Tomlinson, 2015). When investing their resources, organizations usually aim to achieve economic results, tangible returns, and to justify their use, they try to calculate the return on investment they will have after a certain time (Bevilacqua et al., 2024).

2.5.1. Tangible returns

ROI is defined as a performance indicator used to assess the financial effectiveness of an investment in generating a return, or to compare the effectiveness of different investments (McGuire-Kuletz & Tomlinson, 2015). It is the relationship established between profit and the investment generating the profit (Lal et al., 2020), the quantification of the profitability or lack of profitability of an investment (McGuire-Kuletz & Tomlinson, 2015). It can be used to measure the return of an organization in general, or of a specific project (Bevilacqua et al., 2024), assist in the qualification of an investment, as well as in evaluating the progress of its goals (McManus et al., 2004).

Traditionally, in general terms, ROI can be calculated simply by the ratio between the net benefits of an investment and its total cost (Bevilacqua et al., 2024; McGuire-Kuletz & Tomlinson, 2015), represented by the simple mathematical expression:

ROI = (Total return on investment-Cost of investment)/(Cost of investment).

To achieve greater accuracy in calculating ROI, the costs of the investment and the benefits generated must be carefully defined. At this point, it is necessary to estimate the financial benefits generated by the investment, isolating them from the influence of other factors and converting them into monetary values (Fu et al., 2018).

Defining return on investment targets and business objectives effectively and in advance can give the managers responsible some credibility in their segments, giving the organization competitive and sustainable advantages in the market. Considering these advantages, companies should incorporate ROI into their decision-making practices not only as a one-off study, but also in determining and demonstrating the value of specific projects, throughout all stages of execution, seeking constant improvements and maximization of results (Fu et al., 2018).

Bearing in mind that investors' return expectations can determine the size of the investment, it is essential to understand that successful ROI measurement is sensitive to how investment costs and benefits are considered in the project. Benefits have uncertainties and, just as an investment can take place through monetary or non-monetary values, in the same way, the benefits generated can be financial or non-financial (McGuire-Kuletz & Tomlinson, 2015), highlighting the importance of additionally measuring and evaluating intangible returns.

2.5.2. Intangible returns

The literature suggests that, in many cases, ROI should not only be measured in financial terms, considering the tangible profit of the investment, giving managers the task of also considering intangible returns, defining new metrics focused on objectives aimed at generating value for the project or organization (Lal et al., 2020). These intangible benefits influence the organization's stakeholders in different ways, such as social, cultural, behavioral and psychological. They can be expressed in terms of consumer engagement and loyalty, word of mouth, improved brand awareness, social responsibility, reputation and authority, positioning against competitors, encouraging innovation, optimizing decision-making, increasing productivity, staff satisfaction and retention (Bevilacqua et al., 2024; Fu et al., 2018).

It should be noted that intangible ROI can add to the overall value improvement for organizations and their stakeholders, since the benefits mentioned can influence increasing revenue, also impacting economic ROI (Bevilacqua et al., 2024).

2.5.3. Social return on investment (SROI)

Given the need to also quantify intangible benefits, which can result in several different ways, the concept of social return on investment is a method used to understand, measure and report the social and economic value of an organization's initiative. In addition to economic results, SROI determines the broader social value of a project. It is possible to estimate the non-financial costs and benefits that are not included in the traditional ROI, by assigning a monetary value to these results, which are generally inherent to the well-being of stakeholders such as customers, investors and the organization (McGuire-Kuletz & Tomlinson, 2015).

The focus of an investment is to create value for a project or the organization, but the nature of the value generated can be classified using two different concepts, economic value and social value. Emerson et al. (2001) distinguishes between these concepts by defining that economic value is created by using resources to create processes that increase their value, or that produce a product or service with greater market value. On the other hand, social value is created when resources are used to generate processes or policies that improve the lives of individuals or society in general. However, quantifying the social value generated by an investment can be one of the main challenges for the organization, since many results are complex to monetize (Hutchinson et al., 2019).

In this light, Hohler (2010) describes SROI as a specialized type of cost-benefit analysis that attempts to monetarily quantify outcomes that affect or are affected by a program's stakeholders. At the same time, Nicholls et al. (2012) summarize SROI as recognizing the social value that has been generated and for whom. In practice, social value can be expressed in the form of various intangible benefits, such as consumer loyalty, customer and employee satisfaction, increased productivity, brand reputation, competitive advantages in the market, fostering innovation, improving organizational culture, investor confidence, among others (Bevilacqua et al., 2024).

Mathematically, SROI is expressed as the ratio between the adjusted value of the benefits and the total investment. There are two types of SROI and both are related to when they are approached. SROI can be evaluative, when it is calculated after an intervention, considering existing results. It can also be classified as predictive, when it is considered in investment planning, to foresee how much social value can be created by achieving the expected results (Nicholls et al., 2012).

2.5.4. ROI in Marketing

By measuring the effectiveness of marketing, companies are able to understand the influence of different areas on the return obtained, so they can identify strengths and weaknesses in the project that will be used to support decisions and implement future initiatives (Skačkauskienė et al., 2023).

Based on the need to develop solid metrics to define marketing's contribution to company profitability, the concept of Marketing Return on Investment (MROI) was developed (Farris et al., 2015). Generally speaking, MROI is an indicator used to measure the effectiveness of marketing within an organization and understand how it contributes to the overall success of the business (Skačkauskienė et al., 2023), and is increasingly the metric used to evaluate organizations' marketing investments, guide strategic decisions (Farris et al., 2015) and has been applied for various purposes, such as assessing the cost of capital to be invested, the progress of marketing projects, the productivity of marketing and its potential to generate revenue, supporting the review and definition of the budget, as well as the proper allocation of resources in projects (Farris et al., 2015).

Despite its derivation, MROI is not calculated in the same way as traditional ROI, since marketing is a different and specific type of investment. MROI is the ratio between the value attributed to one or a set of marketing initiatives, net of their cost, and the marketing "invested". MROI can therefore be represented by the expression (Farris et al., 2015):

$$\text{MROI} = \frac{(\text{Financial value generated by marketing} - \text{Cost of marketing investment})}{\text{Cost of marketing investment}}$$

MROI can evaluate the return generated by a single marketing initiative or for a set of combinations of actions, such as the entire marketing mix. While ROI is generally used to measure a company's performance, MROI assesses the effectiveness of the marketing investment it has made. Companies may overlook the fact that marketing returns should be measured based on investment targets, considering a specific timeframe. In this way, they tend to include marketing initiatives in the overall calculation of the organization's ROI, without obtaining the real value generated by them. As a result, they categorize these actions as general expenses, rather than investments with specific return targets (Farris et al., 2015).

Although the importance of determining return on investment is compelling in marketing, many professionals still struggle to demonstrate the value they generate through their strategies (Fu et al., 2018). Following, an elaborate discussion on Return on Marketing challenges is presented.

2.5.5. Challenges in calculating MROI

Kumar and Reinartz (2016) state three factors that weaken the demonstration of marketing value: i) failure to adopt effective performance metrics that consider both financial, attitudinal, and behavioral aspects; ii) inability of marketers to establish causal links between the success of these metrics and the investment made; and iii) ineffective communication in presenting the return obtained to investors and other stakeholders. However, marketing is circumvented by market uncertainties, which makes its operation complex and makes it impossible to create standards on when to collect and manipulate data, how to analyze it, how to estimate costs and how to report the necessary information (Fu et al., 2018).

Determining ROI considers tangible and intangible benefits, where the latter are as important to the organization as achieving a positive ROI. Usually, some companies tend to avoid projects whose ROI encompasses intangible returns, but they can fall into the trap of neglecting significant benefits that may even justify the investment. Furthermore, in many cases, working with non-monetary returns may be unavoidable, so realizing and measuring these benefits becomes extremely relevant.

2.5.6. Artificial Intelligence and ROI

Although organizations are willing to invest such high amounts in their AI ventures, it is still a challenge to assess the real impact and ROI of these initiatives (Fu et al., 2018). In many cases, a careless approach to ROI can jeopardize the implementation, maintenance, or health of the project.

Usually, executives perceive AI as a tool to increase the results of their organizations and achieve a significant ROI, however, they still face difficulties in determining how and when. Thus, when considering that AI can have an impact on business objectives in the short and long term, organizations need to perceive AI projects as isolated investments and not expenses included in the company's overall budget. Therefore, the ROI of these projects must be calculated in isolation, based on the specific timeframe of each one, to know the value actually generated and measure the return attributed to the investment (Farris et al., 2015; Lal et al., 2020).

To measure the return on investments made in technology, in this case in AI, it is important to reconsider the traditional ROI calculation, since in order to measure the return on investment, intangible and indirect returns must be weighted (Bevilacqua et al., 2024; Lal et al., 2020). Intangible value is not easily measured, but it impacts the organization in terms of its culture, customer relations and competitiveness.

Several factors can be decisive in measuring the effective return of an AI project, such as the impact generated on the quality of the product or service, the improvement of technology and processes, brand differentiation and even the speed of value creation (Slalom, 2020).

To better understand the intangible returns on AI investments, it is essential to adopt methods or indicators that can measure these returns in various areas. The following table presents a selection of these indicators, organized into key categories: culture, process efficiency, customer experience, innovation, productivity, quality, investor relations, brand reputation, staff satisfaction, safety, sustainability, and decision-making. Each area represents a critical aspect where AI can generate value, but which often escapes traditional financial metrics, offering a more holistic and strategic view of the impacts of such investments.

Table 3. Methods or indicators for measuring intangible returns

Intangible returns	**Method/Indicator**	**References**
Culture	Employee feedback surveys Participation in development programs Organizational climate surveys Performance evaluations Involvement rate in related projects Cultural fit rating scale Uptake rate of new technologies Number of innovation ideas	Auh et al., 2019; Bammens, 2016; Lee & Jeung, 2016; Manzoor et al., 2011; Schneider et al., 2017; Yan, 2022
Process efficiency	Average Cycle Time Error or rework rate Automation rate (reduction of manual processes) Resource utilization rate Process standardization index	Daudelin et al., 2015; Griffin, 1997; Sarkar et al., 2013
Consumer experience	Net Promoter Score (NPS) Customer Satisfaction Score Conversion rate Number of positive reviews and comments Abandonment rate Return rate Number of interactions with the technology Average session time Problem resolution time Customer retention rate User Engagement Scale	Fornell et al., 2010; Haleem et al., 2022 Koladycz et al., 2018; Lariviere et al., 2014; Saura et al., 2021

continued on following page

Table 3. Continued

Intangible returns	Method/Indicator	References
Innovation	Number of new patents registered Launch rate of new products or services Development time for new products or services Adoption rate of new technologies and methodologies Success rate of innovations	Adams et al., 2006; Brau et al., 2013; Laforest, 2014; Mounir & Gardoni, 2020
Productivity	Error or rework rate Problem-solving time Learning and adaptation time Production volume per time Average task completion time	Bracci & Maran, 2011; Flynn et al., 1995; Li & Kim, 2021; Sickles & Zelenyuk, 2019
Quality	Complaints rate Customer satisfaction index Number of positive reviews and comments Defect or error rate Process quality index Process and service standardization index Net Promoter Score (NPS) Deadline compliance rate Average problem resolution time Customer response time	Abdelkader, 2023; Flynn et al., 1995; Koladycz et al., 2018; Li & Kim, 2021; Restrepo & Lis-Gutiérrez, 2023
Investor relations	Investor retention rate Investor satisfaction rate Participation rate in actions and events Conversion rate from leads to investors Communication rating scale	Bushee & Miller, 2007; Ramassa & Fabio, 2016
Brand reputation	Number of awards and recognitions Number of media and press mentions Brand reputation index Brand perception survey Brand recognition index Online presence index Digital authority or influence index Customer loyalty index Customer life cycle time	Al-Tuama & Nasrawi, 2022; Liu, 2023; Mir-Bernal, 2019; Rizard et al., 2022

continued on following page

Table 3. Continued

Intangible returns	Method/Indicator	References
Team satisfaction	Retention rate Internal customer satisfaction rate Cross-training rate Participation rate in events Participation rate in institutional projects Rate of involvement in institutional actions Cultural fit rating scale	Bevilacqua et al., 2024; Hopp & Van Oyen, 2004; Tomei & Russo, 2016)
Security	Average time to resolve information security incidents Average threat detection time Success rate of security tests Unauthorized access prevention rate Financial fraud rate	Hernández & Hidalgo, 2020; Varshini & Latha, 2023
Sustainability	Resource efficiency index Operating cost reduction rate Associated carbon footprint index Corporate social responsibility index Financial sustainability index Socially Responsible Investment Index	Azad et al., 2018; Feng et al., 2017; Gleißner et al., 2022; Mill, 2006; Mulrow et al., 2019
Decision-making	Average decision-making time Organizational learning index Decision conflict resolution rate Information reliability index Stakeholder satisfaction index Decision transparency rate Decision accuracy index	Dowding & Thompson, 2003; Karaulova et al., 2012; Li et al., 2013; Oliver & Roos, 2005

3. CONCLUSIONS

The rapid and significant advances in AI have substantially shaped the business landscape, imposing on organizations the imperative need to integrate with this technological revolution to reap the benefits arising from these innovations. The intrinsic capacity of AI, defined as the ability of a system to accurately interpret external data, learn from that data, and employ that learning to achieve specific goals, is proving to be a strategic differentiator, especially in the context of digital marketing, where different types of AI play crucial roles.

In this context, evaluating the ROI of AI projects emerges as a multifaceted challenge, as it transcends traditional tangible returns, expressed in financial values, to encompass intangible returns, which permeate social, cultural, and behavioral spheres. The literature points out that ROI should not be restricted to financial metrics, but should consider intangible benefits, which influence stakeholders in different dimensions.

Larger, more mature companies may be more likely to prioritize intangible returns when investing in AI projects, but in general, the most perceived intangible returns are related to optimizing operations, such as improvements in productivity, process efficiency and decision-making. In terms of ROI, the results point to cost reduction as the third most perceived benefit, revealing the positive impact that implementing AI can have on organizations.

The results also show a more holistic and strategic view of the impacts of such investments, as follows.

An important conclusion suggests that most of the benefits and improvements derived from AI technology investments are related to business processes: e.g., efficiency, productivity and quality standards assurance. AI and service automation enables many companies to improve their processes and increase workers' productivity. Therefore, companies are integrating AI models and applications into their business models as a critical efficiency component, reporting that AI fosters revenue in sales and marketing while reducing costs in supply chain management and manufacturing functions.

Another major conclusion suggests that management decision making and Marketing "Agile" will greatly benefit from faster and robust predictive ML algorithms.

Nowadays, everything around us, from culture to consumer products, is a product of intelligence. With the increasing use of AI-assisted channels, people are progressively more dependent on these technologies, e.g. assisted by chatbot applications.

The role that AI can take in decision-making processes, giving certain predictions or suggestions based on past consumer behaviors patterns, as a base for sales forecasting, entails accurate ML algorithms results to avoid costly mistakes for business performance.

Therefore, for companies, AI technologies entail several benefits for business: increased revenues, sales reinforcement, price segmentation from the customer database, customer satisfaction, lower product returns, and cost reduction.

Finally, the chapter concludes that AI intangibles ROI are related to important business non-financial assets. For instance, organizational culture, customer's and employee's satisfaction are important indicators to measure decent work in happy organizations, empowered employees. This will be reflected in a positive organizational brand image, which in turns attracts and retains collaborators and customers increasing long lasting relationships. These are important business's non-financial assets affecting positively long-term business results and performance.

Despite the benefits from business AI investments there are also some challenges to tackle driving future research avenues: Issues concerning data reliability, cybersecurity, data privacy, "job losses", Upskilled and more skilled and educated collaborators, are among the hot topics of research mainstream.

Also, the dependency on AI can raise a significant risk for organizations and customers.

For instances, AI emerges as an effective marketing tool and a powerful manipulation tool to price discriminate against customers by using different messages and prices based on customers' specific profiles. However, there is a considerable reputational risk that AI-enabled aggressive strategies can generate that could provoke major financial and operational problems and that could damage brand trust and the benefits associated with AI technologies.

Additionally, organizations use AI to maintain good customer service and optimize costs and the delivery of services. This way, the customer service is less personalized, might lack transparency, and can raise concerns about privacy and security issues, resulting in unhappy and frustrated customers. Furthermore, using AI applications in some contexts can result in client harm, especially when AI is applied to medicine and healthcare.

Future research initiatives can help to address the shortcomings of this chapter.

REFERENCES

Abbott, D. (2014). *Applied predictive analytics: Principles and techniques for the professional data analyst.* John Wiley & Sons, Inc.

Abdelkader, O. A. (2023). ChatGPT's influence on customer experience in digital marketing: Investigating the moderating roles. *Heliyon*, 9(8), e18770. Advance online publication. DOI: 10.1016/j.heliyon.2023.e18770 PMID: 37576290

Adams, R., Bessant, J., & Phelps, R. (2006). Innovation management measurement: A review. In *International Journal of Management Reviews*, 8(1), 21–47). DOI: 10.1111/j.1468-2370.2006.00119.x

Al-Tuama, A. T., & Nasrawi, D. A. (2022). A survey on the impact of chatbots on marketing activities. *2022 13th International Conference on Computing Communication and Networking Technologies, ICCCNT 2022.* DOI: 10.1109/ICCCNT54827.2022.9984635

Auh, S., Menguc, B., Imer, P., & Uslu, A. (2019). Frontline employee feedback-seeking behavior: How is it formed and when does it matter? *Journal of Service Research*, 22(1), 44–59. DOI: 10.1177/1094670518779462

Azad, A. M. S., Raza, A., & Zaidi, S. S. Z. (2018). Empirical relationship between operational efficiency and profitability (Evidence from Pakistan exploration sector). *Journal of Accounting. Business and Finance Research*, 2(1), 7–11. DOI: 10.20448/2002.21.7.11

Bammens, Y. P. M. (2016). Employees' innovative behavior in social context: A closer examination of the role of organizational care. *Journal of Product Innovation Management*, 33(3), 244–259. DOI: 10.1111/jpim.12267

Bellman, R. (1978). *An Introduction to Artificial Intelligence: Can Computers Think?* Boyd & Fraser Publishing Company.

Bevilacqua, M., Berente, N., Domin, H., Goehring, B., & Rossi, F. (2024). The return on investment in AI ethics: A holistic framework. *Hawaii International Conference on System Sciences (HICSS) 2024.*

Bracci, E., & Maran, L. (2011). *Performance measurement in the public sector: some theoretical and practical reflections*. https://www.unife.it/dipartimento/economia/pubblicazioni/quaderni-del-

Brau, E., Reinhardt, R., & Gurtner, S. (2013). Measuring the success of open innovation. In *Evolution of Innovation Management* (pp. 52–74). Palgrave Macmillan UK. DOI: 10.1057/9781137299994_3

Bughin, J., Hazan, E., Ramaswamy, S., Chui, M., Allas, T., Dahlström, P., Henke, N., & Trench, M. (2017). *Artificial Intelligence: The next digital frontier?*www.mckinsey.com/mgi

Bushee, B. J., & Miller, G. S. (2007). Investor relations, firm visibility, and investor following. SSRN *Electronic Journal*. DOI: 10.2139/ssrn.643223

Chintalapati, S., & Pandey, S. K. (2022). Artificial intelligence in marketing: A systematic literature review. *International Journal of Market Research*, 64(1), 38–68. DOI: 10.1177/14707853211018428

Daudelin, D. H., Selker, H. P., & Leslie, L. K. (2015). Applying process improvement methods to clinical and Translational research: Conceptual framework and case examples. *Clinical and Translational Science*, 8(6), 779–786. DOI: 10.1111/cts.12326 PMID: 26332869

Daugherty, P. R., & Wilson, H. J. (2018). *Human + machine: reimagining work in the age of AI*. Harvard Business Review Press.

de Luca, L. M., Herhausen, D., Troilo, G., & Rossi, A. (2021). How and when do big data investments pay off? The role of marketing affordances and service innovation. *Journal of the Academy of Marketing Science*, 49(4), 790–810. DOI: 10.1007/s11747-020-00739-x

Deggans, J., Krulicky, T., Kovacova, M., Valaskova, K., & Poliak, M. (2019). Cognitively enhanced products, output growth, and labor market changes: Will artificial intelligence replace workers by automating their jobs? *Economics, Management, and Financial Markets*, 14(1), 38. DOI: 10.22381/EMFM14120194

Dowding, D., & Thompson, C. (2003). Measuring the quality of judgement and decision-making in nursing. *Journal of Advanced Nursing*, 44(1), 49–57. DOI: 10.1046/j.1365-2648.2003.02770.x PMID: 12956669

Dumitriu, D., & Popescu, M. A. M. (2020). Artificial intelligence solutions for digital marketing. *Procedia Manufacturing*, 46, 630–636. DOI: 10.1016/j.promfg.2020.03.090

Dwivedi, Y. K., Hughes, L., Ismagilova, E., Aarts, G., Coombs, C., Crick, T., Duan, Y., Dwivedi, R., Edwards, J., Eirug, A., Galanos, V., Ilavarasan, P. V., Janssen, M., Jones, P., Kar, A. K., Kizgin, H., Kronemann, B., Lal, B., Lucini, B., & Williams, M. D. (2021). Artificial Intelligence (AI): Multidisciplinary perspectives on emerging challenges, opportunities, and agenda for research, practice and policy. *International Journal of Information Management*, 57, 101994. Advance online publication. DOI: 10.1016/j.ijinfomgt.2019.08.002

Dwivedi, Y. K., Ismagilova, E., Hughes, D. L., Carlson, J., Filieri, R., Jacobson, J., Jain, V., Karjaluoto, H., Kefi, H., Krishen, A. S., Kumar, V., Rahman, M. M., Raman, R., Rauschnabel, P. A., Rowley, J., Salo, J., Tran, G. A., & Wang, Y. (2021). Setting the future of digital and social media marketing research: Perspectives and research propositions. *International Journal of Information Management*, 59, 102168. Advance online publication. DOI: 10.1016/j.ijinfomgt.2020.102168

Emerson, J., Wachowicz, J., & Chun, S. (2001, January 29). *Social return on investment (SROI): Exploring aspects of value creation*. Harvard Business School Working Knowledge. https://hbswk.hbs.edu/archive/social-return-on-investment-sroi-exploring-aspects-of-value-creation

Endert, A., Hossain, M. S., Ramakrishnan, N., North, C., Fiaux, P., & Andrews, C. (2014). The human is the loop: New directions for visual analytics. *Journal of Intelligent Information Systems*, 43(3), 411–435. DOI: 10.1007/s10844-014-0304-9

Erevelles, S., Fukawa, N., & Swayne, L. (2016). Big Data consumer analytics and the transformation of marketing. *Journal of Business Research*, 69(2), 897–904. DOI: 10.1016/j.jbusres.2015.07.001

Farris, P. W., Hanssens, D. M., Lenskold, J. D., & Reibstein, D. J. (2015). Marketing return on investment: Seeking clarity for concept and measurement. *Applied Marketing Analytics: The Peer-Reviewed Journal*, 1(3), 267–282. DOI: 10.69554/FFOM1594

Feng, Y., Zhu, Q., & Lai, K. H. (2017). Corporate social responsibility for supply chain management: A literature review and bibliometric analysis. *Journal of Cleaner Production*, 158, 296–307. DOI: 10.1016/j.jclepro.2017.05.018

Flavián, C., Pérez-Rueda, A., Belanche, D., & Casaló, L. V. (2022). Intention to use analytical artificial intelligence (AI) in services – the effect of technology readiness and awareness. *Journal of Service Management*, 33(2), 293–320. DOI: 10.1108/JOSM-10-2020-0378

Flynn, B. B., Schroeder, R. G., & Sakakibara, S. (1995). The impact of quality management practices on performance and competitive advantage. *Decision Sciences*, 26(5), 659–691. DOI: 10.1111/j.1540-5915.1995.tb01445.x

Fornell, C., Rust, R. T., & Dekimpe, M. G. (2010). The Effect of Customer Satisfaction on Consumer Spending Growth. *JMR, Journal of Marketing Research*, 47(1), 28–35. DOI: 10.1509/jmkr.47.1.28

Fu, F. Q., Phillips, J. J., & Phillips, P. P. (2018). ROI Marketing: Measuring, Demonstrating, and Improving Value. *Performance Improvement*, 57(2), 6–13. DOI: 10.1002/pfi.21771

Gandomi, A., & Haider, M. (2015). Beyond the hype: Big data concepts, methods, and analytics. *International Journal of Information Management*, 35(2), 137–144. DOI: 10.1016/j.ijinfomgt.2014.10.007

Gleißner, W., Günther, T., & Walkshäusl, C. (2022). Financial sustainability: Measurement and empirical evidence. *Journal of Business Economics*, 92(3), 467–516. DOI: 10.1007/s11573-022-01081-0

Griffin, A. (1997). The effect of project and process characteristics on product development cycle time. *JMR, Journal of Marketing Research*, 34(1), 24–35. DOI: 10.1177/002224379703400103

Hair, J. F.Jr, Harrison, D. E., & Risher, J. J. (2018). Marketing research in the 21st century: Opportunities and challenges. *Revista Brasileira de Marketing*, 17(5), 666–699. DOI: 10.5585/bjm.v17i5.4173

Haleem, A., Javaid, M., & Singh, R. P. (2022). An era of ChatGPT as a significant futuristic support tool: A study on features, abilities, and challenges. *BenchCouncil Transactions on Benchmarks. Standards and Evaluations*, 2(4), 100089. DOI: 10.1016/j.tbench.2023.100089

Haugeland, J. (1985). *Artificial intelligence: The very idea*. MIT Press.

Hernández, A. B., & Hidalgo, D. B. (2020). Detection of fraud patterns in accounting accounts using data mining techniques. *Open Journal of Business and Management*, 08(04), 1609–1618. DOI: 10.4236/ojbm.2020.84102

Hildebrand, C. (2019). The machine age of marketing: How artificial intelligence changes the way people think, act, and decide. *NIM Marketing Intelligence Review*, 11(2), 10–17. DOI: 10.2478/nimmir-2019-0010

Hohler, A. (2010, March 1). *Measuring the bang of every donated buck*. The Wall Street Journal. https://www.wsj.com/articles/SB10001424052748703787304575075340954767332

Hopp, W. J., & Van Oyen, M. P. (2004). Agile workforce evaluation: A framework for cross-training and coordination. [Institute of Industrial Engineers]. *IIE Transactions*, 36(10), 919–940. DOI: 10.1080/07408170490487759

Huang, M. H., & Rust, R. T. (2018). Artificial Intelligence in Service. *Journal of Service Research*, 21(2), 155–172. DOI: 10.1177/1094670517752459

Huang, M. H., & Rust, R. T. (2021). A strategic framework for artificial intelligence in marketing. *Journal of the Academy of Marketing Science*, 49(1), 30–50. DOI: 10.1007/s11747-020-00749-9

Hutchinson, C. L., Berndt, A., Forsythe, D., Gilbert-Hunt, S., George, S., & Ratcliffe, J. (2019). Valuing the impact of health and social care programs using social return on investment analysis: How have academics advanced the methodology? A systematic review. *BMJ Open*, 9(8), e029789. Advance online publication. DOI: 10.1136/bmjopen-2019-029789 PMID: 31446413

Illescas-Manzano, M. D., López, N. V., González, N. A., & Rodríguez, C. C. (2021). Implementation of chatbot in online commerce, and open innovation. *Journal of Open Innovation*, 7(2), 125. Advance online publication. DOI: 10.3390/joitmc7020125

Jacobs, B. J. D., Donkers, B., & Fok, D. (2016). Model-Based Purchase Predictions for Large Assortments. *Marketing Science*, 35(3), 389–404. DOI: 10.1287/mksc.2016.0985

Jain, P., & Aggarwal, K. (2020). Transforming Marketing with Artificial Intelligence. *International Research Journal of Engineering and Technology, 07*(07), 3964–3976. DOI: 10.13140/RG.2.2.25848.67844

Jarrahi, M. H. (2018). Artificial intelligence and the future of work: Human-AI symbiosis in organizational decision making. *Business Horizons*, 61(4), 577–586. DOI: 10.1016/j.bushor.2018.03.007

Javaid, M., Haleem, A., Singh, R. P., & Suman, R. (2022). Artificial intelligence applications for industry 4.0: A literature-based study. *Journal of Industrial Integration and Management*, 07(01), 83–111. DOI: 10.1142/S2424862221300040

Kaplan, A., & Haenlein, M. (2019). Siri, Siri, in my hand: Who's the fairest in the land? On the interpretations, illustrations, and implications of artificial intelligence. *Business Horizons*, 62(1), 15–25. DOI: 10.1016/j.bushor.2018.08.004

Karaulova, T., Kostina, M., & Shevtshenko, E. (2012). Reliability assessment of manufacturing processes. *International Journal of Industrial Engineering and Management*, 3(3), 143–151. DOI: 10.24867/IJIEM-2012-3-118

Koladycz, R., Fernandez, G., Gray, K., & Marriott, H. (2018). The Net Promoter Score (NPS) for Insight Into Client Experiences in Sexual and Reproductive Health Clinics. *Global Health, Science and Practice*, 6(3), 413–424. DOI: 10.9745/GHSP-D-18-00068 PMID: 30072372

Kotler, P., & Armstrong, G. (2006). *Principles of Marketing* (3rd ed.). Pearson.

Kumar, L. (2017). State of The Art-Intense Review on Artificial Intelligence Systems Application in Process Planning and Manufacturing. *Engineering Applications of Artificial Intelligence*, 65, 294–329. DOI: 10.1016/j.engappai.2017.08.005

Kumar, V., Rajan, B., Venkatesan, R., & Lecinski, J. (2019). Understanding the role of artificial intelligence in personalized engagement marketing. *California Management Review*, 61(4), 135–155. DOI: 10.1177/0008125619859317

Kumar, V., & Reinartz, W. (2016). Creating enduring customer value. *Journal of Marketing*, 80(6), 36–68. DOI: 10.1509/jm.15.0414

Laforest, V. (2014). Assessment of emerging and innovative techniques considering best available technique performances. *Resources, Conservation and Recycling*, 92, 11–24. DOI: 10.1016/j.resconrec.2014.08.009

Lal, B., Ismagilova, E., Dwivedi, Y. K., & Kwayu, S. (2020). Return on investment in social media marketing: Literature review and suggestions for future research. In *Digital and social media marketing: Advances in theory and practice of emmerging markets* (pp. 3–17). Springer., DOI: 10.1007/978-3-030-24374-6_1

Lariviere, B., Keiningham, T. L., Cooil, B., Aksoy, L., & Malthouse, E. C. (2014). A longitudinal examination of customer commitment and loyalty. *Journal of Service Management*, 25(1), 75–100. DOI: 10.1108/JOSM-01-2013-0025

Lee, J. Y., & Jeung, W. (2016). Differential effects of person-organization and person-team cultural fit on work-related attitudes and job performance. *Proceedings - Academy of Management*, 1. Advance online publication. DOI: 10.5465/ambpp.2016.13447abstract

Li, J., & Kim, J. E. (2021). The effect of task complexity on time estimation in the virtual reality environment: An eeg study. *Applied Sciences (Basel, Switzerland)*, 11(20), 9779. Advance online publication. DOI: 10.3390/app11209779

Li, T. H. Y., Ng, S. T., & Skitmore, M. (2013). Evaluating stakeholder satisfaction during public participation in major infrastructure and construction projects: A fuzzy approach. *Automation in Construction*, 29, 123–135. DOI: 10.1016/j.autcon.2012.09.007

Liu, Y. (2023). The impact of social media influencers on Generation Z online consumer behavior. *Advances in Economics. Management and Political Sciences*, 41(1), 19–24. DOI: 10.54254/2754-1169/41/20232026

Luo, X., Tong, S., Fang, Z., & Qu, Z. (2019). Frontiers: Machines vs. humans: The impact of artificial intelligence chatbot disclosure on customer purchases. *Marketing Science*, 38(6), 937–947. DOI: 10.1287/mksc.2019.1192

Manzoor, S. R., Ullah, H., Hussain, M., & Ahmad, Z. M. (2011). Effect of teamwork on employee performance. *International Journal of Learning and Development*, 1(1), 110. DOI: 10.5296/ijld.v1i1.1110

Mazurek, G., & Małagocka, K. (2019). Perception of privacy and data protection in the context of the development of artificial intelligence. *Journal of Management Analytics*, 6(4), 344–364. DOI: 10.1080/23270012.2019.1671243

McAfee, A., & Brynjolfsson, E. (2012). Big data: The management revolution. *Harvard Business Review*, 90(10), 60–68. PMID: 23074865

McGuire-Kuletz, M., & Tomlinson, P. (2015). *Return on investment and economic impact: Determining and communicating the value of vocational rehabilitation.*

McManus, D. J., Wilson, L. T., & Snyder, C. A. (2004). Assessing the business value of knowledge retention projects - Results of four case studies. *IFIP International Conference on Decision Support Systems.*

Mill, G. A. (2006). The financial performance of a socially responsible investment over time and a possible link with corporate social responsibility. *Journal of Business Ethics*, 63(2), 131–148. DOI: 10.1007/s10551-005-2410-7

Mir-Bernal, P. (2019). Brand reputation in the Facebook era: The impact of user generated content in brand reputation management brand reputation in the Facebook era. In *Brand Culture and Identity* (pp. 1544–1556). IGI Global., DOI: 10.4018/978-1-5225-7116-2.ch083

Mounir, I., & Gardoni, M. (2020, November 18). Front-end of innovation metrics: Research question and literature review. *X Congreso Internacional de Conocimiento e Inovación (CIKI).* DOI: 10.48090/ciki.v1i1.913

Mulrow, J., Machaj, K., Deanes, J., & Derrible, S. (2019). The state of carbon footprint calculators: An evaluation of calculator design and user interaction features. *Sustainable Production and Consumption*, 18, 33–40. DOI: 10.1016/j.spc.2018.12.001

Nicholls, J., Lawlor, E., Neitzert, E., & Goodspeed, T. (2012). *A guide to social return on investment.* http://www.socialvaluelab.org.uk/wp-content/uploads/2016/09/SROI-a-guide-to-social-return-on-investment.pdf

Oliver, D., & Roos, J. (2005). Decision-making in high-velocity environments: The importance of guiding principles. *Organization Studies*, 26(6), 889–913. DOI: 10.1177/0170840605054609

Overgoor, G., Chica, M., Rand, W., & Weishampel, A. (2019). Letting the computers take over: Using AI to solve marketing problems. *California Management Review*, 61(4), 156–185. DOI: 10.1177/0008125619859318

Oxford Internet Institute. (2020, January). *Human in the loop.* https://atozofai.withgoogle.com/intl/pt-BR/human-in-the-loop/

Rabby, F., Chimhundu, R., & Hassan, R. (2021). Artificial intelligence in digital marketing influences consumer behaviour: A review and theoretical foundation for future research. *Academy of Marketing Studies Journal*, 25(5), 1–7.

Ramassa, P., & Di Fabio, C. (2016). Social media for investor relations: A literature review and future directions. *The International Journal of Digital Accounting Research*, 5, 117–134.

Restrepo, A. N. R., & Lis-Gutiérrez, J. P. (2023). A review of GPT Chat applications in Marketing. *Salud, Ciencia y Tecnologia - Serie de Conferencias, 2*. DOI: 10.56294/sctconf2023514

Rich, E., & Knight, K. (1991). *Artificial Intelligence* (2nd ed.). McGraw-Hill.

Rizard, S. R., Waluyo, B., & Jaswir, I. (2022). Impact of brand equity and service quality on the reputation of universities and students' intention to choose them: The case of IIUM and UIN. *F1000 Research*, 11, 1412. DOI: 10.12688/f1000research.122386.1 PMID: 37767070

Russell, S. J., & Norvig, P. (2009). *Artificial Intelligence: A Modern Approach* (3rd ed.). Prentice-Hall.

Sajid, S., Haleem, A., Bahl, S., Javaid, M., Goyal, T., & Mittal, M. (2021). Data science applications for predictive maintenance and materials science in context to Industry 4.0. *Second International Conference on Aspects of Materials Science and Engineering (ICAMSE 2021), 45*, 4898–4905. DOI: 10.1016/j.matpr.2021.01.357

Sarkar, S. A., Mukhopadhyay, A. R., & Ghosh, S. K. (2013). Improvement of claim processing cycle time through lean six sigma methodology. *International Journal of Lean Six Sigma*, 4(2), 171–183. DOI: 10.1108/20401461311319347

Saura, J. R., Ribeiro-Soriano, D., & Palacios-Marqués, D. (2021). Setting B2B digital marketing in artificial intelligence-based CRMs: A review and directions for future research. *Industrial Marketing Management*, 98, 161–178. DOI: 10.1016/j.indmarman.2021.08.006

Schneider, B., González-Romá, V., Ostroff, C., West, M., & Management Labs, T. (2017). Organizational climate and culture: Reflections on the history of the constructs in Journal of Applied Psychology. *The Journal of Applied Psychology*, 102(3), 468–482. DOI: 10.1037/apl0000090 PMID: 28125256

Shahid, M. Z., & Li, G. (2019). Impact of Artificial Intelligence in Marketing: A Perspective of Marketing Professionals of Pakistan. *Global Journal of Management and Business Research*, 19(2), 27–33.

Sharma, A. K., & Sharma, R. (2023). The role of generative pre-trained transformers (GPTs) in revolutionising digital marketing: A conceptual model. *Journal of Cultural Marketing Strategy*, 8(1), 80–92. DOI: 10.69554/TLVQ2275

Shovo, N. (2021). Marketing with artificial intelligence and predicting consumer choice. *AI & Society*, 1(1), 6–18.

Sickles, R. C., & Zelenyuk, V. (2019). Measurement of productivity and efficiency: Theory and practice. In *Measurement of Productivity and Efficiency*. Cambridge University Press., DOI: 10.1017/9781139565981

Skačkauskienė, I., Nekrošienė, J., & Szarucki, M. (2023). A review on marketing activities effectiveness evaluation metrics. *13th International Scientific Conference "Business and Management 2023"*. DOI: 10.3846/bm.2023.1037

Sterne, J. (2017). *Artificial intelligence for marketing: Practical applications*. Wiley. DOI: 10.1002/9781119406341

Sujan, M. (1985). Consumer knowledge: Effects on evaluation strategies mediating consumer judgments. *The Journal of Consumer Research*, 12(1), 31–46. DOI: 10.1086/209033

Swami, V. I., & Naidu, D. (2020). Social media marketing: Gateway to success for homepreneurs. *International Journal of Innovative Technology and Exploring Engineering*, 9(4S), 66–70. DOI: 10.35940/ijitee.D1011.0394S20

Taecharungroj, V. (2023). "What can ChatGPT do?" Analyzing early reactions to the innovative AI chatbot on Twitter. *Big Data and Cognitive Computing*, 7(1), 35. Advance online publication. DOI: 10.3390/bdcc7010035

Teradata. (2017, October 11). *Survey: 80 Percent of enterprises investing in AI, but cite significant challenges ahead*. Terada. https://www.teradata.com/Press-Releases/2017/Survey-80-Percent-of-Enterprises-Invest-in-AI

Thiraviyam, T. (2018). Artificial Intelligence Marketing. *International Journal of Recent Research Aspects*, 449–452.

Tomei, P. A., & Russo, G. (2016). Cultural fit and desired organizational values: The case of ARFCO. *Organizational Cultures: An International Journal*, 16(3), 27–49. DOI: 10.18848/2327-8013/CGP/v16i03/27-49

Varsha, P. S., Akter, S., Kumar, A., Gochhait, S., & Patagundi, B. (2021). The impact of artificial intelligence on branding: A bibliometric analysis (1982-2019). In *Journal of Global Information Management* (Vol. 29, Issue 4, pp. 221–246). IGI Global. DOI: 10.4018/JGIM.20210701.oa10

Varshini, G. Y. S., & Latha, S. (2023). Detection of data integrity attack using model and data-driven-based approach in CPPS. *International Transactions on Electrical Energy Systems*, 2023, 1–24. Advance online publication. DOI: 10.1155/2023/6098519

Vimalkumar, M., Sharma, S. K., Singh, J. B., & Dwivedi, Y. K. (2021). 'Okay google, what about my privacy?': User's privacy perceptions and acceptance of voice based digital assistants.

Wedel, M., & Kannan, P. K. (2016). Marketing analytics for data-rich environments. *Journal of Marketing*, 80(6), 97–121. DOI: 10.1509/jm.15.0413

Wilson, H. J., Daugherty, P. R., & Morini-Bianzino, N. (2017). The jobs that artificial intelligence will create. *MIT Sloan Management Review*, 58(4).

Wirtz, J., Patterson, P. G., Kunz, W. H., Gruber, T., Lu, V. N., Paluch, S., & Martins, A. (2018). Brave new world: Service robots in the frontline. *Journal of Service Management*, 29(5), 907–931. DOI: 10.1108/JOSM-04-2018-0119

Yan, N. (2022). Research on the relationship between employee mental health and enterprise work performance. *Journal of Healthcare Engineering*, 2022, 1–9. DOI: 10.1155/2022/3008947 PMID: 35265296

Yang, S., Yang, S., & Evans, C. (2019). Opportunities and Challenges in Using AI Chatbots in Higher Education. *The 3rd International Conference on Education and E-Learning (ICEEL 2019)79*, 79–83. DOI: 10.1145/3371647.3371659

Yau, K. L. A., Saad, N. M., & Chong, Y. W. (2021). Artificial Intelligence Marketing (AIM) for enhancing customer relationships. *Applied Sciences (Basel, Switzerland)*, 11(18), 1–17. DOI: 10.3390/app11188562

Yenduri, G., Ramalingam, M., Selvi, G. C., Supriya, Y., Srivastava, G., Maddikunta, P. K. R., Raj, G. D., Jhaveri, R. H., Prabadevi, B., Wang, W., Vasilakos, A. V., & Gadekallu, T. R. (2024). Gpt (generative pre-trained transformer) – a comprehensive review on enabling technologies, potential applications, emerging challenges, and future directions. *IEEE Access : Practical Innovations, Open Solutions*, 12, 54608–55464. DOI: 10.1109/ACCESS.2024.3389497

Zerfass, A., Hagelstein, J., & Tench, R. (2020). Artificial intelligence in communication management: A cross-national study on adoption and knowledge, impact, challenges and risks. *Journal of Communication Management (London)*, 24(4), 377–389. DOI: 10.1108/JCOM-10-2019-0137

Zhao, H., Lyu, F., & Luo, Y. (2022). Research on the Effect of Online Marketing Based on Multimodel Fusion and Artificial Intelligence in the Context of Big Data. *Security and Communication Networks*, 2022, 1–9. Advance online publication. DOI: 10.1155/2022/1516543

ADITTIONAL READING

Phillips, P. P. (2023). *Return on investment (ROI) basics*. Association for Talent Development.

Pires, P. B., Santos, J. D., & Pereira, I. V. (2025). Artificial Neural Networks: History and State of the Art. In M. Khosrow-Pour, D.B.A. (Ed.), *Encyclopedia of Information Science and Technology, Sixth Edition*. DOI: 10.4018/978-1-6684-7366-5.ch037

Pires, P. B., Santos, J. D., Pereira, I. V., & Torres, A. I. (Eds.). (2023). *Confronting Security and Privacy Challenges in Digital Marketing*. IGI Global., DOI: 10.4018/978-1-6684-8958-1

Torres, A. I., & Beirão, G. (2024). Artificial Intelligence Technologies: Benefits, Risks, and Challenges for Sustainable Business Models. In *Artificial Intelligence Approaches to Sustainable Accounting* (pp. 229-248). IGI Global.

KEY TERMS AND DEFINITIONS

Artificial Intelligence: Computer science discipline whose goal is to develop systems and algorithms that can carry out tasks that would typically need human intelligence.

Chatbot: A chatbot is artificial intelligence software that can simulate a conversation with human users.

Customer Experience: Describes how consumers feel about a business or brand, considering all the interactions and touchpoints they encounter along their customer journey.

Data analysis: The act of examining, purifying, converting, and modeling data to find relevant information, draw conclusions, and facilitate well-informed decision-making.

Digital Marketing: The collection of tactics and methods that uses of digital platforms and media to promote goods, services, brands, or causes.

Machine Learning: A branch of artificial intelligence whose goal is to create models and algorithms that let computers learn from data and make predictions or judgments.

Predictive analysis: A sort of data analytics that uses machine learning, artificial intelligence, statistics, pattern matching, and prediction modeling to find pertinent data trends.

ROI (Return on Investment): It is an essential tool for businesses and investors to use when deciding how best to use their resources.

Chapter 13

Social Media Analytics for Effective Customer Brand Engagement Assessment: A Theoretical Exploration

Lhoussaine Alla
https://orcid.org/0000-0002-7238-1792
Sidi Mohamed Ben Abdellah University, Fez, Morocco

Naoual Bouhtati
Sidi Mohamed Ben Abdellah University, Fez, Morocco

Mourad Aarabe
https://orcid.org/0009-0003-9772-6683
Sidi Mohamed Ben Abdellah University, Fez, Morocco

Nouhaila Ben Khizzou
Sidi Mohamed Ben Abdellah University, Fez, Morocco

ABSTRACT

Customer engagement has become a critical component of business success in the digital age. Challenges to this commitment include creating personalized experiences, building trust, and using data to anticipate customer needs. Our study aims to analyze the impact of social media analytics on online customer engagement assessment. We propose an analysis model integrating key dimensions of customer engagement, such as interaction, satisfaction and social influence. The expected results of this study are to provide a solid analysis model to assess customer engagement on social media and practical recommendations to improve the marketing strategies of companies on social media.

DOI: 10.4018/979-8-3693-5340-0.ch013

1. INTRODUCTION

The social media landscape continues to grow exponentially over the past decade, transforming the way brands interact with their customers. Social media platforms offer businesses a powerful way to promote their brand and connect directly with their target audience.

Such growth has created new opportunities for brands to build closer relationships with their customers. Social media platforms such as Facebook, Twitter, Instagram and LinkedIn offer two-way communication channels, allowing brands to receive instant feedback, respond to customer concerns and provide effective customer service.

In particular, the evaluation of customer engagement with the brand on social networks presents major challenges to monitor and actively evaluate this engagement in order to measure the impact of marketing actions and adjust strategies accordingly. This requires the ability to analyze customer interactions in real time, understand their feelings and expectations, as well as identify opportunities for improvement and strengthen the brand-customer relationship to foster loyalty and positive experience.

More than ever, customer engagement has become an essential component of social media marketing strategies, attracting considerable interest from professional researchers and marketing academicians (Vinerean & Opreana, 2021).

In this sense, our study is primarily motivated by the lack of clear understanding of how brands can effectively assess customer engagement on these platforms. Similarly, traditional marketing performance indicators, such as sales and conversion rates, are no longer sufficient on their own to assess the impact of social media on brand building and customer engagement. The research issue in this article is to analyze how brands can effectively use social media analytics to effectively assess customer engagement.

To do this, we will adopt a mixed qualitative methodological approach, combining bibliometric analysis via VOSviewer and textual analysis through the NVIVO V14 software post. In this chapter, we will begin by presenting the theoretical framework of the research, to identify the key concepts, an overview on the state of the art of the research question and the theories mobilized. Then, we will explain our methodological approach? Finally, we will develop the results of the study and their discussion.

2. THEORETICAL BACKGROUND

The rise of social media has transformed the way brands interact with their customers. These platforms offer a space for direct exchange and allow companies to measure the commitment of customers to their brand. The analysis of this engagement is crucial to understand customer perceptions, attitudes and behaviors, and thus adapt marketing strategies.

2.1. From brand to customer commitment to brand

2.1.1. The company's online brand

Online brand development levers are similar to the quality and relevance of shared content (Ashley & Tuten, 2015), the quality of the company's engagement with consumers (Brodie et al., 2013), and the quality of the customer experience (Bleier et al., 2019).

The targeted brand represents the online image that the company wants to project, while the perceived brand is the one actually perceived by consumers (Lane Keller, 2013). The gap in terms of perception of the company's brand image is often due to the lack of consistency of communication on the various channels (Fournier & Avery, 2011), its personalization while preserving the brand identity (De Vries et al., 2017) and online reputation management (Kietzmann et al., 2011).

A range of indicators can be distinguished to measure the effectiveness of online brand management, including engagement rates (Dessart et al., 2015), sentiment analysis (Liu, 2012), brand equity (Aaker, 1996), and net promoter score (Reichheld, 2003).

2.1.2. Customer commitment to brand

Customer Commitment to the Brand or simply Brand Engagement (BE) remains a multidimensional concept encompassing multiple cognitive, emotional and behavioral interactions of customers with a brand (Hollebeek, 2011). BE is a psychological process leading to the formation of fidelity (Bowden, 2009), a behavioral manifestation (Bijmolt et al., 2010; Van Doorn et al., 2010; Verhoef et al., 2010), or even a psychological state characterized by a degree of vigor, dedication, absorption and interaction (Patterson et al., 2006). In addition to this integrated approach, the BE is formed by continuous interactions between customers and a brand (Daqar & Smoudy 2019).

According to Dessart et al. (2016), BE stimulates consumer affiliate behavior and is expressed through various levels of emotional, cognitive and behavioral manifestations that go beyond immediate exchange relationships.

In summary, brand engagement refers to cognitive, emotional and behavioral activities that revolve around a consumer's focus and interaction with a brand (Chairy, 2020; Wulandari et al., 2022). On social media, it manifests itself through actions such as mentions, comments, shares and reactions.

2.2. Online Brand Engagement Assessment

The Online Customer Engagement Assessment (OCEA) refers to the analysis and measurement of the level of customer engagement with a company or brand on digital channels (Hollebeek et al., 2014). According to In the Online Context, this translates into customer interactions and behaviors towards a brand on digital channels, such as social media, websites, and mobile apps. This assessment identifies the strengths and weaknesses of the online experience to optimize customer engagement and retention (Brodie et al., 2013).

The assessment of online customer engagement with a brand can be done through a holistic approach (Brodie et al. (2013) incorporating cognitive, emotional and behavioral dimensions (Hollebeek et al. (2014). The implementation of actions of such a man oeuvre must meet several challenges inherent to the multiplicity of online channels (Voorveld et al., 2018), arbitrage in terms of quality vs quantity of interactions with the customer (Pansari & Kumar, 2017), data privacy issues (Malthouse et al., 2013) and the issue of rapid technological change (Wirtz et al., 2013).

The evaluation of online customer engagement necessitates the measurement and analysis of interactions and behaviors in order to ascertain the extent of customer engagement with the brand. Table 1 presents a summary of the principal key performance indicators utilized to assess online customer engagement with the brand.

Table1. KPI for effective OCEA

Indicator	Description	Reference
Interaction rate	This KPI measures the number of user interactions with brand content on social media (likes, shares, comments).	Hoffman & Fodor (2010); Mangold & Faulds (2009); Chaffey & Ellis-Chadwick (2019)
Conversion rate	The conversion rate measures the percentage of customers who perform a desired action, such as a purchase, registration or download. It is important to track the conversion rate for each digital channel in order to determine which ones are most effective in generating concrete results.	Zook & Smith (2016); Kumar & Reinartz (2016).
Commitment rate	It measures the percentage of followers or followers that interact with brand content.	Sabate et al. (2014)
Sentiment of online mentions	Sentiment analysis assesses customers' attitudes and emotions towards the brand based on their online comments and mentions.	Pang & Lee (2008); Liu (2022); Xiang et al (2015)
Client Retention Rate	This KPI measures the brand's ability to maintain lasting relationships with its online customers	Bijmolt et al. (2010)

continued on following page

Table1. Continued

Indicator	Description	Reference
Customer Lifetime Value	Estimates the potential value of a customer over the duration of their relationship with the brand, based on their interactions and purchases.	Gupta et al. (2004)
Net Promoter Score	This score measures the likelihood that customers will recommend the brand to others, which is a key indicator of engagement and loyalty.	Reichheld (2003); Kumar & Reinartz (2018)

Source: Authors.

On social networks in particular, the issue of evaluation of customer engagement with the brand is confronted with multiple issues:

- First, the issue of measuring engagement, and therefore the need for a range of metrics such as the number of likes, shares, comments ... (Coulter & Roggeveen, 2012; Hollebeek et al., 2014).
- Second, the role of feedback sentiment analysis in translating engagement (Schivinski & Dabrowski, 2016).
- In addition, the understanding of customers' motivations to interact with the brand on social media, including self-image, community belonging, etc. (Marbach et al., 2016; Muntinga et al., 2011).
- Also, integrating analysis of the influence of opinion leaders and its impact on other consumers (Chu & Kim, 2011; Munnukka et al., 2016).
- In addition, the relationship with strategy personalization, to the extent that such an assessment allows tailoring content and interactions with each customer segment (Hollebeek & Macky, 2019).
- Finally, the link with performance, where the level of customer engagement is generally associated with that of the brand's marketing and financial performance (Appel et al., 2020; Jayachandran et al., 2005).

It is evident that these issues underscore the significance of comprehending and quantifying customer engagement on social media in order to optimize the efficacy of brand strategies. Nevertheless, these issues simultaneously illustrate the intricacy of the approach, the proliferation of data, and the proliferation of methodologies. The integration of smart solutions, including social media analytics, is strongly encouraged.

2.3. Social Media Analytics for Brand Engagement

Social Media Analytics (SMA) is part of Social Marketing Analytics, approached as social marketing analysis is the discipline that helps companies measure, assess and explain the performance of social media initiatives in the context of specific business objectives (Owyang et al., 2010).

As summarized in Table 2, there is a suite of actionable SMA solutions to better assess customer engagement with the brand. Such solutions constitute a set of devices to monitor and analyze data collected in social networks, blogs, forums, to identify relevant information related to consumer perceptions, competitors, products, brands, and helping with marketing decisions through real-time feedback and actionable insights it provides (Anjanita, 2017; Sivarajah et al., 2019).

Table 2. Main SMA for evaluation brand commitment

Solution	Description	References
Sentiment Analysis	This technique uses natural language processing algorithms to detect and classify emotions and opinions expressed in online messages.	Liu (2022)
Social Network Analysis	It allows to study the interactions and relationships between users, influencers and online communities.	Wasserman & Faust (1994)
Trend Tracking	This approach involves monitoring and analyzing popular topics, keywords and hashtags to identify emerging trends and topics of interest.	Holsapple et al. (2018)
Online Reputation Analysis	It aims to monitor and manage the perception of the brand or company on social networks.	Pang & Lee (2008)
Predictive Analytics	Using machine learning and modeling techniques, this approach help predict future customer behaviors and trends.	Sivarajah et al. (2017)

Source: Authors.

According to Batrinca and Treleaven (2015), the SMA refers to the analysis of data generated by interactions on social networks to understand and optimize the engagement of customers and prospects. It is a set of techniques and tools that extract valuable information from conversations, comments, mentions, shares and other online activities (Batrinca & Treleaven, 2015).

2.4. State of the art

Social media analytics have become an essential tool for assessing customer engagement with the brand (Järvinen & Karjaluoto, 2015; Sano & Sano, 2020). According to Hollebeek et al. (2014), customer engagement with a brand is manifested through cognitive, emotional and behavioral interactions. These interactions can be measured through the analysis of data from social media (Dessart et al., 2016).

Many conceptual models have been proposed to assess customer engagement with a brand on social media. For example, the model of Hollebeek et al. (2019) identifies three dimensions of engagement: cognitive engagement, emotional engagement, and behavioral engagement. This model has been empirically validated in the context of social media by Harrigan et al. (2018).

Muntinga et al. (2011) also developed a model that distinguishes three levels of consumer engagement on social media: consumption, contribution, and content creation. This model was taken over and refined by Schivinski et al. (2016) in the context of the commitment to the brand.

In summary, the theoretical framework of this research builds on existing models of customer engagement with the brand on social media, with an emphasis on the cognitive, emotional and behavioral dimensions of that engagement (Harrigan et al., 2018; Hollebeek et al., 2019) and the different levels of engagement (Muntinga et al., 2011; Schivinski et al., 2016).

3. METHODOLOGY

3.1. Epistemological and methodological choices

To better base our theoretical study on the impact of SMA on Effective OCEA, we made rigorous epistemological and methodological choices.

On the one hand, we opt for pragmatism as a research paradigm and interpretivism as an epistemological posture. First, by conducting a literature review focused more on the usefulness and applicability of the knowledge produced rather than on ontological or epistemological debates. Then, seeking to understand in depth how ADMs influence the assessment of client engagement, analyzing the different perspectives and interpretations of the authors.

On the other hand, we make methodological choices centered on the review of exploratory literature as a research strategy, the systematic approach for data collection, thematic analysis for data analysis.

3.2. Data Collection Framework

To identify and select relevant sources, we have adopted a keyword-based approach (Dhamija & Bag, 2020). The main keywords included are combined in an equation to refine and increase the reach of the identified publications: ("Social Media Analytics" OR "Social Media Analysis" OR "Social Media Monitoring")

AND ("Customer Commitment" OR "Customer Engagement" OR "Brand Loyalty") AND ("Brand Assessment" OR "Brand Evaluation" OR "Brand Perception"). Since each database has its advantages and limitations, we searched the AI dimension database as an alternative to these reputable databases such as SCOPUS, WOS or Google Scholar (Dallas et al., 2018; Krauskopf, 2017; Martín-Martín et al., 2021; Singh et al., 2022), to centralize research and facilitate literature analysis.

To refine the initial results, we followed the PRISMA protocol (Preferred Reporting Items for Systematic Reviews and Meta-Analyses) (Mateo, 2020; Moher et al., 2009; Moher, PRISMA-P Group et al., 2015) to ensure relevance comprehensiveness and transferability of results. Dimension AI allows spreading the period of research from 1975 to the date of data extraction (2 may 2024), while the first identified publications return to the year 2009 when social networks began to gain momentum. This period makes it possible to identify a wide scope of publications in the field.

Using our search equation on the AI dimension database, we were able to identify 947 publications from various databases. Then, after removing duplicates and filtering results by search domain, we limited our corpus to 469 sources that are part of the «Commerce, Management, Tourism and Services» domain. This corpus serves as a basis for quantitative (bibliometric) analysis. Using other filters, we included 207 research articles with the exclusion of other types of publication, to finally include 90 open access articles for possible in-depth qualitative analysis. The following figure illustrates the different phases of the PRISMA protocol.

Figure 1. PRISMA flowchart (Adapted from Moher et al., 2009)

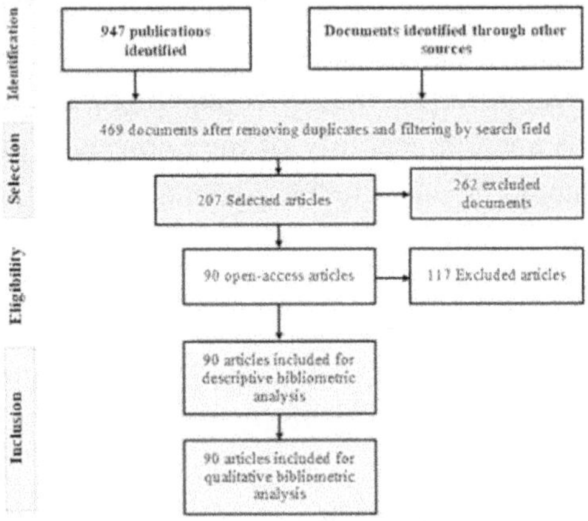

3.3. Data Analysis Approach

A mixed analysis of our corpus will be approached in two stages to understand the context and existing links between the solutions of the social media analysis and the evaluation of the customer's commitment to the brand (Kamila & Jasrotia, 2023a). Bibliometric (descriptive and qualitative) analysis serves as a basis to show the directions of the evolution of the field of study, so the literature review serves to summarize the state of the art on the subject.

4. RESULTS AND DISCUSSION

4.1. Descriptive bibliometric analysis

An analysis of descriptive statistics was conducted on the 469 references selected for quantitative analysis to understand trends in scientific production in the field. Using the VOSviewer bibliometric analysis software, we represented the scientific contribution in our subject by country, by year of publication and by journal of publication (Van Eck & Waltman, 2010).

4.1.1. Analysis by years of publication

The following visualization (Figure 2) shows the number of references published each year on social media analytics solutions for effective customer engagement with brand evaluation from 2015 to the extraction date.

Figure 2. Contributions published annually (Authors)

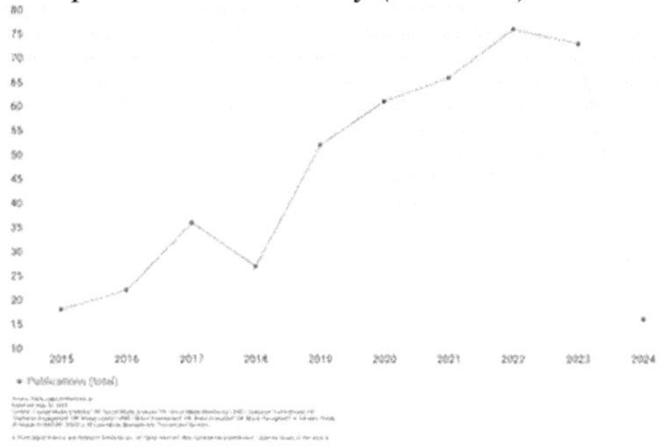

Over the years, scientific production has grown significantly with an increase in the number of publications each year. This trend can be explained by the increased importance given in recent years to social networks and their impact on consumer behavior and the brand image of companies. Although the first publication identified in this corpus returns to 2009, the number of publications remains low, and it is from 2015 that the volume of contributions begins to exceed 10 publications per year. A significant increase in the number of publications was observed from 2019 until the date of extraction thus representing 73% of the total of our corpus. This may be due to hyperconnectivity, caused by the increased use of social networks due to the effects of the Covid 19 pandemic. A slight decrease is observed in 2024 compared to the previous year, which is normal, given that we are still at the beginning of the year.

After evaluating the scientific contribution over the years according to the number of publications, a more qualitative approach was adopted by the reference assessment according to the overall number of citations (Kamila & Jasrotia, 2023b; Kumar et al., 2020). This is to assess the number of times publications have been cited by other publications in the database (Figure 3).

Figure 3. Citations by year (Authors)

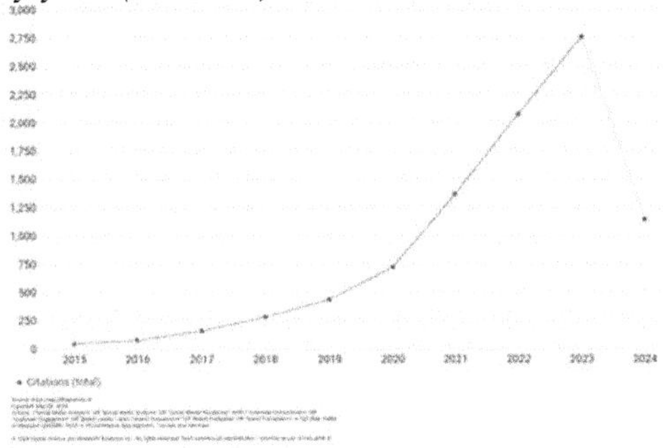

An increasing number of citations per year was observed. This indicates the growing interest of the scientific community in the existing literature in this field. A very significant attention needs to be highlighted from 2021, the year in which the publications reached a number of citations exceeding 1000 with a distinction of the years 2022 and 2023. This explains the relevance and importance of new publications among researchers in the field. The drop in the number of publications in 2024 is normal due to possible delays in indexing and considering citations of new publications.

4.1.2. Analysis of publications by journal title:

For the distribution of publications by source, we provided a list of the top 20 journals in which the publications in our sample were published, ranking them according to the relevance of the work published by each source (Table 3). The data will greatly assist researchers working on social media analytics and their importance to the consumer and brand. "International journal of information management has 912 citations, journal of marketing has 665 citations, Journal of retailing and consumer services has 479 citations, international journal of research in marketing has 427 citations, and the list goes on. They are the most contributing journals in this field.

Table 3. Main publication sources

Source	Documents	Citations
International Journal of Information Management	2	912
Journal of Marketing	2	665
Journal of Retailing and Consumer Services	5	479
International Journal of Research in Marketing	5	427
Journal of Business Research	9	377
International Journal of Advertising	4	333
Journal of the Academy of Marketing Science	2	319
Tourism Management	6	240
Journal of Advertising	2	230
International Journal of Contemporary Hospitality Management	3	167
International Journal of Production Economics	1	161
Information Technology and People	3	135
Psychology and Marketing	3	133
Journal of Destination Marketing & Management	2	127
Journal of Brand Management	6	107
European Journal of Marketing	5	102
International Journal of Event and Festival Management	1	102
Journal of Marketing Management	3	93
Australasian Marketing Journal (AMJ)	1	87
Journal of Travel Research	2	85

Source: Authors.

4.1.3. Analysis of publications by country:

The distribution of publications by country makes it possible to bring several insights to researchers. The Table 4 presents a state of the top performing countries in scientific research in our field.

Table 4. Scientific contributions by country

Country	Documents	Citations		Country	Documents	Citations
United States	49	2845		Spain	9	441
United Kingdom	34	2173		Malaysia	11	373
Finland	6	1883		Italy	14	353
Australia	27	1801		Portugal	6	170
India	26	1626		Netherlands	7	158
Germany	14	1342		Taiwan	6	141
France	7	1006		Turkey	7	126
Canada	9	998		South Africa	5	89
China	27	595		South Korea	7	59
Cyprus	6	445		Iran	5	44

Source: Authors.

4.2. Qualitative bibliometric analysis

Bibliometric analysis is possible with several software available, the choice of «VOSviewer: simple application and mediated by the scientific community» because it implies a wide acceptance (Van Eck & Waltman, 2010). It can analyze information from Scopus, Web of Science, dimensions or any other program. The current study aims to analyze and interpret a large amount of data for a literature review. The following subsections will cover the author's influence, the most cited documents in the world, data on the most popular keywords and search terms regarding social media analytics and customer brand evaluation.

4.2.1 Analysis of keyword occurrences

Keywords are one of the essential components of search engines. Proper keyword selection is crucial to getting more contributions. Here is a list of the main search terms for which «brand» is the main keyword. The frequency of occurrence of the most listed keywords is revealed by the following word cloud. Terms such as "social media"; "Marketing"; "Customer"; "Consumer"; "Engagement"; "Content" and others were highlighted (Figure 4). These keywords highlight the main terms addressed by the literature; the predominance of these keywords shows the relevance of our corpus.

Figure 4. Word cloud (Authors)

4.2.2. Citation network analysis and co-citations

Through matrices and visualizations established by the software, a network analysis of citations, co-citations, co-occurrence of keywords was conducted. To do this, we used the dimensions database to meet our search criteria, and then we used the VOSviewer tool by importing the sources exported from AI dimension. Results include citation analysis, co-citation analysis, and co-occurrence network.

- *Citation analysis*

Citation analysis involves examining the intellectual links between the publications of one article referring to another (Appio et al., 2014). The evaluation of the impact of the publication in the eyes of the scientific community can be measured by the number of citations it receives from other works. Based on the analysis of citations and contributions from previous years of our corpus, the following table presents the top 20 most influential authors.

Table 5. Author performance analysis

Authors	Documents	Citations		Authors	Documents	Citations
Dwivedi, Yogesh K.	4	938		Rosenberger, Philip J.	2	132
Rauschnael, Philipp A.	2	926		Moro, Sérgio	2	126
Filieri, Raffaele	2	912		Lim, Weng Marc	2	111
Salo, Jari	2	906		Shankar, Venkatesh	2	95
Larimo, Jorma	2	334		Akkiraju, Rama	2	75
Leonidou, Leonidas C.	2	334		Gal, David	2	75
Li, Fangfang	2	334		Hong, Yili	2	75
Cheung, Man Lai	4	224		Hu, Yuheng	2	75
Leung, Wilson K.S.	4	224		Akter, Shahriar	3	70
Aw, Eugene Cheng-Xi	2	133		Moon, Sangkil	3	41

Source: Authors.

With 938 citations and 4 publications, (Arora et al., 2019; Dwivedi et al., 2021; P. Kumar et al., 2021; Varela-Neira et al., 2022) tops the list. Other authors then arrive with very close citations and fewer publications (Bazi et al., 2023; Cripps et al., 2020; Filieri et al., 2023; Rauschnabel et al., 2019) are among the authors who have contributed significantly to research in the field.

- *Co-citation analysis*

Co-citation analysis examines the relationship between existing works between references, sources or authors. The studied network that links two publications when they appear simultaneously in the references of another article makes it possible to highlight the link between the collaboration of the authors and the network of co-citations between the authors (Kaur et al., 2024). The following visualization illustrates the kinship of the researchers according to the number of times they cite each other. With the help of VOSviewer, we created a co-citation network between the authors of this study. The minimum number of citations for an author is set at 20. Of the 44,391 authors, VOSviewer has identified 338 that meet these thresholds.

Figure 5. Main author co-citations network (Compiled by authors using VOSviewer Dimensions AI)

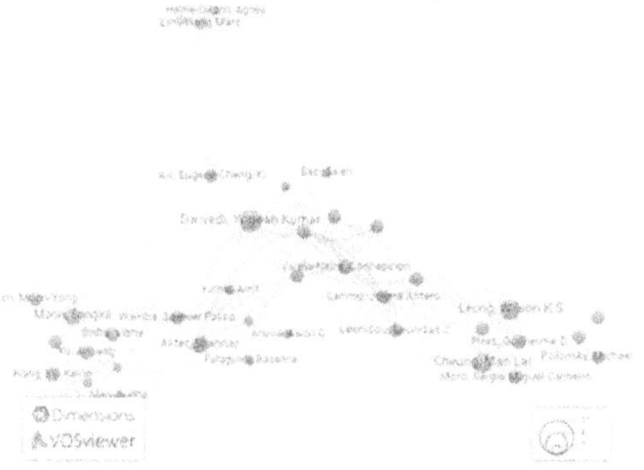

4.2.3. Keyword cooccurrence analysis

Using VOSviewer network analysis, we performed a clustering of data with similar characteristics in a single location called Cluster (Goel et al., 2022). We set the limit of the minimum number of occurrences of a keyword to "10"; the result shows that out of 9,492 keywords, 253 reach the threshold. The VOSviewer separates the 152 items into 3 clusters, 7843 links. Then, these knowledge groups are explored using cognition, in which the keywords of each group are logically arranged to reveal the subjects of previous studies.

Figure 6. Connecting keywords (Authors)

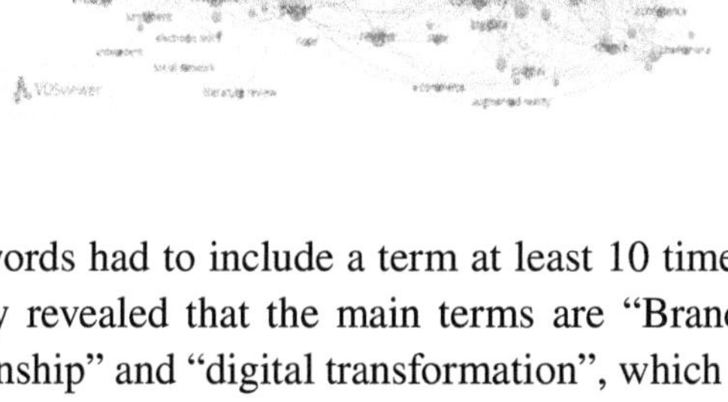

The article keywords had to include a term at least 10 times to be included in Figure 6. The study revealed that the main terms are "Brand", "management", "Content", "Relationship" and "digital transformation", which explains the significant intersection between the different terms that constitute our research object.

Recalling that the co-occurrence of keywords measures the most popular and frequent keywords in the same references (Kraus et al., 2020; Vallaster et al., 2019), this visualization suggests that the link of this term is significant. The importance of the term is underlined by its frequent co-occurrence with other popular keywords.

4.3 Literature Review

The Table 6 presents the main contributions of the top 10 most cited works.

Table 6. Literature review

Authors	Main conclusions	Number of citations
Dwivedi et al. (2021)	The use of the internet and social media has disrupted business practices and consumer behavior.	882
Arora et al. (2019)	Social and digital marketing offer allows organizations to reduce costs, build awareness and increase sales.	329
Li et al. (2020)	Negative word of mouth and intrusion are major challenges in the presence of an online brand.	314
Moro & Rita (2018)	This study proposes mechanisms and indices (engagement, reach, sentiment and growth) to measure the popularity of social media platforms such as Facebook, Twitter and Instagram.	112
Vermeer et al. (2019)	This study offers insights for e-commerce, viral marketing, social media marketing, brand management	98
Aydin (2019)	This study presents the definition, conceptualization and taxonomy of SMMSs	78
Giglio et al. (2020)	This study details the SMMSs development process including engines, inputs, flows and outputs.	72
Roma & Aloini (2019)	The study reveals a strong link between social media and brand building stages, but other brand strategies like co-branding and franchising require special attention. A concentration also on the tourism and hotel sector is important.	70
Helme-Guizon & Magnoni, (2019)	Marketers have difficulty tracking and analyzing eWOM on social media.	61
Poulis et al. (2019)	Sentiment analysis allows companies to identify eWOM content that is relevant to the response and commitment to the brand.	61

Source: Authors.

Following a more in-depth analysis of the full-text articles, we were able to identify the following synthesis of the main SMA Solutions and PKI of brand commitment (Table 7).

Table 7. Summary of results

SMA Solution	KPI for Effective OCEA
Classical Solutions: • Social Media Monitoring Platforms • Text Analysis Tools • Data Visualization Tools • Social Listening Tools • Social Media Analytics Dashboards • Social Media Advertising Platforms • Social Network Analysis	**Scope of commitment:** • Brand Mentions or Discussions • Likes, Shares or Comments on Brand-Related Posts • Virality of User-Generated Content • Interaction Between Users and Brand-Generated Content • Likes, Shares or Comments on Brand Posts • Frequency and Regularity of Consumer Interaction with the Brand on Social Media • Brand Awareness
Smart Solutions: • Text Mining And Topic Modeling • Machine Learning • Semantic Analysis • Computer Vision • Natural Language Processing • Sentiment Analysis • Social Media Analytics	**Depth of commitment:** • Level of Emotional Brand Commitment • Diversity and Relevance of User-Generated Content • Consumer Identification and Emotional Attachment to the Brand • Consumer Participation in Interactive Brand Activities • Brand Loyalty • Electronic Word-Of-Mouth (eWOM) • Purchase Intent

Source: Authors.

In fact, the appreciation of the scale and breadth of the commitment of customers to the brand on social networks, under these aspects both quantitative and qualitative, requires the combination of a range of Social Media Analytics solutions, both traditional and smart.

4.4. Discussion and analysis model sketch

Social media analytics solutions play a critical role in assessing online customer engagement. These tools allow companies to track, analyze and optimize their social media communication efforts to improve customer interaction and loyalty (Aral et al., 2013; Gao et al., 2018). The content, sentiment and influence analyses offered by these solutions help marketers better understand their customers' preferences and behaviors online (Batrinca & Treleaven, 2015; Chaffey & Patron, 2012). This allows them to adapt their customer engagement strategies and optimize the user experience on their digital channels (Lamberton & Stephen, 2016; Tuten & Solomon, 2017). Companies that use these solutions effectively are able to increase customer satisfaction, retention and lifetime value (Kumar et al., 2016; Trainor et al., 2014).

Based on the results of our theoretical study (Table 3 and Table 4), we can propose a framework of analysis of the impact of social media analytics solutions on the effectiveness of the evaluation of customer engagement with the brand on social networks (Figure 7).

Figure 7. Analysis model sketch (Authors)

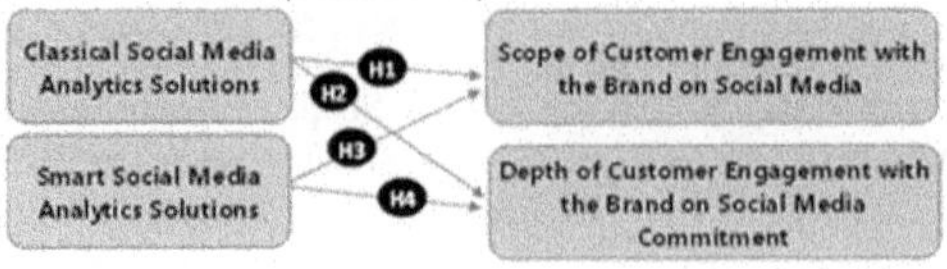

The following main hypotheses are based on such a model framework:

Hypothesis 1: The use of Classical Social Media Analytics Solutions (CSMAS) helps improve the effectiveness of the Scope of Customer Engagement with the Brand on Social Media (SCEB) assessment.

To this end, Peters et al. (2013) point out that traditional social media analytics solutions track reach metrics such as mentions, shares and audience size, helping to assess the Scope of Customer Engagement. Similarly, Luo et al. (2013) showed that the volume of online conversations (buzz) around a brand is related to the value of the company, reinforcing the importance of evaluating the SCEB.

Using this data, companies can identify trends and patterns in online conversations, allowing them to adjust their marketing strategies to maximize their reach and engagement (Batrinca & Treleaven, 2015).

Hypothesis 2: The use of Classical Social Media Analytics Solutions (CSMAS) helps improve the effectiveness of the Depth of Customer Engagement with the Brand on Social Media Commitment (DCEB) assessment.

Ghiassi et al. (2016) developed a hybrid sentiment analysis system for social media that combined n-gram analysis and neural networks to assess the depth of emotional engagement. Also, Rambocas and Pacheco (2018) treated negation and intensifiers in sentiment analysis, improving the accuracy of the DCEB assessment. By understanding these qualitative aspects, companies can better understand the strength and nature of their customers' engagement, allowing them to tailor their communications and offerings accordingly (Schweidel & Moe, 2014).

Hypothesis 3: The use of Smart Social Media Analytics Solutions (SSMAS) helps improve the effectiveness of the Scope of Customer Engagement with the Brand on Social Media (SCEB) assessment.

Accordingly, He et al. (2015) emphasize that intelligent analytics solutions are capable of analyzing unstructured data, including text, images, and videos. This enables the capture of a more comprehensive range of interactions, thereby reflecting the SCEB. Furthermore, Stieglitz et al. (2018) identified the challenges of topic discovery, data collection, and data preparation in SSMAS, which are crucial for an accurate assessment of SCEB. Consequently, SSMAS provides a more precise and comprehensive evaluation of the extent of customer engagement on social media.

Hypothesis 4: The use of Smart Social Media Analytics Solutions (SSMAS) helps improve the effectiveness of the Depth of Customer Engagement with the Brand on Social Media Commitment (DCEB) assessment.

In this regard, Ruan et al. (2019) used deep learning and advanced sentiment analysis on Twitter to better understand users' intentions and motivations, contributing to the assessment of DCEB. Also, Schweidel and Moe (2014) proposed a model that combines feelings and social media formats, offering a richer perspective on the depth of emotional engagement (DCEB).

This framework of analysis model, after possible purification and adaptations about specificities (sector, size of the company, level of customer empowerment, maturity of digital transformation, evolution of data analysis technologies, ...), provides a basis for future quantitative studies to test research hypotheses.

Table 8. Prospective analysis

Future trends **• Increased use of AI, augmented reality, digital marketing and content** **• Growing use of social media influence indexes** **• Social media marketing strategy (SMMS)** **• Use of machine learning to analyze relevant eWOM on social networks** **• Increased engagement with lively, interactive content on social media**	**Opportunities** **• Cost reduction** **• Improved brand awareness** **• Increase sales** **• Identification of key information multipliers** **• Social media promotion and engagement** **• Strategic development based on SMMS maturity** **• Increased efficiency in social marketing** **• Improved identification of relevant eWOM through industry-specific classifiers** **• Increased subscriber interaction through effective organic posts** **• Identification of key success factors in branding strategies**
Challenges • Dealing with negative online reviews • presence of intrusive brands • Accuracy in measuring influence through various algorithms • Complexity of implementing machine learning techniques for accurate analysis • Create content that captures attention and stimulates user engagement • Analyze the vast amount of data generated by interactions on social networks	**Practical implications** • Improved reach and effectiveness of e-commerce, viral marketing, social media marketing, and brand management through the analysis of influencers. • Improved marketing strategy through the systematic classification and empirical validation of SMMS. • The implementation of automated analysis techniques is enabling the identification of relationships between social media and branding. • Improved efficiency of eWOM tracking and analysis through the application of machine learning techniques to identify relevant comments requiring a response. • Enhancing the efficacy of organic publications by concentrating on dynamic, interactive content. • Employing text analytics to comprehend the influence of social media on brand strategies, thereby facilitating the formulation of more efficacious communication strategies.

Source: Authors.

5. CONCLUSION

Online customer engagement assessment is a complex process that requires the use of multiple KPIs. By tracking these metrics, companies can better understand how customers interact with their brand and identify areas for improvement.

Online customer engagement has become a crucial element for companies looking to stand out in an increasingly competitive market. It is an ongoing process of building strong and lasting relationships with customers across all digital channels.

Assessing online customer engagement is key to measuring the effectiveness of marketing strategies and identifying areas for improvement. It allows companies to understand how customers interact with their brand on social networks, websites and other digital platforms.

By developing a robust conceptual model, this research will help close the current gap in understanding the impact of social media on brand development and customer engagement. This knowledge will help marketers make more informed decisions to improve their social media marketing strategies.

This research makes an important contribution to understanding the evaluation of online customer engagement, especially on social media. Indeed, after the conceptual and theoretical framing of the question, the chapter proposed a framework of solid conceptual analysis model to evaluate online customer engagement, by integrating key dimensions such as interaction, satisfaction and social influence (justified by the abstract). This allowed us to highlight the crucial importance of online customer engagement for business success in a competitive digital environment (Vinerean & Opreana, 2021). The research also highlighted challenges related to evaluating online customer engagement, including the need to analyze interactions in real time, understand customer feelings and expectations, and identify opportunities for improvement.

Similarly, the mixed methodological approach, combining bibliometric and textual analysis, made it possible to study the subject in depth.

The initial challenge of this research was to analyze how brands can effectively use social media analytics to assess online customer engagement (justified by the introduction). In response to this issue, the study's results propose a conceptual analysis model that integrates key dimensions of customer engagement, such as interaction, satisfaction and social influence. This model will allow companies to understand customer interactions with their brand better and identify areas for improvement, thus bridging the current lack of understanding of the impact of social media on brand building and customer engagement (justified by the conclusion).

Although the research is intended to be exploratory, the limits of research must be mentioned. Particularly at the methodological level,

The proposed conceptual model may need to be revised in its ability to capture the full complexity of online customer engagement, requiring refinements and integration of other relevant dimensions. Similarly, the mixed methodological approach combining bibliometric and textual analysis could have limitations in terms of data representativeness and generalization of results.

To deepen the research on the subject, this study offers valuable perspectives. Indeed, the integration of technological developments and interdisciplinary perspectives makes it possible to respond to the evolving nature of social media analysis in a holistic approach. Thus, the comparative analysis of the various social media analysis tools (ADMs) will provide practical insights to professionals while focusing on ethical considerations to promote responsible data protection practices. Future research could explore case studies and concrete applications with suitable methodologies and possible empirical validations.

REFERENCES

Aaker, D. A. (1996). Measuring brand equity across products and markets. *California Management Review*, 38(3), 102–120. DOI: 10.2307/41165845

Appel, G., Grewal, L., Hadi, R., & Stephen, A. T. (2020). The future of social media in marketing. *Journal of the Academy of Marketing Science*, 48(1), 79–95. DOI: 10.1007/s11747-019-00695-1 PMID: 32431463

Appio, F. P., Cesaroni, F., & Di Minin, A. (2014). Visualizing the structure and bridges of the intellectual property management and strategy literature: A document co-citation analysis. *Scientometrics*, 101(1), 623–661. DOI: 10.1007/s11192-014-1329-0

Aral, S., Dellarocas, C., & Godes, D. (2013). Introduction to the special issue - social media and business transformation: A framework for research. *Information Systems Research*, 24(1), 3–13. DOI: 10.1287/isre.1120.0470

Arora, A., Bansal, S., Kandpal, C., Aswani, R., & Dwivedi, Y. (2019). Measuring social media influencer index-insights from Facebook, Twitter and Instagram. *Journal of Retailing and Consumer Services*, 49, 86–101. DOI: 10.1016/j.jretconser.2019.03.012

Ashley, C., & Tuten, T. (2015). Creative strategies in social media marketing: An exploratory study of branded social content and consumer engagement. *Psychology and Marketing*, 32(1), 15–27. DOI: 10.1002/mar.20761

Aydin, G. (2020). Social media engagement and organic post effectiveness: A roadmap for increasing the effectiveness of social media use in hospitality industry. *Journal of Hospitality Marketing & Management*, 29(1), 1–21. DOI: 10.1080/19368623.2019.1588824

Batrinca, B., & Treleaven, P. C. (2015). Social media analytics: A survey of techniques, tools and platforms. *AI & Society*, 30(1), 89–116. DOI: 10.1007/s00146-014-0549-4

Bazi, S., Filieri, R., & Gorton, M. (2023). Social media content aesthetic quality and customer engagement: The mediating role of entertainment and impacts on brand love and loyalty. *Journal of Business Research*, 160, 113778. DOI: 10.1016/j.jbusres.2023.113778

Bijmolt, T. H., Leeflang, P. S., Block, F., Eisenbeiss, M., Hardie, B. G., Lemmens, A., & Saffert, P. (2010). Analytics for customer engagement. *Journal of Service Research*, 13(3), 341–356. DOI: 10.1177/1094670510375603

Bleier, A., Harmeling, C. M., & Palmatier, R. W. (2019). Creating effective online customer experiences. *Journal of Marketing*, 83(2), 98–119. DOI: 10.1177/0022242918809930

Bowden, J. L. H. (2009). The process of customer engagement: A conceptual framework. *Journal of Marketing Theory and Practice*, 17(1), 63–74. DOI: 10.2753/MTP1069-6679170105

Brodie, R. J., Ilic, A., Juric, B., & Hollebeek, L. (2013). Consumer engagement in a virtual brand community: An exploratory analysis. *Journal of Business Research*, 66(1), 105–114. DOI: 10.1016/j.jbusres.2011.07.029

Chaffey, D., Ellis-Chadwick, F., & Mayer, R. (2009). *Internet marketing: strategy, implementation and practice*. Pearson Education.

Chaffey, D., & Patron, M. (2012). From web analytics to digital marketing optimization: Increasing the commercial value of digital analytics. *Journal of Direct, Data and Digital Marketing Practice*, 14(1), 30–45. DOI: 10.1057/dddmp.2012.20

Chu, S. C., & Kim, Y. (2011). Determinants of consumer engagement in electronic word-of-mouth (eWOM) in social networking sites. *International Journal of Advertising*, 30(1), 47–75. DOI: 10.2501/IJA-30-1-047-075

Coulter, K. S., & Roggeveen, A. (2012). "Like it or not" Consumer responses to word-of-mouth communication in on-line social networks. *Management Research Review*, 35(9), 878–899. DOI: 10.1108/01409171211256587

Cripps, H., Singh, A., Mejtoft, T., & Salo, J. (2020). The use of Twitter for innovation in business markets. *Marketing Intelligence & Planning*, 38(5), 587–601. DOI: 10.1108/MIP-06-2019-0349

Dallas, T., Gehman, A. L., & Farrell, M. J. (2018). Variable bibliographic database access could limit reproducibility. *Bioscience*, 68(8), 552–553. DOI: 10.1093/biosci/biy074

De Vries, L., Gensler, S., & Leeflang, P. S. (2017). Effects of traditional advertising and social messages on brand-building metrics and customer acquisition. *Journal of Marketing*, 81(5), 1–15. DOI: 10.1509/jm.15.0178

Dessart, L., Veloutsou, C., & Morgan-Thomas, A. (2015). Consumer engagement in online brand communities: A social media perspective. *Journal of Product and Brand Management*, 24(1), 28–42. DOI: 10.1108/JPBM-06-2014-0635

Dessart, L., Veloutsou, C., & Morgan-Thomas, A. (2016). Capturing consumer engagement: Duality, dimensionality and measurement. *Journal of Marketing Management*, 32(5-6), 399–426. DOI: 10.1080/0267257X.2015.1130738

Dhamija, P., & Bag, S. (2020). Role of artificial intelligence in operations environment: A review and bibliometric analysis. *The TQM Journal*, 32(4), 869–896. DOI: 10.1108/TQM-10-2019-0243

Dwivedi, Y. K., Ismagilova, E., Hughes, D. L., Carlson, J., Filieri, R., Jacobson, J., Jain, V., Karjaluoto, H., Kefi, H., Krishen, A. S., Kumar, V., Rahman, M. M., Raman, R., Rauschnabel, P. A., Rowley, J., Salo, J., Tran, G. A., & Wang, Y. (2021). Setting the future of digital and social media marketing research: Perspectives and research propositions. *International Journal of Information Management*, 59, 102168. DOI: 10.1016/j.ijinfomgt.2020.102168

Filieri, R., Alguezaui, S., Galati, F., & Raguseo, E. (2023). Customer experience with standard and premium Peer-To-Peer offerings: A mixed-method combining text analytics and qualitative analysis. *Journal of Business Research*, 167, 114128. DOI: 10.1016/j.jbusres.2023.114128

Fournier, S., & Avery, J. (2011). The uninvited brand. *Business Horizons*, 54(3), 193–207. DOI: 10.1016/j.bushor.2011.01.001

Gao, G. Y., Xie, E., & Zhou, K. Z. (2015). How does technological diversity in supplier network drive buyer innovation? Relational process and contingencies. *Journal of Operations Management*, 36(1), 165–177. DOI: 10.1016/j.jom.2014.06.001

Ghiassi, M., Skinner, J., & Zimbra, D. (2013). Twitter brand sentiment analysis: A hybrid system using n-gram analysis and dynamic artificial neural network. *Expert Systems with Applications*, 40(16), 6266–6282. DOI: 10.1016/j.eswa.2013.05.057

Giglio, S., Pantano, E., Bilotta, E., & Melewar, T. C. (2020). Branding luxury hotels: Evidence from the analysis of consumers' "big" visual data on TripAdvisor. *Journal of Business Research*, 119, 495–501. DOI: 10.1016/j.jbusres.2019.10.053

Goel, P., Garg, A., Walia, N., Kaur, R., Jain, M., & Singh, S. (2021). Contagious diseases and tourism: A systematic review based on bibliometric and content analysis methods. *Quality & Quantity*, 56(5), 3085–3110. DOI: 10.1007/s11135-021-01270-z PMID: 34697508

Gupta, S., Lehmann, D. R., & Stuart, J. A. (2004). Valuing customers. *JMR, Journal of Marketing Research*, 41(1), 7–18. DOI: 10.1509/jmkr.41.1.7.25084

He, W., Shen, J., Tian, X., Li, Y., Akula, V., Yan, G., & Tao, R. (2015). Gaining competitive intelligence from social media data: Evidence from two largest retail chains in the world. *Industrial Management & Data Systems*, 115(9), 1622–1636. DOI: 10.1108/IMDS-03-2015-0098

Helme-Guizon, A., & Magnoni, F. (2019). Consumer brand engagement and its social side on brand-hosted social media: How do they contribute to brand loyalty? *Journal of Marketing Management*, 35(7-8), 716–741. DOI: 10.1080/0267257X.2019.1599990

Hoffman, D. L., & Fodor, M. (2010). Can you measure the ROI of your social media marketing? *MIT Sloan Management Review*. https://sloanreview.mit.edu/article/can-you-measure-the-roi-of-your-social-media-marketing/

Hollebeek, L. D. (2011). Demystifying customer brand engagement: Exploring the loyalty nexus. *Journal of Marketing Management*, 27(7-8), 785–807. DOI: 10.1080/0267257X.2010.500132

Hollebeek, L. D., Glynn, M. S., & Brodie, R. J. (2014). Consumer brand engagement in social media: Conceptualization, scale development and validation. *Journal of Interactive Marketing*, 28(2), 149–165. DOI: 10.1016/j.intmar.2013.12.002

Hollebeek, L. D., & Macky, K. (2019). Digital content marketing's role in fostering consumer engagement, trust, and value: Framework, fundamental propositions, and implications. *Journal of Interactive Marketing*, 45(1), 27–41. DOI: 10.1016/j.intmar.2018.07.003

Holsapple, C. W., Hsiao, S. H., & Pakath, R. (2018). Business social media analytics: Characterization and conceptual framework. *Decision Support Systems*, 110, 32–45. DOI: 10.1016/j.dss.2018.03.004

Jayachandran, S., Sharma, S., Kaufman, P., & Raman, P. (2005). The role of relational information processes and technology use in customer relationship management. *Journal of Marketing*, 69(4), 177–192. DOI: 10.1509/jmkg.2005.69.4.177

Kamila, M. K., & Jasrotia, S. S. (2023a). Ethics and marketing responsibility: A bibliometric analysis and literature review. *Asia Pacific Management Review*, 28(4), 567–583. DOI: 10.1016/j.apmrv.2023.04.002

Kamila, M. K., & Jasrotia, S. S. (2023b). Ethics in product marketing: A bibliometric analysis. *Asian Journal of Business Ethics*, 12(2), 151–174. DOI: 10.1007/s13520-023-00168-3

Kaur, A., Kumar, V., Sindhwani, R., Singh, P. L., & Behl, A. (2024). Public debt sustainability: A bibliometric co-citation visualization analysis. *International Journal of Emerging Markets*, 19(4), 1090–1110. DOI: 10.1108/IJOEM-04-2022-0724

Kietzmann, J. H., Hermkens, K., McCarthy, I. P., & Silvestre, B. S. (2011). Social media? Get serious! Understanding the functional building blocks of social media. *Business Horizons*, 54(3), 241–251. DOI: 10.1016/j.bushor.2011.01.005

Kraus, S., Li, H., Kang, Q., Westhead, P., & Tiberius, V. (2020). The sharing economy: A bibliometric analysis of the state-of-the-art. *International Journal of Entrepreneurial Behaviour & Research*, 26(8), 1769–1786. DOI: 10.1108/IJEBR-06-2020-0438

Krauskopf, E. (2017). Call for caution in the use of bibliometric data. *Journal of the Association for Information Science and Technology*, 68(8), 2029–2032. DOI: 10.1002/asi.23809

Kumar, P., Polonsky, M., Dwivedi, Y. K., & Kar, A. (2021). Green information quality and green brand evaluation: The moderating effects of eco-label credibility and consumer knowledge. *European Journal of Marketing*, 55(7), 2037–2071. DOI: 10.1108/EJM-10-2019-0808

Kumar, S., Sureka, R., & Colombage, S. (2020). Capital structure of SMEs: A systematic literature review and bibliometric analysis. *Management Review Quarterly*, 70(4), 535–565. DOI: 10.1007/s11301-019-00175-4

Kumar, V., Dixit, A., Javalgi, R. G., & Dass, M. (2016). Research framework, strategies, and applications of intelligent agent technologies (IATs) in marketing. *Journal of the Academy of Marketing Science*, 44(1), 24–45. DOI: 10.1007/s11747-015-0426-9

Kumar, V., & Reinartz, W. (2018). *Customer Relationship Management: Concept, Strategy, and Tools*. Springer. DOI: 10.1007/978-3-662-55381-7

Lamberton, C., & Stephen, A. T. (2016). A thematic exploration of digital, social media, and mobile marketing: Research evolution from 2000 to 2015 and an agenda for future inquiry. *Journal of Marketing*, 80(6), 146–172. DOI: 10.1509/jm.15.0415

Lane Keller, K. (2013). *Strategic Brand Managment: Building, Measuring, and Managing Brand Equity*. Pearson Education Limited.

Li, F., Larimo, J., & Leonidou, L. C. (2021). Social media marketing strategy: Definition, conceptualization, taxonomy, validation, and future agenda. *Journal of the Academy of Marketing Science*, 49(1), 51–70. DOI: 10.1007/s11747-020-00733-3

Liu, B. (2022). *Sentiment analysis and opinion mining*. Springer Nature.

Luo, X., Zhang, J., & Duan, W. (2013). Social media and firm equity value. *Information Systems Research*, 24(1), 146–163. DOI: 10.1287/isre.1120.0462

Malthouse, E. C., Haenlein, M., Skiera, B., Wege, E., & Zhang, M. (2013). Managing customer relationships in the social media era: Introducing the social CRM house. *Journal of Interactive Marketing*, 27(4), 270–280. DOI: 10.1016/j.intmar.2013.09.008

Mangold, W. G., & Faulds, D. J. (2009). Social media: The new hybrid element of the promotion mix. *Business Horizons*, 52(4), 357–365. DOI: 10.1016/j.bushor.2009.03.002

Marbach, J., Lages, C. R., & Nunan, D. (2016). Who are you and what do you value? Investigating the role of personality traits and customer-perceived value in online customer engagement. *Journal of Marketing Management*, 32(5-6), 502–525. DOI: 10.1080/0267257X.2015.1128472

Martín-Martín, A., Thelwall, M., Orduna-Malea, E., & Delgado López-Cózar, E. (2021). Google Scholar, Microsoft Academic, Scopus, Dimensions, Web of Science, and OpenCitations' COCI: A multidisciplinary comparison of coverage via citations. *Scientometrics*, 126(1), 871–906. DOI: 10.1007/s11192-020-03690-4 PMID: 32981987

Mateo, S. (2020). Procédure pour conduire avec succès une revue de littérature selon la méthode PRISMA. *Kinésithérapie, la Revue*, 20(226), 29–37. DOI: 10.1016/j.kine.2020.05.019

Moher, D., Liberati, A., Tetzlaff, J., & Altman, D. G. (2009). Preferred reporting items for systematic reviews and meta-analyses: The PRISMA statement. *Annals of Internal Medicine*, 151(4), 264–269. DOI: 10.7326/0003-4819-151-4-200908180-00135 PMID: 19622511

Moher, D., Shamseer, L., Clarke, M., Ghersi, D., Liberati, A., Petticrew, M., Shekelle, P., & Stewart, L. A.Prisma-P Group. (2015). Preferred reporting items for systematic review and meta-analysis protocols (PRISMA-P) 2015 statement. *Systematic Reviews*, 4(1), 1–9. DOI: 10.1186/2046-4053-4-1 PMID: 25554246

Moon, S., & Iacobucci, D. (2022). Social media analytics and its applications in marketing. *Foundations and Trends® in Marketing, 15*(4), 213-292.

Moro, S., & Rita, P. (2018). Brand strategies in social media in hospitality and tourism. *International Journal of Contemporary Hospitality Management*, 30(1), 343–364. DOI: 10.1108/IJCHM-07-2016-0340

Munnukka, J., Uusitalo, O., & Toivonen, H. (2016). Credibility of a peer endorser and advertising effectiveness. *Journal of Consumer Marketing*, 33(3), 182–192. DOI: 10.1108/JCM-11-2014-1221

Muntinga, D. G., Moorman, M., & Smit, E. G. (2011). Introducing COBRAs: Exploring motivations for brand-related social media use. *International Journal of Advertising*, 30(1), 13–46. DOI: 10.2501/IJA-30-1-013-046

Owyang, J., Lovett, J., Peterson, E. T., Li, C., & Tran, C. (2010). *Social marketing analytics: A new framework for measuring results in social media*. Altimeter Group.

Pang, B., & Lee, L. (2008). Opinion mining and sentiment analysis. *Foundations and Trends® in Information Retrieval, 2*(1-2), 1-135.

Pansari, A., & Kumar, V. (2017). Customer engagement: The construct, antecedents, and consequences. *Journal of the Academy of Marketing Science*, 45(3), 294–311. DOI: 10.1007/s11747-016-0485-6

Patterson, P., Yu, T., & De Ruyter, K. (2006, December). Understanding customer engagement in services. In *Advancing theory, maintaining relevance, proceedings of ANZMAC 2006 conference*, Brisbane (Vol. 4, No. 6, pp. 1-8).

Peters, K., Chen, Y., Kaplan, A. M., Ognibeni, B., & Pauwels, K. (2013). Social media metrics—A framework and guidelines for managing social media. *Journal of Interactive Marketing*, 27(4), 281–298. DOI: 10.1016/j.intmar.2013.09.007

Poulis, A., Rizomyliotis, I., & Konstantoulaki, K. (2019). Do firms still need to be social? Firm generated content in social media. *Information Technology & People*, 32(2), 387–404. DOI: 10.1108/ITP-03-2018-0134

Ramadhan, A. I. (2020). Pengaruh Brand Image, Product Involvement, dan Brand Engagement Terhadap Purchase Intention Teh Pucuk di Kota Jakarta. *Jurnal Manajemen Bisnis dan Kewirausahaan, 4*(1), 42-47.

Rambocas, M., & Pacheco, B. G. (2018). Online sentiment analysis in marketing research: A review. *Journal of Research in Interactive Marketing*, 12(2), 146–163. DOI: 10.1108/JRIM-05-2017-0030

Rauschnabel, P. A., Felix, R., & Hinsch, C. (2019). Augmented reality marketing: How mobile AR-apps can improve brands through inspiration. *Journal of Retailing and Consumer Services*, 49, 43–53. DOI: 10.1016/j.jretconser.2019.03.004

Reichheld, F. F. (2003). The one number you need to grow. *Harvard Business Review*, 81(12), 46–55. PMID: 14712543

Reichheld, F. F. (2004). The one number you need to grow. *Harvard Business Review*, 82(6), 133–133. PMID: 14712543

Roma, P., & Aloini, D. (2019). How does brand-related user-generated content differ across social media? Evidence reloaded. *Journal of Business Research*, 96, 322–339. DOI: 10.1016/j.jbusres.2018.11.055

Ruan, Y., Durresi, A., & Alfantoukh, L. (2018). Using Twitter trust network for stock market analysis. *Knowledge-Based Systems*, 145, 207–218. DOI: 10.1016/j.knosys.2018.01.016

Sabate, F., Berbegal-Mirabent, J., Cañabate, A., & Lebherz, P. R. (2014). Factors influencing popularity of branded content in Facebook fan pages. *European Management Journal*, 32(6), 1001–1011. DOI: 10.1016/j.emj.2014.05.001

Schivinski, B., & Dabrowski, D. (2016). The effect of social media communication on consumer perceptions of brands. *Journal of Marketing Communications*, 22(2), 189–214. DOI: 10.1080/13527266.2013.871323

Schweidel, D. A., & Moe, W. W. (2014). Listening in on social media: A joint model of sentiment and venue format choice. *JMR, Journal of Marketing Research*, 51(4), 387–402. DOI: 10.1509/jmr.12.0424

Singh, A., Rana, N. P., & Parayitam, S. (2022). Role of social currency in customer experience and co-creation intention in online travel agencies: Moderation of attitude and subjective norms. International. *Journal of Information Management Data Insights*, 2(2), 100114. DOI: 10.1016/j.jjimei.2022.100114

Sivarajah, U., Irani, Z., Gupta, S., & Mahroof, K. (2020). Role of big data and social media analytics for business to business sustainability: A participatory web context. *Industrial Marketing Management*, 86, 163–179. DOI: 10.1016/j.indmarman.2019.04.005

Sivarajah, U., Kamal, M. M., Irani, Z., & Weerakkody, V. (2017). Critical analysis of Big Data challenges and analytical methods. *Journal of Business Research*, 70, 263–286. DOI: 10.1016/j.jbusres.2016.08.001

Stieglitz, S., Mirbabaie, M., Ross, B., & Neuberger, C. (2018). Social media analytics–Challenges in topic discovery, data collection, and data preparation. *International Journal of Information Management*, 39, 156–168. DOI: 10.1016/j.ijinfomgt.2017.12.002

Trainor, K. J., Andzulis, J. M., Rapp, A., & Agnihotri, R. (2014). Social media technology usage and customer relationship performance: A capabilities-based examination of social CRM. *Journal of Business Research*, 67(6), 1201–1208. DOI: 10.1016/j.jbusres.2013.05.002

Tuten, T. L. (2023). *Social media marketing*. Sage Publications Limited.

Vallaster, C., Kraus, S., Lindahl, J. M. M., & Nielsen, A. (2019). Ethics and entrepreneurship: A bibliometric study and literature review. *Journal of Business Research*, 99, 226–237. DOI: 10.1016/j.jbusres.2019.02.050

Van Doorn, J., Lemon, K. N., Mittal, V., Nass, S., Pick, D., Pirner, P., & Verhoef, P. C. (2010). Customer engagement behavior: Theoretical foundations and research directions. *Journal of Service Research*, 13(3), 253–266. DOI: 10.1177/1094670510375599

Van Eck, N., & Waltman, L. (2010). Software survey: VOSviewer, a computer program for bibliometric mapping. *Scientometrics*, 84(2), 523–538. DOI: 10.1007/s11192-009-0146-3 PMID: 20585380

Varela-Neira, C., Dwivedi, Y. K., & Camoiras-Rodriguez, Z. (2023). Social media marketing system: Conceptualization, scale development and validation. *Internet Research*, 33(4), 1302–1330. DOI: 10.1108/INTR-06-2021-0393

Verhoef, P. C., Reinartz, W. J., & Krafft, M. (2010). Customer engagement as a new perspective in customer management. *Journal of Service Research*, 13(3), 247–252. DOI: 10.1177/1094670510375461

Vermeer, S. A., Araujo, T., Bernritter, S. F., & van Noort, G. (2019). Seeing the wood for the trees: How machine learning can help firms in identifying relevant electronic word-of-mouth in social media. *International Journal of Research in Marketing*, 36(3), 492–508. DOI: 10.1016/j.ijresmar.2019.01.010

Vinerean, S., & Opreana, A. (2021). Measuring customer engagement in social media marketing: A higher-order model. *Journal of Theoretical and Applied Electronic Commerce Research*, 16(7), 2633–2654. DOI: 10.3390/jtaer16070145

Vivek, S. D., Beatty, S. E., & Morgan, R. M. (2012). Customer engagement: Exploring customer relationships beyond purchase. *Journal of Marketing Theory and Practice*, 20(2), 122–146. DOI: 10.2753/MTP1069-6679200201

Voorveld, H. A., Van Noort, G., Muntinga, D. G., & Bronner, F. (2018). Engagement with social media and social media advertising: The differentiating role of platform type. *Journal of Advertising*, 47(1), 38–54. DOI: 10.1080/00913367.2017.1405754

Wang, Z., & Yang, X. (2024). Building brand loyalty through value co-creation practices in brand communities: the role of affective commitment and psychological brand ownership. *Journal of Research in Interactive Marketing, Vol. ahead-of-print No*. ahead-of-print. doi:DOI: 0.1108/JRIM-10-2023-0359

Wasserman, S., & Faust, K. (1994). *Social network analysis: Methods and applications*. Cambridge University Press. DOI: 10.1017/CBO9780511815478

Wirtz, J., Den Ambtman, A., Bloemer, J., Horváth, C., Ramaseshan, B., Van De Klundert, J., Gurhan Canli, Z., & Kandampully, J. (2013). Managing brands and customer engagement in online brand communities. *Journal of Service Management*, 24(3), 223–244. DOI: 10.1108/09564231311326978

Wulandari, A., Suryawardani, B., & Marcelino, D. (2022). Create Brand Loyalty of Indonesıan Facebook User Through Brand Engagement: Utılızatıon the Role of Socıal Medıa Marketıng Elements. *Asia Pacific Management and Business Application*, 10(3), 377–394. DOI: 10.21776/ub.apmba.2022.010.03.10

Xiang, Z., Schwartz, Z., Gerdes, J. H.Jr, & Uysal, M. (2015). What can big data and text analytics tell us about hotel guest experience and satisfaction? *International Journal of Hospitality Management*, 44, 120–130. DOI: 10.1016/j.ijhm.2014.10.013

Zook, Z., & Smith, P. R. (2016). *Marketing communications: offline and online integration, engagement and analytics*. Kogan Page Publishers.

ADDITIONAL READING

Barklamb, A. M., Molenaar, A., Brennan, L., Evans, S., Choong, J., Herron, E., Reid, M., & McCaffrey, T. A. (2020). Learning the language of social media: A comparison of engagement metrics and social media strategies used by food and nutrition-related social media accounts. *Nutrients*, 12(9), 2839. DOI: 10.3390/nu12092839 PMID: 32948033

Drivas, I. C., Kouis, D., Kyriaki-Manessi, D., & Giannakopoulou, F. (2022). Social media analytics and metrics for improving users engagement. *Knowledge (Beverly Hills, Calif.)*, 2(2), 225–242.

Duncan, S. Y., Chohan, R., & Ferreira, J. J. (2019). What makes the difference? Employee social media brand engagement. *Journal of Business and Industrial Marketing*, 34(7), 1459–1467. DOI: 10.1108/JBIM-09-2018-0279

Fletcher, K. A., & Gbadamosi, A. (2022). Examining social media live stream's influence on the consumer decision-making: A thematic analysis. *Electronic Commerce Research*, 1–31.

Ghareeb, N. B., Aboutabl, A. E., Shalash, S. O., & Mostafa, A. M. (2024, March). Using Data Analytics Techniques for Enhancing Social Media Marketing Processes. In *2024 6th International Conference on Computing and Informatics (ICCI)* (pp. 443-451). IEEE. DOI: 10.1109/ICCI61671.2024.10485047

Jaitly, R. C., & Gautam, O. (2021). Impact of social media influencers on customer engagement and brand perception. *International Journal of Internet Marketing and Advertising*, 15(2), 220–242. DOI: 10.1504/IJIMA.2021.114336

Liu, Y., Liu, X., Wang, M., & Wen, D. (2021). How to catch customers' attention? A study on the effectiveness of brand social media strategies in digital customer engagement. *Frontiers in Psychology*, 12, 800766. DOI: 10.3389/fpsyg.2021.800766 PMID: 34975700

Xu, Z., Vail, C., Kohli, A. S., & Tajdini, S. (2021). Understanding changes in a brand's core positioning and customer engagement: A sentiment analysis of a brand-owned Facebook site. *Journal of Marketing Analytics*, 9(1), 3–16. DOI: 10.1057/s41270-020-00099-z

KEY TERMS AND DEFINITIONS

Bibliometric Approach: A quantitative research methodology that uses statistical techniques to extract scientific publications and identify trends in terms of research perspectives (by year, by most influential authors, by country, by type of publication ...) and scientific collaborations (by citation and co-citation occurrences).

Brand Awareness: A brand's presence in the marketplace market, measured by its ability to be recognized or recalled by the consumer.

Brand Commitment Engagement Assessment: Measures a customer's attachment to a specific brand by analyzing interactions, mentions and positive attitudes on different platforms.

Brand Customer Commitment: The deep psychological and emotional commitment developed between the consumer and the brand, increasing loyalty, repeat purchases and the predisposition to recommend the brand to others.

Classical Solutions Social Media Analytics: Use of metric tools to collect and analyze data from social platforms, including mentions, likes, shares and comments.

Electronic Word of Mouth (eWOM): All online opinions, recommendations and reviews of a product or brand, influencing consumer attitudes and purchasing behavior.

Online Company's Brand: An organization's digital footprint on websites, social networks and online interactions with customers, including visual, textual and experiential content.

Qualitative Analysis: Research method focusing on the interpretation of non-measurable data from interviews, observations and documentary analysis, aimed at understanding stakeholder behavior, experiences and perspectives.

Smart Solutions Social Media Analytics: Use of emerging technologies (AI, Machine Learning, ...) to conduct accurate and predictive analysis of users' behaviors, trends, feelings and emotions on social media.

Social Media Analytics: The process of collecting, measuring and interpreting social media data to understand user behavior, market trends and online communication strategies.

Chapter 14

Mediation Effect of Customer Loyalty in Relationship Between Market Orientation, Entrepreneurial Orientation, and Firm Performance in Ethiopia

Tafese Niguse
Bule Hora University, Ethiopia

Shashi Kant
https://orcid.org/0000-0003-4722-5736
Bule Hora University, Ethiopia

Metasebia Adula
https://orcid.org/0000-0001-5732-2850
Bule Hora University, Ethiopia

ABSTRACT

This study focused on the mediating role of customer loyalty between market orientation, entrepreneurial orientation and Ethiopian hotel performance. It was aimed: To see effect of market orientation and entrepreneurial orientation on business performance, to see effect market orientation and entrepreneurial orientation on customer loyalty, and to find mediation effect of customer loyalty between market

DOI: 10.4018/979-8-3693-5340-0.ch014

orientation, entrepreneurial orientation and business performance. Descriptive research design and non-probability, particularly convenience sampling was used. Structured questionnaire was used. For data analysis, percentage, mean, standard deviations were employed. Structural equation modeling by EFA and CFA was employed using SPSS and AMOS.23. The finding showed there is positive significant relationship between MO, CL, and FP. However, there is negative relationship between EO and FP. But, with the mediation of CL, the relationship between EO and FP was found.

1. INTRODUCTION

The hotel industry faces several challenges, including fluctuating demand, a competitive business climate and high fixed costs, exerting pressure on hotel performance (Sampaio et al., 2021). This changing and uncertain environment necessitates improving hotel performance via appropriate strategy and practice for present success and for future competitive advantage (Presutti et al., 2020). Consequently, it is essential to investigate hotel performance and the most effective practices and strategies for enhancing performance. Since every hotel business serves its consumers and competes with others, Market Orientation (MO) and Entrepreneurial Orientation (EO) is essential to achieving high performance (Dabrowski et al., 2019).

Market orientation is company's method to create superior performance, and the behaviors needed to improve the performance of the firm. The performance is accomplished by applying a market-oriented culture that is how the company understands the needs, wants and demands of the market (Andriyanto & Sufian, 2017). Market-oriented companies pursue success in the market by meeting customers' demands and need more effectively than their rivals (Hiong et al., 2020; Oduro & Haylemariam, 2019). MO improves a company's understanding of giving higher customer value and boosting corporate performance (Narver & Slater, 1990). Therefore, by embracing MO, hotels would have the opportunity to achieve market orientation and hotel performance environmental changes, allowing them to overcome challenges and improve performance (Ighomereho, 2022).

Customer loyalty is the strength of the relationship between a clients' relative attitude and repurchase trade (Dick & Basu, 1994). Customer loyalty also was described as a strong continued commitment to repurchase or patronize a favored product/service consistently in the future, thereby creating repeated same products/brands purchasing (Dam & Dam, 2021).

Entrepreneurial Orientation concept starts from the Miller (1983) and Miller defines as one that engages in product-market innovation, undertakes somewhat risky ventures, and is first to come up with 'proactive' innovations, beating competitors to the punch. Morris and Paul (1987) expressed the understanding of Entrepreneurial Orientation is one with decision-making norms that emphasize proactive, innovative strategies that contain an element of risk (Tajeddini & Ratten, 2020). Entrepreneurship can offer a way to compete in an increasingly fierce market through innovativeness, pro-activeness and risk-taking. The link between entrepreneurial orientation and company performance has led to an increase in the number of studies that explore how they relate to one another (Oktavio et al, 2019).

Business performance is the operational ability to satisfy the desires of the company's major shareholders, and it must be assessed to measure an organization's accomplishment. There are various methods to measure business performance of enterprises since performance is multidimensional that related to the subject of interest (Rahman et al., 2018). This study provides for future research by adding the knowledge by bridging the gap between market orientation and customer loyalty to augment the hospitality performance in Ethiopia.

The study focused on the following specific objectives:

- ✓ To see the effect of market orientation on business performance.
- ✓ To find out the effect of entrepreneurial orientation on business performance.
- ✓ To see the effect market orientation on customer loyalty in the study area.
- ✓ To analyze the effect of entrepreneurial orientation on customer loyalty.
- ✓ To examine the effect of customer loyalty on business performance.
- ✓ To find out the mediation effect of customer loyalty between market orientation, entrepreneurial orientation and business performance.

2. REVIEW OF RELATED LITERATURE

2.1. Statement of the problem

Researchers in the link between market orientation, entrepreneurial orientation, hotel performance have investigated direct relationship (Alnawas & Hemsley-Brown, 2019; Dabrowski et al, 2019; Sampaio et al., 2019), moderated relationship (Hernández-Linares et al., 2021; Selmi & Chaney, 2018; Tajeddini & Ratten, 2020;

Wang et al., 2019) and mediated effect (Alnawas & Hemsley-Brown, 2019; Chuang, 2018; Oktavio et al., 2019; Sampaio et al., 2021; Santra, 2018).

Even though many researchers have been conducted in marketing regarding to market orientation, entrepreneurial orientation and business performance, there are only limited (Sampaio et al., 2020; Hutagalung et al., 2020) studies regarding to customer loyalty as mediating variable. So, in this research, the researchers used customer loyalty as mediating variable to fill knowledge gap of previous researches.

The researchers also identified geographical gap of previous studies in Ethiopian context since the researchers like Hassen and Singh (2020) and Shiferaw (2018) conducted their studies. However, these were limited studies conducted in Ethiopian context. So, this study fill geographical gap of previous researches.

In this research, the researchers also find out theoretical gap since some researchers, like Joensuu-Salo et al. (2018), Kellermanns et al. (2018) and Al Marzooqi and Abdulla (2020) used resource-based view theory and others like Varadarajan (2020), Rubera and Kirca (2017) used market based view theory. Acosta et al. (2018), Fitriati et al. (2020), Abu-Rumman et al. (2021) and Randhawa et al. (2021) used dynamic capability theory and Line et al. (2019), Su (2018) and Montiel-Campos (2018) used dominant service logic to study market orientation, entrepreneurial orientation and business performance. However, these theories are rather dated and the current study bear the fruit by investigation in terms of combination of these theories and theoretical development will be warranted.

The researchers also identified an apparent evidence gap in prior research (Lekmat, 2018; Oktavio, 2019; Taheri et al., 2019), obtained significant effect of market and entrepreneurial orientation on business performance; While the other researchers (Dabrowski, 2019; Ghantous, 2020; Nuvriasari, 2020) obtained insignificant effect of market orientation and entrepreneurial orientation on business performance. To fill this contradictory evidence, the researchers interested to conduct present study.

Therefore, the primary objective of this study was mediation effect of customer loyalty in relationship between market orientation, entrepreneurial orientation and business performance the case of Ethiopian hotels. The finding of the study was important to provide information to entrepreneurs, hotel owners, managers and employees to maintain customer loyalty by focusing on market orientation and entrepreneurial orientation.

2.2. Concept of market orientation

Market orientation can be defined as company's method to create superior performance, and the behaviors needed to improve the performance of the firm. The performance can be accomplished by applying a market-oriented culture that is how the company understands the needs, wants and demands of the market (Lemma, 2020).

Narver and Slater (1990) adopt developed the concept and define Market Orientation as “the organization culture that most effectively and efficiently creates the necessary behaviors for the creation of superior value for buyers and, thus, continuous superior performance for the business”. In consonance with this approach, these authors propose that Market Orientation features three different dimensions: Customer Orientation, Competitor Orientation, and Inter-functional Coordination.

Narver and Slater (1990) specified that MO involves three cultural components, namely, customer orientation that refers to the sufficient understanding of target buyers to continuously create superior value for them; competitor orientation that refers to the ability of a firm to understand weaknesses, strengths, long-term capabilities and strategies of current and potential competitors; and inter functional component that refers to the firms’ capabilities of integrating their resources to create superior value for target customers.

The elements of market orientation are:

- *Customer Orientation:* Customer orientation is a business approach that puts the needs of the customer over the needs of the business. Customer-oriented companies understand that the business won't thrive unless it consistently improves customer focus (Ismail, 2023).
- *Competitor Orientation:* It is the individual's inclination to perform better than others (Chen et al., 2011), and it has been found to influence unethical decision-making (Li et al., 2018).
- *Cross Functional Integration*: It is the close collaboration of personnel who represent different functional organizations through cross-functional teams or other organizational vehicles (Maharani 2020).

2.3. Concept of entrepreneurial orientation

The Entrepreneurial Orientation concept starts from the Miller (1983) defines as one that engages in product-market innovation, undertakes somewhat risky ventures, and is first to come up with ‘proactive’ innovations, beating competitors to the punch.

Morris and Paul (1987) cited by Criado-Gomis (2018) expressed the understanding of Entrepreneurial Orientation is one with decision making norms that emphasize proactive, innovative strategies that contain an element of risk.

EO is "driving force behind the organizational pursuit of entrepreneurial activities" (Covin & Wales, 2012). EO is reflected in the entrepreneurial practices and firm behavior (Zahra et al., 2014). Originally, EO concept was introduced by Miller (1983) that illustrates as "an entrepreneurial firm that engages in product-market innovation, undertakes somewhat risky ventures, and is first to come up with 'proactive' innovations, beating competitors to the punch". Based on this definition, EO is recognized by three components i.e., innovativeness, reactiveness, and risk-taking (Singh, 2021).

The elements of entrepreneurship orientation are

- *Pro-activeness:* is the propensity to identify event in advance or an act that facilitate future prospect and needs rather than responding later when the incident must have been spread-out. A proactive firm is that firm that adopts an opportunity seeking prospect (Cuevas-Vargas, 2019).
- *Risk Taking:* Is the act or fact of doing something that involves danger or risk in order to achieve a goal. Starting a business always involves some risk-taking (Singh, 2021).
- *Innovativeness:* is the practice of establishing creating new business ideas intending to generate profit, assist their community and accomplish company goals (Ghee, 2018).

2.4. The concept of customer loyalty

The concept of customer loyalty has happened in many discussions in the literature with different definitions. Jacoby and Kyner (1973) were described customer loyalty as the tended (i.e., non-random), behavioral reply (i.e., buying), demonstrated over time, by some decision-making unit, concerning one or more alternative brands out of a collection of such brands, and was a role of psychological (i.e., decision making, evaluation) processes (Jacoby & Kyner, 1973). Customer loyalty was defined as the strength of the relationship between a clients' relative attitude and repurchase trade (Dick & Basu, 1994). Customer loyalty also was described as a strong continued commitment to repurchase or patronize a favored product/

service consistently in the future, thereby creating repeated same products/brands purchasing (Dam & Dam 2021).

Based on the model of Quintana (2004), elements of customer loyalty are:

- *Perceived Quality:* is defined as the consumers' judgment about an entity's services containing overall excellence or superiority.
- *Customer Satisfaction:* is a measure of how well a company's products, services, and overall customer experience meet customer expectations. It reflects your business' health by showing how well your products or services resonate with buyers.
- *Switching Cost:* Switching costs are the costs that a consumer incurs as a result of changing brands, suppliers, or products. Although most prevalent switching costs are monetary in nature, there are also psychological, effort-based, and time-based switching costs.

2.5. The concept of business performance

Business performance is the operational ability to satisfy the desires of the company's major shareholders, and it is assessed to measure an organization's accomplishment. There are various methods to measure business performance of enterprises since performance is multidimensional that related to the subject of interest (Rahman et al., 2018).

The balance scorecard (BSC) model, introduced in 1990, identifies strategic indicators that a company must achieve in order to reach a long-term vision, which means it is oriented towards the future, as well as to the improvement of the business itself. The BSC model combines all these four components. When there is an investment in the training of the employees (learning and development), the quality of business (internal processes) improves, and this positively influences customer satisfaction (customer), which contributes to better business operations (finances) (Dudic et al., 2020).

2.6. Theoretical review

Theories have been examined to see the mediation effect of customer loyalty in relationship between market orientation, entrepreneurship orientation and business performance in selected hotels of Ethiopia. So, Resource based view theory, Dynamic capability theory; Market based view theory and service dominant logic was used depending on their relevance for this study.

2.6.1. Resources based view theory

The RBV was evident in this era especially in the work of Barney (1991) cited by Joensuu-Salo et al. (2018), higher focus was on two key aspects namely logic and firm's resources. From the above discussed aspects of RBV theory, it is confirmed that more than external, the internal components of the organization are essential in determining the effectiveness of the organization. According to RBV theory, market orientation practices are a rare, valuable, and resources that difficult to imitate. Furthermore, it was known as the firm's internal capability, and it aided in the generation of a long-term advantage (Joensuu-Salo et al., 2018). Market orientation in RBV theory lens is a critical organizational capability and a strategic asset that has helped organizations improve their business performance (Al Marzooqi & Abdulla, 2020). Resource Based View Theory (RBV) and Entrepreneurial Orientation as a key resource that enabled the organization to find new methods to improve income, increase success rates in the worldwide market, and make optimal use of all organizational resources (Kellermanns et al., 2018). Entrepreneurial orientation, according to the RBV principle, is a collection of special tools that can be used to channel the creation of new goods in response to evolving environmental patterns.

2.6.2. Market based view theory

According to this theory Competitive strategy is concerned with establishing and defending strategic position in the marketplace. Knowing the economic drivers of the firm, its essential cost position, differentiating itself from its competitors and its chosen position in the market in terms of ability to exploit natural economies of scale and scope is necessary to get competitive advantage (Varadarajan, 2020).

Competitive advantage means the delivery of superior value to customers and economic value to firms. Thus, competitive strategy is largely conceived as a positioning of the firm in its markets and thus is known as the market positioning view or the market-based view (MBV). This contrasts with the resource-based view which focuses on the distinctive nature of the resources and capabilities that are required to underpin and produce competitive advantage. Competitive strategy is concerned with establishing and defending strategic position in the market place. This requires a deep understanding of the economic drivers of the firm, its essential cost position, its approach to differentiating itself in the market from its competitors, and its chosen position in the market in terms of ability to exploit natural economies of scale and scope (Abdul-Halim, 2019).

2.6.3. Dynamic capability theory

DCs are defined as "the capacity of an organization to purposefully create, extend or modify its resource base" (Helfat et al., 2007). Capacity implies the ability to perform a task at an acceptable level, denoting repeatability and intent (Brodie et al., 2019), while a firm's resource base comprises all tangible, intangible and human resources and capabilities that a firm possesses, controls or to which it has preferential access (Kachouie et al., 2018).

The theory of dynamic capability suggests that market orientation is a key capability that allow firm to sense and respond to market changes effectively (Vargo & Lusch, 2004a). It emphasizes the importance of continuous learning adaptation and innovation to maintain a competitive advantage in dynamic markets (Acosta et al., 2018).

2.7. Empirical review and hypothesis development

2.7.1. Market orientation and business performance

Business performance dimensions in this research are the market performance, supplier performance, process performance, people performance, and customer relationship performance. Hotel industry needs to understand the concept of market orientation that can provide performance benefits to their business (Ismail, 2023). Market orientation significantly affects the performance of the hotels (Alnawas & Hemsley-Brown, 2019). According to the research of (Dabrowskiet al., 2019) only customer orientation positively correlates to the hotels' financial performance, while competitor orientation and inter-function coordination partially affect how well the hotels perform financially. Customer orientation and inter-function coordination affect both aspects of hospitality sectors' performances as identified by (Kazemian et al., 2020).

Mitchell et al. (2010) extensively reviewed the literature on market orientation and its impact on entities' performance. They proposed a re-conceptualization of market orientation by including sustainability principles that were considered more applicable, comprehensive and strategic in the modern macroeconomic environment. Market Orientation affects Business Performance positively with Mediating Role of Employee and Customer Satisfaction in Ethiopia Banks (Wakjira & Kant, 2022).

On the base of related empirical literature review following hypothesis is proposed:

H1: There is relationship between market orientation and business performance.

2.7.2. Entrepreneurial orientation and business performance

There is relationship between entrepreneur orientation and business performance Octavia et al. (2020). Entrepreneurial orientation benefits business performance especially when coupled with strong business and social networks. To that end, the authors suggest an integrated approach to entrepreneurship by building a contingent model with sustainable entrepreneurial orientation as an antecedent (Criado-Gomis et al., 2018).

There are also some studies that have been studied in Ethiopian context. While studying Entrepreneurial orientation and business performance: an assessment of start-up companies in Addis Ababa found there is a positive relationship between EO and business performance. This study wants to create awareness and knowledge among startup entrepreneurs to adopt entrepreneurship (Goulap, 2020). A Study of Amhara Region of Ethiopia found positive relationship between entrepreneurial orientation and small and medium enterprise performance (Singh, 2021).

Dimensions of EO are related in different ways to the performance of functions in a firm. A positive relationship is observed between innovativeness and R&D performance and between pro-activeness and marketing and sales performance. A negative relationship exists between risk taking and production performance. The results also show a sequential positive relationship from R&D via production and marketing and sales to overall performance of firms (Rezaei & Ortt, 2018). The following hypothesis is put out in light of the relevant empirical literature review:

H2: There is relationship between Entrepreneurial orientation and business performance.

2.7.3. Market orientation and customer loyalty

Quality of service, service orientation, and strategy of marketing mix applied by the company are not all variables can directly affect customer loyalty but must first going through satisfaction. Which means that companies must first need to understand what the customer needs through variable service quality, service orientation, and marketing mix strategy so that the customers feel loyal when the level of satisfaction is resolved (Maharani, 2020). The service quality provided by the telecommunications industry needs to be improved in order to improve customer satisfaction and loyalty which needs market orientation (Fernandes et al., 2018).

In the current competitive business environment, effective customer-defined market orientation practices can enable organizations to acquire competitive advantage by providing superior value to customers (Rezaei & Ortt, 2018). Effective implementation of customer-defined market orientation practices provides long-term benefit to the organization through market research activities to determine customer need, using customer information to deliver product/services that are in line with customer requirement, responding quickly to competitor's moves, understanding their competition, share customer information with related staff and all department work together to create superior customer value hence, it contributes to building a long-term relationship with satisfied and loyal customers (Khan & Ghouri, 2018).

Customer orientation is a driver for customers" satisfaction, customers" commitment and their degree of loyalty. It is necessary to mention that employing customer-oriented employees does not guarantee economic success but represent an important step in achieving it (Lemma, 2020).

The following hypothesis is put up based on a survey of related empirical literature:

H3: There is relationship between Market orientation and Customer loyalty.

2.7.4. Entrepreneurial orientation and customer loyalty

Significant and positive correlation between entrepreneurship orientation and loyalty found. This fact that there is a strong relationship between entrepreneurship orientation and customer loyalty in business and also according to research findings, customer satisfaction, on loyalty has positive significant effect on customer loyalty, however, it is recommended to increase customer loyalty in companies should increase customer satisfaction (Maharani, 2020).

In continue the binary relationship each of measuring satisfaction variables with dimensions to entrepreneurship orientation and loyalty with customer satisfaction is considered. Customer satisfaction and loyalty have positive correlation together which indicates that consumers are more satisfied they are buying of the center again and have a loyalty to the company (Sampaio et al., 2018). Entrepreneurship orientation has significant and positive correlation with broadcasting company's loyalty in Kermanshah. Therefore, it is naturally that in any amount that these companies tend more to these components; their loyalty will improve perspective of consumers. This study, the relationship between corporate entrepreneurial orientation and consumer loyalty of companies were assessed in different dimension (Arfaei et al., 2012).

Based on an analysis of relevant empirical literature, the following hypothesis is formulated:

H4: There is relationship between Entrepreneurship orientation and Customer loyalty.

2.7.5. Customer loyalty and business performance

Customer satisfaction and service quality are positively and directly related to customer loyalty as hypothesized. Every satisfied customer can be a loyal one if he feels that the service is quality. The only missing link in this final model is the direct effect of perceived value on loyalty. The sole feeling of the value does not create loyalty on customers (Omoregie et al., 2019).

As loyal customers are always viewed as profitable, many retailers try to invest considerable sums of money to provide incentives, in many forms such as coupons or store loyalty cards, to loyal customer to retain them (Bustos-Reyes & Gozalez-Benito, 2008).

The greater the loyalty of employees causes greater the performance and competitiveness of the company. The greater business performance is a direct consequence of employee loyalty (Stojanovic et al., 2020. Customer loyalty is increased with augmented employee performance apropos the demands of the customers (Wongleedee, 2020).

The following hypothesis is put out in light of the relevant empirical literature review:

H5: There is relationship between customer loyalty and business performance.

2.7.6. Market Orientation, Entrepreneurial Orientation and Business Performance through Customer Loyalty

Customer loyalty was found to mediate the influence of customer orientation and business performance (Ismail, 2023). The company strives to measure customer satisfaction" were found to have more impact on customer loyalty. This means that small businesses understand the importance of customer satisfaction and invest more in providing better customer service that is in line with the needs of the customers. This further explains that SMEs have proper practices to develop customer commitment. Since customer commitment is mostly connected with customer loyalty, SMEs striving to create customer value have higher chances of converting indifferent customers into loyal ones (Ismail, 2023). Customers' loyalty is an entity that always turns into the favor of an organization. Therefore, organizations having greater volume of customers' loyalty enjoy more business gains and easily win competitive advantages which ultimately enhance business performance of the organization (Boonmalert, 2020).

Based on an analysis of relevant empirical literature, the following hypotheses are formulated:

H6a: Customer loyalty significantly mediates the relationship between market orientation and business performance.

H6b: Customer loyalty significantly mediates the relationship between entrepreneurial orientation and business performance.

2.8. Conceptual framework

The key hypothesis is that the success of businesses is directly impacted by both market orientation and entrepreneurial orientation (H1, H2). Furthermore, these orientations affect the loyalty of customers (H3, H4), which affects the success of businesses (H5). The framework further suggests that the link between market/entrepreneurial attitudes and real company success outcomes is explained or transmitted by customer loyalty, which is considered a mediating element (H6a, H6b). This conceptual framework mentioned under Figure 1, which places a strong emphasis on customer loyalty as a key mediating factor, essentially aims to unravel the processes and channels via which market and entrepreneurial orientations propel corporate success. The specific linkages are established by the hypotheses, and a more complete view of these intricate dynamics is offered by the broader framework.

Figure 1. Conceptual framework

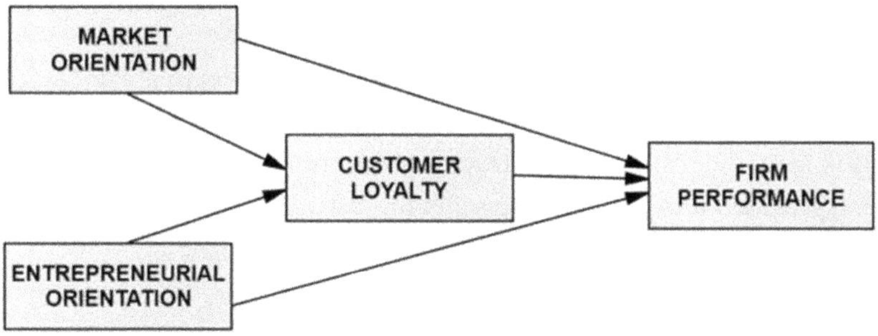

(Authors)

3. RESEARCH METHODOLOGY

Research design is the blueprint for fulfilling research objectives and answering research questions John et al. (2007). For this study, the researchers used descriptive and explanatory research designs. The purpose of descriptive research design is describing the state of affairs as it exists at present and the goal of exploratory research is to formulate problems, clarify concepts, and form hypotheses.

3.1. Target population

A population is a group of individuals, objects or items from which samples are taken for measurement. It refers to an entire group of persons or elements that have at least one thing in common (Kombo & Tromp, 2006). The population for this study comprises owners, managers, and employees of the Ethiopian hotels.

3.2. Sampling technique and sample size determination

Sampling is the process of selecting a number of individuals or objects from a population such that the selected group contains elements that are representative of the characteristics that are found in the entire group (Orodho & Kombo, 2002). For this study, the researchers used selected hotels judgmentally and 384 workers selected by non-probability particularly convenience sampling.

3.3. Data collection methods

In order to achieve the objectives of this research and effectively undertake data analysis in the later stage of the research, a structured questionnaire was used to collect information from the respondents. Structured questionnaires are important as they could be aggregated into a composite scale for statistical analysis (Kothari, 2004).

3.4. Methods of data analysis

Data obtained via a questionnaire was coded and converted to the structured format from the questionnaires. For the quantitative data, the researchers used software called SPSS and AMOS version-23. Descriptive statistical analysis such as frequency, percentage, means, standard deviation, and Structural Equation Modeling (with the help of EFA and CFA) was used to analyze data. Researchers used SPSS 23 and AMOS 23 in this chapter to perform various statistical techniques for analyzing the results. Data was initially coded in Excel sheet and exported for further analysis to Statistical Tools. Exploratory factor analysis, Confirmatory factor analysis and Cross Tabulation methods were used for analysis. Analysis was performed in which principal component method was selected with rotation of varimax to reduce and summarize the results.

3.4.1. Exploratory Factor Analysis (EFA)

The objective of exploratory factor analysis according to Kinnear and Gray (2010) is to find the independent factors that explain the correlations. In this case, items are typically reduced to specific interrelated and relevant dimensions with a very small amount of information loss describing as much variation as possible on the original items.

Table 1. KMO and Bartlett's test

Kaiser-Meyer-Olkin Measure of Sampling Adequacy.		**.817**
Bartlett's Test of Sphericity	Approx. Chi-Square	1905.082
	Df	66
	Sig.	.000

Source: Authors.

Moreover, table1 shows two statistical measures are also generated by SPSS to help assess the factorability of the data (i.e. suitability of the dataset for factor analysis): Bartlett's test of sphericity should be significant ($p<0.05$) for the factor analysis to be considered appropriate and Kaiser Meyer Olkin (KMO) measure of sampling adequacy the value of KMO should be greater than 0.5 if sample is adequate (Hair et al., 2022) to proceed factor analysis. For current study, the KMO values for all of the factors was >0.5 and the Bartlett's test was significant ($p=0.00$), indicating that the data were suitable for factor analysis.

Table 2. Communalities

	Initial	Extraction
CG	1.000	.763
EM	1.000	.708
BH	1.000	.699
FN	1.000	.661
NF	1.000	.644
SAT	1.000	.677
CO	1.000	.843
COP	1.000	.636
IC	1.000	.786
INN	1.000	.680
RT	1.000	.744

continued on following page

Table 2. Continued

	Initial	Extraction
PRO	1.000	.752

Extraction Method: Principal Component Analysis.
Source: Authors.

Table 2 shows communalities of constructs are calculated to check reliability of data. Communalities indicate the amount of variance in each variable that is accounted for. Principal component analysis works on the initial assumption that all variance is common therefore before the extraction the communalities are all 1. The amount of variance in each variable that can be explained by the retained factors is represented by the communalities after extraction. Small values (average <0.60 at cases >250) indicate variables that do not fit well with the factor solution and should possibly be dropped from the analysis. For current study, the communalities values for all of the factors were greater than 0.5 indicating that the data were suitable for factor analysis.

Table 3: Total variance explained

Component	Initial Eigenvalues			Extraction Sums of Squared Loadings			Rotation Sums of Squared Loadings		
	Total	% Variance	Cumulative %	Total	% Variance	Cumulative %	Total	% Variance	Cumulative %
1	4.444	37.033	37.033	4.444	37.033	37.033	3.242	27.021	27.021
2	2.739	22.824	59.857	2.739	22.824	59.857	3.204	26.698	53.719
3	1.409	11.746	71.603	1.409	11.746	71.603	2.146	17.884	71.603
4	.639	5.323	76.926						
5	.524	4.364	81.290						
6	.482	4.020	85.310						
7	.427	3.557	88.866						
8	.383	3.194	92.061						
9	.307	2.559	94.620						
10	.250	2.083	96.703						
11	.230	1.918	98.621						
12	.165	1.379	100.000						

Extraction Method: Principal Component Analysis.
Source: Authors.

All 3 variables in Table 3 reflected 71.603% of the variance. The overall variance described by these 3 components 71.603%) is more than the level of 50 percent widely used in the social sciences (Hair et al., 2022). Therefore, going through the study is reasonable enough. We can also see from the above table that the Eigen values of the first 3 components are more than 1.044, so these components are important for the analysis because they contribute positively to the analysis.

Table 4. Rotated component matrix

	Component		
	1	2	3
CG		.842	
EM		.745	
BH		.833	
FN			.802
NF			.724
SAT			.811
CO	.911		
COP	.756		
IC	.877		
INN		.706	
RT		.856	
PRO		.831	

Extraction Method: Principal Component Analysis.
Rotation Method: Varimax with Kaiser Normalization.
a. Rotation converged in 4 iterations.
Source: Authors.

Rotated component matrix Table 4 reflects the relationship strength under one factor between the item and element, and the item's membership. Here it is determined the membership of the item in factor by identifying the highest load in one factor. The load values range from 0 to 1. Value close to 1 suggested maximum loading factor. Generally, loading factor greater than 0.5 is acceptable as (Hair et al., 2022).

3.4.2. Convergent validity

Depicted by validly test specified in Table 5, Factor loadings are significant and greater than 0.5 and Average Variance Extracted (AVE) for each of the factors > 0.5 indicates good convergent validity assumption. Accordingly, as result of current final study in table 6 above shows; all of items have greater than 0.50 loads on their predicted construct that demonstrate a higher degree of association between the latent items and that constructs; thus, convergent validity is confirmed. Discriminant validity as depicted under Table 5 is the degree to which one construct is truly different from the other construct. According to Hair et al. (2022), Average AVE of two constructs must be greater than the square of their correlation to satisfy the condition of discriminant validity. In Table 6, AVE and square correlation of all constructs satisfy the condition. Hence, it can be concluded that discriminant validity of the factor structure is confirmed.

Table 5. Validity test

	CR	AVE	MSV	MaxR(H)	EO	MO	CL	FP
EO	0.818	0.602	0.537	0.851	**0.776**			
MO	0.870	0.693	0.238	0.899	0.088	**0.833**		
CL	0.757	0.589	0.537	0.851	0.733	0.423	**0.723**	
FP	0.737	0.535	0.238	0.743	0.179	0.488	0.357	**0.731**

Source: Authors.

3.5. Assumptions of Structural Equation Modeling

3.5.1. Observed Variables Have Multivariate Normality:

Neglecting the assumption of multivariate normal distribution of observed variables leads to a high CMIN/DF value and a significant test outcome. The skewness and kurtosis values are examined to determine whether the variables in the data set are normally distributed. In this case values between -2 and +2 are considered normal as depicted by Table 6.

Table 6. Assessment of normality

Variable	Min	Max	Skew	c.r.	kurtosis	c.r.
EM	1.600	5.000	-.904	-7.229	1.013	4.052
BH	2.200	5.000	-.560	-4.482	.167	.667
SAT	2.333	5.000	-.192	-1.536	-.393	-1.573
NF	2.000	5.000	-.081	-.652	-.925	-3.702
FN	2.200	4.800	-.162	-1.299	-.557	-2.227
RT	1.600	5.000	-1.256	-10.046	1.855	7.419
INN	1.400	4.800	-.852	-6.815	.785	3.141
PRO	1.000	5.000	-.765	-6.119	.264	1.056
CO	2.200	5.000	-.563	-4.508	.430	1.721
COP	1.400	5.000	-.371	-2.967	-.119	-.474
IC	1.600	5.000	-.195	-1.557	.531	2.124
Multivariate					5.848	3.388

Source: Authors.

3.5.2. Linearity

Structural equation modeling is a component of factor and regression analysis. Therefore, linearity, which is the most important assumption of regression analysis, also applies to structural equation modeling. In the structural equation model, it is assumed that there are linear relationships between latent variables and also between observed and latent variables.

3.5.3. Multicollinearity test

Multicollinearity exists if there is a high correlation between independent variables when regressed against each other, which is generally accepted as 0.80 or higher as harmful (Field, 2005). It was tested under Table 7 by using tolerance value and Variance Inflation Factor (VIF) (Field, 2005) and no multicollinearity problem was found because tolerance level for all items founded below 1 and VIF below 10.

Table 7. Collinearity statistics

Model		Collinearity Statistics	
		Tolerance	**VIF**
1	**(Constant)**		
	CG	.338	2.958
	EM	.363	2.757
	BH	.411	2.433
	CO	.278	3.594
	COP	.530	1.887
	IC	.340	2.942
	INN	.446	2.244
	RT	.376	2.659
	PRO	.477	2.097

Source: Authors.

3.6. Structural Equation Model

SEM is a potent multivariate statistical method that enables the evaluation of several related dependent relationships at once. It works well for examining intricate models with several components (market orientation, entrepreneurial orientation, customer loyalty, and business success) and potential connections between them, such as the one you presented. In order to thoroughly examine the conceptual model and clarify the intricate interactions that exist between market orientation, entrepreneurial orientation, customer loyalty, and business success, SEM offers a thorough analytical framework as depicted under Figure 2. The findings may provide insightful information for theoretical advancement as well as real-world applications.

Figure 2. Structural equation model for first order CFA

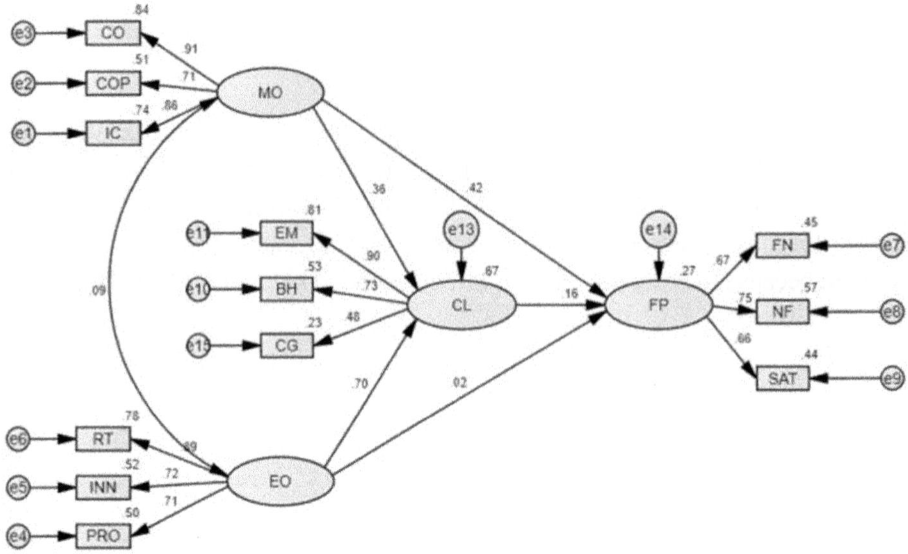

(Authors)

Table 8. Standardized regression weights

			Estimate
IC	**<---**	**MO**	**.858**
COP	**<---**	**MO**	.713
CO	**<---**	**MO**	.914
PRO	**<---**	**EO**	.707
INN	**<---**	**EO**	.721
RT	**<---**	**EO**	.886
FN	**<---**	**FP**	.668
NF	**<---**	**FP**	.752
SAT	**<---**	**FP**	.664

continued on following page

Table 8. Continued

			Estimate
IC	<---	**MO**	**.858**
BH	<---	**CL**	.726
EM	<---	**CL**	.901
CG	<---	**CL**	.481

Source: Authors.

The factor loading of observed variables listed in Table 8 are reliability estimates of individual constructs. All factor loadings by Kline (1998) are above the suggested limit of 0.50. Looking at their level of significance 0.05 above, the weight of regression is significant except CG to CL which is .481.

3.6.1. First order confirmatory analysis

Usually, the initial phase in SEM is the initial-Order CFA, where the validation of the measurement models for each of the conceptual framework's distinct latent components is the main goal. Before moving on to the whole structural equation model, the researchers made sure the measurement characteristics of the important constructs are sound by doing this First-Order CFA. This establishes the foundation for precisely verifying the correlations that are proposed in the conceptual framework under Table 9.

Table 9. Model fit summary

CMIN					
Model	**NPAR**	**CMIN**	**DF**	**P**	**CMIN/DF**
MO	30	654.866	48	.000	13.643
Saturated model	78	.000	0		
Independence model	12	2538.133	66	.000	38.457

Source: Authors.

In the Table 10, the CMIN value 654.866 reflects the difference between the unrestricted sample covariance matrix S and the restricted covariance matrix Σ (θ) hierarchy and, in essence, reflects the statistics of the Likelihood Ratio Test, most generally represented as a statistic of $\chi 2$. The test of HO, the Market Orientation Model does not fit the data yielded a value of CMIN 654.866, with 48 degrees of freedom. One of the first fit statistics to address this problem was the $\chi 2$/degrees of freedom ratio (summers, 1977), which appears as CMIN / DF is 13.643 (Standard Recommended value is $< = 5$). So, based on CMIN criteria, the first order CFA model is not fitted.

Table 10. Model fit summary

Model	RMR	GFI	AGFI	PGFI
MO	.057	.778	.640	.479
Saturated model	.000	1.000		
Independence model	.132	.391	.280	.331

Source: Authors.

Table 10 shows that GFI is .778, AGFI is .640 and RMR .057. For the model fitness GFI and AGFI must be greater than 0.9 and PGFI greater than 0.5 is acceptable as Hair et al. (2022). Based on this table, the model is not well fitted.

Table 11. Baseline comparisons for first order confirmatory analysis

Baseline Comparisons					
Model	**NFI Delta1**	**RFI rho1**	**IFI Delta2**	**TLI rho2**	**CFI**
MO	.742	.645	.756	.662	.755
Saturated model	1.000		1.000		1.000
Independence model	.000	.000	.000	.000	.000

Source: Authors.

According to Marsh et al. (1993), baseline comparisons can be categorized as incremental or comparative fit indices. The value of more than 0.90 is known to be a good fit model (Bentler, 1992). For this study the value mentioned under table 11 is 0.755 for CFI and 0.742 for NFI which suggests the model's good fit is not well. RFI and NFI derivative, values ranging from 0 to 1, with values close to .95 suggesting superior fit (Hu & Bentler, 1999). In this case, the value is 0.645 for CFI and 0.742 for NFI, which suggests the model is not well fitted.

Table 12. RMSEA for first order confirmatory analysis

RMSEA				
Model	**RMSEA**	**LO 90**	**HI 90**	**PCLOSE**
MO	.182	.169	.194	.000
Independence model	.313	.302	.323	.000

Source: Authors.

According to Browne and Cudeck (1993), values depicted under Table 12 for RMSEA 0.05 indicate good fit and values as high as 0.08 reflect acceptable approximation errors in the population. In this analysis the RMSEA value is 0.182 which indicates the model is not fit well. So, it can be concluded on the basis of goodness-of-fit, the hypothesized model fit not reasonably well and needs further analysis which is second order CFA.

3.6.2. Second order confirmatory factor analysis

By examining the constructions' higher-order factor structure, the Second-Order CFA expands on the first-order CFA. The first-order latent variables (market orientation, entrepreneurial orientation, customer loyalty, and company success, for example) are seen to be markers of more abstract, higher-order characteristics by the academics. The researchers were able to comprehend the conceptual framework underpinning the important variables in the model more thoroughly by carrying out this Second-Order CFA under Figure 3. The suggested conceptual framework received stronger empirical support and stronger theoretical underpinnings from these extra layers of investigation.

Figure 3. Model for second order confirmatory analysis

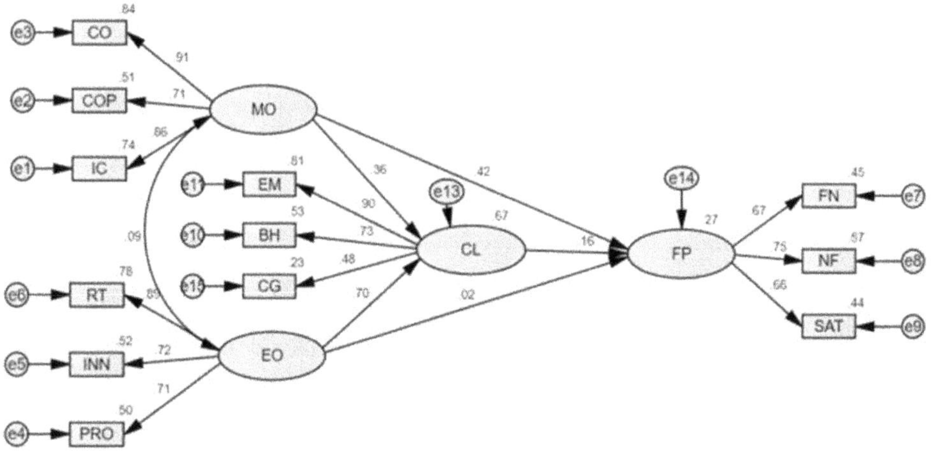

(Authors)

In this model under figure 3, from customer loyalty construct, (CG) is removed because of fewer factors loading which is 0.481. Standardized Regression Weights are manifested under Table 13.

Table 13. Standardized regression weights

			Estimate
IC	<---	MO	.856
COP	<---	MO	.712
CO	<---	MO	.917
PRO	<---	EO	.721
INN	<---	EO	.714
RT	<---	EO	.877
FN	<---	FP	.668
NF	<---	FP	.751
SAT	<---	FP	.665
BH	<---	CL	.800
EM	<---	CL	.836

Source: Authors.

Table 14. CMIN for second order

CMIN					
Model	**NPAR**	**CMIN**	**DF**	**P**	**CMIN/DF**
MO	28	302.141	38	.000	7.951
Saturated model	66	.000	0		
Independence model	11	2112.077	55	.000	38.401

Source: Authors.

In the Table 14, the test of HO, the Market Orientation Model not fits the data yielded value as CMIN is 302.141, with DF 38 and CMIN / DF is 13.643 (Standard Recommended value < = 5).

Table 15. RMR and GFI test

RMR, GFI				
Model	**RMR**	**GFI**	**AGFI**	**PGFI**
MO	.044	.869	.773	.501
Saturated model	.000	1.000		
Independence model	.131	.429	.315	.358

Source: Authors.

As Table 15, the value of GFI increased is 0.869. AGFI is 0.773 and RMR is 0.044. For the model fitness GFI and AGFI must greater than 0.9 and PGFI greater than 0.5 is acceptable. Since GFI and AGFI is less than 0.9, the model is not fitted well.

Table 16. Baseline comparisons model

Baseline Comparisons					
Model	**NFI Delta1**	**RFI rho1**	**IFI Delta2**	**TLI rho2**	**CFI**
MO	.857	.793	.873	.814	.872
Saturated model	1.000		1.000		1.000
Independence model	.000	.000	.000	.000	.000

Source: Authors.

As Table 16, for the second order confirmatory factor analysis, for baseline, CFI = 0.872 and NFI is 0.857. However, the value of CFI and NFI more than 0.90 is known to be a good fit for model (Bentler, 1992). So, the second order CFA is not well fitted, based on baseline comparison.

Table 17. RMSEA for second order confirmatory analysis

RMSEA				
Model	**RMSEA**	**LO 90**	**HI 90**	**PCLOSE**
MO	.135	.121	.149	.000
Independence model	.312	.301	.324	.000

Source: Authors.

As shown in Table 17, the RMSEA value is 0.135. However, the model is not well fitted since the value should less than 0.05. So, it can be concluded on the basis of goodness-of-fit the hypothesized model fits is not reasonably well and needs further analysis.

3.6.3. Last order confirmatory factor analysis

According to previous research on the Structural Equation Modeling (SEM) technique, "Last Order Confirmatory Factor Analysis" is not usually performed as a separate phase. In this procedure carried out under figure 4, there is normally no distinct "Last Order" CFA phase. Prior to analyzing the structural links, the CFA as mentioned in Figure 4, studies are centered on verifying the validity and reliability of the measurement models.

Figure 4. Last order confirmatory analysis

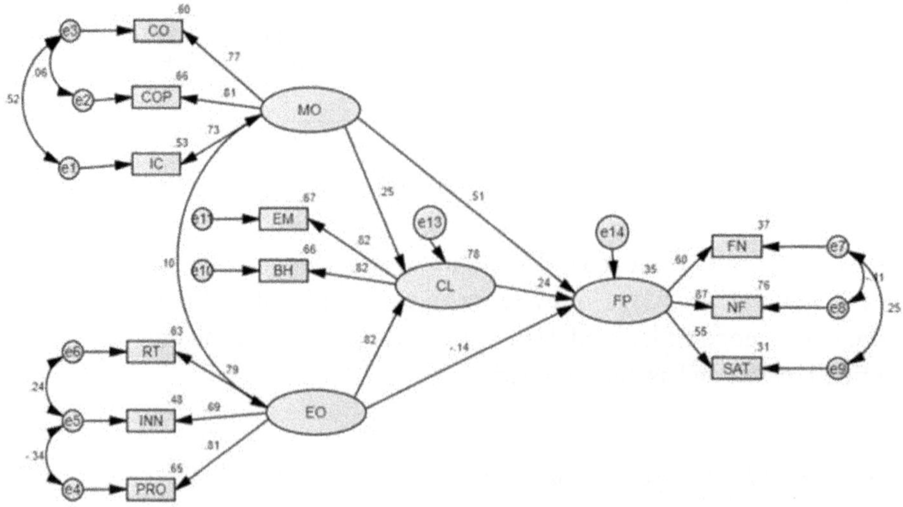

(Authors)

Table 18. CMIN for lasted order confirmatory analysis by AMOS

Model	NPAR	CMIN	DF	P	CMIN/DF
MO	37	33.922	29	.242	1.170
Saturated model	66	.000	0		
Independence model	11	2036.401	55	.000	37.025

Source: Authors.

In the Table 18, by last order CFA, the value CMIN is 33.922, DF is 29 and CMIN / DF is 1.170 (Standard Recommended value is < = 5) in which the model is well fitted.

Table 19. RMR and GFI test for last order confirmatory analysis

Model	RMR	GFI	AGFI	PGFI
MO	.012	.985	.965	.433
Saturated model	.000	1.000		
Independence model	.133	.429	.314	.357

Source: Authors.

As Table 19 shows the value of GFI= 0.985 and AGFI=0.965, for the model fitness GFI and AGFI must greater than 0.9. The RMR value in this table is 0.012 and it is acceptable since its value is less than 0.8. Based on this evidence, fitness for the model fit is well.

Table 20. Baseline comparisons for last order confirmatory model

Model	NFI Delta1	RFI rho1	IFI Delta2	TLI rho2	CFI
MO	.983	.968	.998	.995	.998
Saturated model	1.000		1.000		1.000
Independence model	.000	.000	.000	.000	.000

Source: Authors.

For this last order confirmatory factor analysis, the value of baseline comparison has been checked. As we can see on the Table 20, CFI value is 0.998 and NFI is 0.983. As Bentler (1992), acceptable value of CFI and NFI is more than 0.90. So, the last order CFA fitness is well based on baseline comparison.

Table 21. RMSEA for the last order confirmatory analysis

Model	RMSEA	LO 90	HI 90	PCLOSE
MO	.021	.000	.046	.975
Independence model	.307	.295	.318	.000

Source: Authors.

As per Table 21 output, the last order CFA the RMSE value is 0.021. Since the value 0.021 is less than 0.05, RMSEA value is acceptable for this model. So, it can be concluded that on the basis of our goodness-of-fit results, the hypothesized model fits is reasonably well fitted in the last CFA.

3.7. Testing direct and mediation effect by AMOS

To establish mediation, the following three conditions must hold: First, the independent variable (IV) (tested at step1) must affect the mediator (M); second, the independent variable (tested at step2) must be shown to affect the dependent variable (DV) and third, the mediator must affect the dependent variable. If effect of independent variables (Market orientation and entrepreneurship orientation) on DV significant also after IV+M (*Customer* loyalty in this study) has significant, the mediator partially mediates the relationship between IV and DV but if effect of independent variable (MO and EO) on DV not significant and after IV+M has significant as shown in Table 22, the mediation fully mediates the relationship between IV and DV (Baron & Kenny, 1986).

Table 22. Testing mediation effect by standardized coefficients (r)

	Standardized total Effect	Standardized direct Effect	Standardized in direct effect	Indirect/Total
EO→ CL	.822	.822	.000	
MO→ CL	.247	.247	.000	
MO→ FP	.570	.512	.058	.058/.570=.102
EO→ FP	.054	-.141	.194	.194/.054= 3.6
CL→ FP	.236	.236	.000	

Source: Authors.

The standardized indirect (mediated) effect of MO on FP is .058. when MO goes up by 1 standard deviation, FP goes up by 0.058 standard deviations. This is in addition to any direct (unmediated) effect that MO may have on FP. The standardized indirect (mediated) effect of EO on FP is .194. when EO goes up by 1 standard deviation, FP goes up by 0.194 standard deviations. As finding showed, CL partially metiates the relation between MO and FP. However, CL fully mediates the relation ship between EO and firm performance.

4. DISCUSSION

This research is related with the thematic area of present book customer loyalty and present chapter wants to address the issue related to customer loyalty in hospitality industry with augmentation of market orientation. In the discussion part authors tested the hypothesis as discussed below.

H1: There is relationship between market orientation and business performance. The standardized direct effect of MO on FP is 0.512. When MO goes up by 1 standard deviation, FP goes up by 51.2% standard deviations. Hence, H1 is accepted. This finding supports the findings of Wakjira and Kant (2022).

H2: There is a relationship between entrepreneurial orientation and business performance. The standardized direct (unmediated) effect of EO on FP is -.141. When EO goes up by 1 standard deviation, FP goes down by 14.1% standard deviations. Hence, H2 is rejected. This finding supports the finding of Singh (2021).

H3: There is a relationship between market orientation and customer loyalty. The standardized direct (unmediated) effect of MO on CL is .247. When MO goes up by 1 standard deviation, CL goes up by 24.7% standard deviations. Hence, H3 is accepted. This finding is similar to the finding of Lemma, (2020).

H4: There is a significant positive relationship between entrepreneurial orientation and customer loyalty. The standardized direct (unmediated) effect of EO on CL is 0.822. When EO goes up by 1 standard deviation, CL goes up by 82.2% standard deviations. Hence, H4 is accepted. This finding is similar to Arfaei et al. (2012).

H5: There is a relationship between customer loyalty and business performance. The standardized direct (unmediated) effect of CL on FP is .236. When CL goes up by 1 standard deviation, FP goes up by 23.6% standard deviations. Hence, H5 is accepted. This is the same finding as Omoregie et al. (2019).

H6a: Customer loyalty significantly mediates the relationship between market orientation and business performance. The standardized indirect (mediated) effect of MO on FP is .058. When MO goes up by 1 standard deviation, FP goes up by 5.8% standard deviations. The direct effect of MO on FP 51.2% is greater than mediated effect of MO on FP which 5.8%. Hence, H6a is rejected. This finding opposes Boonmalert et al. (2021) finding.

H6b: Customer loyalty significantly mediates the relationship between entrepreneurial orientation and business performance. The standardized indirect (mediated) effect of EO on FP is .194. When EO goes up by 1 standard deviation, FP goes up by 19.4% standard deviations. The indirect effect of CL on FP 19.4% is greater than direct effect of CL on FP which is -14.1%. Hence, H6b is accepted. This finding supports the finding of Ismail (2023).

5. CONCLUSION

This study focused on the effect of market orientation and entrepreneurial orientation of hotel performance with mediating role of customer loyalty. The study was based on Narver and Slater (1990), which includes three components of market orientation: customer orientation, competitor orientation, and cross-functional integration for market orientation. For entrepreneurial orientation, the study was focused on Morris and Paul (1987) expressed the understanding of Entrepreneurial Orientation is one with decision-making norms that emphasize proactive, innovative strategies that contain an element of risk. For performance measurement, the study focused on BSC model developed in 1992 by Kaplan and Norton, which includes learning and growth, internal business process, customer satisfaction and financial performance. In this study customer loyalty dimensions were based on the customer loyalty model proposed by Dwyer in 1987, which includes cognitive, affective, and behavioral dimensions.

To fill theoretical gap of previous study, this research included: resource-based view theory, market based view theory, Dynamic capability theory and Service dominant logic model.

To collect data from respondents, a structured questionnaire having five point likert scales has been used. To analyze data SPSS version 23 and AMOS version 22 have been used. Structural equation modeling was used in the study. The reliability of questionnaire was checked by using Cronbach's alpha and the all variables are having its value more than .06. Convergent and divergent validity of the data was checked by principal component analysis and factor loading in the study for suitability of data for CFA.

Moreover, this model is saturated model because it has zero degree of freedom. Saturated model shows perfect fit with data. This research support RBV theory since the resources of the organization are vital for performance of organization. MBV theory also supported by this research because of in addition to resource of an organization, the success is the function of environmental drivers. Dynamic capability theory was also used in this research and the finding of the study supports the theory because learning about customers and their behavior is important to be successful. Service dynamic logic has also been supported by this study finding because of co-creation of value is important to be profitable in organization.

Based on the finding of this study, both MO and EO are important for firm performance in hotel industry since MO and EO affect firm performance directly as the model of the study shows. However, in the incorporation of mediating variable customer loyalty, the result has been changed. As we can see from the study, the indirect effect of customer loyalty between MO and firm performance is significant; however direct effect is more compared with indirect effect. So, customer loyalty can mediate the relationship between market orientation and firm performance in the hotel industry. The indirect effect of EO on firm performance is significant. But with the introduction of Customer loyalty between EO and FP, their relationship increased. So that, we can say, customer loyalty mediates the relationship between MO and EO fully.

Based on the finding the study, hypothesis developed was tested. Hence, H2 and H6 have been rejected and H1, H3, H4 and H5 were rejected.

In this study, the researcher focused only on MO and EO from strategic orientation dimensions. The strategic orientation dimensions are not only limited to MO and EO. So that, the interested researchers should focus on the dimensions not incorporated in this in this study. They have to also focus on green MO and EO since environmental concerns are important in this contemporary business to gain attention of environment sensitive customer. The present study is cross sectional in nature and the further researchers' needs to longitudinal. Present study is quantitative. Therefore, the interested researchers in the area will follow qualitative approach also to get more insight.

This study investigated the issues related with effect of market orientation on business performance, effect of entrepreneurial orientation on business performance, effect market orientation on customer loyalty in the study area, effect of entrepreneurial orientation on customer loyalty, effect of customer loyalty on business performance and mediation effect of customer loyalty between market orientation, entrepreneurial orientation and business performance, which is unique for manifestation of customer loyalty importance and able to fill the existing knowledge gap.

REFERENCES

Abu-Rumman, A., Al Shraah, A., Al-Madi, F., & Alfalah, T. (2021). Entrepreneurial networks, entrepreneurial orientation, and performance of small and medium enterprises: Are dynamic capabilities the missing link? *Journal of Innovation and Entrepreneurship*, 10(1), 1–16. DOI: 10.1186/s13731-021-00170-8

Acosta, A. S., Crespo, Á. H., & Agudo, J. C. (2018). Effect of market orientation, network capability and entrepreneurial orientation on international performance of small and medium enterprises (SMEs). *International Business Review*, 27(6), 1128–1140. DOI: 10.1016/j.ibusrev.2018.04.004

Alnawas, I., & Hemsley-Brown, J. (2019). Market orientation and hotel performance: Investigating the role of high-order marketing capabilities. *International Journal of Contemporary Hospitality Management*, 31(4), 1885–1905. DOI: 10.1108/IJCHM-07-2018-0564

Arfaei, A., Mohammadi, R., & Akbari, P. (2012). Study the effects of corporate entrepreneurial orientation on customer loyalty (Case Study: Broadcasting companies in the food, pharmaceutical and health in Kermanshah, Iran). *International Research Journal of Applied and Basic Sciences*, 3, 2620–2625.

Baron, R. M., & Kenny, D. A. (1986). The moderator–mediator variable distinction in social psychological research: Conceptual, strategic, and statistical considerations. *Journal of Personality and Social Psychology*, 51(6), 1173–1182. DOI: 10.1037/0022-3514.51.6.1173 PMID: 3806354

Bentler, P. M. (1992). On the fit of models to covariances and methodology to the Bulletin. *Psychological Bulletin*, 112(3), 400–404. DOI: 10.1037/0033-2909.112.3.400 PMID: 1438635

Boonmalert, W., Ayasanond, C., Phoothong, B., & Chaitorn, T. (2021). A causal influence model of innovation and digital marketing on the small and medium enterprise (SME) performance in Thailand. *European Journal of Molecular & Clinical Medicine, 8*(03), 63-72. ISSN 2515-8260

Browne, M. W., & Cudeck, R. (1993). *Alternative ways of assessing model fit. Testing structural equation models*. KA Bollen and JS Long.

Bustos-Reyes, C. A., & González-Benito, Ó. (2008). Store and store format loyalty measures based on budget allocation. *Journal of Business Research*, 61(9), 1015–1025. DOI: 10.1016/j.jbusres.2007.03.008

Chuang, S. H. (2018). Facilitating the chain of market orientation to value co-creation: The mediating role of e-marketing adoption. *Journal of Destination Marketing & Management*, 7, 39–49. DOI: 10.1016/j.jdmm.2016.08.007

Covin, J. G., & Wales, W. J. (2019). Crafting high-impact entrepreneurial orientation research: Some suggested guidelines. *Entrepreneurship Theory and Practice*, 43(1), 3–18. DOI: 10.1177/1042258718773181

Criado-Gomis, A., Iniesta-Bonillo, M. Á., & Cervera-Taulet, A. (2018). Sustainable entrepreneurial orientation within an intrapreneurial context: Effects on business performance. *The International Entrepreneurship and Management Journal*, 14(2), 295–308. DOI: 10.1007/s11365-018-0503-x

Cuevas-Vargas, H., Parga-Montoya, N., & Fernández-Escobedo, R. (2019). Effects of Entrepreneurial Orientation on Business Performance: The Mediating Role of Customer Satisfaction - A Formative Reflective Model Analysis. *SAGE Open*, 9(2). Advance online publication. DOI: 10.1177/2158244019859088

Dabrowski, D., Brzozowska-Woś, M., Gołąb-Andrzejak, E., & Firgolska, A. (2019). Market orientation and hotel performance: The mediating effect of creative marketing programs. *Journal of Hospitality and Tourism Management*, 41, 175–183. DOI: 10.1016/j.jhtm.2019.10.006

Dam, S. M., & Dam, T. C. (2021). Relationships between service quality, brand image, customer satisfaction, and customer loyalty. *The Journal of Asian Finance. Economics and Business*, 8(3), 585–593.

Dick, A. S., & Basu, K. (1994). Customer loyalty: Toward an integrated conceptual framework. *Journal of the Academy of Marketing Science*, 22(2), 99–113. DOI: 10.1177/0092070394222001

Dudic, Z., Dudic, B., Gregus, M., Novackova, D., & Djakovic, I. (2020). The innovativeness and usage of the balanced scorecard model in SMEs. *Sustainability (Basel)*, 12(8), 3221. DOI: 10.3390/su12083221

Field, A. P. (2005). Is the meta-analysis of correlation coefficients accurate when population correlations vary? *Psychological Methods*, 10(4), 444–467. DOI: 10.1037/1082-989X.10.4.444 PMID: 16392999

Fitriati, T. K., Purwana, D., Buchdadi, A. D., & Subagja, I. K. (2020). Entrepreneurial orientation and SME performance: Dynamic capabilities as mediation study on SMEs in Indonesia. *KnE Social Sciences*, 74-89. .DOI: 10.18502/kss.v4i14.7860

Ghee, W. Y. (2018). An application of Timmons model in the mini entrepreneurial logistics project. *Advances in Social Sciences Research Journal*, 5(10). Advance online publication. DOI: 10.14738/assrj.510.5541

Goulap, J. B. (2020). Entrepreneurial orientation and business performance: An assessment of start-up companies. *International Journal of Engineering and Management Research*, 10(2), 151–163. DOI: 10.31033/ijemr.10.2.18

Hair, J. F., Hult, G. T. M., Ringle, C. M., & Sarstedt, M. (2022). *A Primer on Partial Least Squares Structural Equation Modeling (PLS-SEM)* (3rd rd.). Thousand Oaks: Sage.

Halim, H. A., Ahmad, N. H., & Ramayah, T. (2019). Sustaining the innovation culture in SMEs: The importance of organisational culture, organisational learning and market orientation. *Asian Journal of Business Research*, 9(2), 14–33. DOI: 10.14707/ajbr.190059

Hassen, Y., & Singh, A. (2020). The effect of market orientation on the performance of small and medium enterprises in case of Amhara Region, Ethiopia. *Journal of New Business Ventures*, 1(1-2), 92–109. DOI: 10.1177/2632962X20961051

Helfat, C. E., Finkelstein, S., Mitchell, W., Peteraf, M. A., Singh, H., Teece, D. J., & Winter, S. G. (2007). *Dynamic Capabilities: Understanding Strategic Change in Organizations*. Blackwell Publishing., DOI: 10.1287/orsc.1120.0810

Hernández-Linares, R., López-Fernández, M. C., García-Piqueres, G., Pina e Cunha, M., & Rego, A. (2023). How knowledge-based dynamic capabilities relate to firm performance: The mediating role of entrepreneurial orientation. *Review of Managerial Science*, •••, 1–33. DOI: 10.1007/s11846-023-00691-4

Hiong, L. S., Ferdinand, A. T., & Listiana, E. (2020). Techno-resonance innovation capability for enhancing marketing performance: A perspective of RA-theory. *Business: Theory and Practice*, 21(1), 329–339. https://hdl.handle.net/10419/248033. DOI: 10.3846/btp.2020.12117

Hu, L. T., & Bentler, P. M. (1999). Cutoff criteria for fit indexes in covariance structure analysis: Conventional criteria versus new alternatives. *Structural Equation Modeling*, 6(1), 1–55. DOI: 10.1080/10705519909540118

Hutagalung, L., Sinaga, P., Tan, J., & Tukiran, M. (2020). The Role of e-marketing and Customer Oriented on Business Performance Through Customer Loyalty and Hotels Competitive Advantage. *Kontigensi: Jurnal Ilmiah Manajemen*, 8(2), 202–217. DOI: 10.56457/jimk.v8i2.163

Ighomereho, S. (2022). Market and Entrepreneurial Orientations as Predictors of Small and Medium Enterprises' Performance in the Covid-19 Era. *Innovative Marketing*, 18(2), 161–173. DOI: 10.21511/im.18(2).2022.14

Ismail, I. J. (2023). Speaking to the hearts of the customers! The mediating effect of customer loyalty on customer orientation, technology orientation and business performance. *Technological Sustainability*, 2(1), 44–66. DOI: 10.1108/TECHS-03-2022-0016

Jacoby, J., & Kyner, D. B. (1973). Brand loyalty vs. repeat purchasing behavior. *JMR, Journal of Marketing Research*, 10(1), 1–9. DOI: 10.1177/002224377301000101

Javalgi, R. R. G., Martin, C. L., & Young, R. B. (2018). Marketing research, market orientation and customer relationship management: A framework and implications for service providers. *Journal of Services Marketing*, 20(1), 12–23. DOI: 10.1108/08876040610646545

Jeong, G. Y. (2017). The effect of entrepreneurial orientation on marketing capability. *Korean Corp. Manag. Rev.*, 24(4), 75–106. Advance online publication. DOI: 10.21052/KCMR.2017.24.4.04

Jercinovic, S., & Ham, M. (2022, October). The Significance of Social Benefit Orientation in Market Orientation for the Realization of The Strategic Marketing Concept of Sustainability. In *Economic and Social Development (Book of Proceedings), 88th International Scientific Conference on Economic and Social Development* (p. 320). DOI: 10.22616/ESRD.2018.105

Joensuu-Salo, S., Sorama, K., Viljamaa, A., & Varamäki, E. (2018). Firm performance among internationalized SMEs: The interplay of market orientation, marketing capability and digitalization. *Administrative Sciences*, 8(3), 31. DOI: 10.3390/admsci8030031

Kachouie, R., Mavondo, F., & Sands, S. (2018). Dynamic marketing capabilities view on creating market change. *European Journal of Marketing*, 52(5/6), 1007–1036. DOI: 10.1108/EJM-10-2016-0588

Kazemian, S., Djajadikerta, H. G., Said, J., Roni, S. M., Trireksani, T., & Alam, M. M. (2021). Corporate governance, market orientation and performance of Iran's upscale hotels. *Tourism and Hospitality Research*, 21(3), 344–357. DOI: 10.1177/14673584211003644

Kellermanns, F. W., Hernández-Linares, R., & López-Fernández, M. C. (2018). A note on the relationships between learning, market, and entrepreneurial orientations in family and nonfamily firms. *Journal of Family Business Strategy*, 9(3), 192–204. DOI: 10.1016/j.jfbs.2018.08.001

Khan, M., & Ghouri, A. M. (2018). Enhancing customer satisfaction and loyalty through customer-defined market orientation and customer inspiration: A critical literature review. *International Business Education Journal*, 11(1), 25–39. DOI: 10.37134/ibej.vol11.1.3.2018

Kinnear, P. R., & Gray, C. D. (2010). *PASW statistics 17 made simple*. Psychology Press.

Kohli, A. K., Jaworski, B. J., & Kumar, A. (1993). MARKOR: A measure of market orientation. *JMR, Journal of Marketing Research*, 30(4), 467–477. DOI: 10.1177/002224379303000406

Kombo, D. K., Tromp, D. L., & DL, A. (2006). *Proposal and thesis writing*. Paulines Publication Africa.

Lekmat, L., Selvarajah, C., & Hewege, C. (2018). Relationship between Market Orientation, Entrepreneurial Orientation, and Firm Performance in Thai SMEs: The Mediating Role of Marketing Capabilities. *European Journal of Pediatric Dermatology : PD*, 28(4).

Lemma, S. (2020). *Impact of customer orientation of service employees on relationship quality and customer loyalty (case study of commercial bank of Ethiopia in Addis Ababa)*. Doctoral dissertation, St. Mary's University.

Maharani, B. P., & Saroso, D. S. (2020). Analysis of Service Quality an Empirical Study of Customer Satisfaction in Information and Technology Service Companies. *Dinasti International Journal of Digital Business Management*, 1(2), 200–209. DOI: 10.31933/dijdbm.v1i2.152

Marsh, H. W., Balla, J. R., & Hau, K. T. (2013). An evaluation of incremental fit indices: A clarification of mathematical and empirical properties. In *Advanced structural equation modeling* (pp. 315–353). Psychology Press.

Miller, D. (1983). The correlates of entrepreneurship in three types of firms. *Management Science*, 29(7), 770–791. DOI: 10.1287/mnsc.29.7.770

Montiel-Campos, H. (2018). Entrepreneurial orientation and market orientation: Systematic literature review and future research. *Journal of Research in Marketing and Entrepreneurship*, 20(2), 292–322. DOI: 10.1108/JRME-09-2017-0040

Morris, M. H., & Paul, G. W. (1987). The relationship between entrepreneurship and marketing in established firms. *Journal of Business Venturing*, 2(3), 247–259. DOI: 10.1016/0883-9026(87)90012-7

Narver, J. C., & Slater, S. F. (1990). The effect of a market orientation on business profitability. *Journal of Marketing*, 54(4), 20–35. DOI: 10.1177/002224299005400403

Narver, J. C., Slater, S. F., & MacLachlan, D. L. (2004). Responsive and proactive market orientation and new-product success. *Journal of Product Innovation Management*, 21(5), 334–347. DOI: 10.1111/j.0737-6782.2004.00086.x

Nuvriasari, A., Ishak, A., Hidayat, A., Mustafa, Z., & Haryono, S. (2020). The effect of market and entrepreneurship orientation on SME's business performance: The role of entrepreneurial marketing in Indonesian Batik industries. *European Journal of Business and Management*, 12(5), 29–37.

Octavia, A., Indrawijaya, S., Sriayudha, Y., & Hasbullah, H. (2020). Impact on E-commerce adoption on entrepreneurial orientation and market orientation in business performance of SMEs. *Asian Economic and Financial Review*, 10(5), 516–525. DOI: 10.18488/journal.aefr.2020.105.516.525

Oduro, S., & Haylemariam, L. G. (2019). Market orientation, CSR and financial and marketing performance in manufacturing firms in Ghana and Ethiopia. *Sustainability Accounting. Management and Policy Journal*, 10(3), 398–426. DOI: 10.1108/SAMPJ-11-2018-0309

Omoregie, O. K., Addae, J. A., Coffie, S., Ampong, G. O. A., & Ofori, K. S. (2019). Factors influencing consumer loyalty: Evidence from the Ghanaian retail banking industry. *International Journal of Bank Marketing*, 37(3), 798–820. DOI: 10.1108/IJBM-04-2018-0099

Orodho, A. J., & Kombo, D. K. (2002). Research methods. Nairobi: Kenyatta University, Institute of Open Learning. *International Journal of Economics, Commerce and Management, 39*(7), 48-50.

Presutti, M., Savioli, M., & Odorici, V. (2020). Strategic orientation of hotels: Evidence from a contingent approach. *Tourism Economics*, 26(7), 1212–1230. DOI: 10.1177/1354816619868886

Quintana, C., Reiser, B. J., Davis, E. A., Krajcik, J., Fretz, E., Duncan, R. G., & Soloway, E. (2018). A scaffolding design framework for software to support science inquiry. In *Scaffolding* (pp. 337–386). Psychology Press.

Rahman, M. M., & Saima, F. N. (2018). Efficiency of board composition on firm performance: Empirical evidence from listed manufacturing firms of Bangladesh. *The Journal of Asian Finance. Economics and Business*, 5(2), 53–61. DOI: 10.13106/jafeb.2018.vol5.no2.53

Randhawa, K., Wilden, R., & Gudergan, S. (2021). How to innovate toward an ambidextrous business model? The role of dynamic capabilities and market orientation. *Journal of Business Research*, 130, 618–634. DOI: 10.1016/j.jbusres.2020.05.046

Rezaei, J., & Ortt, R. (2018). Entrepreneurial orientation and firm performance: The mediating role of functional performances. *Management Research Review*, 41(7), 878–900. DOI: 10.1108/MRR-03-2017-0092

Rubera, G., & Kirca, A. H. (2017). You gotta serve somebody: The effects of firm innovation on customer satisfaction and firm value. *Journal of the Academy of Marketing Science*, 45(5), 741–761. DOI: 10.1007/s11747-016-0512-7

Sampaio, C. A. F., Hernández, J. M. H., & de Rodrigues, R. J. A. G. (2020). The relationship between market orientation, customer loyalty and business performance: A sample from the Western Europe hotel industry. *Tourism and Hospitality Research*, 20(2), 131–143. DOI: 10.1177/1467358419829179

Santra, I. K. (2018). Entrepreneurial orientation and marketing performance of budget hotel smes in Bali Island. *International Journal of Entrepreneurship*, 22(4), 1–11.

Selmi, N., & Chaney, D. (2018). A measure of revenue management orientation and its mediating role in the relationship between market orientation and performance. *Journal of Business Research*, 89, 99–109. DOI: 10.1016/j.jbusres.2018.04.008

Shiferaw, B. (2018). *The effect of internal marketing on customer orientation of employees: the case of selected star hotels in Addis Ababa.* Published Master Thesis. Department of Marketing Management Addis Ababa University School of Commerce.

Singh, A. (2021). The Effect of Entrepreneurial Orientation on Business Performance of Small and Medium Scale Enterprises: A Study of Amhara Region of Ethiopia. *SSRN*. DOI: 10.2139/ssrn.3769062

Stojanovic, A., Milosevic, I., Arsic, S., Urosevic, S., & Mihajlovic, I. (2020). Corporate social responsibility as a determinant of employee loyalty and business performance. *Journal of Competitiveness*, 12(2), 149–166. DOI: 10.7441/joc.2020.02.09

Taheri, B., Bititci, U., Gannon, M. J., & Cordina, R. (2019). Investigating the influence of performance measurement on learning, entrepreneurial orientation and performance in turbulent markets. *International Journal of Contemporary Hospitality Management*, 31(3), 1224–1246. DOI: 10.1108/IJCHM-11-2017-0744

Tajeddini, K., & Ratten, V. (2020). The moderating effect of brand orientation on inter-firm market orientation and performance. *Journal of Strategic Marketing*, 28(3), 194–224. DOI: 10.1080/0965254X.2017.1293138

Varadarajan, R. (2020). Customer information resources advantage, marketing strategy and business performance: A market resources based view. *Industrial Marketing Management*, 89, 89–97. DOI: 10.1016/j.indmarman.2020.03.003

Vargo, S. L., & Lusch, R. F. (2004). Evolving to a new dominant logic for marketing. *Journal of Marketing*, 68(1), 1–17. DOI: 10.1509/jmkg.68.1.1.24036

Wakjira, G. G., & Kant, S. (2022). Significance of Market Orientation On Business Performance With Mediating Role of Employee And Customer Satisfaction In Ethiopia Banks. *Partners Universal International Research Journal*, 1(4), 118–125. DOI: 10.5281/zenodo.7495221

Wales, W. J., Covin, J. G., & Monsen, E. (2020). Entrepreneurial orientation: The necessity of a multilevel conceptualization. *Strategic Entrepreneurship Journal*, 14(4), 639–660. DOI: 10.1002/sej.1344

Wang, Y., Shi, S., Chen, Y., & Gursoy, D. (2019). An examination of market orientation and environmental marketing strategy: The case of Chinese firms. *Service Industries Journal*, 39(15-16), 1046–1071. DOI: 10.1080/02642069.2018.1551370

Wang, Y., Shi, S., Chen, Y., & Gursoy, D. (2019). An examination of market orientation and environmental marketing strategy: The case of Chinese firms. *Service Industries Journal*, 39(15-16), 1046–1071. DOI: 10.1080/02642069.2018.1551370

Wongleedee, K. (2020). Role of Customer Loyalty on Employee Performance and Productivity in Pharmacy Business in Thailand. *Systematic Reviews in Pharmacy*, 11(2). Advance online publication. DOI: 10.5530/srp.2020.2.91

Yang, Y. I., & Chung, J. H. (2006). The impact of market orientation on marketing capability and performance in the hotel industry. *J. Hosp. Tour. Stud.*, 8, 44–56. DOI: 10.3390/su11030729

ADDITIONAL READING

Baskoro, B. D., Radzi, R. M., & Omar, N. D. (2022). Entrepreneurial Orientation,-Psychological Capital, Entrepreneurial Strategy, and Firm Performance on Private Daycare in Indonesia: A Conceptual Paper. *ESI* Preprints, *12*, 450-492. doi:. 2022. p450.DOI: 10.19044/esipreprint.12

Bekata, A. T., & Kero, C. A. (2024). Customer orientation, open innovation and enterprise performance, evidence from Ethiopian SMEs. *Cogent Business & Management*, 11(1), 2320462. Advance online publication. DOI: 10.1080/23311975.2024.2320462

Pratono, A. H., & Mahmood, R. (2015). Mediating effect of marketing capability and reward philosophy in the relationship between entrepreneurial orientation and firm performance. *Journal of Global Entrepreneurship Research*, 5(1), 1–12. DOI: 10.1186/s40497-015-0023-x

Wakjira, G. G. (2023). Assessments of CFA Measurement Model of Digital Marketing Success with Business Performance: The Mediating role of Customer Loyalty: The Case of Commercial Banks of Ethiopia (CBE), Ethiopia. *International Journal of Social Science. Management and Economics Research*, 1(2), 38–47. DOI: 10.61421/IJSSMER.2023.1204

KEY TERMS AND DEFINITIONS

Confirmatory Factor Analysis: A statistical method for confirming a collection of observed variables' component structure and determining if the data matches a proposed measurement model.

Convergent Validity: The degree of correlation between a measure and other measures that the measure is theoretically expected to correlate with, indicating the efficacy of the measurement of the concept.

Discriminant Validity: A measure's uniqueness is demonstrated by how different it is from other measures that it is not logically supposed to correlate with.

Goodness-of-Fit Indices: Measures of statistical significance that show how well a collection of observable data fits a theoretical model; these metrics are used to assess how well a structural equation model fits data overall.

Latent Construct: An inferred theoretical variable from a collection of observable variables that are thought to reflect the construct but cannot be explicitly seen or measured.

Measurement Model: The part of a structural equation model that describes how the underlying latent constructs that the observable variables are intended to assess relate to each other.

Structural Equation Modeling: A multivariate statistical method for examining the connections among observable and latent variables by fusing elements of factor analysis and multiple regressions.

Chapter 15
Customer Orientation and Ethiopian Bank Performance With Mediation of Competitive Advantage

Dawit Jabo
https://orcid.org/0009-0002-1828-1982
Bule Hora University, Ethiopia

Shashi Kant
https://orcid.org/0000-0003-4722-5736
Bule Hora University, Ethiopia

Brehanu Borji
Independent Researcher, Ethiopia

ABSTRACT

The impact of competitive advantage in mitigating the detrimental impacts of customer orientation on business performance was examined in this chapter. Few research have examined the relationship between competitive advantage and customer orientation and how it influences business success in emerging economies, particularly in sub-Saharan Africa. This article attempted to investigate the matter from an Ethiopian perspective in order to bridge that gap. a response obtained from the 383 Commercial Bank of Ethiopia (CBE) customers in the Dilla area of southern Ethiopia using a survey questionnaire. Employing SPSS and AMOS edition 26 together with the Structure Equation Model (SEM) technique, the collected

DOI: 10.4018/979-8-3693-5340-0.ch015

data was analysed to see if the two proposed variables were related. The results showed that customer orientation has a positive, significant influence on business performance through the competitive advantage negotiating process. The results of this study suggest that commercial banks should use client orientation to obtain a competitive advantage.

1. INTRODUCTION

Customers are a limited resource in the competitive circumstances of today. The banking industry's performance depends on its ability to recognize the regular changes in the needs and wishes of its consumers. Typically, banks must also be aware of their competitors as their products and services are more likely to appeal to customers' preferences and choices (Aqmala & Putra, 2021).

According to certain research customer orientation is a strategy that attempts to provide the banking sector with a clear objective and unique viewpoint while also increasing knowledge and accessibility (Gonu et al., 2023; Rahman et al., 2021). It is the clients, and it is thought to result in services that offer greater value to the client and help the banking sector outperform (Muis & Isyanto, 2021; Puspaningrum, 2020). A competitive advantage that the banking industry may use is client orientation in customer knowledge (Bankole et al., 2022; Yuliantari & Pramuki, 2022). For this reason, it is anticipated that client orientation would be advantageous for bank sectors as well as other business kinds.

The tactic and practice of consistently evaluating the needs and preferences of customers in order to attract and satisfy them is known as customer orientation. If client orientation is used, the business sector will function more efficiently (Domi & Musabelliu, 2020). Studying and investigating this subject is essential as customer orientation is a critical topic of discussion that will determines competitive advantage and produces high performance (Aqmala & Putra, 2021; Gontur et al., 2022). An operational concept known as "customer orientation" centers all business activities around the needs and wants of the customer.

Customer orientation is also significant since it is linked to company performance, as it generates a critical performance element for business performance (Domi & Musabelliu, 2020; Dos Santos et al., 2020). Thus, the ability of the industry to service its consumers is ultimately what determines a business's performance, meaning that in order to become more competitive, the sector needs to adopt more strategies like client orientation (Muis & Isyanto, 2021). If businesses in the banking industry can get a competitive advantage, their performance will improve (Bankole et al., 2022). A competitive advantage makes a company operate more efficiently and performance fully (Hendi & Arafah, 2022; Priyanto & Murwaningsari, 2022). According to

Sampaio and Régio (2022), there is a possibility that competitive advantage acts as a mediator between the impact of client orientation and firm efficiency.

This inquiry is also predicted to provide several results. This study initially looks at a number of business parameters in order to support performance improvement at the commercial bank of Ethiopia's selected locations in the Dilla area, which are now quite competitive. Additionally, the goal of this study is to close any gaps in the literature about the influence of customer orientation on business performance. Finally, this study aims to show how a competitive advantage might mediate customer focus and improve the business performance of selected commercial bank branches in the Dilla area of Ethiopia.

2. REVIEW OF LITERATURE

2.1. Performance of business

One way to conceptualize corporate performance is as a complex concept that encompasses elements beyond income (Ghlichlee & Bayat, 2021). According to Abuzid and Abbas (2017), business performance is the culmination of all company activities and processes. Rahman et al. (2021) on the other hand, defined business performance as the degree to which an industry has reached its objective. According to Domi and Musabelliu (2020), customer orientation refers to how customers characterize performance variations between companies. A company's performance is enhanced by customer orientation as it gives it a competitive edge.

There is a wealth of empirical data linking corporate performance with client orientation. Previous studies have found a relationship between customer orientation and business performance that is either direct (Amegavie et al., 2019; Hanaysha & Mehmood, 2022; Rahman et al., 2021); indirect (Abuzid & Abbas, 2017; Kelvin & Joyce, 2019; Sampaio & Régio, 2022) or dual (Ghlichlee & Bayat, 2021; Hanafi & Yahia, 2022).

According to Rahman et al. (2021), corporate performance is the extent to which an industry can meet the needs of its customers as well as its own survival requirements. The definition that the researcher for this study would adopt is the one provided by Ghlichlee and Bayat (2021) and Oluwatoyin et al. (2018) for the operationalization of firm performance. Market share for non-financial performance and sales growth for financial performance are two ways to measure the monetary and non-monetary performance of a company's components (Enad & Gerinda, 2022; Mokhtaran & Komeilian, 2016). His client focus is therefore one of the most important business performance indicators in the banking industry.

2.2. Competitive Advantage

According to Abdigolbaghi and Sehhat (2018), advantage in the context of competition is an improvement that an industry achieves in a rivalry by providing a more substantial benefit than competitors. If an industry has a competitive resource advantage that allows it to manufacture goods of higher value at lower cost, then it is considered to be in a competitive position.

Understanding competitive advantage requires a comprehensive understanding of competitors' and businesses' performance (Islam & Qamari, 2021; Yang et al., 2022). Competitive advantage stems from a variety of diverse activities, including product quality (Hanaysha & Mehmood, 2022; Rahman et al., 2021), service quality (Bankole et al., 2022; Puspaningrum, 2020), technological capability (Dos Santos et al., 2020; Yuliantari & Pramuki, 2022), and time (Al-Dulaimi et al, 2016; Raewf et al., 2021). Competitive advantage can be measured in a variety of ways, including cost leadership, time of delivery, and technology capability (Aqmala & Putra, 2021; Tarabieh, 2015; Yang et al., 2022). Others include product quality, service quality, and technology capability.

The competitive advantage of the banking industry is seen in the superior quality of their products and services, their advanced technology, and their cheap costs. According to Nyoman et al. (2020), customer orientation produces advantage in the competitive sense. Thus, this study concentrates on the quality of the product, service, technical capability, and time. Based on the aforementioned, that leaves customer orientation as their primary system for establishing competitive advantage.

2.3. Customer orientation

Customer orientation is a basic subordinate concept of market orientation. In general, it is a major worry for all companies, but service-oriented companies particularly so. In order to gather market data, predict future consumer wants, and meet those needs by providing goods and services that are more valuable and improving corporate performance, a concept known as “customer orientation” focuses on the client, the employee, and the industry (Hanaysha & Mehmood, 2022; Muis & Isyanto, 2021). Furthermore, customer-oriented behavior may foster a positive relationship between service providers and clients, which in turn can improve corporate performance (Islam & Qamari, 2021).

Customers are the source of buyer worth in the corporate sector, and buyer worth is produced and preserved through client preference, satisfaction, and engagement (Abuzid & Abbas, 2017; Sampaio & Régio, 2022). Product, preference, retention, and satisfaction—the cores dimensions of customer orientation—are therefore seen as important strategic orientation. These days, an organization's ability to endure in a competitive market is based on how customer-focused it is. Stated differently, the ultimate objectives of sustaining and operating a business or industry are to uphold customer preferences, guarantee them of their contact with their anticipated offerings in the shortest amount of time, and provide the highest quality of product (Abdigolbaghi & Sehhat, 2018; Digdowiseiso & Lestari, 2021; Mosa, 2022).

Despite this, client orientation is defined as preference (Islam & Zhe, 2022), quality in customer service (Gonu et al., 2023), customer happiness (Mistrean, 2021), and goods with distinctive features. Hence, demonstrate the importance of client focus in the banking sector.

3. EMPIRICAL LITERATURE AND DEVELOPMENT OF HYPOTESIS

3.1. Customer orientation and performance of business

Business performance is one of the measures used to examine the performances of the sector's approach since every sector is fascinated with figuring out how to assess the performance of the goods or services that customers purchase (Dos Santos et al., 2020). The performance of the company is based on how well banks promote a client-focused culture (Puspaningrum, 2020). Mokhtaran and Komeilian (2016) and Gonu et al. (2023) provide evidence that a customer-focused approach enhances corporate performance.

A business that prioritises customer needs should be able to anticipate changes in those needs and develop new products and services (Hanaysha & Mehmood, 2022). Consequently, the adoption of a customer-oriented approach ought to augment an organization's ability to modify its operational protocols in reaction to the modifications (Rahman et al., 2021). The "customer orientation" strategy of a corporation puts the needs of the customer ahead of its own (Amegavie et al., 2019). Businesses that put their customers first understand that they cannot prosper unless they constantly increase their customer focus (Sampaio & Régio, 2022). It's a way of thinking that links your business's goals with those of your customers (Kelvin & Joyce, 2019). In view of these considerations, the following hypothesis is formulated:

H1 - Customer orientation positively impacts business performance.

3.2. Customer orientation and competitive advantage

Furthermore, the more customer-focused a company is, the more capable it is of developing a competitive edge through innovation and industry uniqueness (Mosa, 2022). Conversely, a competitor's orientation might be damaging to a company's ability to stand out in the market. Customer satisfaction is the primary objective of customer orientation, which is believed to create more value for customers and give the business a competitive edge by helping it outperform the competition (Digdowiseiso & Lestari, 2021). When implemented properly, market orientation may help a company grow into new markets and retain consumers (Abdigolbaghi & Sehhat, 2018).

In order to obtain a competitive advantage over competitors, market focus may occasionally make known buyer needs that are just too expensive or difficult to fulfil (Bankole et al., 2022). Narver and Slater (1990) identify three main components of market orientation: an opponent orientation that helps an organization understand what its competitors anticipate in a constantly changing market; and a customer orientation that helps an organization understand its target clients (Yuliantari & Pramuki, 2022). In view of these considerations, the following hypothesis is formulated:

H2 - Customer orientation positively impacts competitive advantage.

3.3. Competitive advantage and performance of business

The capacity of a business to create goods or services faster, more efficiently, or cheaper than its rivals is a point of difference (Puspaningrum, 2020). These elements enable the manufacturing facility to outperform its competitors in terms of sales or profit margins (Raewf et al., 2021). Al-Dulaimi et al. (2016) research indicates a strong correlation between corporate performance and competitive advantage. Businesses that have a competitive edge might make more money since they are unique and hard for competitors to imitate. Firm rivalry in the market drives companies to enhance their products, which are then presented to customers as more efficient, effective, and customized choices (Dos Santos et al., 2020).

The most evident benefits of competition for users are lower expenses and increased buying power. The company has an edge over competitors as it can provide customers with reduced price (Yang et al., 2022). When a business offers customers unique or exceptional products or services that are thought to be more value than those offered by its rivals, it has an advantage over them (Aqmala & Putra, 2021). A company may increase its market share, boost earnings, and break into new markets with the aid of a competitive advantage (Cakir et al., 2022; Tarabieh, 2015). Furthermore, it might help shield a business from the potential for competitors to have access to its trade (Kimiti et al., 2021). In view of these considerations, the following hypothesis is formulated:

H3 - Competitive advantage positively impacts business performance.

3.4. Mediation of competitive advantage amongst business performance and customer orientation

The marketplace's emphasis on customer satisfaction has the potential to provide it a competitive advantage. According to Puspaningrum (2020), increasing competitive advantage is impacted by the efficacy of industrial customer orientation. According to Islam and Zhe (2022) and Rahman et al. (2021), a business's ability to focus on its customers enhances performance metrics including market share and sales growth. According to research findings by El Saghier (2021), Puspaningrum (2020), Milani and Salavati (2018), and Abuzid and Abbas (2017), competitive advantage contributes to enhanced corporate performance.

Utilizing competitors can either directly impact business efficiency or function as a bridge between operations performance and customer orientation (Bhandari & Amponstira, 2021; Hendi & Arafah, 2022; Puspaningrum, 2020; Priyanto & Murwaningsari, 2022; Sampaio & Régio, 2022; Suandi & Yulihasri, 2022). Customer attention helps increase business income through competitive advantage, according to Suandi and Yulihasri (2022), Dos Santos et al. (2020), Milani and Salavati (2018), and Allaoui et al. (2017). Based on the results of previous studies, the hypothesis is:

H4: The impact of competitive advantage mediation on corporate performance may be observed in the customer orientation.

Considering the hypotheses formulated, we present the conceptual model (Figure 1).

Figure 1. Research framework

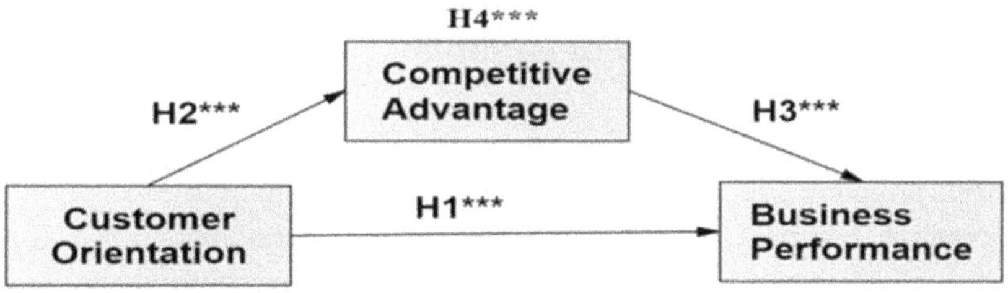

(Authors)

4. METHOD OF RESEARCH

4.1. Sampling and population

The 210,039 clients of the Commercial Bank of Ethiopia, which operates six bank branches in the Dilla area, comprise the population under study. The study used an arithmetical technique, as suggested by Dillaman (2000), to determine the sample size using a sampling formula.

$n = [(N)(p)(1\text{-}p)] / [(N\text{-}1)(B/C)^2 + (P)(1\text{-}P)]$,

Where N = 210,039, P = 0.5, B = 0.05, C = 1.96

$n = [(210{,}039)(0.5)(1\text{-}0.5)] / [(210{,}039\text{-}1)(0.05/1.96)2 + (0.5)(1\text{-}0.5)]$

$n = 383$

This sampling strategy is essential for reducing the likelihood of systematic error and biases in the sample process. Finding a representative sample is also desirable in order to draw conclusions about the population that may be applied to a larger population. Because of this, the sample size used in the proportionate stratified approach for each strata matches the population size of that stratum in the bank branches. Following the reduction of the sample size to 383 samples, samples are collected using convenience sampling methods. Through convenience sampling, a type of non-probability sampling, members of the population under study who meet specific practical criteria—such as easy access, close proximity, and availability for involvement at a specific time—are included for the investigation.

4.2. Operational definition of variable

A focus on the customer (X1): the process and initiatives an organization takes to foster client preference, retention, and satisfaction are known as customer orientation.

The industry's product quality, customer service, technological prowess, and reduced costs relative to competitors are reflected in competitive advantage (X2).

Business performance (X3): business performance is a gauge of an industry's ability to performance fully sells its goods and services, as seen by increase in sales and market share.

Operational definition of variables and indicators are presented under Table 1.

Table 1. Operational definition of variables and indicators

Determinant	Proxies	Reference
Customer Orientation	I. Product	Bhandari & Amponstira, 2021; Hendi & Arafah, 2022; Priyanto & Murwaningsari, 2022; Puspaningrum, 2020; Sampaio & Régio, 2022; Suandi & Yulihasri, 2022.
	II. Preference	
	III. Retention	
	IV. Satisfaction	
Competitive Advantage	I. Product quality	Abdigolbaghi & Sehhat, 2018; Digdowiseiso & Lestari, 2021; Mosa, 2022.
	II. Customer service	
	III. Technology capability	
	IV. Lower cost	
Performance of business	I. Sale growth	Hendi & Arafah, 2022; Priyanto & Murwaningsari, 2022; Sampaio & Régio 2022
	II. Market share	

Source: Authors.

4.3. Method for data analysis

The data-driven methodology employed in this work is structural equation modelling, or SEM. The t-test is used to determine if direct affect exists or not, using a 5% relevance threshold. The following criteria must be met in order to evaluate a hypothesis as either accepting or rejecting it: if the likelihood value is greater than 5%, then either H0 is accepted or H1 is declined; if the probability value is 5%, then either H0 is denied or H0 is acknowledged. When using full or partial mediation, the mediation test is conducted.

4.4. Data adequacy test

The KMO presented under table 2, establishes the minimum sufficiency of data that must be more than 0.5 in order for a factor analysis to be deemed both acceptable and integer.

Table 2. Sample adequacy teat

"Kaiser-Meyer-Olkin" evaluate of data sufficiency.		.810
"Bartlett's investigation for Sphericity"	Likelihood value	1036.271
	Degree of freedpm	21
	P-Value	.000

Source: Authors.

The data result as an output of software IBM SPSS demonstrated sphericity under table 2 results, as seen by the established KMO value of 0.810, which falls between 0.6 and 1. This allowed factor analysis to produce unique and dependable factors. The KMO assesses sample adequacy; a value of more than 0.5 is required for the recognition of an adequate factor evaluation. Rewards for employees take into account both incentives and appreciation. Using KMO and Bartlett's Test to determine the sphericity of the data, the result was KMO=0.810. KMO findings thus demonstrated that the data were sufficient. Table 3 below illustrates the total variance of the explained outcome.

Table 3. Total variance explained

	Eigen-values preliminary			drawing out arithmetic Squared Loadings			turning round arithmetic Squared Loadings		
	Sum	% of discrepancy	collective %	Sum	% of discrepancy	collective %	Sum	% of inconsistency	collective %
1	3.619	51.698	51.698	3.61	51.698	51.698	1.91	27.404	27.404
2	1.040	14.850	66.548	1.04	14.850	66.548	1.83	26.214	53.619
3	1.001	9.859	76.407	.690	9.859	76.407	1.59	22.788	76.407
4	.610	8.719	85.127						

Source: Authors.

The sum of variances was recognized by the total variance, which also established the three distinct major components. The proportion of variance accounted for by a principal component that is 76.407% signifies that this percentage is equal to the ratio between the discrepancy of the main component and the overall variance. Divide the overall variance by the sum of the variances of the primary elements. The entire amount of variation that may be explained by each of the main three parts was represented by their Eigenvalues.

In theory, they may be positive or negative, but in practice, they always account for favorable variance. Eigen-values larger than zero are a positive indication. The interaction for each item was represented by the eigenvalue of the three principal components. The eigenvalue for a single component was expressed as the sum of squared component loadings over all items. The overall variance was calculated as the sum of the Eigenvalues that were for all three elements, which came to 76.407.

4.5. Confirmatory factor analysis

A form of statistics called confirmatory factor analysis is used to confirm the factor structure of a collection of observed variables. Researchers can test hypotheses using CFA based on correlations between variables that are seen and the foundational framework. The researcher can use CFA under figure 2 to test the idea that there is a connection between the variables that are being observed and the latent notions that underlie them (Luong & Flake, 2022).

Figure 2. Confirmatory factor analyses

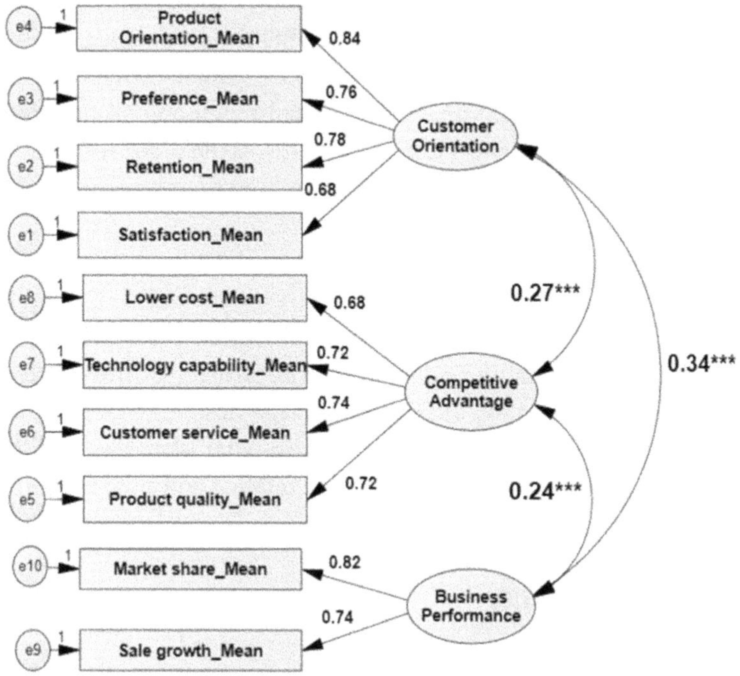

(Authors)

Table 4. Covariances

Covariance			Estimate	S.E.	C.R.	P	Hy.
Competitive advantage	<-->	Customer orientation	.299	.036	8.390	***	**H2**
Competitive advantage	<-->	performance of business	.265	.035	7.507	***	**H3**
Customer orientation	<-->	performance of business	.294	.037	7.876	***	**H1**

Source: Authors.

According to estimates results of table 4, there is a.299 correlation between customer focus and competitive advantage. The standard error of the covariance estimate, 0.299, is roughly 0.036. Z =.299/.036 = 8.390 is obtained by dividing the covariance assessment by the estimation of its standard error. The covariance estimate is, in other words, 8.39 standard errors above zero. There is a less than 0.001 percent chance of obtaining a crucial ratio with an absolute value of 8.39. In other words, at the 0.001 level (two-tailed), the correlation between Competitive advantage and Customer orientation differs significantly from zero. Under reasonable assumptions, these claims are roughly true for large samples.

The calculated covariance among competitive advantage with company performance is 0.265. The standard error of the covariance estimate, 0.265, is roughly 0.035. Z =.265/.035 = 7.507 is obtained by scaling the covariance assessment by the projection of its standard error. The covariance estimate is thus 7.507 standard errors above zero. Less than 0.001 percent of the time, a crucial ratio as great as 7.507 in the absolute sense will occur. In other words, at the 0.001 level (two-tailed), the correlation among competitive advantage with company performance differs appreciably over zero.

The calculated covariance between customer orientation and business performance is 0.294. The usual error of the covariance estimate 0.294, is roughly 0.037. Z =.294/.037 = 7.876 is obtained by scaling the covariance calculation by the estimate of the standard error of the estimate. The covariance estimate is thus 7.876 standard errors higher than zero. It is very unlikely (less than 0.001) to obtain a critical fraction with an absolute value of 7.876. In other words, at the 0.001 level (two-tailed), the correlation between customer orientation and business performance is considerably distinct over zero.

4.5. Discriminant validity

Confirmation that measurements of dimensions that conceptually ought not to be substantially linked with one another are actually not discovered to be significantly correlated with one another serves as proof of discriminant validity as showed under Table 5. In reality, convergent coefficients of validity should be substantially larger with discriminant validity coefficients.

Table 5. Validity concern

	CR	AVE	MSV	MaxR(H)	CO	CA	OP
CO	0.825	0.641	0.117	0.828	**0.664**		
CA	0.764	0.602	0.024	0.798	0.142	**0.634**	
OP	0.822	0.636	0.117	0.830	0.342	0.154	**0.661**

Note: CO= Customer orientation; CA= Competitive advantage; OP= Organization performance
Source: Authors.

Since the square root of the AVE is greater than every other correlation values, discriminant validity is established. Since the AVE for customer orientation is greater than 0.50, convergence validity was attained. The fact that the AVE is for competitive advantage is greater than 0.50; that led to convergence validity. Since the AVE for business performance is exceeding 0.50, convergence validity was attained.

4.6. Mediation analysis

Based on the information provided, Figure 3 likely represents the structural equation model or path model that depicts the relationships between the key variables in this study. This structural equation model allows for the examination of the direct effects of MO and EO on Firm Performance, as well as the indirect or mediated effects through Customer Loyalty. The mediation analysis can provide insights into the mechanisms by which MO and EO influence Firm Performance in the Ethiopian context.

Figure 3. Equation of structure

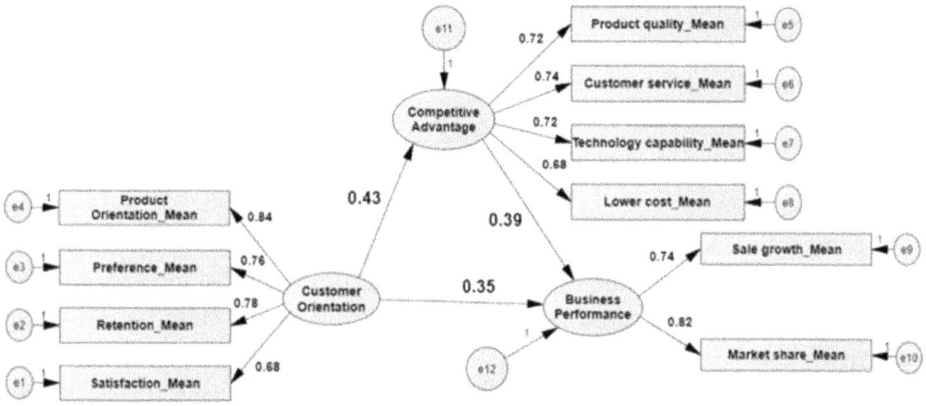

(Authors)

4.7. Model fit indices

The Table 6 outcomes demonstrate that the CMIN/DF value of 2.213, a value that is a minimum or not more than 3, demonstrates an excellent model fit. Additionally, the root mean of the remaining is below the threshold of 0.05 by 0.021, and the goodness and comparative fit indices are both greater than 0.90. As a result, the model's overall fit is good. The GFI for the standard design is the value that is significant here; therefore that was the primary area of attention. GFI, which is more than 0.90 and indicates the Goodness of Fit Index for the researchers' suggested Model, is 0.972.

Table 6. Indices for model fit

Sig.	Chi-Sq	R-M-R	Fitness Goodness	Fitness Confirmatory	T-L-I	RMSEA
0.371	2.123	.021	0.972	0.941	0.963	.025

Source: Authors.

As per results of table 7, Competitive advantage rises by 0.977 when customer orientation rises by 1. The standard error of the regression weight estimate, 0.977, is roughly.104. Z =.977/.104 = 9.373 is obtained by dividing the regression weight estimate by the estimate of its standard error. The regression weight estimate is thus 9.373 standard errors above zero. Less than 0.001 percent of the time, a crucial ratio as great as 9.373 in absolute value will occur. In other words, at the two-tailed 0.001 level, the regression weight for Customer orientation in the anticipated outcome of Competitive advantage is substantially distinct from zero.

Table 7. Influences for regression

Relation			Approx.	S.E.	C.R.	P	Ass.
Competitive advantage	<---	Customer orientation	.977	.104	9.373	***	H2
performance of business	<---	Competitive advantage	.285	.136	2.366	***	H3
performance of business	<---	Customer orientation	1.143	.197	5.793	***	H1

Source: Authors.

As competitive advantage increases by 1, company performance increases by 0.285. The performance of the firm increases by 1.173 for every increase in customer orientation. The standard error of the regression weight estimate, 1.143, is roughly.197. Z = 1.143/.197 = 5.793 is obtained by splitting the regression weight estimate by the calculated value of its standard error. The regression weight estimate is thus 5.793 standard errors above zero. There is a less than 0.001 percent chance of obtaining a crucial ratio with an absolute value of 5.793.

In other words, at the two-tailed significance level of 0.001, the coefficient of regression for customer orientation in the forecast of company performance differs substantially from zero. Under reasonable assumptions, these claims are roughly true for huge amounts of data.

Table 8. Mediation analysis

	Customer orientation	Competitive advantage
Competitive advantage	.877	.000
performance of business	.592	.285

Source: Authors.

As Table 8 depicted that, Customer orientation has a 0.592 overall (directly as well as indirectly) impact on business performance. This means that when customer orientation increases by 1, business performance increases by 0.592 owing to both immediate (unmediated) and secondary (mediated) benefits of customer orientation on company performance. Competitive advantage has a 0.285 overall (direct and indirect) impact on business performance. That is, when Competitive advantage increases by 1, performance of business increases by 0.285. This is because Competitive advantage has both direct (unmediated) and indirect (mediated) effects on business performance.

Customer orientation has an overall (directly as well as indirectly) competitive advantage impact of 0.877. That is, when Customer orientation increases by 1, Competitive advantage increases by 0.877 as a result of both the direct (unmediated) and indirect (mediated) impacts of Customer orientation on Competitive advantage.

5. CONCLUSION

The study's main objective was to get a better understanding of how competitive advantage affects organizational performance and personnel compensation structures. Based on data analysis utilizing the AMOS program system, it was shown that, in the absence of a competitive advantage serving as a mediator, the link between customer orientation and organizational performance is relatively minimal in the context of a standardized direct impact. However, due to the inclusion of competitive advantage as a mediator, the association between customer orientation and organizational performance is fairly strong in the form of a standardized total impact. The likelihood of mediation was investigated using scaling (ten thousand runs). Both tests showed that competitive advantage mediates the association between the bank performance and customer orientation. It showed that competitive advantage serves as a moderator of this connection to some extent. Consequently, in the study domain, it may be claimed that competitive advantage mediates the link between customer orientation and organizational performance.

5.1. Academic implications

According to study, a bank's competitive advantage acts as a mediator between client orientation and performance, with the former having a considerable beneficial effect on the latter. This suggests that banks that place a high priority on comprehending and satisfying the demands of their clients are better equipped to create distinctive skills and tactics that provide them a competitive advantage in the market, which eventually improves their financial and operational results. This research adds to the body of knowledge about market orientation, competitive strategy, and performance in the banking business, especially in emerging nations like Ethiopia where the sector is undergoing fast change. It underscores the significance of customer-focused business models and the part unique capabilities play in creating long-term competitive advantage.

5.2. Managerial implications

The results highlight for bank management how important it is for the entire company to have a strong client focus. This entails having a thorough grasp of the demands of the client, creating specialized goods and services, and providing exceptional value. Creating this customer-focused culture may help a bank stand out from rivals in terms of cost-effectiveness, product innovation, or service quality. To gain a competitive edge and boost financial performance, bank management should place a high priority on educating staff, doing market research, and fostering cross-functional cooperation. In order to keep their advantage in the market, managers must also constantly assess how the competitive environment is changing and modify their plans as necessary.

REFERENCES

Abdigolbaghi, M., & Sehhat, S. (2018). The Impact of Customer Relationship Management on an Organization's Competitive Advantage Considering the Mediating Variable of Customer Loyalty. *International Journal of Business and Management*, 3(2), 76–92.

Abuzid, H. F., & Abbas, M. (2017). Banks Performance and Impact of Market Orientation Strategy: Do Employee Satisfaction and Customer Loyalty Augment this Relationship? Teamwork View project International Review of Management and Marketing Banks Performance and Impact of Market Orientation. *International Review of Management and Marketing*, 7(2), 60–66.

Al-Dulaimi, Z. Y. S., Muhammad, Z. G., & Abbas, B. (2019). Customer orientation and organizational performance in Iraqi private banks. In *International Conference on Marketing and Business*, Bucharest, Romania.

Allaoui, M. E., Ouddane, B., & Tidjani, C. (2017). The Importance of Training Programs in the Improvement of the Performance of Employees In The Petroleum Companies - Case of Sonatrach Company - The Regional Directorate of BERKAOUI (Ouargla-Algeria). *Saudi Journal of Business and Management Studies*, 2(7), 693–699. DOI: 10.21276/sjbms

Amegavie, L. O., Mensah, N. M. D., & Jephthah Kwame, A. (2019). Consumer Relationship Management and Its Effect On Organizational Performance Within the Telecommunication Industry of Ghana. *European Journal of Business and Management Research*, 4(6), 1–10. DOI: 10.24018/ejbmr.2019.4.6.166

Aqmala, D., & Putra, F. I. F. S. (2021). Rayu : A Competitive Strategy Model of Wood Craft Business in Soloraya Post Covid-19 Pandemic. *Journal of Management and Entrepreneurship Research*, 2(2), 74–87. DOI: 10.34001/jmer.2021.12.02.2-19

Bankole, O. A., Olaremu, Y. B., & Oghogho, V. O. (2022). Customer Orientation and Firm Competitiveness of Selected Banks in Ekiti State, Nigeria. *Turk Turizm Arastirmalari Dergisi*, 5(1), 15–25. DOI: 10.26677/TR1010.2022.996

Bhandari, P., & Amponstira, F. (2021). Model of Entrepreneurial Orientation, Competitive Advantage and Performance of Women-Owned Enterprises in Gandaki Province, Nepal. *Open Journal of Business and Management*, 09(06), 2854–2865. DOI: 10.4236/ojbm.2021.96159

Bhardwaj, P. (2019). Types of sampling in research. *Journal of the Practice of Cardiovascular Sciences*, 5(3), 157. DOI: 10.4103/jpcs.jpcs_62_19

Cakir, F. S., Aslan, B., & Adiguzel, Z. (2022). The Bank's Effect on Digital Capability and Knowledge Acquisition Within the Performance and Digital Native's Perception of Mobile Banking. *Revista de Estudios Empresariales*, 2, 292–313.

Daengs, G. S. A., Kurniasih, N., Reni, A., Istanti, E., Zuhroh, D., & Qomariah, N. (2019). The effect of business sphere on competitive advantage and performance of business of SMEs. *Management Science Letters*, 9(8), 1153–1160. DOI: 10.5267/j.msl.2019.4.025

Digdowiseiso, K., & Lestari, R. (2021). Determinants of Competitive Advantage and Their Impact on Consumer Satisfaction at Chicken Restaurants in South Jakarta. *Budapest International Research and Critics Institute-Journal (BIRCI-Journal), 4*(4), 12047-12053.

Domi, S., & Musabelliu, B. (2020). Customer orientation and SME performance in Albania: A case study of the mediating role of innovativeness and innovation behavior. *Journal of Vacation Marketing*, 26(1), 130–146. DOI: 10.1177/1356766719867374

dos Santos, M. J., Perin, M. G., Simões, C., & Sampaio, C. H. (2020). Customer orientation and financial performance relationship: The mediating role of innovative capability. *Gestão & Produção*, 27(4), e4706. DOI: 10.1590/0104-530x4706-20

El Saghier, N. (2021). The Effect of E-marketing Orientation on E-business Strategy: E-trust as a Mediator. *Journal of Alexandria University for Administrative Sciences*, 58(2), 193–242. DOI: 10.21608/acj.2021.167937

Enad, O. M. A., & Gerinda, S. M. A. (2022). Enhancing financial performance of the banks: The role of customer response and operations management. *Journal of Innovation and Entrepreneurship*, 11(1), 28. DOI: 10.1186/s13731-022-00211-w

Ghlichlee, B., & Bayat, F. (2021). Frontline employees' engagement and performance of business: The mediating role of customer-oriented behaviors. *Management Research Review*, 44(2), 290–317. DOI: 10.1108/MRR-11-2019-0482

Gontur, S., Vem, L. J., Goyit, M. G., & Davireng, M. (2022). Entrepreneurial marketing, corporate reputation, corporate creativity and competitive advantage: A research framework and proposition. *International Journal of Business. Management and Economics*, 3(1), 52–80.

Gonu, E., Agyei, P. M., Richard, O. K., & Asare-Larbi, M. (2023). Customer orientation, service quality and customer satisfaction interplay in the banking sector: An emerging market perspective. *Cogent Business and Management*, 10(1), 2163797. Advance online publication. DOI: 10.1080/23311975.2022.2163797

Hanafi, H. M., & Yahia, M. A. (2022). Customer Orientation of Service Employees in the Banking Sector in Sudan. *International Journal of Scientific Research*, 11(8), 312–317. DOI: 10.21275/SR22804022752

Hanaysha, J., & Mehmood, K. K. (2022). An Exploration of the Effect of Customer Relationship Management on Organizational Performance in the Banking Sector. *International Journal of Customer Relationship Marketing and Management*, 13(1), 1–16. Advance online publication. DOI: 10.4018/IJCRMM.2022010101

Hariandi, M. S. I., Gumanti, T. A., & Wahyudi, E. (2019). E-commerce, competitive advantage and performance of business of banyuwangi small and medium-sized enterprises. *International Journal of Scientific and Technology Research*, 8(8), 1216–1220.

Hashem, T., Hashem, T. N., & Alqirem, A. A. (2019). the Impact of Quality Culture on Competitive Advantage in Financial Services Companies. *IJRRAS, 38*(1). www.arpapress.com/Volumes/Vol38Issue1/IJRRAS_38_1_08.pdf

Hendi, Y. Z. B., & Arafah, W. (2022). Analysis of Improving Competitive Advantage for Startup Business in Indonesia. *International Journal of Economics. Business and Management Research*, 6(2), 223–231. DOI: 10.51505/IJEBMR.2022.6216

Islam, A. M., & Qamari, I. N. (2021). Effect of Supply Chain Management on Competitive Advantage and Organizational Performance. Studies on the Batik Industry in Yogyakarta City. In *4th International Conference on Sustainable Innovation 2020-Accounting and Management (ICoSIAMS 2020)* (pp. 334–339). DOI: 10.2991/aer.k.210121.047

Islam, M. Z., & Zhe, Z. (2022). The effect of customer orientation on financial performance in service firms: The mediating role of service innovation. *Management Science Letters*, 12(2), 101–116. DOI: 10.5267/j.msl.2021.10.003

Kelvin, E. A., & Joyce, E. (2019). Effect of Market Orientation on Organizational Performance (A Study of the Nigerian Banking Industry). *International Journal of Business and Social Science*, 10(12), 93–102. DOI: 10.30845/ijbss.v10n12a9

Kimiti, P., Muathe, S., & Murigi, E. M. (2020). Cost Leadership Strategy, Competitive Advantage, and Performance: A Cross-Sectional Study in the Context of Milk Processing Firms in Kenya. International *Journal of Management. Innovation & Entrepreneurial Research*, 6(2), 64–76. DOI: 10.18510/ijmier.2020.627

Kimiti, P. G., Muathe, S. M. A., & Murigi, E. M. (2021). Cost Leadership Strategy: A New Game Strategy for Competitive Advantage in Milk Processing Firms in Kenya. *European Scientific Journal*, 17(23), 296–306. DOI: 10.19044/esj.2021.v17n23p296

Kwak, J., & Moon, J. (2021). The Effect of Self-Leadership on Job Satisfaction and Customer Orientation: The Role of Supervisor Support. *East Asian Journal of Business Economics*, 9(2), 75–84.

Milani, A. M., & Salavati, S. (2018). The role of Market Orientation and Innovation in Improving performance of business of the Banking Industry. *European Journal of Sustainable Development*, 7(4), 556–571. DOI: 10.14207/ejsd.2018.v7n4p556

Mishra, C. S. (2017). *Mishra, C. S. (2017). Creating and Sustaining Competitive Advantage: Management Logics, Business Models, and Entrepreneurial Rent.* Springer. DOI: 10.1007/978-3-319-54540-0

Mistrean, L. (2021). Customer Orientation As a Basic Principle in the Contemporary Activity of the Bank. *Journal of Public Administration. Finance and Law*, 21(21), 39–51. DOI: 10.47743/jopafl-2021-21-05

Mohiuddin Babu, M. (2018). Impact of firm's customer orientation on performance: The moderating role of interfunctional coordination and employee commitment. *Journal of Strategic Marketing*, 26(8), 702–722. DOI: 10.1080/0965254X.2017.1384037

Mokhtaran, M., & Komeilian, B. (2016). Exploring the effect of customer orientation on Dana insurance performance considering the intermediary role of customer relations and service quality management. *International Review (Steubenville, Ohio)*, 2(3–4), 51–61. DOI: 10.5937/intrev1604051M

Mosa, R. A. (2022). The Influence of E-Customer Relationship Management on Customer Experience in E-Banking Service. *International Journal of Academic Research in Business & Social Sciences*, 12(2), 193–215. DOI: 10.6007/IJARBSS/v12-i2/12195

Muis, I., & Isyanto, P. (2021). Market Orientation, Transformational Leadership, Partnership Effects on Organizational Performance: Competitive Advantage as a Mediator. *Binus Business Review*, 12(3), 263–277. DOI: 10.21512/bbr.v12i3.7284

Murerwa, F. K., Onditi, A. L., & Nyagol, M. (2022). Influence of Product Differentiation Strategy on Performance of Commercial Banks in Lodwar, Kenya. *International Journal of Business and Management*, VII(9), 554–565. DOI: 10.24940/theijbm/2022/v10/i10/BM2210-017

Nyoman, N., Yasa, K., Giantari, I. G. A. K., & Setini, M. (2020). The role of competitive advantage in mediating the effect of promotional strategy on marketing performance. *Management Science Letters*, 10, 2845–2848. DOI: 10.5267/j.msl.2020.4.024

Oluwatoyin, A. M., Olufunke, A. P., & Salome, I. O. (2018). The Impact of Market Orientation on Performance of Selected Hotels in Ondo State, Nigeria. *Open Journal of Business and Management*, 06(03), 616–631. DOI: 10.4236/ojbm.2018.63047

Othman, B. (2020). The Influence of Total Quality Management on Competitive Advantage towards Bank Organizations: Evidence from Erbil/Iraq. *International Journal of Psychosocial Rehabilitation*, 24(5), 3427–3439. DOI: 10.37200/IJPR/V24I5/PR202053

Park, J. H., Chung, H., Kim, K. H., Kim, J. J., & Lee, C. (2021). The impact of technological capability on financial performance in the semiconductor industry. *Sustainability*, 13(2), 1–20. DOI: 10.3390/su13020489 PMID: 34123411

Priyanto, P., & Murwaningsari, E. (2022). The Effect of Sustainability Innovation, Organizational Learning on Firm Performance with Competitive Advantage as Moderation. *International Journal of Academic Research in Accounting. Finance and Management Sciences*, 12(1), 257–275. DOI: 10.6007/IJARAFMS/v12-i1/10832

Puspaningrum, A. (2020). Market Orientation, Competitive Advantage and Marketing Performance of Small Medium Enterprises (SMEs). *Journal of Economics, Business, &. Accountancy Ventura*, 23(1), 19–27. DOI: 10.14414/jebav.v23i1.1847

Raewf, M., Aissa, S. A. H., & Thabit, T. (2021). The impact of quality, cost, and lead time on competitive advantage: Case of SMEs operating in Iraq. *Economic Studies Journal, 19*(03).

Rahman, M. M., Hussain, M. T., Moon, S. P., Tisha, M. M., & Lima, M. T. (2021). Impact of Customer Relationship Management (CRM) on Organizational Performance: A Study from the Perspective of Bangladesh. *American Journal of Trade and Policy*, 8(3), 225–230. DOI: 10.18034/ajtp.v8i3.609

Sampaio, C., & Régio, M. (2022). Market Orientation and Hotel Industry: Literature Review and Implications for Periods of Market Turmoil. *Journal of Risk and Financial Management*, 15(11), 497. DOI: 10.3390/jrfm15110497

Suandi, E., & Yulihasri, H. (2022). Evaluating the relationship among entrepreneurial marketing, competitive advantage, and Islamic banks performance. *Journal of Financial Services Marketing*, 28(3), 599–614. DOI: 10.1057/s41264-022-00169-6

Tarabieh, S. (2015). The Impact of Customer Orientation and Supplementary Services in Gaining Competitive Advantage and Organizational Performance in the Jordanian Banking Industry. *International Review of Social Sciences*, 3(2), 47–59.

Tarabieh, S. M. Z. A., Ahmad, Z. A., & Siron, R. (2015). The Synergistic Impact of Customer Orientation and Supplementary Services on Competitive Advantage and Organizational Performance (Pilot Survey). *International Review of Management and Business Research*, 4(2), 484–498.

Yang, M., Jaafar, N., Al Mamun, A., Salameh, A. A., & Nawi, N. C. (2022). Modelling the significance of strategic orientation for competitive advantage and economic sustainability: The use of hybrid SEM–neural network analysis. *Journal of Innovation and Entrepreneurship*, 11(1), 44. Advance online publication. DOI: 10.1186/s13731-022-00232-5 PMID: 35754704

Yuliantari, N. P. Y., & Pramuki, N. M. W. A. (2022). The Role of Competitive Advantage in Mediating the Relationship Among Digital Transformation and MSME Performance in Bali. *Jurnal Ekonomi & Bisnis Jagaditha*, 9(1), 66–75. DOI: 10.22225/jj.9.1.2022.66-75

Zaini, A., Hadiwidjojo, D., Rohman, F., & Maskie, G. (2014). Effect Of Competitive Advantage As A Mediator Variable Of Entrepreneurship Orientation To Marketing Performance. *IOSR Journal of Business and Management*, 16(5), 5–10. DOI: 10.9790/487X-16510510

ADDITIONAL READING

Cruz Rincon, M. L., Agredo Diaz, M. L., & Puente, R. C. (2023). Is entrepreneurship enough to achieve superior performance in SMEs in emerging countries? Multiple mediation of market orientation and marketing capabilities. *Journal of Entrepreneurship in Emerging Economies*, 15(5), 945–966. DOI: 10.1108/JEEE-03-2021-0115

Kosa, A., Mohammad, I., & Ajibie, D. (2018). Entrepreneurial orientation and venture performance in Ethiopia: The moderating role of business sector and enterprise location. *Journal of Global Entrepreneurship Research*, 8(1), 1–17. DOI: 10.1186/s40497-018-0110-x

Oduro, S., & Haylemariam, L. G. (2019). Market orientation, CSR and financial and marketing performance in manufacturing firms in Ghana and Ethiopia. *Sustainability Accounting. Management and Policy Journal*, 10(3), 398–426.

Wakjira, G. G., & Kant, S. (2023). Significance of Market Orientation on Business Performance with Mediating Role of Employee and Customer Satisfaction in Ethiopia Banks. *Journal of Entrepreneurship, Management, and Innovation*, 5(1), 144–158.

KEY TERMS AND DEFINITIONS

Competitive Advantage: The unique market position that allows a firm to outperform competitors and deliver superior customer value.

Customer Loyalty: The degree to which customers exhibit repeat purchasing, have a positive attitude towards the firm, and consider the firm as their primary provider. Customer loyalty is an important driver of firm performance.

Dynamic Capabilities: A firm's ability to integrate, build, and reconfigure internal and external competencies to address rapidly changing environments.

Entrepreneurial Orientation (EO): A firm's strategic orientation characterized by entrepreneurial decision-making styles, methods, and practices such as innovativeness, proactiveness, and risk-taking. Strong EO can contribute to competitive advantage and superior performance.

Firm Performance: The overall effectiveness and efficiency of a firm in achieving its goals, measured through financial (e.g., profitability, sales growth) and non-financial (e.g., customer satisfaction, market share) indicators. Firm performance is the key dependent variable.

Market Intelligence: Information about current and future customer needs; competitor actions, and broader market trends and developments.

Market Orientation (MO): A firm's ability to generate, share, and respond to market intelligence about customer needs, competitor actions, and the broader business environment. High market orientation is linked to better firm performance.

Mediation Effect: The process by which an independent variable (e.g., MO, EO) influences a dependent variable (e.g., firm performance) through an intervening or mediating variable (e.g., customer loyalty). Understanding mediation provides insights into the pathways of impact.

Organizational Innovativeness: A firm's capacity to engage in and support the development of new ideas, experimentation, and creative processes that lead to new products, services, or processes.

Organizational Learning: The process of acquiring, disseminating, and utilizing knowledge to enhance competitive advantage and performance.

Compilation of References

Aaker, D. A. (1991). *Managing brand equity: capitalizing on the value of a brand name*. Free Press.

Aaker, D. A. (1996). Measuring brand equity across products and markets. *California Management Review*, 38(3), 102–120. DOI: 10.2307/41165845

Abbott, D. (2014). *Applied predictive analytics: Principles and techniques for the professional data analyst*. John Wiley & Sons, Inc.

Abdelkader, O. A. (2023). ChatGPT's influence on customer experience in digital marketing: Investigating the moderating roles. *Heliyon*, 9(8), e18770. Advance online publication. DOI: 10.1016/j.heliyon.2023.e18770 PMID: 37576290

Abdigolbaghi, M., & Sehhat, S. (2018). The Impact of Customer Relationship Management on an Organization's Competitive Advantage Considering the Mediating Variable of Customer Loyalty. *International Journal of Business and Management*, 3(2), 76–92.

Abdullah, I., Mahmood, W. H. W., Fauadi, H. F. M., Rahman, M. N. A., & Mohamed, S. B. (2017). Sustainable manufacturing practices in Malaysian palm oil mills: Priority and current performance. *Journal of Manufacturing Technology Management*, 28(3), 278–298. DOI: 10.1108/JMTM-09-2016-0128

Abhirup, G. (2024, Jul 09). *The Role of AI and Machine Learning in E-Commerce Personalization.* https://www.codilar.com/the-role-of-ai-and-machine-learning-in-e-commerce-personalization/

Abhishek, D., A., & Gupta, N. (2021). A systematic review of techniques, tools and applications of machine learning. *3rd International Conference on Intelligent Communication Technologies and Virtual Mobile Networks, ICICV 2021* (pp. 764-768). Tirunelveli: Institute of Electrical and Electronics Engineers Inc. DOI: 10.1109/ICICV50876.2021.9388637

Abu-Rumman, A., Al Shraah, A., Al-Madi, F., & Alfalah, T. (2021). Entrepreneurial networks, entrepreneurial orientation, and performance of small and medium enterprises: Are dynamic capabilities the missing link? *Journal of Innovation and Entrepreneurship*, 10(1), 1–16. DOI: 10.1186/s13731-021-00170-8

Abutaleb, S., & El-Bassiouny, N. (2020). Assessing sustainability marketing from macromarketing perspective: A multistakeholder approach. *World Journal of Entrepreneurship, Management and Sustainable Development*, 16(4), 287–305. DOI: 10.1108/WJEMSD-02-2019-0017

Abuzid, H. F., & Abbas, M. (2017). Banks Performance and Impact of Market Orientation Strategy: Do Employee Satisfaction and Customer Loyalty Augment this Relationship? Teamwork View project International Review of Management and Marketing Banks Performance and Impact of Market Orientation. *International Review of Management and Marketing*, 7(2), 60–66.

Accenture. (2018). Personalization Pulse Check. https://www.accenture.com/content/dam/accenture/final/a-com-migration/pdf/pdf-83/accenture-making-personal.pdf

Accenture. (2022). *Creating value in all directions*. https://www.accenture.com/content/dam/accenture/final/capabilities/corporate-functions/growth-and-strategy/document/Accenture-Fiscal-2022-Annual-Report.pdf#zoom=50

Acebo, E., Miguel-Dávila, J.-Á., & Nieto, M. (2021). External stakeholder engagement: Complementary and substitutive effects on firms' eco-innovation. *Business Strategy and the Environment*, 30(5), 2671–2687. DOI: 10.1002/bse.2770

Acosta, A. S., Crespo, Á. H., & Agudo, J. C. (2018). Effect of market orientation, network capability and entrepreneurial orientation on international performance of small and medium enterprises (SMEs). *International Business Review*, 27(6), 1128–1140. DOI: 10.1016/j.ibusrev.2018.04.004

Acquisti, A., Brandimarte, L., & Loewenstein, G. (2015). Privacy and Human Behavior in the Age of Information. *Science*, 347(6221), 509–514. DOI: 10.1126/science.aaa1465 PMID: 25635091

Adams, R., Bessant, J., & Phelps, R. (2006). Innovation management measurement: A review. In *International Journal of Management Reviews*, 8(1), 21–47). DOI: 10.1111/j.1468-2370.2006.00119.x

Adams, D., Donovan, J., & Topple, C. (2023). Sustainability in large food and beverage companies and their supply chains: An investigation into key drivers and barriers affecting sustainability strategies. *Business Strategy and the Environment*, 32(4), 1451–1463. DOI: 10.1002/bse.3198

Agarwal, T., Gopalkrishnan, S., Kale, V., Periwal, D., Kulkarni, A. A., & Tharkude, D. (2023). Transforming Advertising: Harnessing AI for Personalised Customer-Centricity. *IEEE International Conference on Technology Management, Operations and Decisions, ICTMOD 2023.* Rabat: Institute of Electrical and Electronics Engineers Inc. DOI: 10.1109/ICTMOD59086.2023.10438160

Ahmed, S., Sharif, T., Ting, D. H., & Sharif, S. J. (2024). Crafting emotional engagement and immersive experiences: Comprehensive scale development for and validation of hospitality marketing storytelling involvement. *Psychology and Marketing*, 41(7), 1514–1529. DOI: 10.1002/mar.21994

Ahn, R. J., Cho, S. Y., & Sunny Tsai, W. (2022). Demystifying computer-generated imagery (CGI) influencers: The effect of perceived anthropomorphism and social presence on brand outcomes. *Journal of Interactive Advertising*, 22(3), 327–335. DOI: 10.1080/15252019.2022.2111242

Aka, D., Kehinde, O., & Ogunnaike, O. (2016). Relationship marketing and customer satisfaction: A conceptual perspective. *Binus Business Review*, 7(2), 185–190. DOI: 10.21512/bbr.v7i2.1502

Akila, D., Jeyalaksshmi, S., & Padmapriya, D. Devipriya, Prithika, P., & Elangovan, V. R. (2022). Significance of Machine Learning and Deep Learning in Development of Artificial Intelligence. In (pp. 25-44). DOI: 10.1201/9780367816414-2

Aksu, O. (2019). Artificial Intelligence in the Era of Transhumanism Smart Phones. In *Handbook of Research on Learning in the Age of Transhumanism* (pp. 157–170). IGI Global., DOI: 10.4018/978-1-5225-8431-5.ch010

Akter, S. (2024a). Exploring Cutting-Edge Frontiers in Artificial Intelligence: An Overview of Trends and Advancements. *Journal of Artificial Intelligence General science (JAIGS), 2*(1). https://ojs.boulibrary.com/index.php/JAIGS/article/view/43/28

Akter, S. (2024b). Investigating State-of-the-Art Frontiers in Artificial Intelligence: A Synopsis of Trends and Innovations. *Journal of Artificial Intelligence General science (JAIGS), 2*(1). https://jaigs.org/index.php/JAIGS/article/view/19/11

Akter, S., Dwivedi, Y. K., Biswas, K., Michael, K., Bandara, R. J., & Sajib, S. (2021). Addressing algorithmic bias in AI-driven customer management. [JGIM]. *Journal of Global Information Management*, 29(6), 1–27. DOI: 10.4018/JGIM.20211101.oa3

Al-Dulaimi, Z. Y. S., Muhammad, Z. G., & Abbas, B. (2019). Customer orientation and organizational performance in Iraqi private banks. In *International Conference on Marketing and Business*, Bucharest, Romania.

Allaoui, M. E., Ouddane, B., & Tidjani, C. (2017). The Importance of Training Programs in the Improvement of the Performance of Employees In The Petroleum Companies - Case of Sonatrach Company - The Regional Directorate of BERKAOUI (Ouargla-Algeria). *Saudi Journal of Business and Management Studies*, 2(7), 693–699. DOI: 10.21276/sjbms

Allil, K. (2024). Integrating AI-driven marketing analytics techniques into the classroom: pedagogical strategies for enhancing student engagement and future business success. *Journal of Marketing Analytics*, 1–27. doi:.DOI: 10.1057/S41270-023-00281-Z/METRICS

Allison, K. (2024). Data-Driven Customer Relationship Management (CRM) Modeling: Humanistic Connection in Predictive Analytics. In *Revolutionizing the AI-Digital Landscape* (pp. 244-262). Productivity Press.

Almahairah, M. S. (2023). Artificial Intelligence Application for Effective Customer Relationship Management. In *2023 International Conference on Computer Communication and Informatics (ICCCI)* (pp. 1-7). IEEE. DOI: 10.1109/ICCCI56745.2023.10128360

Al-Mulla, S., Ari, I., & Koç, M. (2022). Social media for sustainability education: Gaining knowledge and skills into actions for sustainable living. *International Journal of Sustainable Development and World Ecology*, 29(5), 455–471. DOI: 10.1080/13504509.2022.2036856

Alnawas, I., & Hemsley-Brown, J. (2019). Market orientation and hotel performance: Investigating the role of high-order marketing capabilities. *International Journal of Contemporary Hospitality Management*, 31(4), 1885–1905. DOI: 10.1108/IJCHM-07-2018-0564

Alnofeli, K., Akter, S., & Yanamandram, V. (2023). Understanding the Future trends and innovations of AI-based CRM systems. In *Handbook of Big Data Research Methods* (pp. 279–294). Edward Elgar Publishing. DOI: 10.4337/9781800888555.00021

Al, S. W. E. (2021). How artificial intelligence transforms the experience of employees. *Türk Bilgisayar Ve Matematik Eğitimi Dergisi*, 12(10), 7116–7135. DOI: 10.17762/turcomat.v12i10.5603

Alsiehemy, A. (2023). Emergence of {Digital} {Marketing} in {Current} {Scenario} and {Implementation} of {AI} to {Improve} the {Productivity} of a {Concern}. *Pacific Business Review International*, 15(7), 19–27.

Al-Surmi, A., Bashiri, M., & Koliousis, I. (2022). AI based decision making: Combining strategies to improve operational performance. *International Journal of Production Research*, 60(14), 4464–4486. DOI: 10.1080/00207543.2021.1966540

Al-Tuama, A. T., & Nasrawi, D. A. (2022). A survey on the impact of chatbots on marketing activities. *2022 13th International Conference on Computing Communication and Networking Technologies, ICCCNT 2022*. DOI: 10.1109/ICCCNT54827.2022.9984635

Alvarez-Milán, A., Felix, R., Rauschnabel, P. A., & Hinsch, C. (2018). Strategic customer engagement marketing: A decision making framework. *Journal of Business Research*, 92, 61–70. DOI: 10.1016/j.jbusres.2018.07.017

Alzahrani, M. E., Aldhyani, T. H. H., Alsubari, S. N., Althobaiti, M. M., & Fahad, A. (2022). Developing an Intelligent System with Deep Learning Algorithms for Sentiment Analysis of E-Commerce Product Reviews. *Computational Intelligence and Neuroscience*, 2022, 1–10. Advance online publication. DOI: 10.1155/2022/3840071 PMID: 35669644

Amazon (2024). Leadership Principles. https://www.amazon.jobs/content/en/our-workplace/leadership-principles

Ameen, N., Tarhini, A., Reppel, A., & Anand, A. (2021). Customer experiences in the age of artificial intelligence. *Computers in Human Behavior*, 114, 106548. DOI: 10.1016/j.chb.2020.106548 PMID: 32905175

Amegavie, L. O., Mensah, N. M. D., & Jephthah Kwame, A. (2019). Consumer Relationship Management and Its Effect On Organizational Performance Within the Telecommunication Industry of Ghana. *European Journal of Business and Management Research*, 4(6), 1–10. DOI: 10.24018/ejbmr.2019.4.6.166

Anjelita, M., Juniwati, J., Purmono, B. B., Pebrianti, W., & Saputra, P. (2023). How Does Personalization by AI on TikTok Influence Purchase Intention? *Jurnal Mantik*, 7(3), 2513–2523.

Anute, N., Paliwal, M., Patel, M., & Kandale, N. (2021). Impact of artificial intelligence and machine learning on business operations. *Journal of Management Research and Analysis*, 8(2), 69–74. DOI: 10.18231/j.jmra.2021.015

Appel, G., Grewal, L., Hadi, R., & Stephen, A. T. (2020). The future of social media in marketing. *Journal of the Academy of Marketing Science*, 48(1), 79–95. DOI: 10.1007/s11747-019-00695-1 PMID: 32431463

Appio, F. P., Cesaroni, F., & Di Minin, A. (2014). Visualizing the structure and bridges of the intellectual property management and strategy literature: A document co-citation analysis. *Scientometrics*, 101(1), 623–661. DOI: 10.1007/s11192-014-1329-0

Aqle, A., Islam, F., Rezk, E., & Jaoua, A. (2016). Mobile app conceptual browser: Online marketplaces information extraction. *13th IEEE/ACS International Conference of Computer Systems and Applications, AICCSA 2016*. 0. Agadir: IEEE Computer Society. DOI: 10.1109/AICCSA.2016.7945671

Aqmala, D., & Putra, F. I. F. S. (2021). Rayu : A Competitive Strategy Model of Wood Craft Business in Soloraya Post Covid-19 Pandemic. *Journal of Management and Entrepreneurship Research*, 2(2), 74–87. DOI: 10.34001/jmer.2021.12.02.2-19

Aral, S., Dellarocas, C., & Godes, D. (2013). Introduction to the special issue - social media and business transformation: A framework for research. *Information Systems Research*, 24(1), 3–13. DOI: 10.1287/isre.1120.0470

Araujo, T. (2018). Living up to the chatbot hype: The influence of anthropomorphic design cues and communicative agency framing on conversational agent and company perceptions. *Computers in Human Behavior*, 85, 183–189. DOI: 10.1016/j.chb.2018.03.051

Arfaei, A., Mohammadi, R., & Akbari, P. (2012). Study the effects of corporate entrepreneurial orientation on customer loyalty (Case Study: Broadcasting companies in the food, pharmaceutical and health in Kermanshah, Iran). *International Research Journal of Applied and Basic Sciences*, 3, 2620–2625.

Arora, S. (2018). *Brand Image And Its Impact on Buying Behaviour*. Medium. https://medium.com/business2change/brand-image-and-its-impact-on-buying-behaviour-faa61776664

Arora, A., Bansal, S., Kandpal, C., Aswani, R., & Dwivedi, Y. (2019). Measuring social media influencer index-insights from Facebook, Twitter and Instagram. *Journal of Retailing and Consumer Services*, 49, 86–101. DOI: 10.1016/j.jretconser.2019.03.012

Arthur, W. B., & Polak, W. (2006). The Evolution of Technology within a Simple Computer Model. *Complexity*, 11(5), 23–31. DOI: 10.1002/cplx.20130

Aryee, R., & Adaku, E. (2023). The reverse logistics resource matrix: A novel classification scheme. *Journal of Manufacturing Technology Management*, 34(3), 435–454. DOI: 10.1108/JMTM-06-2022-0226

Ashfaq, M., Yun, J., Yu, S., & Loureiro, S. M. (2020). I, Chatbot: Modeling the determinants of users' satisfaction and continuance intention of AI-powered service agents. *Telematics and Informatics*, 54, 101473. DOI: 10.1016/j.tele.2020.101473

Ashley, C., & Tuten, T. (2015). Creative strategies in social media marketing: An exploratory study of branded social content and consumer engagement. *Psychology and Marketing*, 32(1), 15–27. DOI: 10.1002/mar.20761

Assabil, M. R., Yusliani, N., & Darmawahyuni, A. (2023). Text Generation using Long Short Term Memory to Generate a LinkedIn Post. *Sriwijaya Journal of Communication*, 4(2), 10–19. DOI: 10.36706/sjia.v4i2.64

Astuti, E., Harsono, I., Uhai, S., Muthmainah, H. N., & Vandika, A. Y. (2024). Application of artificial intelligence technology in customer service in the hospitality industry in Indonesia: A literature review on improving efficiency and user experience. *Sciences Du Nord Nature Science and Technology*, 1(01), 28–36.

Atabekova, N. K., Dzedik, V. A., Troyanskaya, M. A., & Matytsin, D. E. (2022). The role of education and social policy in the development of responsible production and consumption in the AI economy. *Frontiers in Environmental Science*, 10, 929193. Advance online publication. DOI: 10.3389/fenvs.2022.929193

Atli, Q. (2024). How Tesco Uses Data to Personalize the Shopping Experience: A Deep Dive. https://www.atliq.ai/how-tesco-uses-data-to-personalize-the-shopping-experience/

Auh, S., Menguc, B., Imer, P., & Uslu, A. (2019). Frontline employee feedback-seeking behavior: How is it formed and when does it matter? *Journal of Service Research*, 22(1), 44–59. DOI: 10.1177/1094670518779462

Awad, E., Dsouza, S., Kim, R., Schulz, J., Henrich, J., Shariff, A., Bonnefon, J.-F., & Rahwan, I. (2018). The moral machine experiment. *Nature*, 563(7729), 59–64. DOI: 10.1038/s41586-018-0637-6 PMID: 30356211

Aw, E. C. X., & Chuah, S. H. W. (2021). "Stop the unattainable ideal for an ordinary me!" Fostering parasocial relationships with social media influencers: The role of self- discrepancy. *Journal of Business Research*, 132, 146–157. DOI: 10.1016/j.jbusres.2021.04.025

Aydin, G. (2020). Social media engagement and organic post effectiveness: A roadmap for increasing the effectiveness of social media use in hospitality industry. *Journal of Hospitality Marketing & Management*, 29(1), 1–21. DOI: 10.1080/19368623.2019.1588824

Azad, A. M. S., Raza, A., & Zaidi, S. S. Z. (2018). Empirical relationship between operational efficiency and profitability (Evidence from Pakistan exploration sector). *Journal of Accounting. Business and Finance Research*, 2(1), 7–11. DOI: 10.20448/2002.21.7.11

Azhar, D. (2023). Desain Model Artificial Intelligence Untuk Peningkatan Customer Experience & Penjualan Tenaga Listrik Melalui Penambahan Fitur Virtual Customer Support Pada Aplikasi PLN Mobile. *Jurnal Energi dan Ketenagalistrikan, 1*(2), 157-165. .DOI: 10.33322/juke.v1i2.33

Baah, C., Opoku-Agyeman, D., Acquah, I. S. K., Issau, K., & Moro Abdoulaye, F. A. (2021). Understanding the influence of environmental production practices on firm performance: A proactive versus reactive approach. *Journal of Manufacturing Technology Management*, 32(2), 266–289. DOI: 10.1108/JMTM-05-2020-0195

Bacalhau, L. S. M. (2020). *Capital das Marcas Organizacionais (B2B): Uma Abordagem em Contexto de Ingredient Branding - Os Casos da Shimano, Inc. e Órbita - Bicicletas Portuguesas, Lda.* [PhD Thesis, Universidade do Porto]. https://hdl.handle.net/10216/130411

Baesens, B., Verstraeten, G., Van den Poel, D., Egmont-Petersen, M., Van Kenhove, P., & Vanthienen, J. (2004). Bayesian network classifiers for identifying the slope of the customer lifecycle of long-life customers. *European Journal of Operational Research*, 156(2), 508–523. DOI: 10.1016/S0377-2217(03)00043-2

Bager, S. L., & Lambin, E. F. (2020). Sustainability strategies by companies in the global coffee sector. *Business Strategy and the Environment*, 29(8), 3555–3570. DOI: 10.1002/bse.2596

Bai, C., Dallasega, P., Orzes, G., & Sarkis, J. (2020). Industry 4.0 technologies assessment: A sustainability perspective. *International Journal of Production Economics*, 229, 107776. DOI: 10.1016/j.ijpe.2020.107776

Bain. (2023). *Case Study | The Complete Playbook for Generative AI in Fashion.* https://www.businessoffashion.com/case-studies/technology/generative-ai-playbook-machine-learning-emerging-technology/

Bakan, J. (2016). Social marketing: Thoughts from an empathetic outsider. *Journal of Marketing Management*, 32(11–12), 1183–1189. DOI: 10.1080/0267257X.2016.1171035

Balakrishnan, J., Cheng, C.-H., Wong, K.-F., & Woo, K.-H. (2018). Product Recommendation Algorithms in the Age of Omnichannel Retailing – An Intuitive Clustering Approach. *Computers & Industrial Engineering*, 115, 133–150. DOI: 10.1016/j.cie.2017.12.005

Ball, T., & Zorn, B. (2015). Teach foundational language principles. *Communications of the ACM*, 58(5), 30–31. DOI: 10.1145/2663342

Bammens, Y. P. M. (2016). Employees' innovative behavior in social context: A closer examination of the role of organizational care. *Journal of Product Innovation Management*, 33(3), 244–259. DOI: 10.1111/jpim.12267

Banerjee, S. R., Mohapatra, S., & Bharati, M. (2022). *AI in Fashion Industry*. Emerald Publishing Limited eBooks. .DOI: 10.1108/9781802626339

Bankole, O. A., Olaremu, Y. B., & Oghogho, V. O. (2022). Customer Orientation and Firm Competitiveness of Selected Banks in Ekiti State, Nigeria. *Turk Turizm Arastirmalari Dergisi*, 5(1), 15–25. DOI: 10.26677/TR1010.2022.996

Barile, S., Grimaldi, M., Loia, F., & Sirianni, C. A. (2020). Technology, value co-creation and innovation in service ecosystems: Toward sustainable co-innovation. *Sustainability (Basel)*, 12(7), 2759. DOI: 10.3390/su12072759

Baron, R. M., & Kenny, D. A. (1986). The moderator–mediator variable distinction in social psychological research: Conceptual, strategic, and statistical considerations. *Journal of Personality and Social Psychology*, 51(6), 1173–1182. DOI: 10.1037/0022-3514.51.6.1173 PMID: 3806354

Basker, E. (2016). The evolution of technology in the retail sector. In Basker, E. (Ed.), *Handbook on the Economics of Retailing and Distribution* (pp. 38–53). Edward Elgar Publishing. DOI: 10.4337/9781783477388.00010

Batin, M., Turchin, A., Markov, S., Zhila, A., & Denkenberger, D. (2017). Artificial Intelligence in Life Extension: From Deep Learning to Superintelligence. *Informatica-Journal of Computing and Informatics*, 41(4), 401–417.

Batley, M. M. (2021). AI adoption accelerated during the pandemic, but many say it's moving too fast: KPMG survey. https://info.kpmg.us/news-perspectives/technology-innovation/thriving-in-an-ai-world/aiadoption-accelerated-during-pandemic.html

Batrinca, B., & Treleaven, P. C. (2015). Social media analytics: A survey of techniques, tools and platforms. *AI & Society*, 30(1), 89–116. DOI: 10.1007/s00146-014-0549-4

Bayerl, P. S., & Jacobs, G. (2022). Who is responsible for customers' privacy? Effects of first versus third party handling of privacy contracts on continuance intentions. *Technological Forecasting and Social Change*, 185, 122039. DOI: 10.1016/j.techfore.2022.122039

Bazi, S., Filieri, R., & Gorton, M. (2023). Social media content aesthetic quality and customer engagement: The mediating role of entertainment and impacts on brand love and loyalty. *Journal of Business Research*, 160, 113778. DOI: 10.1016/j.jbusres.2023.113778

BBC. (2014). Sydney siege sees Uber raise prices before backtracking. https://www.bbc.com/news/technology-30478008

Bedué, P., & Fritzsche, A. (2022). Can we trust AI? An empirical investigation of trust requirements and guide to successful AI adoption. *Journal of Enterprise Information Management*, 35(2), 530–549. DOI: 10.1108/JEIM-06-2020-0233

Behare, N., & Jeet, D. (2024). The art and science of user engagement: Personalization and recommendations in the OTT era. In *The Rise of Over-the-Top (OTT) Media and Implications for Media Consumption and Production* (pp. 130-159). IGI Global. DOI: 10.4018/979-8-3693-0116-6.ch009

Belarbi, H., Tajmouati, A., Bennis, H., & Tirari, M. E. (2016). Predictive Analysis of Big Data in Retail Industry: Literature Review. *Proceedings of the International Conference on Computing Wireless and Communication Systems*, 560-562.

Belk, R. (2020). Ethical issues in service robotics and artificial intelligence. *Service Industries Journal*, 41(13–14), 860–876. DOI: 0.1080/02642069.2020.1727892

Bellman, R. (1978). *An Introduction to Artificial Intelligence: Can Computers Think?* Boyd & Fraser Publishing Company.

Bentler, P. M. (1992). On the fit of models to covariances and methodology to the Bulletin. *Psychological Bulletin*, 112(3), 400–404. DOI: 10.1037/0033-2909.112.3.400 PMID: 1438635

Bernasconi, C., & Blume, L. B. (2023). Theorizing architectural research and practice in the metaverse: The meta-context of virtual community engagement. *Archnet-IJAR: International Journal of Architectural Research* (ahead-of-print). .DOI: 10.1108/ARCH-08-2023-0203

Berne-Manero, C., & Marzo-Navarro, M. (2020). Exploring How Influencer and Relationship Marketing Serve Corporate Sustainability. *Sustainability (Basel)*, 12(11), 4392. Advance online publication. DOI: 10.3390/su12114392

Bertsimas, D., & Kallus, N. (2019). From Predictive to Prescriptive Analytics. *Management Science*, 66(3), 1025–1044. DOI: 10.1287/mnsc.2018.3253

Bevilacqua, M., Berente, N., Domin, H., Goehring, B., & Rossi, F. (2024). The return on investment in AI ethics: A holistic framework. *Hawaii International Conference on System Sciences (HICSS) 2024.*

Bhandari, P., & Amponstira, F. (2021). Model of Entrepreneurial Orientation, Competitive Advantage and Performance of Women-Owned Enterprises in Gandaki Province, Nepal. *Open Journal of Business and Management*, 09(06), 2854–2865. DOI: 10.4236/ojbm.2021.96159

Bhardwaj, P. (2019). Types of sampling in research. *Journal of the Practice of Cardiovascular Sciences*, 5(3), 157. DOI: 10.4103/jpcs.jpcs_62_19

Bhardwaj, S., Nair, K., Tariq, M. U., Ahmad, A., & Chitnis, A. (2023). The State of Research in Green Marketing: A Bibliometric Review from 2005 to 2022. *Sustainability (Basel)*, 15(4), 2988. Advance online publication. DOI: 10.3390/su15042988

Bhatia, L., Jha, H., Sarkar, T., & Sarangi, P. K. (2023). Food Waste Utilization for Reducing Carbon Footprints towards Sustainable and Cleaner Environment: A Review. *International Journal of Environmental Research and Public Health*, 20(3), 2318. DOI: 10.3390/ijerph20032318 PMID: 36767685

Bhima, B., Zahra, A. R. A., Nurtino, T., & Firli, M. Z. (2023). Enhancing organizational efficiency through the integration of artificial intelligence in management information systems. *APTISI Transactions on Management*, 7(3), 282–289. DOI: 10.33050/atm.v7i3.2146

Bhutto, R. A., & Maqsood, A. (2007). Customer services: a case study of cellular phone companies in Pakistan. *JISR management and social sciences & economics, 5*(1), 19-23.

Bialkova, S. (2024). AI Transforming Business and Everyday Life. In Bialkova, S. (Ed.), *The Rise of AI User Applications: Chatbots Integration Foundations and Trends* (pp. 143–165). Springer Nature Switzerland., DOI: 10.1007/978-3-031-56471-0_9

Bijmolt, T. H., Leeflang, P. S., Block, F., Eisenbeiss, M., Hardie, B. G., Lemmens, A., & Saffert, P. (2010). Analytics for customer engagement. *Journal of Service Research*, 13(3), 341–356. DOI: 10.1177/1094670510375603

Bilal, M., Zhang, Y., Cai, S., Akram, U., & Halibas, A. S. (2024). Artificial intelligence is the magic wand making customer-centric a reality! An investigation into the relationship between consumer purchase intention and consumer engagement through affective attachment. *Journal of Retailing and Consumer Services*, 77(March), 103674. DOI: 10.1016/j.jretconser.2023.103674

Birou, L. M., Green, K. W., & Inman, R. A. (2019). Sustainability knowledge and training: Outcomes and firm performance. *Journal of Manufacturing Technology Management*, 30(2), 294–311. DOI: 10.1108/JMTM-05-2018-0148

Bizz-O-Tech. (2024, Jul 03). *The Role of AI-Driven Recommendation Systems in E-Commerce and Their Impact on Consumer Behavior and Sales.* https://www.linkedin.com/pulse/role-ai-driven-recommendation-systems-e-commerce-impact-consumer-a8oof/

Bleier, A., Harmeling, C. M., & Palmatier, R. W. (2019). Creating effective online customer experiences. *Journal of Marketing*, 83(2), 98–119. DOI: 10.1177/0022242918809930

Blut, M., Wang, C., Wünderlich, N. V., & Brock, C. (2021). Understanding anthropomorphism in service provision: A meta-analysis of physical robots, chatbots, and other AI. *Journal of the Academy of Marketing Science*, 49(4), 1–27. DOI: 10.1007/s11747-020-00762-y

Bogicevic, V., Seo, S., Kandampully, J. A., Liu, S. Q., & Rudd, N. A. (2019). Virtual reality presence as a preamble of tourism experience: The role of mental imagery. *Tourism Management*, 74, 55–64. DOI: 10.1016/j.tourman.2019.02.009

Boguda, S. K., & Shailaja, A.Satish Kumar Boguda. (2019). The Future of Customer Experience in the Information Age of Artificial Intelligence-Get Ready for Change. *International Journal of Engineering Research & Technology (Ahmedabad)*, 8(6), 1141–1150. DOI: 10.17577/IJERTV8IS060622

Bolesnikov, M., Popović Stijačić, M., Keswani, A. B., & Brkljač, N. (2022). Perception of Innovative Usage of AI in Optimizing Customer Purchasing Experience within the Sustainable Fashion Industry. *Sustainability (Basel)*, 14(16), 10082. Advance online publication. DOI: 10.3390/su141610082

Bolton, R. N., McColl-Kennedy, J. R., Cheung, L., Gallan, A., Orsingher, C., Witell, L., & Zaki, M. (2018). Customer experience challenges: Bringing together digital, physical and social realms. *Journal of Service Management*, 29(5), 776–808. DOI: 10.1108/JOSM-04-2018-0113

Bolze, J. D., & Engles, E. (2018). Artificial intelligence based service implementation. https://patents.google.com/patent/AU2018274927A1/en

Bonfanti, A., Mion, G., Brunetti, F., & Vargas-Sánchez, A. (2023). The contribution of manufacturing companies to the achievement of sustainable development goals: An empirical analysis of the operationalization of sustainable business models. *Business Strategy and the Environment*, 32(4), 2490–2508. DOI: 10.1002/bse.3260

Boonmalert, W., Ayasanond, C., Phoothong, B., & Chaitorn, T. (2021). A causal influence model of innovation and digital marketing on the small and medium enterprise (SME) performance in Thailand. *European Journal of Molecular & Clinical Medicine, 8*(03), 63-72. ISSN 2515-8260

Boonsirisumpun, N., Okafor, E., & Surinta, O. (2024). Vehicle image datasets for image classification. *Data in Brief*, 53, 110133. DOI: 10.1016/j.dib.2024.110133 PMID: 38348321

Botha, E., & Reyneke, M. (2016). The influence of social presence on online purchase intention: An experiment with different product types. In C. Campbell & J. Ma (Eds.), *Looking forward, looking back: Drawing on the past to shape the future of marketing,proceedings of the 2013 World Marketing Congress* (pp. 180-183). Springer. DOI: 10.1007/978-3-319-24184-5_49

Bounatirou, M., & Lim, A. (2020). A case study on the impact of artificial intelligence on a hospitality company. In *Sustainable Hospitality Management: Designing Meaningful Encounters With Talent and Technology* (pp. 179-187). Emerald Publishing Limited. DOI: 10.1108/S1877-636120200000024013

Bouras, C., Diasakos, D., Katsigiannis, C., Kokkinos, V., Gkamas, A., Karacapilidis, N., & Alexopoulos, C. (2023). On the Development of a Novel Chatbot Generator Architecture: Design and Assessment Issues. *8th International Conference on Mathematics and Computers in Sciences and Industry, MCSI 2023* (pp. 83-88). Athens: Institute of Electrical and Electronics Engineers Inc. DOI: 10.1109/MCSI60294.2023.00021

Bowden, J. L. H. (2009). The Process of Customer Engagement: A Conceptual Framework. *Journal of Marketing Theory and Practice*, 17(1), 63–74. DOI: 10.2753/MTP1069-6679170105

Bowen, J. T., & Chen, S. L. (2001). The relationship between customer loyalty and customer satisfaction. *International Journal of Contemporary Hospitality Management*, 13(5), 213–217. DOI: 10.1108/09596110110395893

Bowman, J. (2023, November 21). *How artificial intelligence is used in customer service*. The Motley Fool. https://www.fool.com/investing/stock-market/market-sectors/information-technology/ai-stocks/ai-in-customer-service/

Box, G. E. P., Jenkins, G. M., & Reinsel, G. C. (2015). *Time Series Analysis: Forecasting and Control*. John Wiley & Sons.

Bracci, E., & Maran, L. (2011). *Performance measurement in the public sector: some theoretical and practical reflections*. https://www.unife.it/dipartimento/economia/pubblicazioni/quaderni-del-

Bramer, M. (2013). *Principles of Data Mining*. Springer. DOI: 10.1007/978-1-4471-4884-5

Brandon Ginsberg. *Artificial Intelligence In Fashion*. Forbes. https://www.forbes.com/sites/theyec/2023/02/21/artificial-intelligence-in-fashion

Brau, E., Reinhardt, R., & Gurtner, S. (2013). Measuring the success of open innovation. In *Evolution of Innovation Management* (pp. 52–74). Palgrave Macmillan UK. DOI: 10.1057/9781137299994_3

Britannica, E. (2018). Rapid transit: https://www. britannica. com/technology/rapid-transit

Brodie, R. J., Benson-Rea, M., & Medlin, C. J. (2016). Branding as a dynamic capability. *Marketing Theory*, 17(2), 183–199. DOI: 10.1177/1470593116679871

Brodie, R. J., Ilic, A., Juric, B., & Hollebeek, L. D. (2013). Consumer engagement in a virtual brand com- munity: An exploratory analysis. *Journal of Business Research*, 66(1), 105–114. DOI: 10.1016/j.jbusres.2011.07.029

Browne, M. W., & Cudeck, R. (1993). *Alternative ways of assessing model fit. Testing structural equation models*. KA Bollen and JS Long.

Brown, T. B., Mann, B., Ryder, N., Subbiah, M., Kaplan, J., Dhariwal, P., Neelakantan, A., Shyam, P., Sastry, G., Askell, A., Agarwal, S., Herbert-Voss, A., Krueger, G., Henighan, T., Child, R., Ramesh, A., Ziegler, D. M., Wu, J., Winter, C., & Amodei, D. (2020). Language Models are Few-Shot Learners. *ArXiv*. https://arxiv.org/abs/2005.14165

Brynjolfsson, E., Hu, Y. J., & Rahman, M. S. (2013). Competing in the Age of Omnichannel Retailing. *MIT Sloan Management Review*, 54(4), 23–29.

Bryson, D., Atwal, G., & Hultén, P. (2013). Towards the conceptualisation of the antecedents of extreme negative affect towards luxury brands. *Qualitative Market Research*, 16(4), 393–405. DOI: 10.1108/QMR-06-2013-0043

Bughin, J., Hazan, E., Ramaswamy, S., Chui, M., Allas, T., Dahlström, P., Henke, N., & Trench, M. (2017). *Artificial Intelligence: The next digital frontier?*www .mckinsey.com/mgi

Bushee, B. J., & Miller, G. S. (2007). Investor relations, firm visibility, and investor following. SSRN *Electronic Journal*. DOI: 10.2139/ssrn.643223

Bustos-Reyes, C. A., & González-Benito, Ó. (2008). Store and store format loyalty measures based on budget allocation. *Journal of Business Research*, 61(9), 1015–1025. DOI: 10.1016/j.jbusres.2007.03.008

Buttle, F., & Maklan, S. (2019). *Customer relationship management: Concepts and technologies* (4th ed.). Taylor and Francis Inc., DOI: 10.4324/9781351016551

Cakir, F. S., Aslan, B., & Adiguzel, Z. (2022). The Bank's Effect on Digital Capability and Knowledge Acquisition Within the Performance and Digital Native's Perception of Mobile Banking. *Revista de Estudios Empresariales*, 2, 292–313.

Caldarini, G., Jaf, S., & McGarry, K. (2022). A Literature Survey of Recent Advances in Chatbots. *Information (Basel)*, 13(1), 41. Advance online publication. DOI: 10.3390/info13010041

Calderón-Fajardo, V., Anaya-Sánchez, R., & Rejón-Guardia, F. (2024). Neurotourism Insights: Eye Tracking and Galvanic Analysis of Tourism Destination Brand Logos and AI Visuals. *Tourism &amp. Tourism & Management Studies*, 20(3), 53–78. DOI: 10.18089/tms.20240305

Camaréna, S. (2021). Engaging with Artificial Intelligence (AI) with a Bottom-Up Approach for the Purpose of Sustainability: Victorian Farmers Market Association, Melbourne Australia. *Sustainability*, 13(16). Advance online publication. DOI: 10.3390/su13169314

Cambria, E. (2016). Affective computing and sentiment analysis. *IEEE Intelligent Systems*, 31(2), 102–107. DOI: 10.1109/MIS.2016.31

Cammarano, A., Perano, M., Michelino, F., Del Regno, C., & Caputo, M. (2022). SDG-Oriented Supply Chains: Business Practices for Procurement and Distribution. *Sustainability (Basel)*, 14(3), 1325. Advance online publication. DOI: 10.3390/su14031325

Campbell, C., Sands, S., Ferraro, C., Tsao, H., & Mavrommatis, A. (2020). From data to action: How marketers can leverage AI. *Business Horizons*, 63(2), 227–243. DOI: 10.1016/j.bushor.2019.12.002

Campbell, M., Hoane, A. J.Jr, & Hsu, F. (2002). Deep Blue. *Artificial Intelligence*, 134(1), 57–83. DOI: 10.1016/S0004-3702(01)00129-1

Carbonneau, R., Laframboise, K., & Vahidov, R. (2008). Application of machine learning techniques for supply chain demand forecasting. *European Journal of Operational Research*, 184(3), 1140–1154. DOI: 10.1016/j.ejor.2006.12.004

Carlucci, D., Renna, P., & Materi, S. (2023). A Job-Shop Scheduling Decision-Making Model for Sustainable Production Planning With Power Constraint. *IEEE Transactions on Engineering Management*, 70(5), 1923–1932. DOI: 10.1109/TEM.2021.3103108

Carole, K. S., Theodore Armand, T. P., & Kim, H. C. (2024). Enhanced Experiences: Benefits of AI-Powered Recommendation Systems. *26th International Conference on Advanced Communications Technology, ICACT 2024* (pp. 216-220). Pyeong Chang: Institute of Electrical and Electronics Engineers Inc. DOI: 10.23919/ICACT60172.2024.10471918

Caroline (2022). Easier to Sell More Products with Gucci Shoe AR Try-on. https://tryon.kivisense.com/blog/gucci-sneaker-ar-try-on

Casarejos, F., Frota, M. N., Rocha, J. E., Da Silva, W. R., & Barreto, J. T. (2016). Corporate Sustainability Strategies: A Case Study in Brazil Focused on High Consumers of Electricity. *Sustainability (Basel)*, 8(8), 791. Advance online publication. DOI: 10.3390/su8080791

Cavoukian, A. (2020). Understanding how to implement privacy by design, one step at a time. *IEEE Consumer Electronics Magazine*, 9(2), 78–82. DOI: 10.1109/MCE.2019.2953739

Chaffey, D. (2020). *Digital Marketing: Strategy, Implementation and Practice*. Pearson Education.

Chaffey, D., & Ellis-Chadwick, F. (2019). *Digital Marketing: Strategy, Implementation, and Practice*. Pearson.

Chaffey, D., Ellis-Chadwick, F., & Mayer, R. (2009). *Internet marketing: strategy, implementation and practice*. Pearson Education.

Chaffey, D., & Patron, M. (2012). From web analytics to digital marketing optimization: Increasing the commercial value of digital analytics. *Journal of Direct, Data and Digital Marketing Practice*, 14(1), 30–45. DOI: 10.1057/dddmp.2012.20

Chai, J. C. Y., Malhotra, N. K., & Alpert, F. (2015). A two-dimensional model of trust-value-loyalty in service relationships. *Journal of Retailing and Consumer Services*, 26, 23–31. DOI: 10.1016/j.jretconser.2015.05.005

Chandgude, V., & Kawade, B. (2023). Role of Artificial Intelligence and Machine Learning in Decision Making for Business Growth. *International Journal of Advanced Research in Science. Tongxin Jishu*, 54-58, 54–58. Advance online publication. DOI: 10.48175/IJARSCT-8556

Chandra, S., Shirish, A., & Srivastava, S. C. (2022). To be or not to be… human? Theorizing the role of human-like competencies in conversational artificial intelligence agents. *Journal of Management Information Systems*, 39(4), 969–1005. DOI: 10.1080/07421222.2022.2127441

Chandra, S., Verma, S., Lim, W. M., Kumar, S., & Donthu, N. (2022). Personalization in personalized marketing: Trends and ways forward. *Psychology and Marketing*, 39(8), 1529–1562. DOI: 10.1002/mar.21670

Chatfield, C. (2003). *The Analysis of Time Series: An Introduction* (6th ed.). Chapman and Hall/CRC. DOI: 10.4324/9780203491683

Chatterjee, S., Chaudhuri, R., & Vrontis, D. (2022). AI and digitalization in relationship management: Impact of adopting AI-embedded CRM system. *Journal of Business Research*, 150, 437–450. DOI: 10.1016/j.jbusres.2022.06.033

Chaturvedi, R., Verma, S., & Srivastava, V. (2024). Empowering AI Companions for Enhanced Relationship Marketing. *California Management Review*, 66(2), 65–90. DOI: 10.1177/00081256231215838

Chaudhary, P., Kurariya, P., Singh, S. P., Bodhankar, J., Singh, L., & Kumar, A. (2022). Intelligent virtual research environment for natural language processing (IvrE-NLP). In *Smart Trends in Computing and Communications* [Springer Nature Singapore.]. *Proceedings of SmartCom*, 2022, 453–465.

Chaudhuri, R., Chatterjee, S., Vrontis, D., & Chaudhuri, S. (2022). Innovation in SMEs, AI Dynamism, and Sustainability: The Current Situation and Way Forward. *Sustainability (Basel)*, 14(19), 12760. Advance online publication. DOI: 10.3390/su141912760

Chen, H., & Magramo, K. (2024, February 4). Finance worker pays out $25 million after video call with deepfake 'chief financial officer'. *CNN*. https://edition.cnn.com/2024/02/04/asia/deepfake-cfo-scam-hong-kong-intl-hnk/index.html

Chen, J., Ganguly, B., Kanade, S. G., & Duffy, V. G. (2023). Impact of AI on Mobile Computing: A Systematic Review from a Human Factors Perspective. *25th International Conference on Human-Computer Interaction, HCII 2023. 14059 LNCS* (pp. 24-38). Copenhagen: Springer Science and Business Media Deutschland GmbH. DOI: 10.1007/978-3-031-48057-7_2

Chen, Y., & Feng, S. (2021). Artificial Intelligence: Creating More Possibilities for Programmatic Advertising. In *Proceedings of the AHFE 2021 Virtual Conferences on Human Factors in Software and Systems Engineering, Artificial Intelligence and Social Computing, and Energy* (pp. 148–155), July 25-29, 2021, USA. Springer. DOI: 10.1007/978-3-030-80624-8_19

Cheng, Z. (2024). *Interpretable and generative AI for actionable insights from textual data*. Phd Thesis. Boston University. https://hdl.handle.net/2144/48748

Cheng, C. F., Huang, C. C., Lin, M. C., & Chen, T. C. (2023). Exploring Effectiveness of Relationship Marketing on Artificial Intelligence Adopting Intention. *SAGE Open*, 13(4), 21582440231222760. Advance online publication. DOI: 10.1177/21582440231222760

Cheng, Y., & Jiang, H. (2020). How Do AI-driven Chatbots Impact User Experience? Examining Gratifications, Perceived Privacy Risk, Satisfaction, Loyalty, and Continued Use. *Journal of Broadcasting & Electronic Media*, 64(4), 592–614. DOI: 10.1080/08838151.2020.1834296

Cheng, Y., & Jiang, H. (2022). Customer–brand relationship in the era of artificial intelligence: Understanding the role of chatbot marketing efforts. *Journal of Product and Brand Management*, 31(2), 252–264. DOI: 10.1108/JPBM-05-2020-2907

Chen, H., Mao, S., & Liu, Y. (2014). Big Data: A Survey. *Mobile Networks and Applications*, 19(2), 171–209. DOI: 10.1007/s11036-013-0489-0

Chen, M. C., Chiu, A. L., & Chang, H. H. (2005). Mining changes in customer behavior in retail marketing. *Expert Systems with Applications*, 28(4), 773–781. DOI: 10.1016/j.eswa.2004.12.033

Chen, Q., Lu, Y., Gong, Y., & Xiong, J. (2023). Can AI chatbots help retain customers? Impact of AI service quality on customer loyalty. *Internet Research*, 33(6), 2205–2243. DOI: 10.1108/INTR-09-2021-0686

Chen, Y. L., Huang, T. C. K., & Chang, S. K. (2008). A novel approach for discovering retail knowledge with price information from transaction databases. *Expert Systems with Applications*, 34(4), 2350–2359. DOI: 10.1016/j.eswa.2007.03.006

Chen, Y., & Prentice, C. (2024). Integrating artificial intelligence and customer experience. *Australasian Marketing Journal*, 14413582241252904, 14413582241252904. Advance online publication. DOI: 10.1177/14413582241252904

Chen, Y., Prentice, C., Weaven, S., & Hisao, A. (2022). The influence of customer trust and artificial intelligence on customer engagement and loyalty–The case of the home-sharing industry. *Frontiers in Psychology*, 13, 912339. DOI: 10.3389/fpsyg.2022.912339 PMID: 35992434

Chenying, Y. (2023). A Case Study of Netflix's Marketing Strategy. *International Conference on Advances in Internet Marketing and Business Management (ICAMM 2023)* (pp. 185-192). DOI: 10.54691/bcpbm.v42i.4580

Chintalapati, S., & Pandey, S. K. (2021). Artificial intelligence in marketing: A systematic literature review. *International Journal of Market Research*, 64(1), 38–68. DOI: 10.1177/14707853211018428

Chong, T., Yu, T., Keeling, D. I., & de Ruyter, K. (2021). AI-chatbots on the services frontline addressing the challenges and opportunities of agency. *Journal of Retailing and Consumer Services*, 63, 102735. DOI: 10.1016/j.jretconser.2021.102735

Chopdar, P. K., Paul, J., & Prodanova, J. (2022). Mobile shoppers' response to Covid-19 phobia, pessimism and smartphone addiction: Does social influence matter? *Technological Forecasting and Social Change*, 174, 121249. DOI: 10.1016/j.techfore.2021.121249 PMID: 36540714

Chopra, R., & Sharma, G. D. (2021). Application of Artificial Intelligence in Stock Market Forecasting: A Critique, Review, and Research Agenda. *Journal of Risk and Financial Management*, 14(11), 526. DOI: 10.3390/jrfm14110526

Chowdhary, C. L., Alazab, M., Chaudhary, A., Hakak, S., & Gadekallu, T. R. (2024). Computer Vision and Recognition Systems Using Machine and Deep Learning Approaches: Fundamentals, technologies and applications. In *Computer Vision and Recognition Systems Using Machine and Deep Learning Approaches: Fundamentals, technologies and applications* (pp. 1-483). Institution of Engineering and Technology. DOI: 10.1049/PBPC042E

Christodoulides, G. (2009). Branding in the post-internet era. *Marketing Theory*, 9(1), 141–144. DOI: 10.1177/1470593108100071

Christodoulides, G., Athwal, N., Boukis, A., & Semaan, R. W. (2021). New forms of luxury consumption in the sharing economy. *Journal of Business Research*, 137, 89–99. DOI: 10.1016/j.jbusres.2021.08.022

Chuang, S. H. (2018). Facilitating the chain of market orientation to value co-creation: The mediating role of e-marketing adoption. *Journal of Destination Marketing & Management*, 7, 39–49. DOI: 10.1016/j.jdmm.2016.08.007

Chung, K. C. (2020). Green marketing orientation: Achieving sustainable development in green hotel management. *Journal of Hospitality Marketing & Management*, 29(6), 722–738. DOI: 10.1080/19368623.2020.1693471

Chung, M., Ko, E., Joung, H., & Kim, S. J. (2020). Chatbot e-service and customer satisfaction regarding luxury brands. *Journal of Business Research*, 117, 587–595. DOI: 10.1016/j.jbusres.2018.10.004

Chung, S.-Y., & Byrom, J. (2020). Co-creating consistent brand identity with employees in the hotel industry. *Journal of Product and Brand Management*, 30(1), 74–89. DOI: 10.1108/JPBM-08-2019-2544

Chu, S. C., & Kim, Y. (2011). Determinants of consumer engagement in electronic word-of-mouth (eWOM) in social networking sites. *International Journal of Advertising*, 30(1), 47–75. DOI: 10.2501/IJA-30-1-047-075

Chutcheva, Y. V., Kuprianova, L. M., Seregina, A. A., & Kukushkin, S. N. (2022). Environmental management of companies in the oil and gas markets based on AI for sustainable development: An international review. *Frontiers in Environmental Science*, 10, 952102. DOI: 10.3389/fenvs.2022.952102

Claffey, E., & Brady, M. (2017). Examining consumers' motivations to engage in firm-hosted virtual communities. *Psychology and Marketing*, 34(4), 356–375. DOI: 10.1002/mar.20994

Claffey, E., & Brady, M. (2019). An empirical study of the impact of consumer emotional engagement and affective commitment in firm-hosted virtual communities. *Journal of Marketing Management*, 35(11–12), 1047–1079. DOI: 10.1080/0267257X.2019.1601125

CMAPL. C. M. (2022, Aug 22). *Visual Search Market Key Players & Growth Rate and Forecasts to 2028.* https://www.linkedin.com/pulse/visual-search-market-key-players-growth-rate-forecasts-/

Cook, G. O. K., & Olsanova, K. (2024). Luxury brand management in the world of evolving technologies. *The Journal of Business Leadership*, 31(1), 58–68. DOI: 10.69847/Ip4X5VDf

Copeland, B. J. (2018). Artificial intelligence. https://www.britannica.com/technology/artificialintelligence

Cordero, J., Barba-Guaman, L., & Guaman, F. (2022). *Use of chatbots for customer service in MSMEs*. Applied Computing and Informatics., DOI: 10.1108/ACI-06-2022-0148

Corner, A., & Randall, A. (2011). Selling climate change? The limitations of social marketing as a strategy for climate change public engagement. *Global Environmental Change*, 21(3), 1005–1014. DOI: 10.1016/j.gloenvcha.2011.05.002

Cortese, D., Rainero, C., & Cantino, V. (2021). Stakeholders' social dialogue about responsibility and sustainability in the food sector. *British Food Journal*, 123(3), 1287–1301. DOI: 10.1108/BFJ-11-2019-0826

Coulter, K. S., & Roggeveen, A. (2012). "Like it or not" Consumer responses to word-of-mouth communication in on-line social networks. *Management Research Review*, 35(9), 878–899. DOI: 10.1108/01409171211256587

Covin, J. G., & Wales, W. J. (2019). Crafting high-impact entrepreneurial orientation research: Some suggested guidelines. *Entrepreneurship Theory and Practice*, 43(1), 3–18. DOI: 10.1177/1042258718773181

Criado-Gomis, A., Iniesta-Bonillo, M. Á., & Cervera-Taulet, A. (2018). Sustainable entrepreneurial orientation within an intrapreneurial context: Effects on business performance. *The International Entrepreneurship and Management Journal*, 14(2), 295–308. DOI: 10.1007/s11365-018-0503-x

Cripps, H., Singh, A., Mejtoft, T., & Salo, J. (2020). The use of Twitter for innovation in business markets. *Marketing Intelligence & Planning*, 38(5), 587–601. DOI: 10.1108/MIP-06-2019-0349

Crutzen, R., Ygram Peters, G.-J., & Mondschein, C. (2019). Why and how we should care about the General Data Protection Regulation. *Psychology & Health*, 34(11), 1347–1357. DOI: 10.1080/08870446.2019.1606222 PMID: 31111730

Cuevas-Vargas, H., Parga-Montoya, N., & Fernåndez-Escobedo, R. (2019). Effects of Entrepreneurial Orientation on Business Performance: The Mediating Role of Customer Satisfaction - A Formative Reflective Model Analysis. *SAGE Open*, 9(2). Advance online publication. DOI: 10.1177/2158244019859088

Cukier, K. (2021). Commentary: How AI shapes consumer experiences and expectations. *Journal of Marketing*, 85(1), 152–155. DOI: 10.1177/0022242920972932

D'Cruz, J. R., Kidder, W., & Varshney, K. R. (2022). The empathy gap: Why AI can forecast behavior but cannot assess trustworthiness. In *Proceedings of the AAAI fall symposium series symposium on thinking fast and slow and other cognitive theories in AI.*

Dabiran, E., Farivar, S., Wang, F., & Grant, G. (2024). Virtually human: Anthropomorphism in virtual influencer marketing. *Journal of Retailing and Consumer Services*, 79, 103797. DOI: 10.1016/j.jretconser.2024.103797

Dabrowski, D., Brzozowska-Woś, M., Gołąb-Andrzejak, E., & Firgolska, A. (2019). Market orientation and hotel performance: The mediating effect of creative marketing programs. *Journal of Hospitality and Tourism Management*, 41, 175–183. DOI: 10.1016/j.jhtm.2019.10.006

Daengs, G. S. A., Kurniasih, N., Reni, A., Istanti, E., Zuhroh, D., & Qomariah, N. (2019). The effect of business sphere on competitive advantage and performance of business of SMEs. *Management Science Letters*, 9(8), 1153–1160. DOI: 10.5267/j.msl.2019.4.025

Dagan, A., Guy, I., & Novgorodov, S. (2021). An Image is Worth a Thousand Terms Analysis of Visual E-Commerce Search. *44th International ACM SIGIR Conference on Research and Development in Information Retrieval, SIGIR 2021* (pp. 102-112). Virtual, Online: Association for Computing Machinery, Inc. DOI: 10.1145/3404835.3462950

Dalal, T., Chaudhary, P., Rawat, S. S., & Metha, Y. (2022). Artificial Intelligence (AI) Powered Customer Care. In Pillai, R. K., Singh, B. P., & Murugesan, N. (Eds.), *ISUW 2021. Lecture Notes in Electrical Engineering* (Vol. 843). Springer., DOI: 10.1007/978-981-16-8727-3_42

Dallas, T., Gehman, A. L., & Farrell, M. J. (2018). Variable bibliographic database access could limit reproducibility. *Bioscience*, 68(8), 552–553. DOI: 10.1093/biosci/biy074

Damasio, A. R. (1994). *Descartes' error: emotion, reason, and the human brain.* G.P. Putnam.

Dam, S. M., & Dam, T. C. (2021). Relationships between service quality, brand image, customer satisfaction, and customer loyalty. *The Journal of Asian Finance. Economics and Business*, 8(3), 585–593.

Dam, T. C.DAM. (2020). Influence of Brand Trust, Perceived Value on Brand Preference and Purchase Intention. *Journal of Asian Finance. Economics and Business*, 7(10), 939–947. DOI: 10.13106/jafeb.2020.vol7.no10.939

Daniel, E. J. (2024). *AI-Enabled Retail: Crafting the Future of Shopping Experiences.* Medium. https://medium.com/@daniel.erinj2/ai-enabled-retail-crafting-the-future-of-shopping-experiences-4aa275e5f5cb

Dash, G., Sharma, C., & Sharma, S. (2023). Sustainable Marketing and the Role of Social Media: An Experimental Study Using Natural Language Processing (NLP). *Sustainability (Basel)*, 15(6), 5443. Advance online publication. DOI: 10.3390/su15065443

Daskou, S., & Mangina, E. E. (2003). Artificial Intelligence in Managing Market Relationships: The Use of Intelligence Agents. *Journal of Relationship Marketing*, 2(1-2), 85–102. DOI: 10.1300/J366v02n01_06

Daudelin, D. H., Selker, H. P., & Leslie, L. K. (2015). Applying process improvement methods to clinical and Translational research: Conceptual framework and case examples. *Clinical and Translational Science*, 8(6), 779–786. DOI: 10.1111/cts.12326 PMID: 26332869

Daugherty, P. R., & Wilson, H. J. (2018). *Human + machine: reimagining work in the age of AI.* Harvard Business Review Press.

Dave, M., & Patel, N. (2023, May 26). Artificial intelligence in healthcare and education. *British Dental Journal*, 234(10), 761–764. DOI: 10.1038/s41415-023-5845-2 PMID: 37237212

Davenport, T. H., & Ronanki, R. (2018). Artificial Intelligence for the Real World. Harvard Business Review (HBR). https://www.bizjournals.com/boston/news/2018/01/09/hbr-artificial-intelligence-for-the-real-world.html

Davenport, T. H. (2018). *The AI Advantage: How to Put the Artificial Intelligence Revolution to Work.* MIT Press. DOI: 10.7551/mitpress/11781.001.0001

Davenport, T. H., & Glaser, J. (2022). Factors governing the adoption of artificial intelligence in healthcare providers. *Discover Health Systems*, 1(1), 4. Advance online publication. DOI: 10.1007/s44250-022-00004-8 PMID: 37521111

Davenport, T. H., Guha, A., Grewal, D., & Bressgott, T. (2020). How Artificial Intelligence Will Change the Future of Marketing. *Journal of the Academy of Marketing Science*, 48(1), 24–42. DOI: 10.1007/s11747-019-00696-0

Davenport, T. H., & Ronanki, R. (2018). Artificial intelligence for the real world. *Harvard Business Review*, 96(1), 108–116.

Davenport, T. H., & Ronanki, R. (2018). Artificial Intelligence for the Real World. *Harvard Business Review*, 96(1), 108–116.

Davenport, T., & Harris, J. (2017). *Competing on analytics: Updated, with a new introduction: The new science of winning*. Harvard Business Press.

De Bruyn, A., Viswanathan, V., Beh, Y. S., Brock, J. K. U., & Von Wangenheim, F. (2020). Artificial intelligence and Marketing: Pitfalls and opportunities. *Journal of Interactive Marketing*, 51(1), 91–105. DOI: 10.1016/j.intmar.2020.04.007

De Buck, A. J., Hendrix, E. M. T., & Schoorlemmer, H. B. (1999). Analysing production and environmental risks in arable farming systems: A mathematical approach. *European Journal of Operational Research*, 119(2), 416–426. DOI: 10.1016/S0377-2217(99)00143-5

de Chernatony, L. (2010). *From Brand Vision to Brand Evaluation: The Strategic Process of Growing and Strengthening Brand* (3rd ed.). Routledge. DOI: 10.4324/9780080966649

De Keyser, A., Köcher, S., Alkire, L., Verbeeck, C., & Kandampully, J. (2019). Frontline service technology infusion: Conceptual archetypes and future research directions. *Journal of Service Management*, 30(1), 156–183. DOI: 10.1108/JOSM-03-2018-0082

de Luca, L. M., Herhausen, D., Troilo, G., & Rossi, A. (2021). How and when do big data investments pay off? The role of marketing affordances and service innovation. *Journal of the Academy of Marketing Science*, 49(4), 790–810. DOI: 10.1007/s11747-020-00739-x

de Sá Siqueira, M. A., Müller, B. C., & Bosse, T. (2023). When do we accept mistakes from chatbots? The impact of human-like communication on user experience in chatbots that make mistakes. *International Journal of Human-Computer Interaction*, 40(11), 2862–2872. DOI: 10.1080/10447318.2023.2175158

De Sousa, J. R., & dos Santos, S. C. (2020). Análise de conteúdo em pesquisa qualitativa: modo de pensar e de fazer. *Pesquisa e debate em Educação, 10(*2), 1396-1416.

De Vries, L., Gensler, S., & Leeflang, P. S. (2017). Effects of traditional advertising and social messages on brand-building metrics and customer acquisition. *Journal of Marketing*, 81(5), 1–15. DOI: 10.1509/jm.15.0178

Deepa, S., & Abirami, A. (2024). The Impact of AI on Customer Experience. In *Balancing Automation and Human Interaction in Modern Marketing* (pp. 263–285). IGI Global., DOI: 10.4018/979-8-3693-2276-5.ch014

Deggans, J., Krulicky, T., Kovacova, M., Valaskova, K., & Poliak, M. (2019). Cognitively enhanced products, output growth, and labor market changes: Will artificial intelligence replace workers by automating their jobs? *Economics, Management, and Financial Markets*, 14(1), 38. DOI: 10.22381/EMFM14120194

Dehdashti, Y., Lotfi, N., & Karami, N. (2012). Analyzing factors effective on the development of relationship commitment. Proceedings of the *2012 International Conference on Artificial Intelligence*, ICAI 2012.

Demessie, G. T., & Shukla, A. (2024). Drivers and outcomes of sustainable marketing strategy in the African context: The role of competitive advantage and strategic proactivity as mediating and moderating variables. *Cogent Business & Management*, 11(1), 2348442. DOI: 10.1080/23311975.2024.2348442

Deng, S., Wang, D., Li, Y., Cao, B., Yin, J., Wu, Z., & Zhou, M. (2016). A Recommendation System to Facilitate Business Process Modeling. *IEEE Transactions on Cybernetics*, 47(6), 1380–1394. DOI: 10.1109/TCYB.2016.2545688 PMID: 27076482

Deng, Z. (2023). Research on the Development Trend of Artificial Intelligence Led by ChatGPT. *Highlights in Science. Engineering and Technology*, 56, 112–116. DOI: 10.54097/hset.v56i.9822

Deryl, M. D., Verma, S., & Srivastava, V. (2023). How does AI drive branding? Towards an integrated theoretical framework for AI-driven branding. *International Journal of Information Management Data Insights*, 3(2), 100205. DOI: 10.1016/j.jjimei.2023.100205

Desai, P. (2021). A Strategic Approach to Enrich Brand Through Artificial Intelligence. In *Machine Learning for Predictive Analysis* [Springer Singapore.]. *Proceedings of ICTIS*, 2020, 579–587.

Dessart, L., Veloutsou, C., & Morgan-Thomas, A. (2015). Consumer engagement in online brand communities: A social media perspective. *Journal of Product and Brand Management*, 24(1), 28–42. DOI: 10.1108/JPBM-06-2014-0635

Dessart, L., Veloutsou, C., & Morgan-Thomas, A. (2016). Capturing consumer engagement: Duality, dimensionality and measurement. *Journal of Marketing Management*, 32(5-6), 399–426. DOI: 10.1080/0267257X.2015.1130738

Devi, K. V., Manjula, V., & Pattewar, T. (2023). *ChatGPT: Comprehensive study on generative AI tool.* Academic Guru Publishing House.

Devlin, J., Chang, M. W., Lee, K., & Toutanova, K. (2018). BERT: Pre-training of Deep Bidirectional Transformers for Language Understanding. https://arxiv.org/abs/1810.04805v2

Dhaliwal, A. (2022). Towards AI-driven transport and logistics. In *Workshop on e-Business* (pp. 119-131). Springer Nature.

Dhamija, P., & Bag, S. (2020). Role of artificial intelligence in operations environment: A review and bibliometric analysis. *The TQM Journal*, 32(4), 869–896. DOI: 10.1108/TQM-10-2019-0243

Di Vaio, A., Palladino, R., Hassan, R., & Escobar, O. (2020). Artificial intelligence and business models in the sustainable development goals perspective: A systematic literature review. *Journal of Business Research*, 121, 283–314. DOI: 10.1016/j.jbusres.2020.08.019

Dick, A. S., & Basu, K. (1994). Customer loyalty: Toward an integrated conceptual framework. *Journal of the Academy of Marketing Science*, 22(2), 99–113. DOI: 10.1177/0092070394222001

Digdowiseiso, K., & Lestari, R. (2021). Determinants of Competitive Advantage and Their Impact on Consumer Satisfaction at Chicken Restaurants in South Jakarta. *Budapest International Research and Critics Institute-Journal (BIRCI-Journal), 4*(4), 12047-12053.

Dilmegani, C. (2024, March 22). *11 AI use cases in customer service: In-depth guide in 2024*. AIMultiple. https://research.aimultiple.com/customer-service-ai/

Dinakar, J. R., & Vagdevi, S. (2023). Real-time streaming analytics using big data paradigm and predictive modelling based on deep learning. *International Journal on Recent and Innovation Trends in Computing and Communication*, 11(4s), 161–165. DOI: 10.17762/ijritcc.v11i4s.6323

Ding, Y., Tu, R., Xu, Y., & Park, S. K. (2022). Repurchase intentions of new e-commerce users in the COVID-19 context: The mediation role of brand love. *Frontiers in Psychology*, 13, 823456. DOI: 10.3389/fpsyg.2022.968722 PMID: 35978786

Dinner, I. M., Heerde Van, H. J., & Neslin, S. A. (2014). Driving Online and Offline Sales: The Cross-Channel Effects of Traditional, Online Display, and Paid Search Advertising. *JMR, Journal of Marketing Research*, 51(5), 527–545. DOI: 10.1509/jmr.11.0466

Dinu, V. (2021). Artificial Intelligence in Wholesale and Retail. *Bucharest Academy of Economic Studies, 23*(56), 5-5. DOI: 10.24818/EA/2021/56/5

Djamaludin, M. D., & Fahira, A. (2023). The Influence of Brand Trust and Satisfaction towards Consumer Loyalty of a Local Cosmetic Products Brand X among Generation Z. *Journal of Consumer. The Sciences*, 7(1), 27–44.

Do, D. K. X., Rahman, K., Robinson, L. J., & Bowden, J. (2023). Negative customer engagement in emerging markets: Cognitive dimension. *Journal of Strategic Marketing*, 31(2), 370–402. DOI: 10.1080/0965254X.2021.1919180

Dolan, R., Conduit, J., & Fahy, J. (2016). Social media engagement: A construct of positively and negatively valenced engagement behaviours. In Brodie, R., Hollebeek, L., & Conduit, J. (Eds.), *Customer engagement: Contemporary issues and challenges* (pp. 96–117). Routledge.

Domingos, P. (2012). A Few Useful Things to Know About Machine Learning. *Communications of the ACM*, 55(10), 78–87. DOI: 10.1145/2347736.2347755

Domi, S., & Musabelliu, B. (2020). Customer orientation and SME performance in Albania: A case study of the mediating role of innovativeness and innovation behavior. *Journal of Vacation Marketing*, 26(1), 130–146. DOI: 10.1177/1356766719867374

Dong, Y., Yang, Y., Tang, J., Yang, Y., & Chawla, N. V. (2014, August). Inferring user demographics and social strategies in mobile social networks. In *Proceedings of the 20th ACM SIGKDD international conference on Knowledge discovery and data mining* (pp. 15-24). DOI: 10.1145/2623330.2623703

dos Santos, M. J., Perin, M. G., Simões, C., & Sampaio, C. H. (2020). Customer orientation and financial performance relationship: The mediating role of innovative capability. *Gestão & Produção*, 27(4), e4706. DOI: 10.1590/0104-530x4706-20

Dotsika, F., & Watkins, A. (2017). Identifying potentially disruptive trends by means of keyword network analysis. *Technological Forecasting and Social Change*, 119, 114–127. DOI: 10.1016/j.techfore.2017.03.020

Dowding, D., & Thompson, C. (2003). Measuring the quality of judgement and decision-making in nursing. *Journal of Advanced Nursing*, 44(1), 49–57. DOI: 10.1046/j.1365-2648.2003.02770.x PMID: 12956669

Draws, T., Szlávik, Z., Timmermans, B., Tintarev, N., Varshney, K. R., & Hind, M. (2021, April). Disparate impact diminishes consumer trust even for advantaged users. In *International Conference on Persuasive Technology* (pp. 135-149). Cham: Springer International Publishing. DOI: 10.1007/978-3-030-79460-6_11

Duan, Y., Edwards, J. S., & Dwivedi, Y. K. (2019). Artificial intelligence for decision making in the era of Big Data – evolution, challenges and research agenda. *International Journal of Information Management*, 48, 63–71. DOI: 10.1016/j.ijinfomgt.2019.01.021

Dudic, Z., Dudic, B., Gregus, M., Novackova, D., & Djakovic, I. (2020). The innovativeness and usage of the balanced scorecard model in SMEs. *Sustainability (Basel)*, 12(8), 3221. DOI: 10.3390/su12083221

Dumitriu, D., & Popescu, M. A. M. (2020). Artificial intelligence solutions for digital marketing. *Procedia Manufacturing*, 46, 630–636. DOI: 10.1016/j.promfg.2020.03.090

Durai, S., Manoharan, G., & Priya, T. S. R., J., Razak, A., & Ashtikar, S. P. (2024). Quantifying the impacts of artificial intelligence implementations in marketing. In *Smart and Sustainable Interactive Marketing* (pp. 120-144). IGI Global. DOI: 10.4018/979-8-3693-1339-8.ch008

Durmaz, Y., Güvenç, H., & Kaymaz, S. (2020). The importance and benefits of relationship marketing concept. *European Journal of Business and Management Research*, 5(4). Advance online publication. DOI: 10.24018/ejbmr.2020.5.4.483

Dwivedi, D. N., & Mahanty, G. (2023). AI-Powered Employee Experience: Strategies and Best Practices. In *Exploring the Intersection of AI and Human Resources Management* (pp. 166-181). IGI Global. DOI: 10.4018/979-8-3693-0039-8.ch009

Dwivedi, Y. K., Balakrishnan, J., Baabdullah, A. M., & Das, R. (2023a). Do chatbots establish "humanness" in the customer purchase journey? An investigation through explanatory sequential design. *Psychology and Marketing*, 40(11), 2244–2271. DOI: 10.1002/mar.21888

Dwivedi, Y. K., Hughes, L., Ismagilova, E., Aarts, G., Coombs, C., Crick, T., Duan, Y., Dwivedi, R., Edwards, J., Eirug, A., Galanos, V., Ilavarasan, P. V., Janssen, M., Jones, P., Kar, A. K., Kizgin, H., Kronemann, B., Lal, B., Lucini, B., & Williams, M. D. (2021). Artificial Intelligence (AI): Multidisciplinary perspectives on emerging challenges, opportunities, and agenda for research, practice and policy. *International Journal of Information Management*, 57, 101994. DOI: 10.1016/j.ijinfomgt.2019.08.002

Dwivedi, Y. K., Ismagilova, E., Hughes, D. L., Carlson, J., Filieri, R., Jacobson, J., Jain, V., Karjaluoto, H., Kefi, H., Krishen, A. S., Kumar, V., Rahman, M. M., Raman, R., Rauschnabel, P. A., Rowley, J., Salo, J., Tran, G. A., & Wang, Y. (2021). Setting the future of digital and social media marketing research: Perspectives and research propositions. *International Journal of Information Management*, 59, 102168. Advance online publication. DOI: 10.1016/j.ijinfomgt.2020.102168

Dwivedi, Y. K., Kshetri, N., Hughes, L., Rana, N. P., Baabdullah, A. M., Kar, A. K., Koohang, A., Ribeiro-Navarrete, S., Belei, N., Balakrishnan, J., Basu, S., Behl, A., Davies, G. H., Dutot, V., Dwivedi, R., Evans, L., Felix, R., Foster-Fletcher, R., Giannakis, M., & Yan, M. (2023b). Exploring the darkverse: A multi-perspective analysis of the negative societal impacts of the metaverse. *Information Systems Frontiers*, 25(5), 2071–2114. DOI: 10.1007/s10796-023-10400-x PMID: 37361890

Eagle, L., Osmond, A., McCarthy, B., Low, D., & Lesbirel, H. (2017). Social Marketing Strategies for Renewable Energy Transitions. *Australasian Marketing Journal*, 25(2), 141–148. DOI: 10.1016/j.ausmj.2017.04.006

Earley, S. (2018). The role of a customer data platform. *IT Professional*, 20(1), 69–76. DOI: 10.1109/MITP.2018.011301803

Eastin, M. S., Brinson, N. H., Doorey, A., & Wilcox, G. (2016, May 01). Living in a big data world: Predicting mobile commerce activity through privacy concerns. *Computers in Human Behavior*, 58, 214–220. DOI: 10.1016/j.chb.2015.12.050

Echeberria, A. L. (2022). The Impact of AI on Business, Economics and Innovation. In *Artificial Intelligence for Business: Innovation, Tools and Practices* (pp. 67-96). Springer International Publishing. DOI: 10.1007/978-3-030-88241-9_3

Ekwunife, M. (2023). *Technology Manufacturing Leaders' Innovation Strategies to Improve Users' Choice Capabilities in a Fast-Changing Markets*. Walden University.

El Saghier, N. (2021). The Effect of E-marketing Orientation on E-business Strategy: E-trust as a Mediator. *Journal of Alexandria University for Administrative Sciences*, 58(2), 193–242. DOI: 10.21608/acj.2021.167937

El Youbi, R., Messaoudi, F., & Loukili, M. (2023). Machine Learning-driven Dynamic Pricing Strategies in E-Commerce. *14th International Conference on Information and Communication Systems, ICICS 2023*. Irbid: Institute of Electrical and Electronics Engineers Inc. DOI: 10.1109/ICICS60529.2023.10330541

Emerson, J., Wachowicz, J., & Chun, S. (2001, January 29). *Social return on investment (SROI): Exploring aspects of value creation*. Harvard Business School Working Knowledge. https://hbswk.hbs.edu/archive/social-return-on-investment-sroi-exploring-aspects-of-value-creation

Enad, O. M. A., & Gerinda, S. M. A. (2022). Enhancing financial performance of the banks: The role of customer response and operations management. *Journal of Innovation and Entrepreneurship*, 11(1), 28. DOI: 10.1186/s13731-022-00211-w

Endert, A., Hossain, M. S., Ramakrishnan, N., North, C., Fiaux, P., & Andrews, C. (2014). The human is the loop: New directions for visual analytics. *Journal of Intelligent Information Systems*, 43(3), 411–435. DOI: 10.1007/s10844-014-0304-9

Erevelles, S., Fukawa, N., & Swayne, L. (2016). Big Data consumer analytics and the transformation of marketing. *Journal of Business Research*, 69(2), 897–904. DOI: 10.1016/j.jbusres.2015.07.001

Etemad-Sajadi, R., & Ghachem, L. (2015). The impact of hedonic and utilitarian value of online avatars on e-service quality. *Computers in Human Behavior*, 52, 81–86. DOI: 10.1016/j.chb.2015.05.048

European Comission. (2018). Ethics guidelines for trustworthy AI. https://digital-strategy.ec.europa.eu/en/library/ethics-guidelines-trustworthy-ai

Evans, M., & Ghafourifar, A. (2019). Build A 5-star customer experience with artificial intelligence. Forbes. https://www.forbes.com/sites/allbusiness/2019/02/17/customer-experience-artificial-intelligence

Fader, P. (2020). *Customer centricity: Focus on the right customers for strategic advantage*. University of Pennsylvania Press.

Farayola, O. A., Abdul, A. A., Irabor, B. O., & Okeleke, E. C. (2023). Innovative business models driven by ai technologies: A review. *Computer Science & IT Research Journal*, 4(2), 85–110.

FareIntelligence. (2023, Nov 09). *Dynamic Pricing in Airlines: The Science Behind Airfare Fluctuations*. https://www.linkedin.com/pulse/dynamic-pricing-airlines-science-behind-airfare-fluctuations-pydqf/

Farris, P. W., Bendle, N. T., Pfeifer, P. E., & Reibstein, D. J. (2010). *Marketing Metrics: The Definitive Guide to Measuring Marketing Performance*. Pearson Education.

Farris, P. W., Hanssens, D. M., Lenskold, J. D., & Reibstein, D. J. (2015). Marketing return on investment: Seeking clarity for concept and measurement. *Applied Marketing Analytics: The Peer-Reviewed Journal*, 1(3), 267–282. DOI: 10.69554/FFOM1594

Fatima, S., Alqahtani, H., Naim, A., & Alma'alwi, F. (2022). E-CRM through social media marketing activities for brand awareness, brand image, and brand loyalty. In *Building a brand image through electronic customer relationship management* (pp. 109–138). IGI Global. DOI: 10.4018/978-1-6684-5386-5.ch006

Feng, Y., Zhu, Q., & Lai, K. H. (2017). Corporate social responsibility for supply chain management: A literature review and bibliometric analysis. *Journal of Cleaner Production*, 158, 296–307. DOI: 10.1016/j.jclepro.2017.05.018

Fenwick, A., Molnar, G., & Frangos, P. (2023). Revisiting the role of HR in the age of AI: Bringing humans and machines closer together in the workplace. *Frontiers in Artificial Intelligence*, 6, 1272823. DOI: 10.3389/frai.2023.1272823 PMID: 38288334

Fernandes, D. (2022). How chatbot is transforming the fashion retail industry in the future of fashion. https://helloyubo.com/chatbot/how-retail-chatbots-is-transforming-the-future-of-fashion

Ferraro, C., Demsar, V., Sands, S., Restrepo, M., & Campbell, C. (2024). The paradoxes of generative AI-enabled customer service: A guide for managers. *Business Horizons*, 67(5), 549–559. Advance online publication. DOI: 10.1016/j.bushor.2024.04.013

Ferreira, A. G., Crespo, C. F., Ribeiro, F. M., & Barreiros, P. (2024). The social media theatre: New guidelines to foster parasocial interactions with followers and improve influencer marketing communication effectiveness. *Journal of Marketing Communications*, 1–25. DOI: 10.1080/13527266.2024.2318696

Ferreira, D., Goncalves, J., Kostakos, V., Barkhuus, L., & Dey, A. K. (2014). Contextual experience sampling of mobile application micro-usage. *16th ACM International Conference on Human-Computer Interaction with Mobile Devices and Services, MobileHCI 2014* (pp. 91-100). Toronto: Association for Computing Machinery. DOI: 10.1145/2628363.2628367

Fianto, A. Y. A., & Dutahatmaja, A. (2023). Artificial Intelligence and Novel Services: Exploring Opportunities in the Marketing Landscape. *Journal of Applied Management and Business*, 4(1), 49–59.

Field, A. P. (2005). Is the meta-analysis of correlation coefficients accurate when population correlations vary? *Psychological Methods*, 10(4), 444–467. DOI: 10.1037/1082-989X.10.4.444 PMID: 16392999

Figueiredo, J., Oliveira, I., Silva, S., Pocinho, M., Cardoso, A., & Pereira, M. (2023). Artificial intelligence in relational marketing practice: CRM as a loyalty strategy. In *The Use of Artificial Intelligence in Digital Marketing: Competitive Strategies and Tactics* (pp. 73-96). IGI Global. DOI: 10.4018/978-1-6684-9324-3.ch003

Figueiredo, J., Oliveira, I., Silva, S., Pocinho, M., Cardoso, A., & Pereira, M. (2024). From Personalisation to Satisfaction: New Communication Strategies in Web Marketing. In J. Remondes, P. Madeira, & C. Alves (Eds.), *Connecting With Consumers Through Effective Personalization and Programmatic Advertising* (pp. 52–74). IGI Global. DOI: 10.4018/978-1-6684-9146-1.ch003

Filieri, R., Alguezaui, S., Galati, F., & Raguseo, E. (2023). Customer experience with standard and premium Peer-To-Peer offerings: A mixed-method combining text analytics and qualitative analysis. *Journal of Business Research*, 167, 114128. DOI: 10.1016/j.jbusres.2023.114128

Filiputti, E., Quattrin, R., & Brusaferro, S. (2013). Social marketing for health promotion and prevention: a review of literature: Elisa Filiputti. *European Journal of Public Health, 23*(suppl_1), ckt124.012. .DOI: 10.1093/eurpub/ckt124.012

Firestone, R., Rowe, C. J., Modi, S. N., & Sievers, D. (2017). The effectiveness of social marketing in global health: A systematic review. *Health Policy and Planning*, 32(1), 110–124. DOI: 10.1093/heapol/czw088 PMID: 27476502

Fishman. (2023). How Artificial Intelligence is changing the fashion industry. https://immago.com/ai-fashion-industry

Fitriati, T. K., Purwana, D., Buchdadi, A. D., & Subagja, I. K. (2020). Entrepreneurial orientation and SME performance: Dynamic capabilities as mediation study on SMEs in Indonesia. *KnE Social Sciences*, 74-89. .DOI: 10.18502/kss.v4i14.7860

Flavián, C., & Casaló, L. V. (2021). Artificial intelligence in services: Current trends, benefits and challenges. *Service Industries Journal*, 41(13-14), 853–859. DOI: 10.1080/02642069.2021.1989177

Flavián, C., Pérez-Rueda, A., Belanche, D., & Casaló, L. V. (2022). Intention to use analytical artificial intelligence (AI) in services – the effect of technology readiness and awareness. *Journal of Service Management*, 33(2), 293–320. DOI: 10.1108/JOSM-10-2020-0378

Floridi, L. (2020). Artificial intelligence as a public service: Learning from Amsterdam and Helsinki. *Philosophy & Technology*, 33(4), 541–546. DOI: 10.1007/s13347-020-00434-3

Flynn, B. B., Schroeder, R. G., & Sakakibara, S. (1995). The impact of quality management practices on performance and competitive advantage. *Decision Sciences*, 26(5), 659–691. DOI: 10.1111/j.1540-5915.1995.tb01445.x

Fobbe, L. (2020). Analysing Organisational Collaboration Practices for Sustainability. *Sustainability (Basel)*, 12(6), 2466. Advance online publication. DOI: 10.3390/su12062466

Følstad, A., & Skjuve, M. (2019). Chatbots for customer service: user experience and motivation. In *Proceedings of the 1st international conference on conversational user interfaces* (pp. 1-9). DOI: 10.1145/3342775.3342784

Fornell, C., Rust, R. T., & Dekimpe, M. G. (2010). The Effect of Customer Satisfaction on Consumer Spending Growth. *JMR, Journal of Marketing Research*, 47(1), 28–35. DOI: 10.1509/jmkr.47.1.28

Fountaine, T., McCarthy, B., & Saleh, T. (2019). Building the AI-Powered Organization. *Harvard Business Review*.https://hbr.org/2019/07/building-the-ai-powered-organization

Fournier, S., & Avery, J. (2011). The uninvited brand. *Business Horizons*, 54(3), 193–207. DOI: 10.1016/j.bushor.2011.01.001

Fredricks, J. A., Blumenfeld, P. C., & Paris, A. H. (2004). School engagement: Potential of the concept, state of the evidence. *Review of Educational Research*, 74(1), 59–109. DOI: 10.3102/00346543074001059

Frey, R. M., Xu, R., Ammendola, C., Moling, O., Giglio, G., & Ilic, A. (2017, November). Mobile recommendations based on interest prediction from consumer's installed apps–insights from a large-scale field study. *Information Systems*, 71, 152–163. DOI: 10.1016/j.is.2017.08.006

Fronczek, L. P., Mende, M., Scott, M. L., Nenkov, G. Y., & Gustafsson, A. (2023). Friend or foe? Can anthropomorphizing self-tracking devices backfire on marketers and consumers? *Journal of the Academy of Marketing Science*, 51(5), 1075–1097. DOI: 10.1007/s11747-022-00915-1

Frow, P., & Payne, A. (2009). Customer relationship management: A strategic perspective. *Journal of Business Market Management*, 3(1), 7–28. DOI: 10.1007/s12087-008-0035-8

Fu, F. Q., Phillips, J. J., & Phillips, P. P. (2018). ROI Marketing: Measuring, Demonstrating, and Improving Value. *Performance Improvement*, 57(2), 6–13. DOI: 10.1002/pfi.21771

Gabriel, A., Ajriya, A. D., Fahmi, C. Z., & Handayani, P. W. (2023). The influence of AR on E-commerce: A case study on fashion and beauty products. *Cogent Business and Management*, 7(3), 2513–2523.

Gaffney, J. S., & Marley, N. A. (2018). Chemical measurements and instrumentation. In *General Chemistry for Engineers* (pp. 493–532). Elsevier., DOI: 10.1016/B978-0-12-810425-5.00015-1

Gajapathy, V. (2023). Role of Artificial Intelligence Across various media platforms: A quantitative investigation of media. In *Futuristic Trends in Management* (Vol. 2, pp. 1–10). IIP Series., DOI: 10.58532/V2BS7P1CH1

Galdolage, B. S. (2021). Customer value co-creation intention, practices and experience in self-service technologies. *Journal of Scientific Research and Reports*, 27(4), 12–26. DOI: 10.9734/jsrr/2021/v27i430375

Gandomi, A., & Haider, M. (2015). Beyond the hype: Big data concepts, methods, and analytics. *International Journal of Information Management*, 35(2), 137–144. DOI: 10.1016/j.ijinfomgt.2014.10.007

Ganjavi, N., & Fazlollahtabar, H. (2023). Integrated Sustainable Production Value Measurement Model Based on Lean and Six Sigma in Industry 4.0 Context. *IEEE Transactions on Engineering Management*, 70(6), 2320–2333. DOI: 10.1109/TEM.2021.3078169

Gankidi, N., & Gundu, S. viqar Ahmed, M., Tanzeela, T., Prasad, C. R., & Yalabaka, S. (2022, June). Customer segmentation using machine learning. In *2022 2nd International Conference on Intelligent Technologies (CONIT)* (pp. 1-5). IEEE.

Gao, G. Y., Xie, E., & Zhou, K. Z. (2015). How does technological diversity in supplier network drive buyer innovation? Relational process and contingencies. *Journal of Operations Management*, 36(1), 165–177. DOI: 10.1016/j.jom.2014.06.001

Gao, Y., & Liu, H. (2022). Artificial intelligence-enabled personalization in interactive marketing: A customer journey perspective. *Journal of Research in Interactive Marketing*, 17(5), 663–680. DOI: 10.1108/JRIM-01-2022-0023

Garner, B., & Mady, A. (2023). Social media branding in the food industry: Comparing B2B and B2C companies' use of sustainability messaging on Twitter. *Journal of Business and Industrial Marketing*, 38(11), 2485–2504. DOI: 10.1108/JBIM-09-2022-0418

Gartner. (2020). Drive growth in times of disruption.

Gelderman, C. J., Schijns, J., Lambrechts, W., & Vijgen, S. (2021). Green marketing as an environmental practice: The impact on green satisfaction and green loyalty in a business-to-business context. *Business Strategy and the Environment*, 30(4), 2061–2076. DOI: 10.1002/bse.2732

Gentsch, P. (2019). *AI in Marketing, Sales and Service: How Marketers without a Data Science Degree can use AI, Big Data and Bots*. Springer. DOI: 10.1007/978-3-319-89957-2

Ghadimi, P., Ghassemi Toosi, F., & Heavey, C. (2018). A multi-agent systems approach for sustainable supplier selection and order allocation in a partnership supply chain. *European Journal of Operational Research*, 269(1), 286–301. DOI: 10.1016/j.ejor.2017.07.014

Ghali, Z., Rather, R. A., & Khan, I. (2024). Investigating metaverse marketing-enabled consumers' social presence, attachment, engagement and (re)visit intentions. *Journal of Retailing and Consumer Services*, 77, 103671. DOI: 10.1016/j.jretconser.2023.103671

Ghee, W. Y. (2018). An application of Timmons model in the mini entrepreneurial logistics project. *Advances in Social Sciences Research Journal*, 5(10). Advance online publication. DOI: 10.14738/assrj.510.5541

Ghiassi, M., Skinner, J., & Zimbra, D. (2013). Twitter brand sentiment analysis: A hybrid system using n-gram analysis and dynamic artificial neural network. *Expert Systems with Applications*, 40(16), 6266–6282. DOI: 10.1016/j.eswa.2013.05.057

Ghlichlee, B., & Bayat, F. (2021). Frontline employees' engagement and performance of business: The mediating role of customer-oriented behaviors. *Management Research Review*, 44(2), 290–317. DOI: 10.1108/MRR-11-2019-0482

Ghosh, S., Ness, S., & Salunkhe, S. (2024). The Role of AI Enabled Chatbots in Omnichannel Customer Service. *Journal of Engineering Research and Reports*, 26(6), 327–345. DOI: 10.9734/jerr/2024/v26i61184

Gibson, K. (2022). Lyft and Uber criticized for surge pricing after Brooklyn subway shooting. Online. https://www.cbsnews.com/news/brooklyn-subway-shooting-lyft-uber-surge-pricing/

Giglio, S., Pantano, E., Bilotta, E., & Melewar, T. C. (2020). Branding luxury hotels: Evidence from the analysis of consumers' "big" visual data on TripAdvisor. *Journal of Business Research*, 119, 495–501. DOI: 10.1016/j.jbusres.2019.10.053

Giovanni Zúñiga Vásquez, F. (2023). La importancia de la inteligencia artificial en las comunicaciones en los procesos marketing. *Vivat Academia*, 156, 19–39. DOI: 10.15178/va.2023.156.e1474

Giri, C., Jain, S., Zeng, X., & Bruniaux, P. (2019). A detailed review of artificial intelligence applied in the fashion and apparel industry. *IEEE Access : Practical Innovations, Open Solutions*, 7, 95376–95396. DOI: 10.1109/ACCESS.2019.2928979

Gleißner, W., Günther, T., & Walkshäusl, C. (2022). Financial sustainability: Measurement and empirical evidence. *Journal of Business Economics*, 92(3), 467–516. DOI: 10.1007/s11573-022-01081-0

Goel, P., Garg, A., Walia, N., Kaur, R., Jain, M., & Singh, S. (2021). Contagious diseases and tourism: A systematic review based on bibliometric and content analysis methods. *Quality & Quantity*, 56(5), 3085–3110. DOI: 10.1007/s11135-021-01270-z PMID: 34697508

Gołąb-Andrzejak, E. (2023). AI-powered Digital Transformation: Tools, Benefits and Challenges for Marketers – Case Study of LPP. *Procedia Computer Science*, 219, 397–404. DOI: 10.1016/j.procs.2023.01.305

Golbeck, J. (2017). The importance of consent in user comfort with personalization. *9th International Conference on Social Informatics, SocInfo 2017. 10540 LNCS* (pp. 469-476). Oxford: Springer Verlag. DOI: 10.1007/978-3-319-67256-4_37

Gonçalves, A. R., Pinto, D. C., Rita, P., & Pires, T. (2023). Artificial Intelligence and Its Ethical Implications for Marketing. *Emerging Science Journal*, 7(2), 313–327. DOI: 10.28991/ESJ-2023-07-02-01

Gontur, S., Vem, L. J., Goyit, M. G., & Davireng, M. (2022). Entrepreneurial marketing, corporate reputation, corporate creativity and competitive advantage: A research framework and proposition. *International Journal of Business. Management and Economics*, 3(1), 52–80.

Gonu, E., Agyei, P. M., Richard, O. K., & Asare-Larbi, M. (2023). Customer orientation, service quality and customer satisfaction interplay in the banking sector: An emerging market perspective. *Cogent Business and Management*, 10(1), 2163797. Advance online publication. DOI: 10.1080/23311975.2022.2163797

Goodfellow, I., Bengio, Y., & Courville, A. (2016). Deep Learning. *MIT Press.* https://mitpress.mit.edu/9780262035613/deep-learning/

Goodfellow, I., Pouget-Abadie, J., Mirza, M., Xu, B., Warde-Farley, D., Ozair, S., Courville, A., & Bengio, Y. (2014). *Generative Adversarial Nets*https://proceedings.neurips.cc/paper_files/paper/2014/file/5ca3e9b122f61f8f06494c97b1afccf3-Paper.pdf

Goodfellow, I. J., Pouget-Abadie, J., Mirza, M., Xu, B., Warde-Farley, D., Ozair, S., Courville, A., & Bengio, Y. (2014). Generative Adversarial Networks. *Science Robotics*, 3(January), 2672–2680. https://arxiv.org/abs/1406.2661v1

Google. (2024). Help your users take action with Google Assistant. https://developers.google.com/assistant/why-build

Gordon, R., Bádéǰ, F. A., & Gurrieri, L. (2022). Towards a framework for critical social marketing: What is to be done for emancipation? *Journal of Marketing Management*, 38(17–18), 2135–2163. DOI: 10.1080/0267257X.2022.2086286

Gordon, R., Russell-Bennett, R., & Lefebvre, R. C. (2016). Social marketing: The state of play and brokering the way forward. *Journal of Marketing Management*, 32(11–12), 1059–1082. DOI: 10.1080/0267257X.2016.1199156

Gori, E., Romolini, A., Fissi, S., & Contri, M. (2020). Toward the Dissemination of Sustainability Issues through Social Media in the Higher Education Sector: Evidence from an Italian Case. *Sustainability (Basel)*, 12(11), 4658. Advance online publication. DOI: 10.3390/su12114658

Goulap, J. B. (2020). Entrepreneurial orientation and business performance: An assessment of start-up companies. *International Journal of Engineering and Management Research*, 10(2), 151–163. DOI: 10.31033/ijemr.10.2.18

Govender, O. V. (2017). *An investigation into the challenges faced by a mobile service provider in meeting customer needs* (Doctoral dissertation). DOI: 10.51415/10321/2561

Grand View Research. (2023). *Customer relationship management market size, share, & trends analysis report, by component, by solution, by deployment, by enterprise size, by end use, and segment forecasts, 2024–2030*. https://www.grandviewresearch.com/industry-analysis/customer-relationship-management-crm-market

Greenstein-Messica, A., Rokach, L., & Shabtai, A. (2017). Personal-discount sensitivity prediction for mobile coupon conversion optimization. *Journal of the Association for Information Science and Technology*, 68(08), 1940–1952. DOI: 10.1002/asi.23838

Grewal, D., Guha, A., Satornino, C. B., & Schweiger, E. B. (2021). Artificial intelligence: The light and the darkness. *Journal of Business Research*, 136, 229–236. DOI: 10.1016/j.jbusres.2021.07.043

Grewal, D., Hulland, J., Kopalle, P. K., & Karahanna, E. (2020). The Future of Technology and Marketing: A Multidisciplinary Perspective. *Journal of the Academy of Marketing Science*, 48(1), 1–8. DOI: 10.1007/s11747-019-00711-4

Grewal, D., Roggeveen, A. L., & Nordfält, J. (2017). The Future of Retailing. *Journal of Retailing*, 93(1), 1–6. DOI: 10.1016/j.jretai.2016.12.008

Griffin, A. (1997). The effect of project and process characteristics on product development cycle time. *JMR, Journal of Marketing Research*, 34(1), 24–35. DOI: 10.1177/002224379703400103

Groshek, J., Cutino, C., & Walsh, J. (2020). People hate phone menus and don't trust virtual assistants like Siri. *PhysOrg*. https://phys.org/news/2016-04-people-menus-dont-virtual-siri.html

Gubbi, J., Buyya, R., Marusic, S., & Palaniswami, M. (2013). Internet of Things (IoT): A Vision, Architectural Elements, and Future Directions. *Future Generation Computer Systems*, 29(7), 1645–1660. DOI: 10.1016/j.future.2013.01.010

Guerola-Navarro, V., Gil-Gomez, H., Oltra-Badenes, R., & Sendra-García, J. (2021). Customer relationship management and its impact on innovation: A literature review. *Journal of Business Research*, 129, 83–87. DOI: 10.1016/j.jbusres.2021.02.050

Guest, B. (2023, Jul 04). *Personalization: Role of AI in Consumer Engagement.* https://www.determ.com/blog/the-power-of-personalization-role-of-ai-in-consumer-engagement/

Gugerty, L. (2006). Newell and Simon's Logic Theorist: Historical Background and Impact on Cognitive Modeling. *Proceedings of the Human Factors and Ergonomics Society Annual Meeting*, 50(9), 880–884. DOI: 10.1177/154193120605000904

Guliyev, S. M. (2023). The Impact of Brand Perception and Brand Image on Consumer Purchasing Behavior in Azerbaijan. *Science, Education and Innovations in the context of modern problems, 6*(1), 137-144. .DOI: 10.56334/sei/6.1.5

Guo, G. (2022). Application of E-commerce Personalized Recommendation Algorithm Based on Collaborative Filtering. In *Lecture Notes on Data Engineering and Communications Technologies* (pp. 959–966). Springer Science and Business Media Deutschland GmbH., DOI: 10.1007/978-3-030-97874-7_140

Gupta, Y., & Khan, F. M. (2024). Role of artificial intelligence in customer engagement: A systematic review and future research directions. *Journal of Modelling in Management* (ahead-of-print). .DOI: 10.1108/JM2-01-2023-0016

Gupta, A., & Agarwal, N. (2016, August). Streaming Analytics. In *Proceedings of the 22nd ACM SIGKDD International Conference on Knowledge Discovery and Data Mining* (pp. 2123-2123). DOI: 10.1145/2939672.2945395

Gupta, R., Nair, K., Mishra, M., Ibrahim, B., & Bhardwaj, S. (2024). Adoption and impacts of generative artificial intelligence: Theoretical underpinnings and research agenda. *International Journal of Information Management Data Insights*, 4(1), 100232. DOI: 10.1016/j.jjimei.2024.100232

Gupta, S., & Joshi, S. (2022, November). Predictive analytic techniques for enhancing marketing performance and personalized customer experience. In *2022 International Interdisciplinary Humanitarian Conference for Sustainability (IIHC)* (pp. 16-22). IEEE. DOI: 10.1109/IIHC55949.2022.10060286

Gupta, S., Lehmann, D. R., & Stuart, J. A. (2004). Valuing customers. *JMR, Journal of Marketing Research*, 41(1), 7–18. DOI: 10.1509/jmkr.41.1.7.25084

Hacker, P. (2021). A legal framework for AI training data - from first principles to the Artificial Intelligence Act. *Law, Innovation and Technology*, 13(2), 257–301. DOI: 10.1080/17579961.2021.1977219

Hackley, C. (2023). Crap detecting. Autoethnographic reflections on critical practice in marketing pedagogy. *Journal of Marketing Management*, 39(1–2), 20–31. DOI: 10.1080/0267257X.2022.2132754

Haigh, T. (2023). There Was No 'First AI Winter'. *Communications of the ACM*, 66(12), 35–39. DOI: 10.1145/3625833

Haigh, T. (2024). How the AI Boom Went Bust. *Communications of the ACM*, 67(2), 22–26. DOI: 10.1145/3634901

Hair, J. F., Hult, G. T. M., Ringle, C. M., & Sarstedt, M. (2022). *A Primer on Partial Least Squares Structural Equation Modeling (PLS-SEM)* (3rd rd.). Thousand Oaks: Sage.

Hair, J. F.Jr. (2007). Knowledge creation in marketing: The role of predictive analytics. *European Business Review*, 19(4), 303–315. DOI: 10.1108/09555340710760134

Hair, J. F.Jr, Harrison, D. E., & Risher, J. J. (2018). Marketing research in the 21st century: Opportunities and challenges. *Revista Brasileira de Marketing*, 17(5), 666–699. DOI: 10.5585/bjm.v17i5.4173

Halachmi, A., Hardy, W. P., & Rhoades, B. L. (1993). Demographic data and strategic analysis. *Public Administration Quarterly*, •••, 159–174.

Haldorai, A., Murugan, S., & Ramu, A. (2021). Evolution, challenges, and application of intelligent ICT education: An overview. *Computer Applications in Engineering Education*, 29(3), 562–571. DOI: 10.1002/cae.22217

Haleem, A., Javaid, M., & Singh, R. P. (2022). An era of ChatGPT as a significant futuristic support tool: A study on features, abilities, and challenges. *BenchCouncil Transactions on Benchmarks. Standards and Evaluations*, 2(4), 100089. DOI: 10.1016/j.tbench.2023.100089

Halim, H. A., Ahmad, N. H., & Ramayah, T. (2019). Sustaining the innovation culture in SMEs: The importance of organisational culture, organisational learning and market orientation. *Asian Journal of Business Research*, 9(2), 14–33. DOI: 10.14707/ajbr.190059

Hanafi, H. M., & Yahia, M. A. (2022). Customer Orientation of Service Employees in the Banking Sector in Sudan. *International Journal of Scientific Research*, 11(8), 312–317. DOI: 10.21275/SR22804022752

Hanaysha, J. R., Al Shaikh, M. E., & Alzoubi, H. M. (2021). Importance of marketing mix elements in determining consumer purchase decision in the retail market. [IJSSMET]. *International Journal of Service Science, Management, Engineering, and Technology*, 12(6), 56–72. DOI: 10.4018/IJSSMET.2021110104

Hanaysha, J., & Mehmood, K. K. (2022). An Exploration of the Effect of Customer Relationship Management on Organizational Performance in the Banking Sector. *International Journal of Customer Relationship Marketing and Management*, 13(1), 1–16. Advance online publication. DOI: 10.4018/IJCRMM.2022010101

Han, B., Deng, X., & Fan, H. (2023). Partners or opponents? How mindset shapes consumers' attitude toward anthropomorphic artificial intelligence service robots. *Journal of Service Research*, 26(3), 441–458. DOI: 10.1177/10946705231169674

Han, H., Li, Z., & Li, Z. (2023). Using Machine Learning Methods to Predict Consumer Confidence from Search Engine Data. *Sustainability (Basel)*, 15(4), 3100. DOI: 10.3390/su15043100

Harguess, J., & Ward, C. M. (2022). Is the Next Winter Coming for AI? Elements of Making Secure and Robust AI. In *Proceedings - Applied Imagery Pattern Recognition Workshop*, 2022-October. DOI: 10.1109/AIPR57179.2022.10092230

Hariandi, M. S. I., Gumanti, T. A., & Wahyudi, E. (2019). E-commerce, competitive advantage and performance of business of banyuwangi small and medium-sized enterprises. *International Journal of Scientific and Technology Research*, 8(8), 1216–1220.

Harms, J.-G., Kucherbaev, P., Bozzon, A., & Houben, G.-J. (2019, March-April). Approaches for dialog management in conversational agents. *IEEE Internet Computing*, 23(02), 13–22. DOI: 10.1109/MIC.2018.2881519

Haron, R., & Subar, N. A. (2020). Service quality of Islamic banks, loyalty and the mediating role of trust. *Islamic Economic Studies*, 28(1), 3–23. DOI: 10.1108/IES-12-2019-0041

Harreis, H., Koullias, T., Roberts, R., & Te, K. (2023). Generative AI: Unlocking the future of fashion. McKinsey & Company. https://www.mckinsey.com/industries/retail/our-insights/generative-ai-unlocking-the-future-of-fashion

Hasan, R., Weaven, S., & Thaichon, P. (2021). Blurring the line between physical and digital environment: The impact of artificial intelligence on customers' relationship and customer experience. In Thaichon, P., & Ratten, V. (Eds.), *Developing Digital Marketing* (pp. 135–153). Emerald Publishing Limited., DOI: 10.1108/978-1-80071-348-220211008

Hashem, T., Hashem, T. N., & Alqirem, A. A. (2019). the Impact of Quality Culture on Competitive Advantage in Financial Services Companies. *IJRRAS, 38*(1). www.arpapress.com/Volumes/Vol38Issue1/IJRRAS_38_1_08.pdf

Hassabis, D., Kumaran, D., Summerfield, C., & Botvinick, M. (2017). Neuroscience-Inspired Artificial Intelligence. *Neuron*, 95(2), 245–258. DOI: 10.1016/j.neuron.2017.06.011 PMID: 28728020

Hassen, Y., & Singh, A. (2020). The effect of market orientation on the performance of small and medium enterprises in case of Amhara Region, Ethiopia. *Journal of New Business Ventures*, 1(1-2), 92–109. DOI: 10.1177/2632962X20961051

Haugeland, J. (1985). *Artificial intelligence: The very idea*. MIT Press.

He, A., & Zhang, Y. (2022). AI-powered touch points in the customer journey: A systematic literature review and research agenda. *Journal of Research in Interactive Marketing*, 17(4), 620–639. DOI: 10.1108/JRIM-03-2022-0082

Heath, R. (2009). Emotional engagement: How television builds big brands at low attention. *Journal of Advertising Research*, 49(1), 62–73. DOI: 10.2501/S0021849909090060

Hegner, S. M., Fetscherin, M., & van Delzen, M. (2017). Determinants and outcomes of brand hate. *Journal of Product and Brand Management*, 26(1), 13–25. DOI: 10.1108/JPBM-01-2016-1070

He, K., Zhang, X., Ren, S., & Sun, J. (2015). Delving deep into rectifiers: Surpassing human-level performance on imagenet classification. In *Proceedings of the IEEE international conference on computer vision* (pp. 1026-1034). DOI: 10.1109/ICCV.2015.123

Helfat, C. E., Finkelstein, S., Mitchell, W., Peteraf, M. A., Singh, H., Teece, D. J., & Winter, S. G. (2007). *Dynamic Capabilities: Understanding Strategic Change in Organizations*. Blackwell Publishing., DOI: 10.1287/orsc.1120.0810

Helme-Guizon, A., & Magnoni, F. (2019). Consumer brand engagement and its social side on brand-hosted social media: How do they contribute to brand loyalty? *Journal of Marketing Management*, 35(7-8), 716–741. DOI: 10.1080/0267257X.2019.1599990

Hendi, Y. Z. B., & Arafah, W. (2022). Analysis of Improving Competitive Advantage for Startup Business in Indonesia. *International Journal of Economics. Business and Management Research*, 6(2), 223–231. DOI: 10.51505/IJEBMR.2022.6216

Hengstler, M., Enkel, E., & Duelli, S. (2016). Applied AI and trust—The case of autonomous vehicles and medical assistance devices. *Technological Forecasting and Social Change*, •••, 105–120. DOI: 10.1016/j.techfore.2015.12.014

Hermann, E. (2022). Leveraging artificial intelligence in marketing for social good—An ethical perspective. *Journal of Business Ethics*, 179(1), 43–61. DOI: 10.1007/s10551-021-04843-y PMID: 34054170

Hern, A. (2017, October 24). Facebook translates 'good morning' into 'attack them', leading to arrest. *The Guardian*. https://www.theguardian.com/technology/2017/oct/24/facebook-palestine-israel-translates-good-morning-attack-them-arrest

Hernández, A. B., & Hidalgo, D. B. (2020). Detection of fraud patterns in accounting accounts using data mining techniques. *Open Journal of Business and Management*, 08(04), 1609–1618. DOI: 10.4236/ojbm.2020.84102

Hernández-Linares, R., López-Fernández, M. C., García-Piqueres, G., Pina e Cunha, M., & Rego, A. (2023). How knowledge-based dynamic capabilities relate to firm performance: The mediating role of entrepreneurial orientation. *Review of Managerial Science*, •••, 1–33. DOI: 10.1007/s11846-023-00691-4

Hernández-Ortega, B., Aldas-Manzano, J., & Ferreira, I. (2022). Relational cohesion between users and smart voice assistants. *Journal of Services Marketing*, 36(5), 725–740. DOI: 10.1108/JSM-07-2020-0286

He, S. (2023). Do you reap what you sow? Driving mechanism of supply chain transparency on consumers' indirect reciprocity. *Frontiers in Psychology*, 14, 1081297. DOI: 10.3389/fpsyg.2023.1081297 PMID: 36844304

He, W., Shen, J., Tian, X., Li, Y., Akula, V., Yan, G., & Tao, R. (2015). Gaining competitive intelligence from social media data: Evidence from two largest retail chains in the world. *Industrial Management & Data Systems*, 115(9), 1622–1636. DOI: 10.1108/IMDS-03-2015-0098

Hicham, N., Nassera, H., & Karim, S. (2023). Strategic framework for leveraging artificial intelligence in future marketing decision-making. *Journal of Intelligent and Management Decision*, 2(3), 139–150. DOI: 10.56578/jimd020304

Hidayat, K., & Idrus, M. I. (2023). The effect of relationship marketing towards switching barrier, customer satisfaction, and customer trust on bank customers. *Journal of Innovation and Entrepreneurship*, 12(1), 29. DOI: 10.1186/s13731-023-00270-7 PMID: 37193581

Hildebrand, C. (2019). The machine age of marketing: How artificial intelligence changes the way people think, act, and decide. *NIM Marketing Intelligence Review*, 11(2), 10–17. DOI: 10.2478/nimmir-2019-0010

Hinton, G. E., Osindero, S., & Teh, Y. W. (2006). A fast learning algorithm for deep belief nets. *Neural Computation*, 18(7), 1527–1554. DOI: 10.1162/neco.2006.18.7.1527 PMID: 16764513

Hiong, L. S., Ferdinand, A. T., & Listiana, E. (2020). Techno-resonance innovation capability for enhancing marketing performance: A perspective of RA-theory. *Business: Theory and Practice*, 21(1), 329–339. https://hdl.handle.net/10419/248033. DOI: 10.3846/btp.2020.12117

Hoffman, D. L., & Fodor, M. (2010). Can you measure the ROI of your social media marketing? *MIT Sloan Management Review*. https://sloanreview.mit.edu/article/can-you-measure-the-roi-of-your-social-media-marketing/

Hohler, A. (2010, March 1). *Measuring the bang of every donated buck*. The Wall Street Journal. https://www.wsj.com/articles/SB10001424052748703787304575075340954767332

Hollebeek, L. (2011). Exploring customer brand engagement: Definition and themes. *Journal of Strategic Marketing*, 19(7), 555–573. DOI: 10.1080/0965254X.2011.599493

Hollebeek, L. D. (2011). Demystifying customer brand engagement: Exploring the loyalty nexus. *Journal of Marketing Management*, 27(7-8), 785–807. DOI: 10.1080/0267257X.2010.500132

Hollebeek, L. D., & Chen, T. (2014). Exploring positively-versus negatively-valenced brand engagement: A conceptual model. *Journal of Product and Brand Management*, 23(1), 62–74. DOI: 10.1108/JPBM-06-2013-0332

Hollebeek, L. D., Glynn, M. S., & Brodie, R. J. (2014). Consumer brand engagement in social media: Conceptualization, scale development and validation. *Journal of Interactive Marketing*, 28(2), 149–165. DOI: 10.1016/j.intmar.2013.12.002

Hollebeek, L. D., & Macky, K. (2019). Digital content marketing's role in fostering consumer engagement, trust, and value: Framework, fundamental propositions, and implications. *Journal of Interactive Marketing*, 45(1), 27–41. DOI: 10.1016/j.intmar.2018.07.003

Hollebeek, L. D., Sprott, D. E., & Brady, M. K. (2021). Rise of the machines? Customer engagement in automated service interactions. *Journal of Service Research*, 24(1), 3–8. DOI: 10.1177/1094670520975110

Holsapple, C. W., Hsiao, S. H., & Pakath, R. (2018). Business social media analytics: Characterization and conceptual framework. *Decision Support Systems*, 110, 32–45. DOI: 10.1016/j.dss.2018.03.004

Hopp, W. J., & Van Oyen, M. P. (2004). Agile workforce evaluation: A framework for cross-training and coordination. [Institute of Industrial Engineers]. *IIE Transactions*, 36(10), 919–940. DOI: 10.1080/07408170490487759

Hossain, M. S., Rahman, M. M., Abresham, A. E., Pranto, A. J., & Rahman, M. R. (2023). AI and machine learning applications to enhance customer support. In *Handbook of Research on AI and Machine Learning Applications in Customer Support and Analytics* (pp. 300–324). IGI Global., DOI: 10.4018/978-1-6684-7105-0.ch015

Hou, M., & Tang, Y. (2023, August). The Influence of Visual Features in Product Images on Sales Volume: A Machine Learning Approach to Extract Color and Deep Learning Super Sampling Features. *TS. Traitement du Signal*, 40(04), 1469–1477. DOI: 10.18280/ts.400415

Howard, J. A., & Sheth, J. (1969). The Theory of Buyer Behavior. In *Research Policy*. John Wiley & Sons., http://www.people.umass.edu/aizen/pdf/tpb.intervention.pdf

Howard, J., & John Howard, C. (2019). Artificial intelligence: Implications for the future of work. *American Journal of Industrial Medicine*, 62(11), 917–926. DOI: 10.1002/ajim.23037 PMID: 31436850

Howarth, J. (2024, July 25). 57 new artificial intelligence statistics (Aug 2024). Exploding Topics. https://explodingtopics.com/blog/ai-statistics#ai-in-marketing

Hsieh, S. H., & Lee, C. T. (2021). Hey Alexa: Examining the effect of perceived socialness in usage intentions of AI assistant-enabled smart speaker. *Journal of Research in Interactive Marketing*, 15(2), 267–294. DOI: 10.1108/JRIM-11-2019-0179

Huang, C., Zhang, Z., Mao, B., & Yao, X. (2023). An Overview of Artificial Intelligence Ethics. *IEEE Transactions on Artificial Intelligence*, 4(4), 799–819. DOI: 10.1109/TAI.2022.3194503

Huang, M. H., & Rust, R. T. (2018). Artificial intelligence in service. *Journal of Service Research*, 21(2), 155–172. DOI: 10.1177/1094670517752459

Huang, M. H., & Rust, R. T. (2021). A strategic framework for artificial intelligence in marketing. *Journal of the Academy of Marketing Science*, 49(1), 30–50. DOI: 10.1007/s11747-020-00749-9

Huang, S. (2024). Exploring the Influence of Natural Language Processing Technology on Marketing Strategy Innovation Management in Emerging Markets for Multinational Corporations. *Journal of Logistics. Informatics and Service Science*, 11(3), 399–411. DOI: 10.33168/JLISS.2024.0326

Huang, W., Liu, B., & Tang, H. (2019). Privacy Protection for Recommendation System: A Survey. *Journal of Physics: Conference Series*, 1325(1), 012087. DOI: 10.1088/1742-6596/1325/1/012087

Huggard, E., & Särmäkari, N. (2023). How digital-only fashion brands are creating more participatory models of fashion co-design. *Fashion, Style & Popular Culture*, 10(4), 583–600. DOI: 10.1386/fspc_00176_1

Hu, L. T., & Bentler, P. M. (1999). Cutoff criteria for fit indexes in covariance structure analysis: Conventional criteria versus new alternatives. *Structural Equation Modeling*, 6(1), 1–55. DOI: 10.1080/10705519909540118

Hu, P., & Wei, Q. (2020, April 1). Research on Personal Data Protection of EU General Data Protection Regulation. *IOP Conference Series. Materials Science and Engineering*, 806(1), 012003–012003. DOI: 10.1088/1757-899X/806/1/012003

Hutagalung, L., Sinaga, P., Tan, J., & Tukiran, M. (2020). The Role of e-marketing and Customer Oriented on Business Performance Through Customer Loyalty and Hotels Competitive Advantage. *Kontigensi: Jurnal Ilmiah Manajemen*, 8(2), 202–217. DOI: 10.56457/jimk.v8i2.163

Hutchinson, C. L., Berndt, A., Forsythe, D., Gilbert-Hunt, S., George, S., & Ratcliffe, J. (2019). Valuing the impact of health and social care programs using social return on investment analysis: How have academics advanced the methodology? A systematic review. *BMJ Open*, 9(8), e029789. Advance online publication. DOI: 10.1136/bmjopen-2019-029789 PMID: 31446413

Hutter, F., Kotthoff, L., & Vanschoren, J. (2019). *Automated Machine Learning: Methods, Systems, Challenges*. Springer. DOI: 10.1007/978-3-030-05318-5

Ianenko, M., Stepanov, M., & Mironova, L. (2020). Brand identity development. *E3S Web of Conferences, 164*, 09015. .DOI: 10.1051/e3sconf/202016409015

Iatsyshyn, A. V., Kovach, V. O., Romanenko, Y. O., Deinega, I. I., Iatsyshyn, A. V., Popov, O. O., & Lytvynova, S. H. (2019). Application of AR technologies for preparation of specialists of new technological era. *2nd International Workshop on AR in Education*, (pp. 181-200). Kryvyi Rih, Ukraine.

Ibegbulam, C. M., Olowonubi, J. A., Fatounde, S. A., & Oyegunwa, O. A.Ibegbulam C.MOlowonubi, J.AFatounde, S.AOyegunwa, O.A. (2023). Artificial intelligence in the era of 4IR: Drivers, challenges and opportunities. *Engineering Science & Technology Journal*, 4(6), 473–488. DOI: 10.51594/estj.v4i6.668

Idnay, B., Cordoba, E., Ramirez, S. O., Xiao, E., Wood, O. R., Batey, D. S., Garofalo, R., & Schnall, R. (2024). Social Marketing Perspective on Participant Recruitment in Informatics-Based Intervention Studies. *AIDS and Behavior*, 28(9), 1–14. DOI: 10.1007/s10461-024-04355-6 PMID: 38703337

Ighomereho, S. (2022). Market and Entrepreneurial Orientations as Predictors of Small and Medium Enterprises' Performance in the Covid-19 Era. *Innovative Marketing*, 18(2), 161–173. DOI: 10.21511/im.18(2).2022.14

Iglesias, O., Landgraf, P., Ind, N., Markovic, S., & Koporcic, N. (2020). Corporate brand identity co-creation in business-to-business contexts. *Industrial Marketing Management*, 85, 32–43. DOI: 10.1016/j.indmarman.2019.09.008

Illescas-Manzano, M. D., López, N. V., González, N. A., & Rodríguez, C. C. (2021). Implementation of chatbot in online commerce, and open innovation. *Journal of Open Innovation*, 7(2), 125. Advance online publication. DOI: 10.3390/joitmc7020125

Inavolu, S. M. (2024). *Exploring AI-Driven Customer Service: Evolution, Architectures, Opportunities, Challenges and Future Directions*. DOI: 10.13140/RG.2.2.19937.31841

Ind, N., & Coates, N. (2013). The meanings of co-creation. *European Business Review*, 25(1), 86–95. DOI: 10.1108/09555341311287754

Indurkhya, B. (2019). Is morality the last frontier for machines? *New Ideas in Psychology*, 54, 107–111. DOI: 10.1016/j.newideapsych.2018.12.001

Ingole, A., Khude, P., Kittad, S., Parmar, V., & Ghotkar, A. (2024, 22-23 Feb. 2024). Competitive Sentiment Analysis for Brand Reputation Monitoring. In *2024 Second International Conference on Emerging Trends in Information Technology and Engineering (ICETITE)*. DOI: 10.1109/ic-ETITE58242.2024.10493574

Islam, A. M., & Qamari, I. N. (2021). Effect of Supply Chain Management on Competitive Advantage and Organizational Performance. Studies on the Batik Industry in Yogyakarta City. In *4th International Conference on Sustainable Innovation 2020-Accounting and Management (ICoSIAMS 2020)* (pp. 334–339). DOI: 10.2991/aer.k.210121.047

Islam, M. Z., & Zhe, Z. (2022). The effect of customer orientation on financial performance in service firms: The mediating role of service innovation. *Management Science Letters*, 12(2), 101–116. DOI: 10.5267/j.msl.2021.10.003

Ismail, I. J. (2023). Speaking to the hearts of the customers! The mediating effect of customer loyalty on customer orientation, technology orientation and business performance. *Technological Sustainability*, 2(1), 44–66. DOI: 10.1108/TECHS-03-2022-0016

Issalillah, F., Darmawan, D., & Khairi, M. (2022). The Role of Brand Image and Brand Communications on Brand Trust. *Journal of Science* [SICO]. *Technology in Society*, 3(1), 1–6.

Isyanto, H., Arifin, A. S., & Suryanegara, M. (2020). Performance of Smart Personal Assistant Applications Based on Speech Recognition Technology using IoT-based Voice Commands. *11th International Conference on Information and Communication Technology Convergence, ICTC 2020. Volume 2020-October* (pp. 640-645). Jeju Island: IEEE Computer Society. DOI: 10.1109/ICTC49870.2020.9289160

Itani, O. S., Kassar, A. N., & Loureiro, S. M. C. (2019). Value get, value give: The relationships among perceived value, relationship quality, customer engagement, and value consciousness. *International Journal of Hospitality Management*, 80, 78–90. DOI: 10.1016/j.ijhm.2019.01.014

Itechnolab. (2021). *How Sephora is using technology like AI and AR to engage with consumers?*https://itechnolabs.ca/sephora-using-technology-like-ai-and-ar/

Iyer, P., Davari, A., Zolfagharian, M., & Paswan, A. (2019). Market orientation, positioning strategy and brand performance. *Industrial Marketing Management*, 81, 16–29. DOI: 10.1016/j.indmarman.2018.11.004

Jacobs, B. J. D., Donkers, B., & Fok, D. (2016). Model-Based Purchase Predictions for Large Assortments. *Marketing Science*, 35(3), 389–404. DOI: 10.1287/mksc.2016.0985

Jacoby, J., & Kyner, D. B. (1973). Brand loyalty vs. repeat purchasing behavior. *JMR, Journal of Marketing Research*, 10(1), 1–9. DOI: 10.1177/002224377301000101

Jacovi, A., Marasović, A., Miller, T., & Goldberg, Y. (2021). Formalizing trust in artificial intelligence: Prerequisites, causes and goals of human trust in AI. In *Proceedings of the 2021 ACM conference on fairness, accountability, and transparency* (pp. 624-635). Association for Computing Machinery. DOI: 10.1145/3442188.3445923

Jain, P., & Aggarwal, K. (2020). Transforming Marketing with Artificial Intelligence. *International Research Journal of Engineering and Technology, 07*(07), 3964–3976. DOI: 10.13140/RG.2.2.25848.67844

Jain, R., Luck, E., Mathews, S., & Schuster, L. (2023). Creating Persuasive Environmental Communicators: Spokescharacters as Endorsers in Promoting Sustainable Behaviors. *Sustainability (Basel)*, 15(1), 335. Advance online publication. DOI: 10.3390/su15010335

Jain, S., Bruniaux, J., Zeng, X., & Bruniaux, P. (2017). Big data in fashion industry. *IOP Conference Series. Materials Science and Engineering*, 254, 152005. DOI: 10.1088/1757-899X/254/15/152005

James, L. (2018, Jan 24). *Pinterest's Visual Lens: How computer vision explores your taste-The science behind personalized visual recommendations*. https://towardsdatascience.com/pinterests-visual-lens-how-computer-vision-explores-your-taste-5470f87502ad

Jang, Y., Liu, A. Y., & Ke, W. Y. (2023). Exploring smart retailing: Anthropomorphism in voice shopping of smart speaker. *Information Technology & People*, 36(7), 2894–2913. DOI: 10.1108/ITP-07-2021-0536

Jankovic, S. D., & Curovic, D. M. (2023). Strategic integration of artificial intelligence for sustainable businesses: Implications for data management and human user engagement in the digital era. *Sustainability (Basel)*, 15(21), 15208. DOI: 10.3390/su152115208

Jarrahi, M. (2018). AI and the Future of Work: Human-AI Symbiosis in Organizational Decision Making. *Business Horizons*, 61(4), 577–586. DOI: 10.1016/j.bushor.2018.03.007

Javaid, M., Haleem, A., Singh, R. P., & Suman, R. (2022). Artificial intelligence applications for industry 4.0: A literature-based study. *Journal of Industrial Integration and Management*, 07(01), 83–111. DOI: 10.1142/S2424862221300040

Javalgi, R. R. G., Martin, C. L., & Young, R. B. (2018). Marketing research, market orientation and customer relationship management: A framework and implications for service providers. *Journal of Services Marketing*, 20(1), 12–23. DOI: 10.1108/08876040610646545

Jayachandran, S., Sharma, S., Kaufman, P., & Raman, P. (2005). The role of relational information processes and technology use in customer relationship management. *Journal of Marketing*, 69(4), 177–192. DOI: 10.1509/jmkg.2005.69.4.177

Jayawardena, N. S., Behl, A., Thaichon, P., & Quach, S. (2022). Artificial intelligence (AI)-based market intelligence and customer insights. In *Artificial intelligence for marketing management* (pp. 120–141). Routledge. DOI: 10.4324/9781003280392-10

Jeong, G. Y. (2017). The effect of entrepreneurial orientation on marketing capability. *Korean Corp. Manag. Rev.*, 24(4), 75–106. Advance online publication. DOI: 10.21052/KCMR.2017.24.4.04

Jerbi, D. (2023). Exploring the Latest Frontiers of Artificial Intelligence: A Review of Trends and Developments. *TechRxiv*. DOI: 10.36227/techrxiv.22717327

Jercinovic, S., & Ham, M. (2022, October). The Significance of Social Benefit Orientation in Market Orientation for the Realization of The Strategic Marketing Concept of Sustainability. In *Economic and Social Development (Book of Proceedings), 88th International Scientific Conference on Economic and Social Development* (p. 320). DOI: 10.22616/ESRD.2018.105

Jiang, T., & Tuzhilin, A. (2008). Improving personalization solutions through optimal segmentation of customer bases. *IEEE Transactions on Knowledge and Data Engineering*, 21(3), 305–320. DOI: 10.1109/TKDE.2008.163

Joensuu-Salo, S., Sorama, K., Viljamaa, A., & Varamäki, E. (2018). Firm performance among internationalized SMEs: The interplay of market orientation, marketing capability and digitalization. *Administrative Sciences*, 8(3), 31. DOI: 10.3390/admsci8030031

Johnson, D., & Grayson, K. (2005). Cognitive and affective trust in service relationships. *Journal of Business Research*, 58(4), 500–507. DOI: 10.1016/S0148-2963(03)00140-1

Jones, L. D., Golan, D., Hanna, S. A., & Ramachandran, M. (2018). Artificial intelligence, machine learning and the evolution of healthcare: A bright future or cause for concern? *Bone & Joint Research*, 7(3), 223–225. DOI: 10.1302/2046-3758.73.BJR-2017-0147.R1 PMID: 29922439

Juniper. (2021, Aug). *Voice Assistant Transaction Values to Grow by Over 320% by 2023*. https://www.juniperresearch.com: https://www.juniperresearch.com/press/voice-assistant-transaction-values-grow-by-320

Jurafsky, D., & Martin, J. H. (2021). *Speech and Language Processing*. Prentice Hall.

Kaartemo, V., & Helkkula, A. (2018). A Systematic Review of Artificial Intelligence and Robots in Value Co-creation: Current status and Future research avenues. *Journal of Creating Value*, 4(2), 211–228. DOI: 10.1177/2394964318805625

Kachouie, R., Mavondo, F., & Sands, S. (2018). Dynamic marketing capabilities view on creating market change. *European Journal of Marketing*, 52(5/6), 1007–1036. DOI: 10.1108/EJM-10-2016-0588

Kamila, M. K., & Jasrotia, S. S. (2023a). Ethics and marketing responsibility: A bibliometric analysis and literature review. *Asia Pacific Management Review*, 28(4), 567–583. DOI: 10.1016/j.apmrv.2023.04.002

Kamila, M. K., & Jasrotia, S. S. (2023b). Ethics in product marketing: A bibliometric analysis. *Asian Journal of Business Ethics*, 12(2), 151–174. DOI: 10.1007/s13520-023-00168-3

Kaminski, J. (2009, October). Editorial: Join the Co-Creation Wave! [OJNI]. *On-Line Journal of Nursing Informatics*, 13(3). http://ojni.org/13_3/june.pdf

Kang, W., Shao, B., Du, S., Chen, H., & Zhang, Y. (2024). How to improve voice assistant evaluations: Understanding the role of attachment with a socio-technical systems perspective. *Technological Forecasting and Social Change*, 200, 123171. DOI: 10.1016/j.techfore.2023.123171

Kapferer, J. N. (2012). *The New Strategic Brand Management: Advanced Insights and Strategic Thinking*. Kogan Page.

Kaplan, A., & Haenlein, M. (2019). Siri, Siri, in my hand: Who's the fairest in the land? On the interpretations, illustrations, and implications of artificial intelligence. *Business Horizons*, 62(1), 15–25. DOI: 10.1016/j.bushor.2018.08.004

Kaplan, L., Gerzon, N., Mislove, A., & Sapiezynski, P. (2022, October). Measurement and analysis of implied identity in ad delivery optimization. In *Proceedings of the 22nd ACM Internet Measurement Conference* (pp. 195-209). DOI: 10.1145/3517745.3561450

Karaulova, T., Kostina, M., & Shevtshenko, E. (2012). Reliability assessment of manufacturing processes. *International Journal of Industrial Engineering and Management*, 3(3), 143–151. DOI: 10.24867/IJIEM-2012-3-118

Kasula, B. Y. (2024). Ethical implications and future prospects of artificial intelligence in healthcare: A research synthesis. *International Meridian Journal*, 6(6), 1–7.

Kaul, V., Enslin, S., & Gross, S. A. (2020). History of artificial intelligence in medicine. *Gastrointestinal Endoscopy*, 92(4), 807–812. DOI: 10.1016/j.gie.2020.06.040 PMID: 32565184

Kaur, A., Kumar, V., Sindhwani, R., Singh, P. L., & Behl, A. (2024). Public debt sustainability: A bibliometric co-citation visualization analysis. *International Journal of Emerging Markets*, 19(4), 1090–1110. DOI: 10.1108/IJOEM-04-2022-0724

Kawai, M., & Nogami, S. (2016, June). A hybrid recommender system of collaborative and content based filtering. *Information (Japan)*, 19(6B), 2177–2183.

Kazemian, S., Djajadikerta, H. G., Said, J., Roni, S. M., Trireksani, T., & Alam, M. M. (2021). Corporate governance, market orientation and performance of Iran's upscale hotels. *Tourism and Hospitality Research*, 21(3), 344–357. DOI: 10.1177/14673584211003644

Keegan, B. J., Canhoto, A. I., & Yen, D. A. (2022). Power negotiation on the tango dancefloor: The adoption of AI in B2B marketing. *Industrial Marketing Management*, 100, 36–48. DOI: 10.1016/j.indmarman.2021.11.001

Keerthika, M., Abilash, K., Vasanth, M. S., Kuralamudhu, M., & Abbirooban, S. (2024). Emotional AI: Computationally intelligent devices for education. In *Emotional AI and Human-AI Interactions in Social Networking* (pp. 87-99). Academic Press.

Keller, K. L. (1993). Conceptualizing, Measuring, and Managing Customer-Based Brand Equity. *Journal of Marketing*, 57(1), 1–22. DOI: 10.1177/002224299305700101

Keller, K. L., & Lehmann, D. R. (2006). Brands and Branding: Research Findings and Future Priorities. *Marketing Science*, 25(6), 740–759. DOI: 10.1287/mksc.1050.0153

Kellermanns, F. W., Hernández-Linares, R., & López-Fernández, M. C. (2018). A note on the relationships between learning, market, and entrepreneurial orientations in family and nonfamily firms. *Journal of Family Business Strategy*, 9(3), 192–204. DOI: 10.1016/j.jfbs.2018.08.001

Kelly, R. c. (2023). *How Do Brand Image and Marketing Affect Market Share?* Investopedia. https://www.investopedia.com/ask/answers/032615/how-does-brand-image-and-marketing-affect-market-share.asp

Kelvin, E. A., & Joyce, E. (2019). Effect of Market Orientation on Organizational Performance (A Study of the Nigerian Banking Industry). *International Journal of Business and Social Science*, 10(12), 93–102. DOI: 10.30845/ijbss.v10n12a9

Kenwright, B. (2023). Exploring the power of creative ai tools and game-based methodologies for interactive web-based programming. *arXiv preprint arXiv:2308.11649.*

Keusch, F., Struminskaya, B., Antoun, C., Couper, M. P., & Kreuter, F. (2019). Willingness to Participate in Passive Mobile Data Collection. *Public Opinion Quarterly*, 83(S1), 210–235. DOI: 10.1093/poq/nfz007 PMID: 31337924

Khan, M. S. U., Hasan, M. F., Islam, M. S., & Hassan, S. T. (2021). Artificial intelligenc e in the banking sector of Bangladesh: Applicability and the challenges. *Roundtabl e discussion series-2021. Keynote Paper of Roundtable Discussion of BIBM, 6*(2).

Khan, A. W., & Pandey, J. (2023). Consumer psychology for food choices: A systematic review and research directions. *European Journal of Marketing*, 57(9), 2353–2381. DOI: 10.1108/EJM-07-2021-0566

Khan, M. A., Saleh, A. M., Waseem, M., & Sajjad, I. A. (2023). Artificial Intelligence Enabled Demand Response: Prospects and Challenges in Smart Grid Environment. *IEEE Access : Practical Innovations, Open Solutions*, 11, 1477–1505. DOI: 10.1109/ACCESS.2022.3231444

Khan, M. A., Saqib, S., Alyas, T., Ur Rehman, A., Saeed, Y., Zeb, A., Zareei, M., & Mohamed, E. M. (2020). Effective Demand Forecasting Model Using Business Intelligence Empowered with Machine Learning. *IEEE Access : Practical Innovations, Open Solutions*, 8, 116013–116023. DOI: 10.1109/ACCESS.2020.3003790

Khan, M., & Ghouri, A. M. (2018). Enhancing customer satisfaction and loyalty through customer-defined market orientation and customer inspiration: A critical literature review. *International Business Education Journal*, 11(1), 25–39. DOI: 10.37134/ibej.vol11.1.3.2018

Khan, R. U., Salamzadeh, Y., Iqbal, Q., & Yang, S. (2022). The impact of customer relationship management and company reputation on customer loyalty: The mediating role of customer satisfaction. *Journal of Relationship Marketing*, 21(1), 1–26. DOI: 10.1080/15332667.2020.1840904

Khokhar, P., & Chitsimran. (2019). Evolution of AI in Marketing, Comparison With. *Our Heritage*, 67, 375–389.

Kietzmann, J. H., Hermkens, K., McCarthy, I. P., & Silvestre, B. S. (2011). Social media? Get serious! Understanding the functional building blocks of social media. *Business Horizons*, 54(3), 241–251. DOI: 10.1016/j.bushor.2011.01.005

Kim, H. (2022). Keeping up with influencers: Exploring the impact of social presence and parasocial interactions on Instagram. *International Journal of Advertising*, 41(3), 414–434. DOI: 10.1080/02650487.2021.1886477

Kim, H., & Park, M. (2024). When digital celebrity talks to you: How human-like virtual influencers satisfy consumer's experience through social presence on social media endorsements. *Journal of Retailing and Consumer Services*, 76, 103581. DOI: 10.1016/j.jretconser.2023.103581

Kim, H., So, K. K. F., Shin, S., & Li, J. (2024). Artificial intelligence in hospitality and tourism: Insights from industry practices, research literature, and expert opinions. *Journal of Hospitality & Tourism Research (Washington, D.C.)*, 10963480241229235, 10963480241229235. Advance online publication. DOI: 10.1177/10963480241229235

Kimiti, P. G., Muathe, S. M. A., & Murigi, E. M. (2021). Cost Leadership Strategy: A New Game Strategy for Competitive Advantage in Milk Processing Firms in Kenya. *European Scientific Journal*, 17(23), 296–306. DOI: 10.19044/esj.2021.v17n23p296

Kimiti, P., Muathe, S., & Murigi, E. M. (2020). Cost Leadership Strategy, Competitive Advantage, and Performance: A Cross-Sectional Study in the Context of Milk Processing Firms in Kenya. International *Journal of Management. Innovation & Entrepreneurial Research*, 6(2), 64–76. DOI: 10.18510/ijmier.2020.627

Kim, J., Kang, S., & Bae, J. (2021). The effects of customer consumption goals on artificial intelligence driven recommendation agents: Evidence from stitch fix. *International Journal of Advertising*, 41(6), 997–1016. DOI: 10.1080/02650487.2021.1963098

Kim, J., Thomas, P., Sankaranarayana, R., Gedeon, T., & Yoon, H.-J. (2016, November 01). Understanding eye movements on mobile devices for better presentation of search results. *Journal of the Association for Information Science and Technology*, 67(11), 2607–2619. DOI: 10.1002/asi.23628

Kim, S. H. (2015). Mobile Marketing: Focusing on the Impact of Value, Privacy, and Trust. *International Journal of Mobile Marketing*, 10(1), 14–31.

Kim, Y., & Sundar, S. S. (2012). Anthropomorphism of computers: Is it mindful or mindless? *Computers in Human Behavior*, 28(1), 241–250. DOI: 10.1016/j.chb.2011.09.006

Kindylidi, I., & Cabral, T. S. (2021). Sustainability of AI: The Case of Provision of Information to Consumers. *Sustainability (Basel)*, 13(21), 12064. Advance online publication. DOI: 10.3390/su132112064

Kinnear, P. R., & Gray, C. D. (2010). *PASW statistics 17 made simple*. Psychology Press.

Kishore, R. (2023, Jul 05). *Amazon's Dynamic Pricing Strategy: How It Balances Customer Trust and Profitability*. https://www.linkedin.com: https://www.linkedin.com/pulse/amazons-dynamic-pricing-strategy-how-balances-trust-kishore-rajgopal/

Knox, S., Maklan, S., Payne, A., Peppard, J., & Ryals, L. (2003). A strategic framework for CRM. In Knox, S., Maklan, S., Payne, A., Peppard, J., & Ryals, L. (Eds.), *Customer relationship management* (pp. 17–41). Butterworth-Heinemann. DOI: 10.1016/B978-0-7506-5677-1.50006-4

Koay, K. Y., Lim, W. M., Kaur, S., Soh, K., & Poon, W. C. (2023). How and when social media influencers' intimate self-disclosure fosters purchase intentions: The roles of congruency and parasocial relationships. *Marketing Intelligence & Planning*, 41(6), 790–809. DOI: 10.1108/MIP-06-2023-0246

Koehler, J., Fux, E., Herzog, F. A., Lötscher, D., Waelti, K., Imoberdorf, R., & Budke, D. (2018). Towards intelligent process support for customer service desks: Extracting problem descriptions from noisy and multi-lingual texts. In Business Process Management Workshops: BPM 2017 International Workshops, Barcelona, Spain, September 10-11, 2017, Revised Papers 15 (pp. 36-52). Springer International Publishing.

Kohli, A. K., Jaworski, B. J., & Kumar, A. (1993). MARKOR: A measure of market orientation. *JMR, Journal of Marketing Research*, 30(4), 467–477. DOI: 10.1177/002224379303000406

Koladycz, R., Fernandez, G., Gray, K., & Marriott, H. (2018). The Net Promoter Score (NPS) for Insight Into Client Experiences in Sexual and Reproductive Health Clinics. *Global Health, Science and Practice*, 6(3), 413–424. DOI: 10.9745/GHSP-D-18-00068 PMID: 30072372

Kolasani, S. (2023). Optimizing natural language processing, large language models (LLMs) for efficient customer service, and hyper-personalization to enable sustainable growth and revenue. *Transactions on Latest Trends in Artificial Intelligence, 4*(4).

Kolla, N., & Kumar, M. G. (2019). Meta-synthesis on artificial intelligence (AI): Imperatives for branding. *International Journal of Recent Technology and Engineering*, 8(3), 2251–2255. DOI: 10.35940/ijrte.B3268.098319

Kombo, D. K., Tromp, D. L., & DL, A. (2006). *Proposal and thesis writing*. Paulines Publication Africa.

Konina, N. Y. (2023). Artificial intelligence in the Fashion Industry—Reality and Prospects. In *Approaches to global sustainability, markets, and governance* (pp. 273–280). DOI: 10.1007/978-981-99-2198-0_29

Kopalle, P. K., Gangwar, M., Kaplan, A., Ramachandran, D., Reinartz, W., & Rindfleisch, A. (2022). Examining artificial intelligence (AI) technologies in marketing via a global lens: Current trends and future research opportunities. *International Journal of Research in Marketing*, 39(2), 522–540. DOI: 10.1016/j.ijresmar.2021.11.002

Koren, Y., Bell, R., & Volinsky, C. (2009). Matrix Factorization Techniques for Recommender Systems. *Computer*, 42(8), 30–37. DOI: 10.1109/MC.2009.263

Kostadinov, S. (2021, December 11). Understanding Backpropagation Algorithm - towards Data science. *Medium*. https://towardsdatascience.com/understanding -backpropagation-algorithm- 7bb3aa2f95fd

Kotler, P., Kartajaya, H., & Hooi, D. H. (2019). Marketing 4.0: moving from traditional to digital. *World Scientific Book Chapters*, 99-123.

Kotler, P. (2000). *Marketing Management: Millennium Edition*. Prentice Hall.

Kotler, P., & Armstrong, G. (2006). *Principles of Marketing* (3rd ed.). Pearson.

Kotras, B. (2020). Mass personalization: Predictive marketing algorithms and the reshaping of consumer knowledge. *Big Data & Society*, 7(2), 2053951720951581. DOI: 10.1177/2053951720951581

Krauskopf, E. (2017). Call for caution in the use of bibliometric data. *Journal of the Association for Information Science and Technology*, 68(8), 2029–2032. DOI: 10.1002/asi.23809

Kraus, S., Li, H., Kang, Q., Westhead, P., & Tiberius, V. (2020). The sharing economy: A bibliometric analysis of the state-of-the-art. *International Journal of Entrepreneurial Behaviour & Research*, 26(8), 1769–1786. DOI: 10.1108/IJEBR-06-2020-0438

Kraus, S., Oshrat, Y., Aumann, Y., Hollander, T., Maksimov, O., Ostroumov, A., & Shechtman, N. (2023, September). Customer service combining human operators and virtual agents: a call for multidisciplinary AI Research. In *Proceedings of the AAAI Conference on Artificial Intelligence* (Vol. 37, No. 13, pp. 15393-15401). DOI: 10.1609/aaai.v37i13.26795

Kreijns, K., Xu, K., & Weidlich, J. (2022). Social presence: Conceptualization and measurement. *Educational Psychology Review*, 34(1), 139–170. DOI: 10.1007/s10648-021-09623-8 PMID: 34177204

Kreps, J., Narkhede, N., & Rao, J. (2011, June). Kafka: A distributed messaging system for log processing. In *Proceedings of the NetDB* (Vol. 11, No. 2011, pp. 1-7).

Krijger, J., Thuis, T., de Ruiter, M., Ligthart, E., & Broekman, I. (2023). The AI ethics maturity model: A holistic approach to advancing ethical data science in organizations. *AI and Ethics*, 3(2), 355–367. DOI: 10.1007/s43681-022-00228-7

Krishna, S. H., Vijayanand, N., Suneetha, A., Basha, S. M., Sekhar, S. C., & Saranya, A. (2022, December). Artificial Intelligence Application for Effective Customer Relationship Management. In *2022 5th International Conference on Contemporary Computing and Informatics (IC3I)* (pp. 2019-2023). IEEE. DOI: 10.1109/IC3I56241.2022.10073038

Krisnanto, U., Juharsah, J., Putra, P., Achmad, A. D., & Timotius, E. (2022). Utilizing Apriori Data Mining Techniques on Sales Transactions. *Webology*, 19(1), 5581–5590. DOI: 10.14704/WEB/V19I1/WEB19376

Kristi, K. M., & Kusumawati, N. (2021). Technology acceptance and customer perception of AR in Indonesian beauty industry. *ICE-BEES 2020: Proceedings of the 3rd International Conference on Economics, Business and Economic Education Science*, (p. 134). Semarang, Indonesia: European Alliance for Innovation.

Kronemann, B., Kizgin, H., Rana, N. P., & Dwivedi, Y. (2023). How AI encourages consumers to share their secrets? The role of anthropomorphism, personalisation, and privacy concerns and avenues for future research. *Spanish Journal of Marketing - ESIC, 27*(1), 2–19. DOI: 10.1108/SJME-10-2022-0213

Krupka, Z. (2023). Exploring the Influence of Sensory Marketing on Brand Perception. *Naše gospodarstvo/Our economy, 69*(3), 45-55. .DOI: 10.2478/ngoe-2023-0017

Kuanr, A., Pradhan, D., Lyngdoh, T., & Lee, M. S. (2022). Why do consumers subvert brands? Investigating the influence of subjective well-being on brand avoidance. *Psychology and Marketing*, 39(3), 612–633. DOI: 10.1002/mar.21606

Kubacki, K., & Szablewska, N. (2019). Social marketing targeting Indigenous peoples: A systematic review. *Health Promotion International*, 34(1), 133–143. DOI: 10.1093/heapro/dax060 PMID: 28973158

Kucuk, S. U. (2016). *Brand hate: Navigating consumer negativity in the digital world*. Springer. DOI: 10.1007/978-3-319-41519-2

Kucuk, S. U. (2019a). Consumer brand hate: Steam rolling whatever I see. *Psychology and Marketing*, 36(5), 431–443. DOI: 10.1002/mar.21175

Kucuk, S. U. (2019b). What is brand hate? In *Brand Hate: Navigating Consumer Negativity in the Digital World* (pp. 23–48). Springer International Publishing. DOI: 10.1007/978-3-030-00380-7_2

Kull, A. J., Romero, M., & Monahan, L. (2021). How may I help you? Driving brand engagement through the warmth of an initial chatbot message. *Journal of Business Research*, 135, 840–850. DOI: 10.1016/j.jbusres.2021.03.005

Kumar, L., & Jindal, S. (2018). Role of Artificial Intelligence in Intellectual Property Rights. In *Shivam Jindal Artificial Intelligence* (pp. 609-614).

Kumar, A., Tejaswini, P., Nayak, O., Kujur, A. D., Gupta, R., Rajanand, A., & Sahu, M. (2022). A Survey on IBM Watson and Its Services. *Journal of Physics: Conference Series*, 2273(1), 012022. DOI: 10.1088/1742-6596/2273/1/012022

Kumar, J., & Gupta, S. S. (2023). Impact of artificial intelligence towards customer relationship in Indian banking industry. *Gyan Manag. J*, 17(1), 105–115. DOI: 10.48165/gmj.2022.17.1.12

Kumar, J., & Gupta, S. S. (2023). Impact of artificial intelligence towards customer relationship in Indian banking industry. *Gyan Management.Journal*, 17(1), 105–115.

Kumar, L. (2017). State of The Art-Intense Review on Artificial Intelligence Systems Application in Process Planning and Manufacturing. *Engineering Applications of Artificial Intelligence*, 65, 294–329. DOI: 10.1016/j.engappai.2017.08.005

Kumar, M., Raut, R. D., Mangla, S. K., Ferraris, A., & Choubey, V. K. (2022). The adoption of artificial intelligence powered workforce management for effective revenue growth of micro, small, and medium scale enterprises (MSMEs). *Production Planning and Control*, •••, 1–17. DOI: 10.1080/09537287.2022.2131620

Kumar, P., Polonsky, M., Dwivedi, Y. K., & Kar, A. (2021). Green information quality and green brand evaluation: The moderating effects of eco-label credibility and consumer knowledge. *European Journal of Marketing*, 55(7), 2037–2071. DOI: 10.1108/EJM-10-2019-0808

Kumar, S., Sureka, R., & Colombage, S. (2020). Capital structure of SMEs: A systematic literature review and bibliometric analysis. *Management Review Quarterly*, 70(4), 535–565. DOI: 10.1007/s11301-019-00175-4

Kumar, V., Ashraf, A. R., & Nadeem, W. (2024). AI-powered marketing: What, where, and how? *International Journal of Information Management*, 77, 102783. DOI: 10.1016/j.ijinfomgt.2024.102783

Kumar, V., Dixit, A., Javalgi, R. G., & Dass, M. (2016). Research framework, strategies, and applications of intelligent agent technologies (IATs) in marketing. *Journal of the Academy of Marketing Science*, 44(1), 24–45. DOI: 10.1007/s11747-015-0426-9

Kumar, V., & Pansari, A. (2016). Competitive Advantage through Engagement. *JMR, Journal of Marketing Research*, 53(4), 497–514. DOI: 10.1509/jmr.15.0044

Kumar, V., Rajan, B., Gupta, S., & Pozza, I. D. (2021). Customer Engagement in Service. *Journal of the Academy of Marketing Science*, 49, 304–325.

Kumar, V., Rajan, B., Venkatesan, R., & Lecinski, J. (2019). Understanding the role of artificial intelligence in personalized engagement marketing. *California Management Review*, 61(4), 135–155. DOI: 10.1177/0008125619859317

Kumar, V., Ramachandran, D., & Kumar, B. (2021). Influence of new-age technologies on marketing: A research agenda. *Journal of Business Research*, 122, 864–877. DOI: 10.1016/j.jbusres.2020.01.007

Kumar, V., & Reinartz, W. (2016). Creating enduring customer value. *Journal of Marketing*, 80(6), 36–68. DOI: 10.1509/jm.15.0414

Kumar, V., & Reinartz, W. (2018). *Customer Relationship Management: Concept, Strategy, and Tools*. Springer. DOI: 10.1007/978-3-662-55381-7

Kushwaha, A. K., Kumar, P., & Kar, A. K. (2021). What impacts customer experience for B2B enterprises on using AI-enabled chatbots? Insights from Big data analytics. *Industrial Marketing Management*, 98, 207–221. DOI: 10.1016/j.indmarman.2021.08.011

Kutz, J., Neuhüttler, J., Spilski, J., & Lachmann, T. (2022, July). Implementation of AI Technologies in manufacturing-success factors and challenges. In The Human Side of Service Engineerin, Proceedings of the 13th International Conference on Applied Human Factors and Ergonomics (AHFE 2022), New York, NY, USA (pp. 24-28).

Kwak, J., & Moon, J. (2021). The Effect of Self-Leadership on Job Satisfaction and Customer Orientation: The Role of Supervisor Support. *East Asian Journal of Business Economics*, 9(2), 75–84.

Kwon, H. J., & Lim, H. K. (2021). A Study on the Prospects of the Korea Beauty Industry. [TURCOMAT]. *Turkish Journal of Computer and Mathematics Education*, 12(5), 382–386.

Laforest, V. (2014). Assessment of emerging and innovative techniques considering best available technique performances. *Resources, Conservation and Recycling*, 92, 11–24. DOI: 10.1016/j.resconrec.2014.08.009

Lal, B., Ismagilova, E., Dwivedi, Y. K., & Kwayu, S. (2020). Return on investment in social media marketing: Literature review and suggestions for future research. In *Digital and social media marketing: Advances in theory and practice of emmerging markets* (pp. 3–17). Springer., DOI: 10.1007/978-3-030-24374-6_1

Lalit, S. (2023, Sept 06). *Top 13 eCommerce Trends in 2024*. https://www.netsolutions.com/hub/ecommerce/trends

Lamberton, C., & Stephen, A. T. (2016). A thematic exploration of digital, social media, and mobile marketing: Research evolution from 2000 to 2015 and an agenda for future inquiry. *Journal of Marketing*, 80(6), 146–172. DOI: 10.1509/jm.15.0415

Lambrecht, A., & Tucker, C. (2013). When Does Retargeting Work? Information Specificity in Online Advertising. *JMR, Journal of Marketing Research*, 50(5), 561–576. DOI: 10.1177/002224371305000508

Lan, D. H., & Tung, T. M. (2024). AI-Powered Customer Experience: Personalization, engagement, and intelligent Decision-Making in CRM. *Deleted Journal*, 20(5s), 55–71. DOI: 10.52783/jes.1832

Lane Keller, K. (2013). *Strategic Brand Managment: Building, Measuring, and Managing Brand Equity*. Pearson Education Limited.

Lariviere, B., Keiningham, T. L., Cooil, B., Aksoy, L., & Malthouse, E. C. (2014). A longitudinal examination of customer commitment and loyalty. *Journal of Service Management*, 25(1), 75–100. DOI: 10.1108/JOSM-01-2013-0025

Lau, O., & Ki, C. W. (2021). Can consumers' gamified, personalized, and engaging experiences with VR fashion apps increase in-app purchase intention by fulfilling needs? *Fashion and Textiles*, 8(1), 1–22. DOI: 10.1186/s40691-021-00270-9

Lavidge, R., & Steiner, G. (1961). A Model of Predictive Measurements of Advertising Effectiveness. *Journal of Marketing*, 25(6), 59–62. DOI: 10.1177/002224296102500611

LeCun, Y., Bengio, Y., & Hinton, G. (2015). Deep Learning. *Nature*, 521(7553), 436–444. DOI: 10.1038/nature14539 PMID: 26017442

LeCun, Y., Bottou, L., Bengio, Y., & Haffner, P. (1998). Gradient-based learning applied to document recognition. *Proceedings of the IEEE*, 86(11), 2278–2323. DOI: 10.1109/5.726791

Ledro, C., Nosella, A., & Dalla Pozza, I. (2023). Integration of AI in CRM: Challenges and guidelines. *Journal of Open Innovation*, 9(4), 100151. DOI: 10.1016/j.joitmc.2023.100151

Ledro, C., Nosella, A., & Vinelli, A. (2022). Artificial intelligence in customer relationship management: Literature review and future research directions. *Journal of Business and Industrial Marketing*, 37(13), 48–63. DOI: 10.1108/JBIM-07-2021-0332

Lee, A., & Chung, T.-L. D. (2023). Transparency in corporate social responsibility communication on social media. *International Journal of Retail & Distribution Management*, 51(5), 590–610. DOI: 10.1108/IJRDM-01-2022-0038

Lee, H. M., Chen, T., Chen, Y. S., Lo, W. Y., & Hsu, Y. H. (2021). The effects of consumer ethnocentrism and consumer animosity on perceived betrayal and negative word-of-mouth. *Asia Pacific Journal of Marketing and Logistics*, 33(3), 712–730. DOI: 10.1108/APJML-08-2019-0518

Lee, J. Y., & Jeung, W. (2016). Differential effects of person-organization and person-team cultural fit on work-related attitudes and job performance. *Proceedings - Academy of Management*, 1. Advance online publication. DOI: 10.5465/ambpp.2016.13447abstract

Lee, M., & Park, J. S. (2022). Do parasocial relationships and the quality of communication with AI shopping chatbots determine middle-aged women consumers' continuance usage intentions? *Journal of Consumer Behaviour*, 21(4), 842–854. DOI: 10.1002/cb.2043

Lee, S. M., & Lee, D. (2020). "Untact": A new customer service strategy in the digital age. *Service Business*, 14(1), 1–22. DOI: 10.1007/s11628-019-00408-2

Lee, T. C., & Peng, M. Y. P. (2021). Green experiential marketing, experiential value, relationship quality, and customer loyalty in environmental leisure farm. *Frontiers in Environmental Science*, 9, C7–C657523. DOI: 10.3389/fenvs.2021.657523

Lefkeli, D., Karataş, M., & Gürhan-Canli, Z. (2024). Sharing information with AI (versus a human) impairs brand trust: The role of audience size inferences and sense of exploitation. *International Journal of Research in Marketing*, 41(1), 138–155. DOI: 10.1016/j.ijresmar.2023.08.011

Lekmat, L., Selvarajah, C., & Hewege, C. (2018). Relationship between Market Orientation, Entrepreneurial Orientation, and Firm Performance in Thai SMEs: The Mediating Role of Marketing Capabilities. *European Journal of Pediatric Dermatology : PD*, 28(4).

Lemma, S. (2020). *Impact of customer orientation of service employees on relationship quality and customer loyalty (case study of commercial bank of Ethiopia in Addis Ababa)*. Doctoral dissertation, St. Mary's University.

Lemon, K. N., & Verhoef, P. C. (2016). Understanding customer experience throughout the customer journey. *Journal of Marketing*, 80(6), 69–96. DOI: 10.1509/jm.15.0420

Leocádio, D., Guedes, L., Oliveira, J., Reis, J., & Melão, N. (2024). Customer service with AI-powered human-robot collaboration (HRC): A literature review. *Procedia Computer Science*, 232, 1222–1232. DOI: 10.1016/j.procs.2024.01.120

Letheren, K., Jetten, J., Roberts, J., & Donovan, J. (2021). Robots should be seen and not heard... sometimes: Anthropomorphism and AI service robot interactions. *Psychology and Marketing*, 38(12), 2393–2406. DOI: 10.1002/mar.21575

Levy, M. (2020). *Customer Data Platforms: A Marketer's Guide*. MarketingProfs.

Liao, C., Chen, J. L., & Yen, D. C. (2007). Theory of planning behavior (TPB) and customer satisfaction in the continued use of e-service: An integrated model. *Computers in Human Behavior*, 23(6), 2804–2822. DOI: 10.1016/j.chb.2006.05.006

Li, B., Liu, L., Mao, W., Qu, Y., & Chen, Y. (2023). Voice artificial intelligence service failure and customer complaint behavior: The mediation effect of customer emotion. *Electronic Commerce Research and Applications*, 59, 101261. DOI: 10.1016/j.elerap.2023.101261

Liebers, N., & Schramm, H. (2019). Parasocial interactions and relationships with media characters–an inventory of 60 years of research. *Communication Research Trends*, 38(2), 4–31.

Li, F., Larimo, J., & Leonidou, L. C. (2021). Social media marketing strategy: Definition, conceptualization, taxonomy, validation, and future agenda. *Journal of the Academy of Marketing Science*, 49(1), 51–70. DOI: 10.1007/s11747-020-00733-3

Li, G., Li, N., & Sethi, S. P. (2021). Does CSR Reduce Idiosyncratic Risk? Roles of Operational Efficiency and AI Innovation. *Production and Operations Management*, 30(7), 2027–2045. DOI: 10.1111/poms.13483

Li, J., & Kim, J. E. (2021). The effect of task complexity on time estimation in the virtual reality environment: An eeg study. *Applied Sciences (Basel, Switzerland)*, 11(20), 9779. Advance online publication. DOI: 10.3390/app11209779

Lim, J. S., Hwang, Y., Kim, S., & Biocca, F. A. (2015). How social media engagement leads to sports channel loyalty: Mediating roles of social presence and channel commitment. *Computers in Human Behavior*, 46, 158–167. DOI: 10.1016/j.chb.2015.01.013

Lindecrantz, E., Gi, M. T. P., & Zerbi, S. (2018). Personalizing the Customer Experience: Driving Differentiation in Retail. https://www.mckinsey.com/industries/retail/our-insights/personalizing-the-customer-experience-driving-differentiation-in-retail

Lin, J. S., & Hsieh, P. L. (2006). The role of technology readiness in customers' perception and adoption of self-service technologies. *International Journal of Service Industry Management*, 17(5), 497–517. DOI: 10.1108/09564230610689795

Link, M., Dukino, C., Ganz, W., Hamann, K., & Schnalzer, K. (2020). The Use of AI-Based Assistance Systems in the Service Sector: opportunities, challenges and applications. In *Advances in Human Factors and Systems Interaction:Proceedings of the AHFE 2020 Virtual Conference on Human Factors and Systems Interaction,July 16-20, 2020,USA* (pp. 10-16). Springer International Publishing. DOI: 10.1007/978-3-030-51369-6_2

Lin, Y., Wang, H., Li, J., & Gao, H. (2019). Data source selection for information integration in big data era. *Information Sciences*, 479, 197–213. DOI: 10.1016/j.ins.2018.11.029

Lisa Bertagnoli. (2022). Artificial Intelligence In Fashion. Built In. https://builtin.com/artificial-intelligence/ai-fashion

Li, T. H. Y., Ng, S. T., & Skitmore, M. (2013). Evaluating stakeholder satisfaction during public participation in major infrastructure and construction projects: A fuzzy approach. *Automation in Construction*, 29, 123–135. DOI: 10.1016/j.autcon.2012.09.007

Liu, B. (2022). *Sentiment analysis and opinion mining*. Springer Nature.

Liu, J., Kong, X., Xia, F., Bai, X., Wang, L., Qing, Q., & Lee, I. (2018). Artificial intelligence in the 21st century. *IEEE Access : Practical Innovations, Open Solutions*, 6, 34403–34421. DOI: 10.1109/ACCESS.2018.2819688

Liu, M. W., & Keh, H. T. (2015). Consumer delight and outrage: Scale development and validation. *Journal of Service Theory and Practice*, 25(6), 680–699. DOI: 10.1108/JSTP-08-2014-0178

Liu-Thompkins, Y., & Malthouse, E. C. (2017). A primer on using behavioral data for testing theories in advertising research. *Journal of Advertising*, 46(1), 213–225. DOI: 10.1080/00913367.2016.1252289

Liu-Thompkins, Y., Okazaki, S., & Li, H. (2022). Artificial empathy in marketing interactions: Bridging the human-AI gap in affective and social customer experience. *Journal of the Academy of Marketing Science*, 50(6), 1198–1218. DOI: 10.1007/s11747-022-00892-5

Liu, X., Singh, P. V., & Srinivasan, K. (2016). A structured analysis of unstructured big data by leveraging cloud computing. *Marketing Science*, 35(3), 363–388. DOI: 10.1287/mksc.2015.0972

Liu, Y. (2023). The impact of social media influencers on Generation Z online consumer behavior. *Advances in Economics. Management and Political Sciences*, 41(1), 19–24. DOI: 10.54254/2754-1169/41/20232026

Liu, Y., & Chen, M. (2023). The Knowledge Structure and Development Trend in Artificial Intelligence Based on Latent Feature Topic Model. *IEEE Transactions on Engineering Management*, •••, 1–12. DOI: 10.1109/TEM.2022.3232178

Li, Y., Xu, S., Luo, X., & Lin, S. (2014, December 01). A new algorithm for product image search based on salient edge characterization. *Journal of the Association for Information Science and Technology*, 65(12), 2534–2551. DOI: 10.1002/asi.23136

Li, Z., Kong, D., Niu, Y., Peng, H., Li, X., & Li, W. (2023, January 1). An Overview of AI and Blockchain Integration for Privacy-Preserving. Cornell University. doi:DOI: 10.48550/arXiv.2305

Lohit, V. S., Mujahid, M. M., & Sai, G. K. (2022). Use of machine learning for continuous improvement and handling multi-dimensional data in service sector. *Comput. Intell. Mach. Learn*, 3(2), 39–46. DOI: 10.36647/CIML/03.02.A006

Lo, S. C. (2012). A study of relationship marketing on customer satisfaction. *Journal of Social Sciences (New York, N. Y.)*, 8(1), 91–94. DOI: 10.3844/jssp.2012.91.94

Lo, V. S. Y. (2005). Marketing Data Mining. In *Encyclopedia of Data Warehousing and Mining* (pp. 698–704). Idea Group Reference. DOI: 10.4018/978-1-59140-557-3.ch133

Luce, L. (2018). *Artificial Intelligence for Fashion: How AI is Revolutionizing the Fashion Industry*. Apress.

Lu, L., Rui-Ying, C., & Gürsoy, D. (2019). Developing and validating a service robot integration willingness scale. *International Journal of Hospitality Management*, 80, 36–51. DOI: 10.1016/j.ijhm.2019.01.005

Luo, X., Tong, S., Fang, Z., & Qu, Z. (2019). Frontiers: Machines vs. humans: The impact of artificial intelligence chatbot disclosure on customer purchases. *Marketing Science*, 38(6), 937–947. DOI: 10.1287/mksc.2019.1192

Luo, X., Zhang, J., & Duan, W. (2013). Social media and firm equity value. *Information Systems Research*, 24(1), 146–163. DOI: 10.1287/isre.1120.0462

Lv, X., Yang, Y., Qin, D., Cao, X., & Xu, H. (2022). Artificial intelligence service recovery: The role of empathic response in hospitality customers' continuous usage intention. *Computers in Human Behavior*, 126, 106993. DOI: 10.1016/j.chb.2021.106993

Lyulyov, O., Chygryn, O., Pimonenko, T., & Kwilinski, A. (2023). Stakeholders' Engagement in the Company's Management as a Driver of Green Competitiveness within Sustainable Development. *Sustainability (Basel)*, 15(9), 7249. Advance online publication. DOI: 10.3390/su15097249

Machado, L., & Goswami, S. (2023). Marketing sustainability within the jewelry industry. *Journal of Marketing Communications*, •••, 1–16. DOI: 10.1080/13527266.2023.2166566

Magno, F., & Dossena, G. (2023). The effects of chatbots' attributes on customer relationships with brands: PLS-SEM and importance–performance map analysis. *The TQM Journal*, 35(5), 1156–1169. DOI: 10.1108/TQM-02-2022-0080

Maharani, B. P., & Saroso, D. S. (2020). Analysis of Service Quality an Empirical Study of Customer Satisfaction in Information and Technology Service Companies. *Dinasti International Journal of Digital Business Management*, 1(2), 200–209. DOI: 10.31933/dijdbm.v1i2.152

Maj, A. (2021). The Rise of Conversational AI Platforms. In *The AI Book: The Artificial Intelligence Handbook for Investors, Entrepreneurs and FinTech Visionaries* (pp. 111-112). Wiley. DOI: 10.1002/9781119551966.ch31

Makhija, P., & Chacko, E. (2021). Efficiency and Advancement of Artificial Intelligence in Service Sector with Special Reference to Banking Industry. In Nasser Rashad Al Mawali & Anis Moosa Al Lawati & Ananda S (Ed.), *Fourth Industrial Revolution and Business Dynamics* (pp. 21-35), Springer.DOI: 10.1007/978-981-16-3250-1_2

Makridakis, S. (2017). The forthcoming Artificial Intelligence (AI) revolution: Its impact on society and firms. *Futures*, 90, 46–60. DOI: 10.1016/j.futures.2017.03.006

Ma, L., Ou, W., & Lee, C. (2022). Investigating Consumers' Cognitive, Emotional, and Behavioral Engagement in Social Media Brand Pages: A Natural Language Processing Approach. *Electronic Commerce Research and Applications*, 54, 101179. DOI: 10.1016/j.elerap.2022.101179

Ma, L., & Sun, B. (2020). Machine Learning and AI in Marketing – Connecting Computer Power to Human Insights. *International Journal of Research in Marketing*, 37(3), 481–504. DOI: 10.1016/j.ijresmar.2020.04.005

Malthouse, E. C., Haenlein, M., Skiera, B., Wege, E., & Zhang, M. (2013). Managing customer relationships in the social media era: Introducing the social CRM house. *Journal of Interactive Marketing*, 27(4), 270–280. DOI: 10.1016/j.intmar.2013.09.008

Mangold, W. G., & Faulds, D. J. (2009). Social media: The new hybrid element of the promotion mix. *Business Horizons*, 52(4), 357–365. DOI: 10.1016/j.bushor.2009.03.002

Mangtani, N., Bajpai, N., Sahasrabudhe, S., & Wasule, D. (2020). Importance of AI and AR in cosmetic and beauty industry post Covid 19. *World Journal of Pharmaceutical Research*, 9(8), 2296–2308.

Manjula, R., & Chilambuchelvan, A. (2016). Content based filtering techniques in recommendation system using user preferences. *Int. J. Innov. Eng. Technol*, 7(4), 151.

Manzoor, S. R., Ullah, H., Hussain, M., & Ahmad, Z. M. (2011). Effect of teamwork on employee performance. *International Journal of Learning and Development*, 1(1), 110. DOI: 10.5296/ijld.v1i1.1110

Maras, E. (2020, July 11). Beauty retailers embrace AR, AI. www.digitalsignagetoday.com. https://www.digitalsignagetoday.com/articles/beauty-retailers- embrace-ar-ai/

Marbach, J., Lages, C. R., & Nunan, D. (2016). Who are you and what do you value? Investigating the role of personality traits and customer-perceived value in online customer engagement. *Journal of Marketing Management*, 32(5-6), 502–525. DOI: 10.1080/0267257X.2015.1128472

Marissa, J. (2023, Jul 21). *Voice commerce, AI, and the future of shopping*. https://www.bazaarvoice.com/blog/voice-commerce-ai/

Markets and Markets. (2022). AI in Fashion Market by Solutions & Services. Retrieved from https://www.marketsandmarkets.com/Market-Reports/ai-in-fashion-market-144448991.html#:~:text=AI%20in%20fashion%3F-The%20global%20AI%20in%20fashion%20market%20size%20is%20expected%20to,40.8%25%20during%20the%20forecast%20period

Marr, B. (2019). *How Fashion Retailer H&M Is Betting On Artificial Intelligence And Big Data To Regain Profitability*. Forbes. https://www.forbes.com/sites/bernardmarr/2018/08/10/how-fashion-retailer-hm-is-betting-on-artificial-intelligence-and-big-data-to-regain-profitability/

Marsh, H. W., Balla, J. R., & Hau, K. T. (2013). An evaluation of incremental fit indices: A clarification of mathematical and empirical properties. In *Advanced structural equation modeling* (pp. 315–353). Psychology Press.

Martínez-Falcó, J., Marco-Lajara, B., Sánchez-García, E., & Millan-Tudela, L. A. (2023). Sustainable Development Goals in the Business Sphere: A Bibliometric Review. *Sustainability (Basel)*, 15(6), 5075. Advance online publication. DOI: 10.3390/su15065075

Martín-Martín, A., Thelwall, M., Orduna-Malea, E., & Delgado López-Cózar, E. (2021). Google Scholar, Microsoft Academic, Scopus, Dimensions, Web of Science, and OpenCitations' COCI: A multidisciplinary comparison of coverage via citations. *Scientometrics*, 126(1), 871–906. DOI: 10.1007/s11192-020-03690-4 PMID: 32981987

Maslow, A. H. (1943). A theory of human motivation. *Psychological Review*, 50(4), 370–396. DOI: 10.1037/h0054346

Masnita, Y., Ramadina, A. A., Zahra, A., & Bakiewicz, A. (2024). The World Of AI: Strategies In The Beauty Industry. In M. Ali Tarar, M. Saghir Ahmad, & L. Walambuka (Eds.), *Social Green Behaviour, AI and Business Strategies and Perspectives in Global Digital Society* (Vol. 13, p. 34). NCM Publishing House.

Mateo, S. (2020). Procédure pour conduire avec succès une revue de littérature selon la méthode PRISMA. *Kinésithérapie, la Revue*, 20(226), 29–37. DOI: 10.1016/j.kine.2020.05.019

Matosas-López, L. (2024). The influence of brand credibility and brand loyalty on customer satisfaction and continued use intention in new voice assistance services based on AI. *Journal of Marketing Analytics*, 1-22.

Mazhar, M., Hooi Ting, D., Zaib Abbasi, A., Nadeem, M. A., & Abbasi, H. A. (2022). Gauging customers' negative disconfirmation in online post-purchase behaviour: The moderating role of service recovery. *Cogent Business & Management*, 9(1), 2072186. DOI: 10.1080/23311975.2022.2072186

Mazurek, G., & Małagocka, K. (2019). Perception of privacy and data protection in the context of the development of artificial intelligence. *Journal of Management Analytics*, 6(4), 344–364. DOI: 10.1080/23270012.2019.1671243

Mbete, G. S., & Tanamal, R. (2020). Effect of easiness, service quality, price, trust of quality of information, and brand image of consumer purchase decision on Shopee online purchase. *Jurnal Informatika Universitas Pamulang*, 5(2), 100–110. DOI: 10.32493/informatika.v5i2.4946

McAfee, A., & Brynjolfsson, E. (2012). Big data: The management revolution. *Harvard Business Review*, 90(10), 60–68. PMID: 23074865

McAlindon, K. (2017). Selling Innovations Like Soap: The Interactive Systems Framework and Social Marketing. *American Journal of Community Psychology*, 60(1–2), 242–256. DOI: 10.1002/ajcp.12157 PMID: 28815622

McCarthy, J., Minsky, M. L., Rochester, N., & Shannon, C. E. (1955). A proposal for the Dartmouth summer research project on artificial intelligence. http://www-formal.stanford.edu/jmc/history/dartmouth/dartmouth.html

McCarthy, E. J. (1960). *Basic marketing: A managerial approach.*

McGuire-Kuletz, M., & Tomlinson, P. (2015). *Return on investment and economic impact: Determining and communicating the value of vocational rehabilitation.*

McKinsey & Company. (2020). The Value of Getting Personalization Right—or Wrong—is Multiplying. McKinsey & Company. https://www.mckinsey.com/capabilities/growth-marketing-and-sales/our-insights/the-value-of-getting-personalization-right-or-wrong-is-multiplying

McManus, D. J., Wilson, L. T., & Snyder, C. A. (2004). Assessing the business value of knowledge retention projects - Results of four case studies. *IFIP International Conference on Decision Support Systems.*

Mello-Klein, C. (2022). Facebook's ad delivery algorithm is discriminating based on race, gender and age in photos, Northeastern researchers find. https://news.northeastern.edu/2022/10/25/facebook-algorithm-discrimination/

Mentzas, G., Hribernik, K., Stahre, J., Romero, D., & Soldatos, J. (2024). Editorial: Human-Centered Artificial Intelligence in Industry 5.0. *Frontiers in Artificial Intelligence*, 7, 1429186. Advance online publication. DOI: 10.3389/frai.2024.1429186 PMID: 38915905

Meurisch, C., & Mühlhäuser, M. (2021, March 5). Data Protection in AI Services. *ACM Computing Surveys*, 54(2), 1–38. DOI: 10.1145/3440754

Miklosik, A., Kuchta, M., Evans, N., & Zak, S. (2019). Towards the adoption of machine learning-based analytical tools in digital marketing. *IEEE Access : Practical Innovations, Open Solutions*, 7, 85705–85718. DOI: 10.1109/ACCESS.2019.2924425

Milana, C., & Ashta, A. (2021). Artificial intelligence techniques in finance and financial markets: A survey of the literature. *Strategic Change*, 30(3), 189–209. DOI: 10.1002/jsc.2403

Milani, A. M., & Salavati, S. (2018). The role of Market Orientation and Innovation in Improving performance of business of the Banking Industry. *European Journal of Sustainable Development*, 7(4), 556–571. DOI: 10.14207/ejsd.2018.v7n4p556

Miles, L. (2023). *How L'Oréal developed better content and customer experiences online*. AdAge. https://adage.com/article/digital-marketing-ad-tech-news/how-loreal-developed-better-content-and-customer-experiences-online/2486346

Miller, D. (1983). The correlates of entrepreneurship in three types of firms. *Management Science*, 29(7), 770–791. DOI: 10.1287/mnsc.29.7.770

Mill, G. A. (2006). The financial performance of a socially responsible investment over time and a possible link with corporate social responsibility. *Journal of Business Ethics*, 63(2), 131–148. DOI: 10.1007/s10551-005-2410-7

Mim, K. B., Jai, T., & Lee, S. H. (2022). The Influence of Sustainable Positioning on eWOM and Brand Loyalty: Analysis of Credible Sources and Transparency Practices Based on the S-O-R Model. *Sustainability (Basel)*, 14(19), 12461. Advance online publication. DOI: 10.3390/su141912461

Mir-Bernal, P. (2019). Brand reputation in the Facebook era: The impact of user generated content in brand reputation management brand reputation in the Facebook era. In *Brand Culture and Identity* (pp. 1544–1556). IGI Global., DOI: 10.4018/978-1-5225-7116-2.ch083

Mirwan, S. H., Ginny, P. L., Darwin, D., Ghazali, R., & Lenas, M. N. J. (2023). Using Artificial Intelligence (AI) in Developing Marketing Strategies. [IJARSS]. *International Journal of Applied Research and Sustainable Sciences*, 1(3), 225–238. DOI: 10.59890/ijarss.v1i3.896

Mirzajani, Z., Nikoofal, M. E., & Zolfaghari, S. (2024). Sustainable sourcing contracts under supplier capital constraints and information asymmetry. *Omega*, 125, 103035. DOI: 10.1016/j.omega.2024.103035

Mishra, A., Shukla, A., Rana, N. P., & Dwivedi, Y. K. (2021). From "touch" to a "multisensory" experience: The impact of technology interface and product type on consumer responses. *Psychology and Marketing*, 38(3), 385–396. DOI: 10.1002/mar.21436

Mishra, C. S. (2017). *Mishra, C. S. (2017). Creating and Sustaining Competitive Advantage: Management Logics, Business Models, and Entrepreneurial Rent.* Springer. DOI: 10.1007/978-3-319-54540-0

Mishra, S., & Tripathi, A. (2020). *AI Business Model: An Integrative Business Approach. Research Square*. DOI: 10.21203/rs.3.rs-90687/v1

Mishra, S., & Tripathi, A. R. (2021). AI business model: An integrative business approach. *Journal of Innovation and Entrepreneurship*, 10(1), 18. DOI: 10.1186/s13731-021-00157-5

Misic, M., Đurđević, Đ., & Tomasevic, M. (2012). Evolution and trends in GPU computing. In *Proceedings of the 35th International Convention MIPRO,* 21-25 may 2012.

Misischia, C. V., Poecze, F., & Strauss, C. (2022). Chatbots in customer service: Their relevance and impact on service quality. *Procedia Computer Science*, 201, 421–428. DOI: 10.1016/j.procs.2022.03.055

Mistrean, L. (2021). Customer Orientation As a Basic Principle in the Contemporary Activity of the Bank. *Journal of Public Administration. Finance and Law*, 21(21), 39–51. DOI: 10.47743/jopafl-2021-21-05

Mitchell, T. M. (1997). *Machine Learning*. McGraw-Hill.

Mogaji, E. (2021). *Brand Management: An introduction through storytelling*. Palgrave Macmillan. DOI: 10.1007/978-3-030-66119-9

Moher, D., Liberati, A., Tetzlaff, J., & Altman, D. G. (2009). Preferred reporting items for systematic reviews and meta-analyses: The PRISMA statement. *Annals of Internal Medicine*, 151(4), 264–269. DOI: 10.7326/0003-4819-151-4-200908180-00135 PMID: 19622511

Moher, D., Liberati, A., Tetzlaff, J., & Altman, D. G.Prisma Group. (2009). Preferred reporting items for systematic reviews and meta-analyses: The PRISMA statement. *PLoS Medicine*, 6(7), e1000097. DOI: 10.1371/journal.pmed.1000097 PMID: 19621072

Moher, D., Shamseer, L., Clarke, M., Ghersi, D., Liberati, A., Petticrew, M., Shekelle, P., & Stewart, L. A.Prisma-P Group. (2015). Preferred reporting items for systematic review and meta-analysis protocols (PRISMA-P) 2015 statement. *Systematic Reviews*, 4(1), 1–9. DOI: 10.1186/2046-4053-4-1 PMID: 25554246

Mohiuddin Babu, M. (2018). Impact of firm's customer orientation on performance: The moderating role of interfunctional coordination and employee commitment. *Journal of Strategic Marketing*, 26(8), 702–722. DOI: 10.1080/0965254X.2017.1384037

Mokhtaran, M., & Komeilian, B. (2016). Exploring the effect of customer orientation on Dana insurance performance considering the intermediary role of customer relations and service quality management. *International Review (Steubenville, Ohio)*, 2(3–4), 51–61. DOI: 10.5937/intrev1604051M

Molina, M. D., & Sundar, S. S. (2022). Does distrust in humans predict greater trust in AI? Role of individual differences in user responses to content moderation. *New Media & Society*, 26(6), 3638–3656. DOI: 10.1177/14614448221103534

Mondal, B. (2019). Artificial intelligence: state of the art. In *Intelligent systems reference library* (pp. 389–425). DOI: 10.1007/978-3-030-32644-9_32

Monica, R., & Soju, A. V. (2024). Artificial Intelligence and Service Marketing Innovation. In *AI Innovation in Services Marketing* (pp. 150–172). IGI Global., DOI: 10.4018/979-8-3693-2153-9.ch007

Montes, G. A., & Goertzel, B. (2019). Distributed, decentralized, and democratized artificial intelligence. *Technological Forecasting and Social Change*, 141, 354–358. DOI: 10.1016/j.techfore.2018.11.010

Montgomery, D. C. (2015). *Design and Analysis of Experiments*. John Wiley & Sons.

Montiel-Campos, H. (2018). Entrepreneurial orientation and market orientation: Systematic literature review and future research. *Journal of Research in Marketing and Entrepreneurship*, 20(2), 292–322. DOI: 10.1108/JRME-09-2017-0040

Moon, S., & Iacobucci, D. (2022). Social media analytics and its applications in marketing. *Foundations and Trends® in Marketing, 15*(4), 213-292.

Mordor Intelligence. (2024). *CRM industry size & share analysis - growth trends & forecasts (2024 - 2029)*. https://www.mordorintelligence.com/industry-reports/customer-relationship-management-market

Mori, M., MacDorman, K. F., & Kageki, N. (2012). The uncanny valley [from the field]. *IEEE Robotics & Automation Magazine*, 19(2), 98–100. DOI: 10.1109/MRA.2012.2192811

Moriuchi, E. (2021). An empirical study on anthropomorphism and engagement with disembodied AIs and consumers' re-use behavior. *Psychology and Marketing*, 38(1), 21–42. DOI: 10.1002/mar.21407

Moro, S., & Rita, P. (2018). Brand strategies in social media in hospitality and tourism. *International Journal of Contemporary Hospitality Management*, 30(1), 343–364. DOI: 10.1108/IJCHM-07-2016-0340

Morris, M. H., & Paul, G. W. (1987). The relationship between entrepreneurship and marketing in established firms. *Journal of Business Venturing*, 2(3), 247–259. DOI: 10.1016/0883-9026(87)90012-7

Morrow, E., Zidaru, T., Ross, F., Mason, C., Patel, K. D., Ream, M., & Stockley, R. (2023). Artificial intelligence technologies and compassion in healthcare: A systematic scoping review. *Frontiers in Psychology*, 13, 971044. DOI: 10.3389/fpsyg.2022.971044 PMID: 36733854

Mosa, R. A. (2022). The Influence of E-Customer Relationship Management on Customer Experience in E-Banking Service. *International Journal of Academic Research in Business & Social Sciences*, 12(2), 193–215. DOI: 10.6007/IJARBSS/v12-i2/12195

Mostafa, R. B., & Kasamani, T. (2022). Antecedents and consequences of chatbot initial trust. *European Journal of Marketing*, 56(6), 1748–1771. DOI: 10.1108/EJM-02-2020-0084

Mostafa, R. B., Lages, C. R., & Shaalan, A. (2024). The dark side of virtual agents: Ohhh no! *International Journal of Information Management*, 75, 102721. DOI: 10.1016/j.ijinfomgt.2023.102721

Motadi, M. S. (2024). Harnessing AI for Ethical Digital Consumer Behavior Analysis. In Enhancing and Predicting Digital Consumer Behavior with AI (pp. 211-237). IGI Global. DOI: 10.4018/979-8-3693-4453-8.ch012

Mounir, I., & Gardoni, M. (2020, November 18). Front-end of innovation metrics: Research question and literature review. *X Congreso Internacional de Conocimiento e Inovación (CIKI)*. DOI: 10.48090/ciki.v1i1.913

Mourtzis, D., Angelopoulos, J., & Panopoulos, N. (2023). The future of the human–machine interface (HMI) in society 5.0. *Future Internet*, 15(5), 162. DOI: 10.3390/fi15050162

Mozafari, N., Weiger, W. H., & Hammerschmidt, M. (2022). Trust me, I'm a bot–repercussions of chatbot disclosure in different service frontline settings. *Journal of Service Management*, 33(2), 221–245. DOI: 10.1108/JOSM-10-2020-0380

Muis, I., & Isyanto, P. (2021). Market Orientation, Transformational Leadership, Partnership Effects on Organizational Performance: Competitive Advantage as a Mediator. *Binus Business Review*, 12(3), 263–277. DOI: 10.21512/bbr.v12i3.7284

Mukonza, C., & Swarts, I. (2020). The influence of green marketing strategies on business performance and corporate image in the retail sector. *Business Strategy and the Environment*, 29(3), 838–845. DOI: 10.1002/bse.2401

Mulrow, J., Machaj, K., Deanes, J., & Derrible, S. (2019). The state of carbon footprint calculators: An evaluation of calculator design and user interaction features. *Sustainable Production and Consumption*, 18, 33–40. DOI: 10.1016/j.spc.2018.12.001

Muniz, F., Stewart, K., & Magalhães, L. (2023). Are they humans or are they robots? The effect of virtual influencer disclosure on brand trust. *Journal of Consumer Behaviour*, 23(3), 1234–1250. DOI: 10.1002/cb.2271

Munnukka, J., Uusitalo, O., & Toivonen, H. (2016). Credibility of a peer endorser and advertising effectiveness. *Journal of Consumer Marketing*, 33(3), 182–192. DOI: 10.1108/JCM-11-2014-1221

Muntinga, D. G., Moorman, M., & Smit, E. G. (2011). Introducing COBRAs: Exploring motivations for brand-related social media use. *International Journal of Advertising*, 30(1), 13–46. DOI: 10.2501/IJA-30-1-013-046

Murerwa, F. K., Onditi, A. L., & Nyagol, M. (2022). Influence of Product Differentiation Strategy on Performance of Commercial Banks in Lodwar, Kenya. *International Journal of Business and Management*, VII(9), 554–565. DOI: 10.24940/theijbm/2022/v10/i10/BM2210-017

Murtarelli, G., Gregory, A., & Romenti, S. (2021). A conversation-based perspective for shaping ethical human–machine interactions: The particular challenge of chatbots. *Journal of Business Research*, 129, 927–935. DOI: 10.1016/j.jbusres.2020.09.018

Mustak, M., Salminen, J., Plé, L., & Wirtz, J. (2021). Artificial intelligence in marketing: Topic modeling, scientometric analysis, and research agenda. *Journal of Business Research*, 124, 389–404. DOI: 10.1016/j.jbusres.2020.10.044

Nadanyiova, M., Gajanova, L., & Majerova, J. (2020). Green Marketing as a Part of the Socially Responsible Brand's Communication from the Aspect of Generational Stratification. *Sustainability (Basel)*, 12(17), 7118. Advance online publication. DOI: 10.3390/su12177118

Nalbant, K. G., & Aydin, S. (2023). Development and Transformation in Digital Marketing and Branding with AI and Digital Technologies Dynamics in the Metaverse Universe. *Journal of Metaverse*, 3, 9–18. DOI: 10.57019/jmv.1148015

Nanda, A. P., & Banerjee, R. (2020). Binge watching: An exploration of the role of technology. *Psychology and Marketing*, 37(9), 1212–1230. DOI: 10.1002/mar.21353

Nandyala, L. (2024). Ethical implications of artificial intelligence in marketing. *Indian Scientific Journal Of Research In Engineering And Management*, 08(05), 1–5. DOI: 10.55041/IJSREM33275

Nardini, F. M., Trani, R., & Venturini, R. (2019). Fast approximate filtering of search results sorted by attribute. *42nd International ACM SIGIR Conference on Research and Development in Information Retrieval, SIGIR 2019* (pp. 815-824). Paris: Association for Computing Machinery, Inc. DOI: 10.1145/3331184.3331227

Narver, J. C., & Slater, S. F. (1990). The effect of a market orientation on business profitability. *Journal of Marketing*, 54(4), 20–35. DOI: 10.1177/002224299005400403

Narver, J. C., Slater, S. F., & MacLachlan, D. L. (2004). Responsive and proactive market orientation and new-product success. *Journal of Product Innovation Management*, 21(5), 334–347. DOI: 10.1111/j.0737-6782.2004.00086.x

Nass, C., & Moon, Y. (2000). Machines and mindlessness: Social responses to computers. *The Journal of Social Issues*, 56(1), 81–103. DOI: 10.1111/0022-4537.00153

Naumann, K., Bowden, J., & Gabbott, M. (2020). Expanding customer engagement: The role of negative engagement, dual valences and contexts. *European Journal of Marketing*, 54(7), 1469–1499. DOI: 10.1108/EJM-07-2017-0464

Nayak, A., Patnaik, A., Satpathy, I., & Khang, A. (2024). The Power of Artificial Intelligence in Management Education. In *Digital Talent Management Strategies* (pp. 54–70). Springer.

Naz, F., Agrawal, R., Kumar, A., Gunasekaran, A., Majumdar, A., & Luthra, S. (2022). Reviewing the applications of artificial intelligence in sustainable supply chains: Exploring research propositions for future directions. *Business Strategy and the Environment*, 31(5), 2400–2423. DOI: 10.1002/bse.3034

Newman, D. (2019). 5 ways AI is transforming the customer experience. *Forbes*. https://www.forbes.com/sites/danielnewman/2019/04/16/5-ways-ai-is-transforming-the-customer-experience/

Nezami, M. A., & Rukham, R. (2022). Crowdsourced NLP Retraining Engine in Chatbots. *International Conference on Emerging Technologies and Intelligent Systems, ICETIS 2021Al.* 322 (pp. 311-320). Buraimi: Springer Science and Business Media Deutschland GmbH. DOI: 10.1007/978-3-030-85990-9_26

Nguyen, Q. (2023). AI Representation in Cinema: A Quantitative Content Analysis. https://www.researchgate.net/profile/Quynh-Nguyen-431/publication/377410844_AI_REPRESENTATION_IN_CINEMA_A_Quantitative_Content_Analysis/links/65a56a5a5582153a6828704d/AI-REPRESENTATION-IN-CINEMA-A-Quantitative-Content-Analysis.pdf

Nguyen, B., & Mutum, D. (2012). A Review of Customer Relationship Management: Successes, Advances, Pitfalls and Futures. *Business Process Management Journal*, 18(3), 400–419. Advance online publication. DOI: 10.1108/14637151211232614

Nicholls, J., Lawlor, E., Neitzert, E., & Goodspeed, T. (2012). *A guide to social return on investment*. http://www.socialvaluelab.org.uk/wp-content/uploads/2016/09/SROI-a-guide-to-social-return-on-investment.pdf

Noranee, S., & bin Othman, A. K. (2023). Understanding consumer sentiments: Exploring the role of artificial intelligence in marketing. *JMM17: Jurnal Ilmu ekonomi dan manajemen, 10*(1), 15-23. .DOI: 10.30996/jmm17.v10i1.8690

Nunes, P. M. D. (2023). *A Inteligência Artificial e o direito da propriedade intelectual*. Edições Almedina.

Nuvriasari, A., Ishak, A., Hidayat, A., Mustafa, Z., & Haryono, S. (2020). The effect of market and entrepreneurship orientation on SME's business performance: The role of entrepreneurial marketing in Indonesian Batik industries. *European Journal of Business and Management*, 12(5), 29–37.

Nygaard, S., Kokholm, A. R., & Huulgaard, R. D. (2022). Incorporating the sustainable development goals in small- to medium-sized enterprises. *Journal of Urban Economics*, 8(1), juac022. Advance online publication. DOI: 10.1093/jue/juac022

Nyoman, N., Yasa, K., Giantari, I. G. A. K., & Setini, M. (2020). The role of competitive advantage in mediating the effect of promotional strategy on marketing performance. *Management Science Letters*, 10, 2845–2848. DOI: 10.5267/j.msl.2020.4.024

O'Neil, C. (2017). *Weapons of math destruction: How big data increases inequality and threatens democracy*. Crown.

Oanh, V. T. K. (2024). Evolving Landscape of E-Commerce, Marketing, and Customer Service: The Impact of Ai Integration. *Journal of Electrical Systems*, 20(3s), 1125–1137. Advance online publication. DOI: 10.52783/jes.1426

Obilo, O. O., Chefor, E., & Saleh, A. (2021). Revisiting the consumer brand engagement concept. *Journal of Business Research*, 126, 634–643. DOI: 10.1016/j.jbusres.2019.12.023

Obrenovic, B., Gu, X., Wang, G., Godinic, D., & Jakhongirov, I. (2024). Generative AI and human–robot interaction: Implications and future agenda for business, society and ethics. *AI & Society*, 1–14. DOI: 10.1007/s00146-024-01889-0

Octavia, A., Indrawijaya, S., Sriayudha, Y., & Hasbullah, H. (2020). Impact on E-commerce adoption on entrepreneurial orientation and market orientation in business performance of SMEs. *Asian Economic and Financial Review*, 10(5), 516–525. DOI: 10.18488/journal.aefr.2020.105.516.525

Odekerken-Schröder, G., Mennens, K., Steins, M., & Mahr, D. (2022). The service triad: An empirical study of service robots, customers and frontline employees. *Journal of Service Management*, 33(2), 246–292. DOI: 10.1108/JOSM-10-2020-0372

Oduro, S., & Haylemariam, L. G. (2019). Market orientation, CSR and financial and marketing performance in manufacturing firms in Ghana and Ethiopia. *Sustainability Accounting. Management and Policy Journal*, 10(3), 398–426. DOI: 10.1108/SAMPJ-11-2018-0309

Oh, H. J., Kim, J., Chang, J. J., Park, N., & Lee, S. (2023). Social benefits of living in the metaverse: The relationships among social presence, supportive interaction, social self-efficacy, and feelings of loneliness. *Computers in Human Behavior*, 139, 107498. DOI: 10.1016/j.chb.2022.107498

Oliver, D., & Roos, J. (2005). Decision-making in high-velocity environments: The importance of guiding principles. *Organization Studies*, 26(6), 889–913. DOI: 10.1177/0170840605054609

Olson, E. M., & Olson, K. C. (2024). Exploring the Feasibility of AI-Generated Logo Concepts. *Design Management Review*, 35(2), 20–27. DOI: 10.1111/drev.12394

Oluwatoyin, A. M., Olufunke, A. P., & Salome, I. O. (2018). The Impact of Market Orientation on Performance of Selected Hotels in Ondo State, Nigeria. *Open Journal of Business and Management*, 06(03), 616–631. DOI: 10.4236/ojbm.2018.63047

Omoregie, O. K., Addae, J. A., Coffie, S., Ampong, G. O. A., & Ofori, K. S. (2019). Factors influencing consumer loyalty: Evidence from the Ghanaian retail banking industry. *International Journal of Bank Marketing*, 37(3), 798–820. DOI: 10.1108/IJBM-04-2018-0099

Ooi, K.-B., Tan, G. W.-H., Al-Emran, M., Al-Sharafi, M. A., Capatina, A., Chakraborty, A., Dwivedi, Y. K., Huang, T.-L., Kar, A. K., Lee, V.-H., Loh, X.-M., Micu, A., Mikalef, P., Mogaji, E., Pandey, N., Raman, R., Rana, N. P., Sarker, P., Sharma, A., & Wong, L.-W. (2023). The potential of generative artificial intelligence across disciplines: Perspectives and future directions. *Journal of Computer Information Systems*, 1–32. DOI: 10.1080/08874417.2023.2261010

Oppenheim, M. (2018, October 11) Amazon scraps 'sexist AI' recruitment tool. *Independent*. https://www.independent.co.uk/tech/amazon-ai-sexist-recruitment-tool-algorithm-a8579161.html

Ordonez-Ponce, E., Clarke, A., & MacDonald, A. (2021). Business contributions to the sustainable development goals through community sustainability partnerships. *Sustainability Accounting. Management and Policy Journal*, 12(6), 1239–1267. DOI: 10.1108/SAMPJ-03-2020-0068

Orodho, A. J., & Kombo, D. K. (2002). Research methods. Nairobi: Kenyatta University, Institute of Open Learning. *International Journal of Economics, Commerce and Management, 39*(7), 48-50.

Ortega-Bolaños, R., Bernal-Salcedo, J., Ortiz, M. G., Sarmiento, J. G., Ruz, G. A., & Tabares-Soto, R. (2024). Applying the ethics of AI: A systematic review of tools for developing and assessing AI- based systems. *Artificial Intelligence Review*, 57(5), 110. Advance online publication. DOI: 10.1007/s10462-024-10740-3

Osifo, O. C. (2023). Transparency and its roles in realizing greener AI. *Journal of Information. Communication and Ethics in Society*, 21(2), 202–218. DOI: 10.1108/JICES-11-2022-0097

Othman, B. (2020). The Influence of Total Quality Management on Competitive Advantage towards Bank Organizations: Evidence from Erbil/Iraq. *International Journal of Psychosocial Rehabilitation*, 24(5), 3427–3439. DOI: 10.37200/IJPR/V24I5/PR202053

Ouaddi, C., Benaddi, L., Souha, A., & Jakimi, A. (2024, 24-26 April 2024). A comparative and analysis study for recommending a chatbot development tool. *2024 International Conference on Global Aeronautical Engineering and Satellite Technology (GAST)*. DOI: 10.1109/GAST60528.2024.10520754

Overgoor, G., Chica, M., Rand, W., & Weishampel, A. (2019). Letting the computers take over: Using AI to solve marketing problems. *California Management Review*, 61(4), 156–185. DOI: 10.1177/0008125619859318

Owyang, J., Lovett, J., Peterson, E. T., Li, C., & Tran, C. (2010). *Social marketing analytics: A new framework for measuring results in social media*. Altimeter Group.

Oxford Internet Institute. (2020, January). *Human in the loop*. https://atozofai.withgoogle.com/intl/pt-BR/human-in-the-loop/

Oyeniyi, L. D., Ugochukwu, C. E., & Mhlongo, N. Z.Lawrence Damilare OyeniyiChinonye Esther UgochukwuNoluthando Zamanjomane Mhlongo. (2024). Implementing AI in banking customer service: A review of current trends and future applications. *International Journal of Science and Research Archive*, 11(2), 1492–1509. DOI: 10.30574/ijsra.2024.11.2.0639

P&G. (2022). Leveraging Technology to Improve The Lives of P&G Consumers. https://us.pg.com/blogs/executive-talks-innovation-vittorio-cretella/

Pal, A., Parhi, P., & Aggarwal, M. (2017). An improved content based collaborative filtering algorithm for movie recommendations. *10th International Conference on Contemporary Computing, IC3 2017. 2018-January* (pp. 01-03). Noida: Institute of Electrical and Electronics Engineers Inc. DOI: 10.1109/IC3.2017.8284357

Pala, E., Kapitan, S., & van Esch, P. (2022). Simulated satiation through reality-enhancing technology. *Psychology and Marketing*, 39(3), 483–494. DOI: 10.1002/mar.21582

Pancras, J., & Sudhir, K. (2007). Optimal marketing strategies for a customer data intermediary. *JMR, Journal of Marketing Research*, 44(4), 560–578. DOI: 10.1509/jmkr.44.4.560

Pang, B., & Lee, L. (2008). Opinion mining and sentiment analysis. *Foundations and Trends® in Information Retrieval, 2*(1-2), 1-135.

Pang, B., & Lee, L. (2008). Opinion Mining and Sentiment Analysis. *Foundations and Trends in Information Retrieval*, 2(1-2), 1–135. DOI: 10.1561/1500000011

Pankaj, K. (2022, Sept 07). *Google Lens: For the Constantly Inquisitive.* Retrieved Jun 20, 2024, from https://www.copperpodip.com: https://www.copperpodip.com/post/what-is-google-lens

Pansare, P. (2024). Futuristic trends in artificial intelligence. In *Futuristic trends in management* (Vol. 3, Book 27, pp. 81-102). IIP Series. DOI: 10.58532/V3BH-MA27P2CH3

Pansare, R., Yadav, G., Garza-Reyes, J. A., & Raosaheb Nagare, M. (2023). Assessment of Sustainable Development Goals through Industry 4.0 and reconfigurable manufacturing system practices. *Journal of Manufacturing Technology Management*, 34(3), 383–413. DOI: 10.1108/JMTM-05-2022-0206

Pansari, A., & Kumar, V. (2017). Customer engagement: The construct, antecedents, and consequences. *Journal of the Academy of Marketing Science*, 45(3), 294–311. DOI: 10.1007/s11747-016-0485-6

Pantano, E., Carlson, J., Spanaki, K., & Christodoulides, G. (2024). Guest editorial: More supportive or more distractive? Investigating the negative effects of technology at the customer interface. *International Journal of Information Management*, 75, 102752. DOI: 10.1016/j.ijinfomgt.2023.102752

Pantano, E., Pedeliento, G., & Christodoulides, G. (2022). A strategic framework for technological innovations in support of the customer experience: A focus on luxury retailers. *Journal of Retailing and Consumer Services*, 66, 102959. DOI: 10.1016/j.jretconser.2022.102959

Pantano, E., & Scarpi, D. (2022). I, robot, you, consumer: Measuring artificial intelligence types and their effect on consumers emotions in service. *Journal of Service Research*, 25(4), 583–600. DOI: 10.1177/10946705221103538

Parise, S., Guinan, P. J., & Kafka, R. (2016). Solving the crisis of immediacy: How digital technology can transform the customer experience. *Business Horizons*, 59(4), 411–420. DOI: 10.1016/j.bushor.2016.03.004

Park, G., Yim, M. C., Chung, J., & Lee, S. (2023). Effect of AI chatbot empathy and identity disclosure on willingness to donate: The mediation of humanness and social presence. *Behaviour & Information Technology*, 42(12), 1998–2010. DOI: 10.1080/0144929X.2022.2105746

Park, J. H., Chung, H., Kim, K. H., Kim, J. J., & Lee, C. (2021). The impact of technological capability on financial performance in the semiconductor industry. *Sustainability*, 13(2), 1–20. DOI: 10.3390/su13020489 PMID: 34123411

Parmar, A., & Rajgor, A. (2023). Enhancing fashion recommendations: Deep neural networks for personalized outfit suggestions. *International Journal of Scientific Research in Science and Technology*, 10(3), 576–581. DOI: 10.32628/IJSRST523103117

Pataranutaporn, P., Liu, R., Finn, E., & Maes, P. (2023). Influencing human–AI interaction by priming beliefs about AI can increase perceived trustworthiness, empathy and effectiveness. *Nature Machine Intelligence*, 5(10), 1076–1086. DOI: 10.1038/s42256-023-00720-7

Patil, S. R., Jadhav, S. N., & Nimbagal, S. (2024). A study on ethical implications of using technology in ESG investing and ensuring unbiased decision making. *Multidisciplinary Science Journal*, 6(8), 2024153. DOI: 10.31893/multiscience.2024153

Patterson, P., Yu, T., & De Ruyter, K. (2006, December). Understanding customer engagement in services. In *Advancing theory, maintaining relevance, proceedings of ANZMAC 2006 conference*, Brisbane (Vol. 4, No. 6, pp. 1-8).

Payne, A., & Frow, P. (2017). Relationship marketing: Looking backwards towards the future. *Journal of Services Marketing*, 31(1), 11–15. DOI: 10.1108/JSM-11-2016-0380

Payne, E. H. M., Dahl, A. J., & Peltier, J. W. (2021). Digital servitization value co-creation framework for AI services: A research agenda for digital transformation in financial service ecosystems. *Journal of Research in Interactive Marketing*, 15(2), 200–222. DOI: 10.1108/JRIM-12-2020-0252

Peddie, J. (2017). *Augmented Reality: Where We Will All Live*. Springer. DOI: 10.1007/978-3-319-54502-8

Peltier, J. W., Dahl, A. J., & Schibrowsky, J. A. (2024). Artificial intelligence in interactive marketing: A conceptual framework and research agenda. *Journal of Research in Interactive Marketing*, 18(1), 54–90. DOI: 10.1108/JRIM-01-2023-0030

Peltier, J., Schibrowsky, J. A., Schultz, D. E., & Zahay, D. (2006). Interactive IMC: The relational-transactional continuum and the synergistic use of customer data. *Journal of Advertising Research*, 46(2), 146–159. DOI: 10.2501/S0021849906060193

Peng, C., van Doorn, J., Eggers, F., & Wieringa, J. E. (2022). The effect of required warmth on consumer acceptance of artificial intelligence in service: The moderating role of AI-human collaboration. *International Journal of Information Management*, 66, 102533. DOI: 10.1016/j.ijinfomgt.2022.102533

Pentina, I., Hancock, T., & Xie, T. (2023). Exploring relationship development with social chatbots: A mixed-method study of replika. *Computers in Human Behavior*, 140, 107600. DOI: 10.1016/j.chb.2022.107600

Perez-Vega, R., Hopkinson, P., Singhal, A., & Waite, K. (2020). Special session: relationship intelligence: affordance of AI in practice: an abstract. In *Developments in Marketing Science:Proceedings of the Academy of Marketing Science* (pp. 141-142). Springer Nature. DOI: 10.1007/978-3-030-42545-6_35

Perry, A. (2023). AI will never convey the essence of human empathy. *Nature Human Behaviour*, 7(11), 1808–1809. DOI: 10.1038/s41562-023-01675-w PMID: 37474839

Pessach, D., & Shmueli, E. (2020, January 1). *Algorithmic Fairness*. doi:/arXiv.2001.09784DOI: 10.48550

Petersen, J. A., & Kumar, V. (2015, April 01). Perceived risk, product returns, and optimal resource allocation: Evidence from a field experiment. *JMR, Journal of Marketing Research*, 52(02), 268–285. DOI: 10.1509/jmr.14.0174

Peters, K., Chen, Y., Kaplan, A. M., Ognibeni, B., & Pauwels, K. (2013). Social media metrics—A framework and guidelines for managing social media. *Journal of Interactive Marketing*, 27(4), 281–298. DOI: 10.1016/j.intmar.2013.09.007

Petrescu, M., & Krishen, A. S. (2023). Hybrid intelligence: Human–AI collaboration in marketing analytics. *Journal of Marketing Analytics*, 11(3), 263–274. DOI: 10.1057/s41270-023-00245-3

Petrescu, M., Krishen, A. S., Kachen, S., & Gironda, J. T. (2022). AI-based innovation in B2B marketing: An interdisciplinary framework incorporating academic and practitioner perspectives. *Industrial Marketing Management*, 103, 61–72. DOI: 10.1016/j.indmarman.2022.03.001

Petzer, D. J., & Roberts-Lombard, M. (2021). Delight and Commitment—Revisiting the Satisfaction-Loyalty Link. *Journal of Relationship Marketing*, 20(4), 282–318. DOI: 10.1080/15332667.2020.1855068

Pfeffer, J., Zorbach, T., & Carley, K. M. (2014). Understanding online firestorms: Negative word-of- mouth dynamics in social media networks. *Journal of Marketing Communications*, 20(1-2), 117–128. DOI: 10.1080/13527266.2013.797778

Pillai, M. C. (2024). The Evolution of Customer Service: Identifying the Impact of Artificial Intelligence on Employment and Management in Call Centres. *Journal of Business Management and Information Systems*. .DOI: 10.48001/jbmis.2024.si1010

Pillarisetty, R., & Mishra, P. (2022). A Review of AI Tools and Customer Experience in Online Fashion Retail. *E-Business Research, 18*, 0-12.

Pinto, F. M., Marques, A., & Santos, M. F. (2009). Ontology-supported database marketing. *Journal of Database Marketing and Customer Strategy Management*, 16(2), 76–91. DOI: 10.1057/dbm.2009.9

Piotrowicz, W., & Cuthbertson, R. (2014). Introduction to the Special Issue Information Technology in Retail: Toward Omnichannel Retailing. *International Journal of Electronic Commerce*, 18(4), 5–16. DOI: 10.2753/JEC1086-4415180400

Pires, P. B., Santos, J. D., & Pereira, I. V. (2024). Artificial Neural Networks: History and State of the Art. In Encyclopedia of Information Science and Technology, Sixth Edition (pp. 1-25). IGI Global. DOI: 10.4018/978-1-6684-7366-5.ch037

Pitardi, V., & Marriott, H. R. (2021). Alexa, she's not human but… Unveiling the drivers of consumers' trust in voice-based artificial intelligence. *Psychology and Marketing*, 38(4), 626–642. DOI: 10.1002/mar.21457

Pizoń, J., & Gola, A. (2023). Human–machine relationship—Perspective and future roadmap for Industry 5.0 solutions. *Machines (Basel)*, 11(2), 203. DOI: 10.3390/machines11020203

Pol, L. G. (1986). Marketing and the demographic perspective. *Journal of Consumer Marketing*, 3(1), 57–65. DOI: 10.1108/eb008153

Poole, D. L., & Mackworth, A. K. (2010). *Artificial Intelligence: Foundations of Computational Agents*. Cambridge University Press. DOI: 10.1017/CBO9780511794797

Poornima, S., Mohanavalli, S., Swarnalatha, S., & Kesavarthini, I. (2021). Dynamic Pricing of Products Based on Visual Quality and E-Commerce Factors. *International Conference on Mathematical Analysis and Computing, ICMAC 2019* (pp. 413-427). Springer. DOI: 10.1007/978-981-33-4646-8_34

Porter, M. E. (1985). *The Competitive Advantage: Creating and Sustaining Superior Performance*. Free Press.

Poulis, A., Rizomyliotis, I., & Konstantoulaki, K. (2019). Do firms still need to be social? Firm generated content in social media. *Information Technology & People*, 32(2), 387–404. DOI: 10.1108/ITP-03-2018-0134

Pöyry, E., Hietaniemi, N., Parvinen, P., Hamari, J., & Kaptein, M. (2017). Personalized product recommendations: Evidence from the field. In S. R. Bui T.X. (Ed.), *50th Annual Hawaii International Conference on System Sciences, HICSS 2017. 2017-January* (pp. 3859-3867). Big Island: IEEE Computer Society. https://www.scopus.com/record/display.uri?eid=2-s2.0-85068324707&origin=scopusAI

Prahalad, C. K., & Ramaswamy, V. (2004). Co-creation experiences: The next practice in value creation. *Journal of Interactive Marketing*, 18(3), 5–14. DOI: 10.1002/dir.20015

Prasad, R., & Choudhary, P. (2021). State-of-the-Art of Artificial Intelligence. Journal of Mobile Multimedia. DOI: 10.13052/jmm1550-4646.171322

Prasad, N. S. (2024). A Study to Know the Impact of AI on Sustainability of Products in the Carbonated Beverages. *International Journal of Scientific Research in Engineering and Management*, 08(03), 1–15. DOI: 10.55041/IJSREM29113

Prassas, G., Pramataris, K. C., & Papaemmanouil, O. (2001). Dynamic recommendations in internet retailing. *Global Co-Operation in the New Millennium*, (pp. 368-379). Slovenia.

Prataviera, L. B., Creazza, A., Perotti, S., & Rodrigues, V. S. (2023). How to align logistics environmental sustainability with corporate strategy? An Italian perspective. *International Journal of Logistics Research and Applications*, 1–23. .DOI: 10.1080/13675567.2023.2230916

Prates, M. O. R., Avelar, P. H., & Lamb, L. C. (2020). Assessing gender bias in machine translation: A case study with Google Translate. *Neural Computing & Applications*, 32(10), 6363–6381. DOI: 10.1007/s00521-019-04144-6

Prentice, C., & Nguyen, M. (2020). Engaging and retaining customers with AI and employee service. *Journal of Retailing and Consumer Services*, 56, 102186. DOI: 10.1016/j.jretconser.2020.102186

Presutti, M., Savioli, M., & Odorici, V. (2020). Strategic orientation of hotels: Evidence from a contingent approach. *Tourism Economics*, 26(7), 1212–1230. DOI: 10.1177/1354816619868886

Prey, R. (2020). Locating Power in Platformization: Music Streaming Playlists and Curatorial Power. *Social Media + Society*, 6(2), 2056305120933291. DOI: 10.1177/2056305120933291

Primožič, L., & Kutnar, A. (2022). Sustainability Communication in Global Consumer Brands. *Sustainability (Basel)*, 14(20), 13586. Advance online publication. DOI: 10.3390/su142013586

Prior, D. D., Buttle, F., & Maklan, S. (2024). *Customer relationship management: Concepts, applications and technologies.* Taylor & Francis.

Priscille Biehlmann. (2023, October 1). 'You've got to be data-driven': The fashion forecasters using AI to predict the next trend. The Guardian. https://www.theguardian.com/technology/2023/oct/01/ai-artificial-intelligence-fashion-trend-forecasting-style

Priyanto, P., & Murwaningsari, E. (2022). The Effect of Sustainability Innovation, Organizational Learning on Firm Performance with Competitive Advantage as Moderation. *International Journal of Academic Research in Accounting. Finance and Management Sciences*, 12(1), 257–275. DOI: 10.6007/IJARAFMS/v12-i1/10832

Puntoni, S., Reczek, R. W., Giesler, M., & Botti, S. (2020). Consumers and Artificial intelligence: An Experiential perspective. *Journal of Marketing*, 85(1), 131–151. DOI: 10.1177/0022242920953847

Puspaningrum, A. (2020). Market Orientation, Competitive Advantage and Marketing Performance of Small Medium Enterprises (SMEs). *Journal of Economics, Business, &. Accountancy Ventura*, 23(1), 19–27. DOI: 10.14414/jebav.v23i1.1847

Pykett, J., Jones, R., Welsh, M., & Whitehead, M. (2014). The art of choosing and the politics of social marketing. *Policy Studies*, 35(2), 97–114. DOI: 10.1080/01442872.2013.875141

Qiu, J., Liu, J., & Shen, Y. (2021). Computer Vision Technology Based on Deep Learning. .DOI: 10.1109/ICIBA52610.2021.9687873

Quintana, C., Reiser, B. J., Davis, E. A., Krajcik, J., Fretz, E., Duncan, R. G., & Soloway, E. (2018). A scaffolding design framework for software to support science inquiry. In *Scaffolding* (pp. 337–386). Psychology Press.

Rabata, R. (2024). *Case studies: Successful AI implementations in various industries.* Capella Solutions. https://www.capellasolutions.com/blog/case-studies-successful-ai-implementations-in-various-industries

Rabby, F., Chimhundu, R., & Hassan, R. (2021). Artificial intelligence in digital marketing influences consumer behaviour: A review and theoretical foundation for future research. *Academy of Marketing Studies Journal*, 25(5), 1–7.

Radford, A., & Narasimhan, K. (2018). Improving Language Understanding by Generative Pre-Training. https://hayate-lab.com/wp-content/uploads/2023/05/43372bfa750340059ad87ac8e538c53b.pdf

Raewf, M., Aissa, S. A. H., & Thabit, T. (2021). The impact of quality, cost, and lead time on competitive advantage: Case of SMEs operating in Iraq. *Economic Studies Journal, 19*(03).

Rahman, M. S., Bag, S., Gupta, S., & Sivarajah, U. (2023). Technology readiness of B2B firms and AI-based customer relationship management capability for enhancing social sustainability performance. *Journal of Business Research, 156*, 113525. .DOI: 10.1016/j.jbusres.2022.113525

Rahman, M. M., Hussain, M. T., Moon, S. P., Tisha, M. M., & Lima, M. T. (2021). Impact of Customer Relationship Management (CRM) on Organizational Performance: A Study from the Perspective of Bangladesh. *American Journal of Trade and Policy*, 8(3), 225–230. DOI: 10.18034/ajtp.v8i3.609

Rahman, M. M., & Saima, F. N. (2018). Efficiency of board composition on firm performance: Empirical evidence from listed manufacturing firms of Bangladesh. *The Journal of Asian Finance. Economics and Business*, 5(2), 53–61. DOI: 10.13106/jafeb.2018.vol5.no2.53

Rahman, S. M., Carlson, J., & Chowdhury, N. H. (2022a). SafeCX: A framework for safe customer experience in omnichannel retailing. *Journal of Services Marketing*, 36(4), 499–529. DOI: 10.1108/JSM-04-2021-0114

Rahman, S. M., Carlson, J., Gudergan, S. P., Wetzels, M., & Grewal, D. (2022b). Perceived Omnichannel Customer Experience (OCX): Concept, measurement, and impact. *Journal of Retailing*, 98(4), 611–632. DOI: 10.1016/j.jretai.2022.03.003

Raikwar, P. P., Bhandari, G. M., Patil, S. S., & Shivale, N. M. (2024). Robust Cloth Warping via Multi-Scale Patch Adversarial Loss for Virtual Try-On Framework. *Jisuanji Yanjiu Yu Fazhan*, 24(4), 89–92.

Rajendran, R. K., Priya, T. M., & Chitrarasu, K. (2024). Natural Language Processing (NLP) in chatbot design: NLP's impact on chatbot architecture. In *Design and Development of Emerging Chatbot Technology* (pp. 102-113). IGI Global. DOI: 10.4018/979-8-3693-1830-0.ch006

Raji, M. A., Olodo, H. B., Oke, T. T., Addy, W. A., Ofodile, O. C., & Oyewole, A. T. (2024). E-commerce and consumer behavior: A review of AI-powered personalization and market trends. *GSC Advanced Research and Reviews, 18*(3), 066-077. .DOI: 10.30574/gscarr.2024.18.3.0090

Rakib, M. A., Chang, H. J., & Jones, R. P. (2022). Effective Sustainability Messages Triggering Consumer Emotion and Action: An Application of the Social Cognitive Theory and the Dual-Process Model. *Sustainability (Basel)*, 14(5), 2505. Advance online publication. DOI: 10.3390/su14052505

Ramadhan, A. I. (2020). Pengaruh Brand Image, Product Involvement, dan Brand Engagement Terhadap Purchase Intention Teh Pucuk di Kota Jakarta. *Jurnal Manajemen Bisnis dan Kewirausahaan, 4*(1), 42-47.

Ramassa, P., & Di Fabio, C. (2016). Social media for investor relations: A literature review and future directions. *The International Journal of Digital Accounting Research*, 5, 117–134.

Rambocas, M., & Pacheco, B. G. (2018). Online sentiment analysis in marketing research: A review. *Journal of Research in Interactive Marketing*, 12(2), 146–163. DOI: 10.1108/JRIM-05-2017-0030

Rana, J. (2024, July 15). *AI in customer service: Ways to use it for amazing support.* ReveChat. https://www.revechat.com/blog/ai-in-customer-service/

Rana, J., Gaur, L., Singh, G., Awan, U., & Rasheed, M. I. (2022). Reinforcing customer journey through artificial intelligence: A review and research agenda. *International Journal of Emerging Markets*, 17(7), 1738–1758. DOI: 10.1108/IJOEM-08-2021-1214

Randhawa, K., Wilden, R., & Gudergan, S. (2021). How to innovate toward an ambidextrous business model? The role of dynamic capabilities and market orientation. *Journal of Business Research*, 130, 618–634. DOI: 10.1016/j.jbusres.2020.05.046

Rashid, S. M., Ali, K. A. A., Mousa, K. M., & Pooyanmehr, M. (2024). Developing Business Management Concepts in the Economic Field Based on Artificial Intelligence in Light of Increasing Data. In *Preprints*: *Preprints*.

Rather, R. A. (2021). Monitoring the impacts of tourism-based social media, risk perception and fear on tourist's attitude and revisiting behaviour in the wake of COVID-19 pandemic. *Current Issues in Tourism*, 24(23), 3275–3283. DOI: 10.1080/13683500.2021.1884666

Rather, R. A., & Hollebeek, L. D. (2021). Customers' service-related engagement, experience, and behavioral intent: Moderating role of age. *Journal of Retailing and Consumer Services*, 60, 102453. DOI: 10.1016/j.jretconser.2021.102453

Rather, R. A., Hollebeek, L. D., & Rasoolimanesh, S. M. (2022). First-time versus repeat tourism customer engagement, experience, and value cocreation: An empirical investigation. *Journal of Travel Research*, 61(3), 549–564. DOI: 10.1177/0047287521997572

Rathi, T., & Ravi, V. (2016). Customer lifetime value measurement using machine learning techniques. In Artificial Intelligence: Concepts, Methodologies, Tools, and Applications (Vol. 4, pp. 3013-3022). IGI Global. DOI: 10.4018/978-1-5225-1759-7.ch124

Rauschnabel, P. A., Felix, R., & Hinsch, C. (2019). Augmented reality marketing: How mobile AR-apps can improve brands through inspiration. *Journal of Retailing and Consumer Services*, 49, 43–53. DOI: 10.1016/j.jretconser.2019.03.004

Reddy, S. R. (2021). Predictive Analytics in Customer Relationship Management: Utilizing Big Data and AI to Drive Personalized Marketing Strategies. *Australian Journal of Machine Learning Research and Applications*, 1(1), 1–12.

Reichheld, F. F. (2001). *The Loyalty Effect: The Hidden Force Behind Growth, Profits, and Lasting Value*. Harvard Business Review Press.

Reichheld, F. F. (2003). The one number you need to grow. *Harvard Business Review*, 81(12), 46–55. PMID: 14712543

Reis, J. (2024). Customer service through AI-powered human-robot relationships: Where are we now? The case of Henn na cafe, Japan. *Technology in Society*, 77, 102570. DOI: 10.1016/j.techsoc.2024.102570

Reis, J., Amorim, M., Cohen, Y., & Rodrigues, M. (2020). Artificial intelligence in service delivery systems: A systematic literature review. In *Trends and Innovations in Information Systems and Technologies* (Vol. 1, pp. 222–233). Springer. DOI: 10.1007/978-3-030-45688-7_23

Restiana, L. (2021). Customer Perceived Service Quality, Product Quality, Satisfaction and Loyalty in Beauty IPTEK Journal of Proceedings SeriesBusiness. *IPTEK Journal of Proceedings Series*, 1, 288–291. DOI: 10.12962/j23546026.y2020i1.10858

Restrepo, A. N. R., & Lis-Gutiérrez, J. P. (2023). A review of GPT Chat applications in Marketing. *Salud, Ciencia y Tecnologia - Serie de Conferencias, 2*. DOI: 10.56294/sctconf2023514

Rezaei, J., & Ortt, R. (2018). Entrepreneurial orientation and firm performance: The mediating role of functional performances. *Management Research Review*, 41(7), 878–900. DOI: 10.1108/MRR-03-2017-0092

Rezig, E. K., Cafarella, M., & Gadepally, V. (2021). Technical Report on Data Integration and Preparation. https://arxiv.org/pdf/2103.01986

Ricca, F., Marchetto, A., & Stocco, A. (2021). AI-based test automation: A grey literature analysis. In *Proceedings - 2021 IEEE 14th International Conference on Software Testing, Verification and Validation Workshops, ICSTW 2021* (pp. 263–270). DOI: 10.1109/ICSTW52544.2021.00051

Rice, D. M. (2014). Neural calculus. In *Calculus of Thought Neuromorphic Logistic Regression in Cognitive Machines* (pp. 125–144). Elsevier., DOI: 10.1016/B978-0-12-410407-5.00005-2

Rich, E., & Knight, K. (1991). *Artificial Intelligence* (2nd ed.). McGraw-Hill.

Rigby, D. (2011). The Future of Shopping. *Harvard Business Review*. https://hbr.org/2011/12/the-future-of-shopping

Rizard, S. R., Waluyo, B., & Jaswir, I. (2022). Impact of brand equity and service quality on the reputation of universities and students' intention to choose them: The case of IIUM and UIN. *F1000 Research*, 11, 1412. DOI: 10.12688/f1000research.122386.1 PMID: 37767070

Roba, G. B., & Maric, P. (2023). AI in Customer Relationship Management. In *Developments in Information and Knowledge Management Systems for Business Applications* (pp. 469–487). Springer., DOI: 10.1007/978-3-031-25695-0_21

Rodak, O. (2020). Hashtag hijacking and crowdsourcing transparency: Social media affordances and the governance of farm animal protection. *Agriculture and Human Values*, 37(2), 281–294. DOI: 10.1007/s10460-019-09984-5

Rodgers, W., & Nguyen, T. (2022). Advertising benefits from ethical AI algorithmic purchase decision pathways. *Journal of Business Ethics*, 178(4), 1043–1061. DOI: 10.1007/s10551-022-05048-7

Roess, M. (2016). Old answers to new questions: Turing tests in the era of big data. *PsycCRITIQUES*, •••, 61.

Rohan, D. J., & Banubakode, A. (2024). The Implications of Artificial Intelligence on the Employment Sector. *International Journal For Multidisciplinary Research*, 6(3), 22716. Advance online publication. DOI: 10.36948/ijfmr.2024.v06i03.22716

Rolls-Royce. (2018). *Rolls-Royce's IntelligentEngine Vision Takes Shape*. Retrieved from Rolls-Royce.

Roma, P., & Aloini, D. (2019). How does brand-related user-generated content differ across social media? Evidence reloaded. *Journal of Business Research*, 96, 322–339. DOI: 10.1016/j.jbusres.2018.11.055

Rondonuwu, A. O. R., Freddy. (2024). The Influence of Brand Image Brand Awareness and Promotion on Purchase Decisions for Ubiquiti Brand IT Network Devices in Indonesia. *Co-Value: Jurnal Ekonomi, Koperasi & Kewirausahaan, 14.*

Roozen, I., Raedts, M., & Waetermans, G. (2022). Does a chatbot's location influence consumer attitude and intentions? *International Journal of Internet Marketing and Advertising*, 16(1), 24–38.

Rosário, A. T., & Dias, J. C. (2023b). The New Digital Economy and Sustainability: Challenges and Opportunities. *Sustainability (Switzerland), 15(14 C7 -10902).* .DOI: 10.3390/su151410902

Rosário, A. T., & Dias, J. C. (2023c). Marketing Strategies on Social Media Platforms.International *Journal of e-Business Research, 19(1 C7 - 316969).* .DOI: 10.4018/IJEBR.316969

Rosário, A. T., & Dias, J. C. (2023a). How has data-driven marketing evolved: Challenges and opportunities with emerging technologies. *International Journal of Information Management Data Insights*, 3(2), 100203. DOI: 10.1016/j.jjimei.2023.100203

Rosenblatt, F. (1958). The perceptron: A probabilistic model for information storage and organization in the brain. *Psychological Review*, 65(6), 386–408. DOI: 10.1037/h0042519 PMID: 13602029

Roski, J., Maier, E. J., Vigilante, K., Kane, E. A., & Matheny, M. E. (2021). Enhancing trust in AI through industry self-governance. *Journal of the American Medical Informatics Association : JAMIA*, 28(7), 1582–1590. DOI: 10.1093/jamia/ocab065 PMID: 33895824

Rossi, P. E., McCulloch, R. E., & Allenby, G. M. (1996). The value of purchase history data in target marketing. *Marketing Science*, 15(4), 321–340. DOI: 10.1287/mksc.15.4.321

Rossiter, J. R. (2012). A new C-OAR-SE-based content-valid and predictively valid measure that distinguishes brand love from brand liking. *Marketing Letters*, 23(3), 905–916. DOI: 10.1007/s11002-012-9173-6

Rouhani, S., Ashrafi, A., Zare Ravasan, A., & Afshari, S. (2016). The impact model of business intelligence on decision support and organizational benefits. *Journal of Enterprise Information Management*, 29(1), 19–50. DOI: 10.1108/JEIM-12-2014-0126

Roy, G., Jain, V., & Salunke, P. (2023). Data Processing and AI-Technology Integration for Personalized Services. In *Artificial Intelligence in Customer Service: The Next Frontier to Personalized Engagement* (pp. 205-228). Springer International Publishing. DOI: 10.1007/978-3-031-33898-4_9

Roy, D., Srivastava, R., Jat, M., & Karaca, M. S. (2022). A Complete Overview of Analytics Techniques: Descriptive, Predictive and Prescriptive. In Jeyanthi, P. M., Choudhury, T., Hack-Polay, D., Singh, T. P., & Abujar, S. (Eds.), *Decision Intelligence Analytics and the Implementation of Strategic Business Management* (pp. 20–49). Springer. DOI: 10.1007/978-3-030-82763-2_2

Roy, S. K., Sharma, A., Bose, S., & Singh, G. (2022). Consumer-brand relationship: A brand hate perspective. *Journal of Business Research*, 144, 1293–1304. DOI: 10.1016/j.jbusres.2022.02.065

Ruan, Y., Durresi, A., & Alfantoukh, L. (2018). Using Twitter trust network for stock market analysis. *Knowledge-Based Systems*, 145, 207–218. DOI: 10.1016/j.knosys.2018.01.016

Rubera, G., & Kirca, A. H. (2017). You gotta serve somebody: The effects of firm innovation on customer satisfaction and firm value. *Journal of the Academy of Marketing Science*, 45(5), 741–761. DOI: 10.1007/s11747-016-0512-7

Rumelhart, D. E., Hinton, G. E., & Williams, R. J. (1986). Learning representations by back-propagating errors. *Nature*, 323(6088), 533–536. DOI: 10.1038/323533a0

Russell, S., & Norvig, P. (2021). *Artificial Intelligence, Global Edition: A Modern Approach*. Pearson.

Russell, S. J., & Norvig, P. (2009). *Artificial Intelligence: A Modern Approach* (3rd ed.). Prentice-Hall.

Rusthollkarhu, S., Toukola, S., Aarikka-Stenroos, L., & Mahlamäki, T. (2022). Managing B2B customer journeys in digital era: Four management activities with artificial intelligence-empowered tools. *Industrial Marketing Management*, 104, 241–257. DOI: 10.1016/j.indmarman.2022.04.014

Rust, R. T., & Huang, M. H. (2014). The service revolution and the transformation of marketing science. *Marketing Science*, 33(2), 206–221. DOI: 10.1287/mksc.2013.0836

Ryan, M. (2020). In AI we trust: Ethics, artificial intelligence, and reliability. *Science and Engineering Ethics*, 26(5), 2749–2767. DOI: 10.1007/s11948-020-00228-y PMID: 32524425

Rzepka, C., Berger, B., & Hess, T. (2020). Why another customer channel? Consumers' perceived benefits and costs of voice commerce. In B. T.X. (Ed.), *53rd Annual Hawaii International Conference on System Sciences, HICSS 2020* (pp. 4079-4088). Maui: IEEE Computer Society.

Sabate, F., Berbegal-Mirabent, J., Cañabate, A., & Lebherz, P. R. (2014). Factors influencing popularity of branded content in Facebook fan pages. *European Management Journal*, 32(6), 1001–1011. DOI: 10.1016/j.emj.2014.05.001

Sadriwala, M. F., & Sadriwala, K. F. (2022). Perceived usefulness and ease of use of artificial intelligence on marketing innovation. [IJIDE]. *International Journal of Innovation in the Digital Economy*, 13(1), 1–10. DOI: 10.4018/IJIDE.292010

Saha, S., & Srivastava, A. (2014). Predictive Analytics Using Google Cloud Machine Learning. *International Journal of Computer Applications*, 104(17), 12–17.

Sahlgren, O. (2024). Action-guidance and AI ethics: The case of fair machine learning. *AI and Ethics*. Advance online publication. DOI: 10.1007/s43681-024-00437-2

Sahoo, S. (2022). Big data analytics in manufacturing: A bibliometric analysis of research in the field of business management. *International Journal of Production Research*, 60(22), 6793–6821. DOI: 10.1080/00207543.2021.1919333

Sajid, S., Haleem, A., Bahl, S., Javaid, M., Goyal, T., & Mittal, M. (2021). Data science applications for predictive maintenance and materials science in context to Industry 4.0. *Second International Conference on Aspects of Materials Science and Engineering (ICAMSE 2021), 45*, 4898–4905. DOI: 10.1016/j.matpr.2021.01.357

Salem, S. F. (2021). Do relationship marketing constructs enhance consumer retention? An empirical study within the hotel industry. *SAGE Open*, 11(2), 21582440211009224. DOI: 10.1177/21582440211009224

Samosir, J., Indrawan-Santiago, M., & Haghighi, P. D. (2016). An evaluation of data stream processing systems for data driven applications. *Procedia Computer Science*, 80, 439–449. DOI: 10.1016/j.procs.2016.05.322

Sampaio, C. A. F., Hernández, J. M. H., & de Rodrigues, R. J. A. G. (2020). The relationship between market orientation, customer loyalty and business performance: A sample from the Western Europe hotel industry. *Tourism and Hospitality Research*, 20(2), 131–143. DOI: 10.1177/1467358419829179

Sampaio, C., & Régio, M. (2022). Market Orientation and Hotel Industry: Literature Review and Implications for Periods of Market Turmoil. *Journal of Risk and Financial Management*, 15(11), 497. DOI: 10.3390/jrfm15110497

Sanadi, A. M. B. (2022). A Review Paper on Natural Language Processing (NLP). *International Journal of Advanced Research in Science* [IJARSCT]. *Tongxin Jishu*, 2(2), 23–29. DOI: 10.48175/IJARSCT-2685

Sankar, J. G. (2024). AI-Driven Marketing Success Stories: A Case Note of Industry Pioneers. In *AI-Driven Marketing Research and Data Analytics* (pp. 48-66). IGI Global. DOI: 10.4018/979-8-3693-2165-2.ch003

Santra, I. K. (2018). Entrepreneurial orientation and marketing performance of budget hotel smes in Bali Island. *International Journal of Entrepreneurship*, 22(4), 1–11.

Sarkar, S. A., Mukhopadhyay, A. R., & Ghosh, S. K. (2013). Improvement of claim processing cycle time through lean six sigma methodology. *International Journal of Lean Six Sigma*, 4(2), 171–183. DOI: 10.1108/20401461311319347

Sarwar, B., Karypis, G., Konstan, J., & Riedl, J. (2001, April). Item-based collaborative filtering recommendation algorithms. In *Proceedings of the 10th international conference on World Wide Web* (pp. 285-295). DOI: 10.1145/371920.372071

Sasmita, M. T., Arie Yudhistira, P. G., & Aditya Aristana, I. K. G. (2022). The Influence of Brand Image and Brand Trust on Consumer Loyalty (Case Study on Consumers of PT Citilink Indonesia Branch Office Denpasar). *TRJ Tourism Research Journal*, 6(1), 60. Advance online publication. DOI: 10.30647/trj.v6i1.129

Saura, J. R., Ribeiro-Soriano, D., & Palacios-Marqués, D. (2021). Setting B2B digital marketing in artificial intelligence-based CRMs: A review and directions for future research. *Industrial Marketing Management*, 98, 161–178. DOI: 10.1016/j.indmarman.2021.08.006

Schepman, A., & Rodway, P. (2023). The General Attitudes towards Artificial Intelligence Scale (GAAIS): Confirmatory validation and associations with personality, corporate distrust, and general trust. *International Journal of Human-Computer Interaction*, 39(13), 1–18. DOI: 10.1080/10447318.2022.2085400

Schivinski, B., & Dabrowski, D. (2016). The effect of social media communication on consumer perceptions of brands. *Journal of Marketing Communications*, 22(2), 189–214. DOI: 10.1080/13527266.2013.871323

Schlesinger, L. A. (2009). Customer Experience Creation: Determinants, dynamics and management strategies. *Journal of Retailing*, 85(1), 31–41. DOI: 10.1016/j.jretai.2008.11.001

Schneider, B., & Bowen, D. E. (2010). Winning the service game: Revisiting the rules by which people co-create value. In *Handbook of Service Science* (pp. 31–59). Springer US. DOI: 10.1007/978-1-4419-1628-0_4

Schneider, B., González-Romá, V., Ostroff, C., West, M., & Management Labs, T. (2017). Organizational climate and culture: Reflections on the history of the constructs in Journal of Applied Psychology. *The Journal of Applied Psychology*, 102(3), 468–482. DOI: 10.1037/apl0000090 PMID: 28125256

Schroeder, J. E. (2014). Branding in Perspective: The Cultural Code of Branding. *Marketing Theory*, 14(1), 131–143.

Schrotenboer, D. W. (2019). *The impact of artificial intelligence along the customer journey: a systematic literature review*. https://purl.utwente.nl/essays/78520

Schwartz, R., Vassilev, A., Greene, K., Perine, L., Burt, A., & Hall, P. (2022). Towards a standard for identifying and managing bias in artificial intelligence (NIST Special Publication 1270). *National Institute of Standards and Technology, 10.*

Schweidel, D. A., & Moe, W. W. (2014). Listening in on social media: A joint model of sentiment and venue format choice. *JMR, Journal of Marketing Research*, 51(4), 387–402. DOI: 10.1509/jmr.12.0424

Seitz, L., Bekmeier-Feuerhahn, S., & Gohil, K. (2022). Can we trust a chatbot like a physician? A qualitative study on understanding the emergence of trust toward diagnostic chatbots. *International Journal of Human-Computer Studies*, 165, 102848. DOI: 10.1016/j.ijhcs.2022.102848

Selmi, N., & Chaney, D. (2018). A measure of revenue management orientation and its mediating role in the relationship between market orientation and performance. *Journal of Business Research*, 89, 99–109. DOI: 10.1016/j.jbusres.2018.04.008

Semwal, M., Akila, K., Manasa, M., Raj, P. S., Motukuru, Y., & Karthik, P. (2024). Machine Learning-Enabled Business Intelligence For Dynamic Pricing Strategies In E-Commerce. *2nd International Conference on Disruptive Technologies, ICDT 2024* (pp. 116-120). Greater Noida: Institute of Electrical and Electronics Engineers Inc. DOI: 10.1109/ICDT61202.2024.10489724

Sephora. (2017). Sephora Virtual Artist Uses AI to Transform Beauty Shopping Experience. Business Wire. Retrieved from Business Wire.

Seranmadevi, R., Chakraverty, S., Raj, B., Kudapa, V. K., Hepziba, R. E., & Suleimenova, K. (2022, 25-27 May 2022). Utilisation of Virtual Assistant and Its Impact on Retail Industry. In *2022 6th International Conference on Intelligent Computing and Control Systems (ICICCS)*, DOI: 10.1109/ICICCS53718.2022.9788243

Servera-Francés, D., Fuentes-Blasco, M., & Piqueras-Tomás, L. (2020). The Importance of Sustainable Practices in Value Creation and Consumers' Commitment with Companies' Commercial Format. *Sustainability (Basel)*, 12(23), 9852. Advance online publication. DOI: 10.3390/su12239852

Shaalan, A., Eid, R., & Tourky, M. (2022a). De-linking from western epistemologies: Using guanxi-type relationships to attract and retain hotel guests in the Middle East. *Management and Organization Review*, 18(5), 859–891. DOI: 10.1017/mor.2021.21

Shaalan, A., Tourky, M. E., & Ibrahim, K. (2022b). The chatbot revolution: Companies and consumers in a new digital age. In Hanlon, A., & Tuten, T. L. (Eds.), *The SAGE Handbook of Digital Marketing* (Vol. 1, pp. 369–392). SAGE Publications Ltd., DOI: 10.4135/9781529782509.n21

Shahid, M. Z., & Li, G. (2019). Impact of Artificial Intelligence in Marketing: A Perspective of Marketing Professionals of Pakistan. *Global Journal of Management and Business Research*, 19(2), 27–33.

Shankar, V. (2018). How artificial intelligence (AI) is reshaping retailing. *Journal of Retailing*, 94(4), vi–xi. DOI: 10.1016/S0022-4359(18)30076-9

Sharma, S., Baishya, K., Pandey, M., & Rautaray, S. S. (2021). Hybrid Product Recommendation System using Popularity Based and Content-Based Filtering. *nternational Conference on Data Science, Agents and Artificial Intelligence, ICDSAAI 2023.* Chennai: Institute of Electrical and Electronics Engineers Inc. DOI: 10.1109/ICDSAAI59313.2023.10452564

Sharma, V., & Bose, I. (2024). Unlocking AI's Potential in Customer Service Marketing. In *AI Innovations in Service and Tourism Marketing* (pp. 80-103). IGI Global. DOI: 10.4018/979-8-3693-7909-7.ch005

Sharma, A. K., & Sharma, R. (2023). The role of generative pre-trained transformers (GPTs) in revolutionising digital marketing: A conceptual model. *Journal of Cultural Marketing Strategy*, 8(1), 80–92. DOI: 10.69554/TLVQ2275

Sharma, L., & Gera, A. (2013). A Survey of Recommendation System: Research Challenges. [IJETT]. *International Journal of Engineering Trends and Technology*, 4(5), 1989–1992.

Sharma, R. S., Shaikh, A. A., & Li, E. (2021). Designing Recommendation or Suggestion Systems: Looking to the future. *Electronic Markets*, 31(2), 243–252. DOI: 10.1007/s12525-021-00478-z

Sharma, S. (2023). *AI for Small Business: Leveraging Automation to Stay Ahead*. Lead Management Consultant, SKS Consulting & Advisors., DOI: 10.46679/9788195732234

Sheehan, B., Jin, H. S., & Gottlieb, U. (2020). Customer service chatbots: Anthropomorphism and adoption. *Journal of Business Research*, 115, 14–24. DOI: 10.1016/j.jbusres.2020.04.030

Shekhar, S. K. (2022). Social Marketing Plan to Decrease the COVID-19 Vaccine Hesitancy among Senior Citizens in Rural India. *Sustainability (Basel)*, 14(13), 7561. Advance online publication. DOI: 10.3390/su14137561

Shi, M., & Lewis, V. D. (2020). Using artificial intelligence to analyze fashion trends. arXiv (Cornell University). https://arxiv.org/pdf/2005.00986

Shiferaw, B. (2018). *The effect of internal marketing on customer orientation of employees: the case of selected star hotels in Addis Ababa*. Published Master Thesis. Department of Marketing Management Addis Ababa University School of Commerce.

Shin, H., & Kang, J. (2020). Reducing perceived health risk to attract hotel customers in the COVID-19 pandemic era: Focused on technology innovation for social distancing and cleanliness. *International Journal of Hospitality Management*, 91, 102664. DOI: 10.1016/j.ijhm.2020.102664 PMID: 32921871

Shirazi, F., & Mohammadi, M. (2019). A big data analytics model for customer churn prediction in the retiree segment. *International Journal of Information Management*, 48, 238–253. DOI: 10.1016/j.ijinfomgt.2018.10.005

Shmueli, G., & Koppius, O. R. (2011). Predictive Analytics in Information Systems Research. *Management Information Systems Quarterly*, 35(3), 553–572. DOI: 10.2307/23042796

Shoukat, A. A. S. V. K. (2021). AI-Natural Language Processing (NLP). *International Journal for Research in Applied Science & Engineering Technology (IJRASET)*, 9(8), 135-140. https://www.ijraset.com/fileserve.php?FID=37293

Shovo, N. (2021). Marketing with artificial intelligence and predicting consumer choice. *AI & Society*, 1(1), 6–18.

Shrum, L. J. (2012). *The psychology of entertainment media: Blurring the lines between entertainment and persuasion*. Routledge. DOI: 10.4324/9780203828588

Shukla, P., & Shamurailatpam, S. D. (2022). Conceptualizing the Use of Artificial Intelligence in Customer Relationship Management and Quality of Services: A Digital Disruption in the Indian Banking System. In *Adoption and Implementation of AI in Customer Relationship Management* (pp. 177-201). IGI Global. DOI: 10.4018/978-1-7998-7959-6.ch012

Shumanov, M., & Johnson, L. (2021). Making conversations with chatbots more personalized. *Computers in Human Behavior*, 117, 106627. DOI: 10.1016/j.chb.2020.106627

Siau, K., & Wang, W. (2018). Building trust in AI, machine learning, and robotics. *Cutter Business Technology Journal*, 31(2), 47–53.

Sickles, R. C., & Zelenyuk, V. (2019). Measurement of productivity and efficiency: Theory and practice. In *Measurement of Productivity and Efficiency*. Cambridge University Press., DOI: 10.1017/9781139565981

Siems, E., Seuring, S., & Schilling, L. (2023). Stakeholder roles in sustainable supply chain management: A literature review. *Journal of Business Economics*, 93(4), 747–775. DOI: 10.1007/s11573-022-01117-5

Signalytics. (2023, May 29). *Voice activated shopping*. https://medium.com/@Signalytics/reimagining-e-commerce-how-amazons-voice-activated-shopping-is-impacting-brands-1e8a2c15e5bb

Silver, D., Schrittwieser, J., Simonyan, K., Antonoglou, I., Huang, A., Guez, A., Hubert, T., Baker, L., Lai, M., Bolton, A., Chen, Y., Lillicrap, T., Hui, F., Sifre, L., van den Driessche, G., Graepel, T., & Hassabis, D. (2017). Mastering the game of Go without human knowledge. *Nature*, 550(7676), 354–359. DOI: 10.1038/nature24270 PMID: 29052630

Singh, A. (2021). The Effect of Entrepreneurial Orientation on Business Performance of Small and Medium Scale Enterprises: A Study of Amhara Region of Ethiopia. *SSRN*. DOI: 10.2139/ssrn.3769062

Singh, A., Rana, N. P., & Parayitam, S. (2022). Role of social currency in customer experience and co-creation intention in online travel agencies: Moderation of attitude and subjective norms. International. *Journal of Information Management Data Insights*, 2(2), 100114. DOI: 10.1016/j.jjimei.2022.100114

Singh, B., & Kaunert, C. (2024). Future of Digital Marketing: Hyper-Personalized Customer Dynamic Experience with AI-Based Predictive Models. In *Revolutionizing the AI-Digital Landscape: A Guide to Sustainable Emerging Technologies for Marketing Professionals* (pp. 189–208). Taylor and Francis., DOI: 10.4324/9781032688305-14

Singh, C. B., & Ahmed, M. M. (2024). Revolutionizing digital marketing: The impact of AI on personalized campaigns. *International Research Journal of Business and Social Science*, 10(1), 573–585.

Singh, C., Dash, M. K., Sahu, R., & Kumar, A. (2023). Artificial intelligence in customer retention: A bibliometric analysis and future research framework. *Kybernetes*. Advance online publication. DOI: 10.1108/K-02-2023-0245

Sinha, S., Sinha, D., & Dalmia, T. (2024). Role of AI in Enhancing Customer Experience in Online Shopping. *11th International Conference on Reliability, Infocom Technologies and Optimization, ICRITO 2024*. Hybrid, Noida: Institute of Electrical and Electronics Engineers Inc. DOI: 10.1109/ICRITO61523.2024.10522285

Sitecore. (2023). *L'Oréal harnesses the power of Generative AI at scale with Sitecore*. Sitecore. https://www.sitecore.com/customers/consumer-goods/loreal-drives-innovation-with-composable-sitecore-platform

SiteMinder. (2024, Feb 16). *Hotel dynamic pricing: Definition, examples, and best software to use*. https://www.siteminder.com/r/hotel-dynamic-pricing/

Sivadas, E., & Baker-Prewitt, J. (2000). An examination of the relationship between service quality, customer satisfaction, and store loyalty. *International Journal of Retail & Distribution Management*, 28(2), 73–82. DOI: 10.1108/09590550010315223

Sivarajah, U., Irani, Z., Gupta, S., & Mahroof, K. (2020). Role of big data and social media analytics for business to business sustainability: A participatory web context. *Industrial Marketing Management*, 86, 163–179. DOI: 10.1016/j.indmarman.2019.04.005

Sivarajah, U., Kamal, M. M., Irani, Z., & Weerakkody, V. (2017). Critical analysis of Big Data challenges and analytical methods. *Journal of Business Research*, 70, 263–286. DOI: 10.1016/j.jbusres.2016.08.001

Skačkauskienė, I., Nekrošienė, J., & Szarucki, M. (2023). A review on marketing activities effectiveness evaluation metrics. *13th International Scientific Conference "Business and Management 2023"*. DOI: 10.3846/bm.2023.1037

Skjuve, M., Følstad, A., Fostervold, K. I., & Brandtzaeg, P. B. (2021). My chatbot companion - A study of human-chatbot relationships. *International Journal of Human-Computer Studies*, 149, 102601. DOI: 10.1016/j.ijhcs.2021.102601

Sleiman, R., Tran, K. P., & Thomassey, S. (2022). Natural language processing for fashion trends detection. *2022 International Conference on Electrical, Computer and Energy Technologies (ICECET)*. DOI: 10.1109/ICECET55527.2022.9872832

Smeureanu, I., Ruxanda, G., & Badea, L. M. (2013). Customer segmentation in private banking sector using machine learning techniques. *Journal of Business Economics and Management*, 14(5), 923–939. DOI: 10.3846/16111699.2012.749807

Smith, A. (2018). *Starbucks Leverages AI to Personalize Loyalty Program*. Forbes. Retrieved from Forbes.

Smith, W. R. (1956). Product Differentiation and Market Segmentation as Alternative Marketing Strategies. *Journal of Marketing*, 21(1), 3–8. DOI: 10.1177/002224295602100102

Sniecinski, I., & Seghatchian, J. (2018). Artificial intelligence: A joint narrative on potential use in pediatric stem and immune cell therapies and regenerative medicine. *Transfusion and Apheresis Science : Official Journal of the World Apheresis Association : Official Journal of the European Society for Haemapheresis*, 57(3), 422–424. DOI: 10.1016/j.transci.2018.05.004 PMID: 29784537

Söderlund, M., & Oikarinen, E.-L. (2021). Service encounters with virtual agents: An examination of perceived humanness as a source of customer satisfaction. *European Journal of Marketing*, 55(13), 94–121. DOI: 10.1108/EJM-09-2019-0748

Sokolova, K., & Kefi, H. (2020). Instagram and YouTube bloggers promote it, why should I buy? How credibility and parasocial interaction influence purchase intentions. *Journal of Retailing and Consumer Services*, 53, 101742. DOI: 10.1016/j.jretconser.2019.01.011

Song, M., Xing, X., Duan, Y., Cohen, J., & Mou, J. (2022). Will artificial intelligence replace human customer service? The impact of communication quality and privacy risks on adoption intention. *Journal of Retailing and Consumer Services*, 66, 102900. DOI: 10.1016/j.jretconser.2021.102900

Sousa, T. B. (2022, July). Customer Data Platforms: A Pattern Language for Digital Marketing Optimization with First-Party Data. In *Proceedings of the 27th European Conference on Pattern Languages of Programs* (pp. 1-5).

Sreerama, J., & Krishnamoorthy, G. (2022). Ethical Considerations in AI Addressing Bias and Fairness in Machine Learning Models. *Journal of Knowledge Learning and Science Technology ISSN: 2959-6386 (online), 1*, 130-138. DOI: 10.60087/jklst.vol1.n1.p138

Srinivasan, R., & González, B. S. M. (2022). The role of empathy for artificial intelligence accountability. *Journal of Responsible Technology*, 9, 100021. DOI: 10.1016/j.jrt.2021.100021

Srivastava, A., & Dey, D. K. (2016). Brand analysis of global and local banks in India: A study of young consumers. *Journal of Indian Business Research*, 8(1), 4–18. DOI: 10.1108/JIBR-05-2015-0061

Statista. (2023). Apparel market worldwide. https://www.statista.com/topics/5091/apparel-market-worldwide

Steinhoff, L., Arli, D., Weaven, S., & Kozlenkova, I. V. (2019). Online relationship marketing. *Journal of the Academy of Marketing Science*, 47(3), 369–393. DOI: 10.1007/s11747-018-0621-6

Stein, J.-P., Linda Breves, P., & Anders, N. (2022). Parasocial interactions with real and virtual influencers: The role of perceived similarity and human-likeness. *New Media & Society*. Advance online publication. DOI: 10.1177/14614448221102900

Sternberg, R. (2003). A duplex theory of hate: Development and application to terrorism, massacres, and genocide. *Review of General Psychology*, 7(3), 299–328. DOI: 10.1037/1089-2680.7.3.299

Sterne, J. (2017). *Artificial intelligence for marketing: Practical applications*. Wiley. DOI: 10.1002/9781119406341

Sterrett, S. G. (2020). The Genius of the 'Original Imitation Game' Test. *Minds and Machines*, 30(4), 469–486. DOI: 10.1007/s11023-020-09543-6

Steve, N., Ben, K., & Max, M. (2017, Jul 26). *Find It On eBay: Using Pictures Instead of Words*. https://innovation.ebayinc.com/tech/product/find-it-on-ebay-using-pictures-instead-of-words/

Stieglitz, S., Mirbabaie, M., Ross, B., & Neuberger, C. (2018). Social media analytics–Challenges in topic discovery, data collection, and data preparation. *International Journal of Information Management*, 39, 156–168. DOI: 10.1016/j.ijinfomgt.2017.12.002

Stöger, K., Schneeberger, D., Kieseberg, P., & Holzinger, A. (2021). Legal aspects of data cleansing in medical AI. *Computer Law & Security Report*, 42, 105587. DOI: 10.1016/j.clsr.2021.105587

Stoilova, E. (2021). AI chatbots as a customer service and support tool. *ROBONOMICS. The Journal of the Automated Economy*, 2(21).

Stojanovic, A., Milosevic, I., Arsic, S., Urosevic, S., & Mihajlovic, I. (2020). Corporate social responsibility as a determinant of employee loyalty and business performance. *Journal of Competitiveness*, 12(2), 149–166. DOI: 10.7441/joc.2020.02.09

Stone, M., Aravopoulou, E., Ekinci, Y., Evans, G., Hobbs, M., Labib, A., Laughlin, P., Machtynger, J., & Machtynger, L. (2020). AI in Strategic Marketing Decision-Making: A research agenda. *The Bottom Line (New York, N.Y.)*, 33(2), 147–166. DOI: 10.1108/BL-03-2020-0022

Stone, M., Aravopoulou, E., Gerardi, G., Todeva, E., Weinzierl, L., Laughlin, P., & Stott, R. (2017). How platforms are transforming customer information management. *The Bottom Line (New York, N.Y.)*, 30(3), 216–235. DOI: 10.1108/BL-08-2017-0024

Stone, M., & Woodcock, N. (2014). Interactive, Direct and Digital Marketing: A Future that Depends on Better Use of Business Intelligence. *Journal of Research in Interactive Marketing*, 8(1), 4–17. DOI: 10.1108/JRIM-07-2013-0046

Suandi, E., & Yulihasri, H. (2022). Evaluating the relationship among entrepreneurial marketing, competitive advantage, and Islamic banks performance. *Journal of Financial Services Marketing*, 28(3), 599–614. DOI: 10.1057/s41264-022-00169-6

Sudmann, A. (2022). *On Computer creativity. Machine learning and the arts of artificial intelligences*. .DOI: 10.5817/CZ.MUNI.M280-0225-2022-11

Suharto, S., & Yuliansyah, Y. (2023). The influence of customer relationship management and customer experience on customer satisfaction. *Integrated Journal of Business and Economics*, 7(1), 389. DOI: 10.33019/ijbe.v7i1.641

Sujan, M. (1985). Consumer knowledge: Effects on evaluation strategies mediating consumer judgments. *The Journal of Consumer Research*, 12(1), 31–46. DOI: 10.1086/209033

Sundar, S. S., & Nass, C. (2000). Source orientation in human-computer interaction: Programmer, networker, or independent social actor. *Communication Research*, 27(6), 683–703. DOI: 10.1177/009365000027006001

Sung, E., Bae, S., Han, D.-I. D., & Kwon, O. (2021). Consumer engagement via interactive artificial intelligence and mixed reality. *International Journal of Information Management*, 60, 102382. DOI: 10.1016/j.ijinfomgt.2021.102382

Sunita, C. (2023). AI in E-Commerce: Exploring the Purchase Decisions through Logistic Regression Analysis. *International Journal of Commerce and Management*, 3(3), 301–309.

Sun, T. (2019). Artificial Intelligence in Customer Relationship Management. *International Journal of Market Research*, 61(3), 213–226.

Sun, Y., Chen, J., & Sundar, S. S. (2024). Chatbot ads with a human touch: A test of anthropomorphism, interactivity, and narrativity. *Journal of Business Research*, 172, 114403. DOI: 10.1016/j.jbusres.2023.114403

Su, Z., Togay, G., & Côté, A. M. (2021). Artificial intelligence: A destructive and yet creative force in the skilled labour market. *Human Resource Development International*, 24(3), 341–352. DOI: 10.1080/13678868.2020.1818513

Swami, V. I., & Naidu, D. (2020). Social media marketing: Gateway to success for homepreneurs. *International Journal of Innovative Technology and Exploring Engineering*, 9(4S), 66–70. DOI: 10.35940/ijitee.D1011.0394S20

Taecharungroj, V. (2023). "What can ChatGPT do?" Analyzing early reactions to the innovative AI chatbot on Twitter. *Big Data and Cognitive Computing*, 7(1), 35. Advance online publication. DOI: 10.3390/bdcc7010035

Taherdangkoo, M., Ghasemi, K., & Beikpour, M. (2017). The role of sustainability environment in export marketing strategy and performance: A literature review. *Environment, Development and Sustainability*, 19(5), 1601–1629. DOI: 10.1007/s10668-016-9841-4

Taheri, B., Bititci, U., Gannon, M. J., & Cordina, R. (2019). Investigating the influence of performance measurement on learning, entrepreneurial orientation and performance in turbulent markets. *International Journal of Contemporary Hospitality Management*, 31(3), 1224–1246. DOI: 10.1108/IJCHM-11-2017-0744

Tajeddini, K., & Ratten, V. (2020). The moderating effect of brand orientation on inter-firm market orientation and performance. *Journal of Strategic Marketing*, 28(3), 194–224. DOI: 10.1080/0965254X.2017.1293138

Talib, M. A., Majzoub, S., Nasir, Q., & Jamal, D. (2021). A systematic literature review on hardware implementation of artificial intelligence algorithms. *The Journal of Supercomputing*, 77(2), 1897–1938. DOI: 10.1007/s11227-020-03325-8

Tan, C. W., Benbasat, I., & Cenfetelli, R. T. (2017). An exploratory study of the formation and impact of electronic service failures. *Management Information Systems Quarterly*, 40(1), 1–29. DOI: 10.25300/MISQ/2016/40.1.01

Tarabieh, S. (2015). The Impact of Customer Orientation and Supplementary Services in Gaining Competitive Advantage and Organizational Performance in the Jordanian Banking Industry. *International Review of Social Sciences*, 3(2), 47–59.

Tarabieh, S. M. Z. A., Ahmad, Z. A., & Siron, R. (2015). The Synergistic Impact of Customer Orientation and Supplementary Services on Competitive Advantage and Organizational Performance (Pilot Survey). *International Review of Management and Business Research*, 4(2), 484–498.

Tarannum, J., Arfath, J., Madnoor, P., Alekhya, M., & Maltumkar Sri, L. (2024). A Study on Importance of Branding and Its Effects on Products in Business. [IRJAEM]. *International Research Journal on Advanced Engineering and Management*, 2(04), 656–661. DOI: 10.47392/IRJAEM.2024.0091

Tarka, P., & Łobiński, M. (2014). Decision Making in Reference to Model of Marketing Predictive Analytics–Theory and Practice. *Management and Business Administration.Central Europe*, 22(1), 60–69.

Taufique, K. M. R. (2022). Integrating environmental values and emotion in green marketing communications inducing sustainable consumer behaviour. *Journal of Marketing Communications*, 28(3), 272–290. DOI: 10.1080/13527266.2020.1866645

Teixeira, S., & Remondes, J. (2023). *The Use of Artificial Intelligence in Digital Marketing: Competitive Strategies and Tactics: Competitive Strategies and Tactics*. IGI Global., DOI: 10.4018/978-1-6684-9324-3

Temporal, P. (2014). *Branding for the Public Sector: Creating, Building and Managing Brands People will Value*. John Wiley and Sons Ltd. DOI: 10.1002/9781119176824

Teradata. (2017, October 11). *Survey: 80 Percent of enterprises investing in AI, but cite significant challenges ahead*. Terada. https://www.teradata.com/Press-Releases/2017/Survey-80-Percent-of-Enterprises-Invest-in-AI

Thamik, H., & Wu, J. (2022). The Impact of Artificial Intelligence on Sustainable Development in Electronic Markets. *Sustainability (Basel)*, 14(6), 3568. Advance online publication. DOI: 10.3390/su14063568

Thiraviyam, T. (2018). Artificial Intelligence Marketing. *International Journal of Recent Research Aspects*, 449–452.

Thontirawong, P., & Chinchanachokchai, S. (2021). Teaching artificial intelligence and machine learning in marketing. *Marketing Education Review*, 31(2), 58–63. DOI: 10.1080/10528008.2021.1871849

Tiutiu, M., & Dabija, D. C. (2023). Improving Customer Experience Using Artificial Intelligence in Online Retail. In *Proceedings of the International Conference on Business Excellence, 17*(1), 1139-1147. DOI: 10.2478/picbe-2023-0102

Tomei, P. A., & Russo, G. (2016). Cultural fit and desired organizational values: The case of ARFCO. *Organizational Cultures: An International Journal*, 16(3), 27–49. DOI: 10.18848/2327-8013/CGP/v16i03/27-49

Trainor, K. J., Andzulis, J. M., Rapp, A., & Agnihotri, R. (2014). Social media technology usage and customer relationship performance: A capabilities-based examination of social CRM. *Journal of Business Research*, 67(6), 1201–1208. DOI: 10.1016/j.jbusres.2013.05.002

Tran, M. T. (2024). Unlocking the AI-Powered Customer Experience: Personalized Service, Enhanced Engagement, and Data-Driven Strategies for E-Commerce Applications. In *Enhancing and Predicting Digital Consumer Behavior with AI* (pp. 375–382). IGI Global., DOI: 10.4018/979-8-3693-4453-8.ch019

Trawnih, A., Al Masaeed, S., Alsoud, M., & Alkufahy, A. (2022). Understanding AI experience: A customer perspective. *International Journal of Data and Network Science*, 6(3), 1471–1484. DOI: 10.5267/j.ijdns.2022.5.004

Tripathi, A., Singh, A. K., Singh, K. K., Choudhary, P., & Vashist, P. C. (2021). Machine learning architecture and framework. In *Machine Learning and the Internet of Medical Things in Healthcare* (pp. 1–22). Elsevier., DOI: 10.1016/B978-0-12-821229-5.00005-7

Triznova, M., Maťova, H., Dvoracek, J., & Sadek, S. (2015). Customer relationship management based on employees and corporate culture. *Procedia Economics and Finance*, 26, 953–959. DOI: 10.1016/S2212-5671(15)00914-4

Truong, V. D., & Hall, C. M. (2017). Corporate social marketing in tourism: To sleep or not to sleep with the enemy? *Journal of Sustainable Tourism*, 25(7), 884–902. DOI: 10.1080/09669582.2016.1201093

Tsai, W. H. S., Liu, Y., & Chuan, C. H. (2021). How chatbots' social presence communication enhances consumer engagement: The mediating role of parasocial interaction and dialogue. *Journal of Research in Interactive Marketing*, 15(3), 460–482. DOI: 10.1108/JRIM-12-2019-0200

Tsang, A. H. C. (2002). Strategic Dimensions of Maintenance Management. *Journal of Quality in Maintenance Engineering*, 8(1), 7–39. DOI: 10.1108/13552510210420577

Tuten, T. L. (2023). *Social media marketing*. Sage Publications Limited.

Tzou, H., Tseng, J., & CTO, P. (2022). How AI and AR can help beauty industry. *NCT, 1*, 7-14.

Uber. (2020, Mar). *How Uber's dynamic pricing model works.* https://www.uber.com/en-GB/blog/uber-dynamic-pricing/

Uysal, E., Alavi, S., & Bezençon, V. (2023). Anthropomorphism in Artificial Intelligence: A review of empirical work across domains and insights for future research. In Sudhir, K., & Toubia, O. (Eds.), *Artificial Intelligence in Marketing* (Vol. 20, pp. 273–308). Emerald Publishing Limited., DOI: 10.1108/S1548-643520230000020015

Uzir, M. U., Bukari, Z., Al Halbusi, H. L., Wahab, S. N., Rasul, T., & Eneizan, B. (2023). Applied AI: Acceptance-intention-purchase and satisfaction on smartwatch usage in a Ghanaian context. *Heliyon*, 9(1), e14532.

Vallaster, C., Kraus, S., Lindahl, J. M. M., & Nielsen, A. (2019). Ethics and entrepreneurship: A bibliometric study and literature review. *Journal of Business Research*, 99, 226–237. DOI: 10.1016/j.jbusres.2019.02.050

Van Doorn, J., Lemon, K. N., Mittal, V., Nass, S., Pick, D., Pirner, P., & Verhoef, P. C. (2010). Customer engagement behavior: Theoretical foundations and research directions. *Journal of Service Research*, 13(3), 253–266. DOI: 10.1177/1094670510375599

Van Doorn, J., Mende, M., Noble, S. M., Hulland, J., Ostrom, A. L., Grewal, D., & Petersen, J. A. (2017). Domo Arigato Mr. Roboto: Emergence of automated social presence in organizational frontlines and customers' service experiences. *Journal of Service Research*, 20(1), 43–58. DOI: 10.1177/1094670516679272

Van Eck, N., & Waltman, L. (2010). Software survey: VOSviewer, a computer program for bibliometric mapping. *Scientometrics*, 84(2), 523–538. DOI: 10.1007/s11192-009-0146-3 PMID: 20585380

Van Esch, P., & Stewart Black, J. (2021). Artificial intelligence (AI): Revolutionizing digital marketing. *Australasian Marketing Journal*, 29(3), 199–203. DOI: 10.1177/18393349211037684

Van Melle, W. (1978). MYCIN: A knowledge-based consultation program for infectious disease diagnosis. *International Journal of Man-Machine Studies*, 10(3), 313–322. DOI: 10.1016/S0020-7373(78)80049-2

Van Pinxteren, M. M., Wetzels, R. W., Rüger, J., Pluymaekers, M., & Wetzels, M. (2019). Trust in humanoid robots: Implications for services marketing. *Journal of Services Marketing*, 33(4), 507–518. DOI: 10.1108/JSM-01-2018-0045

Vanek, J., King, K., & Bigelow, M. (2018). Social presence and identity: Facebook in an English language classroom. *Journal of Language, Identity, and Education*, 17(4), 236–254. DOI: 10.1080/15348458.2018.1442223

Vapnik, V., & Lerner, A. (1963). Pattern Recognition Using Generalized Portrait Method. *Automation and Remote Control*, 24(06).

Varadarajan, R. (2020). Customer information resources advantage, marketing strategy and business performance: A market resources based view. *Industrial Marketing Management*, 89, 89–97. DOI: 10.1016/j.indmarman.2020.03.003

Varela-Neira, C., Dwivedi, Y. K., & Camoiras-Rodriguez, Z. (2023). Social media marketing system: Conceptualization, scale development and validation. *Internet Research*, 33(4), 1302–1330. DOI: 10.1108/INTR-06-2021-0393

Vargo, S. L., Koskela-Huotari, K., Baron, S., Edvardsson, B., Reynoso, J., & Colurcio, M. (2017). A systems perspective on markets – Toward a research agenda. *Journal of Business Research*, 79, 260–268. DOI: 10.1016/j.jbusres.2017.03.011

Vargo, S. L., & Lusch, R. F. (2004). Evolving to a new dominant logic for marketing. *Journal of Marketing*, 68(1), 1–17. DOI: 10.1509/jmkg.68.1.1.24036

Vargo, S. L., & Lusch, R. F. (2017). Service-dominant logic 2025. *International Journal of Research in Marketing*, 34(1), 46–67. DOI: 10.1016/j.ijresmar.2016.11.001

Varsha, P. S., Akter, S., Kumar, A., Gochhait, S., & Patagundi, B. (2021). The Impact of Artificial Intelligence on Branding. *Journal of Global Information Management*, 29(4), 221–246. DOI: 10.4018/JGIM.20210701.oa10

Varshini, G. Y. S., & Latha, S. (2023). Detection of data integrity attack using model and data-driven-based approach in CPPS. *International Transactions on Electrical Energy Systems*, 2023, 1–24. Advance online publication. DOI: 10.1155/2023/6098519

Vasundhara, S., & Venkatesh, K. S. V., M., P., S., S., S., & Boopathi, S. (2024). AI-powered marketing revolutionizing customer engagement through innovative strategies. In *Cases on AI Ethics in Business* (pp. 21-46). IGI Global. doi:DOI: 10.4018/9798369326435.ch002

Vaswani, A., Shazeer, N., Parmar, N., Uszkoreit, J., Jones, L., Gomez, A. N., Kaiser, Ł., & Polosukhin, I. (2017). Attention Is All You Need. https://arxiv.org/abs/1706.03762v7

Verhagen, T., Van Nes, J., Feldberg, F., & Van Dolen, W. (2014). Virtual customer service agents: Using social presence and personalization to shape online service encounters. *Journal of Computer-Mediated Communication*, 19(3), 529–545. DOI: 10.1111/jcc4.12066

Verhoef, P. C., Kannan, P. K., & Inman, J. J. (2015). From Multi-Channel Retailing to Omni-Channel Retailing: Introduction to the Special Issue on Multi-Channel Retailing. *Journal of Retailing*, 91(2), 174–181. DOI: 10.1016/j.jretai.2015.02.005

Verhoef, P. C., Reinartz, W. J., & Krafft, M. (2010). Customer engagement as a new perspective in customer management. *Journal of Service Research*, 13(3), 247–252. DOI: 10.1177/1094670510375461

Verifone. (2024, Mar 28). *eCommerce: Trends and Predictions for the Next Decade*. https://blog.2checkout.com/ai-trends-and-predictions-in-ecommerce/

Verma, R. K., & Kumari, N. (2023). Generative AI as a tool for enhancing customer relationship management automation and personalization techniques. *International Journal of Responsible Artificial Intelligence*, 13(9), 1–8.

Verma, S., Sharma, R., Deb, S., & Maitra, D. (2021). Artificial intelligence in marketing: Systematic review and future research direction. *International Journal of Information Management Data Insights*, 1(1), 100002. DOI: 10.1016/j.jjimei.2020.100002

Vermeer, S. A., Araujo, T., Bernritter, S. F., & van Noort, G. (2019). Seeing the wood for the trees: How machine learning can help firms in identifying relevant electronic word-of-mouth in social media. *International Journal of Research in Marketing*, 36(3), 492–508. DOI: 10.1016/j.ijresmar.2019.01.010

Vial, G. (2019). Understanding digital transformation: A review and a research agenda. *The Journal of Strategic Information Systems*, 28(2), 118–144. DOI: 10.1016/j.jsis.2019.01.003

Vimalkumar, M., Sharma, S. K., Singh, J. B., & Dwivedi, Y. K. (2021). 'Okay google, what about my privacy?': User's privacy perceptions and acceptance of voice based digital assistants.

Vinerean, S., & Opreana, A. (2021). Measuring customer engagement in social media marketing: A higher-order model. *Journal of Theoretical and Applied Electronic Commerce Research*, 16(7), 2633–2654. DOI: 10.3390/jtaer16070145

Vinod, N. (2023). Artificial Intelligence. Advances in logistics, operations, and management science book series. In *Cases on Managing Dairy Productive Chains* (pp.226-240). DOI: 10.4018/979-8-3693-0418-1.ch015

Vivek, S. D., Beatty, S. E., & Morgan, R. M. (2012). Customer engagement: Exploring customer relationships beyond purchase. *Journal of Marketing Theory and Practice*, 20(2), 122–146. DOI: 10.2753/MTP1069-6679200201

Vlačić, B., Corbo, L., Silva, S. C. E., & Dabić, M. (2021). The evolving role of artificial intelligence in marketing: A review and research agenda. *Journal of Business Research*, 128, 187–203. DOI: 10.1016/j.jbusres.2021.01.055

Volkmar, G., Fischer, P. M., & Reinecke, S. (2022). AI and Machine Learning: Exploring drivers, barriers, and future developments in marketing management. *Journal of Business Research*, 149, 599–614. DOI: 10.1016/j.jbusres.2022.04.007

Vomberg, A. (2023). Dynamic Pricing Process: How to Transition from Fixed to Dynamic Pricing? In *Digital Pricing Strategy: Capturing Value from Digital Innovations* (pp. 27-38). Taylor and Francis. DOI: 10.4324/9781003226192-5

Voorveld, H. A. M. (2019). Brand Communication in Social Media: A Research Agenda. *Journal of Advertising*, 48(1), 14–26. DOI: 10.1080/00913367.2019.1588808

Voorveld, H. A., Van Noort, G., Muntinga, D. G., & Bronner, F. (2018). Engagement with social media and social media advertising: The differentiating role of platform type. *Journal of Advertising*, 47(1), 38–54. DOI: 10.1080/00913367.2017.1405754

Vo, T. Q., & Nguyen-Anh, T. (2024). Corporate social marketing and brand equity – a case of dairy products in Vietnam. *Cogent Business & Management*, 11(1), 2321795. Advance online publication. DOI: 10.1080/23311975.2024.2321795

Wakjira, G. G., & Kant, S. (2022). Significance of Market Orientation On Business Performance With Mediating Role of Employee And Customer Satisfaction In Ethiopia Banks. *Partners Universal International Research Journal*, 1(4), 118–125. DOI: 10.5281/zenodo.7495221

Wald, R., Heijselaar, E., & Bosse, T. (2021). Make your own: The potential of chatbot customization for the development of user trust. In *Adjunct Proceedings of the 29th ACM Conference on User Modeling, Adaptation and Personalization* (pp. 382-387).

Wales, W. J., Covin, J. G., & Monsen, E. (2020). Entrepreneurial orientation: The necessity of a multilevel conceptualization. *Strategic Entrepreneurship Journal*, 14(4), 639–660. DOI: 10.1002/sej.1344

Wang, P. (2021). Research and Development Trend of Artificial Intelligence Technology Innovation Under the Internet Background. In *Cyber Security Intelligence and Analytics:2021 International Conference on Cyber Security Intelligence and Analytics (CSIA2021),* Volume 1 (pp. 266-273). Springer International Publishing. DOI: 10.1007/978-3-030-70042-3_39

Wang, Z., & Yang, X. (2024). Building brand loyalty through value co-creation practices in brand communities: the role of affective commitment and psychological brand ownership. *Journal of Research in Interactive Marketing, Vol. ahead-of-print No.* ahead-of-print. doi:DOI: 0.1108/JRIM-10-2023-0359

Wang, L., & Liu, S. (2020, July). Research on E-commerce Customer Relationship Management Based on Data Analysis. In *Proceedings of the 2020 11th International Conference on E-business, Management and Economics* (pp. 20-26). DOI: 10.1145/3414752.3414776

Wang, Y. (2021). When artificial intelligence meets educational leaders' data-informed decision-making: A cautionary tale. *Studies in Educational Evaluation*, 69, 100872. DOI: 10.1016/j.stueduc.2020.100872

Wang, Y., Shi, S., Chen, Y., & Gursoy, D. (2019). An examination of market orientation and environmental marketing strategy: The case of Chinese firms. *Service Industries Journal*, 39(15-16), 1046–1071. DOI: 10.1080/02642069.2018.1551370

Waqar, A., Othman, I., Shafiq, N., & Mansoor, M. S. (2023). Applications of AI in oil and gas projects towards sustainable development: A systematic literature review. *Artificial Intelligence Review*, 56(11), 12771–12798. DOI: 10.1007/s10462-023-10467-7 PMID: 37362898

Wasilewski, A., & Przyborowski, M. (2023). Clustering Methods for Adaptive e-Commerce User Interfaces. *International Joint Conference on Rough Sets, IJCRS 2023. 14481 LNAI* (pp. 511-525). Krakow: Springer Science and Business Media Deutschland GmbH. DOI: 10.1007/978-3-031-50959-9_35

Wasserman, S., & Faust, K. (1994). *Social network analysis: Methods and applications*. Cambridge University Press. DOI: 10.1017/CBO9780511815478

Wedel, M., Bigné, E., & Zhang, J. (2020). Virtual and AR: Advancing research in consumer marketing. *International Journal of Research in Marketing*, 37(3), 443–465. DOI: 10.1016/j.ijresmar.2020.04.004

Wedel, M., & Kannan, P. K. (2016). Marketing Analytics for Data-Rich Environments. *Journal of Marketing*, 80(6), 97–121. DOI: 10.1509/jm.15.0413

West, D. M., & Allen, J. R. (2018). How artificial intelligence is transforming the world. https://www.brookings.edu/articles/how-artificial-intelligence-is-transforming-the-world/

Whang, J. B., Song, J. H., Choi, B., & Lee, J. H. (2021). The effect of AR on purchase intention of beauty products: The roles of consumers' control. *Journal of Business Research*, 133, 275–284. DOI: 10.1016/j.jbusres.2021.04.057

Whang, S. E., Roh, Y., Song, H., & Lee, J. G. (2023). Data collection and quality challenges in deep learning: A data-centric ai perspective. *The VLDB Journal*, 32(4), 791–813. DOI: 10.1007/s00778-022-00775-9

Whetten, D. A. (2006). Albert and Whetten Revisited: Strengthening the Concept of Organizational Identity. *Journal of Management Inquiry*, 15(3), 219–234. DOI: 10.1177/1056492606291200

Whig, P., Bhatia, A. B., & Yathiraju, N. (2024). AI-Driven Innovations in Service Marketing Transforming Customer Engagement and Experience. In *AI Innovations in Service and Tourism Marketing* (pp. 17–34). IGI Global. DOI: 10.4018/979-8-3693-7909-7.ch002

Wilkins, J., Sparrow, D. A., Fealing, C. A., Vickers, B. D., Ferguson, K. A., & Wojton, H. (2024). A team-centric metric framework for testing and evaluation of human-machine teams. *Systems Engineering*, 27(3), 466–484. DOI: 10.1002/sys.21730

Wilson, H. J., Daugherty, P. R., & Morini-Bianzino, N. (2017). The jobs that artificial intelligence will create. *MIT Sloan Management Review*, 58(4).

Winder, D. (2024, January 23). Warning as 26 billion records leak: Dropbox, LinkedIn, Twitter named. *Forbes*. https://www.forbes.com/sites/daveywinder/2024/01/23/massive-26-billion-record-leak-dropbox-linkedin-twitterx-all-named/

Winroth, M., Almström, P., & Andersson, C. (2016). Sustainable production indicators at factory level. *Journal of Manufacturing Technology Management*, 27(6), 842–873. DOI: 10.1108/JMTM-04-2016-0054

Wirtz, J., Den Ambtman, A., Bloemer, J., Horváth, C., Ramaseshan, B., Van De Klundert, J., Gurhan Canli, Z., & Kandampully, J. (2013). Managing brands and customer engagement in online brand communities. *Journal of Service Management*, 24(3), 223–244. DOI: 10.1108/09564231311326978

Wirtz, J., Kunz, W. H., Hartley, N., & Tarbit, J. (2023). Corporate digital responsibility in service firms and their ecosystems. *Journal of Service Research*, 26(2), 173–190. DOI: 10.1177/10946705221130467

Wirtz, J., Patterson, P. G., Kunz, W. H., Gruber, T., Lu, V. N., Paluch, S., & Martins, A. (2018). Brave new world: Service robots in the frontline. *Journal of Service Management*, 29(5), 907–931. DOI: 10.1108/JOSM-04-2018-0119

Wittorski, R. (2012). Professionalisation and the Development of Competences in Education and Training. In Valerie Cohen-Scali, V. (Ed.), *Competence and Competence Development* (pp. 31–51). Barbara Budrich Publishers. DOI: 10.2307/j.ctvbkk2h9.6

Woessner, M. N., Tacey, A., Levinger-Limor, A., Parker, A. G., Levinger, P., & Levinger, I. (2021). The Evolution of Technology and Physical Inactivity: The Good, the Bad, and the Way Forward. *Frontiers in Public Health*, 9, 655491. DOI: 10.3389/fpubh.2021.655491 PMID: 34123989

Wolniak, R., & Grebski, W. (2023). Functioning of predictive analytics in business. *Silesian University of Technology Scientific Papers. Organization and Management Series, 175*, 631-649.

Wongleedee, K. (2020). Role of Customer Loyalty on Employee Performance and Productivity in Pharmacy Business in Thailand. *Systematic Reviews in Pharmacy*, 11(2). Advance online publication. DOI: 10.5530/srp.2020.2.91

Wu, H. C., Wei, C. F., Tseng, L. Y., & Cheng, C. C. (2018). What drives green brand switching behavior? *Marketing Intelligence & Planning*, 36(6), 694–708. DOI: 10.1108/MIP-10-2017-0224

Wulandari, A., Suryawardani, B., & Marcelino, D. (2022). Create Brand Loyalty of Indonesıan Facebook User Through Brand Engagement: Utılızatıon the Role of Socıal Medıa Marketıng Elements. *Asia Pacific Management and Business Application*, 10(3), 377–394. DOI: 10.21776/ub.apmba.2022.010.03.10

Xiang, Z., Schwartz, Z., Gerdes, J. H.Jr, & Uysal, M. (2015). What can big data and text analytics tell us about hotel guest experience and satisfaction? *International Journal of Hospitality Management*, 44, 120–130. DOI: 10.1016/j.ijhm.2014.10.013

Xie, M., Michelinakis, F., Dreibholz, T., Pujol-Roig, J. S., Malacarne, S., Majumdar, S., & Elmokashfi, A. M. (2021, June). An exposed closed-loop model for customer-driven service assurance automation. In *2021 Joint European Conference on Networks and Communications & 6G Summit (EuCNC/6G Summit)* (pp. 419-424). IEEE. DOI: 10.1109/EuCNC/6GSummit51104.2021.9482533

Xinxing, S., Sarkar, A., Yue, D., Hongbin, Z., & Fangyuan, T. (2023). The influences of the advancement of green technology on agricultural CO2 release reduction: A case of Chinese agricultural industry. *Frontiers in Sustainable Food Systems*, 7, 1096381. DOI: 10.3389/fsufs.2023.1096381

Xu, X., Wen, N., & Liu, J. (2023). Empathic accuracy in artificial intelligence service recovery. *Tourism Review* (ahead-of-print). .DOI: 10.1108/TR-06-2023-0394

Xu, K., & Lombard, M. (2017). Persuasive computing: Feeling peer pressure from multiple computer agents. *Computers in Human Behavior*, 74, 152–162. DOI: 10.1016/j.chb.2017.04.043

Xu, R., & Wunsch, D.II. (2005). Survey of Clustering Algorithms. *IEEE Transactions on Neural Networks*, 16(3), 645–678. DOI: 10.1109/TNN.2005.845141 PMID: 15940994

Xu, Y., Liu, X., Cao, X., Huang, C., Liu, E., Qian, S., Liu, X., Wu, Y., Dong, F., Qiu, C., Qiu, J., Hua, K., Su, W., Wu, J., Xu, H., Han, Y., Fu, C., Yin, Z., Liu, M., & Zhang, J. (2021). Artificial intelligence: A powerful paradigm for scientific research. *Innovation (Cambridge (Mass.))*, 2(4), 100179. DOI: 10.1016/j.xinn.2021.100179 PMID: 34877560

Xu, Y., Shieh, C. H., van Esch, P., & Ling, I. L. (2020). AI customer service: Task complexity, problem-solving ability, and usage intention. *Australasian Marketing Journal*, 28(4), 189–199. DOI: 10.1016/j.ausmj.2020.03.005

Xu, Z., Liu, X., Bai, C., & Hu, L. (2015). Green Marketing: A Grey-based Rough Set Theory Analysis of Activities. *International Journal of Innovation Science*, 7(1), 27–38. DOI: 10.1260/1757-2223.7.1.27

Yamagiwa, A., & Goto, M. (2022). Evaluation of Analysis Model for Products with Coefficients of Binary Classifiers and Consideration of Way to Improve. *14th International Conference on Social Computing and Social Media, SCSM 2022 Held as Part of the 24th HCI International Conference, HCII 2022. 13316 LNCS* (pp. 388-402). Virtual, Online: Springer Science and Business Media Deutschland GmbH. DOI: 10.1007/978-3-031-05064-0_29

Yamane, T., & Kaneko, S. (2022). The Sustainable Development Goals as new business norms: A survey experiment on stakeholder preferences. *Ecological Economics*, 191, 107236. DOI: 10.1016/j.ecolecon.2021.107236

Yang, S., Yang, S., & Evans, C. (2019). Opportunities and Challenges in Using AI Chatbots in Higher Education. *The 3rd International Conference on Education and E-Learning (ICEEL 2019)79*, 79–83. DOI: 10.1145/3371647.3371659

Yang, C., & Hu, J. (2022). When do consumers prefer AI-enabled customer service? The interaction effect of brand personality and service provision type on brand attitudes and purchase intentions. *Journal of Brand Management*, 29(2), 167–189. DOI: 10.1057/s41262-021-00261-7

Yang, M., Jaafar, N., Al Mamun, A., Salameh, A. A., & Nawi, N. C. (2022). Modelling the significance of strategic orientation for competitive advantage and economic sustainability: The use of hybrid SEM–neural network analysis. *Journal of Innovation and Entrepreneurship*, 11(1), 44. Advance online publication. DOI: 10.1186/s13731-022-00232-5 PMID: 35754704

Yang, Q., Hayat, N., Al Mamun, A., Makhbul, Z. K. M., & Zainol, N. R. (2022). Sustainable customer retention through social media marketing activities using hybrid SEM-neural network approach. *PLoS One*, 17(3), e0264899. DOI: 10.1371/journal.pone.0264899 PMID: 35245323

Yang, X. (2023). The effects of AI service quality and AI function-customer ability fit on customer's overall co-creation experience. *Industrial Management & Data Systems*, 123(6), 1717–1735. DOI: 10.1108/IMDS-08-2022-0500

Yang, X., Li, H., Ni, L., & Li, T. (2021). Application of Artificial Intelligence in Precision Marketing. *Journal of Organizational and End User Computing*, 33(4), 209–219. DOI: 10.4018/JOEUC.20210701.oa10

Yang, Y. I., & Chung, J. H. (2006). The impact of market orientation on marketing capability and performance in the hotel industry. *J. Hosp. Tour. Stud.*, 8, 44–56. DOI: 10.3390/su11030729

Yang, Y., Gong, Y., Land, L. P. W., & Chesney, T. (2020). Understanding the effects of physical experience and information integration on consumer use of online to offline commerce. *International Journal of Information Management*, 51, 102046. DOI: 10.1016/j.ijinfomgt.2019.102046

Yan, N. (2022). Research on the relationship between employee mental health and enterprise work performance. *Journal of Healthcare Engineering*, 2022, 1–9. DOI: 10.1155/2022/3008947 PMID: 35265296

Yao, L., & Guan, Y. (2018, 10-12 Dec. 2018). An Improved LSTM Structure for Natural Language Processing. *2018 IEEE International Conference of Safety Produce Informatization (IICSPI)*, DOI: 10.1109/IICSPI.2018.8690387

Yau, K. L. A., Saad, N. M., & Chong, Y. W. (2021). Artificial Intelligence Marketing (AIM) for enhancing customer relationships. *Applied Sciences (Basel, Switzerland)*, 11(18), 1–17. DOI: 10.3390/app11188562

Yenduri, G., Ramalingam, M., Selvi, G. C., Supriya, Y., Srivastava, G., Maddikunta, P. K. R., Raj, G. D., Jhaveri, R. H., Prabadevi, B., Wang, W., Vasilakos, A. V., & Gadekallu, T. R. (2024). Gpt (generative pre-trained transformer) – a comprehensive review on enabling technologies, potential applications, emerging challenges, and future directions. *IEEE Access : Practical Innovations, Open Solutions*, 12, 54608–55464. DOI: 10.1109/ACCESS.2024.3389497

Yildirim, M. B., & Mouzon, G. (2012). Single-machine sustainable production planning to minimize total energy consumption and total completion time using a multiple objective genetic algorithm. *IEEE Transactions on Engineering Management*, 59(4), 585–597. DOI: 10.1109/TEM.2011.2171055

Yildiz Çankaya, S., & Sezen, B. (2019). Effects of green supply chain management practices on sustainability performance. *Journal of Manufacturing Technology Management*, 30(1), 98–121. DOI: 10.1108/JMTM-03-2018-0099

Ying, S., Sindakis, S., Aggarwal, S., Chen, C., & Su, J. (2021). Managing big data in the retail industry of Singapore: Examining the impact on customer satisfaction and organizational performance. *European Management Journal*, 39(3), 390–400. DOI: 10.1016/j.emj.2020.04.001

Ying, T., Tang, J., Ye, S., Tan, X., & Wei, W. (2022). Virtual reality in destination marketing: Telepresence, social presence, and tourists' visit intentions. *Journal of Travel Research*, 61(8), 1738–1756. DOI: 10.1177/00472875211047273

Yuan, C., Wang, S., Liu, Y., & Ma, J. W. (2023). Factors influencing parasocial relationship in the virtual reality shopping environment: The moderating role of celebrity endorser dynamism. *Asia Pacific Journal of Marketing and Logistics*, 35(2), 398–413. DOI: 10.1108/APJML-06-2021-0402

Yuan, Y., & Zhu, J. (2023). Intelligent Intercommunicating Multiscale Engineering: The Engineering of the Future. *Engineering (Beijing)*, 30, 13–19. DOI: 10.1016/j.eng.2023.03.021

Yu, J., Dickinger, A., So, K. K. F., & Egger, R. (2024). Artificial intelligence-generated virtual influencer: Examining the effects of emotional display on user engagement. *Journal of Retailing and Consumer Services*, 76(January), 103560. DOI: 10.1016/j.jretconser.2023.103560

Yüksel, H. M., Mut, A. D., & Ozpinar, A. (2023). Enhancing Image Content Analysis in B2C Online Marketplaces. *The European Journal of Research and Development*, 3(4), 229–239. DOI: 10.56038/ejrnd.v3i4.381

Yuliantari, N. P. Y., & Pramuki, N. M. W. A. (2022). The Role of Competitive Advantage in Mediating the Relationship Among Digital Transformation and MSME Performance in Bali. *Jurnal Ekonomi & Bisnis Jagaditha*, 9(1), 66–75. DOI: 10.22225/jj.9.1.2022.66-75

Zahay, D., Peltier, J., Schultz, D. E., & Griffin, A. (2004). The role of transactional versus relational data in IMC programs: Bringing customer data together. *Journal of Advertising Research*, 44(1), 3–18. DOI: 10.1017/S0021849904040188

Zaini, A., Hadiwidjojo, D., Rohman, F., & Maskie, G. (2014). Effect Of Competitive Advantage As A Mediator Variable Of Entrepreneurship Orientation To Marketing Performance. *IOSR Journal of Business and Management*, 16(5), 5–10. DOI: 10.9790/487X-16510510

Zarantonello, L., Romani, S., Grappi, S., & Bagozzi, R. P. (2016). Brand hate. *Journal of Product and Brand Management*, 25(1), 11–25. DOI: 10.1108/JPBM-01-2015-0799

Zerbino, P., Aloini, D., Dulmin, R., & Mininno, V. (2018). Big data-enabled customer relationship management: A holistic approach. *Information Processing & Management*, 54(5), 818–846. DOI: 10.1016/j.ipm.2017.10.005

Zerfass, A., Hagelstein, J., & Tench, R. (2020). Artificial intelligence in communication management: A cross-national study on adoption and knowledge, impact, challenges and risks. *Journal of Communication Management (London)*, 24(4), 377–389. DOI: 10.1108/JCOM-10-2019-0137

Zhang, A., & Yang, Q. (2022). To be human-like or machine-like? An empirical research on user trust in AI applications in service industry. *8th International Conference on Automation, Robotics and Applications* (ICARA).

Zhang, C., & Laroche, M. (2020). Brand hate: A multidimensional construct. *Journal of Product and Brand Management*, 30(3), 392–414. DOI: 10.1108/JPBM-11-2018-2103

Zhang, C., & Lu, Y. (2021). Study on artificial intelligence: The state of the art and future prospects. *Journal of Industrial Information Integration*, 23, 1–9. DOI: 10.1016/j.jii.2021.100224

Zhang, H., Zhao, L., & Gupta, S. (2018, February). The role of online product recommendations on customer decision making and loyalty in social shopping communities. *International Journal of Information Management*, 38(01), 150–166. DOI: 10.1016/j.ijinfomgt.2017.07.006

Zhang, S., Meng, Z., Chen, B., Yang, X., & Zhao, X. (2021). Motivation, Social Emotion, and the Acceptance of Artificial Intelligence Virtual Assistants-Trust-Based Mediating Effects. *Frontiers in Psychology*, 12, 728495. DOI: 10.3389/fpsyg.2021.728495 PMID: 34484086

Zhang, Y. (2015). The Impact of Brand Image on Consumer Behavior: A Literature Review. *Open Journal of Business and Management*, 03(01), 58–62. DOI: 10.4236/ojbm.2015.31006

Zhao, H., Lyu, F., & Luo, Y. (2022). Research on the Effect of Online Marketing Based on Multimodel Fusion and Artificial Intelligence in the Context of Big Data. *Security and Communication Networks*, 2022, 1–9. Advance online publication. DOI: 10.1155/2022/1516543

Zhao, J., & Gómez Fariñas, B. (2023). Artificial Intelligence and Sustainable Decisions. *European Business Organization Law Review*, 24(1), 1–39. DOI: 10.1007/s40804-022-00262-2

Zhao, L., Lee, S. H., Li, M., & Sun, P. (2022). The Use of Social Media to Promote Sustainable Fashion and Benefit Communications: A Data-Mining Approach. *Sustainability (Basel)*, 14(3), 1178. Advance online publication. DOI: 10.3390/su14031178

Zhao, Y. (2023). Exploring the Transformation of Movie Publicity Strategies under the Perspective of New Media Communication. *Communications in Humanities Research*, 22(1), 257–262. DOI: 10.54254/2753-7064/22/20231773

Zheng, Y. (2023). An Analysis of the Technical Trend of Semantic Search in Natural Language Processing. *9th Annual International Conference on Network and Information Systems for Computers, ICNISC 2023* (pp. 51-53). Virtual, Online: Institute of Electrical and Electronics Engineers Inc. DOI: 10.1109/ICNISC60562.2023.00033

Zheng, Y., Mobasher, B., & Burke, R. (2015). Carskit: A java-based context-aware recommendation engine. In *2015 IEEE International Conference on Data Mining Workshop (ICDMW)* (pp. 1668-1671). DOI: 10.1109/ICDMW.2015.222

Zhong, M., & Wang, M. (2023). Corporate sustainability disclosure on social media and its difference from sustainability reports: Evidence from the energy sector. *Frontiers in Environmental Science*, 11, 1147191. https://www.frontiersin.org/articles/10.3389/fenvs.2023.1147191. DOI: 10.3389/fenvs.2023.1147191

Zhou, Q., Simmhan, Y., & Prasanna, V. (2017). Knowledge-infused and consistent Complex Event Processing over real-time and persistent streams. *Future Generation Computer Systems*, 76, 391–406. DOI: 10.1016/j.future.2016.10.030

Zhou, Z., Zhan, G., & Zhou, N. (2019). How does negative experience sharing influence happiness in online brand community? A dual-path model. *Internet Research*, 30(2), 575–590. DOI: 10.1108/INTR-12-2018-0531

Zhu, C. (2022). Construction and Risk Analysis of Marketing System Based on AI. *Scientific Programming*, 2022(1), 2839834. DOI: 10.1155/2022/2839834

Zhu, Q., & Luo, J. (2024). Toward artificial empathy for human-centered design. *Journal of Mechanical Design*, 146(6), 061401. DOI: 10.1115/1.4064161

Ziakis, C., & Vlachopoulou, M. (2023). Artificial intelligence in digital marketing: Insights from a comprehensive review. *Information (Basel)*, 14(12), 664. DOI: 10.3390/info14120664

Zohny, H., McMillan, J., & King, M. (2023). Ethics of generative AI. *Journal of Medical Ethics*, 49(2), 79–80. DOI: 10.1136/jme-2023-108909 PMID: 36693706

Zook, Z., & Smith, P. R. (2016). *Marketing communications: offline and online integration, engagement and analytics*. Kogan Page Publishers.

About the Contributors

José Duarte da Rocha Santos received his PhD in Management from Vigo University. He also holds MSc in Marketing and a bachelor's degree in Business Sciences. Between 1987 and 2002, he played various roles in sales, marketing, and management of companies in the information technology sector. From 2003 to 2018, he performed the functions of a management and marketing consultant. Since 1999, he has been a professor in higher education in Portugal in the fields of management and marketing. He is currently a marketing professor at the Accounting and Business School of the Polytechnic of Porto (ISCAP/P.PORTO). He is also a senior researcher at the CEOS.PP – Center for Organizational and Social Studies of the Polytechnic of Porto, Portugal. His main areas of research are strategic marketing, relational marketing and digital relationship strategies.

Paulo Botelho Pires holds a Ph.D. in Management, a Master's degree in Marketing, and a degree in Systems Engineering and Computer Science. He has edited several books and academic journals and published several papers, chapters and books. He has taught marketing at the university level, with interests in e-commerce, digital strategy, customer experience, and artificial neural networks applied to marketing. Currently, he is a professor of marketing at Accounting and Business School of the Polytechnic of Porto (ISCAP/IPP) and a senior researcher at CEOP.PP - Center for Organizational and Social Studies of the Polytechnic of Porto, Portugal.

Nicholas Grigoriou has over 30 years of academic and practical marketing and international marketing experience in the banking, furniture, petroleum and education industries. Prior to entering academia, Nicholas held marketing roles in the banking, commercial furniture, and petroleum refining industries. Nicholas was awarded a doctorate degree in philosophy from Swinburne University in 2013. His doctoral. research investigated how packaged food and beverage exporters make product customisation and standardisation decisions for export to China.

His academic research interests are in new product development and branding. Nicholas has represented the Monash brand name in and administrative capacity in Guangzhou, China and as an academic in Kuala Lumpur, Malaysia. Nicholas has published peer reviewed research in top ranking academic journals, and has served as a Visiting Professor at IESEG (Lille, France) March 2006, October 2011, February 2012 and 2014 (Lille and Paris) teaching "Doing Business in China" course.

* * *

Mourad Aarabe is a PhD student at the National School of Business and Management of Fez, Sidi Mohamed de Ben Abdellah University. His research focuses on tourism, marketing, digital marketing, and management.

Luzia Arantes has a PhD in Applied Psychology from the University of Minho, which she completed in 2023. She is currently studying for a PhD in Marketing and Strategy at the same institution. She holds a Master's degree in Communication Sciences from the University of Minho in 2018, a Master's degree in Organisational Management from the Polytechnic Institute of Cávado and Ave in 2021, and a degree in Communication Sciences from the University of Beira Interior in 2015. She works as a student evaluator for the External Evaluation Commissions at the Higher Education Evaluation and Accreditation Agency (A3ES). She is also a lecturer and trainer in marketing and communication, teaching various digital marketing subjects at the University of Aveiro and the Polytechnic Institute of Cávado and Ave. She is also a member of the Sustainable Development Research Group at EKA, Riga, Latvia. His professional experience covers the areas of Social Sciences, Business Organisation and Management, Psychology, Communication Sciences, Digital Marketing, Sustainability, and Artificial Intelligence.

Zev Asch is a distinguished marketing executive and successful entrepreneur with over 30 years of experience across various industries, including IT, Retail, and medical device manufacturing. Mr. Asch served as a Graduate Marketing Professor and Director of Innovation and entrepreneurship at Touro University in New York City. He is also a distinguished marketing, leadership, and entrepreneurship professor at Amity Education Group's Long Island campus.

Lara Bacalhau is a Ph.D. in Management - Specialization in Marketing and Strategy from the Faculty of Economics of the University of Porto, where she also completed a Master's degree in Data Analysis and Decision Support Systems. Her academic journey includes also two Bachelor's degrees: one in Mathematics from the University of Coimbra and another in Business Management from the Coimbra

Business School (CBS|ISCAC). Since 2003, she has been a lecturer at CBS|ISCAC, teaching courses in Marketing, Business Management, Accounting, and Taxation. Lara's teaching experience extends to the Coimbra Business School Executive, Viseu School of Technology and Management, and ISLASantarém. Currently, she coordinates the Bachelor's program in Marketing and International Business. She actively contributes to research in Marketing and Business Management, with expertise in areas such as Branding, Digital Marketing, Social Media Marketing, E-commerce, and Relationship Marketing. Lara participates in national and international research projects, serves as a peer reviewer, and co-authors scientific publications.

Yavuz Selim Balcıoğlu is a lecturer at the University of Gebze Technical. He holds a BS in Economics from the University of Kocatepe, an MS in Business Administration from the University of Yasar (2005), and completed his Ph.D. in Business Analytics at the University of Gebze Technical. With a robust academic background, he has authored over 150 journal papers and received 13 international awards in robotics. His research interests span computer vision, robotics, and neural networks.

Nitesh Behare is an accomplished author with a wealth of knowledge and 15 years of experience in the academic field. He currently holds the position of Associate Professor at the Balaji Institute of International Business (BIIB), Sri Balaji University Pune (SBUP). Throughout his career, Dr. Behare has made significant contributions to the academic world through the publication of numerous research papers and book chapters, establishing himself as a recognized authority in his field.

Nouhaila Ben Khizzou is a PhD student at the National School of Business and Management of Fez, Sidi Mohamed de Ben Abdellah University National School of Business and Management of Fez, Morocco.

Naoual Bouhtzati is a PhD student at the LAREMEF laboratory, National School of Commerce and Management, Sidi Mohamed Ben Abdellah University, Fez, Morocco.

Joaquim Casaca is Assistant Professor at IADE, Universidade Europeia, since 2010. He holds a Ph.D. in Management from Universidade Lusíada de Lisboa, a Master's in Management from ISEG - Lisbon School of Economics and Management at the University of Lisbon, a MBA (ISEG), a postgraduate degree in "Technologies and Information Sciences for Organizations" (ISEG) and a degree in Economics (ISEG). He has developed his teaching activity in the scientific areas of Management, Marketing and Statistics in the Marketing and Advertising degree and several masters in the field of marketing, and in the supervision of master's dissertations. He is an integrated member of UNIDCOM/IADE research center and is a member of the scientific committee of the Observatório do Consumo Consciente – Forúm do Consumo (Conscious Consumption Observatory – Consumer Forum), currently developing research on marketing performance, behavior and development sustainable and conscious consumption. Experienced user in statistical analysis programs such as IBM SPSS Statistics, IBM SPSS AMOS and SmartPLS (structural equation models).

Amrish Kumar Choubey is a distinguished professional with over 20 years of experience in both academia and industry. He holds an MBA in Information Technology and Human Resource Management and has earned a Ph.D. in a related field. Dr. Choubey is renowned for his expertise in cloud computing, computer networks, and ERP system development and implementation. Throughout his career, Dr. Choubey has made significant contributions to his areas of expertise, publishing numerous research papers in IEEE and Scopus-indexed journals. His scholarly work reflects a deep commitment to advancing technology and its applications. Dr. Choubey's academic influence extends globally, having participated in academic exchange programs in the USA, UK, France, and Singapore. These international experiences have enriched his teaching and research perspectives, benefiting students and colleagues alike. In addition to his technical and research accomplishments, Dr. Choubey has substantial experience in academic management, including the conduct of examinations. His leadership and administrative skills have been instrumental in fostering educational excellence and innovation.

|**Sandra Barbosa Costa** is a PhD student at Beira Interior University, Portugal, specialising in Marketing and Strategy. Additionally, she has more than 20 years of experience in Management and Marketing in the Business Industry. She holds a Master of Marketing and Communication from the Polytechnic University of Guarda, and her research interests are centred on Marketing, Branding, Sustainability and Management.

Astha Gupta, M.B.A., Ph.D., NET Qualified having overall 20 years of experience in Industry and Academia. Currently working with Amity University since 2010. She is a passionate researcher in the fields of Consumer Behavior, Artificial Intelligence, Machine Learning, and Human Intelligence. She has been session chair and featured speaker at international conferences of repute. She has 4 books on HR to her credit and has published research work in Scopus-indexed journals. She has experience organizing Springer and IEEE Conferences in

Singapore and India. She carries extensive experience in internationalization and organizing conferences in the U.S.A., Singapore, and Australia]

Khaled Ibrahim is a Lecturer in Digital Marketing and Branding at Unitec Institute of Technology and a branding consultant. His research interests are primarily focused on brand management, brand generosity, consumer perception, and AI-based branding, developing concepts such as moral brand machines. His consultancy experience spans several industries, including healthcare, fashion, and gaming.

Md. Touhidul Islam serving as an Assiatant Professor at "NPI University of Bangladesh" and also an adjunct faculty at Army Institute of Business Administration (AIBA) Savar. He got his MPhil and PhD from University of Dhaka, Bangladesh. He has earn BBA & MBA degree under Business Administration from Pabna University of Science and Technology, Bangladesh. He has more than 17 research and conference papers published by various renowned international Journals. He also published a book named "Human Resource Information System (HRIS): The Business Student's Guide" published by LAP Lambert Academic Publishing. Mr. Touhid served as a reviewer for a number of journals. He has research experience on Sustainable Online Business, Agile Marketing, Neuro-Marketing, Sustainable Marketing, Online Shopping, Services Marketing, Customer satisfaction.

Dawit Jabo is a PhD Scholar in Department of Marketing Management, Bule Hora University, Ethiopia.

Chitra Krishnan, Ph.D., Symbiosis Centre for Management Studies, Noida, Symbiosis International (Deemed University) India Teaching professional with over 16 years of national and International experience. She possesses excellence in teaching and research. Before her academic career, she worked in industry in various positions of responsibility. She has been actively involved in rigorous academic pursuits in the field of higher professional education to enhance skill sets that promote the holistic development of learners. She has a number of publications in acclaimed journals at the National and International level and has also participated in many national and international conferences. She is passionate about writing and has six books to her credit with International publishers. She has been empaneled as a member of the review committee for conferences and journals of repute. Her area of interest includes Human Resource Management, Organization Behavior, Talent Management, Diversity Management, Employee Satisfaction, Knowledge Management, Artificial Intelligence, and Emotional Intelligence.

Sunita Kumar is a passionate educationist with 17+ years of experience (Industry: 5+ years and Teaching: 12+ years) experience. Dr Sunita area of expertise/ specialization including advertising, branding, digital Marketing, consumer behaviour, Marketing Analytics. Over the last 12 years, she has taught and received positive evaluations for many marketing units, including Brand Management, Marketing Research, International Marketing, Fundamental of Marketing, Consumer Behaviour, Marketing Management, Social Media and Digital Marketing, Data Analysis using SPSS both postgraduate and undergraduate level. She has also been actively supervising master's and Ph.D. candidates from Christ university in Bangalore. Dr Sunita also often shares her industry experience and research findings with different audiences and stakeholders, both locally and internationally. she has been actively leading and involved in numerous research project and consultancies projects, as well as published numerous indexed journals/ articles, book, chapters in a book, conference proceedings, and industry reports.

Darkio Lourenço is currently a PhD student in Economic and Business Sciences at the University of Aveiro, specializing in Management. In 2024, Darkio earned a Master's degree in Digital Marketing and Communication from the University of Aveiro, conducting research on the tangible and intangible returns on investments in artificial intelligence projects. Additionally, he holds a Bachelor's degree in Financial Management from Cesumar University in Brazil. In his professional career, Darkio Lourenço has extensive experience in public management, particularly in management of educational institutions. He also has expertise in digital marketing, especially in strategy and growth, as well as content production, social media management, Search Engine Optimization (SEO), and App Store Optimization (ASO).

Joana Neves has a Master's degree in Marketing and International Business at Coimbra Business School, specializing in Marketing strategies, international business dynamics, and consumer behavior. Prior academic achievements include a Bachelor's degree in Applied Communication from Lusofona University - Porto Center, focusing on communication theories, Marketing, and media studies. Practical expertise was gained as a Cisco Certified Network Associate through the Cisco Networking Academy, where skills in networking principles and system security were developed. Complementing the academic background, a three-year Informatic Internship at Lusofona University - Porto provided opportunities to offer technical support and perform system maintenance. Currently engaged in research in marketing and technology, with a focus on Digital Marketing strategies, E-commerce, and the integration of technology in Marketing campaigns. Furthermore, is currently studying for a PhD in Management - specializing in Marketing and Strategy from the Faculty of Economics of the University of Porto.

Tafese Niguse is a PhD scholar, Department of Marketing Management, Bule Hora University, Bule Hora, Ethiopia.

Albérico Travassos Rosário, Ph.D. Marketing and Strategy of the Universities of Aveiro (UA), Minho (UM) and Beira Interior (UBI). With affiliation to the GOVCOPP research center of the University of Aveiro. Master in Marketing and Degree in Marketing, Advertising and Public Relations, degree from ISLA Campus Lisbon-European University lLaureate International Universities. Has the title of Marketing Specialist and teaches with the category of Assistant Professor at IADE-Faculty of Design, Technology and Communication of the European University and as a visiting Associate Professor at the Santarém Higher School of Management and Technology (ESGTS) of the Polytechnic Institute of Santarém. He taught at IPAM-School of Marketing lLaureate International Universities, ISLA- Higher Institute of Management and Administration of Santarém (ISLA-Santarém), was Director of the Commercial Management Course, Director of the Professional Technical Course (TeSP) of Sales and Commercial Management, Chairman of the Pedagogical Council and Member of the Technical Council and ISLA-Santarém Scientific Researcher. He is also a marketing and strategy consultant for SMEs.

Ahmed Shaalan is an Associate Professor in Marketing at the University of Birmingham, Dubai and a Visiting Fellow at the School of Management, Cranfield University, UK. He is best known for his work on relationship marketing and social networks, including Chinese guanxi and Arab wasta. He is also interested in tourism marketing. His research has been published in leading scientific journals such as the Journal of Business Ethics, Journal of Business Research, Journal of Sustainable Tourism, International Journal of Contemporary Hospitality Management, and Management and Organizational Review.

Ana Isabel Torres holds a PhD in Management Science and MSc in Marketing and Strategy, both from University of Porto, Faculty of Economics. She is a Professor at the Accounting and Business Administration Institute, University of Aveiro and a researcher at the Laboratory of Artificial Intelligence and Decision Support, Institute for Systems and Computer Engineering, Technology and Science - INESC TEC. Her teaching areas include Marketing Strategy, Digital Economy, Services Management and Digital Consumer Behaviour. She has participated in international projects on the fields of Education Force, Next Generation Technologies for Networked Europe (NEXT NET) and SELF: Solo-entrepreneurship in Post-pandemic Europe (in progress). Her main research interests are focused on education technology, digital service design (Ux), entrepreneurship, innovation and sustainability. She engages in multidisciplinary research that bridges managerial and design-related fields such as digital services management with technology-oriented fields. Her academic work, including a book, book chapters and scientific articles, has been published in several leading international scientific publications, such as the British Journal of Educational Technology, Journal of Intellectual Capital, Electronic Commerce Research, Journal of Small Business Strategy, Journal of Revenue and Pricing Management, Management Research, as well in proceedings of international conferences.

Marwa E. Tourky is an Associate Professor of Marketing and Brand Management at Cranfield School of Management, UK. Her research is focused on areas such as corporate brand, identity and reputation, communications and CSR. Marwa serves on the editorial board of Journal of Marketing Communication. She works hand in hand with non-academic partners, including charities and the public sector, such as Devon and Cornwall Police, as a researcher, advisor and board member. Her research has appeared in leading scientific journals such as Journal of Business Research, European Journal of Marketing, Qualitative Market Research, Management and Organization Review, Journal of Business and Industrial Marketing. She is the co-author of Integrated Marketing Communications: A Global Brand Driven Approach, published by Palgrave Macmillan. She has contributed chapters to edited books, reports for funded projects, and popular accounts of her work has appeared in The Times, The Daily Mail, Devon Live, Palm FM, PlymouthLive, and CornwallLive.

Shrikant Waghulkar is an accomplished academic with a Ph.D. in Business Management from Savitribai Phule Pune University, awarded in March 2020, and SET qualification from the same university in 2017. With 10 years of teaching experience and six years in various challenging roles, he is dedicated to leveraging his skills and knowledge for organizational and personal growth. Known for his confidence, politeness, and motivational abilities, Dr. Waghulkar is an innovative, result-driven team player adept at achieving exceptional results in demanding environments. He is quick to learn and apply new technologies, enhancing his teaching and research capabilities. Dr. Waghulkar is a prolific researcher with numerous publications in international and Scopus-indexed journals, along with authored books and book chapters. Proficient in MS Office, internet technologies, and SPSS, he is highly enthusiastic about research work. Dr. Waghulkar seeks to contribute in the academic and industry knowledge that offer opportunities by utilizing his skills.

Index

A

B

C

D

E

F

G

I

K

L

M

N

O

P

R

S

T

U

V

Milton Keynes UK
Ingram Content Group UK Ltd.
UKHW051834211024
450061UK00009B/120